D0205847

Stuttering and Cluttering

Stuttering and Cluttering provides a comprehensive overview of both theoretical and treatment aspects of disorders of fluency: stuttering (also known as stammering) and the lesser known cluttering.

The book demonstrates how treatment strategies relate to the various theories as to why stuttering and cluttering arise, and how they develop. Uniquely, it outlines the major approaches to treatment alongside alternative methods, including drug treatment and recent auditory feedback procedures. Part 1 looks at different perspectives on causation and development, emphasizing that in many cases these apparently different approaches are inextricably intertwined. Part 2 covers the assessment, diagnosis, treatment, and evaluation of stuttering and cluttering. In addition to chapters on established approaches, there are sections on alternative therapies, including drug therapy, and auditory feedback, together with a chapter on counselling. Reference is made to a number of established treatment programs, but the focus is on the more detailed description of specific landmark approaches. These provide a framework from which the reader may not only understand others' treatment procedures, but also a perspective from which they can develop their own.

Offering a clear, accessible and comprehensive account of both the theoretical underpinning of stammering therapy and its practical implications, the book will be of interest to speech language therapy students, as well as qualified therapists, psychologists, and to those who stutter and clutter.

David Ward is Director of the Speech Research Laboratory at the University of Reading, and a specialist fluency clinician within the NHS. He qualified as a speech language therapist in 1987, and later received an MA in linguistics and phonetics and a PhD in motor control and stuttering. He has lectured extensively on disorders of fluency, and is involved in research into both theoretical and clinical aspects of stuttering and cluttering.

Stuttering and Cluttering
Frameworks for understanding and treatment

David Ward

Psychology Press
Taylor & Francis Group

HOVE AND NEW YORK

First published 2006
by Psychology Press
27 Church Road, Hove, East Sussex BN3 2FA

Simultaneously published in the USA and Canada
by Psychology Press
270 Madison Avenue, New York, NY 10016

*Psychology Press is an imprint of the Taylor & Francis Group,
an informa business*

Typeset in Times by RefineCatch Limited, Bungay, Suffolk
Printed and bound in Great Britain by
TJ International, Padstow, Cornwall
Cover design by Sandra Heath

British Library Cataloguing in Publication Data
A catalogue record for this book is available from the British Library

Library of Congress Cataloging-in-Publication Data
Ward, David, 1956 Dec. 9–
   Stuttering and cluttering: frameworks for understanding and
treatment / David Ward
      p.   ;   cm
   Includes bibliographical references and index.
   ISBN-13: 978–1–84169–334–7
   ISBN-10: 1–84169–334–0
   1. Stuttering.   2. Cluttering (Speech pathology)   3. Speech
Disorders.   I. Title.
   [DNLM: 1. Stuttering.   2. Speech Disorders.   WM 475 W257s 2006]
RC424.W37 2006
616.85′5406—dc22   2006010954

ISBN 13: 978–1–84169–334–7
ISBN 10: 1–84169–334–0

This book is dedicated to those who stutter and clutter

Contents

3   Stuttering and auditory processing   46

4   Motor speech control and stuttering   60

5   Linguistic aspects of stuttering   81

10   Treating early stuttering

11   The treatment of stuttering in school age children

12   The treatment of stuttering in adults

17   Assessment, diagnosis and treatment of cluttering   351

Figures

Tables

Preface

My motivation for writing this book comes from my experiences as a lecturer and researcher in both theoretical and clinical aspects of the subject, and as a specialist clinician in disorders of fluency over the last 13 years. Also, as someone who has more than just a tendency to clutter, I can claim a direct and vested interest in at least the two chapters devoted to this subject.

The purpose of this book

There are already a number of excellent books on stuttering, written by eminent authors, and whose findings are still current. These books, for the large part, can be divided into two types: on the one hand, we have heavily theoretical books with each chapter written by acknowledged experts within their fields comprising impressive amounts of state-of-the-art data within their subject area. On the other, there is the different approach taken in single-authored books, which tend to cover theoretical issues more briefly, instead, focusing more on therapeutic processes.

In a recent survey, Yaruss and Quesal (2002) reported that decreasing teaching time is being made available on disorders of fluency courses. Students have little enough time to assimilate the highly detailed and ever-increasing research data reported in the bigger texts at the best of times, and this worrying trend in shorter courses on the subject only exacerbates the problem. Despite this, a thorough grounding in the key theoretical issues is, of course, vital in order to understand the various models and theories as to why stuttering and cluttering arise, and why these perspectives are important when considering therapeutic options. The purpose of this book, therefore, is to draw together the available theoretical evidence and, wherever appropriate, to relate its relevance to the practicing clinician. While an in-depth coverage of the theoretical issues is prerequisite for this, the aim in this book has been to carefully rationalize the breadth and depth of debate to provide a text which is sufficiently comprehensive to allow properly informed evaluations, but at the same time remaining accessible and concise.

Of course, in attempting to tread the middle ground between the more weighty and advanced texts and the more practical ones, there is always the risk of ultimately failing on the two counts, resulting in a book which is neither practical enough, nor thorough enough, and finding the appropriate balance between necessary detail and clarity and relevance has been a challenging task. It is all too easy to become drawn ever deeper into a level of discussion that has already been presented in a different type of textbook, but underrepresentation of the various arguments is even less acceptable. It is fair to say that there is "robust debate" amongst experts on many aspects of stuttering and cluttering. Inevitably there will be those who will argue that greater emphasis should have been placed on such and such an area, or that another area lacks coverage. Generally, I am happy with the balance of opinion represented in the book, but acknowledge that keeping all parties and all opinions satisfied will be nigh-on impossible. I certainly recognize that some new readers coming to the subject for the first time will want to look further into particular areas discussed in the book; indeed I hope that this will be the case, and that the book will stimulate interest in the subject. To this end, those who wish to know more about a particular area can find references that will direct him or her quickly to alternative sources by use of the suggested reading sections at the end of each chapter.

About the book

The book is divided into two parts: the first on theoretical perspectives, the second on more practical and clinical issues. Throughout, the aim is to help the reader identify links not only between theory and therapy, but relationships between one theory and another, and one therapy and another. Part 1 begins with an overview on stuttering and is designed to provide a general orientation to some of the major features and issues of the stuttering. Unusually for a book of this kind, chapter 1 ends by describing a model of stuttering. The reason for introducing Starkweather and colleagues' Demands and Capacities model at this early stage is to offer the reader a framework which will help put into focus the subsequent information in the book. Regardless of the apparent discontinuities between theoretical and therapeutic stances that arise in remaining chapters, this model allows for incorporation of a range of perspectives, and provides one tangible way of integrating the various and often apparently contradictory data between the different theoretical stances.

Part 2 focuses on the practical aspects of assessments and treatment. In one sense, I have taken a deliberately broad stance on what can be viewed as therapy, including short sections on various counselling techniques, alternative procedures such as altered feedback, drug therapy, as well as nonclinician-led therapy. I think this reflects the changing nature of what is meant by "therapy" and the changing expectations of those seeking help with stuttering. Whether or not clinicians endorse the use of various nonmainstream approaches to treatment or not, it is important that students at least have some basic knowledge of alternative treatment procedures. When it comes to mainstream therapies, I have focused attention on a rather limited number of clinician-led approaches. Why? There are already a great number of publications which outline a range of high-profile programs, and more books are underway. Instead, the purpose of the current book is to provide the reader with examples of significantly different therapeutic programs, underpinned by opposing models and theories as to the nature of the disorder, and consequently how it can best be treated. By outlining a limited number of (mostly) reference point programs, the reader will ultimately have a better framework from which to evaluate and understand the ever-increasing range of integrated treatment options now on offer.

I have not yet mentioned a second focus of the book. Suffice to say, here, that the inclusion of two chapters on cluttering (still very much the poor relation to stuttering when it comes to research on both theory and therapy) reflects my belief that this disorder requires more time than is often devoted to it on fluency disorders courses. It is because of the comparatively small amount published on the subject that I have added my own clinical experience on treatment issues to the few that currently exist in the literature.

A word on terminology

At some point, someone, sometime will do everybody a big favour and come up with some adequate terminology to describe the people that speech professionals see in clinics. For a start, we have to deal with our own cumbersome handle of either "speech language therapist" or "speech language pathologist", depending on which part of the English-speaking world we are practising in. This is bad enough, particularly in Britain, where we sometimes get abbreviated to the awful SALT (speech [and] language therapist). But this rather awkward title pales into insignificance compared to the apparently unsolvable problem of how to describe the people who we aim to help. The term "stutterer" is understandably unacceptable to many, "person who stutters" is more unwielding, and to a great number, its abbreviation PWS is even worse. Then there is the issue as to whether to refer to a hypothetical client as he or she or s/he. Even if I am not totally at ease with my eventual decisions, I refer, throughout this book, to those who seek help with their fluency as "clients" (rather than patients), and those who see them for "therapy" (another word I am somewhat uncomfortable with in the context of fluency management) as clinicians. Also, I will follow the lead of Marty Jezer (1997; who considers the same dilemmas from a consumer's perspective in his superb book *Stuttering: A life bound up in words*) and refer to those with stutters as "people who stutter", rather than use the abbreviated form. I depart from this policy only on a small number of occasions, when failure to do so would result in a particularly unwieldy sentence. Finally, as the majority of clinicians are female, and the majority of clients are male, I use the terms "she" and "he" respectively, in these contexts.

Acknowledgements

First, I owe a debt of gratitude to all those in the stuttering and cluttering community whose work has influenced my thinking over the years, and which has led to the preparation of this text. I would also like to offer my appreciation to the editorial team at Taylor and Francis/Psychology Press; in particular to Lizzie Catford, Tara Stebnicky and Penelope Allport. Without their support, enthusiasm and patience I doubt this book would have ever been completed.

Finally, I would like to thank my family. My wife, Gillian, has been a constant source of encouragement throughout, despite being made a "book widow" for far too long. And to my sons Alex and Nicholas – yes, it really is finished, and yes, we can play football now.

Part I

The aetiology of stuttering and cluttering

1 Definitions and epidemiology

Introduction: What is stuttering?

It is sometimes hard when called upon to explain to a lay person about the types of disorders we see in speech language therapy clinics and exactly what it is that speech language therapists and speech language pathologists actually do. People generally know that a carpenter works with wood; a lawyer deals in settling legal issues; a heart surgeon operates on hearts. Even with professions allied to medicine, many people have some basic understanding of some roles and may have a reasonable idea, for example, as to what a physiotherapist does. But within our more abstract field, our role still remains comparatively unknown and poorly understood. For some (usually older) people, we may still be seen simply as elocutionists, but even those who appreciate that we deal with physical disability, such as "helping people with sore throats to speak", may be unaware that we also deal with more abstract matters, such as language comprehension and psychological profiling. Despite this, there is one area within our profession which provides a notable exception to our comparative obscurity. Mention the word "stuttering" and the lay person's face lights up with instant recognition. In some cases, there follows an enthusiastic monologue of their experiences with people they know or have known who stutter. Alongside this, it also seems that a substantial number have the answer to the nature of the disorder, and/or how it can be cured. "It's all to do with his nerves", ... or "she doesn't think enough before she speaks", or "If Tom just takes a deep breath before he speaks/ drinks two pints of beer/ then he doesn't have any problems at all."

The irony of all this is, of course, that despite having probably received more attention than any other speech language disorder, stuttering is arguably the one whose aetiology is least understood. For clinicians and researchers in the field, it is perhaps the ultimate abstract disorder within an abstract discipline. Over many decades we have accrued huge amounts of information on the subject, yet we still do not know what causes a developmental stutter, and we have still have no cure for the chronic condition. In fact, we struggle even to define stuttering succinctly. Perhaps we shouldn't be surprised at this, given that stuttering implicates, in varying degree, motor speech, language and psychological and environmental components. We return to these issues later in the book, but for the present some background information on stuttering is required. At the outset, this requires us to be aware of two different types of stuttering: these are the developmental and acquired versions, and a further fluency disorder, cluttering.

Developmental stuttering

This is by far the most common type of stuttering, and the one that forms the basis of discussion for all but three chapters of this book. This version, also sometimes called idiopathic stuttering, refers to stuttering that arises in childhood, usually in the preschool years, and for multifactorial reasons. Throughout this book, the term stuttering is used to refer exclusively to the developmental condition, unless explicitly stated otherwise.

Acquired stuttering

Acquired stuttering is a cover term for two types of onset: neurogenic stuttering which occurs following neurological trauma of varying aetiologies (for example, stroke, head injury, tumour, drug use and misuse); and psychogenic stuttering which may be related to a distressing event (for example, bereavement, divorce). Van Riper (1982) has also argued that there is a third type, called occult stuttering. This refers to the appearance of stuttering in adulthood with no apparent neurological or psychological onset that Van Riper argues is actually the re-emergence of a developmental stutter which may have gone undiagnosed in early life, and has subsequently been in some state of remission. We return to the issue of acquired stuttering, specifically, in chapter 16.

Cluttering

Cluttering is a disorder of fluency characterized by two strands of breakdown: those relating to motor speech and those relating to linguistic variables. It has received less coverage in the literature than stuttering, and is comparatively poorly understood. Typically, speech is characterized by fast bursts of jerky speech which may also sound slurred and misarticulated. In addition, language may be poorly organized with evidence of poor word finding together with excessive number of revised sentences, restarts and filler words and phrases. Unlike stuttering, cluttering is characterized by a lack of concern and awareness on behalf of the speaker. We discuss cluttering from an aetiological perspective in chapter 8, and consider therapeutic aspects of the disorder in chapter 17.

Normal nonfluency and stuttering

Levels of fluency vary from person to person, and one thing we can say for certain is that no one is completely fluent. Even the most eloquent and articulate speaker will from time to time make speech errors. The nature of these will vary, but common ones include hesitation and phrase revisions. There may also be single word repetitions, or perhaps the insertion of an interjection, such as "um" or "er". Listeners tend not to pay too much attention to most breaks of fluency that occur in speech, and even if there are a substantial number of certain types of disfluency in a person's speech, they may still not be perceived as having a "speech problem" if those disfluencies are of a particular type.

To understand the nature of stuttering disfluencies, we first need to consider the range of disfluencies that may occur in speech. Campbell and Hill (1987) have identified a number of major disfluency types:

1 Hesitation (of one second or longer).
2 Interjection (such as "um" and "er").
3 Phrase/sentence revision (where a speaker goes back to rephrase the sentence or phrase).
4 Unfinished word.
5 Phrase/sentence repetition.
6 Word repetition.
7 Part-word repetition (which can be either sound, syllable or multisyllabic repetitions).
8 Prolongations (the unnatural stretching of a sound).
9 Block (a session of sound, which can either be momentary or lasting, arising from an occlusion in the vocal tract which is either at an inappropriate location; at an appropriate location, but mistimed; or both). Blocks are usually accompanied by increased localized tension.
10 Other (amongst other possibilities, this may include inappropriate breathing patterns).

Notice that Campbell and Hill (1987) make no distinction here between stuttering disfluencies and normal disfluencies. Leaving aside the necessarily vague "other" category, this is because all of these behaviours could be stuttering, but at the same time, it is equally possible that all categories except blocking could be characteristic of normal disfluency. So what indicates the difference between normal and abnormal fluency if there is such an overlap?

First, the severity of each moment of disfluency will be a factor. A person producing a single repetition of a single syllable word ten times in five minutes of talking, is unlikely to be considered as stuttering; on the other hand, a person repeating the same word eight times will likely to be perceived as having a speech problem, even if such an event occurs only twice in a five-minute speech sample.

Second, the frequency of disfluency will also be a factor: the greater the number of disfluent moments, over a given period of time, the greater the likelihood of perception of stuttering. Third, those disfluencies which contain extra effort (or carry extra tension) are far more likely to be perceived as stuttering (Starkweather, 1987). Blocking, for example, is the only listed disfluency on Campbell and Hill's list which intrinsically carries excessive tension, and it is similarly the only type which (assuming the block is long enough to be noticed) is not characteristic of normal disfluency. Excessive tension goes hand in hand with stuttering, not with normal speech, and the greater its presence, the greater the likelihood of an association with stuttering.

Fourth, disfluency within a word, such as blocking, prolonging, phoneme and part-word repetitions, is regarded as characteristic of stuttering, rather than normal disfluency, whilst the repetition of larger units, particularly phrase repetition and phrase revision is more likely to be associated with normal disfluency. Wyrick (1949) discovered that the majority of repetitions in stuttered speech (63 percent) were typified by part-word repetitions, a finding later corroborated by Soderberg (1967). Conversely, McClay and Osgood (1959) recorded that 71 percent of the disfluencies found in nonstuttered speech were made up of word repetitions, with phrase repetitions accounting for 17 percent; and part-word repetitions for 12 percent. These findings have been corroborated in a number of other studies (Boehmler, 1958; Johnson, 1959). More recent findings have indicated that prolongations and blocks (the other two other types of core behaviours) tend to be associated with stuttering, and not normal disfluency (Gregory & Hill, 1984), and it is highly unusual to find prolongations in nonstuttered speech (Williams & Kent, 1958; Young, 1961). If they do occur, prolongations are likely to be associated with a hesitancy as the speaker considers forming a phrase, such as "W . . . e . . . ll, I'm not too sure . . ." or "Y . . . e . . . s, but on the other hand . . .". Unlike stuttering, these prolongations are under the speaker's control. Silent blocks are almost never encountered in normally disfluent speech. The presence of even one fleeting block in among 500 fluent words may still lead a clinician to suspect a stutter. The presence of one longer block is likely confirmation of the diagnosis.

In sum, sublexical disfluencies are more consistent with stuttering than normal disfluency. The greater the size of the repeated unit, the more likely this will be perceived as normal disfluency (see also Gregory & Hill, 1999).

Primary and secondary stuttering

Thus far, we have noted that stuttering comprises a range of core behaviours. These may also be referred to as primary stuttering: a term which relates directly to the observable sublexical speech fluency breakdowns (although single syllable word repetition is also sometimes included in the definition). Secondary stuttering is characterized by learned behaviours which become attached to the primary activity, including concomitant features such as sudden loss of eye contact, rapid eye blinking, hand tapping, head nodding, jaw jerk, tongue thrust, nostril flaring. These behaviours may be used as a means of avoiding primary stuttering, for example, by the use of starter phrases ("OK, well . . .") or interjections ("um . . . um . . .") to help run up to difficult words,[1] or may be used to help initiate speech. We return to this area in more detail when we talk about the assessment of stuttering in part 2.

We have just seen that the physical act of eye avoidance in association with a moment of stuttering may be regarded as secondary stuttering, but other devices, most commonly a range of avoidance strategies, are often used by those with an established stutter. These may include word avoidance, as well as the avoidance of people and situations that are perceived as difficult for the speaker. However, there is a subgroup for whom avoidance becomes the most significant part of the stutter, and this often continual use of avoidance to conceal stuttering is known as interiorized stuttering (Douglas & Quarrington, 1952) or covert stuttering (Gregory, 2003; Guitar, 1998). These terms apply to a subgroup of individuals who are dominated by their (negative) perceptions of their stutter. People with this type of stutter may present with little or no problem to the listener, but maintain fluency only through the extensive use of circumlocution to avoid difficult words or sounds. Covert stuttering is associated with very high levels of concern, and sometimes an extreme fear of making even the most fleeting speech error. Despite what is quite often normal sounding fluency, such individuals often remain fixed by a sense of acute anxiety that, at any moment, they could block on a word unexpectedly. In many cases, a cognitive approach to therapy, which explores with the client the feelings and associations that underpin these concerns, can bring about a substantial change in that person's self-perceptions (see chapter 12), and a change toward more confident "exteriorized" stuttering, which is the necessary first step in the therapeutic process.

A defining characteristic of stuttering is its heterogeneity, and clearly stuttering can mean very different things to those who suffer from it. It can also mean very different things to those who attempt to describe it, and this has directly led to problems when it comes to a definition of the disorder.

Definitions of stuttering

The stuttering elephant

So what is stuttering? There have been many attempts at a definition, and all are flawed in some way. A basic but very awkward problem is the fact that

---

1 This is a good example of how the same behaviour may be regarded as stuttering or normal disfluency, depending on context. "Um" may be a device used by a person who does not stutter to gain some thinking time. In the context here, however, it is being used to avoid (or at least postpone) an upcoming word which is perceived as difficult.

stuttering combines two distinct but intertwined elements: the observable features of the disrupted speech output, and the reactions and experiences of the individual, relating to those disruptions. A fundamental problem, therefore, has been whether to describe the observable characteristics of the disorder, or the psychological ramifications, and often the route taken reflects a particular researcher's perspective on the disorder. We can see this problem somewhat caricatured in the scenario of the "stuttering elephant", noted by Wendell Johnson nearly 50 years ago. The idea here is that researchers' efforts to define stuttering can be likened to the efforts of a number of blind men examining an elephant. These learned men each rigorously analyze different areas of the animal, one noting the trunk, another the ears, and so on. They subsequently all arrive at completely different and incorrect conclusions as to the animal's identity, based on their close examination of only one part of the anatomy. OK, this is perhaps a little unfair on researchers who necessarily focus their investigations of stuttering within a particular area of expertise, and stuttering is certainly not the only field to suffer from this malaise. Related to this is the very legitimate excuse that stuttering behaviour covers such a wide range of activity that definitions can either seem underspecified, or, in an attempt to capture the breadth of the disorder, to over-elaborate. Let us consider a range of attempts to illustrate the point.

Psychologically based definitions

We begin with a brief mention of four definitions of stuttering, each focusing on a specific presumed underlying psychological cause (although we return to these areas in chapter 6 in more depth):

1   In 1943, Coriat offered a Freudian explanation of stuttering as "a psychoneurosis caused by the persistence into later life of early pregenital oral nursing, oral sadistic and anal sadistic components".
2   Rather little credence is given to such a notion nowadays, but at a similar point in time Johnson's (1946) diagnosogenic perspective of stuttering was the prevailing theory: "Stuttering," Johnson claimed, "is an evaluational disorder. It is what results when normal dysfluency is evaluated as something to be feared and avoided; it is, outwardly, what the stutterer does in an attempt to avoid dysfluency" (Johnson, 1946, p. 452). Nearly 60 years later, the diagnosogenic theory continues to generate heated debate amongst researchers and clinicians, as we see in chapter 7.
3   A little more recently, Brutten and Shoemaker (1967) asserted that "stuttering is that form of fluency failure that results from conditioned negative emotion" (1967, p. 61).
4   Sheehan (1970) took stuttering to be ". . . not a speech disorder but a conflict revolving around self and role, and identity problem" (Sheehan, 1970, p. 4).

It is noteworthy that these references are all rather old. As we will come to see, few would deny the crucial factor of psychological factors in the development of stuttering, and undoubtedly the impact of a range of psychological perspectives on stuttering has been hugely significant, but the explanation of stuttering as arising (solely) due to some underlying psychological deficit or difference has fallen from favour as increases in technology have allowed organic explanations and definitions to predominate.

Symptom-led definitions

In contrast, we can have alternative definitions based more on the physical aspects of stuttering. For example The World Health Organization (WHO) defines stuttering as "disorders in the rhythm of speech in which the individual knows precisely what he wishes to say, but at the same time is unable to say it because of an involuntary, repetitive prolongation or cessation of sound" (WHO, 1992). Van Riper (1982) appears to be taking a similar line when he states: "Stuttering occurs when the forward flow of speech is interrupted by a motorically disrupted sound, syllable, or word" but continues with the important caveat ". . . or by the speaker's reaction thereto" (p. 15). Perkins, Kent, and Curlee (1991), in their neuropsychological perspective, state simply that "stuttering is a disruption of speech experienced by the speaker as loss of control" (p. 734), although this statement could equally apply to those suffering from acquired apraxia of speech, dysarthrias, or even spasmodic dysphonia. That said, there is considerable merit in considering the speaker's perspective in a definition of the disorder.

Wingate's definition

Finally, we come to Wingate's (1964) seminal "definition". In many ways this is really more a description of symptoms than a definition of the disorder. But it does differentiate stuttering from a range of other disorders, and makes an attempt to categorize secondary speech characteristics that can in many cases make up the more significant part of the disorder. Since the mid-1960s it has been quoted very widely, and 40 years later Wingate still provides us with the best reference point from which to consider the disorder of stuttering.

> The term "stuttering" means: I. (a) Disruption in the fluency of verbal expression, which is (b) characterized by involuntary, audible or silent, repetitions or prolongations in the utterance of short speech elements, namely: sounds, syllables, and words of one syllable. These disruptions (c) usually occur frequently or are marked in character and (d) are not readily controllable. II. Sometimes the disruptions are (e) accompanied by accessory activities involving the speech apparatus, related or unrelated body structures, or stereotyped speech utterances. These activities give

the appearance of being speech-related struggle. III. Also, there are not infrequently (f) indications or report of the presence of an emotional state, ranging from a general condition of "excitement" or "tension" to more specific emotions of a negative nature such as fear, embarrassment, irritation, or the like. (g) The immediate source of stuttering is some incoordination expressed in the peripheral speech mechanism; the ultimate cause is presently unknown and may be complex or compound.

(Wingate, 1964, p. 498)

Prevalence and incidence

Prevalence of stuttering refers to the number of cases that will be observed within any defined population and age group. In the UK and USA this has generally been reported as around 1.0 percent (Andrews, 1984; Bloodstein, 1995), although a more recent estimate (Craig, Hancock, Tran, Craig, & Peters, 2002) puts the figure at around 0.75 percent. The 1.0 percent figure roughly equates to 580,000 people of all ages in the UK and 2,740,000 in the USA who stutter. Similar prevalence percentage figures have been quoted in many of the developed countries.

There is evidence from a number of earlier studies that stuttering has been recognized worldwide (see Van Riper, 1982). However, while reports that stuttering simply does not exist in some cultures have yet to be substantiated, there do seem to be communities where stuttering is less common (Stewart, 1960). Some claim that stuttering might be more likely in countries, particularly those in the western world, where there is greater importance placed on verbal acuity, and consequently increased pressure on articulate speech. For example, Lemert (1962) found a lower incidence of stuttering amongst Polynesian societies, as compared to Japanese; an effect considered to reflect the different social pressures between the two cultures. In fact, the idea that stuttering is related to increased linguistic demands is one that is still current. We see this with reference to the theory in chapter 5, and in a number of therapeutic approaches which control for the length and/or complexity of language output. Nonetheless, despite associations between increased linguistic "demand" and stuttering, subsequent findings have shown that stuttering does appear across all known languages, albeit with slightly differing prevalence figures.

The prevalence figures need to be taken alongside incidence data. Incidence here, refers to the appearance of new cases of stuttering within a certain time period. Andrews and Harris' (1964) seminal longitudinal study followed the developmental progress of 1000 children over a 16-year period in Newcastle-upon-Tyne, England and found that stuttering most commonly started between ages 3 to 4 (22 percent of all those whose stutters did not resolve quickly) and that 50 percent of those with persistent stutters had begun by the age of 5. Although stuttering is predominantly a disorder associated with a preschool onset, a significant minority (25 percent) of children will start after the age of 6 (Andrews, 1984). A recent study on over 3000 preschool children in the USA has determined preschool prevalence figures of 2.43 percent (Proctor, Duff, & Yairi, 2002; Yairi & Ambrose, 2005), a statistic that held constant across ethnic minorities. As Yairi and Ambrose (2005) have argued, this puts a slightly different complexion on the idea that stuttering is a rare phenomenon. If these findings are verified in subsequent studies, this means that, although many of the preschoolers who stutter will go on to recover spontaneously, around 2.25 percent of all preschool children and their parents will still need help from fluency therapists. Although some children will only commence stuttering after the preschool years, the estimate is that prevalence drops to those seen amongst adults (Bloodstein, 1995). In the Andrews and Harris (1964) study, a further 37 percent of those diagnosed with stuttering recovered within six months.

Who is at risk of stuttering?

Related to the lack of a single cause to stuttering is the fact that there are a number of factors that place an individual at increased risk of developing the disorder. These are discussed from a number of theoretical perspectives in part 1, and within the therapeutic context in part 2. Below is a brief summary of some of these factors.

Age

The incidence figures show that preschool children are at greatest risk of developing a stutter. Three-quarters of all who stutter will have started before the age of 6, and nearly all stuttering starts before age 12.

Genetic predisposition

Stuttering tends to run in families. Children who have first-degree relatives who stutter are three times as likely to go on to develop a stutter. It is possible that there may be a genetic strain which leads to an intractable condition, and that males may be more at risk to this variety.

Male–female ratio

The ratio of stuttering males to females is around 2:1 in very young preschool children (Ambrose & Yairi, 1999; Yairi & Ambrose, 1992a, 1992b; chapter 6 this volume). Spontaneous recovery is common in both males and females, but the gender ratio in adults is around 4:1, indicating that more females than males spontaneously recover.

Children with co-occuring speech and language problems

Some research has shown that children who have concomitant language delay are at greater risk of stuttering than those who do not (Andrews & Harris, 1964; St Louis & Hinzman, 1988). Similarly, some experts believe that those with a phonological disorder are placed at increased risk of stuttering (Louko, Edwards, & Conture, 1990). However, there are some researchers who have questioned these claims, arguing that better controlled studies are needed to confirm these findings (Nippold, 1990). A recent study found that a third of all children who stuttered also had co-occurring articulation disorders, while just under 13 percent of the 2628 children also presented with phonological disorders. In total, around two-thirds of all the children who stuttered also had some form of speech language or nonspeech disorder (Blood, Ridenour, Qualls, & Hammer, 2004).

Learning disorders

Stuttering appears to be more prevalent amongst the learning disabled (LD). Blood et al. (2004) found that LD children made up 15 percent of their large sample of children who stuttered. Specific issues as how best to manage stuttering amongst such individuals goes beyond the scope of this book, but Bray (2003) has articulated the complexities of the problems, not least those associated with the lack of awareness that stutterers with Down's syndrome often demonstrate, even when there is visible speech-related struggle (Bray, 2005).

Children with poor motor control

Children who stutter are more likely to be late in achieving speech milestones, and may have depressed articulatory skills (Wolk, Edwards, & Conture, 1993).

Environmental factors

In addition to a genetic component, stuttering can be imitative, and it is possible in some cases that a child who stutters may be picking up on a disfluent model. Some researchers have claimed that the extra pressure (for example, increased time pressure on verbal responses; being told to respond using advanced language; generally high level of expectation) can lead to increased risk of stuttering (Rustin, Botterill, & Kelman, 1996; Stewart, 1960), as can negative listener reactions (Johnson et al., 1959).

Increased number of stuttering-like disfluencies

We have already seen that certain types of disfluency are more characteristic of stuttering behaviour than of the normal disfluencies that commonly occur alongside the development of speech and language skills in the preschool years. These include an increase in the number of repeated part-word units, decrease in rhythmic stress patterns in repetitions, increase in speed of repetitions (Yairi, 1997; Yairi & Lewis, 1984).

Development of stuttering

The various factors that have been implicated in stuttering development form the basis of a number of chapters throughout the book. Here, we provide a preamble to some of the major issues.

As we have just seen, stuttering mostly commonly arises in the preschool years. Although there can be variability in speech behaviours at onset (see chapters 6 and 10), stuttering at this time typically comprises only word or syllable repetition (Bloodstein, 1995; Howell, Au Yeung, & Sackin, 1999) and is usually void of struggle, avoidance, or speech-related anxiety. Relatedly, there are usually no signs of the "tricks" such as head nodding and foot tapping that many older children and adults who stutter develop in an effort to control the disorder. Yet the transition from easy and relaxed repetitions to effortful struggle-related blocks and prolongations can take place quickly and such changes signal the likelihood that the stutter will go on to become chronic, and that spontaneous recovery is less likely. For some this may develop slowly and over a long period of time, but for others it may happen over a matter of days or months. Some believe that parental reaction may play a large part in this process. Parent and child verbal and nonverbal exchanges may change as the child becomes aware that something is different and as the parent tries not to draw attention to the child's disfluencies. Alternatively, the parent may tell the child to slow down, take a deep breath and try saying the word again, thus indicating to the child that something is wrong (Rustin et al., 1996). As Starkweather (1999) points out, far from promoting fluency, this can often lead to the establishment of struggle as over time the child (and parents) find that, rather than helping with fluency, these instructions result in increased anxiety and struggle, disrupted breath control and fixed postures associated with an established or chronic stutter. This in turn leads to more fear, anxiety and expectance to stutter, which helps perpetuate the motoric disruptions to speech. So the vicious cycle is completed and the stutter develops.

Phenomena associated with stuttering

Stuttering is variable, and there are a number of situations under which even those with severe stutters experience significantly increased fluency. Some examples include: talking in unison with another speaker (choral speech); copying the speech of another speaker (shadowed speech); whispered speech; when singing or acting; when talking to pets or to babies; when talking aloud to themselves (one example might be when reminding themselves of a shopping list).

Choral speech and shadowed speech may improve fluency through adjusting the way the individual hears his or her own voice (we discuss this in chapters 3 and 14) and it is the related notion that one perceives one's own speech signal as exogenous (or created externally) that may result in the increased fluency that some experience when acting. Whispered speech involves the maintenance of a constant position of the vocal folds, and therefore does away with the continuous online adjustments required in normal speech when switching between voiced and unvoiced sounds (see chapter 4). Conture (2001) suggests that the increase in fluency arising when speaking to babies, pets and oneself all reflect the fact that stuttering is associated with bidirectional speech. Therefore, speech is more fluent when it is unidirectional; when there is no likelihood of a response (or that the response will be limited to an unchallenging gurgle, or nonthreatening bark from a dog). But we also tend to speak in a different way when talking to babies and pets, using uncomplicated language and altered intonation patterns. It is further likely that fluency will fluctuate, depending on the levels of anxiety, more generally. Giving a talk to 1000 people might be considered unidirectional, yet giving a presentation to a large group of people is generally amongst the most feared of scenarios, and one where many claim their stutter is at their worst. Similarly, many fear the answerphone more than the response of a real speaker, although admittedly this also introduces the feature of time pressure into the equation. As for singing, which is one of the most powerful of fluency enhancing phenomena, there may be a number of explanations and we come to these shortly.

Causes of stuttering

There are many theories about stuttering, and some commentators have unkindly suggested that there are as many theories as there are researchers. Bloodstein (1995) suggests that these theories can all eventually be distilled down to three categories: those that relate to the stuttering moment itself; those attempting to explain the aetiology of stuttering; and those attempting to find new frames of reference from which to examine the disorder. Here we have a replication of the problem we first encountered a few sections ago when talking about definitions, and once again the spectre of our stuttering elephant lumbers into view. To attempt to deal with these theories here would be to open far too many cans of worms. Rather, we will come to discuss a range of current perspectives alongside our attempt to unravel the various strands of inquiry in the forthcoming chapters. What can be said at this point is that while there are theories of stuttering as a genetic, motoric, linguistic, neurological, psychological, auditory processing, and environmental phenomenon, no single one can explain its own data, and at the same time answer in sufficient depth the important questions raised in other areas of investigation.

While a unitary cause to stuttering remains to be found, the primary identifying features of the disorder can be quite clearly identified as an output that is motorically disrupted, as Wingate's (1964) definition claims. The difficulty is that there are a number of different explanations as to what underlies the blocks, prolongations and repetitions that typify stuttered speech. Is this the result of faulty neuromotor processing? Are the disruptions peripheral reflections of difficulties with processing phonological, syntactic or lexical aspects of language? Maybe stuttering comes about as a result of genetic component, or perhaps again it is a psychological disorder, or related to environmental factors?

Consider this concrete example of the problem in relation to fluency enhancement. We have already touched on the idea that singing is a strong fluency enhancing factor. But why exactly is this? From an auditory feedback perspective we can argue that singing with others might be likened to a type of chorus speech, and when singing amongst other instruments there might also be some type of masking effect (see chapter 3). From a cerebral dominance perspective, we note that speech tends to be processed in the left hemisphere, whilst singing is a product of the right hemisphere, and that those who stutter often present with increased right hemisphere activity. When singing, though, this right hemisphere activity is now appropriate. Indeed, one method of treating some cases of aphasia, where there has been damage to left-sided language centres, is to encourage compensatory activity from the unaffected right hemisphere precisely by using the medium of music (melodic intonation therapy; see also chapter 2). Another perspective is that fluency increases when a rhythmic stimulus is applied, and of course this is intrinsic in music. From a physiological perspective, the phonation patterning is much simpler when singing, and the airflow does not need to be controlled as precisely as when speaking (see chapter 4). Linguistically, singing might be easier because the words are either written down or already well learned. Finally, when singing, people often perceive themselves to be taking on a different role, and this sense of "stepping out of oneself" can also have a fluency enhancing effect. So, here are a number of different and plausible reasons as to why fluency is enhanced when singing. Does fluency come about as a result of one of these effects? Two of these effects? All of these effects? Perhaps it is due to a combination of some of these effects? If so, would it be the same combination for each person, or would there be different effects? There are no simple answers, and we discuss these issues in the forthcoming chapters. For the present, all we can say is that there is no single cause that can be identified, and that stuttering is likely to involve the interrelationship of a number of influences.

As we will see over the next few chapters, there is no shortage of models of stuttering. In the final section of the present chapter, we outline a model that can deal with the variability and uncertainty that exists within the disorder of stuttering.

Spontaneous recovery

Once stuttering has persisted into adulthood, there is no known cure. Although this is not to say that a range of therapeutic techniques cannot control the disorder to the point where individuals may no longer consider themselves as stuttering, many prefer the term recovered stutterer. It also seems that on very rare occasions an established stutter may permanently disappear in the absence of any therapy whatsoever, and for reasons which mostly appear uncorrelated with any significant life event. The spontaneous recovery from stuttering in childhood, however, is a different matter, and remains one of the more perplexing features of the disorder. Although figures differ (and we look at these in chapter 10) it seems that around 74 percent of all children who stutter will cease to do so by the time they reach their early teens (Mansson, 2000; Yairi & Ambrose, 1999). Spontaneous recovery is more likely if the onset of the disorder is early, and may be as high as 89 percent for girls who have been stuttering for less than a year (Yairi & Ambrose, 1992b). Preliminary evidence suggests the outlook may be less favourable for boys who have a later onset, particularly if they also have delayed speech and language (Yairi, Ambrose, Paden, & Throneburg, 1996). While there is little dispute as to the fact that spontaneous recovery is a common occurrence in the early years, what exactly constitutes both "spontaneous" and "recovery" is not as clear.

With regard to "spontaneous", it may be, in some cases at least, that therapy has played a significant part in the remission, and even where there has been no direct therapy, changes in the way in which the parents interact with their disfluent child (whether done knowingly or unknowingly) may have affected the child's recovery. The term "recovery" raises more difficulties. Does recovery have to involve complete and total cessation of all stuttering behaviour? And if so, over what period of time must this be sustained? One of the features of stuttering, particularly in childhood, is that it is often cyclical, and it is not uncommon for symptoms to disappear for extended periods at a time. So it may not be clear that a recovered child who stutters is not merely going through a period of fluency. There is also the question of "recovery from what?" Different studies have utilized different measures as to the definition of stuttering. We cannot be sure that these studies are actually comparing like with like. Of course, we can see that properly determining accurate levels of spontaneous recovery are of central importance when looking at treatment planning. We return to the issue of spontaneous recovery in this context in chapter 7.

Making sense of the data: Stuttering as a balance between capacity and demand

We comment throughout this book on how stuttering is characterized by variability, and highlight the difficulty in making sense of all the various strands of knowledge in any integrated way concerning linguistic, motoric, neurological, auditory, genetic, psychological and environmental influences. Consider, also, that within many of these areas there are either seemingly contradictory data, insufficient data, or not unusually both, before attempting to synthesize the information into a single integrated theory that, in addition, also explains all the phenomenological data associated with the disorder. Finally, we may think, also, about the fact that, despite the vast array of knowledge that has been accrued on the subject, when asked what causes stuttering, ultimately we still have to say "I don't know", and one might begin to question exactly how far this vast body of research has taken us.

Well, it is true that there are many perspectives on stuttering and no single integrated account, but there are ways in which the various data can be explained using models which allow for the heterogeneity of the disorder. One such is the demands and capacities perspective. The model is usually credited to Starkweather and colleagues (Starkweather, 1987; Starkweather, Gottwald, & Halfond, 1990), although Sheehan had, some time ago already used the term "demand" with reference to the effect of external pressures that could negatively effect a child's fluency. Sheehan had also considered the likelihood that there could be a predisposition to stuttering, which would thus reflect a potential for reduced "capacity" (Sheehan, 1970). The premise is that for every individual (whether a person who stutters, or not), and for each individual's speaking situation, speech performance will vary, depending on: (a) the inherent *capacity* that an individual's speech and language system may have to produce fluent speech; (b) the *demands* under which that system is placed. With stuttering, then, the severity of the disorder is likely to increase when the balance between demands placed on the system and the ability of the system to deal with the level of demand is exceeded. Capacity, for example may reflect a predisposition to the disorder, although as we see in chapter 6 it is not yet clear as to what that genetic component (or components) might code for. This increased likelihood is then acted on by demands. These variables may be internal to the speaker, such as vary levels of self-perception and confidence, the need to be able to express ever more complex thoughts, which in turn requires more advanced language skills. External influences such as increased time pressure, poor parental interaction models and negative peer group reaction to speech may also be factors (see Figure 1.1).

Although descriptive (and as Starkweather emphasizes this is most definitely a model rather than a theory), it is useful because it goes some way toward characterizing the heterogeneity of the disorder, why stuttering arises in the first place; why it develops and why (in some cases) it persists. It also goes some way to explaining its unpredictability, and the range of phenomena associated with it. People who stutter may indeed have some predisposing factors toward stuttering, but it may require the interaction of this predisposition with myriad precipitating and perpetuating factors that gives rise to the different levels of stuttering (and periods of remission) for any given individual.

When increased DEMAND outweighs the reduced CAPACITY, there will be increased stuttering.

DEMANDS

Environmental influences
• Peer group pressure (and reactions to nonfluency)
• Teasing
• Insistence on perfect speech (either by adults, i.e., external pressure; or by the child, internal pressure)
• Increased rate of adult speech
• Advanced language used by adults
• Time pressure
• Stressful speaking situations

Language skills
• Phonology
• Syntax
• Semantics/pragmatics

CAPACITIES

Predisposition to stuttering

Auditory processing deficits

Motor speech instability

Neurologal differences

Affective issues
• Emotional and social capacity to cope with new demands and challenges
• Child's ability to cope with his nonfluency

Cognitive development
• Specifically, the child's meta-linguistic awareness (i.e., his ability to describe his speech processes, and to make sense of his difficulties

Some of these factors will relate more to the appearance and development of stuttering, and others more to its maintenance. Note that the degree of stuttering will depend on the changing balance between increased demands against reduced capacity.

Figure 1.1 Example of some possible demands and capacities.

Take, for example, the finding reported in chapter 7 that identical twins have been found to show extremely high concordance (similarity between both twins) for stuttering, but not 100 percent. This means that although there is a strong likelihood that a genetic component is involved, some also appear to require the interaction of environmental influences in order to result in stuttering. Thus, for these speakers, the reduced capacity (genetic predisposition) only results in stuttering under certain environmental contingencies which increase demand.

While multifactorial accounts of stuttering have met with general approval, the demands and capacities model has not been without its critics, and in the year 2000 a devotion of nearly an entire edition of *Journal of Fluency Disorders* provided an opportunity for experts to discuss some concerns. Most notably these centred on the adequacy of the definition of the terms involved, although opinions varied as to how these issues could be resolved. Siegel (2000), for example, suggested that the model should more accurately be described as demands and performance because capacities are not specifically addressed. Both Bernstein-Ratner (1997, 2000) and Yaruss (2000) argued that replacing capacity with performance does not solve the problem, instead proposing that there needs to be a reframing of the conceptual notions of both "demand" and "capacity" through the use of "measurable aspects of a child's speaking performance and speaking abilities" (p. 347). Bernstein-Ratner (2000), on the other hand, argued that the lack of sufficiently constrained definitions results in a degree of circularity. In one sense, the model's strength then can also be viewed as a weakness: the model stretches to fit all possibilities, but this is at the cost of underspecification in its definitions, which in turn restricts interpretation. In response to these criticisms, Starkweather and Gottwald (2000) contend that Siegel (2000) may have failed to take into account the range of evidence published on the subject.

Six years on from this debate, the demands and capacities model still provides a useful framework from which to explain why stuttering is so variable from one person to another; why people stutter in different ways, and under different circumstances, and indeed, why stuttering occurs in some people, and not in others. For some there may be limited capacity for speech production, but favourable environmental factors; for others there may be a normal capacity but, for example, also exposure to an environment which serves to increase the stuttering.

The approach has also led to the development of a therapeutic model of early intevention (Gottwald & Starkweather, 1995; Starkweather & Gottwald, 1990; Starkweather et al., 1990). In addition, there are strong similarities between the demands and capacities perspective and the multifactorial model of stuttering and the parent–child interaction (PCI) therapy approach taken by a number of therapists (for example, Rustin et al., 1996; see chapter 10). With PCI, stuttering is seen as reflecting the summation of the effects of a number of influences: physiological, linguistic, environmental and neurological. The indirect parent–child interaction approach involves adjusting the family dynamics, paying particular note of the interactive style of the parent with the young child to create a more favourable environment for the development of fluent speech. We spend some time describing PCI in chapter 10, and return to consider a Demands and Capacities perspective throughout this book in regard to both theoretical issues and clinical practice.

Summary

The establishment and maintenance of fluent speech comes about as a result of the successful integration of a number of complex task-specific biological systems, achieved during childhood. The breakdown of speech fluency as evidenced in stuttering can at present best be viewed as a complex multifactorial problem, resulting in a breakdown within and between these systems. Thus it is probable that the heterogeneity which is characteristic of stuttering comes about through the interplay of genetic, linguistic, motor speech, environmental and psychological factors, all of which will carry different weightings for different individuals. It is also likely that the complex interplay of these varying factors not only gives rise to the appearance of stuttering in the first place, but also affects whether the disorder will develop, how it will develop, and the likelihood that it will spontaneous resolve.

There is at present no proper "integrated theory" on stuttering, but the demands and capacities model does offer a simple but useable way of both capturing and making sense of the variability seen in stuttering. The reader is encouraged to view the material in both part 1 and part 2 of this book in the light of this perspective on stuttering, and to keep in mind (even when the data become complicated and even contradictory) the simple idea that the speech breakdown that characterizes stuttering can be viewed as an elaborate balance between a system's capacity to produce fluency, and demands which compromise that ability.

Key points

- This book covers three disorders of fluency: developmental stuttering (which is the most common and comprises the main focus of the book), acquired stuttering and cluttering.
- Acquired stuttering can be caused either by neurological disturbance (neurogenic stuttering) or by psychological trauma (psychogenic stuttering). Acquired stuttering and cluttering are covered in separate chapters, later in the book.
- Approximately 1 percent of the world's population stutters, but the prevalence may be slightly lower in cultures which do not place such critical importance on verbal acuity.
- The onset of stuttering is usually preschool, coincident with the acquisition of language and speech motor skills.
- Over two-thirds of all children who stutter will stop, either with or without therapy before puberty.
- At onset, there are two males to every female that is diagnosed, but more females recover. By the end of elementary school this ratio has changed to 4:1, a figure which stays constant throughout life.
- There is no single integrated account as to why stuttering arises, but there are a number of factors which appear to increase the likelihood that stuttering will develop. These factors may form the basis of a multifactorial account.
- A demands and capacities approach is offered as a useful model from which to understand the heterogeneity associated with stuttering.

In this conception, the likelihood of stuttering is seen as a delicate balance between the inherent ability that a person has to produce fluent speech and the difficulties presented by the constantly changing demands of different environments and external pressures.

Further reading

Conture, E. G. (2001). *Stuttering: Its nature, diagnosis, and treatment* (pp. 4–27). Boston: Allyn & Bacon.
Another excellent introduction to the major issues which underlie stuttering.

Gregory H.H., & Hill, D. (1999). Differential evaluation-differential therapy for stuttering children. In R. F. Curlee (ed.) *Stuttering and related disorders of fluency* (pp. 23–44). New York: Theime.
This provides a very good introduction to the evaluation of stuttering in children, and includes an updated version of Gregory and Hill's stuttering continuum.

Jezer, M. (1997). *Stuttering: A life bound up in words*. New York: Basic Books.
I could have included this excellent book as suggested reading in any number of chapters. Quite simply, Marty Jezer's book on growing up and living with a stutter is an unmissable read from just about every perspective. Superbly written, it is at once informative, funny, moving and, throughout, thought provoking. This book should be read by every student speech and language therapist/pathologist.

Starkweather, C. W. and Gottwald, S. R. (1990) The demands and capacities model II: Clinical application. *Journal of Fluency Disorders, 15*, 143–157.
An original source for the demands and capacities model. It also shows how the model can be of practical help clinically, as well as demonstrating how the sometimes disparate strands of research may be drawn together.

Van Riper, C. (1982). *The nature of stuttering*. Englewood Cliffs, NJ: Prentice-Hall.
This book is nearly 25 years old now, but is still a fascinating read. Any of the first five chapters are of relevance to the areas we have covered, but the first, on the universality of stuttering, is particularly interesting, and for those interested in historical aspects of stuttering, which we have not covered here, it is a must.

2 Brain function and stuttering

Introduction

A commonly asked question is: "Is there something different in the brain that makes people stutter?" There is evidence from a good many sources that links stuttering to neurological anomalies. Some people who stutter may be differentiated from those who do not by lateralization of language function. There may be biochemical factors which distinguish the two groups, and stuttering may be triggered by drugs acting on the central nervous system (CNS). Subcortical processing of linguistic information may be different, and stuttering has been linked to the function of subcortical structures.

Stuttering may also appear subsequent to neurological damage following CNS trauma such as stroke or head injury, and in epilepsy, in the absence of premorbid history of stuttering or any other co-occuring speech or language disorder. There is current disagreement as to the relationship of this "neurogenic stuttering" to the developmental condition we are concerned with here, and this is something we discuss elsewhere (chapter 16).

While we cannot say that stuttering is caused by anomalous CNS functioning, there is mounting evidence to suggest that for a large number of people who stutter, at least, there are subtle differences in the processing of linguistic information that differentiate them from those who do not stutter. For some, also, there are minor but significant neuroanatomical differences.

Cortical studies and cerebral dominance

During the last ten years or so, brain imaging procedures have developed to allow ever more sophisticated analysis of hemispheric functioning. These techniques have led to a resurgence of interest in the pursuit to define CNS functioning in stuttering. Current research, broadly speaking, falls into two categories. One examines cortical structures, most usually with the goal of ascertaining the extent to which cerebral dominance impacts on stuttering or defining structural differences between the brains of those who stutter and those who do not. A second, only studied comparatively recently, looks at subcortical activity. These investigations are more focused on explaining apparent links between stuttering and other disorders which are known to have a subcortically based motor speech component.

Early studies

Aristotle is amongst the earliest scientists to have considered a neurological cause to stuttering. However, his assertion that "the instruments of the tongue itself are weak and cannot exactly follow the concept of the mind" might better fit a diagnosis of dysarthria than stuttering. Whilst there are some early accounts of stuttering arising from a battle for control of speech between the left and right hemispheres (e.g., Sachs & Stier, 1911, reported by Kistler, 1930), the scientific study of CNS activity in stuttering really begins three-quarters of a century ago with the pioneering work of Orton (1927) and subsequently Travis (1931). These researchers developed the first coherent theory of stuttering as a disorder of cerebral imbalance. Their theory was based on the fact that motor innervation for speech muscles is supplied contralaterally. Right-sided muscles receive innervation from the left hemisphere and left-sided muscles receive supply from the right hemisphere. Using neurophysiological tasks such as dichotic listening and tachistoscopic viewing, their thesis was that people who stutter had insufficient margins of dominance of one hemisphere over the other necessary to ensure that the timing of motor impulses from both hemispheres was properly synchronized. This then resulted in disrupted motor speech output. The thalamus was also implicated; the assumption being that varying emotional states could adversely impact on an already impaired cortical system. These findings appeared to corroborate growing empirical evidence that those suffering from a stroke sometimes presented with stuttering-like symptoms, and the cerebral dominance concept was initially embraced with enthusiasm. Findings sparked an increasing interest into cerebral dominance theories and, as we will see, some current theories do not appear that dissimilar to that proposed by Orton and Travis.

However, the theory was not without its problems. First, there remained some question marks as to the interpretation of the available data. For example, Watson and Freeman (1997) argued that the cortical and subcortical areas implicated in the research were not clearly identified. In addition, new research showed that homolateral motor pathways also existed alongside contralateral ones. The biggest difficulty with the cerebral dominance theory was that it remained untestable, with the effect that cerebral dominance became equated more to the somewhat different issue of peripheral sidedness, in turn represented by handedness. The idea here was that people who stuttered had reduced dominance because they had changed from their natural writing hand to the other. Not surprisingly, much research subsequent to Orton and Travis' work lay in determining whether this proposition indeed held true.

Stuttering and handedness

In fact, the relationship between "sidedness" and "dominance" is an awkward one. Dominance is represented peripherally by a number of preferences of which handedness is one of many, and even the issue of what constitutes handedness itself is far from straightforward: individuals may be predominantly right-handed, but perform some tasks left-handedly (or vice versa). Subirana (1964) found only eight out of 600 individuals studied to be completely right-handed and only one of the 600 was completely left-handed. In addition to hand preference, foot and eye preference have been considered when identifying sidedness, and mixed laterality is even more prevalent amongst these preferences.

Findings of handedness amongst people who stutter are equally inconclusive. De Ajuriaguerra, Diatkine, Gobineau, and Stambak (1958) found only 30 percent of their nonstuttering speakers to be thoroughly right-handed, as compared to 68 percent amongst the group who stuttered. There are a number of studies which demonstrate that the performance of many people who stutter more closely approximates that of left-handed or ambidextrous activity than right-handed, supporting the notion that stuttering is associated with left-handedness (Fagan, 1931; Jasper, 1932; Orton & Travis, 1929; Travis 1928; Travis & Herren, 1929; Van Riper, 1935). There is also a substantial body of evidence which does not corroborate these findings (Andrews & Harris, 1964; Daniels, 1940; Johnson, 1959; Johnson & King 1942; Pierce & Lipcon, 1959; Records, Heimbuch, & Kidd, 1977; Spadino, 1941; Streifler & Gumpertz, 1955). There is very little discussion of handedness in the stuttering literature after the 1970s as researchers turned their attention to potential differences in central laterality between people who stutter and nonstutterers, but one recent study (Salihovic & Sinanovic, 2000) found no statistical difference in the incidence of left-handedness of 380 children and adolescents who stutter, and neither were there differences between right- and left-handed people who stutter on a number of variables associated with stuttering, including stuttering severity. Similarly, there is mostly only older and rather limited evidence that a change in peripheral handedness can alter cerebral dominance, or that stuttering can be caused by such a change (Bryngelson & Rutherford, 1937; Haefner, 1929; Hirschberg, 1965; Oates, 1929).

There is, however, some preliminary evidence to suggest that handedness amongst younger children who stutter may be a predictive factor in the development of chronic stuttering. Brosch, Haege, Kalehne, and Johannsen (1999) studied 79 children who stuttered between the ages of 3 and 9 for cerebral dominance via tests of laterality, peripheral hearing and dichotic sound discrimination. Following an 18-month period, the children were evaluated for presence or absence of stuttering, and the results of the laterality tests correlated with the probability of remission. Comparisons showed no relationship between rate of remission and dichotic listening, but left-handed individuals were found to have a significantly poorer chance of attaining fluency. There is no subsequent data to back the findings of this study, and these results should be interpreted with caution, but there is a complicated link between handedness and genetic inheritance, just as there is for stuttering and genetic inheritance, and it is possible there may be some common ground here. As we see from chapter 7, there appears to be preliminary evidence that a genetic component in stuttering may be as much responsible for the persistence of an early stutter toward a chronic condition as for the appearance of stuttering in an individual in the first place. In this sense there is something of a parallel effect to the conclusions drawn by Brosch et al. (1999) who are suggesting the onset of stuttering may not necessarily be linked with given handedness, but rather that handedness may affect the development and continuation of the disorder.

Laterality of auditory function

While foot and eye laterality may not need to be considered when making assertions of laterality of language function, the study of laterality of auditory function commands a study area in its own right, with some researchers claiming that stuttering is not so much a disorder of speech/language production, but one of flawed auditory perception. There is also compelling evidence that altered auditory feedback (AAF) devices can dramatically increase speech fluency, at least in some people who stutter, which further supports the notion of stuttering as a result of disrupted auditory feedback (see chapters 3 and 4).

Dichotic listening studies have shown that stuttering tends to be associated with either a left ear advantage or inconsistent right ear preference for linguistic information, indicating right hemisphere activity for processing (Carr, 1969; Curry & Gregory, 1967; Kimura, 1961, 1967; Sommers, Brady, & Moore, 1975). There is also evidence to suggest that AAF, in both delayed and frequency shifted forms, reduces right hemisphere activity (e.g., Rastatter et al., 1998). One tentative auditory-based theory emanating from AAF laterality studies argues that stuttering is controlled by altered feedback when sensory brain centres perceive a mismatch between auditory and somatic activity. Extra blood flow is fed to these sensory areas, thus correcting the auditory processing deficit. This information is then fed to speech motor integration and activation centres, but the time delay or pitch information, depending on whether delayed or pitch-shifted feedback is used, does not fall within the resolution of these structures' capabilities. (See below regarding the timing capabilities of left and right hemisphere.) The information is therefore passed as normal and speech is not disrupted.

Anaesthesia studies

In 1966 a neurosurgeon, R. K. Jones, used a procedure known as the Wada test (Wada, 1949) in an attempt to determine whether speech/language was lateralized for those who stutter, as it was for nonstutterers (Jones, 1966). The technique requires the injection of an anaesthetic into either the left or right carotid arteries of a subject, while she or he is conscious and talking. Wada and Rasmussen (1960) had already found, using this technique, that a temporary aphasia could be induced, when the anaesthetic was administered to the dominant hemisphere of subjects with normal speech and language. Jones took as his subjects four severe stutterers who had been diagnosed with cerebral tumours, and for whom surgery was a necessity. Prior to surgery, subjects were given the anaesthetic injection. Unlike Wada and Rasmussen's subjects, all stutterers showed aphasia, regardless of which hemisphere had been anaesthetized, leading Jones to conclude that language was represented bilaterally for these individuals. Each of the subjects then underwent surgery to remove the tumour from either the left or right hemisphere. When recovered from their operation, and now only having unilateral representation for speech and language, all subjects had ceased to stutter. Convincing though these results at first appear in support of the argument that stuttering is related to bilateral representation for speech and language, interpretation is complicated by the fact that the majority of the subjects were left-handed, thus it is not known whether this was the cause for bilateral representation. Replications of the study have provided inconclusive data. Andrews, Quinn, and Sorby (1972) reported that two of their three subjects who stuttered had left dominance while Luessenhop, Boggs, Laborwit, and Walle (1973) found that all three of their subjects who stuttered demonstrated normal left-sided dominance.

Electrophysiological studies

The study of brain function has relied on technological advances perhaps more heavily than any other area of investigation of stuttering. There is now a bewildering array of brain imaging techniques and procedures at the researcher's disposal. It is certainly not necessary for clinicians to be familiar with the science behind all of these, although a basic understanding of their strengths and weaknesses is important if we are to be able to make sense of their findings.

We first consider electrophysiological methods. This procedure involves the strategic placement of electrodes, most usually on the surface of the scalp, but occasionally in or even beneath it. Electrical activity in the brain is then picked up by the electrodes and sent, via an amplifier, for permanent record and display on a computer monitor. Alpha waves naturally occur at rest at a rate of around 8–10 waves per second. When stimulated, the brain produces more waves, but of a smaller and more irregular amplitude. Thus, activity in a certain area can be inferred by increased amounts of alpha wave "suppression". This means, rather confusingly, less alpha power across a particular area equates to an increase in activity in that area. Abnormal electroencephalographic (EEG) activity which occurs in brain damage and epilepsy may be identified as short bursts of electrical potential, asynchronies between both hemispheres and dysrythmias in the electrical signal. There are two main drawbacks when analyzing and interpreting alpha data. First, like electromyographic recordings (see chapter 4 for an account of this recording procedure) surface electrodes may be too peripheral to pick up some sub-cutaneous electrical activity and there are examples from at least one CT study of neurogenic stuttering, where site of lesion would have been missed without verification from more advanced single photon emission tomography analysis (Heuer, Sataloff, Mandel, & Travers, 1996). Second, around 10–15 percent of nonstuttering subjects can show abnormal alpha wave activity, particularly when hyperventilating and when subjected to strobe lighting. While we can confidently assume that stuttering subjects were not tested under photic stimulation, we cannot completely rule out the possibility that the less invasive surface electrodes used in the majority of studies mentioned below may have failed to identify subtle changes in alpha wave activity.

This method of examining cortical activity has, in fact, been in existence for a surprisingly long time, although early reports have produced equivocal results. Travis and Knott (1936) found no differences between adults who stuttered and their controls, while Lindsey (1940) found abnormal EEG in the occipital and parietal areas of their stuttering subjects prior to almost every stuttering moment. (See Van Riper, 1982, chapter 14 for an expanded account of early research on EEG.) In an interesting study, Luschsinger and Landolt (1951) found that while the EEGs of the people who stutter were essentially normal, a much greater percentage of the cluttering group had anomalous alpha wave activity; an imbalance which was corroborated in a number of papers subsequently. A more sophisticated version of the EEG procedure is quantitative electroencephalography (QEEG). The main difference to EEG lies in digital data acquisition and processing, and the fact that data can be collected from a greater number of electrode sites. This results in increased resolution of the signals in both frequency and amplitude domains.

The most substantial investigation into cortical anomalies in stuttering did not begin until the late 1970s, specifically through the influential work of the neurologist Walter Moore Jnr. Through a series of papers and reports, Moore and colleagues found systematic evidence that stuttering was associated with a suppression of alpha wave activity over the right temporal-parietal region, thus indicating increased right hemisphere activation in this area (McFarland & Moore, 1982; Moore, Craven, & Faber, 1982; Moore & Haynes, 1980; Moore & Lang, 1977; Moore & Lorendo, 1980). Moore and Haynes (1980, reported in Moore, 1984) concluded:

> Stuttering may emerge when both hemispheric processing of incoming information and motor programming of segmental linguistic units is in the right hemisphere (a non-segmental processor). These processing differences may be related to an inability, under certain circumstances, to handle the segmentation aspects of language. This may suggest the

importance of linguistic segmentation as it relates to motor programming in some stutterers.

(Moore & Haynes, 1980, p. 204)

Boberg, Yeudall, Schopflocher, and Bo-Lassen (1983) provided independent
evidence for this idea in a further alpha suppression study which found a shift
of alpha power from the right hemisphere (again over the right posterior
temporal-parietal region) to the left in those who had successfully completed
fluency treatment programs.

In one sense, these findings support Travis and Orton's theory, in that there
is imbalance of hemispheric functioning in stuttering, but they differ from
earlier reports in that stuttering is now specifically associated with unexpected elevated levels of right hemisphere activity. Also, in linking cerebral
imbalance to a breakdown in linguistic processing and motor programming,
Moore was providing an early neurolinguistic account of stuttering.

Although the research was regarded as sound methodologically, not everyone was convinced by Moore et al.'s interpretation of the data in terms of a
"segmentation disfunction hypothesis". Kent (1984) argued that both hemispheres process segmentally, but that they differ in their preferred temporal
ranges, the left hemisphere having a more narrow temporal resolution than
the right. He supported this model by pointing out that the occurrence of
increased disfluencies on low frequency words, at clause boundaries and
where voicing adjustments need to be made, indicate an increase in fluency
difficulties associated with linguistic variables not typically processed by the
right hemisphere.

Despite claims by some authorities (for example, Starkweather, 1987) that
linguistic processing factors are superfluous when considering brain functioning and stuttering, this is quite clearly not the case. Subsequent work by
Poole, Devous, Freeman, Watson, and Finitzo (1991) has further highlighted
cortical areas associated with language processing whilst Watson, Freeman,
Devons, Chapman, Finitzo, and Pool (1994) observed different language abilities between a subgroup of linguistically impaired people who stuttered and
nonimpaired group across a range of linguistic tasks which could be related
to anomalous cortical areas for language production (see Table 2.1).

Brain imaging studies

Functional neuroanatomy in stuttering

As already mentioned, findings from EEG studies have been regarded as
inconclusive because they have been limited by traditional visual analysis.
Subsequent to advances in nuclear medicine and information technology,
methodology in brain studies of stuttering has expanded and developed
vastly over the last ten years. Methods used now include: quantitative
electroencephalographic (QEEG) techniques (mentioned above); emission

computed tomography (ECT) and its variants – single photon emission computed tomography (SPECT) and positron emission tomography (PET). Functional magnetic resonance imaging (fMRI) has also been used in recent studies.

ECT is a process that detects radionuclides which either emit single photons (as in SPECT) or photons (as in PET). Both PET and SPECT images are built up by recording gamma rays emitted by a radiopharmaceutical agent. Images of the brain are then scanned from multiple directions to develop a cross-sectional image of the scanned area (see Chandra, 1987 for a full discussion of these methodologies). fMRI allows high resolution imaging of cortical and subcortical structures by tracking blood flow and cerebrospinal fluid movement. Unlike ECT, it does not require radiation for its use, so repeated scans are quite safe to undertake (see Moonen, van Zijl, Frank, Le Bihan, & Becker, 1990).

Findings

Table 2.1 shows some key findings from a number of important studies undertaken over the last few years. Generally, the picture we get is of a neural system in stuttering that can be distinguished from that which underlies normal speech, with areas known to be associated with motor speech and language production being found to show differences in levels of activity amongst those who stutter. Although there is no firm consensus as to a

Table 2.1 Selected studies of brain function and stuttering (1991–2005)

Investigators	Method	Task	Findings
Poole, Devous, Freeman, Watson, & Finitzo (1991)	QEEG, SPECT	At rest, only	1 Global reduction in absolute blood flow. 2 Relative blood flow asymmetries (right>left) found in the stuttering group (N = 20) in (a) anterior cingulate; (b) superior temporal; (c) inferior frontal; (d) middle temporal areas relative to the control group.
Ingham, Fox, & Ingham (1994)	PET RCBF	At rest, oral reading, choral reading	1 Stutterers showed increased activity in supplementary area (left>right) and superior lateral premotor cortex (right>left) under oral reading. 2 Almost no activity in these regions under choral condition.

cont.

Table 2.1 continued

Investigators	Method	Task	Findings
Watson, Freeman, Devous, Chapman, Finitzo, & Pool (1994)	RCBF	Discourse production, discourse comprehension, lexical ambiguity decision task	1 No difference in relative blood flow between nonstuttering group and linguistically normal stuttering group. 2 Significant difference (p<0.025) between nonstutterers and linguistically impaired stutterers in rCBF asymmetry (left<right) for both middle temporal and inferior temporal areas. 3 Linguistically impaired stutterers showed lower rCBF in left middle temporal area than linguistically normal group.
Wu et al. (1995)	PET	Oral reading, choral reading	1 Hypoactivity in Broca's area, Wernicke's area, superior frontal cortex and right cerebellum during oral reading. 2 Normal activity resumed under induced fluency task (choral reading). 3 Hyperactivity in substantia nigra and posterior cingulate during induced fluency.
Kroll, DeNil, Kapur, & Houle (1997)	PET	Passive viewing, silent reading, oral reading	1 Subjects (N = 5) who had completed a speak more fluently fluency program showed an absence of activation in the anterior cingulate area. 2 Increased left hemisphere activity following the program.
Ingham, Fox, Costello Ingham, & Zamparripa, (2000)	PET	4 r/handed adults who stuttered and 4 controls during real and imagined oral reading tasks	1 Some parietal regions were activated during imagined stuttering, but not during overt stuttering. 2 Activation in supplementary motor area, anterior insula (bilateral) and cerebellum (bilateral) during overt and imagined stuttering.

Fox, Ingham, Ingham, Zamarripa, Xiong, & Lancaster (2000)	PET blood flow	Oral reading amongst 10 right-handed adults who stuttered and 10 control speakers	1 Brain correlates of stuttering are the speech motor regions of the nondominant hemisphere right (primary motor cortex, supplementary area, inferior lateral premotor area (Broca's area), anterior insula) and nondominant (right cerebellar) hemisphere. 2 Cerebellum seems specifically involved in enabling the fluent utterances occurring in stuttered speech.
De Nil, Kroll, & Houle (2001)	PET	Pre- and post-treatment reading and verb generation tasks	1 Increased cerebellar activity immediately posttreatment – decrease to near normal levels at 1-year posttreatment. 2 During verb generation task resulted in a gradual decrease in cerebellar activity pre-treatment to 1-year post-treatment.
Sommer, Koch, Paulus, Weiller, & Büchel (2002)	Diffusion tensor imaging	15 adults who stuttered and 15 control subjects	Significant differences between experimental and control groups below the laryngeal and tongue representation in the left sensorimotor cortex.
Neumann et al. (2003)	fMRI	Oral reading amongst 9 mostly right-handed adults who stuttered and 16 control speakers. Pre and post therapy	1 Overactivation in precentral sensorimotor and frontal motor regions amongst those who stuttered. Pre therapy, there overactivations were almost exclusively right hemispheric, but more widespread in the left following therapy. 2 After 2-year follow-up period, the overactivations had partially shifted back to the right side. 3 Lower activation levels consistently reported for PWNS throughout the observation periods.

definitive area being implicated in stuttering, there is a growing body of evidence to suggest that the areas identified by Poole et al. (1991) may be of particular importance. Specifically, these are the anterior cingulate, associated with motor initiation; inferior frontal cortex, associated with motor programming; superior temporal and middle temporal areas, associated with language processing. One reasonably consistent finding is of increased activity in motor centres in the nondominant hemisphere. This trend must be taken in context of other studies which indicate a more generalized bilateralization of activity in speech centres (Ingham, Fox, Costello Ingham, & Zamparripa, 2000), but it still represents a strong effect. Of particular interest is that, while a number of studies implicate the anomalous cortical processing of motor speech activity, Ingham et al. (2000) found evidence that motor speech centres are affected even during imaginary stuttering. This, together with the additional finding that parietal regions were activated only during imaginary stuttering, and that subjects' neural activation normalized under fluency enhancing conditions, may be seen as providing an organic explanation in support of Johnson's anticipatory struggle hypothesis and Van Riper's use of preparatory sets (chapter 12) as a means of dealing with the motoric aspects of anticipatory struggle. However, Ingham et al.'s findings currently await corroboration from further research. There is now also preliminary evidence that the cerebellum which is known to be involved in the integration of motor activity does play a part in mediating timing relationships amongst the fluent utterances in stuttered speech. De Nil, Kroll, and Houle (2001) observed that a group of adults who stuttered showed elevated levels of cerebellar activity prior to an intensive fluency training course. Posttreatment, these levels increased further when measured during an oral reading task, but decreased to near normal limits, one year post therapy. Conversely, decreased activation post clinic was observed when the subjects were required to produce verbs post clinic, with further decreases seen at the one-year follow-up. Although confirmation of the exact role of the cerebellum in stuttering awaits the outcome of further investigations, these findings highlight the role that automaticity plays in speech production, and particularly the significance of this with regard to stuttering.

Anomalous anatomy of speech/language centres

There is tentative evidence from a number of earlier studies to indicate that in addition to findings of anomalous function across cortical speech and language centres, the brains of some people who stutter also differ anatomically, with asymmetries noted in the left and right temporal lobes (Benson & Geschwind, 1968; Wada, Clarke, & Hamm, 1975; Witelson & Pallie, 1973). These findings have been corroborated in a recent MRI study (Foundas, Bollich, Corey, Hurley, & Heilman, 2001) which examined the brains of 16 stutterers and 16 controls matched for age, sex, hand preference and education. The primary aim was to determine whether any anomalous neuroanatomy might place an individual at risk for developing stuttering. Frontal areas (pars triangularis and pars opercularis) and temporo-parietal areas (planum temporale and posterior ascending ramus) of both hemispheres were measured, and interhemispheric differences computed. Results showed that both left and right planum temporale were significantly larger for the stuttering group, and there was reduced planar asymmetry. Findings of a second diagonal sulcus and exra gyri along the superior bank of the sylvian fossa were found to be unique to the group who stuttered, and this group was also found to have a greater number of gyral variants. The finding of anatomic subgroups relating to handedness and gender give at least preliminary encouragement to the notion of a possible link between speech fluency and specification of any stuttering subtype. The authors conclude:

> These results provide strong evidence that adults with PDS . . . [persistent developmental stuttering] . . . have anomalous anatomy in perisylvian speech and language areas. No one anatomic feature distinguished the groups, but multiple loci within a widely distributed neural network differed between the groups. These results provide the first evidence that anatomic anomalies within perisylvian speech-language areas may put an individual at risk for the development of stuttering.
>
> (Foundas et al., 2001, p. 207)

These findings certainly appear to provide evidence for an association between anomalous cortical structures and adult stuttering, but it is not very clear as to how the leap from such an identification to association of these differences as "at risk" factors is made. That link really awaits the identification of anomalous perisylvian anatomy in nonstuttering children, who then go on to develop a chronic stutter. There is also preliminary evidence from another study (Sommer, Koch, Paulus, Weiller, & Büchel, 2002) that stuttering is associated with white matter disconnection of motor and premotor areas (left precentral cortex, temporal and frontal language regions respectively). They contend that the finding of right hemisphere overactivation reflects a compensatory mechanism, similar to right hemisphere activation seen in aphasia. Jänke, Hänggi, and Steinmetz (2004) further found that their group of 11 adults who stuttered showed anomolous anatomy in the precentral gyrus perisylvian speech and language centres and also in prefrontal and sensorimotor areas. Increased volume was recorded by MRI in the planum temporale, precentral gryrus, and inferior frontal gyrus. The investigators also noted abnormal structures in areas which implicate auditory processing (see chapter 3).

The findings observed above seem consistent with Neumann et al's (2003) summations of the pathophysiological evidence. Here they suggest that various steps in speech production might be affected in stuttering by a breakdown of neuronal connection between premotor, auditory and speech motor areas, specifically implicating: (a) temporal lobe activation during speech; (b) left interior frontal cortex (affecting articulatory programming) and left premotor and motor cortices (motor preparation); (c) disconnection of white matter between the left precentral cortex (premotor region) and temporal and frontal language areas (motor region).

Brain imaging of young children

Until recently, brain imaging of younger children has not been possible, yet an understanding of the neurological correlates of stuttering at its outset will be crucial to our understanding of the aetiology of the disorder, and the nature of the development of persistent developmental stuttering. There is now, however, greater cause for optimism with the development of near infrared spectroscopy (NIRS; Watanabe et al., 1996; Yamashita, Maki, & Koizumi, 1996). The details of this procedure are beyond the scope of this book, but briefly, the technique involves the tracking of haemoglobin levels by near infrared (optical) lasers. Incident and detection optical probes, all mounted on a single plastic base which is worn by the subject much as a lightweight cap, are then linked via flexible optical fibres to a data acquisition centre. Recordings are made by having the near infrared light penetrate the brain tissue from incident probes, returning through the detection probes. Because all the probes are mounted on a single plastic base, this means setup time is reduced, and that the technique can be applied quickly and to those who might struggle to tolerate more invasive and time-consuming procedures. A recent study has verified the reliability of this procedure with another (magnetoencephalography) imaging technique. Consistent with many data already presented, NIRS confirmed a lack of cerebral dominance amongst a small group of adult males who stuttered (Mori, Sato, Ozama, & Imaizumi, 2004).

Some provisos

Studies of brain function all suffer from the same problem – a lack of subjects. This needs to be remembered particularly when making assertions about subgroups of stutterers. Of the subjects that have been used, the majority have been adult right-handed males, which further limits interpretation. In fact, similar difficulties of interpretation can be seen in a number of studies across the spectrum of stuttering research. To take one example, an electromyographic study found abnormal intrinsic laryngeal muscle activity amongst a small group of adults who stuttered (see chapter 4). One commentator queried whether this finding meant that stuttering was, in part, due to this abnormal muscle activity, or whether the anomalous movement had arisen because the development of the stutter had given rise to chronic abnormal use of the larynx, which then resulted in the anomalous movement. Similarly, we still know very little about CNS activity in children who stutter, and consequently about whether any anomalous activity seen in adults represents a predisposing neural deficit in language processing or a reflection of a brain, which is functioning in a different way, subsequent to many years of stuttering. In other words, we cannot yet say whether hemispheric anomalies really underlie stuttering, or whether they are merely neural representations of the establishment of the disorder. Accordingly, for the moment at least, the language of the link between cortical anomaly and stuttering has to be one of association. Causation has yet to be verified.

CNS and motor speech control

The study of stuttering from a motor speech control perspective is covered in depth elsewhere, but we mention here two recent models of stuttering which directly relate to current models of CNS processing and which both offer arguments as to how theory can be related to clinical practice. Subcortical structures may also be implicated. Alm (2004b) in a review of literature discusses the role of the basal ganglia on fluency, drawing comparisons between the disfluencies of stuttering, and those experienced by those with recognized disorders of the basal ganglia circuits, such as Parkinsonism. In Alm's view, stuttering largely results from an impaired ability of the basal ganglia to produce timing cues necessary for the upcoming motor segments. We return to consider the involvement of the basal ganglia in stuttering and motor control below, but first consider a cortical model of stuttering and motor control (also see Further Reading p. 44).

Webster's two-factor model

One interpretation of impaired CNS control of motor speech has been forwarded by Webster and colleagues in what they call a two-factor model. Here they argue that stuttering is related to a left hemisphere lateralization of neural mechanisms for speech which is similar to that of normal speech, but a left hemisphere system for speech and motor sequencing which is weak (factor 1) and therefore susceptible to interference from other ongoing neural activities, particularly from the right hemisphere (factor 2). (See Figure 2.1.)

The evidence comes in part from research indicating that people who stutter have difficulty in motor control outside the speech domain, particularly in the planning and initiation of new sequences and bimanual coordination (Forster & Webster, 1991, 2001; Webster, 1990). These difficulties implicate the supplementary motor area (SMA), an area situated just above and related to the cingulate cortex, which in turn has been associated with motor speech initiation. Accordingly, Webster (1997) argues that successful treatment must deal with both "factors". First, sources of interference to speech motor control mechanisms need to be removed. Interference can take the form of right hemisphere activated activity, including fear, avoidance, anxiety and other negative emotions, and as these decrease with successful therapy, so there is less interference on the left hemisphere SMA. Dealing with the other factor (the fragility of the left hemisphere system) is achieved by using fluency skills such as such as smooth onsets and controlled airflow (see chapter 12). This,

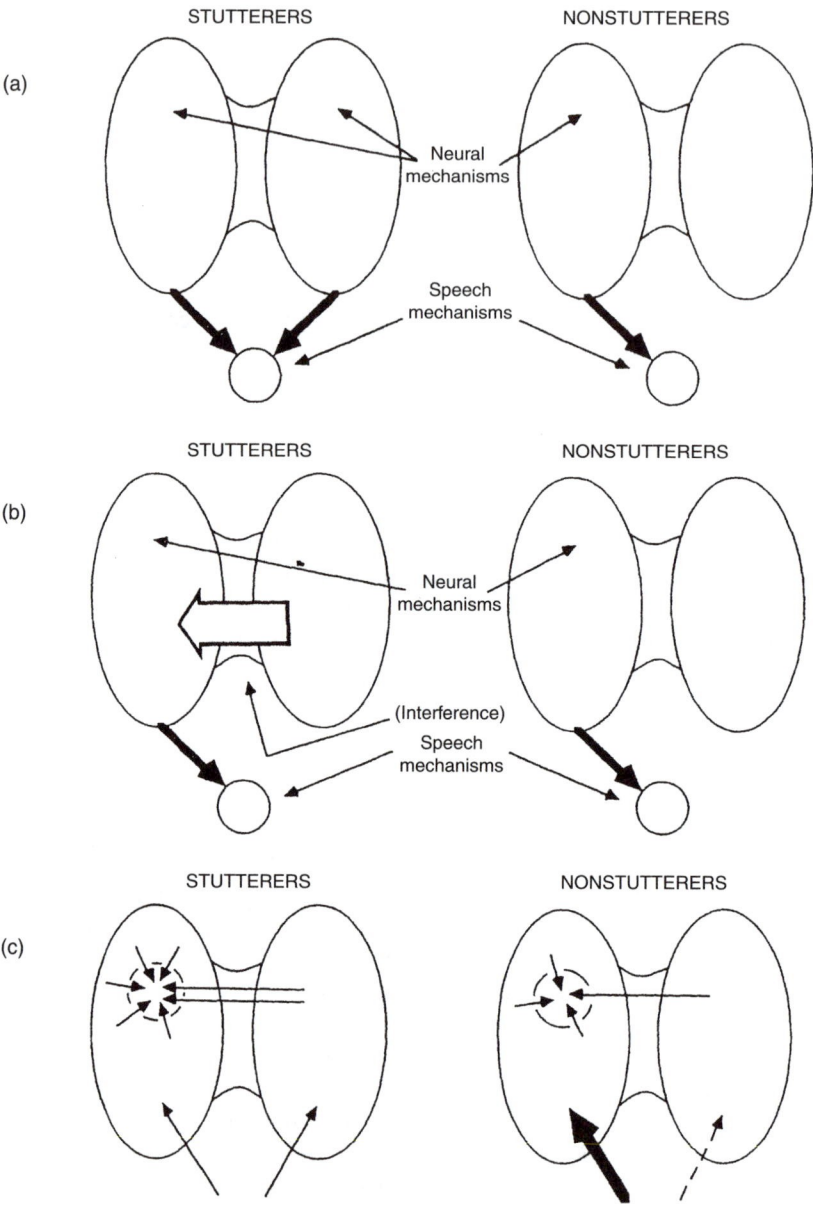

Figure 2.1 Schematic illustration of three models of hemispheric interaction and stuttering: (a) Orton Travis model. Here we see bilateral hemispheric representation of speech, language and fine motor control for stuttering; (b) Interference model. Here stuttering is associated with an overflow of activity from the right to the left hemisphere; (c) Webster's two-factor model (after Webster, 1997). Left hemisphere motor speech control areas are more "porous" and susceptible to other inter-hemisphere and intra-hemisphere brain activity.

Webster believes, simplifies speech and brings it within the capability of the fragile speech motor system.

Goldberg's model

An alternative explanation of CNS anomalies as defective motor control has been proposed by Goldberg (1985), and later developed by Wu and colleagues. This is based on a model of motor control that still underpins the thinking of many concerned with relating neurological functioning to linguistic processing (Goldberg, 1985).

Briefly, in Goldberg's conceptualization there are two premotor systems operating simultaneously (see Figure 2.2). The lateral system consists of the classical cortical areas associated with speech and language processing (including, amongst many others, Broca's area and Wernicke's area). This system is thought to be responsible for conscious but more automatic speech functions such as nonpropositional speech, repetitive and overlearned speech, and such like. It responds online to external stimuli and conditions using feedback information. This system can produce closed loop motor control. This allows the examination and tuning of fine motor activity in a conscious and deliberate manner. We use this system when we are very aware of our motor speech activity (as would be the case when learning fluency shaping approaches to therapy as well as in the examples above).

This is in contrast with the medial system which acts as a control centre for propositional and extended speech. This system would be active when giving a detailed response to a complicated question. It includes subcortical struc-tures such as the striatum, caudate and putamen. The system also has con-nections to the cingulate cortex, The medial system works on a feed forward (or predictive control) basis, based on stored stereotypic actions. Unlike the lateral system, it does not need to wait for feedback, and so it can function more quickly and rapid movements can be produced with little attention. The disadvantage is that because of the lack of sensory feedback, any stuttering may continue, rather than an attempt to correct disfluencies. It is argued that speech motor commands originate at this level, and that these commands eventually control muscle movement sequencing that produces fluent or stuttered speech. To Goldberg's model, Riley, Wu, and Maguire (1997) add a third factor they call a "dopamine 2" (D2) system, which affects the striatum and areas affecting speech motor planning.

Dopamine-based disorders are already likely to be familiar to many speech and language therapy students, particularly with regard to Parkinson's dis-ease (PD) and Tourette's syndrome. Dopamine production occurs in the substantia nigra but its processing influences activity in a number of centres, including the striatum. Riley et al. hypothesize that with stuttering excessive dopamine reaches the striatum and other speech motor planning centres (Wu et al., 1997). This reduces their activation and consequently their effectiveness. So, while speech motor activity (and motor activity generally) in Parkinson's disease is compromised due to decreased dopamine levels, speech motor activity in stuttering is related to increased dopamine levels (see Figure 2.2).

As with Webster's two-factor theory, there are therapeutic implications. Top-down treatments, or those which adopt a cognitive approach such as many stutter-more-fluently approaches, will increase activation in the lateral system. Remembering that both systems operate in parallel, such improvement in the system could then indirectly influence the medial system. A bottom-up or more "motoric" approach to therapy, as seen in fluency shaping programs, would lead to an improved medial system. There is also, potentially the option of drug therapy, specifically D2 antagonist therapy (see section below and chapter 14), and use of auditory masking (also chapter 14), both of which would operate with the medial system. As the authors point out, undertaking a given treatment and then testing to see if changes predicted in the model are confirmed, could help establish or develop the D2 model. We return to therapeutic implications in part 2.

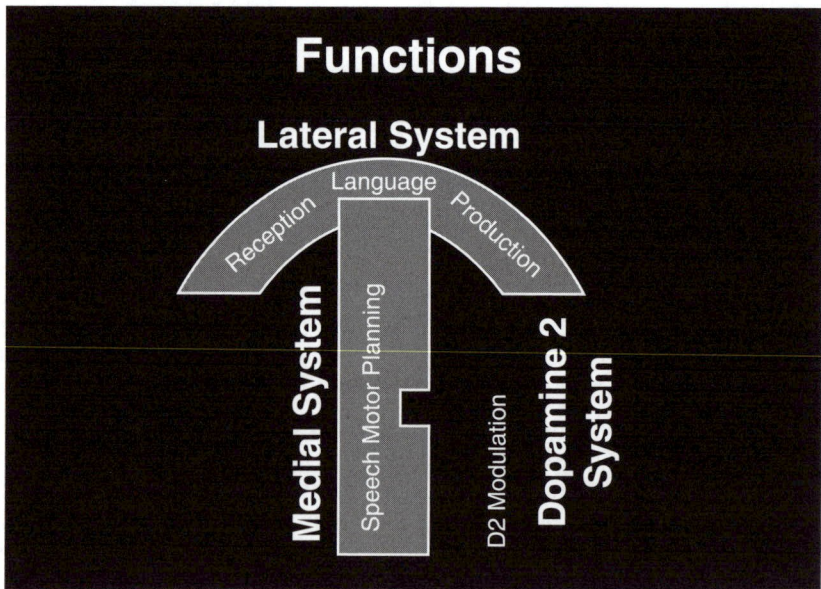

Figure 2.2 Schematic representation of the interaction of the D2 system with speech motor planning function of the medial system (after Wu, Maguire, Riley, Lee, Keator, Tang, et al., 1997. Reprinted with permission).

Stuttering and metabolism

Extrapyramidal function and the role of dopamine

Although there are a number of reports on the use of dopamine in stuttering therapy (see chapter 14), a research study monitoring the effects of therapy on dopamine uptake as suggested by Riley et al. (1997) has yet to be undertaken. There are, however, a number of studies independent of the motor speech model proposed by Wu et al. (1997) that support the idea of stuttering being associated with increased dopamine levels. Because dopamine is produced in structures located in the extrapyramidal system, some researchers are particularly interested in the link between stuttering and other extrapyramidal disorders such as Parkinson's disease and Tourette's syndrome. The idea that stuttering could be associated with altered metabolism and dopamine uptake levels could provide an explanation as to why severity of stuttering varies, for some, in an apparently unpredictable manner. Metabolism is affected by a range of factors, diet being one. It is possible, then, that the fluctuating dopamine levels could interact with other variables such as fear, anxiety, tiredness, which are more easily observable, providing a potential answer to one of the most frustrating and awkward features of stuttering – that of inconsistency of severity. Parkinson's sufferers, like those who stutter, experience fluctuations in ability to control motor control. They both have good days, and bad days.

There is some measure of support for the dopamine hypothesis. Maguire, Gottschalk, Riley, Franklin, and Potkin (1998) observed that the frequency of stuttering decreased by 54 percent across their four subjects. The authors interpreted these findings as evidence for a decreased striatal metabolism amongst people who stutter, and the ability of risperidone (a D2 antagonist) to increase striatal metabolism. Relatedly there is tentative evidence that risperidone can be effective in improving fluency amongst some people who stutter (see chapter 14). Maguire et al. (1998) also draw on some similarities between stuttering and Tourette's syndrome. Both develop in childhood, fluctuate in severity, show similar male to female ratios and have similar hypofunctioning metabolism of the striatum. There is also the claim that both are worsened by stimulants, although there is now equivocal data on this subject with regard to stuttering (see below and chapter 14). A possible link between stuttering and Tourette's syndrome has also been argued by Abwender, Trinidad, Jones, Como, Hymes, and Kurlan (1998). In this study, the subjects were found to demonstrate motor tics and symptoms of obsessive compulsive behaviour at similar rates to those seen in people with Tourette's syndrome. Conversely, while it is often stated that disfluency is a common feature in Tourette's (estimates of incidence vary between 15 percent and 31 percent), there is equivocal evidence as to whether these disfluencies are similar to those seen in stuttering. Van Borsel, Goethals, and Vanryckeghem (2003) found that the greater majority of the disfluencies in their Tourette's speakers could be described as normal disfluencies rather than stuttering, with 70 percent of disfluencies made up of supralexical errors (phrase repetitions, incomplete phrases and interjections). As in a previous study (Van Borsel & Vanryckeghem, 2000) some disfluency seemed more consistent with cluttering, and some consistent with palilalia. A later study (Maguire et al., 1999) showed that ten adult stutterers improved on a measure of severity, but not percentage of time spent stuttering following a six-week period of risperidone (a D2 antagonist) treatment. This finding was in contrast to a control group of stutterers whose fluency remained unchanged during the six-week administration of a placebo. However, a study by Lee, Lee, Kim, Lee, Suh, and Kwak (2001) has failed to support the D2 antagonist model, Lee et al. (2001) found the fluency of their adult stutterers to be adversely affected by risperidone. In addition, Goberman and Blomgren (2003) found similar levels of fluency amongst a group of nine patients with Parkinson's disease either when they were in low dopamine states or high dopamine states, although there was a significant difference between the levels of disfluency of the Parkinson's group and a matched group of control subjects. Goberman and Blomgren (2003) hypothesize, therefore, that speech disfluency may result from either increases or decreases in dopamine levels.

Staying for the moment with the notion that stuttering is associated with elevated dopamine levels, we might predict that levodopa (L-Dopa) therapy, which elevates depressed dopamine levels for PD sufferers, might exacerbate stuttering behaviour. There is some support for this notion. Louis, Winfield, Fahn, and Ford (2001) report findings from two patients diagnosed with PD whose disfluency was exacerbated by levodopa therapy, whilst Ward and Wardman (2005) reported the case of a man diagnosed with PD who developed a severe stutter following administration of a D2 antagonist. Similarly, Anderson, Hughes, Rothi, Crucian, and Heilman (1999) found the fluency of a 44-year-old subject who had a developmental stutter and later developed PD to be related to periods of levodopa medication. During periods of levodopa administration, stuttering increased, and when the medication was withdrawn, stuttering decreased. Against this evidence, Leder (1996) reported a case study of a 29-year-old man whose sudden adult onset of stuttering was initially diagnosed as psychogenic. Despite very severe primary stuttering, including multiple blocks and up to 20 repetitions per word, no secondary symptoms whatsoever were found. Subsequent neurological investigations revealed a number of motoric anomalies, all of which were progressive in nature, and eventually a diagnosis of Parkinson-like syndrome was made. Carbidopa-levodopa resulted in considerable improvement in motor and sensory abilities, including speech fluency. Similarly, Goberman and Blomgren (2003) found no differences in levels of stuttering during periods when dopamine levels were either high and low amongst a group of nine PD clients.

A rather different link between Parkinson's disease and stuttering was noted by Shahed and Jankovic (2001). These researchers provided an interesting account of 12 persons with developmental stuttering whose stutters were resolved in childhood but then reappeared subsequent to the onset of Parkinson's in later life. A consistent finding was that higher Unified Parkinson's Disease Rating Scale scores correlated with more severe stuttering, but severity of premorbid stuttering was not associated with severity of the Parkinson's. The conclusion was that "stuttering may emerge in adulthood with the onset of PD" (p. 114) but the association between the childhood stutter and the PD activated stutter is not clear. That is, it is difficult to say with certainty that it was the childhood stutter rather than disfluency with a neurogenic aetiology that appeared alongside the Parkinson's disease.

Finally, here (as ever) a word of caution: as with brain imaging studies, subject numbers have been small and we must be cautious with our interpretation of all of these studies. Because there are as yet no well-controlled studies with large subject numbers, we cannot predict with real confidence the consistency of the effects of drugs on the heterogeneous population of people who stutter.

Drugs and stuttering

The use of drug therapy in stuttering is becoming one of the biggest issues in stuttering therapy, with increasing numbers of people looking for pharmaceutical answers to control their disfluencies. As stuttering can be contingent on both psychological and organic variables, it would make sense that the disorder could respond both positively and negatively to a variety of drug treatment that acts on both of these variables. Chapter 14 reviews some of the literature on various drug treatments. For the present we focus briefly on drugs which are likely to increase stuttering.

There are a number of drugs that can induce stuttering. In 1998 the *Journal of Psychopharmacology* published a review of the world's medical literature, detailing 22 such cases, with a further two found by the French journal *Prescrire International*. Antidepressants of a number of families were directly linked with stuttering, as were antiepileptics, antipsychotics, mood stabilizers and tranquillizers. In all of the 24 cases, the link between the drug and stuttering was confirmed by the cessation of the stuttering upon withdrawal of the drug (Table 2.2).

Many of these drugs are commonly prescribed by general practitioners, but it is unclear as to what the interaction of these drugs with fluency tell us about CNS functioning in people who stutter, and there are many contradictions. For example, one early study (Guillaume, Mazars, & Mazars, 1957) found anticonvulsants to significantly reduce stuttering in two of their three epileptic subjects, whilst more recently Supprian, Retz, and Deckert (1999) observed epileptic brain activity alongside stuttering subsequent to the administration of clozapine. Confusingly, there are a number of anecdotal reports emanating from the worldwide web, as well as from clinical practice, which confirm that a number of the drugs listed above have led to reduced

Table 2.2 A summary of findings reported in *Journal of Psychopharmacology and Prescrire International* (1998)

Type	Group	Drug and commercial name
Antidepressant	Selective serotonin re-uptake inhibitor (SSRI) family	fluoxetine (Prozac) and sertraline (Zoloft)
Antidepressant	Monoamine oxidase inhibitor (MAOI) family	isocarboxazid (Marplan) and phenelzine (Nardil)
Antiepileptic		abapentin(Neurotonin) and phenytoin (Dilantin)
Antipsychotic groups	Phenothiazine family	chlorpromazine, fluphenazine trifluoperazine and triflupromazine
Mood stabilizers		gabapentin (Neurotonin) lithium (Lithobid, Lithonate)
Tranquillizers	Benzodiazepine family	chlordiazepoxide (Librium) diazepam (Valium), alprazolam (Xanax), temazipam (Restoril)
Other		methylphenidate (Ritalin), theophylline (Slo-Bid, Theo-Dur)

stuttering amongst some people who stutter. These include the benzodiazepine tranquillizers and antidepressants such as Prozac as well as beta blockers such as propranolol (see chapter 14). Even nonprescription drugs such as caffeine, alcohol and nicotine can have completely opposing effects. Of course, most reports lack scientific rigour and need to be considered with caution, but despite this it is clear that responses to drug regimes are very individualistic. In a review of literature on the subject, Brady (1998) asserts that multiple interacting neurotransmitters appear to be involved, and it is these complex interrelationships which may give rise to the variability in impact on fluency. It also seems likely that given the heterogeneous factors involved in stuttering, we are unlikely to find out what variables underlie these apparently individualistic responses until controlled studies are undertaken on a large number of subjects.

Summary

The CNS provides the starting point of processing chains which underpin all aspects of communication, including auditory, motor speech, language and psychological variables. If stuttering is a disorder which affects the function of all of these variables, then the significance of CNS investigations becomes clear. We spend time across a number of chapters in this book discussing the implications of a range of factors involved in the communicative process as it relates to this complex disorder but, as we try to make clear throughout, it is equally important to consider the interrelationships between these subcomponents. None exist in isolation. All have their source in the CNS. Kent (2000) draws the following conclusions from the available data on brain studies:

> First, stuttering can arise from a variety of neurologic disturbances and is not necessarily related to any one structure or neural pathway. Second, stuttering is particularly associated with anomalies in hemispheric asymmetry. Third, stuttering reflects damage to the extrapyramidal motor pathway, especially the basal nuclei, thalamus, or thalamocortical connections.
>
> (Kent, 2000, p. 408)

This book identifies important links between genetic, linguistic and psychological components and stuttering. As we understand more about the neurology of the disorder we will be better placed: (a) more fully to understand the cognitive origins of these fields; (b) to better ascertain how subcomponents within these areas interact with each other; (c) to know how they implicate other areas.

Key points

- From Orton (1927) through to Neumann et al. (2003) there is mounting evidence to suggest that the processing of linguistic information, both for perception and production, differs between those who stutter and their nonstuttering peers. At a cortical level, this presents as increased right hemisphere activation amongst speech, language and auditory processing centres. Subcortically, the striatum appears to be implicated, as does dopamine supply to this and other subcortical structures. Authorities disagree as to the exact processes by which these areas implicate motor speech and language production.
- Many hemispheric anomalies appear linked specifically to the speech act. Studies show more normal brain function under conditions where speech fluency is controlled, for example, following speak-more-fluently type programs. It is not yet clear whether anomalous function is related merely to stuttering, or to any type of disfluency, which may or may not be stuttering. However, Ingham

et al.'s (2000) finding of hemispheric anomalies associated with the anticipation of stuttering suggests that these effects are specific to stuttering. Findings from this study support a neurological explanation of anticipatory struggle and the therapeutic strategy of preparatory set.

- Small subject numbers mean cautious interpretation of all brain function data.
- Webster's interference hypothesis and Wu et al.'s D2 model provide alternative descriptions as to how CNS function could impact on motor speech processing. Although the models offer different explanations of neuromotor processing, both provide justifications for clinical usage of both cognitive and motoric therapeutic strategies.
- The few preliminary reports available show that a diversity of drugs can induce stuttering, including some which may improve fluency. As well as a range of prescription drugs, inconsistency of effect can be seen in responses to alcohol and caffeine.

Further reading

Alm, P. A. (2005). On the causal mechanisms of stuttering. PhD thesis, University of Lund, Sweden.
This volume comprises a collection of recent papers by this author which more fully outlines his perspective on the role of subcortical influences in stuttering.

Brady, J. P. (1998). Drug induced stuttering: A review of the literature. *Journal of Clinical Psychopharmacology*, 18, 50–54.
There is rather little in the way of in-depth analysis of the effects of drugs on stuttering, but this short article offers a useful precis of the literature up to 1998.

De Nil, L. (2004). Recent developments in brain imaging research in stuttering. In B. Maassen, R. D. Kent, H. F. M. Peters, P. H. H. M. van Lieshout, & W. Hulstijn (Eds.), *Speech motor control in normal and disordered speech* (pp. 113–138). Oxford: Oxford University Press.
This chapter provides a very thorough account of the impact of brain imaging on stuttering research. Both procedural matters and findings are covered comprehensively.

Goldberg, G. (1985). Supplemenatry motor area structure and function: Review and hypothesis. *Behavioral and Brain Sciences*, 8, 567–616.
A lengthy but detailed review of the role of the supplementary motor area. A useful read for those wishing to know more about Goldberg's theory of motor control.

Journal of Fluency Disorders (various authors). (2003). Special issue: Brain imaging and stuttering, 28, 4.
An entire edition of *Journal of Fluency Disorders* comprising seven articles, theoretical and experimental, by experts in the field.

Love, G., & Webb, W. (1996). *Neurology for the speech language pathologist*. London: Heinemann Butterworth.

A clearly written and presented introduction to neurology for speech and language. There is no particular focus on the neurology of stuttering, but this is nonetheless a useful resource for those who lack a basic understanding of this field.

Moore, W. H., Jr. (1984). Central nervous system characteristics of stutterers. In R. F. Curlee & W. H. Perkins (Eds.), *Nature and treatment of stuttering: New directions* (pp. 49–72). San Diego, CA: College Hill Press.

Moore is still an influential force with regard to hemispheric functioning and stuttering. This chapter provides an interesting background to earlier brain studies and a particularly useful discussion of Moore's segmentation disfunction hypothesis.

3 Stuttering and auditory processing

Introduction

It is a matter of interest, and potentially considerable clinical significance, that the only population with a reduced prevalence of stuttering is the hearing impaired. Relatedly, one of the most widely researched areas of stuttering in the latter half of the twentieth century has been the relationship between stuttering and auditory processing, and attempting to discover processing differences between those who stutter and those who do not. Findings have led some researchers to argue that stuttering may be related to perceptual, in addition to production, elements. In this chapter we discuss a number of different perspectives on the subject and consider the possibility that stuttering is a disorder of perception rather than production. We have already seen in chapter 2 that stuttering has been associated with differences in hemispheric processing of speech and language, and we will consider the evidence that there are functional neurological differences amongst those who stutter relating to the processing of auditory information.

Stuttering and the hearing impaired

There is evidence dating back almost a century that stuttering is less prevalent among the deaf and hearing impaired than in the general population (e.g., Bleumel, 1913). Backus (1938) found that out of nearly 14,000 deaf or hearing impaired people contacted through schools of the deaf, only 55 or 0.4 percent stuttered. Harms and Malone (1939) found that only 42 out of 14,458 hearing impaired people also stuttered, which represents 0.29 percent of that population, and is significantly lower than the generally quoted prevalence figures of around 1 percent amongst the general population. However, not all studies have supported these findings (Brown, Sambrooks, & MacCulloch, 1975; Gregory, 1964), whilst Ingham (1984) speculated that the figures reported by Harms and Malone could relate to the very high incidence of childhood diseases prevalent at the time of their study.

Where a decreased prevalence of stuttering among the deaf has been found, a number of theories have been argued to account for the findings. Webster and Lubker (1968) believed that the blocking of air conduction was responsible, much in the way that masking of air conducted feedback through white noise has been found to produce similar effects amongst some people who stutter (a phenomenon we will come to below). Some believed, on the other hand, that the hearing impaired modified their speech in much the same way that some people who stutter do in attempts to reduce disfluencies (Wingate, 1970, 1976). This results in a slower rate of speech and extended phonation, both of which have been associated with the type of speech that results from delaying the speaker's auditory feedback (see below). Both slower speech and extended phonation are commonly used as therapeutic strategies in fluency shaping approaches to stuttering (see chapters 11 and 12).

Stuttering and altered auditory feedback

One enduring area of investigation into the auditory processing capabilities of people who stutter has been in the field of altered auditory feedback (AAF), and the influence of such studies has been considerable both theoretically and therapeutically. We discuss therapeutic aspects of altered feedback in chapter 14, but here focus more on the impact altered feedback has made from an aetiological perspective. There are a number of ways in which fluency can be improved by altering the way in which the speaker hears his speech signal. We can discuss these in turn.

Choral and unison speech

Choral or unison speech occurs when a person who stutters either reads aloud or speaks spontaneously in time with a model speaker (or speakers). The fluency enhancing effect of this can be dramatic, in many cases bringing about immediate and normal sounding fluency. In this form, the phenomenon has limited use therapeutically because there is almost no carryover of the effect once the accompanying speaker fades their voice out, but it can be very effective when allied to technology that allows one to hear one's own speech output at a different pitch, thus mimicking the choral speech effect or with delayed feedback.

A variety of early explanations have been launched to explain the effect of choral speech, including distraction (Barber, 1940), reduced meaningfulness (Eisenson & Wells, 1942), slower rate and increased loudness (Wingate, 1969, 1976). Lee (1951) argued that the normal speech signal given by the model speaker could help the person who stutters organize the motor plan for the upcoming word, yet it may not be the speech signal per se that is the significant factor. Kalinowski, Stuart, Rastatter, Snyder, and Dayalu (2000) found that subjects who watched a model speaker silently mouth a text in unison alongside them brought about an 80 percent increase in fluency, in the absence of any auditory stimulus itself. The implication of this finding is that a visual linguistic cue is sufficient to stimulate the auditory cortex. An alternative notion posits that the model speaker, rather than providing a non-distorted motor template for the person who stutters to match, instead provides a pacing or rhythmic one (Johnson & Rosen, 1937); a perspective that would appear consistent with Kalinowski et al's findings. It is worth noting that all of those mentioned above have also been levelled at the fluency enhancing properties of delayed auditory feedback (DAF), which we discuss below. (The relationship between choral speech and DAF is an important one, and we return to this with regard to therapy in chapter 14.)

Shadowed speech

This is a type of cued speech which is very closely related to choral and unison versions. Technically, shadowed speech occurs where there is a slight delay between the speech of the model speaker and the person who stutters, as opposed to the simultaneous output produced during unison and choral speech. The difference is that while with choral speech the speaker knows exactly what the model speaker is going to say, shadowed speech can be used to follow the novel speech of the model speaker. Like choral/unison speech, shadowing can produce dramatic results (Cherry & Sayers, 1956; Kelham & McHale, 1966), but like them the gains in fluency tend to be lost once the stimulus of the model speaker has ended. Because of this, the use of choral or shadowed speech is now rare, and usually confined only to moments in therapy or assessment, where it is considered important to have the client experience a moment of fluency, albeit in the knowledge that this method of producing it will not provide any basis for sustainable improvement. What is interesting from our present perspective, however, is the potential relationship between shadowed speech and delayed auditory feedback. As we will see in chapter 16, the fluency enhancing effect of shadowed and choral speech has been put to use in devices which use DAF and frequency auditory feedback (FAF) to approximate the effects of speaking alongside other speakers.

Delayed auditory feedback

It is now over 40 years since Goldiamond and colleagues first stumbled on the potential fluency enhancing effects of delayed auditory feedback (Flanagan, Goldiamond, & Azrin, 1958, 1959; Goldiamond, 1965). Findings from the earliest experiments centred around the vicarious discovery that some people who stuttered experienced improved fluency when they put on headphones and heard their speech played back to them with a slight time delay. (Some readers may already have experienced DAF as an echo effect when speaking on a poor transcontinental telephone line.) Commonly, DAF also results in reduced fluency in nonstuttering speakers (Fukawa, Yoshioka, Ozawa, & Yoshida, 1988; Stuart, Kalinowski, Rastatter, & Lynch, 2002), although

Fukawa et al. observed that people who stutter were significantly more likely to be affected by DAF than nonstutterers, and that male nonstutterers were more susceptible to the effect than females. Most noticeably, Goldiamond (1965) found a tendency for speakers to slow their rate of speech in an effort to counteract the disruptive influences of the delayed feedback. Particularly, at around 250 ms delay[1] (0.25 of a second) a prolonged speech pattern was produced, where vowels became disproportionately more stretched than consonants. The further finding that the extent of the prolonged speech could be controlled by altering the delay times lead to the development of a number of "prolonged speech" programs which used DAF in a systematic way to elicit fluent speech. (See chapter 12 as to how prolonged speech programs have developed.) During the early stages of therapy, DAF was set to encourage excessive prolongation, usually around 250 ms. When clients were able to demonstrate 100 percent fluency in their speech at this delay setting, the next stepwise decrease in DAF (usually in 50 ms increments) was introduced to encourage a slightly faster rate of speech. Again, the client learned to control fluency using decreased prolongation associated with the reduced DAF. The procedure was then repeated at incrementally reduced delay levels, with clients having to demonstrate completely fluent speech at each one before progressing to the next decreased DAF setting. Eventually, the client reached the point where he was able to maintain fluency without any delay in auditory feedback (e.g., Curlee & Perkins, 1969, 1973). At this time it was thought that the fluency enhancing effects of DAF could be explained simply as by-products of the slower rate speech that it produced. During the mid-1970s and through the 1980s there was a lull in DAF research as clinicians looked to alternative ways of slowing speech for therapy. It was not until the early 1990s when a resurgence of interest occurred, largely driven by findings that increased fluency could indeed result under DAF at normal and even fast rates of speech (e.g., Stuart & Kalinowski, 1996). This finding has led to a new generation of clinicians and researchers becoming interested in DAF as a treatment option for stuttering. We examine the more recent applications in relation to therapy elsewhere (see chapter 14).

Aside from the therapeutic implications, the early findings that DAF could enhance fluency for at least some people who stutter led to a number of theories of stuttering, based on the assumption that timing perception is disturbed.

Masking

Another consistent finding is that people who stutter become more fluent when their own auditory feedback, presented through headphones, is masked by external sound, although this effect only becomes significant if the sound

---

1 Subsequent findings as to the optimal time delay settings have varied widely (see chapter 14).

level of the masking noise is sufficient to block out the speaker's speech signal. Maraist and Hutton (1957) found their 15 subjects who stuttered consistently increased their fluency as the loudness of the masking noise was increased, and there is corroborating evidence from Burke (1969) and Murray (1969) for these findings. Cherry and Sayers (1956) in a series of seminal experiments manipulating auditory feedback found a strong fluency enhancing effect when a pure tone was presented at a level near the threshold of pain. A key finding was that stuttering decreased significantly when the subjects only heard lower frequencies (below 500 Hz) as opposed to only hearing higher frequency sounds (above 500 Hz). This, Cherry and Sayers argued, demonstrated the differential role of bone conduction, which more effectively transmits lower frequency sounds, and air conduction which was assumed to be associated with a broader range of frequencies. In fact, Cherry and Sayers' findings of differential effects in stuttering reduction as dependent on the frequency ranges (high or low) of the masking noise have not been verified in subsequent experiments (Barr & Carmel, 1968; Conture 1974). Nonetheless, the masking effect itself seems to be a consistent one and like DAF and more recently FAF it has found use as a commercially available fluency aid, most notably through the production of the Edinburgh masker, marketed in the 1970s and 1980s (see chapter 14).

Despite the general agreement that masking auditory feedback can be an effective way of reducing moments of stuttering, opinions as to what forces are responsible for the effect differ widely. Some saw the early findings, particularly those of Cherry and Sayers, as evidence for an auditory-perception theory of the disorder. However, findings from a number of early studies have suggested that increased fluency could be attributed to reparameterization of vocal strategies under masking, rather than to factors directly relating to auditory processing. For example (like DAF) masked speech was found to be associated with slower speech rates and slower syllable durations (Hanley & Steer, 1949; Ringel & Steer, 1963), greater vocal intensity (Atkinson, 1952; Garber, Siegel, Pick, & Alcorn, 1976), and increased fundamental frequency or higher pitch of the voice (Atkinson, 1952; Ringel & Steer, 1963). In other words, some claimed that the cause for the increase in fluency lay in changes within the realm of speech production rather than within auditory processing. Interestingly, slower speech rate, increased loudness and increased pitch are all features that have been associated with the speech of the hearing impaired.

Frequency altered feedback

The finding that fluency can be improved when a speaker hears his voice at a different pitch (fundamental frequency) was originally reported by Howell, El-Yaniv, and Powell (1987), and subsequently in a number of papers by Kalinowski, and colleagues (e.g., Kalinowski, Armson, Roland-Mieszowski, & Stuart, 1993; Kalinowski, Armson, Stuart, Hargrave, & MacLeod, 1995).

This finding has been associated with the chorus effect, where, as noted above, increased fluency is thought to arise from having external speech signals provide a type of external speech template, thus tricking the brain into believing that the speech signal is exogenous, or not self-produced. Note also that similar claims have been made for the increased fluency often reported when the speaker adopts a foreign accent, or is acting out a role. Here too the brain may not be recognizing the speech as the primary "self-produced" one. There is evidence to suggest that FAF is more effective in reducing stuttering when used in conjunction with DAF (see chapter 14), and that responses to FAF in isolation can be quite individualistic. Ingham, Moglia, Frank, Ingham, and Cordes (1997) in a series of single subject experiments found one speaker to receive temporary benefit from the technique, whilst another found no change in fluency. Another showed a minimal improvement in fluency, but a deterioration in speech quality; a final speaker made significant and sustained improvement.

Auditory function and cerebral dominance

Structural and functional asymmetries

Ever since Orton and Travis's theory (Orton, 1927; Travis, 1931) of stuttering arising due to incomplete cerebral lateralization, the search for factors linking known differences in hemispheric processing with stuttering has remained a strong research trend (see chapter 2). We also know that where hemispheric imbalance has been confirmed in recent studies using modern brain imaging techniques, areas subserving motor speech and language functions have been implicated (e.g., Fox, Ingham, Ingham, Zamarripa, Xiong, & Lancaster, 2000; Neumann et al., 2003). There is also evidence that differences in the auditory processing capabilities in those who stutter can be traced to differences in cerebral dominance. Dichotic listening studies (see below) indicate that people who stutter may be less able to process linguistic information when presented to the right ear, in the face of a simultaneous competing linguistic message presented to the left ear. The functional neuroanatomy of those who stutter may differ from those who do not stutter with regard to auditory processing factors (Molt, 2003; Rastatter, Stuart, & Kalinowski, 1998; Salmelin, Schnitzler, Schmitz, Jäncke, Witte, & Freund, 1998; and see below). There is recent evidence too that there may be structural differences between brain centres involved in the processing of speech and language (Foundas, Corey, Angeles, Bollich, Crabtree-Hartman, Heilman, 2003; Foundas et al., 2004; Jänke et al., 2004). Using magnetic resonance imaging (MRI; see chapter 2 for a brief outline of this procedure) Jänke et al. (2004) found increased masses in right-sided structures, in contrast to the typical left-sided asymmetry seen in nonstuttering control speakers. The superior temporal gyrus showed increased volume: a hemispheric imbalance that Jänke et al. (2004) believe is related to persistent developmental stuttering.

They conclude that the composition of the auditory cortex is different to that of nonstutterers, but they do add the caveat that (as with neurological studies that have implicated speech processing) it is not known whether these structural differences reflect the cause of stuttering, or an adaptation of the individual to it. Foundas et al. (2004) also noted that some adults who stutter have atypical right-sided planum temporale (PT) anatomy. They subsequently tested two groups of adults who stuttered, one of which had atypical PT anatomy, the other, normal left-sided PT anatomy, against a control group of nonstuttering speakers under both NAF (no altered feedback) and DAF. The group with abnormal PT anatomy was found to have greater stuttering at baseline than the normal PT group, and recorded significantly reduced stuttering under DAF. The normal PT group, on the other hand did not experience any significant improvement in speech fluency. The authors conclude that abnormal PT anatomy might be a risk factor for developmental stuttering in some individuals. They tentatively speculate that this abnormal anatomy may alter speech feedback, allowing DAF to compensate. If this finding is verified in subsequent studies, this could go some way toward explaining the varied successfulness of commercially available altered auditory feedback devices (see chapter 14).

Dichotic listening

Just as most school age children and adults have a hand preference, foot preference, and so on, so we too have an ear preference when it comes to auditory information. One way to test this preference is by having different sounds played through headphones to the left and right ears simultaneously and noting which sound is perceived most readily. This procedure is called dichotic listening. However, just as handedness may be different for different tasks (for example, writing right-handedly and playing golf left-handedly), so too ear preference depends on the nature of the auditory signal. Most right-handed and right-sided adults who do not stutter will more accurately report musical stimuli when it is presented to the left ear, while there is a slight bias towards the right ear for linguistically meaningful information (Kimura, 1963, 1967). Note that due to the decussation (crossing) of the neural pathways involved, a right ear preference indicates left hemisphere dominance and vice versa. This pattern of auditory preference reflects the notion that musical encoding and decoding takes place in the right hemisphere, and linguistic processing takes place in the left in right-sided adults who do not stutter. In saying this, though, we must also acknowledge the complexities we noted in chapter 2 when attempting to link peripheral events, such as handedness, to hemispheric lateralization.

As seems to be the case with hemispheric processing for speech and language (that is, relating to production aspects of communication), there is evidence that there are similar processing differences between the preferences of those who do and do not stutter with regard to auditory perception. Curry and Gregory (1967) found that a group of 20 adults who stuttered showed a significantly reduced right ear preference to dichotically presented common consonant vowel consonant (CVC) words over their matched nonstuttering control group. Quinn (1972) attempted a replication of this research with a larger cohort of subjects (60), and although no significant differences were found, subsequently realized that some of the supposed right-handed people who stutter actually used their left hands for some tasks (for example, a number reportedly played golf left-handed). Rosenfield and Jerger (1984) suggested that this might be a confounding factor in this and other studies and it remains a point of contention today. As we see in chapter 2, there is good evidence that only a very few people are strongly right dominated, and even within the domain of handedness, there are many who switch hands for certain tasks, even if they use their right hand to write. In a more robustly designed experiment, Rosenfield and Goodglass (1980) found that a group of people who stutter showed a right ear preference for linguistic consonant-vowel (CV) stimuli and a left ear preference for melodic stimuli, and that there were no significant differences between this group and a matched group of people who did not stutter. Despite this, a significantly larger proportion of the people who stutter group failed to demonstrate the expected pattern of dominance of either linguistic or melodic stimuli than the control group. What does seem consistent is that when the stimulus becomes less linguistically relevant, the less obvious is the ear preference difference between experimental and control groups. For example, neither Slorach and Noehr (1973) nor Gruber and Powell (1974) found any significant difference between children who stutter and control groups when digit pairs were presented dichotically. A similar effect has been noted when meaningless CV structures have been used (Dorman & Porter, 1975). It is likely, of course, that younger preschool children may have less complete lateralization than older children and adults.

An interesting variation of the dichotic listening paradigm was developed by Sussman and MacNeilage (1975) who asked people who stutter to control the pitch of a tone presented in one ear to match the pitch of a tone presented to the other ear by moving the tongue and jaw up and down accordingly. A right ear advantage was noted for both this group, and a group of matched control speakers. However, the control group, expectedly, were better able to use their tongues to manipulate the tone when the tone that responded to tongue height was presented to the right ear, whereas the group of people who stutter showed a left ear preference for that tone; apparently demonstrating a difficulty with motor and sensory integration rather than with an auditory problem alone. A later replication of the auditory tracking experiment (Neilson, Quinn, & Neilson 1976) found a similar finding for nonstuttering speakers, but no significant difference between this group and a group of adults who stuttered.

Time perception

A number of studies have shown that adults who stutter are likely to perform more poorly than adults who do not stutter when they are required to discriminate between small time differences in auditory signals (Hall & Jerger, 1978; Kramer, Green, & Guitar, 1987). More recently, these findings have been corroborated by Barasch, Guitar, McCauley, and Absher (2000), who found that their group of 20 adults who stuttered were less able to accurately judge the lengths of silent intervals and tones than their nonstuttering peers. Additionally, a negative correlation was found between severity of stuttering and the ability to correctly estimate the length of short tones. Salmelin et al. (1998) compared the neuromagnetic responses of a group of nine people who stuttered to a similar sized control group during mime reading and choral reading. They found that functional organization of the auditory cortices was different amongst the group who stuttered, namely that there were changes in the left auditory cortical representation, which was more strongly noted in the mimed speech than the choral speech. Finally, Molt's (2003) auditory event-related potentials (ERP) analysis found that in addition to ear preference differences a group of 16 adults who stuttered showed greater variability in their ERP responses and waveform shapes, and increased latency of component P300 when subjected to a series of competing auditory stimuli at different intensity levels. (The P300 waveform component reflects cortical recognition on behalf of the speaker that the significant auditory stimulus has taken place. This is opposed to N110 or P200 peaks which are thought to be obligatory products of production.) Consistent with earlier findings, latency of response for the adults who stuttered were longer for competing linguistic stimuli than nonlinguistic stimuli, although these differences were not statistically significant. Molt concedes that there are a number of potential explanations for these findings, but offers reduced language processing ability as one likely factor.

Auditory processing and physiological factors

Thus far, we have looked at the case for an auditory disturbance based on disrupted laterality. However, there is limited evidence that stuttering may also be associated with differences at a more peripheral level. In an often quoted study, Shearer and Simmons (1965) compared electromyographic (EMG) activity in the reaction of the stapedius muscle to vocalization between a small group of people who stutter and control speakers. This tiny muscle contracts as a reflex action at the onset of vocalization (Borg & Zarkrisson, 1975).[2] Shearer and Simmons noted that while the timing of

---

2 In fact, some (e.g., McCall & Rabuzzi, 1973) have argued that this is not merely reflexive action, but rather that the muscle contraction occurs as an integral and centrally mediated part of the vocalization process.

stapedius contraction was consistent within the control group, the group who stuttered showed a greater delay in timing onsets. Further research has proved equivocal though: Hall and Jerger (1978) found no difference between experimental and control two groups with regard to the timing of stapedius contraction, but did find that the scale of contraction was reduced amongst those who stuttered. Subsequently, Hannley and Dorman (1982) found no differences between their two groups, although it is possible that this may be due to a different method used to activate the laryngeal nerves to those used in earlier experiments. A problem with all of these studies is that findings were based on a small numbers of subjects and this, coupled with the range of findings, leaves many questions as to a possible physiological basis to auditory disturbance unanswered.

Another source of data lies in the study of air and bone conduction, and the scientific phenomena that if two pure tones of identical pitch (frequency) and loudness (amplitude) are presented in opposite phase (180 degrees), then they will cancel each other out, and no sound will be heard. An early study (Stromstra, 1957) had a group of people who stutter and a control group subjected to two such tones, one presented through air and the other through bone (via the teeth). The subjects were then asked to manually vary the amplitude and phase until they no longer heard any sound. A significant difference was found between the two groups in the relative phasing of the air and bone conducted tones at 2000 Hz. In a related experiment, Stromstra (1972) had similar groups of subjects adjust amplitude and phase of two air conducted tones presented at either ear until the sounds cancelled themselves out. The phase disparity at several frequencies was found to be twice as wide for the people-who-stutter group as for the controls. Again, small subject numbers call for cautious interpretation, but there is tentative support here for the notion that people who stutter have a reduced capacity to control and manipulate auditory signals.

Stuttering as defective auditory processing

Auditory processing and the role of DAF

The cumulative effect of findings that stuttering can be increased and decreased contingent on changes to auditory feedback have led some authorities to believe that the disorder results, at least in part, from defective auditory processing. One such attempt was made in an innovative study by Harrington (1988). Although the theory argues for a perceptual basis to stuttering, it is also based in part on a cybernetic model of speech production. In this model, motor speech movements are mediated by a feedback system which depends on sensory information in order to maintain error-free speech in which speech performance is measured against a standard template (Fairbanks, 1954). When errors arise, they are recognized by matching the performance with the standard template, and are automatically corrected by searching from the appropriate output until the error has been rectified. Like Fairbanks, Harrington proposed that normal speech was characterized by a cybernetic system, but contended that the basis for error-free ongoing speech output rested on the ability accurately to predict the rhythmic structure which pre-specifies the timing of the ongoing speech output from one stressed vowel to the next. Thus: (a) speech is perceived in terms of a rhythmic structure, based on the speakers predictions as to when the next stressed vowel will come; (b) the person who stutters makes faulty predictions as to the arrival time of the next stressed vowel[3] due to a misperception of auditory information; (c) stuttering results from the attempts to realign the misperceived timing elements. In effect, the person who stutters is trying to correct an error which does not actually exist, and it is the attempt to resolve this perceived but nonexistent timing error that results in the motor speech disruptions identified as stuttering. The argument followed that DAF is effective in increasing fluency amongst people who stutter because the artificial timing delay cancels out the asynchrony between the faulty misperception of when the next stressed vowel is due (see Figure 3.1). The effects of DAF on normal speakers are also explained in this manner in the converse relationship. That is, under DAF the late feedback leads the speaker to miscalculate the arrival of the next stressed vowel, which he had correctly predicted in the first place. The variety of motor-speech consequences of the incorrect vowel percepts, such as repetitions, prolongations and so on, are explained as various attempted repair strategies to rectify the misperceived rhythmic structure.

This elegant theory is not without its problems; not least because it is not easily testable. Perhaps most awkward is the problem that a production theory can account for this data as easily as a perceptually based one. Borden (1988), in a response to Harrington's paper, argues that stuttering occurs not because of a mismatch between the stutterer's perception as to when the following stressed vowel is due and when it actually arrives, but because the production of the relevant timing units is disrupted. In other words, it is perceived as being late because *production* of that sound unit is late.

Despite a body of evidence that suggest that altering auditory feedback can change fluency levels, defining stuttering as a consequence of disrupted auditory feedback processing is far from universally agreed. Postma and Kolk (1992) argued against a theory of stuttering as defective auditory feedback, in an experiment where adults who stutter and control speakers had to detect self-produced speech errors while speaking under normal (NAF) and white noise masked feedback conditions. No significant differences were found between the two groups' ability to detect phonemic errors, leading the authors to conclude that error monitoring skills function normally in those who stutter. They did, however, note that the subjects who stuttered detected

---

3 The significance Harrington places on the perception of stressed vowels are drawn from Ohman's work on the nature of consonant and vowel relationships (e.g., Ohman, 1967).

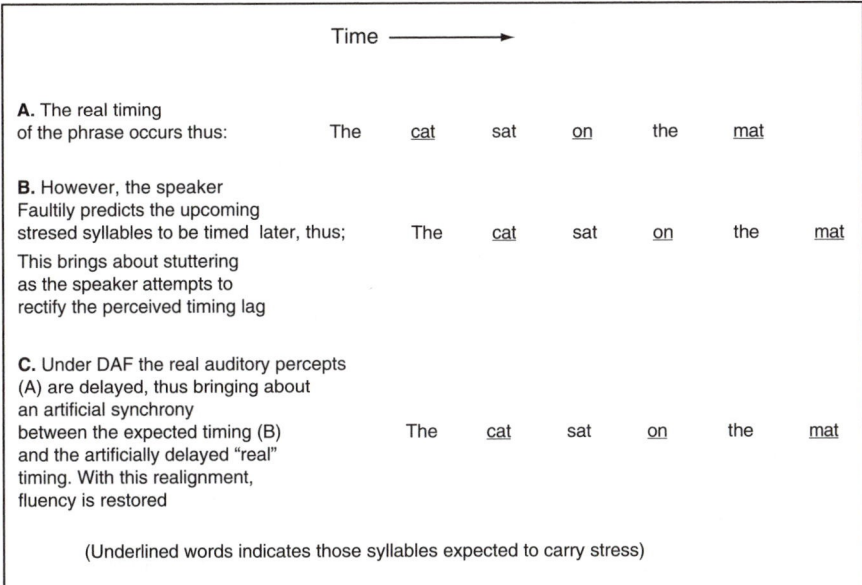

Figure 3.1 A schematic example of Harrington's model of stuttering as the misperception of linguistic rhythm. The figure also demonstrates how introducing an auditory delay artificially restores synchrony between the speaker's
auditory misperception and the "real" timing of the next stressed vowel,
thereby bringing about fluency.

fewer errors when asked to detect errors in others' speech, but as seen in
chapter five, Postma and Kolk favour a production-based phonological processing explanation to the speech errors seen in stuttering.

Summary

There is a range of evidence that points to the notion that stuttering is associated with disrupted auditory processing, although the exact nature of this
disruption remains obscure. Shadowed speech can produce high levels of
fluency, but this may have little to do with any timing misperception induced
by a faulty processing system; we know that unison speech similarly produces
high levels of fluency with no delay. We also know that DAF and FAF can
have dramatic fluency enhancing effects for some people who stutter, yet
others remain DAF and FAF negative, for reasons which are currently
unknown. Also, and as we see in chapter 14, there are reports from some
people who stutter that the effects of altered feedback can wear off over time.
Perhaps these findings suggest that distraction may play as big a part in
inducing fluency as correcting any misperception of a disrupted auditory
timing processing system? As we see in chapter 2, brain studies have shown
differences in functioning between people who stutter and control group

speakers across linguistic and motor areas. The dichotic listening procedure provides one testable method of determining hemispheric dominance for linguistic decoding, and findings from such studies, though far from definitive, lend tentative support to the idea that auditory processing too might be a product of the right hemisphere, at least in some people who stutter. One of the biggest issues faced is that auditory processing is just one part of the communication chain and does not occur in a vacuum. Both production and perception theories must allow for the fact that one is affected by the other. This can lead to a chicken and egg situation, as brought into sharp focus in the criticism of Harrington's theory of linguistic rhythm and auditory feedback: it can be almost impossible to determine what is cause and what is effect.

Key points

- The deaf population is the only one in which stuttering is underrepresented.
- Stuttered speech may be improved under a number of conditions which serve to disrupt or alter auditory feedback, such as masking, delayed auditory feedback (DAF), frequency altered feedback (FAF), choral and unison speech.
- People who stutter may be more reliant on auditory feedback than those who do not stutter.
- The fluency enhancing effects of altered feedback devices may work by convincing the brain that the speaker's speech is actually the product of an external speech source.
- There is evidence that, like processing for speech production, auditory processing for speech may be a product of right hemisphere processing amongst older children and adults who stutter.
- It has been argued that stuttering might result due to misperception of the timing of stressed vowels in speech (Harrington, 1988).
- It is possible that auditory processing anomalies may in fact merely represent "knock-on" effects of a deficit that are in essence production based.

Further reading

Harrington, J. (1988). Stuttering, delayed auditory feedback and linguistic rhythm. *Journal of Speech and Hearing Research, 31*, 36–47.
Aside from the theoretical implications, this thought-provoking paper provides a well-explained introduction into the links between perception and production aspects of speech processing in stuttering.

Kalinowski, J., Armson, J., Roland-Mieszowski, M., & Stuart, A. (1993). Effects of alterations in auditory feedback and speech rate on stuttering frequency. *Language and Speech, 36*, 1–16.

As with the selected reading list from chapter 14 which discusses auditory feedback from a therapeutic perspective, there is a wide range of Kalinowski and colleagues' work that could have been included here. This one is an early but influential article on the discovery that altered feedback could reduce stuttering, without invoking a slowed speech rate.

Rosenfield, D.B., & Jerger, J. (1984). Stuttering and auditory function. In R. Curlee and W. H. Perkins (Eds.), *The nature and treatment of stuttering: New directions* (pp. 73–88). San Diego, CA: College Hill Press.

Much of the work on stuttering and auditory function was undertaken in the 1970s and early 1980s. Despite its age, this is still a very good source for earlier material on the subject of auditory processing and covers a lot of ground. There is currently no similar but more recent publication on the subject.

4 Motor speech control and stuttering

Introduction

Although a unitary definition of stuttering currently evades researchers, its primary expression lies in some incoordination within the three major motor speech subsystems in the vocal tract: those concerned with respiration, phonation and articulation. For some people who stutter, this may result in a difficulty in controlling airflow effectively for speech. For others, there may be problems controlling laryngeal vibration, perhaps in terms of initiating voice, or in controlling pitch, or possibly laryngeal spasms associated with some stuttering blocks. Others still may find fluency compromised by involuntary movement of the articulatory musculature, leading to unexpected or mistimed closure between articulators (resulting in blocks), oscillatory behaviour such as lip or jaw tremor, or spasmodic type posturing (which may result in repetitions and prolongations). Quite often, all three motor speech systems are implicated. Even if the immediate source of the motoric disruption could be traced to a single motor speech subsystem, it is likely that the mistiming will have a knock-on effect on other systems which are linked closely with it.

Perhaps it should not be too great a surprise to find that stuttering presents as a disorder of timing. Clearly, if we were to analyze airflow, phonatory and articulatory characteristics of a speech sample containing repeated silent blocks, we would expect those timing disruptions to be reflected in our findings. But what of the fluent episodes of stuttered speech? Our perception of the speech of all but the most severe stuttering is of an output that is only intermittently interrupted by aberrant motoric activity. In fact, as we will come to see, findings show that while we may perceive nonstuttering speech as fluent, there is evidence for consistent abnormal motor speech activity, even in the absence of observable stuttering.

The purpose throughout this book is to treat stuttering as a problem where systems are integrated, and the particular interrelationship between motor speech and linguistic factors in stuttering is one of the most interesting, but also one of the most awkward to deal with. It is an issue we will return to in both this and the following chapter which considers stuttering from a linguistic perspective. For the moment, we begin by examining the body of evidence for a dyscoordination hypothesis amongst the three systems of respiration, phonation and articulation.

Respiratory control and stuttering

In order to initiate speech, an egressive airstream must be available, and for speech to be fluent and properly coordinated airflow must be controlled with precision. There is a solid body of literature dating back many years which identifies fixations of respiratory muscle systems during stuttering moments (Murray, 1932; Henrickson, 1936) and more recently loss of control of sub-glottal air pressure during stuttering (Zocchi, Estenne, Johnston, del Ferro, Ward, & Macklem, 1990). In contrast to the control speakers, subglottal pressure was found to be unstable amongst their group who stuttered, even during periods of fluency: a finding confirmed in two later studies (Johnston, Watkin, & Macklem, 1993; Peters, Hietkamp, & Boves, 1995). A substantial body of evidence has also noted that muscle groups which normally work reciprocally to ensure effective breathing have instead been found to operate antagonistically. (Lack of muscle reciprocity is an issue which we will return to below.) Empirically, many people who stutter report spasmodic abdominal and thoracic muscle activity coincident with moments of stuttering, and a comparatively common complaint is that this sense of disrupted breathing persists even prior to fluent speech (often accompanied by a fear of impending speech breakdown).

These perceptions have been substantiated in controlled studies. Adams (1974) and Agnello (1975) both found that people who stutter exhibited higher levels of intraoral air pressure during nonstuttered speech than non-stutterers, whilst Huchinson and Navarre (1977) found a similar effect during stuttered episodes. Even prior to a fluent episode, abnormal subglottal air pressure has been identified (Peters & Boves, 1988; Peters, Hietkamp, & Boves, 1993). Further studies have found that people who stutter show greater variability with breath intake over their nonstuttering peers. Within this group, some maintained lung volumes that were consistently above functional residual capacity (FRC), whilst for others lung volumes were consistently below FRC.

Possible control mechanisms

The primary function of the respiratory system is to sustain life, not to provide a flow of air capable of initiating and sustaining speech, and the two modes of breathing are very different. Fairly obviously, the inspiration/ expiration ratio changes between vegetative breathing and breathing for speech. Less obviously, speech constantly requires fast changes in volume and in air pressure. During speech, restrictions to the expiratory airstream vary from open vowels that carry little articulatory constriction, through fricatives, where there is partial articulatory constriction to the complete but momentary cessation of airflow in the case of plosives/stops. Denny and Smith (1997) argue that two structures, the metabolic respiratory controller (MRC) and the periaqueductal grey matter controller (PGMC) may provide competing inputs for control, and that before speech is initiated, there is a shift in control from the MRC which is responsible for vegetative breathing to the PGMC which is better equipped to deal with the variability in breathing needed for speech. In an interesting study, Zhou, Denny, Bachir, and Daubenspeck (1995) found that during normal breathing the glottis automatically widened when a resistance was placed against the inflowing airstream; that is, there was automatic compensation to the change in restriction. However, when a similar restriction was placed on the outgoing airstream, and in marked contrast to the earlier finding, the glottis was found to restrict yet further. Thus it seems that when the MRC is in control it could give motor commands that are totally inappropriate and counterproductive to fluent speech. Denny and Smith stop short of implicating the influence of the MRC over the PGMC as a cause of disrupted breathing in stuttering, but do say "if not suppressed, such a command . . . [to further restrict an already restricted glottis] could easily be disruptive to speech production" (p. 133).

Therapeutic relevance

Many therapeutic programs allow for the readjustment of breathing patterns, and a considerable number encourage breathing from the diaphragm (see chapter 12). The rationale for this varies somewhat from program to program, but it is often in an attempt to provide increased control over exhalation, and to divert attention away from clavicular, or upper chest breathing which is often seen in stuttered speech in combination with excessive upper body tension. The reader may also be interested to learn about the McGuire program and the Valsalva hypothesis; two approaches which have disrupted breathing as the sole target of vocal tract retraining (see chapter 14).

Laryngeal control and stuttering

Voice onset

Voice onset time refers to the time lag between the sudden opening of two articulators following a plosive (or "stop") consonant, and the time taken to initiate periodic vocal cord vibration, subsequently. As we see in the following chapter, the loci of stuttering can be described as linguistically conditioned: for example, consonant sounds are more likely to be stuttered on than vowels, and plosive sounds carry a greater risk of stuttering than any other class of sound production. This is likely due to the fact that the articulators must move with greater precision and within a smaller time frame than for other sounds if the phoneme is not to be misperceived. As such, they carry a greater degree of articulatory difficulty. (Also see Jakielski, 1998 on characterizing articulatory complexity.) The timing of voice onset reflects one part of this subtle set of articulatory timing relationships, and in physiological terms there is much to be done at such times. Take, for example, the initiation of the phrase "Too much". The tongue must be brought up behind the alveolar ridge to form a complete oral closure. At the same time, the lips will be rounding in anticipation of the second and third phonemes (/u/ and /m/). Controlled egressive airflow must allow air pressure to be built up behind the tongue, before the tongue quickly releases the /t/, allowing aspiration. Laryngeal adjustments must be made that allow the correct timing of voice onset. In our example this is likely to be somewhere between 30 and 100 ms after the plosive release. Much less than this and the resulting word will be perceived as "do". So, while voice onset requires precision of laryngeal control, it also, by definition implicates airflow, and in similar measure, articulation.

Voice onset time (VOT) has been one of the most heavily studied areas of motor control in stuttering, particularly during the 1970s and 1980s, using a variety of methodologies; for example, pressure sensor (Agnello & Wingate, 1972), spectrography (Hillman & Gilbert, 1977), electroglottography (Ward, 1990), and X-ray photography (Zimmerman, 1980b). (Also see Adams, 1987; Hand & Luper, 1980; Metz, Conture, & Caruso, 1979.) Findings seem to demonstrate two trends. First, most adults who stutter tend to show longer VOTs than their normally fluent peers. Second, more generally control of VOT is less well constrained in the speech of those who stutter, resulting in a greater range of VOT when compared with those who do not stutter. However, some studies have failed to find statistically significant differences between such groups (for example, Cullinan & Springer, 1980; Viswanath & Rosenfield, 2000). Viswanath and Rosenfield (2000) found that rather than delaying VOT, their group of adults who stuttered displayed plosive pre-voicing across a number of different linguistic contingencies, including rate and consonant identity, thereby demonstrating negative voice onset time. This "full voicing" can sound somewhat similar to the "continuous voicing" sometimes used as a fluency enhancing component in some fluency shaping approaches to therapy. This is a strategy that requires constant vocal fold vibration, even through phonemes which would normally be voiceless.

Voice initiation

Voice initiation time (VIT) is also known as acoustic reaction time, and is similar to VOT in that it describes a period of time that precedes periodic vocal cord vibration, but differs in that the phonatory response, usually either a speech sound (e.g., [a]) or a nonsense syllable (e.g., [pæp, bæb]), is initiated as quickly as possible in response to an external stimulus: this might be a verbal command ("go!"), a nonlinguistic auditory stimulus (buzzing tone) or visual stimulus (presentation of stimulus light). A number of studies have found people who stutter to exhibit slower VIT responses (Adams &

Haydn, 1976; Cross & Luper, 1979; Cross, Shadden, & Luper, 1979; Haydn, 1975; Starkweather, Hirschmann, & Tannenbaum, 1976) than those who do not stutter. As with VOT, this slowness of VIT cannot be explained by any interference of overt stuttering (Cross & Cooke, 1979).

Of particular interest is the fact that the difference in initiation time becomes more apparent as the stimulus becomes more "linguistic". First, there is some evidence to suggest that stutterers' vocal reaction times may more closely resemble those of normal speakers when the stimulus is visual, rather than auditory (Lewis, Ingham, & Gervens, 1979; McFarlane & Shipley, 1981; Prosek, Montgomery, Walden, & Schwartz, 1979). This could be seen as support for the notion that while stuttering presents as a motoric disorder, the nature of the fluency disruptions may lie in disturbed auditory feedback mechanisms. (This possibility is discussed in chapter 3.) However, one study (Murphy & Baumgartner, 1981) found no significant difference in VIT between a group of younger people who stutter and matched group of non-stuttering children (age 4–6) when presented with a pure tone stimulus. It is worthwhile noting that in a number of areas where adults who stutter perform differently to nonstutterers, these differences are not apparent, or at least not as obvious when tested in younger children. We know from a number of studies on dichotic listening (again, see chapter 3) that adults who stutter tend to show a left ear advantage for linguistically meaningful information, implying that, in contrast to nonstuttering speakers, the right side of the brain is involved in processing auditory information, and that lateralization will not be complete in younger children. However, there is little evidence from VIT studies that ear preference is a factor in latency of response; for example, Cross, Shadden, and Luper (1979) found response latencies to be unaffected by which ear was receiving the stimulus auditory signal.

Finally, while there may be equivocal findings with regard to group differences to reaction time studies when giving a simple verbal response, a study by Peters, Hulstijn, and Starkweather (1989) found that people who stutter were markedly slower in their verbal responses than a matched control group when a more complex auditory response was required. This finding was corroborated in a more recent study which found that differences in delay between a group of young adults who stuttered and a group of control subjects became more marked as syntactic complexity increased (Logan, 2003). However, the significance of this finding is not clear. Because increased phonetic complexity is also associated with increased linguistic complexity, it is difficult to make assertions as to whether the marked slowness of response is related to motoric factors, linguistic factors, or a combination of the two. Weber-Fox, Spencer, Spruill, and Smith, (2004) found a group of adults who stutter showed slower reaction times to rhyme judgement task compared with their normally fluent peers only when two orthographically similar words were presented which did not actually rhyme. These findings were interpreted as demonstrating reduced efficiency only in the final stages of phonological processing, and when there is increased cognitive load (also see chapter 5). We will see that difficulty in controlling a range of events related to the timing, both within and outside the speech domain, is a recurring theme throughout this book. It occurs with reference to auditory perception theories (chapter 3), neurological production theories (e.g., Webster and colleagues, chapter 2) as well as neuromotor control perspectives (below).

Given the particular difficulty that many people who stutter report in initiating speech, it is not surprising that having to respond quickly and under time pressure adds significantly to the likelihood of stuttering. We can see how the VIT effect can translate to real life in a number of situations, but particularly in the often feared situation of speaking on the telephone, either when responding to a "hello" (linguistic stimulus), or when leaving a message on an answerphone where there may be instructions to "leave your message after the tone" (nonlinguistic auditory stimulus), whilst in the absence of any mediating properties of visual feedback. The potential theoretical significance of time pressure as a factor in stuttering has been made by Perkins, Kent, and Curlee (1991), who argue for a neuropsychological basis to the disorder, resulting from dyssynchronous activity between linguistic and paralinguistic components. Nonstuttered disfluency (which can include abnormal sounding disfluency) results when there is dyssychrony between these components, but the speaker is not under time pressure. However, when the speaker is under time pressure and experiencing an urgent need to speak, this leads to a sense of loss of control, and alongside this, "genuine" stuttering.

Vowel duration

This refers to the length of time that a vowel stays in a steady state, with the vowel quality remaining consistent, and relatively uninfluenced by the sounds preceding and following it. There is rather less material on this particular area, but it is worth noting that what there is consistently associates either increased or more variable vowel durations amongst those who stutter (Adams, Runyan, & Mallard, 1975; Brayton & Conture, 1978; Colcord & Adams, 1979; De Nil & Brutten, 1991; DiSimoni, 1974; Hand & Luper, 1980; Riley & Ingham, 2000; Starkweather & Myers, 1978). One explanation of these findings, which somewhat echo those from VOT and VIT studies, is that even fluent passages amongst stuttered speech are associated with difficulty in programming vocal tract dynamics within the required temporal ranges, but that is to assume that variability automatically equates to some impairment in motor speech control. Riley and Ingham (2000) observed the acoustic effects of two therapeutic approaches on two groups of young children, one of which underwent a motor speech training approach, the other focusing on extending length of utterance. Following the speech motor therapy, there was a significant increase in vowel duration. The extended length of utterance program resulted in increased fluency over the motor training group, but was not accompanied by the change in vowel duration. Riley and Ingham

(2000) speculated that increased vowel durations allow more time for motor speech planning, and that stuttering is reduced as a byproduct of the longer vowel durations. Here then, we have the notion that longer vowel durations do not indicate an underlying impairment in motor speech organization; rather, that they represent the end product of conscious strategies to control for stuttering, even in young children. It would follow then, that fluency shaping programs, which often combine a slower speech rate with continuous airflow and continuous voicing (see chapter 12), work because they allow the extra time needed to adjust, or to prepare to implement articulatory, phonatory and respiratory control. This may also, in part, explain why fluency is so effortlessly maintained while singing. As mentioned in chapter 1, apart from psychological, situational and rhythmic variables, singing requires both continuous airflow and continuous voicing, as well as natural vowel prolongation.

Electromyographic evidence

Electromyographic (EMG) activity can be recorded when an impulse travels down an axon and causes a temporary reversal of the polarization, called an action potential, of the cell membrane at each muscle fibre. This depolarization and subsequent contraction of the muscle fibre can be seen as fleeting electrical activity which can be recorded via EMG electrodes. By measuring the electrical activity, muscle movement can be inferred, and this technique has been used both in the investigation of movement control in stuttering (e.g., Freeman & Ushijima, 1978; Van Lieshout, 1996) and as a method of monitoring movement responses in therapy (Guitar, 1975). There are three types of electrodes: surface electrodes which are mounted on the skin, and two types of indwelling electrodes (of either needle and hooked wire type) which are inserted directly into the muscle groups. The advantage of indwelling electrodes is that they can pick up very specific activity amongst smaller muscle groups while the surface electrodes are more prone to interference from a number of nearby muscle groups, and can only record activity from more superficial muscle groups. The disadvantage with indwelling electrodes is that they are invasive, and when inserted into the intrinsic muscles of the larynx there is a risk of permanent structural damage.

The investigation of EMG dynamics of the larynx has provided evidence for a mistiming hypothesis in stuttered speech. In a seminal paper, Freeman and Ushijima (1978) found that stuttering, in the four subjects they examined, was characterized by cocontraction of the abductor (posterior cricoid) and at least one adductor (lateral cricoaretynoid, vocalis or interarytenoid) muscles which act reciprocally in normal speech. The group of adults who stutter also consistently showed higher levels of intrinsic laryngeal muscle tone, and abnormal laryngeal activity was also noted in the perceptually normal speech of this group. A subsequent investigation (Shapiro, 1980) described a similar experiment which produced much corroborative evidence for Freeman and Ushijima's (1978) findings of generalized excessive tension. However, this study failed to replicate the finding of antagonist cocontraction of the intrinsic laryngeal musculature for one of the speakers examined when experiencing stuttering moments, and Shapiro was unable to offer any solid reason as to why this should be. The ethical difficulties associated with using invasive hooked wire electrode method required with the investigation of the intrinsic laryngeal muscle groups has meant that follow-up data is scarce. A different view on laryngeal activity has been proposed by Smith, Denny, Shafer, and Kelly (1996) who compared cricothyroid and thyroaretynoid EMG activity between a group of four people who stutter and a control group across a range of vocal contingencies. Key findings were that during fluency enhancing tasks the people who stuttered reduced EMG activity while the control group did not, and that stuttering moments could be associated with either elevated, equal or even suppressed levels of EMG activity.

Therapeutic relevance of a laryngeal component in stuttering

The importance of the VOT time frame is reflected in a number of treatment strategies, where airflow is initiated in a controlled way well in advance of phonation, and the contact between articulators (to take our earlier example of /t/) is lightened to the point where the plosive may be turned into a fricative, that is, a sound which (unlike a plosive) can be stretched without losing its phonetic identity. So, turning our /t/ into something that sounds more like a [s] reduces the articulatory complexity of the sound by removing the need for the constrained time frame of the plosive sound. In addition, and as mentioned earlier, some therapeutic approaches advocate the use of continuous voicing of all speech sounds, reducing complexity even further. Depending on how these techniques are employed, the resulting speech can sound quite unnatural, and this is something we discuss in the second part of this book, but they can produce high levels of fluency. Again, this technique reduces the need for fine control over the coordination of speech apparatus: that is, the switching of voice on and off is simply taken out of the motor speech equation; similarly, the control of the relative timing of airflow is also greatly simplified. Unbroken egressive airflow is constantly sustained during speech, regardless of whether a phone technically demands a complete stoppage of air (such as a plosive or an affricate) or not. EMG studies also have therapeutic ramifications. Although the purpose of Freeman and Ushijima's study was to examine the extent of discoordination of the laryngeal musculature in stuttering, findings have been seen to support the use of Botox (botulinum toxin) in the treatment of stuttering. The technique requires an injection of botulin toxin into the vocal cords to counter excessive laryngeal activity (see chapter 14). As with so many theories that are based on invasive investigatory techniques, only very small numbers of subjects have been used and so the data must be interpreted with caution.

EMG and articulatory timing

EMG research has also been used to examine articulatory timing in PWS. For the most part, these have been studies of lip movement, and have used superficially attached surface electrodes. McClean, Goldsmith, and Cerf (1984) found reciprocal activity in lower lip muscles during stuttering moments and fluent moments alike, although both reciprocal activation and coactivation have been shown to exist simultaneously in some muscle pairings (Humphrey & Reed, 1983).

As we mentioned at the beginning of this chapter, we can accept that primary stuttering presents as a motor speech difficulty. A recurring theme has been that it is specifically related to a difficulty in the sequencing of significant motor speech events. There have been a number of proposals for the exact unit of the mis-sequenced elements.

Muscle movement sequencing

Guitar, Guitar, and Neilson (1988) discovered that people who stuttered were found to start bilabial closure gestures with abnormal lip muscle activity. Nonstuttering speakers were found to consistently activate depressor anguli oris (DAO) muscles prior to depressor labii inferioris (DLI) for bilabial consonantal gesture while those who stuttered frequently reversed the sequence. Although more pronounced during moments of stuttering, reversals were also expressed during perceptually fluent speech. Guitar et al.'s interpretation is also clinically relevant. First, the timing disruptions are seen to take the form of a faulty programming of the procedural aspects of motor sequencing (the reversals), and delays in attempting to correct for the mistimed motor programming resulting in a delay in sound production. This account of mistiming in some ways provides a very similar picture of stuttering to that proposed by Harrington (1988), and described in the previous chapter; the important difference being that Harrington believed these timing misperceptions are related to the perception of the rhythmic structure of speech, whereas Guitar et al. are saying that they are directly related to speech production. Second, stuttering – and specifically secondary stuttering – is seen to arise as a result of anticipatory hypertension. In this theory sequencing reversals represent an active programming decision taken, with the anticipatory contraction occurring as a consequence of attempts to reduce the effects of lip perturbation from the anticipated stutter. Guitar et al. offer an explanation of stuttering where there is a difficulty in evaluating the relationship between afferent and efferent motor activity. They argue that "the persistence of inappropriate efferent activity could produce a vicious cycle effect (positive feedback) leading to progressively increasing levels of cocontraction" (p. 31).

The explanation for adults who stutter is that they are exhibiting a learned response to the involuntary speech behaviours, thus bringing physiological evidence for Van Riper's idea of the preparatory set. (See chapter 12 for a discussion as to how these theories might integrate.) The theory also seems compatible with Bloodstein's (1984) theory of stuttering as fear avoidance. At a physiological level this explanation is also consistent with the findings of Freeman and Ushijima (1978). There is also articulatory EMG evidence from the perceptually fluent speech of adults who stutter to indicate that subtle abnormalities exist, even when there is no visible or audible stuttering (corroborated in a perturbation study by Caruso, Gracco, & Abbs, 1987).

EMG has also been used as a therapeutic biofeedback tool. Levels of tension, as recorded by surface-attached EMG electrodes, are fed back to the client in the form of an auditory signal, the pitch of which changes depending on the degree of muscular tension. The client is taught techniques to gradually reduce tension, and therefore to change the pitch of the auditory signal. Although there are some limited data that this approach can be successful in reducing tension in stuttered speech, it is now nearly 25 years since Van Riper (1982, p. 210) concluded: "Electromyography can give objective measures of [such] tension for research purposes, but it is not very useful in routine clinical practice."

Articulatory kinematics and neuromotor control

Support for a theory of stuttering as a disrupted neuromotor processing deficit goes back many decades, but recent history begins with the pioneering work of Zimmerman. Using cinefluorographic evidence, Zimmerman (1980a, 1980b, 1984) argued that the lower articulatory velocities and smaller articulatory displacements seen in the speech of adults who stutter were associated with processes that ensured brainstem pathway activation was kept below a certain threshold, and that once this threshold was exceeded, stuttering would result. Further, he found that the interarticulator positionings seen in both perceptually fluent and stuttered utterances were dissimilar to those found in the fluent speech of nonstuttering speakers. In implicating the brainstem in the reported behaviour, Zimmerman's notion was again consistent with later brainstem response studies (e.g., Yeudall, Manz, Ridenour, Tani, & Lind, 1991) which linked abnormal subcortical involvement to stuttering (see also chapter 2).

Zimmerman's theory is powerful because it outlines a physiological explanation of stuttering phenomena previously explained psychologically. The effects of anxiety, for example, can be seen in this neuromotor model as being associated with increased activation of brainstem pathways resulting in activity exceeding the "normal" threshold. In turn, this results in aberrant tuning or triggering inputs for the motorneuron pools implicated in the gestural task required, thus altering the relationships of the appropriate muscle groups and leading to stuttered speech. Zimmerman offered two explanations for these data. First, speech breakdowns may be either due to "more variable motorics" resulting from an unstable motor system, or second, that the motor systems of those who stutter are essentially the same as normal speakers but may show less tolerance to variability, which in normal speakers would have no significant effect on either subcortical activation and gestural-motor behaviour. We can also see how Zimmerman's theory is also consistent with findings from both reaction studies and the physiological observations of Freeman and Ushijima (1978) and Shapiro (1980, see earlier in this chapter).

Articulator sequencing and single data-point studies

One way of evaluating the effectiveness of coordinative articulatory systems is by examining the temporal order of movement onsets and peak velocities for combined articulator movements. One of the major findings of the mid-1980s was that nonstuttering speakers produced a highly consistent sequence pattern of upper lip, lower lip, jaw, when these three articulators began to move from a vowel towards a bilabial closure target (/p/) (Gracco, 1986; Gracco & Abbs, 1986). Caruso, Abbs, and Gracco (1988) replicated this result with a group of control subjects, but noticed a remarkable difference in performance from a group of adults who stuttered, whose responses showed many reversals and deviations to this pattern during fluent episodes. At the time, it seemed that this might be the much searched for variant which might separate the speech kinematics of those who stuttered from those who didn't. Unfortunately, a number of subsequent studies failed to replicate this difference, noting that nonstuttering subjects also lack consistency in sequencing patterns (Alfonso, 1991; Max, Gracco, & Caruso, 2004; Ward, 1997a, 1997b). Despite these findings, it does not necessarily follow that adults who stutter do not experience problems with articulatory control, even during fluent episodes, and significant differences between the two groups have been observed. Ward (1997a) found that his group of adults who stuttered reached their articulatory targets with less precision than those of the control speakers, and that this imprecision became more pronounced as greater demands were placed on the speech motor system; for example, when an increased rate of speech or a change in stress pattern was required. One interpretation of this finding is that it might reflect an impairment in intergestural motor timing, albeit one that cannot be characterized in terms of a sequencing deficit. But at what level within the motor output processes is this increased variability occurring? Peters, Hulstijn, and Van Lieshout (2000) argue that the various data point not to an underlying deficit in ability to construct the necessary motor speech plans, but rather to a difference in the parameter settings which are undertaken to adjust the motor programs to the specific demands of each speech situation. That is, although speech movement is controlled in a different way, it may not reflect an impairment with motor speech control so much as either unskilled or perhaps compensatory articulatory strategies. Whether this is found to be true awaits the outcome of further studies. However, one recent study (McClean, Tasko, & Runyan, 2004) analyzed lip, tongue and jaw movement relationships from a group of 37 adults who stuttered and 43 who did not. Results indicated that subgroups of those with more severe stuttering displayed more elevated lip–jaw, and tongue–jaw speed ratios. They suggest that kinematic variables could act as predictors for certain stuttering subgroups.

For the most part, disturbances to motor speech activity have been ascribed to hemispheric anomalies (in the form of functional and structural asymmetries; see chapter 2) but the cerebellum has also been implicated in the (mis)timing of rhythmic speech and nonspeech tasks in those who stutter (Boutsen, Brutten, & Watts, 2000; Howell, AuYeung, & Rustin, 1997). Max and Yudman (2003) on the other hand failed to find either speech or non-speech differences in those who stuttered, thus concluding that the cerebellum was not concerned with the mediation of rhythmic timing in speech.

A speech motor control model of stuttering has not met with universal acclaim (Conture, 2001; Ingham, 1998). Ingham (1998) has forcefully questioned both the motives and the procedures used in motor speech control studies and articulatory dynamics. Citing a study by McClean, Kroll, and Loftus (1990) which failed to find differences between a group of stutterers and nonstutterers across measures of movement amplitude, duration and velocity, Ingham also notes that one study found that the most severe stuttering was associated with the least articulatory variability (McClean, Levandowski, & Cord, 1994). The authors suggest that increased variability might be a sign of a more stable motor system, rather than a less stable one. Ingham (1998, p. 74) asserted: "In short, the concept of variability has become an almost crumbling cornerstone within the original articulatory dynamics model ... Furthermore there is now some suggestion that reduced rather than increased variability characterizes a dysfunctional speech motor system." Ingham (1998) also claims that a motor speech explanation of stuttering cannot hold, in part because not all of those who stutter show these differences to the same extent. As Van Lieshout, Hulstijn, and Peters (2004) point out, speech motor control has already been shown to differ considerably depending on both task level complexity and environmental factors amongst those suffering from a number of disorders implicating motor speech control, including Parkinsonism. It would therefore be expected that a disorder such as stuttering, whose essence is likely to be multicausal (Smith & Kelly, 1997; Starkweather & Gottwald, 1990), would be similarly influenced.

As for the nature of the variability, the issues are complex. There needs to be sufficient variability to perform a complex task, but too much variability will result in a failure of that task. Thus the acceptability of variability may depend on the nature of the linguistic data being collected; more automatic speech results from single point data analyses, whilst more complex data arises from connected speech samples and phrase length data (see section below). It may then be that different levels of variability are needed for different tasks depending on the loading of a range of factors such as different levels of complexity both motorically and linguistically (Grosjean, Van Galen, de Jong, Van Lieshout, & Hulstijn, 1997; Kleinow & Smith, 2000; Van Lieshout, Rutjens, & Spauwen, 2002). As Van Lieshout et al. (2004) put it:

> Variability as such can be a part of a normal speech motor system displaying an element of flexibility to accommodate fast changing demands on the speed and accuracy of individual movements and their couplings ... An overly stable (= rigid) movement pattern would rather impede than facilitate speech motor control under such conditions. On the other hand, in performing highly automatic simple movement patterns, for example repeating the word "apa" repeatedly at the same rate, would not require much movement flexibility, and might actually benefit from a [sic] absolute stable pattern.
>
> (pp. 330–331)

In addition, variability needs to be considered within the context of the methods used to analyze the data. For example, Ward (1997a) found no difference between adults who stuttered and those who did not when analyzing lip and jaw sequencing patterns, but when the same movement traces were analyzed as phase plane trajectories (Kelso & Tuller, 1987) significant differences between the two groups were uncovered when increased linguistic and motoric demands were introduced.

Despite some protestations, research into stuttering and motor variability still continues apace (see section below). Even if the speech of those who stutter is found to be consistently associated with increased variability, and that this variability in turn is shown to correlate with a more stable motor speech system, we would still need to know why such differences exist between those who stutter and those who do not.

The analysis of phrase length data

One limitation of all these studies lies in the fact that the research focus is on very short periods of time. Articulatory movement from vowel to bilabial closure at normal speech rate takes around 200 ms (0.20 second). But speech is a dynamic process, with coarticulation effects extending across a number of phonemes, and some have argued that if we are to fully understand the motor speech control strategies that underlie fluent speech, and any deviance which characterizes stuttered speech, then we need to look at bigger time frames and longer speech sequences. There are now a number of methods that allow the analysis of articulatory patterns across phrase length data (Lucero, Munhall, Gracco, & Ramsey, 1997; Smith, Goffman, Zelaznik, Ying, & McGillem, 1995; Ward & Arnfield, 2001). All work by having subjects repeat a phrase a number of times, whilst the movement of the lower lip is recorded. The variability in the lower lip movement over the phrase is then compared over the repeated trials, resulting in an index of movement variability. In all methods, greater variability in spatio-temporal movement is considered to reflect reduced ability to control motor-speech programming, but different methods of modelling the variability of the movement traces will result in different indices of articulator stability (see Ward & Arnfield, 2001).

Smith et al. (1995) had subjects repeat a phrase a number of times, and then analyze the variability in jaw movement across all the repetitions. A high degree of pattern stability was reflected in low spatial temporal index (STI) score. In a later paper, Smith and Kleinow (2000) found that one-third of an adult PWS group showed abnormal STI instability even under low demand speaking conditions. Surprisingly, they also observed that a slow speech rate did not improve stability, as predicted, and as was the case with the control speakers. There are therapeutic ramifications here: the idea has been implicit, in prolonged speech approaches to therapy that slowing rate improves fluency because motor speech programming and activation have more time to work successfully (Riley & Ingham, 2000, and see section on VIT above). Smith and Kleinow's (2000) findings call into question whether motor speech really does benefit directly in this way, although there is still the possibility that a slower rate allows more time for cognitive and linguistic processing. In addition, they suggest that the very act of changing timing relations (from the unstable habitual speech rate mode to a new slow mode) changes the operating parameters and may help to establish new sets of timing relationships. These, over time, may result in a more stable speech. There may be some limited clinical evidence for the latter in a report by Onslow, Costa, Andrews, Harrison, and Packman (1996) who found that high levels of fluency were maintained following a period of prolonged speech therapy with faster speech rates than those usually targeted by prolonged speech programs. However, there is rather little data to corroborate this finding and as we will see, particularly in part 2, the issue of maintaining high levels of fluency remains a significant problem with all therapies. However, in a further study, Kleinow and Smith (2000) observed that motor control amongst those who stutter showed greater variability with increased syntactic complexity. This does seem consistent with those therapeutic approaches which constrain length of utterance (see chapters 10, 11, 12).

Finally, a word of caution. A problem in almost all of the research on speech kinematics and stuttering is that we only have detailed information from the adult population. Because of this, we can only speculate as to the control mechanisms in place at the onset of stuttering. Equally, we cannot be sure that where group differences have been found between adults who stutter and adults who do not, that these may reflect the use of varied control strategies on behalf of the speakers, rather than the direct effects of the stuttering, itself.

Acoustics

Acoustic studies look at factors relating to the end product of the speech and language processing chain. When speech is produced, changes in air pressure result in the acoustic wave, and it is this continually varying waveform that is decoded in the inner ear and interpreted in the brain via the auditory nerve of the listener. Acoustic properties have been studied extensively amongst those who stutter. As little as 15 years ago, acoustics analysis packages were expensive and belonged solely in the domain of the speech laboratory. Nowadays, acoustic software analysis packages are numerous, powerful, free, and easily downloaded from the worldwide web. The information that can be gained from an examination of the acoustic trace is vast, and we have already seen in earlier sections on voice onset time, voice initiation time and vowel duration how measuring acoustic attributes can allow us to record tiny but significant differences in the timing of significant speech events. Unlike the measurement of physiological/kinematic data, it is perfectly feasible to record acoustic data from young children, and this has led to some interesting findings with regard to the activity of second formant (f2) transitions.[1]

A fairly consistent finding amongst younger children is that formant transitions, which give the listener acoustic cues as to the identity of the upcoming phonetic segments, are different amongst those who stutter (Chang, Ohde, & Conture, 2002; Subramanian, Yairi, & Amir, 2003; Yaruss & Conture, 1993). Chang et al. (2002) argue that organization of the formant transition rate may not be as contrastive, even amongst children as young as 3 years old, than for their nonstuttering peers. Subramanian et al. (2003) found that significantly smaller frequency changes were associated with a group of ten children who went on to develop a persistent stutter than a similar group of young children who eventually recovered. They conclude that this measure should be investigated further as a possible predictor of stuttering. Given these data, it is unsurprising to find that f2 transitions of adults who stutter have also been found to be abnormal (Howell & Vause, 1986; Howell, Williams, & Vause, 1987; Robb & Blomgren, 1997). For example, Howell and Vause (1986) noted that the fluent speech of their group who stuttered was characterized by a lack of f2 transitions between initial consonant and following vowel. As with other areas of motor speech investigation, a significant problem in interpreting these data lies with the possibility that the disruptions observed at a peripheral level may well reflect motor planning and premotor (linguistic) impairment. The need for a better understanding between the relationship between linguistic and motor processing is urgently needed.

---

1 As the articulators move to vary the shape of the vocal tract, so this changes the way that acoustic energy generated by the vocal cords is absorbed or reflected. We hear the note of the fundamental frequency, but above this are unheard formants; bursts of acoustic energy, that reflect the constantly changing shape of the vocal tract and play a significant part in our understanding of speech. Although there are theoretically an infinite number of formants, only the first three (and particularly the first two) are significant for phoneme recognition. Formant 1(f1) frequency changes inversely with tongue height, that is, the lower the tongue, the higher the value of f1, and vice versa. Formant 2 (f2) reflects the front or backness of the tongue; thus a high f2 indicates a front vowel, a low f2 indicates a back vowel. As the articulators change position, so too formant frequencies will change. The time period during which formants associated with one phoneme change to become associated with another is called the formant transition time.

Motor control outside the speech domain

One related and intriguing question is whether the motor disruptions seen in stuttering are limited solely to the speech domain? There have been a number of reports and investigations which suggest that for some, at least, stuttering may be associated with: (a) difficulties in motor control in systems remote from motor speech, (b) difficulties with nonspeech oromotor control; (c) difficulties in coordinating motor speech and nonspeech motor systems.

Motor control in nonspeech tasks

Webster (1985) observed that most people, whether right- or left-handed expressed a right-hand advantage for finger tapping. Regardless of whether the task required single finger-tapping movements or the typing of keys in a particular pattern, the task was achieved more accurately and more quickly with the right hand. This is thought to reflect that the right hand has direct access to the left hemisphere, which is thought to be more capable of dealing with fine levels of motor control (Kinsbourne & McMurray, 1975; see also chapter 2 on brain studies and stuttering) whilst the left hand can only access the commands after they have crossed the corpus callosum. Webster (1986) found that when placed under time pressure, those who stutter were significantly slower in initiating movement of new finger-tapping patterns and made more errors, but that once the patterns were learned, their performance matched those who did not stutter. This finding was substantiated in a subsequent experiment which found a similar effect, even when there was no time pressure (Webster, 1989a). Later experiments also found those who stutter to experience significantly more difficulties than controls when required to finger tap with one hand whilst turning a knob with the other (Webster, 1989b), in further bimanual tasks (Forster & Webster, 2001; Webster, 1988). Despite these differences, there is evidence, however, from another laboratory (Max et al., 2004; Max & Yudman, 2003) that those who stutter tend to use similar motor control strategies (in the shape of similar peak velocity sequencing profiles) to those of their normally fluent peers for some sequential finger-tapping tasks.

Motor control in nonspeech oromotor tasks

If an impairment in motor planning and execution does indeed exist in remote systems such as finger-tapping tasks, we might expect that other motor systems more closely linked to speech would also be implicated. Packman and Onslow (1999) cite the case of an adult who experienced stuttering like motor disruptions whilst playing the trombone, and there are similar cases involving the trumpet, horn and flute. The playing of such instruments in each case involves the controlled use of airflow, and some degree of bilabial constriction, but in the absence of any laryngeal component. In each case, airflow is produced in a manner that is more consistent with singing than speaking, and similarly the degree of articulatory control is much simpler than that required for speech. Clearly, there are a great number of people who stutter who do not experience these motor disruptions whilst playing musical instruments, and it is difficult to make assertions from the small data set currently available on the subject. It may be that there are certain types of stuttering that are particularly susceptible to motor speech disruptions arising in the vocal tract and affecting nonspeech, as well as speech production.

In addition to the data on the so-called musical instrument stuttering, there is also some information as to control strategies used for nonspeech oromotor tasks. Looking at peak velocity sequencing as an index of motor control (see above), Max et al. (2004) found that adults who stuttered and those who did not both performed a bilabial opening and closing task with increased peak velocity sequencing variability when compared to a similar speech-related task, but there was no significant difference between the variability expressed for the two groups. The consistency of data from a number of laboratories now strongly suggests that whether within or outside the speech domain, any anomalies in motor timing related to stuttering cannot be explained in terms of an articulator sequencing deficit. Max (2004) in a review of the literature on nonspeech movement data concludes "differences between stuttering and nonstuttering individuals are indeed not limited to speech movements" (p. 362).

Coordinating motor speech and nonspeech motor systems

The third issue – that of coordinating speech and nonspeech activity – has raised some particularly interesting data, largely through the work of Megan Neilson and colleagues. Briefly, Neilson (1980) had adults who stutter and nonstuttering adults undertake a task where a tone of continually changing frequency presented to one ear had to be matched as closely as possible by a tone, controlled by the subject, presented to the other ear. Response tones were either controlled by hand movement or by jaw movement. A visual tracking task was also completed where a vertically moving point had to be shadowed, again under two conditions: jaw controlled and hand controlled. Findings from this work support those from previous dichotic performance tasks, indicating that there was no difference between the two groups in the visual task, but response to the auditory task was significantly inferior for those who stuttered. Subsequent research (Neilson, O'Dwyer, & Neilson, 1988) found that for a similar task the stutterers' performance differed only marginally from that of the earlier (stuttering) group when no practice time was allowed to become familiar with the experimental task. In comparison, the control group's performance was substantially better in the earlier study than in the later one.

The two main findings that (a) stutterers exhibit inferior performance in auditory tracking tasks, but not for visual tracking, and (b) stutterers have a reduced ability to improve on their auditory tracking performance even when given extended rehearsal periods, led the researchers to the conclusion that the efficiency and accuracy of the underlying sensorimotor integration processes specifically for motor speech are disrupted in stutterers. The theory was refined further in an experiment which required subjects to follow the vertical movements of a cursor in a graphical display with either a light pen or by manipulating a lever. It was predicted that performance would be improved, resulting in more accurate tracking, when the pen was used because of its "highly compatible" control display as compared to the lever's less compatible relationship, and this indeed was shown to be the case. Subjects produced movement patterns that reflected increased delay between the movement of the stimulus and the movement of the response marker when controlled by the lever. Experimental evidence also showed that a normal speaker was able to significantly improve performance with the less compatible arrangement when rehearsed: average delay time was decreased and inappropriate movement patterns associated with the low compatibility control display. More recently, there is evidence from studies where a moving target is tracked by movement of the lower lip that both adults and children who stuttered show greater variability than fluent subjects (Howell et al., 1997).

Taking a rather different approach, Mayberry and Shenker (1997) explored possible links between stuttering and hand gesture. Their findings for both adults and children indicated that increased stuttering was associated with a reduction in gesture. On the few occasions where stuttering and gesture did co-occur, the gesture mirrored the motor speech breakdown, stopping coincident with the moment of stuttering and resuming when fluency was resumed. Their interpretation of this data is that this represents a type of gestural mirroring, and that ". . . the synchronization of dynamic gesture and speech motor patterns during spontaneous language production are all ultimately coordinated with the single linguistic meaning being expressed simultaneously by both modes . . ." (p. 186).

They further hypothesize that the predictable (inverse) relationship between stuttering and gesture comes about because stuttering takes up linguistic processing resources. So, when the spoken aspects of the message use up most of the processing resources, this will mean there is less available for the gestural aspects and therefore that the gesture will be attenuated. In this way, Mayberry and Shenker consider this "gesture-to-speech ratio" to be a reliable and valid indicator of language processing capacity.

Stuttering and internal models

Recently, Max (2004) has suggested that the available data on motor speech, nonspeech motor control and various neurological correlates seen in the stuttering research might best be explained from an "internal model" perspective. Very briefly, this framework holds that, rather than issuing motor speech programs for execution in the vocal tract, the CNS "transforms" cortically generated motor commands, through a number of complex conversions, into movement. In order for these critical transformations to be properly controlled, the CNS maintains internal representations of the properties of the motor systems and environment. There are two internal models, both of which may be implicated in movement control. A forward model works rather like a template, providing a kind of blueprint of the generated motor commands against which the sensory percepts can be compared. An inverse model, on the other hand, takes the sensory consequences of the motor act and maps a route back to the centrally generated commands. Although these notions are established in the study of nonspeech movement, they represent new concepts within the field of stuttering. Although, as Max (2004) concedes, at present the model is mostly speculative, the contention is that stuttering may relate to a failure in childhood to properly acquire or develop the necessary relationships between sensory and motor signals, and/or that during critical periods of craniofacial, neurological and biomechanical changes in childhood, the individual is less able to update these mappings appropriately. See Max's chapter in Maassen, Kent, Peters, Van Lieshout, and Hulstijn (2004) for a full account of internal model concepts.

Summary

Stuttered speech presents as an output which is motorically disrupted or "a limitation in speech motor skill" (Van Lieshout et al., 2004, p. 314). A common finding is that across a range of motor speech tasks which are considered to provide indices of motor control, those who stutter have been found to perform either more slowly or with greater variability (or both) than those who do not stutter. These discrepancies in motor speech performance can be seen at respiratory, laryngeal and articulatory levels, and may also be observed in nonspeech as movements. Neurological evidence, as presented in chapter 2, suggests that areas associated with motor planning such as Broca's area, premotor cortex, supplementary motor area and basal nuclei are likely to be functionally implicated, as are those directly associated with motor execution (the pyramidal and extrapyramidal tracts).

The significance of all of these differences is not easy to define. Some variability at least may represent greater flexibility in coordinated motor activity, but other may be indicative of systems which are compromised in their ability to implement accurate goal directed motor speech output. At present, research into both normal and disordered speech lacks well-defined criteria from which to ascertain the acceptability of motor control variability. More studies are needed to test this notion, and in particular we need kinematic data from younger children who stutter to ascertain whether differences in speech and nonspeech kinematics seen amongst adults hold true for those who have only just begun to stutter. In addition, we lack data as to precisely which aspects of timing are disrupted in those who stutter:

whether these are affecting the timing of individual movements, overlapping articulatory gestures, or the utterance length rhythmical patterning. Whatever the eventual outcome to this, it is clear that, as with the linguistic accounts of stuttering outlined in the following chapter, a motor speech argument alone cannot explain all the phenomena surrounding the disorder. It seems entirely likely that there will be interaction between linguistic, environmental, neurological, psychological and other extraneous variables.

Key points

- It may be helpful to think of the speech production system as comprising three major (but interrelated) motor subsystems: respiration, phonation, articulation. All take their motor commands from higher centres in the cerebral hemispheres via the motor pathways of the pyramidal and extrapyramidal pathways.
- Stuttering is associated with timing anomalies at all three levels of respiration, phonation and articulation. During stuttering there may be antagonist movement of muscles that normally work reciprocally together with inappropriate use of muscular force even when fluent. During fluent episodes, those who stutter are likely to show either longer or more variable motoric behaviour across a range of motor control indices; both acoustic, and physiological/kinematic.
- Some of this more variable motor activity can be explained as the implementation of control strategies on behalf of the speaker, rather than aberrant motor speech planning.
- There is a small but growing body of evidence to suggest that fine motor control outside the speech domain can be compromised in stuttering, whether this is somewhat associated with the speech act, such as vocal tract control when playing a musical instrument, or whether completely independent of speech, as is the case with finger-tapping tasks.
- Disturbances to the speech periphery may reflect underlying premotor deficits. Ascertaining this will in turn require the development of new models of motor speech and linguistic interaction.

Further reading

Conture, E. G. (2001). Motor activity and behaviour. In E. G. Conture *Stuttering: Its nature, diagnosis, and treatment* (pp. 360–337). Boston: Allyn & Bacon.
In this comparatively brief section, Conture skims the literature, but eloquently raises

some of the key issues on the limitations of motor speech research, and the difficulty in interpreting data from this area of investigation.

Kent, R. D. (2000). Research on speech motor control and its disorders: A review and prospective. *Journal of Communication Disorders, 33*, 391–428.

Kent assembles the evidence for a motor control perspective on stuttering, as well as considering other recognized speech disorders, such as dyspraxia and dysarthria. Links are made between stuttering, motor speech and neurological functioning.

Maassen, B., Kent, R., Peters, H. F. M., van Lieshout, P. H. H. M. and Hulstijn, W. (Eds.). (2004). *Speech motor control in normal and disordered speech*. Oxford: Oxford University Press.

As the title implies, this book covers aspects of motor speech control not only in stuttering but in normal speech, as well as across a wide range of disorders. It is extremely thorough and a "must-have" text for anyone interested in gaining an in-depth knowledge on the subject.

Peters, H. F. M., Hulstijn, W., & Van Lieshout, P. H. H. M. (2000). Recent developments in speech motor research into stuttering. *Folia Phoniatrica et Logopaedica, 52*, 103–119.

A paper strongly focused toward the analysis of kinematic data on stuttering, and the need to take on board premotor processing concepts. It is clear and comprehensive in its coverage.

5 Linguistic aspects of stuttering

Introduction

There are a number of findings which point to an association between linguistic variables and stuttering (Blood et al., 2003). Among the most consistent findings in stuttering research is that stuttering most commonly arises in preschool children, and at a time when language development is rapidly emerging (Kloth, Janssen, Kraaimaat, & Brutten, 1995; Yairi et al., 1996). Stuttering is also associated with reduced language processing ability (although the reverse can also sometimes be true as we see, for example, in Van Riper's track theory in chapter 7. Stuttering tends to occur where linguistic demands are high, and as it becomes established severity tends to increase with the emergence of more complex linguistic structures. The problem with all this is that these facts can also be explained in motoric terms. Just as the preschool onset is coincident with an increase in linguistic output, so too motor speech is rapidly developing at exactly this time. It is well known that stuttering is associated with reduced motor speech performance, and it is also the case that moments of linguistic complexity tend to correlate highly with motor speech complexity. To compound the problem, we have at a more theoretical level strong differences of opinion amongst experts as to the exact nature of the phonetics/phonology interface; that is, there is fundamental disagreement as to what might be regarded as motor speech and what is phonological. (See Shockey, 2004 for a very clear account on this last point.)

We begin with an overview of some the classic research in this area, before moving on towards more recent interpretations of these findings and examples of theories of stuttering as a linguistic disorder.

A linguistic basis for stuttering

The loci of stuttering

Table 5.1 lists some of the earlier research into the effects of word position on stuttering. The general conclusions from this body of research are that stuttering is more likely to occur at the beginning of a sentence or clause than in

Table 5.1 Summary of earlier research into the influence of word position on stuttering

Researchers	Findings
Quarrington, Conway, Siegel (1962)	Stuttering was clause initial within a sentence, rather than within a clause.
Soderberg (1967)	Stuttering was mostly clause initial.
Brown (1938)	More stuttering on the first few words of an utterance.
Hejna (1955)	Decrease in stuttering on consecutive words in a sentence (stuttering not predominantly on the first word though).
Bernstein (1981)	Children's stuttering occurs more frequently at sentence initial position.
Trotter (1959)	Conspicuous words carry more severe stuttering.
Quarrington (1965)	More unpredictable words are more likely to be stuttered.
Taylor (1966)	Word position was a more accurate determiner of loci of stuttering than length of word or phonetic identity of the syllables.
Wingate (1979)	More stuttering occurred on the first three words in a sentence.
Griggs & Still (1979)	Stuttering tends to occur at, or near the beginning of a sentence.
Conway & Quarrington (1963)	Initial word more susceptible to stuttering than medial or final words.

the middle or end. (It should be pointed out though that some of the studies which provided these data contained some significant design weaknesses; for example, failing to control for word frequency or potential phonetic influences.)

In addition, there is a considerable body of research to show that the longer the word, the greater the likelihood of stuttering (Griggs & Still, 1979; Hejna, 1955; Silverman, 1972; Soderberg, 1966, 1967). Relatedly, stuttering is also more likely to occur as follows:

1   With increased mean length of utterance (MLU) (Weiss & Zebrowski, 1992; Yaruss, 1999) and particularly on structures which exceed mean length of utterance (Zackheim & Conture, 2003).
2   On structures which are more grammatically complex (Kadi-Hanafi & Howell, 1992; Logan & LaSalle, 1999; Yaruss, 1999). Although some have suggested that this effect diminishes in adults (Logan, 2001).

3   There are higher type-token ratios (TTRs; Bernstein-Ratner, 1997)
4   On sentences which contain grammatical encoding errors (Bernstein-Ratner, 1998; Rommel, 2004).
5   The word is less familiar (Hejna, 1955; Soderberg, 1966) although some researchers have found exceptions. For example, Wingate (1976) found that a word frequency effect was only seen with lists of short rather than longer words. Also see Hubbard and Prins (1994) for an evaluation of the effect of familiarity on fluency.

Lexical retrieval and stuttering

One hypothesis that emerges from time to time is that stuttering may be associated with a difficulty in accessing a word (Gregory & Hill, 1999; Packman, Onslow, Coombes, & Goodwin, 2001; Wingate, 1988). Although difficulties in lexical retrieval are readily recognized as a feature of cluttering (see chapter 8) its acknowledgement as a feature of stuttering is controversial and there have been few well-controlled trials to evaluate this possibility. One of the problems in testing this notion lies in distinguishing differences in response latencies as being due to word fear, rather than difficulties with lexical access (Conture, 1990). The arguments both for and against this possibility have recently been revived in a study which found people who stutter to be disfluent on nonwords as well as real words, thus indicating that the meaning of the word itself was not implicated in any failure in its production (Packman et al., 2001). These findings were subsequently questioned by Au-Yeung and Howell (2002) who pointed out some methodological weaknesses in the study's design, but a subsequent study (Batik, Yaruss, & Bennett, 2003) also found that there was no difference in word-finding ability between a group of 20 children who stuttered (mean age 9 years, 10 months) and a matched control group of nonstuttering children. Batik et al. (2003) concede, however, that their test only required a single word response, and that as the demands of other linguistic factors (such as grammatical complexity, length of utterance) increase in running speech, this could lead to differences in word retrieval between children who stutter and those who do not. (Again, note that this notion is consistent with the Demands and Capacities model of fluency, as outlined in chapter 1.)

Lexical class and stuttering frequency

One area of enduring interest has been the study of stuttering from a word class perspective. Particularly, this relates to the difference noted between stuttering on content words (also known as open class words) comprising nouns, lexical verbs, adjectives and adverbs, and function words (or closed class words) which include pronouns, prepositions, articles, conjunctions and auxiliary verbs. A consistent research finding is that stuttering occurs more commonly on content words amongst the adult population (Brown, 1938,

1945; Hejna, 1955; Howell, Au Yeung, & Pilgrim, 1999; Johnson & Brown, 1935), while stuttering in younger children occurs mostly on function words (Bernstein, 1981; Bloodstein & Gantwerk, 1967; Bloodstein & Grossman, 1981; Howell et al., 1999; Wall, 1977). This change has been said to reflect the growing ability for a child to appropriately use function words within grammatical constituents, which usually occurs by around 8 years of age, although this statement needs some further definition. In a recent study, a group of 26 adult native German speakers, rather than "swapping" stuttering from function words to content words, were found to have significantly increased stuttering rates on both word classes when compared to a group of 6 to 11 year olds (Dworzynski & Howell, 2004). Thus, the increased stuttering seen in the adult group seemed to be related to an increased difficulty with content words, rather than a decrease in difficulty with function words. The notion of stuttering being related to word class forms the basis of a current theory of fluency breakdown, and we return to this issue, below.

The development of linguistic skill and stuttering

A further consistent finding is that stuttering tends to begin at a time of intense language development (Kloth et al., 1995; Yairi et al., 1996; Yaruss, La Salle, & Conture, 1998). Alongside this, children who stutter have been shown to have lower scores for receptive and expressive language (Anderson & Conture, 2000; Byrd & Cooper, 1989; Murray and Reed, 1977; St Louis & Hinzman, 1988), have more immature language (Howell & Au-Yeung, 1995; Wall, 1980), have less well-developed articulatory systems (Melnick & Conture, 2003), and have poorer grammar (Westby, 1974), although findings to the contrary have also been found (Watkins, Yairi, & Ambrose, 1999) and some children who stutter do show advanced linguistic skill.[1] There is evidence too that children who stutter may have reduced abilities to plan, or retrieve sentence level units of speech (Anderson & Conture, 2004; Cuadrado & Weber-Fox, 2003), and that there may be a link between early stuttering and phonological deficit (Kolk & Postma, 1997; Louko et al., 1990; Louko, Conture, & Edwards, 1999; Postma & Kolk, 1993). Louko et al. (1999) claim that around 30 to 40 percent of children who stutter also demonstrate articulation difficulties, as opposed to the figure of 2 to 4 percent expected in the general population, although some research has put this figure as low as 13 percent (Blood et al., 2003). Such findings have in part been responsible for the development of the covert repair hypothesis, which argues that stuttering is related to an unstable phonological system (see below).

---

1 For example, Starkweather (1997) speculates as to whether such children might comprise a specific subgroup of stutterers (see chapter 7).

Models of language processing

Thus far we have determined that the bulk of evidence from motor control studies points to a difficulty in the consistent and accurate coordination of muscle movements for speech amongst those who stutter. What we do not yet know is how to place this data in the context of the whole process of speech and language planning and execution. In other words, at what stage in the speech and language production process do these anomalies appear? The answer to this lies in the model of language processing that one selects. There are a number of alternatives, and the forms which these take reflect the varying standpoints as to how language processing is achieved (Dell & Julliano, 1991; Garrett, 1991; Levelt, 1989, 1992). Translation models (for example, MacNeilage, 1970) posit a hierarchical process from intention to speak, moving down through higher levels of language functioning, such as semantic/ pragmatic levels; down again through grammar and finally to where a notional phonemic form is converted into the articulatory specifications which are then produced and perceived as the final acoustic product. But there are alternative explanations.

One of the most highly regarded models of speech and language production was proposed by Levelt (1989, 1992). To briefly summarize, Levelt divides speech and language production into three processing levels, which for the most part are hypothesized to operate in parallel:

1   *Conceptualization.* Here, intention is created, allowing concepts to be turned into a preverbal message,
2   *Formulation.* At this stage the concepts take on the form of a linguistic plan. Now linguistic identity is achieved via a number of processes: e.g., grammatical encoding involves the selection of lexical items and construction of syntactic frameworks; phonological encoding involves the specification of the final phonetic plan.
3   *Articulation.* This final stage sees the phonetic plan retrieved from a pre-articulatory buffer and then executed as spoken communication.

From a motor control perspective, most of the issues relate to the articulation stage of the model. However, Peters and Starkweather (1990) have argued that there may be three hypotheses that explain the data, and particularly related to the thorny difficulty of the interrelatedness of motoric and linguistic activity. Thus conceptualization and formulation levels will be also be implicated.

The first hypothesis is that there may be separate subgroups of people who stutter; one subgroup may be related to a linguistic deficit, another to a motoric one. It may also be possible that a further subgroup (or subgroups) could arise from a combination of the two. A second possibility is that stuttering arises because of conflict between motoric and linguistic elements. As Peters et al. (2000) have pointed out, stuttering arises at points which are complex, at the same time from both motoric and linguistic perspectives. This is exemplified in a study (Bosshardt, 1998) which found that the greater the cognitive load placed on a person who stutters, the greater the negative effect on stuttering, inspiratory breathing and timing of word repetitions. This is interpreted as demonstrating that increased cognitive load results in slower phonological processing, thus decreasing its effectiveness. It is further speculated that a certain subgroup of people who stutter may be particularly susceptible to cognitive overload. Thus these particular people are placed at increased risk of motor speech disruption. Peters et al. (2000) argue a third hypothesis that stuttering could be adversely affected by a mismatch between language competence and language performance. We know that, as a group, young children who stutter tend to lag behind their normally fluent peers on tests of language performance (although as we have seen with studies of voice onset time and voice initiation time, group performance is also often characterized by a greater spread of ability). One theory is that for young children who stutter who also have depressed performance skills, stuttering could arise due to difficulty with word finding, or reduced ability to construct grammatical sentences, whilst simultaneously maintaining the necessary motor speech control. Conversely, those who have elevated language performance levels might experience difficulty in selecting words from a larger lexicon, and syntactic structures from a greater array that lies at their disposal: in other words, they become "spoiled for choice" and motor speech breaks down as a consequence. Interestingly, this theory fits well with the structuring of a number of therapies, including Ryan's (gradual increase in length and complexity of utterance, GILCU) approach, and more recently, the Lidcombe Program (see chapter 10), although neither approach actually attaches the cause of stuttering to linguistic difficulty. In the earlier stages of Lidcombe therapy, for example, length of utterance is constrained to the point where, during therapy sessions of practice time, a child may only be producing language at a one-word level, and where that word is accessible from a pictorial display, when it is deemed that fluency cannot be maintained with longer structures. We can see how this language restraint fits with the mismatch hypothesis. Those with limited linguistic ability would be saved struggling to access linguistic structures from an inferior array while those with advanced levels of language competence would be helped by having a smaller selection of structures to choose from in the first place. It is of further interest to note that the idea of stuttering onset being associated with two different subgroups – one related to poor linguistic ability in the preschool child and another associated with advanced linguistic skill – has been characterized within Starkweather's nine-track model of stuttering (Starkweather, 1997). We come to this in chapter 7.

Although Levelt's model is well established, there are fundamental problems with models which, in varying ways, translate phonemic (or abstract) units of description which are discrete, context free and exist independently of time, into the concrete, overlapping, context-dependent vocal tract movements which operate in real time to produce the final acoustic product. Van Lieshout (1998) contends that Levelt's (1989, 1992) way of dealing with this through the use of a notional mental store of speech gestures, called syllabary, is unsatisfactory, believing that the evidence for this concept is limited, and that Levelt also fails to solve the basic difficulty of reconciling the abstract linguistic notions of phonology with the concrete dynamical realities implicit with motor speech which operates in real time. One way of attempting to deal with this linguistic expression of the "mind – body problem" has been through the application of action theory concepts (Fowler, 1980) and the related notions associated with articulatory phonology (Browman & Goldstein, 1986, 1995). A detailed explanation of the concepts underlying this dynamical approach to speech processing goes way beyond the scope of this current chapter, but the basic underlying perspective is that linguistic units and the motor representations of speech can be treated as one and the same, therefore doing away with the need to convert a mental process into a physical one.[2]

Linguistic or motor difficulties?

The link between language delay and stuttering in children (Wall, 1977) and specifically the development of stuttering as language begins to emerge (Bernstein-Ratner, 1997; Merits-Patterson & Reed, 1981) all appear consistent with the notion of an underlying problem with linguistic processing. As Starkweather (1987, 1997) points out, however, there are also many children advanced in language development who stutter. Whilst it is known that children who stutter as a group score lower on tests of language than their fluent peers (Andrews, Craig, Feyer, Hoddinott, Howie, & Neilson, 1983) it has been suggested that this may be an artifact of the psychological effects of stuttering itself rather than a reflection of the pure language ability of the child who stutters.

A problem for many areas of research in stuttering is that the data from one area of investigation may be explained equally plausibly in terms of another theory. We see this, for example, in theories of auditory processing which may overlap (to some extent) with theories of central auditory processing as well as with psychological explanations. A similar situation exists for the interpretation of data on linguistic aspects of stuttering. Peters and Starkweather (1989) have suggested that three stuttering subgroups may exist, affected differentially by either motoric deficits, linguistic deficits, or both. Whichever group is implicated, there is an imbalance between language

---

2 Studies taking this dyamical perspective have contended that impairment in articulatory control amongst adults who stutter might be more satisfactorily explained using these models (Alfonso, 1991; Van Lieshout, 1997; Ward, 1997a).

and motor development. A motoric explanation of the linguistic data argues that the increase in stuttering noted at linguistically significant points can be explained by the fact that these points also tend to be motorically significant. For example, longer sentences may produce increased stuttering because they place increased demands on motor programming, not that they are more syntactically complex. It is also possible that both theories hold true. The interference hypothesis proposes that language and speech motor processes interfere with one another during the act of talking. Research on normal speakers by Kinsbourne and Hicks (1978) found that simultaneous performance of language formulation and motor programming resulted in a deterioration of performance in both areas. Separating motor task performance from language performance whilst at the same time being able to compare their relative effects is a difficult task, even in normal speech, not least because, as we have already seen, this precise issue of motor control and its relation to linguistic processing is currently an area under much debate.

Bilingualism and cross-linguistic research

This debate extends into the area of cross-linguistic studies also. There is research to suggest that while bilinguals may stutter on different phonetic loci in their two languages, there is consistency on stuttering loci across syntactic classes (Bernstein-Ratner & Benitez, 1985), although now this notion has been challenged. Howell and colleagues have looked at stuttering loci with a particular focus on the function-content word class distinction already raised above in English and Spanish. Recall that one argument for a motoric explanation of increased stuttering on content words amongst adult stutterers is that these words are stressed, and therefore carry more articulatory effort (Wingate, 1984). They have also been shown to be more motorically complex when measured by instruments such as the Index of Phonetic Complexity (Jakielski, 1998). But while these findings hold true for English, which is considered to have a stress timed metric, stress patterning is very different in Spanish (a so-called syllable timed language), where similar levels of stress are placed on both function and content words. Additionally, function words in English are less complex phonologically than content words. In Spanish, there is a similar level of complexity. All this means that in Spanish similar motor demands are imposed on both function and content words, as opposed to English where increased demands are placed on the production of content words.

In a recent study (Howell, et al., 2004) analyzed patterns of stuttering in an 11-year-old bilingual speaker who, although competent in both Spanish and English, was more fluent in Spanish. Howell et al. found rates of 29.5 percent syllables stuttered (SS) in Spanish compared to 18.4 percent SS in English. Further analysis found that there was less of a difference between function and content word stuttering in Spanish than for English. As stuttering on content words is associated with established stuttering (see sections below) this boy therefore showed a more adult-like pattern of stuttering (located on content rather than function words) in his stronger language. This raises the interesting issue of how two different patterns of stuttering can occur within a single speaker. Howell et al. (2004) contend that different control strategies can be used by the same speaker in different languages. If this finding is corroborated in further research, there are important ramifications for therapy here. Howell and colleagues' model predicts that the language showing stuttering on content words is the one that would need to be targeted in therapy. (See section below on the EXPLAN model of fluency failure.)

Motoric and linguistic models of stuttering

Given the problems in disentangling motor elements from linguistic (language) ones, it is not surprising that there are opposing viewpoints as to whether stuttering is essentially a language or a motor speech based problem. To illustrate this, outlined below are two influential models of stuttering which offer alternative linguistic accounts as to why stuttering errors occur. Both models consider that stuttering results in a pattern of disfluency that can be described in linguistic terms, but they differ in their explanation of the factors underlying these fluency disruptions; one offering a psycholinguistic/ phonologic based theory, the other a motor speech perspective.

The covert repair hypothesis

This is essentially a psycholinguistic theory of error production in nonstuttering speakers, which can also explain the speech errors seen in stuttering from a phonological perspective. Postma and Kolk (1993) and Kolk and Postma (1997) base their covert repair hypothesis theory first and foremost on the assumption that all language production is subject to various self-monitoring procedures, which occur at different stages along the language production process. Early monitoring occurs for the phonetic plan of the utterance whilst the final monitoring stage, occurring fractionally after the speech end-product, is auditory (in fact auditory feedback). The theory contends that the speech flow of those who stutter is interrupted, by an internal feedback loop during prevocalization, just before speech is produced (Levelt, 1998). When an error in the phonetic plan is detected, so speech/language production is halted, and "repairs" are made before the process can continue.

The assumption is that the error type that people who stutter are trying to repair is phonological, and that the phonological encoding which is responsible for developing the articulatory plan is faulty. The theory is based in part on findings that speakers who stutter are slower at phonological encoding than their nonstuttering peers. The timing of the activation of upcoming phonological units is central to the theory. Conture (2001) argues that there may be two strands to the way in which time affects the likelihood of an increase in stuttering:

1   At a normal speech rate the speaker demonstrates a slow activation rate
    of both the target unit and competing targets. This increases the likeli-
    hood of selection error, and consequently the likelihood of stuttering,
    because all the units are equally activated.
2   On the other hand, when speaking rate is increased, the rate of activation
    of the speech units remains normal, but the speaker speeds up the phon-
    eme selection time. This too increases the likelihood that the speaker may
    misselect because both the target and competing units now have similar
    levels of activation.

This leads to the conclusion that both increased speaking rate and slower rate
of target activation may contribute to increased stuttering.

As Conture (2001) explains: "Thus for people who stutter according to
Postma and Kolk, activation of intended sounds or 'target' (sound) units are
delayed or slow to activate for people who stutter. This is thought to result in
a longer period of time during which their intended sounds are in competition with other sounds" (p. 35). However, the problem is compounded when
the speaker tries to increase rate. The implication of this is that the neural
processes underlying phonological processing operate more slowly in those
who stutter. The theory is particularly interesting because there are significant
implications for fluency therapy. For example, prolonged speech therapy, as
outlined in chapter 12, may under this interpretation be successful because it
decreases the time frame during which the target and competing units have
similar levels of activation. As such, this psycholinguistic perspective offers a
very different interpretation to those speech production theories that claim
prolonged speech therapy works on the basis that it gives the person who
stutters the increased time needed to coordinate vocal tract motor speech
subsystems.

In a recent study, Weber-Fox et al. (2004) compared the abilities of adults
who stutter and those who did not to judge rhyme in a reaction time experiment (see also chapter 4). In addition, event related potential (ERP) data was
collected. ERPs are "averaged electrical responses originating from synchronized activity of populations of neurons that are recorded over locations on
the scalp" (Weber-Fox et al., p. 1245). Key components in ERP waveforms
include amplitudes (strength of the signal), scalp distributions, and the polar-
ity of the ERP signal which may be either positive or negative. A number of
ERP studies of rhyme judgements in normally developing children and
adults have been undertaken, where a stimulus word is presented followed by
a second word which the individual has to judge as either rhyming or not
rhyming with the first word. Findings have indicated a negative component in
the signal at around 350–450 ms after the stimulus word had been presented,
and that this was larger when the target word was nonrhyming. Weber-Fox et
al. (2004) found no differences between their two groups on measures of ERP
latencies or amplitudes. However, the adults who stutter were found to exhibit
slower reaction times when demands on phonological processing were at their

highest; for example, when two words appear orthographically similar but do not actually rhyme. In addition, a right hemisphere asymmetry was found for the group that stuttered, suggesting that there is increased right hemisphere activity involved in making rhyme judgements amongst those who stutter. This last finding seems consistent with findings from a number of brain imaging studies which have found increased right hemisphere activity related to linguistic and motor functions in adults who stutter (see chapter 2).

Weber-Fox et al. conclude that findings do not support the idea of stuttering as arising from slowed phonological processing and errors in phonological planning. Instead, they argue that adults who stutter utilize increased right hemisphere involvement when making rhyme decisions. They further suggest that the slowness of the adults who stutter in making the more complex rhyme decisions could be related more to response selection and thus explained as increased vulnerability to higher cognitive loads. As this research group concede, the true significance of this finding awaits the outcome of similar experimentation on younger children, and further studies to confirm or disconfirm differential reaction time (RT) response and ERP patterns when overt speech is required. Work is currently underway to test this.

The EXPLAN model of fluency failure

An alternative model of stuttering has recently been developed by Howell and colleagues (Howell, Au-Yeung, & Sackin, 1999; Howell & Au-Yeung, 2002), which offers an explanation to the long-known association between increased stuttering on function words amongst younger children who stutter, and increased stuttering on content words with adults (Bloodstein & Gantwork, 1967; Brown, 1937). At the core of the EXPLAN model are the following notions:

1   All stuttering is centred around content words.
2   This apparent linguistic effect actually arises due to asynchrony between motor speech planning and motor speech execution.
3   The change from early stuttering on function words to later stuttering on content words reflects different fluency strategies on behalf of the speaker.

In the EXPLAN model, motor execution (EX) and planning (PLAN) are seen as independent processes which take place in parallel. The output of the plan generates from left to right as a motor program and can be represented as a phonetic string, although planning processes can and do continue beyond the immediate program which is represented in the form of syntactic units. Thus the EXPLAN model argues that "fluency failure is then viewed as a sign that planning and execution are out of synchrony" (Dworzynski, Howell, & Natke, 2003, p. 109). To understand EXPLAN we first need to consider two factors central to the model: the notion of the phonological word, and the nature of stalling behaviour in younger children.

Phonological word

Implicit in the EXPLAN model is the notion of the phonological word. This linguistic unit was first proposed by Selkirk (1984) and requires a moment or two by way of explanation. A phonological word comprises a unit of language. It must always contains a content word (e.g., "table"), but may in addition contain a function word or words either (a) as a prefix to the content word (e.g., "the table; on the table") or as a suffix; (b) after (e.g., "hit it"), or both before and after the content word (e.g., "I will hit it"). Thus the phrase "she hit it and ran" comprises two phonological words. "She hit it" (both "she" and "hit" are semantically linked to "it") whilst in the second phonological word, the function word "and" is semantically linked to "ran".

Stalling

Stalling refers to the postponement of upcoming linguistic elements and affects supralexical aspects of language. These include the repetition of words and phrases, together with silent pauses and interjections. (Note that there is an important difference between a silent pause and a silent block: the former may simply be a considered pause in the speech flow; the latter implies occlusion and excessive physical tension at some point, or points in the vocal tract.) Thus, to take our example above, "on the table" may become "on the, the, table" (word repetition) or "on the, on the table" (phrase repetition), "on the [pause] table", or "on the, um, table". As we know, these types of disfluencies are also quite commonly seen amongst normally nonfluent speakers in general, but they are most prevalent amongst preschool children, the population most at risk to develop stuttering. Nonstalling behaviours are seen in sublexical disfluencies such as prolongations, phoneme and syllable repetitions. Howell and colleagues consider both stalling and nonstalling events to be stuttering; a viewpoint that is not universally shared (see, for example, Wingate, 2002 on this subject).

The role of the phonological word and stalling in the EXPLAN model

Howell and colleagues' argument is that content words form the basis of all stuttering. Stuttering in children is associated with stalling on function words, which in effect delays the production of an upcoming content word. The speaker can then use this extra time to prepare for the content word. If a phonological word comprises only a content word (e.g., "Mummy") stalling cannot take place, and where this word might be difficult it might result in a different form of disfluency (e.g., part-word repetitions; mu – mu – mummy).

We already know that others have observed the pattern feature of function words as being more commonly stuttered on than content words in younger children, but Howell and colleagues go on to point out that function words are only affected when they appear as a prefix within a phonological word. So, for example, while we may well get "she, she hit it" within the phonological word "she hit it", we do not find "she hit it, it". There are also examples of this in languages other than English (see Dworzynski & Howell, 2004; Howell et al., 2004).

So, to summarize: when fluency breaks down this is because the motor plan is not ready. This may result in one of two consequences. First, the stalling continues until the motor plan is ready (this results in the word or phrase repetition of function word prefixes in the phonological word). Second, the speaker attempts to continue. If there is insufficient time to complete the motor plan during any function word prefixes then the plan will run out, and the resulting content word may then contain part-word disfluencies. Thus, stalling and nonstalling behaviours are seen as complementary or, put another way, a stalling disfluency prevents nonstalling disfluency (Howell et al., 2004). Recently, Bernstein-Ratner (2005a) criticized the EXPLAN model on a number of accounts; for example, that syntactic components have not been considered as significant factors in the development of stuttering, and that phonetic variables have minor significance for processing models. Howell and Dworzynski (2005) in response counter that if syntax alone was sufficient to account for stuttering then there would not be cases of some specific language-impaired children with syntactic deficit in the absence of stuttering nor any other speech output problems. With regard to the role of phonetic influence, Howell and Dworzynski (2005) argue that speech errors play a significant role in many psycholinguistic models of language processing and that their significance can further be demonstrated in tongue twisters where, for example, there is transposition of the approximants (liquids), but not the vowels (for example, red wellies – yellow wellies), indicating that the two phoneme classes operate independently.

What research into an EXPLAN model of stuttering has demonstrated is that, corroborating earlier evidence (see above), stuttering rates have been found to be associated with increased phonetic complexity (Dworzynski & Howell, 2004). Other laboratories have confirmed that loci of stuttering, stuttering frequencies and type of stuttering behaviours all appear consistent with this model of stuttering (Natke, Sandrieser, van Ark, Pietrowsky, & Kalveram, 2004). Further, the EXPLAN model of stuttering generally appears to be supported by cross-linguistic studies in German (Dworzynski et al., 2003; Rommel, 2001) and Spanish (Au-Yeung, Howell, & Vallejo-Gomez, 1998). Howell et al. (2004) observe, however, that while an exchange between function and content words still takes place in Spanish, these speakers maintain a higher level of stuttering on function words into adulthood than the German and English speakers. They speculate that this may be due to differences in phonetic complexity between the languages.

An integration of motor and linguistic accounts: some final comments

Thankfully, some of the debate as to the relative significance of linguistic/ motor speech influences is now becoming redundant. There seems to be increased recognition from both sides of the argument that their findings must be taken together with those from the other (Smith & Goffman, 2004), but the nature of the interaction between motor speech and linguistic variables, even in normal speech, remains far from clear. In a recent chapter on linguistic variables in stuttering, Conture, Zackheim, Anderson, and Pellowski (2004) suggest that the "physical work" (of respiration, phonation and articulation), while rapid, cannot match the speed involved in changing thought and developing linguistic plans and as such are less likely to be nearer the core of stuttering, although they concede that motor speech variables might exacerbate or perpetuate instances of stuttering:

> If these rapidly changing events which precede motoric planning, control, and/or executions are themselves less efficient, not well integrated, or even slower than typical, is it not possible that they contribute to a person's relative lack of fluent speech?
>
> (Conture et al., 2004, p. 254)

Conture et al.'s conclusion that we will never have answers to this question "until we look outside the motoric lamplight into the linguistic darkness for the keys to stuttering" (p. 254) appears to suggest that this work is not being undertaken. The work emanating from Conture's own laboratory and those of others clearly demonstrates that this is not the case.

To help resolve the issues of the relative influence of motoric and linguistic variables there needs to be both types of data gathered from a task where both are implicated (for example, looking at the influence of syntactic complexity and MLU) from the same subject group(s). As we have seen in the previous chapter, most of the work on motor speech control has been conducted on adults, due in large part to difficulties with younger children tolerating the testing procedures. Work on linguistic processing, on the other hand, has mostly been undertaken on younger children and (less commonly) adolescents. This obviously means that we are collecting data on apples and oranges when we come to make assertions as to what is influencing what. An important step would also be to include data from nonspeech motor control. To properly place a linguistic argument, we need to consider why, for example, some people who stutter also perform hand coordination tasks in a subtly different way to those who do not, and why motor control deficiencies can also be seen amongst some people who stutter when playing wind and brass instruments.

Summary

There is a wealth of evidence to show that stuttering is related to factors that can be explained in linguistic terms. The very early findings that stuttering more commonly arises at linguistically complex loci have been corroborated in a number of more recent studies. Stuttering also usually develops at a time of significant growth in linguistic ability, yet some children with delayed language skills go on to develop a stutter, while others do not, whilst the same is true for children who may be advanced in their language development. Clearly a linguistic explanation cannot be taken in isolation, but the nature of the interaction of motor and linguistic aspects needs to be more fully explored (Conture et al., 2004; Smith & Goffman, 2004).

Of course, it is not just potential motoric influences with which linguistic perspectives need to coexist. For example, it is difficult for linguistic theory alone to explain the unpredictability of stuttering, and that the same word stuttered at one time may not be stuttered the next, and emotional variables may play a significant part in explaining this variability (Conture & Zackheim, 2002). A Demands and Capacities approach might lead us to consider the likelihood that linguistic factors are only one of a number of influences on the development of stuttering; both from a capacity perspective (where there might be some naturally reduced capability amongst young children who stutter) and a demands perspective (where, for example, overexposure to advanced language and an insistence from the parents on complex language usage might combine to outstrip the child's abilities). The therapeutic implications from a parent–child interaction perspective might be to encourage the parents to use simpler linguistic structures to help reduce "demand" on the child's linguistic processing ability, whilst the association between increased linguistic complexity and stuttering give credence to approaches which in their early stages constrain the response length and complexity to help promote fluency, as in Ryan's Gradual Increase in Length and Complexity of Utterance program. (See chapter 10 for details of the management of early stuttering.)

> **Key points**
> - A consistent feature of the disorder of stuttering is that the motoric disruptions perceived as stuttering mostly fall in a manner which can be explained in linguistic terms.
> - Despite this, it is often unclear as to what extent these linguistic factors can be separated from the phonetic (or motoric) correlates. (As we see from chapter 2, brain centres responsible for language processing have been implicated in stuttering, as well as those which subserve motor programming, motor execution and coordination.)

- From a conceptual perspective also, the relationship between language and speech is awkward. Models of language processing cannot easily account for the conversion of abstract (and therefore timeless) linguistic units into the physical realities of motor speech movements which operate in real time. Action theory and articulatory phonology offer alternative explanations of the relationship between linguistic and motor speech activities.
- The covert repair hypothesis (Kolk & Postma, 1997; Postma & Kolk, 1993) and the EXPLAN model of fluency failure (Howell & Au-Yeung, 2002) offer opposing perspectives on stuttering development. The covert repair hypothesis assumes that stuttering is related to an error-prone phonological system, whilst EXPLAN argues that the planning and execution processes are out of synchrony.
- It may be useful to consider linguistic factors in stuttering within the framework of a demands and capacities model of the disorder.

Further reading

Alfonso, P. J. (1991). Implications of the concepts underlying task-dynamic modelling on kinematic studies of stuttering. *Haskins Laboratory Status Report on Speech Research, SR-107–108*, 93–110.
This is quite specialized, but is strongly recommended for those interested in knowing more about action theory and task dynamic modelling, which provides the framework for testing action theory concepts. Although this paper is focused more on speech kinematics, and therefore the articulatory outcome of language processing, it is nonetheless an interesting read from a linguistic perspective as it sets out the case for the idea that linguistic units and motor speech representations do not exist independently, and then places this within the context of stuttering.

Bernstein-Ratner, N. E. (1997). Stuttering: A psycholinguistic perspective. In R. F. Curlee & G. M. Siegel (Eds.), *Nature and treatment of stuttering: New directions* (pp. 99–127). Boston: Allyn & Bacon.
This is the first of two chapters from this edited collection by Curlee and Siegel which are recommended reading. A truly comprehensive read, which in addition to offering a "psycholinguistic perspective" on stuttering also contains a considerable amount of information on "pure" linguistic aspects.

Conture, E. G., Zackheim, C. T., Anderson, J., & Pellowski, M. (2004). Linguistic processes and childhood stuttering: Many's a slip between intention and lip. In B. Maassen, R. D. Kent, H. F. M. Peters, P. H. H. M. van Lieshout and W. Hulstijn (Eds.), *Speech motor control in normal and disordered speech*, (pp. 253–281). Oxford: Oxford University Press.
An up-to-date account of linguistic processing in children, although there is no mention of EXPLAN.

Howell, P., & AuYeung, J. (2002). The EXPLAN theory of fluency control and the diagnosis of stuttering. In E. Fava (Ed.), *Pathology and therapy of speech disorders: Current issues in linguistic theory series* (pp. 75–94). Amsterdam: John Benjamins.
The original source for the EXPLAN model, this chapter also summarizes Howell and coworkers' earlier work on the content and function word distinction in stuttering.

Kolk, H., & Postma, A. (1997). Stuttering as a covert repair phenomenon. In R. F. Curlee & G. M. Siegel (Eds.), *Nature and treatment of stuttering: New directions* (pp. 182–203). Baston: Allyn & Bacon.
Kolk and Postma's covert repair hypothesis is explained in some detail here. Particularly, they expand on the integration of their model within earlier psycholinguistic frameworks.

Smith, A., & Goffman, L. (2004). Interaction of language and motor factors in the development of speech production. In B. Maassen, R. D. Kent, H. F. M. Peters, P. H. H. M. van Lieshout & W. Hulstijn (Eds.), *Speech motor control in normal and disordered speech.* (pp. 227–252). Oxford: Oxford University Press.
This is the second chapter (alongside Conture et al.'s piece) from this volume that is recommended reading. The crucial issue of understanding how speech and linguistic processes coexist and how they need to be considered alongside each other in research is tackled here by two experts in the field.

6 Some psychological perspectives on stuttering

Introduction

In the earlier part of the last century, many of the prevailing theories on stuttering rested on the notion that the disorder was caused by some psychological reaction on behalf of the sufferer. While it is true to say that in recent decades psychological explanations have fallen from favour as a stand-alone answer as to why stuttering arises, a number still offer important frameworks that complement alternative organic explanations. Additionally, it is clear that the development of a stutter is inextricably linked to the environment in which that person (and the stutter) develops. Consequently a number of psychological theories have had a direct and lasting impact on therapeutic practice. Specifically, the importance of recognizing cognitive and affective components in stuttering has been reflected in the success of therapies that target an individual's perception of themselves as a speaker, and in dealing with the belief systems that accompany feelings about their stutter, whilst operant practice has been used extensively in the treatment of both children and adults. It is worth noting that for all the exciting discoveries that continue to be made which strengthen arguments for organic accounts of stuttering, remarkably few translate into a therapeutic framework that directly benefits the person who stutters. In contrast, as we see in part 2 of this book, the vast majority of therapeutic approaches to stuttering have their rationale based in one or other psychological viewpoint, and therapy can be readily translated back to the theory that underlies it.

Learning theory and stuttering

Stuttering – a bad habit?

Perhaps the most basic of all learning theories is that stuttering is a bad habit. There is a long history of stuttering being described and treated as such. Over three centuries ago Amman (1700/1965)) had his patients speak loudly and slowly to break such a habit. Erasmus Darwin (1800), on the other hand, believed stuttering was due to a motoric difficulty which had become habituated, and the fact that over 200 years ago he advocated the use of soft articulatory contact and repeated practice with difficult sounds in order to overcome it might lead us to question whether therapeutic practice really has moved on so greatly. McCormac (1828, cited in Van Riper, 1982) noted that people who stuttered habitually spoke without adequate lung air. Therapy focused on deep breathing and forced exhalation with each word. There have also been a number of subsequent theorists, a noteworthy nineteenth-century example being Alexander Melville Bell (1853) who, in response to those who believed that stuttering had an organic cause, argued that speech was an artificially learned process (through imitation). The habit of stuttering, therefore, was best treated as such. In using controlling techniques, penalizing stuttering and replacing it with overpractised reinforced normal speech, the stuttering habit could be replaced by fluent speech.

Negative practice

The notion that stuttering can be thought of as something as simple as a bad habit may now seem at best naive, but in using fluency enhancing techniques such as rhythmic speech, syllable-timed speech, in addition to the breathing control and soft contact techniques mentioned earlier, these early practitioners were applying speech modification techniques, some of which are still in use today. A rare dissenting voice against the practice of replacing the stuttering habit with a fluent speech habit was raised by Dunlap (1932), who strongly disapproved of this perspective. Dunlap argued that dealing with stuttering as a habit would only affect the stutter within that immediate context. He had a point. Stuttering severity is notoriously variable and therapists today ignore this aspect at their clients' peril.

Instead, Dunlap decided to tackle stuttering through a procedure called "negative practice". Originally, this involved having the speaker stop at a given moment of stuttering, and then consciously trying to imitate the stuttered moment. After using negative practice two or three times, the client would continue in his attempt to produce the stuttered word, but this time fluently. The technique is widely in use today, most commonly as a component of the block modification approach of Van Riper (1973), although there are a number of different ways of using the negative practice technique (now also called pseudo stuttering or voluntary stuttering) therapeutically. For example, some therapists have the client use the technique on words they feel comfortable with, and where there is no danger of genuine stuttering. The idea here being that stuttering, which is usually associated with a sense of loss of control, now becomes a controllable act. (Also see chapter 12 for a description of this process.)

Two-factor theory of stuttering

Another earlier theorist whose work has an enduring effect is Bleumel. Again, taking the premise that speech was a learned behaviour, Bleumel (1935) argued that the disorder of stuttering could be viewed within the contextual framework of Pavlovian (or classical) conditioning, and introduced the notion of primary and secondary stuttering. Some years later, Brutten and Shoemaker (1967) were to redefine the role of conditioning in their two-factor theory of stuttering. This contends that the disorder may be characterized as having a primary stuttering component comprising the physical moments of stuttering such as blocks, repetitions and prolongations, which occur due to classical conditioned negative emotions, and secondary ones, including verbal and nonverbal coping strategies, which are learned through the effects of operant conditioning, associated to the primary ones. These may include loss of eye contact, hand tapping, head nodding, grimacing, and such like. The significance of this interpretation of stuttering in the 1930s is put into sharp context by Van Riper (1982) who recalled severe criticism of his earlier paper (Van Riper, 1937) demonstrating that secondary behaviours were learned and did not represent abnormal neurological dysfunction, as had previously been asserted.

Diagnosogenic theory of stuttering

Johnson and cerebral dominance

Although primarily noted for introducing the world to his diagnosogenic theory of stuttering, as a younger man Wendell Johnson adhered to the prevailing belief of the time that his disorder was, as Travis and Orton proposed, due to lack of cerebral dominance (see chapter 2 for a discussion of this theory). In fact, Johnson became one of Travis' students. Having a severe stutter himself, Johnson looked for ways to re-establish the cerebral dominance which he believed would alleviate his stuttering. Although naturally right-handed, Johnson surmised that he used his right hand in imitation of other family members, and now in a rigorous fashion taught himself how to use his left hand. In doing so, all right-sided and bilateral activity was abandoned. Initially, he reported that his fluency improved, and along with it his attitude towards the stutter, but years later he was forced to concede defeat. Eventually, in 1961 he wrote:

> I put away my left-handed scissors, and with my right hand wrote "Finis" to the experiment, still stuttering splendidly.
>
> (Johnson 1961, p. 27)

Johnson now refocused his efforts to determine the cause of stuttering within a new area. For many years he had been interested in how many authorities had examined only adult stuttering, and yet were making assertions as to how stuttering began. In looking at differences between children who stuttered and those who didn't, Johnson was treading new ground. He began to develop a database of children whose parents considered them to be stuttering and compared this group with others who were not. From his investigations, and particularly through his interviews with parents of children who stuttered, Johnson believed that the many children who stuttered had parents who enforced high levels of expectancy generally, and specifically with regard to speech and language development. Although conducted before his theory became developed, the often-quoted infamous case of the so-called monster study effectively demonstrates the diagnosogenic position.

The monster study

In 1939 one of Johnson's Masters students named Mary Tudor undertook an experiment that now seems rather shocking. Tudor (1939) examined six children with normal speech and language from an orphanage. In the full knowledge that there was nothing wrong with these children, they were nonetheless diagnosed with symptoms of stuttering and told that they were making errors in their speech. In order to deal with this she told them they should speak more carefully. Orphanage staff were also warned that these children should be watched for speech errors, and that any mistakes should be corrected straightaway. Months later, Tudor returned to find that a number of the children she had selected had developed stuttering behaviours. Unfortunately, attempts by her to treat the stuttering were not altogether successful and the disorder, at least in one case, persisted into adulthood.

The diagnosogenic theory

Johnson had already observed that at onset children with stutters and non-stuttering children alike shared the common feature of repetition in their speech. Johnson further speculated that the difference in those children who were diagnosed as stuttering was that the parents (or other significant caregivers) were under the misconception that their child's normal disfluencies were moments of genuine stuttering, hence "diagnosogenic", meaning that the disorder begins with its diagnosis, or more accurately misdiagnosis by the parent. Johnson surmised that the child then picked up on the adverse parental reaction to these disfluencies, which in turn led to struggle and avoidance behaviour as the child attempted to stop the (normal) disfluencies, and genuine stuttering began to develop. The viability of this theory initially depended entirely on evidence that parents of stutterers behaved differently to parents of nonstutterering children, and there is some support for this idea. Moncur (1952) found mothers of stuttering children to be more critical and protective of their offspring than mothers of nonstuttering children. Johnson et al. (1959) found that mothers of stuttering children tended to demand higher standards from their children. Studies have also shown that parents of children who stutter may be more anxious than parents of children who do not stutter (Zenner, Ritterman, Bowen, & Gronhovd, 1978), or more rejecting (Flugel, 1979).

The diagnosogenic theory prevailed through the 1940s and 1950s, largely on the basis of the limited earlier data above. But there are a number of problems. First, not all studies concurred with the above research (Goodstein, 1956; Goodstein & Dahlstrom, 1956). Andrews and Harris (1964) in a rigorous and large-scale longitudinal study of children who stuttered and their environments, found similar personality traits amongst parents of stutterers and parents of nonstutterers, and no indication that there was a difference between the two groups of parents in terms of parental pressure. Generally, the parents of stuttering children were found to be lower achievers and provided more poorly for their children than the parents of nonstuttering children. This does not seem to fit with the notion of insistence on high achievement reported in the earlier studies. Second, if stuttering were a matter of higher levels of expectation being placed on the child, we might expect to see brothers and sisters equally affected. Third, there is debate as to whether any difference in expectation or home environment actually causes stuttering (Yairi, 1997). It is quite possible that anxiety or expectation could signal a response to the onset of stuttering in their children, rather than being the direct cause of it.

By the late 1950s, Johnson was modifying the diagnosogenic theory. Johnson's research had led him to the conclusion that stuttering onset was typified by specific types of fluency errors – syllable repetitions, voiced prolongations and complete blocks – whereas nonstuttering children had phrase repetitions, interjections and pauses. Despite these apparent differences, Johnson argued that there was considerable overlap between the two groups. However, some parents were taking the disfluency types to be normal, while others believed the same disfluency types represented stuttering (Johnson et al., 1959). He now conceded that in addition to listener reaction, the extent of the child's disfluency and the sensitivity of the child to his disfluencies and the listener's reactions were integral parts of the diagnosogenic theory.

Therapeutic perspectives

Therapy, then, focused on modifying parental response and reaction to ensure the child was not receiving the negative feedback which, according to Johnson, was the sole reason for the stutter arising. If stuttering continued in the face of this indirect approach to treatment, Johnson did not advocate attempts to eliminate stuttering, as this would lead to further avoidance. Instead, the child would be taught how to stutter without fear of listener penalty, and without any secondary behaviours. The suggestion, now, that stuttering is a purely psychological phenomenon, arising only because of the negative listener reaction to (initially) normal disfluencies is discredited.

However, some of the therapeutic concepts have been taken up by others, and are still regarded as central in many therapeutic approaches. For example, Sheehan took up Johnson's hypothesis that stuttering was associated to learned fear-motivated behaviour in response to punishment. Sheehan's approach to therapy, however, took a very different path, with confrontation and acute awareness of the stutter being central therapeutic issues (see chapter 12). One can also see some tentative links between the diagnosogenic theory and current treatment approaches such as parent–child interaction (see chapter 10). But while acknowledging that environment, and particularly the interaction between the young child who stutters and the primary care-givers, can be of central importance to the development of the disorder, most clinicians would now want to distance themselves from the idea that adverse parental reaction is at the centre of the cause of stuttering.

Stuttering as an operant behaviour

Subsequent to the publication of B. H. Skinner's *Verbal behavior* (1957), a number of researchers had looked to the proposition that stuttering may be an operant disorder. Recall that Bleumel some 25 years previously had already suggested that there may be a stimulus-response relationship in stuttering. The operant field within learning theory offers a different relationship between stimulus and response, and one which lends itself easily to empirical testing. Those involved in both the study and treatment of stuttering have been sharply divided as to the value of an operant theory, and it remains to this day a contentious issue. Unquestionably, its influence has been wide-ranging; perhaps these days more with regard to therapy than theory, but operant conditioning (and there has been much written about its role with stuttering) does require some detailed attention.

How does operant conditioning work?

"Operant behaviours are those that are controlled – increased, decreased, or changed in form – by their consequences" (Costello, 1984, p. 107). Thus, a given behaviour or response will be affected by the consequences of that behaviour. Central to the theory is the principle of reinforcement. If a reaction (or response) to a behaviour is positive (positive reinforcement), then there is an increased likelihood that the behaviour will occur in the future. Any stimulus that generates an increase in the response frequency is called a positive reinforcer. Conversely, a negative reaction to a stimulus (punishment) is likely to decrease the likelihood of that behaviour occuring again. Simple examples of positive reinforcement would be applauding following a performance, or allowing special privileges to a child who has been particularly helpful. Punishment could be the throwing of rotten fruit at a performance, or sending a child to their room for misbehaving. To these types of reinforcement we can also add two more: the cessation of a negative reinforcer to produce positive reinforcement and conversely the withdrawal of a positive reinforcer to create negative reinforcement, and therefore decrease response rates. In operant terms, response rates may be "extinguished" by judicial manipulation of these stimulus-response relationships, or as they are more generally known, response contingent stimuli (RCS).

Contingent punishment of stuttering

So how does operant conditioning explain stuttering? The working hypothesis of operant theory follows the tenet that (a) stuttering is a learned behaviour. It therefore follows that (b) stuttering occurs in response to interactions between an individual's behaviour and the environment in which that behaviour occurs. So, it should therefore be possible to control levels of stuttering by the manipulation of reinforcement and punishment. This has been attempted in many studies, and there are a number which support the operant standpoint (see Table 6.1).

Aside from the very obvious ethical problems with some of this research, there are also methodological ones. For example, Flanagan, Goldiamond, and Azrin's (1959) research did not distinguish between a rise in disfluency and a rise in stuttering. Also where these techniques formed the basis of a fluency therapy program, there has been a noticeable difficulty in establishing the new controlled levels of fluency outside the laboratory. In many cases, stuttering that had responded to operant procedures returned to baseline levels immediately following the withdrawal of the given stimulus-response relationship, even when operant techniques such as token reinforcement were used. In addition, while many experiments have shown that stuttering can be brought under operant control to some degree, stuttering has very rarely been totally extinguished during these experiments.

Additionally, not all research has supported the operant case. Martin and Siegel (1966) successfully used contingent electric shock to decrease secondary stuttering, but found that at the same time there was an increase in some primary stuttering (prolongations). Biggs and Sheehan (1969) found stuttering to decrease when the individual was presented with a loud tone, regardless of whether the noise was presented together with a moment of stuttering, presented randomly or even withdrawn at a moment of stuttering. There are also a number of replication studies which have failed to corroborate the notion that stuttering is an operant condition. Timmons (1966) found no difference in levels of stuttering between two groups of people who stutter, only one of which received response contingent stimuli in the form of the word "wrong". Similarly, a number of studies (Cady & Robbins, 1968; Cooper, Cady, & Robbins, 1970; Daly & Kimbarrow, 1978) found that positive and neutral verbal contingencies elicited similar decrease in stuttering as did negative verbal stimuli. Similarly, Stevens (1963) and Daly and Cooper (1967) found stuttering failed to respond to electric shock contingencies. Adams and Popelka (1971) found that most

Table 6.1 Summary of early research supporting stuttering as an operant disorder

Researcher	Contingent stimulus	Findings
Flanagan, Goldiamond, & Azrin (1958)	Loud noise	Stuttering increased and decreased contingent on presentation of 105dB tone
Brookshire & Martin (1967)	Stimulus words "wrong"	Reduction in stuttering
Quist & Martin (1967)	The words "wrong", "no" and "uh – uh"	Reduction in stuttering, when "punishing" stimulus words were presented
Crowder & Harbin (1971)	Electric shock	Stuttering decreased by around 85% contingent on use of electric shock
Haroldson, Martin, & Starr (1968)	Time out	Stuttering decreased due to enforced period of silence contingent on stuttering
Martin & Siegel (1975)	Electric shock	Stuttering decrease contingent on use of electric shock
Flanagan, Goldiamond, & Azrin (1959)	Electric shock	Stuttering decreased contingent on use of electric shock
Hedge (1971)	Electric shock	Contingent shock reduced stuttering in oral reading
Gross & Holland (1965)	Electric shock	Decrease in stuttering contingent on electric shock
Goldiamond (1965)	Delayed auditory feedback	Moments of DAF, contingent upon stuttering moments, decreased stuttering

of their subjects who experienced a decrease in stuttering following time-out contingency believed that this was due to the calming effect of not having to speak. For these speakers, at least, the contingency was in fact positively reinforcing, rather than negatively reinforcing. Finally, we should bear in mind that just as some commentators have criticized some of the operant methodology (for example, Sheehan, 1984; Van Riper, 1982), so to concerns have been raised over some experiments that do not support the operant perspective (Ingham, 1984). The subsequent success of operant treatment programs (usually used in conjunction with fluency shaping therapy programs) appears to demonstrate that operant programs can be extremely effective in controlling stuttering in adult stuttering. More recently, the development of the highly successful Lidcombe therapy program for preschool children demonstrates this in striking fashion. Unlike most operant therapy programs which work via the (operant) administration of a range of fluency controlling techniques, this program works simply on the carefully structured administration of verbal praise and (gentle) admonishment of stuttering moments. No techniques or fluency skills are applied. See part 2 of this book for discussion of operant techniques in adult therapy (chapter 12) and the Lidcombe program for preschool children (chapter 10).

An operant explanation of the onset and development of stuttering

In one sense, the above heading is something of a misnomer. Operant theory is atheoretical. Thus, the fact that stuttering can be seen as an operant does not, in theoretical terms, have any ramifications for the underlying cause or causes of the disorder itself. However, although stuttering can certainly be controlled through the use of operant procedures, it cannot be eliminated through the use of operant approaches, particularly with older clients. Some consideration of the nature of the stimulus-response relationships that might be at work is therefore in order.

As we will see elsewhere, a concept common to a number of frameworks of stuttering is that it arises in childhood out of normal disfluency (see also Bloodstein, Alper, & Zisk, 1965) and it can be quite natural for children, when beginning to expand their language and motor speech capabilities, to become nonfluent. One operant stance is that certain forms of these disfluencies then become reinforced, and thereby increase in number (Shames & Sherrick, 1963). But the model does not explain why this occurs, and two issues in particular need clarification. First, why would disfluencies consistent with stuttering such as prolongations and part-word repetitions become reinforced, while others do not? Second, why would such verbal behaviour be rewarded at all? One answer to these questions is that parents unwittingly reward normal disfluency behaviours by giving greater attention to the child's speech; allowing uninterrupted speech (Shames & Sherrick, 1963). This then reinforces the disfluent speech, resulting in more stuttering. It could follow that the more atypical the type of disfluency, the more likely it is to receive parental attention, and also that as stuttering becomes more established, so this can lead to feelings of frustration and rejection. This could then result in the establishment of secondary behaviours such as avoidance and physical escape behaviours such as eye closing, or eye avoidance, stalling behaviour through use of fillers ("um. . .er. . .") all of which serve temporarily to terminate negative listener reactions. Van Riper accepts the possibility that disfluency could at first be positively reinforced and later negatively reinforced:

> On the one hand listener reactions (attention, concern) are so positively reinforcing that they create the stuttering problem by increasing normal disfluencies. On the other hand, listener reactions are so punishing that

successful efforts to escape them are negatively reinforced. This could be true if the child's listeners changed their behavior from attending to rejecting, or from beyond a certain cut-off. This may indeed take place, although we have no evidence that it does.

(Van Riper, 1982, p. 286)

Unfortunately, more than 20 years later, we still lack any consistent and reliable evidence that listeners do respond in this manner. But setting this aside for a moment, the theory can quite elegantly explain how a stutter changes and develops as it becomes more established over a period of many years. But as persistent stuttering becomes more severe over time, so too a wide range of secondary behaviours may increasingly become significant features of the stutter. With the increased severity comes increased punishment in the form of negative listener reaction. Why then is the secondary activity, which can develop into the most noticeable part of the disorder, sustained? There are perhaps two answers, although they are somewhat intertwined.

First, to many people who stutter secondary escape behaviours are quite simply seen as necessary. Although circumlocution, head jerking or knee tapping may not be ideal tools to help fluency, they serve a purpose. If a potential block is avoided by word avoidance, or silent block terminated by a moment of head thrusting, that may be considered by the speaker to be a worthwhile trade. To that extent, these features are reinforcing and self-perpetuating. They may also be modified or exaggerated if they are no longer working. In the same way that, after a period of time, the effect of a prescribed drug may wear off and a higher dose is required to achieve the same effect, so too accessory behaviours may increase over time to become ever more obvious and intrusive features alongside the stutter. Even if the speaker is aware of the abnormality of these self-induced features, it may by now be difficult to extinguish them without specialist help.

The second reason lies in the unreliability of the escape behaviours mentioned above. Operant conditioning laws state that those behaviours which are reinforced intermittently are the hardest ones to extinguish.[1] So, just as the jaw jerk may not prove effective at terminating a block every time, so the behaviour exists in the person's belief that it will help next time. Many people who stutter realize the secondary behaviour may fail to terminate each moment of stuttering, but the association between the stuttering moment and the secondary response becomes automatically linked over time. As such, this

---

1 Gambling on slot machines is a good example of this: we continue gambling even when we are not receiving positive reinforcement (that is, a pay-out) because we cannot predict when we will win. The best slot machines (from their owner's perspective, at least) are the ones that pay out very infrequently but just enough to maintain the gambler's belief, or hope, that she or he will eventually win.

might be seen as habituated behaviour, although this term barely seems to do justice to the association.

Stuttering as an operant disorder – current status

The reality is that while many texts towards the end of the twentieth century have continued to report on psychological perspectives on the development of stuttering, thinking in the late 1970s and 1980s increasingly turned away from any stand-alone idea of stuttering as an operant perspective. Particularly, technological advances in brain imaging and movement measuring devices in the 1980s and 1990s have made brain studies and detailed movement control studies both more viable and more accurate, and specifically many researchers looked to the areas of functional neurology and speech kinematics to explain the disorder. However, it is important that we do not confuse issues relating to the cause of the disorder with those relating to therapy. In one sense, from an operant perspective, it does not matter what the exact nature of stuttering is and what forces underlie it. The more pertinent question is "Can it be effectively treated as an operant"?

The Lidcombe Program provides a good example, here. The program uses operant procedures, yet the ethos behind the program (as we see in chapter 10) is that stuttering at onset is a rather simple problem with motor control. Whether empirical testing eventually bears this theory out or not is in one sense irrelevant. There seems little question that the disorder at onset can be treated as an operant. The issue is more complicated for established stuttering, where operant techniques can provide an effective framework from which to use motor speech control techniques. However, these techniques are controlling stuttering, not eliminating it. Thus, while the establishment of fluency control may be seen to be an operant, the chronic disorder (and thus elimination of the chronic form in adults) cannot be seen to be under operant control.

Thus, we can disassociate the idea of stuttering being operant in nature, as opposed to something that can be helped by an operant approach to treatment.

Stuttering and approach-avoidance conflict

We have already said that "habit" may seem a gross oversimplification to describe a phenomenon such as stuttering, but it is not totally unrelated to more complex theoretical positions, one of which is known as approach-avoidance conflict. Wyneken (1868, cited in Van Riper, 1982) offers an early account of stuttering as a form of inertia, arising from the cancelling out of opposing needs and drives:

> The stutterer is thus a doubter of speech. If he dares the word which seems difficult to him, then however his will, and one which is directly

opposed to the will proper. The muscles which underlie respiration, phonation and articulation are often not sure, if I may express myself thus, whom they should obey, and as a consequence thereof do not fulfill their functions with the necessary synergy, and stuttering occurs.

(p. 21)

Wyneken continues with a further clear example of approach avoidance outside the speech domain:

The relation is similar as when somebody, for example, wants to venture a jump, but in the very moment in which he leaps doubts that he will succeed. Often he can no longer stop the leap, but also does not jump with sufficient assurance (l'aplomb nécessaire), and so does not reach his goal.

(p. 22)

One hundred years later, Sheehan's (1975) approach-avoidance conflict theory viewed stuttering in a somewhat similar light, placing the cause somewhere between psychoanalysis and learning theory. Sheehan's premise was that stuttering, in large part, was due to a build-up of guilt. Original guilt refers to the negative associations and feelings that occur at the onset of stuttering. Later, a secondary cause of guilt may develop alongside the increased self-awareness that the stuttering behaviour (blocks and repetitions) is receiving negative listener reactions. The person who stutters becomes caught in a tug-of-war between two opposing needs: the need to speak and the need to remain silent for fear of stuttering. In approach-avoidance theory, repetitions and blocks reflect attempts to balance out the need to communicate and the fear of failure that might result when attempting to do so. These opposing forces can occur at many different levels, both linguistic (for example, in word avoidance) and affective (e.g., interpersonal relationship level). In every case, the conflict will result in increased anxiety, and it is this anxiety which helps maintain the stutter. Sheehan's indirect therapeutic approach, based on this model of stuttering is described in chapter 12.

Stuttering as anticipatory struggle behaviour

The anticipatory struggle hypothesis (Bloodstein, 1987) has at its basis the idea that stuttering develops when a child becomes frustrated with speech and believes the act of speaking to be difficult. These feelings may initially arise for a variety of reasons, which may not have anything to do with stuttering, but involve factors such as articulation or language difficulties. Bloodstein argues that these, together with environmental influences such as negative listener reaction, may then lead to increased anxiety, which can translate as features such as facial muscle tension. Speech may subsequently become more blocked and disfluent, and stuttering can quickly develop from the typical easy repetitions seen at onset to the increasingly tense blocks and avoidance of an established stutter. A key feature in the anticipatory struggle conception is the child's personality. The individual may set very high standards, which can exacerbate feelings of anxiety, frustration and even inadequacy and shame as the speech problem persists. The family too may set often unrealistically high standards for verbal acuity, and may either knowingly or unknowingly respond negatively when the child does not reach these high goals, both with regard to speech and language and elsewhere.

The idea that the onset of stuttering is characterized by excessive pressure, whether internal or environmental, seems attractive, and many clinicians will be able to identify young clients they have seen whose background is consistent with this pattern. The theory also offers an explanation as to why some children, experiencing nonfluency as is common in preschool speech, go on to develop a stutter while others do not. However, clinicians will also note that a good many children they see do not fit into this pattern. (See for instance the section on tracks of development in the following chapter.) As well, some studies have not found any difference between levels of expectation of parents with children who stutter, and children who do not (Andrews & Harris, 1964).

It may be useful to think of the anticipatory struggle hypothesis as relating to one set of variables which may be of particular significance to a particular subgroup of young stuttering children. The issues concerned here may also seem to fit neatly into Starkweather's Demands and Capacities model of stuttering, which has been outlined in chapter 1.

Summary

Stuttering has a long history of being explained as a psychological disorder. Although some have claimed that those who stutter differ fundamentally in areas such as personality, anxiousness and other variables, evidence is equivocal on the subject. There is also little evidence to substantiate claims made in the early part of the last century that stuttering can be helped by psychoanalysis, as some have claimed (Coriat, 1943; Glauber, 1958). However, stuttering unquestionably does have a significant psychological component associated with its development, and we have seen that this can be modelled in a number of ways. A number of attributes of learning theory and operant theory have contributed substantially to the understanding as to how the disorder develops and, as we see in part 2, these have had a significant impact therapeutically, as well as theoretically. We see this reflected in a number of mainstream approaches described in part 2, as well as in the growing number of psychological approaches now being applied to counselling therapy models (see chapter 13). As with organic explanations, discussed in other chapters, psychological theories may best be seen as part of an integrated perspective on stuttering that includes not only those factors which affect the development of the disorder, but also perspectives which may relate to a predisposition to stutter. This demands and capacities model has been discussed at the end of chapter 1.

Key points

- Stuttering has been described in learning theory terms: including perspectives as a habit, an operant disorder, a disorder arising due to anticipatory struggle behaviour, conflict between approach and avoidance, and a diagnosogenic disorder, where stuttering arises due to a misdiagnosis by parents in the early development.
- Concepts relating to anticipatory struggle and approach-avoidance are interwoven into cognitive-behavioural therapies such as Van Riper's (1973) speech modification approaches. Johnson's diagnosogenic theory has to some degree been discredited, but it has helped generate a greater awareness of the importance of parental reaction (and interaction).
- Operant conditioning principles have formed the underpinning of a number of therapies. Stuttering can be successfully treated as an operant (particularly in the case of the Lidcombe program of early intervention), although the exact nature of this operant is not known.
- These psychological frameworks offer useful perspectives on the development of stuttering, but cannot (of themselves) explain all the phenomena surrounding the disorder. From an aetiological perspective then, they may best be taken as comprising a part of a multifactorial model of stuttering.

Further reading

Ingham, R. J. (1984). *Stuttering and behaviour therapy*. San Diego, CA: College Hill Press.
Twenty years after writing this book, Roger Ingham remains a very influential voice in the field of behaviour therapy, and this book is a huge resource for those interested in this aspect of stuttering. The text is sometimes heavygoing and makes little attempt to hide an operant theory bias, but it is very comprehensive within its field – both for theory and therapy.

Onslow, M. (1996). *Behavioral management of stuttering*. San Diego, CA: Singular Publishing Group.
This book is recommended for gaining a background to learning and behavioural principles, and is also useful for therapeutic implications.

Sheehan, J. (1970). *Stuttering: Research and therapy*, New York: Harper and Row.
There are more recent references to Sheehan's perspective on stuttering as a struggle between approach and avoidance, but this is one of the most comprehensive.

Van Riper, C. (1982). Stuttering as a learned disorder. In C. Van Riper, *The nature of stuttering*. Englewood Cliffs: Prentice-Hall.
Chapter 13 provides a wide coverage of most psychological aspects of stuttering, although Van Riper's scepticism of operant conditioning comes through.

7 The development of stuttering

Introduction

One of the most consistent features of stuttering is that it changes as it becomes established, something we have already seen from a number of perspectives in previous chapters. From a linguistic perspective, for example, we have noted that the focus of stuttering tends to change from function to content words at around age 8 to 10, and also that stuttering commonly begins with part-word repetition, but later tends to expand to include blocks and prolongations. There may be changes between the way that auditory information is processed in very young children who stutter and older children and adults. The development of stuttering is also associated with psychological changes which lead to the development of secondary speech and nonspeech characteristics. We can speculate that functional or (even structural) neurological differences might exist amongst young children who stutter and older primary school children, although this possibility awaits a database of information on the neural correlates of stuttering in young children. Similarly, there is a large gap in current understanding of the motor control capabilities of young children who stutter, largely due to difficulties in children at age 3 or 4 tolerating the measurement procedures involved.

The present chapter explores some more ways in which stuttering changes over time. One obvious factor is the child's environment, but we choose to explore this and related issues within the therapeutic context in part 2. For the present, we are interested in a genetic component; first to the appearance of stuttering and then why, when it does arise, it resolves in the majority of cases, even when untreated, and relatedly we consider the phenomenon of spontaneous recovery. We begin, though, by outlining two opposing track models of stuttering onset and development. Van Riper's (1982) model suggests stuttering is characterized not only by four different onset types, but also different courses of development which affect both primary and secondary stuttering. Starkweather (1997) on the other hand suggests at least nine subgroups at onset.

Track development of stuttering

Subgrouping stuttering

In addition to the recent developments in genetic research which may lead to the discovery of stuttering subgroups based on inheritance, there have been a number of very early attempts to chart the development of stuttering behaviour, from its inception, to its eventual establishment as a chronic and intractable disorder. For example, Bleumel (1913) was one of the first to differentiate between what he later came to call primary and secondary stuttering. Later, Froeshels (1964) noted that stuttering followed a relatively consistent pattern of development, at the start of which the behaviour is dominated by syllable and word repetition; a finding which is consistent with current observations of early onset of stuttering (for example, Howell & Au-Yeung, 2002; Yairi & Ambrose, 1992b; Yairi et al., 1996). But can the progression of stuttering be characterized by distinct stages of development, as opposed to a process of gradual change? There have been a number of attempts to characterize the development of stuttering in this way.

Bloodstein (1960, 1995) looked at behaviour change in stuttering in a group of over 400 children between ages 2 and 16, suggesting that four sequential stages of development could be identified in the disorder. Many of Bloodstein's findings are consistent with more general theories of development of the disorder; for example, the progression from slow easy repetitions, frequent fluent periods and absence of secondary symptoms such as avoidance, anticipation and word substitution as might be expected in 2- to 3-year-old children to a marked increase in avoidance, specific sound fears and word substitution in the 15 to 16 year olds. (Note that the development of stuttering behaviours is also discussed in chapter 9.) However, there are methodological problems with Bloodstein's study, which was cross-sectional and not based on longitudinal data.

Van Riper's four-track model of stuttering development

The track theory of development (Van Riper, 1973) represents a rather different attempt to account for change in stuttering over time. Based on 300 of Van Riper's case histories, 44 of which contained longitudinal information on their progress, Van Riper noted that while there was the heterogeneity of expression that he and others argued confounded attempts to discern a single-stage pattern of development, almost all of his cases could be explained as one of four different initial presentations of the disorder. These four different onsets led to different patterns of development, which Van Riper preferred to call "tracks".

Although old, I believe this model of stuttering development is important because, as Conture (2001) has pointed out, it remains consistent with more recent conceptualizations such as Smith and Kelly's (1997) multifactorial model of stuttering. This model views stuttering as a nonlinear phenomenom whose existence and varied development can be explained as the interaction of a range of environmental and organic factors which are "dynamic", that is, changing in strength over time. A small change in one factor may over time result in new stuttering behaviours, or new associated secondary behaviours. Changes may be great or small depending on the strengths of the factors at any given time and the complex nature of their interrelationships. In placing the heterogeneity of stuttering at the core of the model, and explaining the disorder in terms of the nonlinear interaction of a range of factors, Smith and Kelly's (1997) model bears resemblance to the Demands and Capacities conceptualization (Starkweather, 1987; Starkweather & Gottwald, 1990) discussed in chapter 1; a framework which underpins a range of therapeutic approaches (Conture, 2001; Rustin et al., 1996; Starkweather, 1997; Starkweather & Gottwald, 1990).

Track I

This was the most commonly observed of the four tracks, comprising nearly half of the 44 on whom Van Riper had collected longitudinal data, in addition to just over half of the remaining children who stuttered. Onset, in the form of syllable repetitions which are produced at normal speed, and in the absence of apparent awareness or concern appear between the ages of 2;6 and 4;2, following previously normal speech. Periods of remission are common. There may be substantial inconsistency of stuttering behaviour, with more advanced types of stuttering being seen suddenly and without apparent cause before an equally abrupt return to the milder form, or even another period of remission. Even when not in remission, the children are capable of extended periods of good fluency, with stuttering occuring in clusters, usually in word initial position, or on the most meaningful word in the sentence (all of these are loci which are of linguistic and motoric significance; see chapters 4 and 5).

As the stutter develops, irregular rhythm appears in the stuttered syllables and the number of repetitions per syllable increases from around three at onset, as does frequency of moments of stuttering. Prolongations also start to occur at this point, which Van Riper singles out as a danger sign of established stuttering. Coincident with this the child may start to attempt to force sounds out, in an effort to finish the prolonged sound. Frustration is also now a feature and signs of tension and struggle, initially in the shape of lip and jaw contortions, begin to appear, often followed by secondary head and limb movements. The "cycle of stuttering" begins to take effect now with parental concern being transmitted to the child, which in turn leads to even greater struggle and also fear. Fear almost always leads to avoidance. For the Track I child, Van Riper contends that this results in postponing devices, "ums, ers" and an increase in synonym use to aid word avoidance. Situation fears will also start to appear. The final stages of Track I development sees the stutter become fully established. As Van Riper (1982) puts it: "The stuttering child acquires the self-concept and role of 'stutterer' with all the evil these entail. Personality changes may occur; defenses are set up. The disorder becomes an integral part of his existence" (p. 99).

Track II

This was the most commonly seen track after Track I, comprising 25 percent of the clients with longitudinally data; and around 16.5 percent of the total number. Onset is much earlier than Track I, coincident with the onset of connected speech. As with Track I, disfluencies originally consisted of syllable and single syllable word repetition, but Track II children do not show evenness of pace; their repetitions are quick and dysrhythmic. Note that both unevenness of tempo of repetition and increased speed of repetition have been identified as consistent with incipient stuttering, as opposed to normal nonfluency, in a number of unrelated studies (Campbell & Hill, 1993; Throneburg & Yairi, 1994; Williams, 1978). The majority of this group show marked expressive language delay, with phrase construction not appearing until they are between 3 and 6 years old. Van Riper does not comment on language comprehension abilities, but the implication appears to be that these are within normal limits, and even that the mismatch between an established ability to comprehend complex adult language whilst being unable to produce their own language is a factor in this stuttering subgroup. In the absence of normal verbal skills, communication consists of gesture, jargon and single word level speech. As language abilities slowly progress, poor syntax appears, which leads to disorganized speech, typified by silent pauses, which are not blocks, and hesitations, interjections and retrials, reworking of unfinished sentences and phrase revisions. There may also be a deliberate and sometimes audible intake of breath before a phrase is blurted out at high speed. Articulation too may be affected, with anticipatory errors and phoneme transpositions common. Van Riper also suggests that there may be problems with self-monitoring of speech, and that Track II children do not listen to themselves. (This is somewhat counter to evidence which links early onset stuttering to heightened levels of auditory awareness; see Bernstein-Ratner, 1997; chapter 3 this volume.) He also questions whether this lack of auditory awareness to their own speech might in part be responsible for the delay in the first place.

So now the Track II child is experiencing difficulties with speech, language and fluency, and auditory awareness, yet for all this the child does not usually experience frustration, and avoidance of phonemes or words is rare. With further development, situation fears can arise, however, but even these rarely reach the intensity of fear experienced by children from the other three tracks. Consistent with this lack of awareness and lack of fear, these children do not usually show secondary features, such as abnormal lip or jaw movement, head jerk or other nonspeech body movements. A particular and defining feature of later development of more severe examples of Track II is the perseverative type of stuttering, where the quick and dysrhythmic repetitions take on an almost compulsive quality. It seems almost impossible for the speaker to terminate the rapid and accelerating syllable repetitions, and often only ends when the intake of lung air has run out. There have been some reports of extreme cases where some older Track II children have been known to shout out in the middle of these repetitions in an attempt to stop the uncontrolled repetitions. In cases such as these, the act of stuttering as well as particular speaking situations may become feared. However, the majority of Track II speakers find themselves with speech which Van Riper describes as mildly stuttered but mainly cluttered. Van Riper was very aware of the similarities between Track II stuttering and cluttering (also see chapters 8 and 17), but not all traits are consistent between the two groups. For example, Track II children become aware of their difficulties and may show withdrawal, and use avoidance strategies. Cluttering, on the other hand is associated with a lack of awareness and concern.

Track III

This track was seen in 5 of Van Riper's 44 children who were studied longitudinally, and a total of 18 of the overall total of 300. This track is typically seen in older children who until this point experienced perfectly normal fluency. The Track III children in Van Riper's study were aged 5 to 9, but the pattern has also been observed in children as young as 2, and also in adults. Track III pattern is characterized by an abrupt onset, with the child usually simply being unable to speak. Commonly, attempts are made at vocalization, such as conscious inhalation and appropriate articulatory pre-positioning, which simply result in an inability to produce sound. The child may continue to make repeated attempts to do so, but usually with the same fixed, blocked and silent outcome. If the child is able push through the block and initiate the first phoneme, the remainder of the ensuing sentence is usually fluent. In some cases, there may appear to be some psychological/environmental concomitant to this dramatic change; possibly a frightening experience, shock, physical trauma, sudden change in family dynamics. However, Van Riper argues that when these possibilities are pursued they often appear to have little relevance to the onset of stuttering.

Track III develops quickly with struggle, tension and frustration following rapidly. The blocking, seen initially only in sentence initial position, soon appears in other parts of the utterance and also in other articulatory structures. Lip, tongue and jaw fixations are now also produced with excessive tension and sometimes tremor becoming established. Abnormal breathing patterns, used earlier in an attempt to overcome laryngeal blocking, now appear as ritualized gasping for breath. Van Riper observes that Track III children move from the blocking type of stutter to prolongations. Quickly after the prolongation becomes established, the laryngeal blocking reduces. Coincident with this, struggle reduces and speech output increases. After the prolongations become established, syllabic repetitions begin to appear. Unlike the repetitions that are characteristic of Track I development, these often occur following phoneme prolongation, and each repeated syllable may also be slightly prolonged, for example:

"c———→, c——→ a——→, c——→ a——→, can I have a juice?"

It is interesting to note that in terms of the sequence in which the different types of stuttering develop, Track III presents as almost a mirror of Track I, where syllable initial repetitions later lead to prolongation and blocking. Equally intriguing is that when Track III development reaches the syllable repetition stage, the prognosis for recovery actually increases. For those who do not, however, Van Riper paints a gloomy picture of severe and persistent stuttering accompanied by complex stuttering patterns, high levels of avoidance and anxiety, and increased likelihood of interiorized stuttering. The issue of causation in Track III is an interesting issue, which at first sight might appear to have ramifications for psychogenic stuttering. However, stuttering characteristics do not appear to be consistent with this acquired variant of stuttering. We return to this issue in chapter 16.

Track IV

This was the least commonly observed pattern in Van Riper's group with 4 of the original 44 and 9 of the total 300 showing this pattern of development. Like Track III, this pattern usually begins later than Track I, following a period of normal fluency and with a sudden onset. The initial stuttering behaviour is, however, different to both, being characterized by multiple repetitions of (sometimes) syllables, but more commonly words (including multisyllabic words) and/or phrases. The disfluency appears as a considered and highly conscious pattern on behalf of the child, almost as if there is deliberate stuttering on purpose, yet occurring in the apparent absence of anxiety or concern. It is the very large number of repetitions that tend to distinguish early Track IV stuttering from normal disfluency. Track IV children may quickly move from word repetition to a mixture of part-word and word repetitions, whilst maintaining the large number of repetitions. Thus "It's-It's-It's-It's-It's-It's a nice day" becomes "I-I-I – It's-It's-I-I-it's it's-it's a nice day". This tendency to repeat words that have already been produced fluently is a defining characteristic of this group and is consistent with the very open stuttering seen from the start. In contrast to the other tracks, Track IV stuttering behaviour changes very little from onset to full establishment. Stuttering continues in the absence of fear and avoidance, and without the development of escape behaviours. Van Riper considers Track IV stutterers to use their disfluency as a device to help gain control over the situation, and/or over the listener. As he puts it: "These stutterers suffer less than their listeners. One can sense the controlling, punishing, wheedling, exploitative urges behind the behaviour" (1982, p. 105).

Rather confusingly, Van Riper also considers that there may be some classed as Track IV stutterers who have a rather different onset, with initial behaviours being unfilled pauses rather than repetitions. He cites as an example the case of a young boy who presented with repeated inhalations when speaking, to the point where his chest became distended. Van Riper discovered that the child had used this pattern when frustrated, and long before any fluency difficulties had arisen. It was concluded that this was a controlling tactic over his mother and he was referred to a child psychiatrist. The stutter persisted into adulthood and with it Van Riper describes additional reactions, referring to his behaviours as still "infantile, neurotic" and "controlling".

Summary of track development

Van Riper's track profiles suggest that the majority of stuttering (as in Track I) begins preschool, most commonly begins with repetition, and later ends with blocking, fear and avoidance. Track II in many ways is consistent with cluttering (a point which Van Riper accepts), but as the disorder persists, such children develop awareness of their difficulties as well as linguistic and situational fears and avoidance strategies; all features strongly associated with stuttering and supposedly incompatible with cluttering. Tracks III and IV represent very small subsets amongst the population that stutters (6 percent and 3 percent respectively), and are characterized by distinctive onset patterns and development profiles. (Table 7.1 summarizes how the four tracks can be compared and contrasted at onset of stuttering. Figure 7.1 shows similar information on stuttering development.)

Van Riper makes it clear that these so-called tracks require further data from large-scale longitudinal studies to substantiate the claims he makes. He also admits that there are a number of methodological problems with the study. For example, subjects were not always seen at regular specified intervals and findings may have been influenced by the effects of therapy (although the data collected on the 44 subjects relate exclusively to those who did not do well in therapy). In fact, there is limited evidence from one small longitudinal study which shows findings consistent with those of Van Riper's Track I and Track II (Ohashi, 1973), but to date further data are still lacking. Conture (2001) admits surprise at the lack of research on subgrouping stuttering (although he was not specifically referring to the subgrouping of stuttering development, as we are here), having predicted in an earlier edition of his book that there would be a growth of interest in this area.[1]

---

1 I share Conture's surprise, and can only speculate as to the reasons for the lack of new studies on the subject. Near the top of the list would be the inherent practical difficulties in undertaking longitudinal studies on a sufficient number of people, with reasons ranging from funding sources through subject recruitment and retention to the potentially confounding effects that stuttering therapy might have on track development. Of consideration also would be the potential difficulty in getting data published. Onslow (2004a) has voiced loud and clear the difficulty in finding homes for articles containing long-term follow-up data in respected peer-reviewed journals.

Table 7.1 Tracks of development at onset (adapted from Van Riper, 1982)

Criteria	Track I	Track II	Track III	Track IV
1 Onset	2 ½ to 4 years	Often late, at time of first sentences	Any age after child has consecutive speech	Late, usually after 4 years
2 Fluency	Previously fluent	Never very fluent	Previously fluent	Previously fluent
3 Onset	Gradual	Gradual	Sudden	Sudden
4 Consistency of fluency	Cyclic	Steady	Steady	Erratic
5 Remission	Long remissions	No remission	Few short remissions	No remissions
6 Articulation	Good	Poor	Normal	Normal
7 Speech rate	Normal	Fast spurts	Slow, careful	Normal
8 Type of dysfluencies	Syllabic repetitions	Gaps, revisions, syllable and word repetitions	Unvoiced prolongations, laryngeal blocking	Unusual behaviours
9 Tension levels	No tension, unforced	No tension	Much tension	Variable tension
10 Tremor	No tremors	No	Tremors	Few tremors
11 Loci	First words, function words	First words, long words; scattered throughout sentence; content words	Mostly beginning of utterance	First words; rarely function words; mostly content words
12 Pattern	Variable pattern	Variable	Consistent	Consistent
13 Integration of speech	Normal speech is well integrated	Broken speech; hesitation; gaps even when no dysfluency	Normal speech is very fluent	Normal speech is very fluent
14 Awareness of speech problem	No awareness	No awareness	Highly aware	Highly aware
15 Frustration	No frustration	No frustration	Much frustration	No frustration
16 Fear	No fears, willingness to talk	No fear, willing to talk	Fears speaking; situation and word fears	No evidence of fear; willing to talk

Track I	Track II	Track III	Track IV
Repetitions of syllables increase in frequency and speech, and become irregular.	Revisions and word and syllable repetitions remain the same but the speed increases; their number also increases.	Increase in the frequency of the unvoiced prolongations, but little change otherwise; signs of frustration.	The number of instances increase, and appear in more situations.

Leading to (↓ ↓ ↓ ↓)

Track I	Track II	Track III	Track IV
Syllable repetitions begin to end in prolongations.	Little change in form.	More retrials are seen; lip protrusions and tongue fixations appear; prolongations of initial sounds.	Little change in form; monosymptomatic and symbolic.

Leading to (↓ ↓ ↓ ↓)

Track I	Track II	Track III	Track IV
Prolongations show increased tension, tremors, struggle. Evidence of frustration.	Little change; little awareness; little frustration.	Tremors; struggle, facial contortions; jaw jerk, gasping; marked frustration.	Little change.

Leading to (↓ ↓ ↓ ↓)

Track I	Track II	Track III	Track IV
Overflow of tension, tremors, retrials; speech output decreases; signs of concern.	Duration of nonfluencies increases; more syllabic repetitions; little awareness.	Interrupter devices (e.g., starters, fillers) become more prominent; rate slows; more hesitancy; more refusal to talk.	Little change in type, but duration and visibility increase; no interrupters or new forcing of speech; increased speech output.

Leading to (↓ ↓ ↓ ↓)

Track I	Track II	Track III	Track IV
Word fears and avoidance occur; fears of certain sounds arise; then situation fears develop; repetitions and prolongations turn into silent fixations with struggle (blocking); poor eye contact and tricks to disguise the difficulty are observed; shows hesitancy, embarrassment.	Occasional fears of situations, not of words, or sounds; long strings of syllabic repetitions at fast speed are added to other behaviours; good eye contact; no disguise; output of speech increases; little avoidance; primarily repetitive; unorganized.	Intense fear of words and sounds; many avoidances; patterns change in form and grow more bizarre; much overflow; output of speech decreases; will cease trying to talk; poor eye contact; normal speech becomes hesitant; nonvocalized blockings are frequent; primary tonic blocks with multiple closures.	Very few avoidance or release behaviours; not much evidence of word fears; few consistent loci; very aware of stuttering; stutters very openly; good eye contact; little variability in the stuttering behaviour; normal speech very fluent; talks a lot; consistent pattern; few silent blockings; either tonic or clonic.

Note that Van Riper is not saying that the establishment of new behaviours at each new level are in any way synchronized across the tracks. In each case, the time taken for the disorder to progress will vary.

Figure 7.1 Developmental characteristics of the four tracks of stuttering development (adapted from Van Riper, 1982).

Starkweather's nine tracks of stuttering

More recently, Starkweather (1997) has argued that there may be more than the four tracks that Van Riper originally suggested. Based on a review of around 100 case histories, he offers 9. Although more loosely defined than Van Riper's tracks, they are nonetheless of interest and we outline them briefly below.

"Garden variety"

This track somewhat follows Van Riper's Track I. Onset begins between ages 2 to 5 with syllable and whole word repetitions, and in the absence of any other speech or nonspeech difficulties. This may be distinguished from normal disfluency if there are three or more repetitions. Parental concern is also a defining feature of this track, and counselling is advised to ensure negative listener reaction is not transmitted back to the child, and that struggle and avoidance do not develop.

Slow speech motor skills

Speech is characterized by poor oromotor skills, and sometimes poor gross motor skills, but particularly immature speech motor control. Disordered phonology is often a co-occuring feature, but language skills are normal. Thus speech contains normal length and normally constructed sentences, but with a great deal of articulatory effort. Starkweather suggests that the child and possibly parents also react to this difficulty as being produced too slowly. A second characteristic therefore is attempts to hurry, which translate in speech as "surges of tension" (p. 270). There are some similarities here to Van Riper's Track II (poor articulatory control and elevated speech rate) but there are differences too. For example, the language delay seen in Van Riper's version is missing, as is the lack of awareness of the problem. The perception of time pressure has been cited as a key feature in Perkins, Kent, and Curlee's (1991) neuropsychological theory of stuttering.

Advanced language skills

This group of children have normal motor skills, but from an early age show advanced language abilities. Starkweather observes that these children come from highly verbal families, where parents place a high value on language skills. These children are commonly spoken to by parents who use advanced grammatical structures and a wide range of vocabulary, and this seems to be reflected back in the child's language usage. The suggestion here is that there is a mismatch between motor control and language capabilities, and that stuttering results (particularly on more complex utterances) because motor speech development cannot keep pace with the sophisticated language usage.

It might be expected that therapies which constrain length of utterance (for example, Costello & Ingham, 1999) could be beneficial, in such cases.

Environmental pressures

These children have essentially normal speech and language abilities, but experience an environment which is more conducive to disfluency than fluency. These may include traumatic situations such as frequent house changes, friction within the family, little one-to-one time with parents, hurried and disorganized home environment. Starkweather contends that some parents in this track overtly punish the children for their stuttering whilst others do so unwittingly in their verbal and nonverbal responses to the stuttering. This then can lead to tension and anxiety in the child, and later feelings of shame, embarrassment and avoidance.

Other children included in this track do not appear to encounter unduly stressful environments, but do appear particularly susceptible to stress, and situations which others may deal with easily can become significant problems to such children. According to Starkweather, the resulting severity of stuttering can be highly dependent on a small change in circumstance. The prognosis for these children is usually favourable and stuttering can often be resolved by counselling, and through the instantiation of calming routines at home, for example, improving consistency in bedtime routines. It would be expected that parent–child interaction therapy as described in chapter 10 would be very effective with this type of child.

Children with low self-esteem

Starkweather also identifies a separate track of children who have reduced self-esteem, although he admits that it is often difficult to determine between cause and effect with many in this group. (It is also theoretically possible that low self-esteem may exist alongside but independently of the stuttering.) Stuttering in this group of children may be noticeable when the child is required to initiate (rather than respond to) speech, particularly when a new topic is being introduced, and where the child may perceive that his novel thought as well as increased potential for stuttering will be negatively evaluated. Starkweather suggests there may also be an association with attention deficit hyperactivity disorder (ADHD) children amongst this group.

Shy children

This group of children will experience greater difficulty when talking to strangers than with those they are comfortable with, and moments of more severe stuttering may be specifically related to specific scenarios that trigger their particular anxiety.

Children with specific brain anomaly

This is an interesting one. Children in this track develop stuttering alongside some neurological event such as epilepsy or seizure disorder occurring in childhood. Note that for this track, at least, there is no suggestion of a specific causal relationship, as there would be for a neurogenic or psychogenic stutter. In some cases stuttering precedes the neurological diagnosis and in other cases it appears following it. The pattern of stuttering seen in this track may be unusual, and there may be other behavioural or physical signs which are not usually seen in other tracks of early stuttering. For example, Starkweather also links this group of children to Tourette's syndrome. The grunts, vocal tics and extraneous facial movements seen in Tourette's may in some cases appear consistent with the tension, struggle and avoidance behaviour seen in stuttering. (This is worthy of note: we see in chapter 2 that Tourette's syndrome bears similarity to stuttering in behavioural terms, but some have argued that they may be related in aetiology also both with regard to inheritance and to neurotransmitter underpinnings.) Starkweather also adds, somewhat unscientifically: "Sometimes children who just don't look right end up with this diagnosis" (p. 272). In sum, stuttering occurs alongside signs of mild cognitive difficulty, but lacking significant deficits in any one particular area. Subsequent neurological referral often fails to uncover any specific abnormality, and unfortunately, the stuttering often continues to be highly resistant to therapy.

Language therapy

Starkweather does not go into detail about the relative prevalence of the tracks, but this pattern of stuttering onset is certainly a familiar one. Typically, the child is referred for a fluency assessment by a speech and language therapist or speech language pathologist, who is already seeing this child for language therapy. The child has a history of language delay, and now after a period of therapy improvements are being seen, to the point where abilities are approaching age-appropriate. Unfortunately now though, stuttering is appearing. From a demands and capacities perspective (see chapter 1), this may be due to the increased demand (of higher level language ability focused on in the language therapy) in conjunction with a decreased capacity (that is, an increased susceptibility to stuttering). If language levels are near normal, Starkweather advocates a break from therapy. If fluency improves during this time, the period of nonintervention may be extended to allow stabilization. If language ability is still poor it should continue, preferably with new language forms being introduced at a slow rate in order to minimize the extra demand placed on the child.

Articulation therapy

There may be two subsets of this track. The first has fluency affected by the extra demands placed on the child through therapy, only, unlike the language therapy group where it is the greater cognitive strain on language development that can lead to stuttering, here it is the focus on control of specific muscle groups, and the extra physical tension required to implement new motor control strategies. With this subgroup, Starkweather strongly advises cessation of articulation therapy on the basis that many articulation problems improve over time, and may also be effectively treatable at a later date whereas stuttering is more likely to become chronic and intractable.

The second subtrack relates to children with severe articulation disorders whose stuttering seems to arise because of the articulation disorder rather than any treatment for it. Recommendations here are to continue with articulation therapy in order to avoid the increase in frustration in being unable to communicate, and with the rationale that in reducing concern and anxiety in the child this will indirectly relieve the stuttering.

Summary

Unlike Van Riper's tracks, Starkweather's only provide information as to the onset of each particular track of stuttering, and there is limited information as to how any given track will develop, whether it is resistant to therapy, and in many examples the type of stuttering seen at onset. It is likely that experienced clinicians will readily identify children they have seen with each of the tracks that Starkweather has identified. Of course, equally we can say that there are many more children who grow up with poor motor control, or with advanced linguistic abilities, or with poor self-esteem, but do not develop a stutter. Starkweather's point is that in each individual circumstance the balance of demands and capacities will determine both the existence of stuttering and the efficacy of treatment. Therapy in each case will involve reducing demand and increasing capacity, whether linguistic, motoric, emotional or cognitive, as appropriate to each track and each individual.

Spontaneous recovery

A complicating factor in dealing with stuttering in its earlier years is the fact that many children who are diagnosed as stuttering will cease to stutter, either with or without therapy, by the time they reach puberty. This has in the past given rise to the common call of "he will grow out of it". If this is indeed so, then why should clinicians be concerned about treating the disorder. The answer is that taken out of context, these data can be misleading. Andrews and Harris (1964) found that as many as 80 percent of children who stutter will spontaneously recover before reaching their mid-teens.[2] However, spontaneous recovery rates drop to 40 percent if the stutter persists for more than 1 year, and 18 percent at 5 years post onset (Andrews et al., 1983).

Definitions of spontaneous recovery

Spontaneous recovery has been defined as the disappearance of the disorder without apparent cause, and which results in normal levels of fluency (Ingham, 1984). Nicolosi, Harryman, and Kresheck (1996) add an absence of treatment to these criteria. The problem is that spontaneous recovery has been recorded and explained in a variety of ways. As Finn (1998) points out, some have experienced a slow recovery (Wingate, 1976) while others have had treatment which could have been a confounding factor (Sheehan & Martyn, 1966). Crucially, some who regard themselves as recovered still experience moments of stuttering (Finn, 2003b; Wingate, 1964). The figures for spontaneous recovery arise from either retrospective or longitudinal studies, and are considered more likely to be reliable than those data collected from questionnaires and interviews. When only findings from the former group are taken, a more homogeneous set of figures arise. For example, the following studies reported remission rates, without therapy, of 79 percent (Andrews & Harris, 1964), 80 percent (Panelli, McFarlane, & Shipley, 1978) 65 percent (Ryan, 1990), and 89 percent (Yairi & Ambrose, 1992a, 1996). Both retrospective and longitudinal studies face the same set of problems, namely:

- The problems in lack of consistency in definition of stuttering occurring in the first place: there may be significant differences in the criteria used to define presence or absence of stuttering and some research has shown that some who claim to have recovered from stuttering may well not have had a stutter in the first place (Lankford & Cooper, 1974).
- The possible effects of treatment: indeed, there may be a lack of consistency as to what is actually meant by treatment. There may have been either direct treatment via a speech and language therapist/pathologist, indirect treatment (as discussed in chapter 10), or even self-taught or administered therapeutic procedures, self- or relative-administered treatment.
- The extent to which the recovery is complete: again problems with consistency as to what actually constitutes complete recovery; for example, separating normal nonfluency from stuttering (see chapter 10).

---

2 A recent longitudinal study by Howell, Davis, Cook, and Williams (in preparation) puts this figure as low as 49 percent.

Implications for the treatment of stuttering

Ingham (1984) outlines two models of spontaneous recovery: one which explains the phenomenon as an outgrowing or maturing out of the disorder (Johnson et al., 1959); an alternative position held by Wingate (1976) who argues that recovery comes about through quasi-therapeutic practices administered by parents in the case of children who recover from stuttering, and by self amongst adults who similarly overcome their disorder. These two opposing positions reflect very different views as to the case for early intervention in treatment of the disorder. Onslow (1992) follows Wingate's contention that there are strong arguments to support the case for early intervention. Curlee and Yairi (1997) concur and offer at least five reasons as to why:

1 The figures for remission in untreated children are lower (Martin & Lindamood, 1986; Ramig, 1993).
2 Less than 50 percent of children who recover spontaneously do so without receiving some therapy and, as a number of reports have pointed out, many of those that do stop who have not received clinical intervention have been helped by parents or other caregivers (e.g., Onslow, Andrews, & Lincoln, 1994).
3 Witholding treatment from a child who is beginning to stutter is unethical and places them at increased risk of persistent stuttering (Starkweather, 1997).
4 There is growing evidence that early treatment is highly effective (e.g., Onslow, Packman, & Harrison, 2003; Starkweather, 1997).
5 There is no evidence that early treatment does any harm (e.g., Starkweather, 1997).

On the other hand, some believe that treatment may be justifiably withheld for a period up to and beyond one year post onset for the following reasons:

1 More than 50 percent of children who start to stutter cease to do so within one year, regardless of whether there is any therapy.
2 Further remission continues at decreasing rates even without clinical intervention.
3 Persistence or recovery of stuttering is related to the family history of these outcomes (Ambrose, Cox, & Yairi, 1997; see also below).
4 The effects of parental efforts to help with their child's fluency, either positive or negative, are not known.
5 Curlee (1993) has argued that there is no evidence to show that waiting a year or more will make treatment harder to achieve, less effective or increase the amount of treatment needed.

Probably the key amongst all these data is that although, for some at least, there is the possibility that stuttering will resolve without therapy, the methodological difficulties within the studies that support such claims are such that these data must be treated with great caution. The reality is that very few clinicians nowadays will wait more than a year after diagnosis to begin treatment, and the majority will start as soon as is feasibly possible after a diagnosis of stuttering has been made. At some point in the future, more well-controlled research may indicate that we have been treating some children unnecessarily. For the present, the prevailing decision tends to be to treat, rather than run the opposite risk of potentially failing to deal with a stutter that does not eventually resolve, and having to tackle it in later years when it has become more established and more resistant to therapy.

In recent years, the impact of studies of stuttering from a genetic perspective has contributed significantly to the debate as to who is more likely to recover from stuttering. We now review the evidence below.

A genetic component to stuttering

A commonly asked question of clinicians and reseachers alike is: "Does stuttering run in families?" The short answer to this is yes, in some cases at least. Some authorities suggest that as many of 50 percent of those who stutter have a family history of the disorder (Riaz et al., 2005). Genetic research potentially offers answers as to why this perplexing disorder arises in the first place, and why it continues to develop in some individuals and not others.

There is no question that an advanced understanding of a genetic component in stuttering is of tremendous importance, both theoretically and clinically. From a theoretical perspective, breakthroughs in this area could point toward the very causes of the disorder. We might also learn whether people who stutter with a positive history actually have identical problems to those who stutter with no history, or whether there are subtle differences. A more thorough understanding could also potentially have a huge impact on therapy. Findings could help clinicians to predict whether a child is at increased risk of stuttering, and in the case of a child who is already showing signs of stuttering, the likelihood as to whether the condition will persist into adulthood. Ultimately, there could be the possibility of genetic engineering to reduce the number of people presenting for therapy in the first place.

Recently, Felsenfeld (2002) has pointed out that those researching a genetic explanation to speech disorders are comparative newcomers to the process of gene finding, and that stuttering specifically poses particular problems for those seeking to isolate a gene, or genes which may be responsible for the stuttering phenotype. A fundamental problem, and one we encounter throughout this book, concerns the issue of heterogeneity of the disorder. Identifying subgroups of stuttering is by no means a simple task (see the following section in this chapter for two very different interpretations) and as we have seen in chapter 1, even succinctly defining the disorder poses problems. Yet it is quite possible that subgrouping will occur as a function of increasing genetic research in this area. As Felsenfeld (2002) explains, the identification of subgroups provides a more favourable analysis environment and increases the chances of candidate loci being identified within that specific disorder phenotype.

There have been three major ways in which a genetic component has been investigated in stuttering – twin studies, adoption studies and family studies. We now examine each area in turn.

Twin studies

One way of examining a possible genetic component in stuttering is by comparing the incidence of the disorder in fraternal (dizygotic) and identical (monozygotic) twins. Fraternal twins are genetically only related as siblings resulting from different pregnancies, whilst identical twins have identical genetic makeup. If a behaviour is more consistent between identical twins than fraternal twins, this points to the cause as likely due to the greater genetic similarity. Although many of the early twin studies on stuttering were either poorly controlled or reported, or both, a number of reliable papers have demonstrated that concordance for stuttering is higher amongst identical twins than fraternal twins. (Concordance is the preferred term of genetic scientists to describe the extent to which a phenotype is shared between twins.) Godai, Tatarelli, and Bonanni (1976) found that eight of the nine male identical twins and two of the three female identical twins were concordant for stuttering as opposed to none of the nine male fraternal twins, and only one of the two female fraternal twins was concordant. Howie (1981) observed proband concordances of around 75 percent for both male and female identical twins, but only 45 percent for male fraternal twins and 0 percent for female fraternal twins. The findings of these studies appear to be in general agreement. However, Kidd (1984) makes the point that these (and other studies) run the risk of bias in twin selection because neither used a twin registry, and that concordant identical twins are more likely to come forward as subjects than identical twins who do not share concordance. Notice also that although concordance is high amongst identical twins, it is not 100 percent. This means that nongenetic factors, too must be involved in some cases at least. Felsenfeld (1997) suggests that by careful examination of the histories of each twin we can learn which nonshared variables are significant factors in the different fluency outcomes. She cites as a hypothetical example the possibility that one twin might have experienced a serious medical trauma as an infant. Although twin studies cannot definitively show what these factors are, a more recent study on nearly 4000 unselected twin pairs (Andrews, Morris-Yates, Howie, & Martin, 1990) in a nonclinical study estimated that 71 percent of the variance[3] can be explained by genetic factors, and

---

3 The variance refers to the likelihood as to whether or not one would stutter. The figure of 71 percent means that genetic effects are responsible for 71 percent of the variance.

21 percent by environmental influences. Very similar heritability (70 percent) was found in a more recent twin study which used a similar statistical analysis procedure (Felsenfeld, Kirk, Zhu, Statham, Neale, & Martin, 2000). Clearly, more research is needed, but the body of evidence from twin studies supports the notion that genetic factors play a significant part in the cause of stuttering.

Adoption studies

One very effective way of attempting to limit the potential of environmental influences on genetic studies is to look at the development of children who, having been separated from their natural parents at an early age, have still gone on to develop a stutter. Lack of contact between offspring and parent will mean that any shared stuttering between the two can be attributed to genetic influence. The problem is that adoption studies are few and far between, due largely to the difficulty in accessing adoption records and (like longitudinal studies in treatment efficacy) the time and resources needed to implement a design which is sufficiently well controlled. Felsenfeld (1995) reports some preliminary data from a small cohort of subjects which showed that having a biological parent with a speech language disorder placed the offspring at greater risk for developmental speech disorders (in which stuttering was included) than being raised by a nonbiological parent who had a positive history. However, the fact that small sample sizes were used together with other methodological issues means these data should be interpreted with caution.

Family studies

A number of studies have shown that an individual is at greater risk of stuttering if they have a stuttering relative (Andrews & Harris, 1964; Cox, Kramer, & Kidd, 1984; Gray, 1940; Johnson, 1959; Kant & Ahuja, 1970; Kidd, 1984). In a review of over 20 early family studies compiled by Van Riper (1971) it was discovered that between 24 percent and 80 percent of people who stuttered also reported a family history of the disorder. The often-cited Andrews and Harris (1964) study of 1000 families found a family history of stuttering for 38 percent of the individuals who stuttered as opposed to 1.4 percent among control speakers. They also found that of those with a family history, males were more likely to develop stuttering than females, and that females in this group were more likely to have relatives who stuttered than their male counterparts. These key findings were later substantiated in a series of reports from another respected longitudinal study by Kidd and associates known as the Yale Study (Kidd, 1977; Kidd, Kidd, & Records, 1978; Kidd, Reich, & Kessler, 1973).

More recently too there has been verification of many of Andrews and Harris' (1964) findings. Ambrose, Yairi, and Cox (1993) found that amongst their sample of 69 young children who were beginning to stutter and their families, nearly 70 percent of the children had relatives who stuttered. However, unlike Andrews and Harris (1964) they found that male and females had similar likelihood of having relatives who stuttered. This difference may be explained by the different ages of the probands that were studied. Where Ambrose et al. (1993) looked only at young children, some of Andrews and Harris' children were as old as 11 years. As Guitar (1998) points out, this may mean that the Andrews and Harris study has greater relevance for persistent stuttering, whereas Ambrose and colleagues' study may be pertinent to both transitory stuttering and persistent stuttering because some of these children recovered quickly from stuttering, whilst others did not. Ambrose et al. (1993) also found that the ratio of males to females was 2:1 in the preschool years; significantly lower than the 4:1 (or higher in some studies) reported for the adults. This suggests that girls have a higher recovery rate, which may involve a genetic component. However, findings from a recent study by Howell, Davis, Cook, and Williams (in preparation) indicates the reverse; 53 percent of boys recovered as opposed to 40 percent of girls. In addition, adult females who stutter have also been found to have a higher proportion of relatives who also stutter (Kidd, Heimbuch, & Records, 1981), which also suggests a stronger genetic component for females than for males. However, as Ludlow (1999) has noted, there is evidence that females may be better able to use both left and right hemispheres for language processing (Shaywitz et al., 1995) and might be able to use this increased right hemisphere capability to recover from stuttering.

In a further attempt to determine if recovery from stuttering might be explained as a genetic subgroup, Ambrose et al. (1997) analyzed data from 66 children who stuttered and their extended families. They found that females are far more likely to recover than males, consistent with their idea that similar numbers of male and females start to stutter, but that this ratio changes to around 4:1 (males vs female children) by around the age of 7, after which age the ratio remains unchanged. They also noted that children who had relatives who had a persistent stutter were more likely to be persistent stutterers themselves, and that those children who recovered had a significantly higher number of relatives who themselves had recovered from stuttering (around 4 percent as opposed to 1 percent). These differences led Ambrose et al. (1997) to suggest there may be a genetic link to both recovery and persistence, and that recovery does not appear to be a genetically milder form of stuttering, nor are the two types of disorders genetically independent. Key findings were that (a) persistent and recovered stuttering share a common genetic cause, but also that (b) the persistent variety is, at least in part, the result of additional genetic factors. Guitar (1998) speculates that a single gene model might explain the data of young children, who have a greater likelihood of recovery, whilst a polygenetic model might explain additional factors that increase the likelihood that stuttering will persist into adulthood. Ambrose et al. (1997), on the other hand, argue that both single gene and polygenetic components exist for persistent and recovered stuttering.

Genetic predisposition and environmental factors

One weakness in using family studies to support a genetic hypothesis to the onset of stuttering is that it is difficult to exclude alternative explanations of the data, and particularly nongenetic cultural transmission. Whether stuttering is eventually discovered to reflect a single or multigene disorder, environment too will play a significant part. Some studies have looked not only at a genetic predisposition in stuttering, but also at the relationship between possible genetic components and developmental influences. Eaves, Kendler and Schultz (1986) argued for the possibility of two completely separate bipolar groups. At one end there is a group whose target behaviour can be considered genetically determined with little or no evidence of environmental influence; at the other, a nongenetic (or *sporadic*) group whose behaviour appears strongly related to environmental stressors, in the absence of genetic factors. Within these polar opposites, the expression (or lack of expression) of the disorder might be determined by the interaction of genetic and stress components. Where there are low environmental stress factors, then a higher genetic loading would be needed to activate the disorder. In turn, a weaker susceptibility to a predisposition would require an increase in environmental effects to activate the problem (Monroe & Simmons, 1991).

There is tentative evidence for this type of interaction within the area of stuttering too. Poulos and Webster (1991) divided a group of 169 adolescents and adults who stutter into two: those with a positive family history for stuttering and those without. No between-group differences were found with regard to age of onset, type of stuttering behaviours and emotional factors, but a significantly higher number of the group with negative family history reported physical neurological trauma at birth, or in early childhood (37 percent as opposed to 2 percent). So here the bipolar states are: (a) stuttering with a predisposition and no trauma; (b) stuttering without predisposition but with neurological trauma. However, caution is needed when considering these data, because over 20 percent of all subjects had neither a positive family history nor evidence of trauma.

Family study data are potentially of great value. Of course, there is still the significant unknown factor as to the nature of the genetic components that might underlie the disorder, but already there may be potential clinical benefit to be gained from these studies. If future research confirms that there are two (or perhaps more) strains of stuttering, this would help with both prognosis and treatment of the disorder (Yairi & Ambrose, 1999). Potentially, this information could be used to guide therapy for a child with the natural recovery genetic background. Ultimately, if there is eventual evidence that a particular genetic subtype is correlated with a very high level of spontaneous recovery, it is possible that therapy (perhaps aside from providing advice to parents) might not be indicated at all. This would allow more time and therapeutic resources to be directed for the child with the persistent stuttering genetic background. Of course, we are not even close to this situation yet, and for the present extreme caution is called for when considering genetic history as a factor in the clinical decision-making process of whether an individual is at risk to develop stuttering (see below).

The future

In 1997, Felsenfeld called for work to be done in four key areas, in order to advance knowledge on the subject:

1   The need for development of a standard battery assessment of stuttering across the lifespan: this is an issue that, seven years on, still remains. Accurately comparing data from clinic to clinic remains fraught with difficulty due to the complexity of the disorder. As we see from chapter 9, there are many different ways in which information is captured and recorded. Felsenfeld (1997) suggests that a specialized rating scale could be developed to serve this purpose.
2   The need to identify relationships between family history status and epidemiological variables: this would help determine the probability of spontaneous remission and relapse.
3   The need to examine extrinsic factors which may precipitate or maintain stuttering: areas such as language ability, motor speech ability and parent–child interaction are just a few examples which we discuss in this book.
4   The need to increase the pool of high density pedigrees for genetic modelling and linkage analysis.

Finally, there is cause for optimism that a gene (or genes) for stuttering will be found. Lai, Fisher, Hurst, Vargha-Khadem, and Monaco (2001) have linked the discovery of a mutation of a gene on chromosome 7 to a language disorder that affects grammatical development and articulation. The mutation affects areas of the brain responsible for speech and language functioning.

Very recently, Cox and colleagues have made exciting discoveries that suggest stuttering too may now be linked with specific chromosomes (Cox et al., 2005). The strongest findings were evident on chromosome 9 for the phenotype "ever stuttered" and chromosome 13 for the phenotype "persistent stutter". Families where only females had ever stuttered were associated with strong signals on chromosome 21, whilst families where only males had ever stuttered showed a strong signal for a region on chromosome 7. Linkage analyses (a procedure which finds the general location of genes) was undertaken on the signals from chromosomes 9 and 13 (the primary findings) and on chromosomes 7 and 21 (sex-specific analyses). Findings revealed little of significance conditional on chromosomes 13 and 21, but analyses on chromosomes 7 and 9 were found to replicate some earlier linkage study findings.

Families with the strongest linkage on chromosome 7 also showed a strong pattern of linkage on chromosomes 12 and 18, again replicating findings from earlier studies on the significance of chromosome 12 (Riaz et al., 2005; Yairi, Ambrose, & Cox, 1996). Taken together, these findings led Cox et al. (2005) to suggest that there is a common set of regions implicated in stuttering. In addition, findings support the notion of sex-linked effects in the genetic component to the disorder, and also the possibility of different genetically mediated strains; one of which may be more conducive to therapy and spontaneous recovery, and another which is associated with persistent stuttering. These findings are of particular interest because some of the regions that are implicated have also been associated with other disorders, for example, the association between chromosome 7 with language disorder as earlier observed (Lai et al., 2001) and chromosome X and Down's syndrome.

The potential contribution of genetic research to the understanding of stuttering is considerable. Researchers, clinicians and those who stutter alike await future findings on chromosomal function studies with eager anticipation.

Summary and some words of caution

There is compelling evidence from a number of studies that stuttering can be explained, at least in part, as a genetic disorder. However, the nature of the genetic component remains unclear. Cox et al. (1984) indicated that their data was best explained by a polygenetic model, whilst Ambrose et al. (1993) found evidence for a single major locus. In addition, the risk of stuttering may ultimately depend on the interaction of a number of factors (including environmental, linguistic, neurological, gender) alongside genetic components.

Caution must also be urged when examining even some of the apparently more basic findings in this area of research. First, it would apparently make sense that if we find a child to have no stuttering relatives that this means the individual can be considered at low risk to a genetic component for the disorder, but in fact this is not the case. Research in the field of mental disorders has shown that it is perfectly possible for the proband to be the only person in the family with the disorder, but for there to be a genetic cause (Eaves et al., 1986). Conversely, presence of stuttering among a number of relatives does not guarantee a genetic link to the proband. It is entirely possible that the stuttering observed amongst a number of stuttering relatives relates to nongenetic influences. For this reason and others the family history design requires large sample sizes to ensure that the results noted really do relate directly to the research issue, and cannot be explained by extraneous variables (or "confounding" variables, as statisticians call them.) One simulation study in the area of psychiatry has speculated that in order to run a study with an 80 percent chance of detecting heterogeneity, around 430 probands would be needed, each with reliable evidence of stuttering or nonstuttering from three relatives. In short, unless a very large scale study is undertaken, the chances of finding genetic links using the family history method are remote.

There are also problems in comparing the many research papers on the subject. A substantial number are flawed, some have not used control groups, whilst others may have unwittingly gathered a biased population for their study. Equally difficult is the problem of reliability of the reporting, and relatives' recollections of their stuttering may well be inaccurate. Two relatives, when asked independently at interview or by questionnaire as to whether Cousin John once had a stutter, may well come up with a different interpretation. And while those same two relatives may agree that Aunt Jane used to stutter, they may hold differing views as to whether she actually fully recovered from it. Indeed, as we have seen earlier in this chapter, the very notion of what constitutes recovery is a problem that even experts in the field struggle with, and we still await a consensus as to a definition. Felsenfeld (1997) argues for the development of a standard assessment battery for the diagnosis of stuttering across the lifespan to help reduce the number of these intrusive variables.

A further difficulty is that knowing there may be a genetic component to stuttering does not get us any closer to knowing what that component actually is. Does the genetic predisposition code for a problem with the development of well-coordinated motor speech control, or perhaps it is responsible for some fragility in the development of linguistic skills in the preschool child? Perhaps, alternatively, there is some predisposition toward a psychological profile that is consistent with stuttering, or a central nervous system which is conditioned toward reduced hemispheric dominance for speech and language? There is very little data in this area. However, one study (Janssen, Kraaimaat, & Brutten, 1990) found that a group of people who stuttered and had a family history of stuttering responded similarly when tested across a number of linguistic and psychological variables to a group who had no family history of stuttering. Interestingly though, those with a family history group showed more motoric disruptions in the form of blocks and prolongations than the no-history group. This finding may be seen tentatively to support the notion that genetic predisposition might directly implicate physiological functioning. However, as we continue to argue through the book, many variables associated with stuttering interrelate, making interpretation of findings more difficult.

Finally, clinicians accessing a young child with a stutter cannot access their own twin study data, but they can and often do conduct interviews in an attempt to establish a family history of stuttering. When taken as one of a number of indicators as to the multifactorial background to the disorder that we advocate is so important, this practice seems not just reasonable, but indeed, desirable. However, Felsenfeld (1998) pleads the case for restraint in assigning too much predictive power to this procedure in the strongest possible terms:

> Family history (and recovery) status are complex noncategorical phenomena. Consequently, it must be understood that our attempts to establish "family history" in the clinic through a cursory interview are of questionable sensitivity and are almost certainly inaccurate. Although I am not suggesting that clinicians should stop collecting family history data during assessments, I am arguing that clinical decisions that are based in large part on these constituents should be avoided until we have stronger empirical evidence to support their predictive value. We know precious little about the genetic diathesis, and even less about the "stressors" that we know must be relevant for this diathesis to be activated.
>
> (Felsenfeld, 1998, p. 64)

Summary

We note throughout this book that, from a number of perspectives, stuttering in adulthood is usually very different to the version seen at onset. For example, we have seen in this chapter, as well as in chapters 9, 10 and 11, that during the course of its development primary stuttering changes from the easy part-word repetitions to the blocks and prolongations associated with the more established condition. Consistent with this change in type of stuttering, there is also a change in the linguistic focus of the stuttering and, as we see in chapter 5, a change from stuttering on function words to content words often takes place at around 8 years old. More established stuttering is also associated with an increase in secondary stuttering, tension, struggle behaviour and avoidance (see chapters 11 and 12). Environmental factors will also play a part in determining how a stutter develops (we discuss this within the therapeutic context in chapters 10, 11, 12).

In the present chapter we have considered the likelihood of some of these phenomena being underpinned by genetic predisposition, and the potential influence of hereditary factors on the phenomenon of spontaneous recovery. We have also considered the tentative possibility that there may be a number of different subtypes of stuttering, which comprise different onset types and follow different courses of development. We might further speculate as to whether, if the existence of genuine subgroups is eventually proven, whether some or all of these are genetically conditioned. However, large-scale longitudinal studies would be needed to determine whether functionally different subgroups (which each follow differing courses of development, and potentially with different prognoses) can really be isolated. The disparity between Van Riper's four-track model and Starkweather's nine-track conceptualization suggests that this would not be an easy task, yet the potential gains from both aetiological and therapeutic perspectives are great.

Key points

- A number of attempts have been made to categorize different tracks of stuttering development. While some are still considered to be of both theoretical and therapeutic interest (most notably Van Riper, 1973), it is still unclear whether the gradual change in symptoms and general progression of the disorder over a period of time can really be explained in terms of stages of development through empirical study. There is still no unified "stages of stuttering" framework currently identified.
- The term "spontaneous recovery" is ill-defined and may mean different things to different people. There is no agreed definition as to what the term "recovered" actually means: for some it may refer to a complete recovery from stuttering, while others may consider themselves recovered while still stuttering occasionally.
- Therapeutic efficacy may be difficult to judge due to the phenomenon of spontaneous recovery.
- Over two-thirds of children who stutter will cease to do so by puberty, with females more likely than males to recover.
- Recovery rates drop quickly if stuttering goes untreated for over one year. Most clinicians now favour early diagnosis and early intervention.
- There is evidence from a number of sources that stuttering can be inherited. Although the inheritance cannot be of simple Mendelian pattern, the exact method of transmission is currently not known, and may be either single gene or polygenic. In addition, it is still unclear as to exactly what is inherited; that is what any of the stuttering gene(s) might be coding for. Three major sources of information are twin studies, adoption studies and family history studies.
- There is a need for longitudinal family studies which utilize large sample groups, and whose outcome measures taken across a range of areas are reliably measured.
- The greatest susceptibility to stuttering seems to be a male offspring of a female adult who stutters.
- It is possible that there may be a genetic underpinning to stuttering, with an extra genetic loading being responsible for a more persistent version that is resistant to therapy.
- The chances of any person who stutters having a first-degree relative who also stutters or has stuttered at some time in their life is approximately 15 percent. (The chances of a nonstutterer having a

> first-degree relative who stutters or has stuttered at some time in their life is approximately 1 percent.)
> • The fact that there is not 100 percent concordance for stuttering between identical twins suggests that environmental factors must also play a part in the development of stuttering.

Further reading

Felsenfeld, S., & Drayna, D. (2001). Stuttering and genetics: Our past and our future. In S. E. Gerber (Ed.), *The handbook of genetic communicative disorders.* New York: Academic Press.
This gives very thorough coverage of the study of genetic research into stuttering, including an interesting section on future needs and considerations.

Finn, P. (1998). Recovery without treatment: A review of conceptual and methodological considerations across disciplines. In A. Cordes & R. J. Ingham (Eds.), *Treatment efficacy for stuttering: A search for empirical bases.* San Diego, CA: Singular Publishing Group.
This chapter, written by an acknowledged expert in the area of spontaneous recovery from stuttering, expands on the issues raised above regarding this complex phenomenon.

Van Riper, C. (1982). *The nature of stuttering.* Englewood Cliffs, NJ: Prentice-Hall.
An excellent source for Van Riper's track theory.

Yairi, E., Ambrose, N., & Cox, N. (1996). Genetics of stuttering: A critical review. *Journal of Speech and Hearing Research, 39*, 771–784.
A very useful review of genetic research.

8   The nature of cluttering

Introduction

No one is 100 percent fluent. Even the most eloquent and articulate speaker makes speech errors once in a while, and probably most of us make them rather more frequently than we would like. We might, for example, insert postponing words or sounds "um . . . er . . ." or maybe we will rephrase a sentence that we realized, whilst in the act of speaking, was not going to present our point quite as we had intended. Perhaps we might also repeat words from time to time, or "trip up" over words. I have heard a number of people, when aware and embarrassed at having producing such "muddled" speech, say something like "Oops, I've started stuttering, now!" In fact, none of this is stuttering, but these types of errors in speech and language can be considered as "cluttering-like". When such errors occur consistently and to excess in a person's speech this indeed can be called "cluttering".

Cluttering is a speech and language disorder, which while sharing some characteristics with stuttering, differs in many important respects. Unlike stuttering, it has been surprisingly underresearched (although there are now signs that this is beginning to change), and generally, the disorder has been underrepresented in the literature. Because of this, many clinicians have been unaware of the disorder, mistaking it for stuttering and other disorders. However, like stuttering, it has proved hard to define succinctly, in large part because, as we will see, there is disagreement as to which features are essential for the disorder to be diagnosed and which are coincidental.

Definitions

As is the case with stuttering, defining cluttering presents us with a problem due to differences of opinion as to which of the behaviours associated with the disorder are crucial to its diagnosis and which are peripheral. In an early definition Weiss (1964, p. 1) takes a holistic approach to its description:

> Cluttering is a speech disorder characterized by the clutterer's unaware-ness of his disorder, by short attention span, by disturbances in perception,

articulation and formulation of speech and often speed of delivery. It is a disorder of the thought processes preparatory to speech and based on a hereditary disposition. Cluttering is the verbal manifestation of central language imbalance, which affects all channels of communication (e.g., reading, writing, rhythm, and musicality) and behaviour in general.

St Louis (1992, p. 49) defines cluttering as: "a speech/language disorder", and cites its chief characteristics as "(1) abnormal fluency which is not stuttering and (2) a rapid and/or irregular speech rate". Wohl (1970) on the other hand considered festinant speech (where speech becomes faster and faster) to be the outstanding feature. Although all these definitions cover similar areas, there are significant differences amongst them. Weiss does not mention accelerated speech rate. St Louis provides the only definition that directly implicates loss of fluency. (Interestingly, a little later Daly, 1996 included lack of awareness as a mandatory feature of cluttering: a point we shall return to below and in chapter 17 on cluttering therapy.) More recently, St Louis, Raphael, Myers, and Bakker (2003, p. 4) have offered a reworked definition:

> Cluttering is a syndrome characterized by a speech delivery which is either abnormally fast, irregular or both. In cluttered speech, the person's speech is affected by one or more of the following: (1) failure to maintain normally expected sound, syllable, phrase and pausing patterns (2) evidence of greater than expected incidents of disfluency, the majority of which are unlike those typical of people who stutter.

This provides a comprehensive coverage of motoric and fluency aspects, although I feel that mention should be given to language difficulties that are commonly seen in the disorder. This is something Daly (1992) addresses when describing cluttering as "a disorder of speech and language processing resulting in rapid, dysrhythmic, sporadic, unorganized and frequently unintelligible speech. Accelerated speech is not always present, but an impairment in formulating language almost always is" (Daly, 1992, p. 107). All these differences serve to highlight the multifaceted nature of the disorder, and they bring into focus the difficulties for diagnosis; a process often complicated further by the common presence of co-occurring speech and language disorders.

Aetiology of cluttering

As with stuttering, there is currently no known cause for cluttering. Some have noted a genetic basis and cluttering, like stuttering has been found to run in families where stuttering or cluttering has been observed (Freund, 1952; Luschinger & Arnold, 1965). Freund (1952) found that out of a group of 121 clutterer-stutterers 84 percent reported a family history of either tachylalia (fast speech rate), or tachylalia together with stuttering as opposed to 21 percent among people who stutter. Weiss (1964) went so far as to claim that all cluttering occurred through genetic transmission and that cluttering underpinned all stuttering – an opinion which is not shared by authorities nowadays.

EEG evidence for an organic explanation has found those who clutter to show more abnormal patterns than those who stutter (Langova & Moravek, 1964; Luschinger & Arnold, 1965; Moravek & Langova, 1962). Luschinger and Arnold (1965) found that while a group of people who stutter had essentially normal EEG patterns, 90 percent of those diagnosed with cluttering evidenced deviant EEG traces. Like stuttering, cluttering has been observed as a feature of Tourette's syndrome (Van Borsel & Vanryckeghem, 2000; Van Borsel et al., 2003) and some have observed cluttering subsequent to neurological damage (Hashimoto et al., 1999; Lebrun, 1996; Thacker & De Nil, 1996). Also like stuttering, it occurs more frequently amongst males than females in a ratio of about 4:1 (Arnold, 1960; St Louis & Hinzman, 1988). The motoric component to the disorder has led some to describe cluttering as a type of dyspraxia, and the language component to lead others to link the disorder to a high-level organic dysphasia (De Hirsch, 1961; Luschinger & Landolt, 1951). As with stuttering, some commentators have speculated that cluttering is a disorder of time perception, that is, an auditory based disorder, rather than a speech/language production one (Van Riper, 1992). Molt (1996) found that, in contrast to matched control subjects, three school aged clutterers performed below normal test-established criteria on central auditory processing (CAP) measures and also showed abnormal auditory event potential (AEP) waveform patterns.

Characteristics

One significant problem in trying succinctly to identify the characteristics of a clutter lies in the fact that there may be two basic strands to the disorder; a language component and a motor one. Some researchers (e.g., St Louis et al., 2003) do not include a language component in their definition because there are some people who clutter whose language planning appears intact (although there is acknowledgement that language planning difficulties are often implicated). This may be true, but cases of cluttering in the absence of any language difficulty are rare (Cooperman, 2003; Daly, 1996; Ward, 2004). It is common for cluttering to present more as a language problem than a motoric one. In such cases speech output is more likely to show a lack of linguistic fluency, characterized by poorly constructed language rather than as an output which is motorically disrupted (see below for examples of linguistic and motoric cluttering). St Louis, Myers, Faragasso, Townsend, and Gallaher (2004) explored listeners' perceptions of the speech of two adolescents who cluttered (one severe, one mild-moderate). The two groups of 48 people judged that rate and naturalness were the least acceptable for those who cluttered, followed by articulation. Disfluency and language were considered the most acceptable of the five attributes. One problem with this research is that language difficulties may not have been key features of these two speakers, as they might be for others. Nonetheless, it is significant that disfluency itself is not something that seems prominent to the listener. Though this might at first seem surprising given that cluttering is defined as a disorder of fluency, it actually brings home the point that cluttering tends to present as an output which is primarily disorganized (motorically or linguistically) rather than disfluent. Any loss of fluency comes about primarily because of this disorganization, whether due to a loss of motor control or a lack of linguistic ability.

Table 8.1 Ten significant features of cluttering (after Daly & Cantrell, 2006)

Item	Percentage agreement between the 60 expert raters
1 Telescopes or condenses words (e.g., omits sounds	93.33
2 Lack of effective self-monitoring skills	90.00
3 Lack of pauses between words; run-on sentences	83.33
4 Lack of awareness	83.33
5 Imprecise articulation (e.g., distorts sounds)	82.00
6 Irregular speech rate; speaks in spurts	82.00
7 Interjections; revisions; filler words	80.00
8 Compulsive talker; verbose; circumlocutions common	80.00
9 Language disorganized; confused wording	78.33
10 Seems to verbalize before adequate thought formulation	75.00

Very recently, in an attempt to arrive at some consensus of opinion as to the disorder's significant features, Daly and Cantrell (2006) called on 60 expert researchers and clinicians in cluttering worldwide to respond to a questionnaire containing a number of statements about the disorder. Out of the 50 statements listed on Daly and Cantrell's probe, a significant agreement between the raters (p = <0.05) was arrived at on three items: imprecise articulation (distorts speech sounds); irregular speech rate (speaks in spurts); and demonstrates word-finding difficulties resembling anomia. The ten findings shown in Table 8.1 were rated "Almost always present" or "Frequently present" by the 60 raters.

Ten additional characteristics that the experts thought important for diagnosis were:

1 Excessive "normal" disfluencies.
2 Does not repair mistakes.
3 Difficulty with words of increasing length and complexity.
4 Disfluencies not related to specific sounds/situations.
5 Cluttering co-occurs with ADHD.
6 Great difficulty discriminating vowels.
7 Rapid rate with poor articulation.
8 Irregular fast speech rate, with spurts (which may be interspersed with slower speech and hesitations and pauses).

9   Unaware when communication breakdowns occur.
10 Unwilling to change or to believe treatment is necessary.

We can now look at some of the subcomponents of cluttering which have been considered significant in a little more detail.

Motor components

1   *Tachylalia*. This is perhaps the most often symptom reported by the lay person. "Fred speaks really quickly. I really find it hard to understand him, sometimes." Although a fast rate is a strong feature of the disorder, it is fast *bursts* of speech interspersed with short inappropriate pauses that constitute the defining characteristics. There are very many highly fluent speakers whose habitual speech rate approximates that of many tachylalic clutterers. Froeschels (1955), for example, found only 50 percent of a tachylalic group to be clutterers.

2   *Excessive coarticulation*. This also known as overcoarticulation (Dalton & Hardcastle, 1989). Typically, the person who clutters will display distortions and simplifications similar to those seen in young children when they are developing language. This may include cluster reductions and weak syllable deletion. For the person who clutters, however, this is directly related to the fast speech rate, resulting in a reduced ability to maintain articulatory accuracy at higher speech rates. The resulting lack of precision in the articulation of consonants, particularly, may result in an output that sounds markedly dysarthric.

3   *Articulation errors*. Speech output can also be compromised by the types of articulatory errors seen in apraxia of speech (or verbal apraxia). Indeed, some commentators have likened cluttering to the disorder of apraxia itself (De Hirsch, 1961). Typical speech errors include anticipatory errors (for example, *gleen glass* for *green glass*, and phoneme reversals (or spoonerisms) e.g., *bo gack* for *go back*. Tongue-twisters may be particularly difficult for clutterers, even when speed is reduced. Note that, like the errors made by apraxic speakers, it is only very rarely that clutterers will produce articulatory errors that result in non-native sounds being heard.

4   *Lack of speech rhythm*. Whether accompanied by tachylalia or not, most experts would agree that this is a good diagnostic indicator of cluttering (Daly, 1996; St Louis, 1992; St Louis et al., 2003). Speech may be characterized by jerky bursts of fast speech, interspersed with inappropriate short pauses. These pauses, and subsequent abrupt onset of speech, may give a staccato impression to speech delivery. Because of this, some people who clutter may also have great difficulty in replicating simple phrases (such as children's poems which carry easily maintained rhythmic patterns) even under a slower and controlled rate. When severe, the poor phrasing can greatly reduce intelligibility, and can be difficult to treat.

5   *Monotonous speech.* Difficulties with phrasing may lead to speech that is lacking in pitch range. When there are breaks to the natural flow of speech (as above) this can further reduce intelligibility.

6   *Festinant speech.* Speech may start at a normal pace but become increasingly quick. Coincident with this, speech may become mumbled or over-coarticulated (see above) and may tail off into inaudibility. Wohl (1970) went as far as to suggest that festinant speech was the outstanding feature of cluttering. Although festinant speech may be seen in some who clutter, this view is not commonly shared nowadays.

7   *Fluency disruptions.* With the exception of (3), which directly affects fluency, many of the motoric features tend to affect intelligibility, rather than fluency. Clutterers typically neither block[1] nor prolong, but part-word repetitions are quite common. Word and phrase repetitions are also common, but it may be that these are more related language-based difficulties (see below). Quick phoneme repetitions, free from any struggle behaviour and usually comprising no more than 2–3 per instance, may also be associated with cluttering, but all of these fluency errors will be produced in the absence of any apparent concern, and secondary behaviours.

The box illustrates examples of motoric and linguistic cluttering.

Motoric cluttering

Case A. Male, 18 years. Speech is characterized here by fast rushes of speech, fast phoneme repetitions and inappropriate short pauses (represented by (:)).

Normally I c c come by car, but t t t today I (:) took the bus. My car (:) had to go for a (:) service.

Linguistic cluttering

Case B. Male, 25 years. Speech is characterized by a rate which is mostly within normal limits. However, language is disorganized and confused. Maze behaviour is apparent in excessive phrase revision, excessive number of fillers and sentence revision.

My, favourite – well, the best, best place for my, for a holiday is um, um, is, er, Australia. The heat, well, the er, the er, climate really is. . . . It's it's really great.

---

1   Blocking is not a feature of cluttering, but short inappropriate pauses are, and these can sound somewhat similar to short blocks. If blocks rather than pauses are identified, the clinician would need to consider a stuttering component to the diagnosis.

Language components

Language may be affected at a number of levels:

1 *Grammar and syntax*
   - Excessive amount of phrase repetitions and revisions may occur due to language formulation difficulties.
   - Problems with verb conjugation and incorrect pronoun and pre-position usage.
   - Sentences may be simplified and word order may be incorrect.
   - Function words in particular may be prone to deletion.
   - Incomplete sentences. Sentences may tail off unfinished (St Louis, Hinzman, & Hull, 1985).
2 *Lexical level*
   - Problems with lexical access (word retrieval) may be evident.
   - Frequent and overuse of fillers and interjections such as "um" and "er". Unlike stuttering, where these are used as devices to postpone a difficult word or sound, they are used by the person who clutters to help give time to organize speech. They may also be used to mask word-finding difficulties, which are particularly prevalent amongst this population.
   - There may be substitution of a semantically related item (semantic paraphasia). For example, Saturday may be produced as Sunday, chair as table, and names also may become confused (Paul when meaning Peter). The speaker may or may not be aware of these errors.
   - Maze behaviour: clinicians should be aware of this term, coined by Loban (1976). It refers to an output that, as the title suggests, is indirect, and explores linguistic "dead-ends". Speech may become subject to pause, hesitation and revision as it progresses. This term provides a cover-all for a range of difficulties listed above. The term was originally applied to the language of younger children, but is now frequently used to refer to older children and adults.
3 *Pragmatic level*
   - The person who clutters may experience more generalized difficulties with expressive language, particularly in organizing linguistic infor-mation for discourse and topic maintenance (Teigland, 1996).
   - Summarizing and correctly sequencing information can be problem-atic. Given a front-page newspaper story to recall, a person who clutters might spend time retelling comparatively unimportant details, use tangential speech (becoming sidetracked into unrelated issues) whilst failing to mention that the focus of the story was of a murder.

In sum, if we consider Levelt's (1989, 1992) model of speech and language processing that we use to help describe the levels of linguistic breakdown in stuttering (see chapter 5), we can see that the impact of cluttering can be identified at all three levels: conceptualization, formulation and articulation.

Psychological components

Awareness of cluttering

Consistent across much of the early literature is the idea that, in direct contrast to stuttering, those who clutter tend to be unaware of their speech/ language difficulties, but this notion requires further qualification. Adolescents and adults who clutter may often be aware of the fact that there is a problem, but be unable to do anything about it, or be unaware of the significance of the problem from the listener's perspective. For example, there may be awareness of a fast speech rate and they might even volunteer that, for example, people are always telling them to slow down or to repeat. However, the individual usually has no sense that something is actually pathologically wrong in the way that speech is produced. It is very unusual to find an individual who feels the difficulty actually constitutes a communication "problem". If we consider the fact that many of the speech and language disruptions seen in cluttering are consistent with the speech and language errors that occur in everybody's speech, perhaps this unawareness is unsurprising. We all experience word-finding difficulties from time to time and we may make occasional speech errors without taking any particular mental note of the fact.

Attitudes associated with cluttering

For the most part, avoidance is rare, even amongst the minority of cluttering speakers who are aware of difficulties in controlling their speech or language. Unlike those who stutter, people who clutter do not experience word or sound specific anxieties. Even so, more motorically complex sequences, such as those found in consonant clusters and in longer words, are likely to give more difficulty. Occasionally some speakers report avoiding certain longer words which are harder to pronounce. Also, unlike stuttering, cluttering can usually be temporarily controlled under formal situations, and when greater effort is put into maintaining clarity. As Daly and St Louis (1998) point out, this can create problems at assessment where the client may present with normal sounding speech. (We return to this issue in chapter 17.) In contrast with stuttering, cluttering is relatively unaffected by listener identity and social avoidance is reportedly rare.

Cluttering and personality

Some have argued that there may be a cluttering stereotype. According to Weiss (1964), those who clutter show poor self-monitoring skills that are not just confined to a lack of awareness of speech but are also present in noncommunicative actions, which give rise to inattentiveness and problems with cognitive functions such as high-level short-term memory. This can explain the impression of absentmindedness and the more general lack of awareness that some commentators believe exist amongst this group of speakers. Typically, the poor self-monitoring can translate as poor listening skills and these, together with inattentiveness, may lead to misunderstandings and inappropriate comments and responses. Although a significant number of clients do not exhibit this stereotype my personal experience is that a surprising number do appear to fall within the cluttering stereotype proposed by Weiss, over 40 years ago. Weiss also believed that the cluttering personality was associated with a general lack of organizational skill and untidiness; although these are features which subsequent commentators have been less willing to confirm. It is certainly true to say that the concept of a cluttering stereotype has not been rigorously pursued by researchers in recent years.

Cluttering and normal disfluency

Unlike stuttering, I would argue that much cluttering behaviour sits on a continuum with normal speech. At one end of the continuum we have the highly fluent individual who vary rarely makes any speech/language error. At the other end we have severe cluttering. Clearly, differentially diagnosing these two speakers would not be a problem. However, it could be argued that even the highly fluent speaker "clutters" when interjecting an "um . . ." even though this might occur perhaps once only in 500 words. If we accept then, that everyone has cluttering moments, including people who stutter, the difficulty is in defining a point on the continuum beyond which the individual may be diagnosed as a person who clutters: in other words, the issue of distinguishing between a speaker who demonstrates moments of cluttering and an individual who is "a clutterer". This distinction is often very difficult to make and is in contrast to the situation with stuttering, where differentially diagnosing pathological disfluency at onset can be difficult (see chapter 9) but where even mild stuttering is readily recognized as such when it has become established. (See section below on cluttering spectrum behaviour as one way of characterizing cases of borderline cluttering.)

Development of cluttering

Like stuttering, cluttering usually develops in the preschool years, but it is quite possible for it to go undiscovered or misdiagnosed for many years. In one sense this is understandable because, as mentioned earlier, some aspects of cluttered speech can be regarded as being typical of normal disfluency, and many of the problems associated with the disorder may be seen as part and parcel of the normal speech/language developmental process. Often any delay in any one area is so slight as to go unnoticed, or at least not regarded as needing treatment. For example, as parents we might accept that our child may not be the most skilled for his age at speech motor tasks, and that he may try to talk more quickly than his motor speech abilities allow. Even as clinicians we further acknowledge that in the preschool years processes such as cluster reduction and weak syllable deletion are perfectly natural processes on the way to adult-like phonological representations. We accept that grammar will not be fully established and we accept that attention span and fine motor coordination will also take time to develop. Of course, as clinicians we consider all this information in relation to the times at which the relevant milestones should be achieved, and take action if these are not met within certain time limits. The problem is often that the child who clutters may not show any particular delay in any one area and may simply present with slightly compromised performance across a number of areas. Add to this the fact that most preschool clutterers manage to be understood, and that usually there is no particular sense of concern by the parents (and typically none whatsoever from the child), and this makes for a situation where the speech/language issues may never reach a therapist. Even if they do, there is a danger that the child (in the absence of a diagnosis of cluttering) will not be regarded as a priority for treatment. We return to the issue of therapy in part 2 of this book.

The role of recovery, either with or without therapy, is not known, although, like stuttering, spontaneous recovery once the condition has persisted into adulthood is unlikely. However, it seems reasonable to speculate that if undiagnosed or untreated cluttering is likely to continue into adulthood. In stark contrast to the difficulties experienced by many adolescents who stutter during their secondary school years, the vast majority of these speakers experience few ramifications to their cluttering speech patterns. The speech/language characteristics are also usually taken for granted by peers at school and elsewhere. While there may be some amusement at the features of the clutterer's speech, there are usually only minor (if any) social penalties associated with it, and usually the lack of concern over speech continues. The adolescent who clutters is unlikely to be unaware of any underlying problem at school, and later it seems rare that it causes significant problems during tertiary education either. Often, adult cluttering referrals come via work colleagues and line managers who are concerned that the individual's chances of promotion are being compromised due to that person's lack of clarity in speech. Quite often, the clutterer is surprised that others have difficulty understanding them although, often depending on the severity of the disorder, others are very aware that speech is difficult to follow. There is also variability as to the unawareness of the range of difficulties they have, but to many the clinician's identification of a specific speech/language disorder comes as a surprise.

Cluttering and attention deficit hyperactivity disorder

It is not uncommon for young children who clutter to display behavioural characteristics associated with attention deficit hyperactivity disorder (ADHD; St Louis & Myers, 1997). Such behaviours may include impulsive and uninhibited behaviour and poor attention; problems which tend to become more noticeable as the child starts school when a higher degree of conformity is required. These behaviours may translate as inattentiveness to school work, fidgeting, poor organizational skills or a general inability to concentrate. Consistent with the fact that clutterers tend to have reduced awareness of their speech difficulties, so too unnecessary errors in written work may go unnoticed by the individual. Unlike their stuttering counterparts, children who clutter (and adults too) typically are compulsive talkers. It is not unusual for younger children who clutter to find difficulty in controlling such behaviours and this may lead to disciplinary action for their sometimes disruptive behaviour. Findings such as these have led some to consider the relationship between cluttering and ADHD (Daly, 1992). Cluttering has also been linked with specific learning disorders (SLD). Wiig and Semel (1984) argue that the type of disfluencies that occur in LD children (interjections, pauses, word repetition and word revision) also appear in cluttered speech. St Louis and Myers (1997) state that "some of these disfluent LD children might be regarded more appropriately as clutterers" (p. 317).

Cluttering and stuttering

A complicating factor in identifying cluttering is that it frequently coexists with stuttering; although there is disagreement as to the degree of overlap (Daly, 1986, 1993; Freund, 1952; Myers & St Louis, 1992; Preus, 1992; Weiss, 1964, 1967). Freund reported cluttering in 22 percent of a group of 513 people who stuttered, but a much higher incidence of 47 percent in a subgroup of later onset stutterers. This late onset seems consistent with Van Riper's (1982) track theory (Track III) in which a mixture of cluttering and stuttering-like behaviours were observed. Preus (1981) found that 32 out of a group of 100 people who stutterered studied also showed symptoms of cluttering; a finding consistent with Daly's (1993) report that one in three people who stutter, also clutter. Weiss (1964, 1967) reports a cluttering/stuttering combination in around 67 percent of those referred to him for therapy; the remaining 33 percent being split equally between "pure" clutterers and "pure" stutterers. Pure stutterers themselves made up only 17 percent of his caseload. Daly (1986) indicated that pure cluttering is comparatively rare: less than 5 percent of clients cluttered, compared to 40 percent who both cluttered and stuttered. My own clinical experience concurs with findings of Daly (1986, 1993) and Preus (1981); that is, around one-third of those who are referred for stuttering also present with some cluttering components. I would argue, however, that pure cluttering is not as rare as has previously been reported, but rather that people who only clutter, unlike those who also stutter, are simply less likely to be aware that there is anything pathologically wrong with their speech, and therefore do not refer for therapy.

Weiss (1964), still a respected authority on cluttering, takes a more radical stance on the relationship between stuttering and cluttering, but while his argument that both cluttering and stuttering develop from the same physio-logical anomaly remains viable, his contention that cluttering underpins most stuttering does not stand up to empirical testing. (Were this to be the case fluency clinicians successfully treating stuttering might expect to find cluttering to exist in all of these cases.) All these figures need to be taken with a degree of caution though. For as long as there is no data-based definition of cluttering, we cannot be sure that the groups labelled as clutterers by the various different researchers represent a homogeneous population. Perhaps in the future it will be possible usefully to define cluttering subgroups. In the meantime, even considering the basic strands of the disorder such as lan-guage based, motorically based or mixed, may provide helpful starting points. Below, I suggest an addition to the cluttering terminology which can help with the problem of a cluttering definition, and particularly of describing the coexistence of cluttering with other disorders.

Cluttering spectrum behaviour

I would like to propose the use of the term "cluttering spectrum behaviour" (CSB) as a useful descriptor for those speakers who display some cluttering characteristics, but for whom a diagnosis as "a clutterer" may be less certain. (Of course, this term would not be applied to speakers who only make occa-sional speech and language errors.) Let's take the example of a speaker who does not stutter but does exhibit an excessive number of phrase revisions, together with repeated fillers and word repetitions. This speaker also produces a number of anticipatory speech errors. Speech rate and rhythm is normal, however. So, here the speaker presents with elements of cluttering, but without some of the characteristics that are usually regarded as being at the core of the disorder. Clinical opinion may differ as to whether this person is actually "a person who clutters" but there will be agreement that there is, at least, excessive linguistic nonfluency. Thus, clinicians might agree that such a person could be described as being on the "cluttering spectrum" and, as such, displaying CSB.

This term can also be particularly helpful when describing the speech of those who show elements of other speech or language disorders, which as we have already seen can be a common and confusing element of the disorder. Let's take another example of an adult who attends an assessment with some cluttering symptoms. In addition though, this individual has been diagnosed as clinically depressed and there are elements of his speech and language (low volume and under-articulation and poor pragmatic skills) which can be con-sistent with this diagnosis, also. Applying the term CSB to this person would demonstrate an acknowledgement of the presence of cluttering symptoms. But by avoiding the use of the term "person who clutters" this would also leave room for consideration of the other elements of speech and language, some of which may be difficult to ascribe with certainty to the cluttering or to the depression. Note that this is very different to diagnosing this person as a clutterer, who also has other concomitant speech and language problems. By using the term CSB we avoid making the (implied) assertion that all the cluttering signs are linked causally and exclusively to the disorder of cluttering.

Summary

Is cluttering really a distinct speech and language disorder? This might seem a rather odd question to ask at this late stage in the chapter. I have already spent some time writing about it as such and in part 2 I spend more time discussing how it can be assessed and treated, so presumably I do think it is a genuine and distinct speech/language disorder, which does seem to be the general consensus (e.g., Freund, 1952; Daly & Burnett, 1999; Myers & St Louis, 1992; St Louis, Hinzman, & Hull, 1985; Van Riper, 1992). But let's briefly review some of the evidence. First, as we have already seen, there is some difference of opinion as to the relative importance of the key features that characterize cluttering. Second, there is substantial overlap between behaviours seen in cluttering and a range of other disorders. Specifically, many of the motor speech fluency and language problems regarded as cluttering may also be seen under the headings of articulation and language disorders. In the same way that we would not diagnose acquired cluttering for a person with, say, elements of high-level aphasia and mild dysarthria, could we not then make a case for cluttering to be nothing more than a mixture of (already recognized) speech language difficulties, rather than a separate clinical entity? Weiss' interesting (1964) perspective of cluttering as being just one feature of "central language imbalance" might suggest so. If he is correct in his assertion that cluttering is effectively just one symptom of a larger problem, particularly if this problem is multimodal and ultimately related to thought processing rather than speech or language processing, perhaps we should be looking at cognitive processing to find the core of this problem. Perhaps cluttering can better be described as just one of a number of modular features, alongside lack of rhythmicality (not just within the speech domain) and depressed motor control abilities which may or may not be associated with this more centralized disorder.

The problem is that at the moment cluttering constitutes a broad church, and ultimately cluttering's distinctiveness depends on the narrowness (or breadth) of the definition one employs. Aside from the speech and language issues, we have the notion of the cluttering personality, together with the involvement of such cognitive processes as attention and memory. Yet we still lack verifiable data as to what extent these features really do characterize those who clutter. A consensus needs to be reached as to which other elements are central to the definition, and of course more research is needed. As things currently stand, there are no answers to these questions, and consequently clinicians' opinions differ as to what falls within the umbrella term of cluttering. This in turn means that comparing the research on cluttering is difficult, given the different working definitions that research groups have used to define their cluttering subjects. Equally significantly, this inevitably leads to inconsistent diagnosis of the disorder from clinic to clinic. A survey of expert researchers and clinicians is currently being organized to help determine where the significant diagnostic factors lie (Daly & Cantrell 2006). We must be optimistic that this will lead us toward some better answers. In the meantime, perhaps the use of the term "cluttering spectrum behaviour" can be of use in defining the range of behaviours that clinicians see in their clinics.

Key points

- Cluttering is a disorder of fluency which is related to but different to stuttering. At present, there is no data that supports a single definition of the disorder. The search for a data-based definition must be an urgent priority.
- Cluttering is likely to contain one or more of the following key elements: abnormally fast speech rate, or uncontrolled bursts of fast speech; reduced intelligibility due to overcoarticulation and indistinct articulation; disturbances in language planning; greater than expected number of disfluencies.
- Cluttering commonly exists alongside other disorders including stuttering and, in children, attention deficit hyperactivity disorder. Cluttering behaviours may overlap with those seen in articulation disorders, language disorders, learning difficulty and attention deficit hyperactivity disorders.
- Like stuttering, there may be repetition of sound units, but the other core elements in stuttering, blocking and prolongations, are not present. Also like stuttering, cluttering usually occurs in childhood and there may be a genetic component to its acquisition.
- Unlike stuttering, cluttering is commonly associated with difficulties with higher level language expression, articulation, rhythm, consistency of speech rate and often fast rate of speech, although there is disagreement as to which of these features are required to be present in order to diagnose the disorder. Cluttering may also be associated with reading disorders and poor writing.
- Some claim that, in addition to the speech and language symptoms, there is a cluttering stereotype, characterized by unawareness of any speech/language difficulty, poor organizational skills and poor memory.
- The term cluttering spectrum behaviour is proposed as a descriptor for those who display cluttering characteristics or tendencies but do not warrant a diagnosis of "clutterer".

Further reading

Daly, D. A., & Burnett, M. L. (1999). Cluttering: Traditional views and new perspectives. In R. F. Curlee (Ed.), *Stuttering and related disorders of fluency*. New York: Thieme.
David Daly and Michelle Burnett provide a very readable review of thinking on the subject of cluttering.

Myers, F. L. & St Louis, K. O. (1992). *Cluttering: A clinical perspective*. Kibworth: Far Communications.
This book is now nearly 15 years old, but it is still an excellent source. Despite the emphasis on clinical aspects, there is much of value here with regard to the aetiology of cluttering.

St Louis, K. O. & Myers, F. L. (1997). Management of cluttering and related fluency disorders. In R. F. Curlee & G. M. Siegel (Eds.), *Nature and treatment of stuttering: New directions*. Boston: Allyn & Bacon.
An excellent summary of information on the subject.

Various authors (1996). *Journal of Fluency Disorders, 21*, issues 3–4.
An entire volume of *Journal of Fluency Disorders* consisting of a collection of papers covering aetiological and therapeutic aspects of cluttering.

Weiss, D. (1964). *Cluttering*. Englewood Cliffs, NJ: Prentice-Hall.
It is unusual to single out such an old text for selected reading, but Deso Weiss's work is still influential today. Many of the ideas that he raised still form the basis of current discussion and this text is still frequently referred to by today's authorities.

Part II
The treatment of stuttering and cluttering

9 The measurement and assessment of stuttering

Introduction

Stuttering is a complex multifactorial phenomenon, characterized not only by the disruptions to motor speech which are identified as moments of stuttering, but also the behavioural, cognitive and affective changes that can occur as a consequence of these speech disruptions. It is not surprising then that identification and measurement can both be difficult. In recent years the increasing recognition of the client's point of view as central to the monitoring and evaluation of stuttering has brought with it numerous approaches to the issue of measurement. Importantly, there are now an increasing number of published instruments that probe the client's perception of the disorder, and the effect that it has in the "real world" away from the fluency enhancing environment of the speech clinic.

Stuttering is usually identified via the assessment of two basic strands of the disorder: the examination of motor speech activity in the form of speech rate data and fluency counts; and a cognitive perspective in the form of attitudinal questionnaires (and by more informal measures and discussion in the case of younger children). We could say that the former approach deals with stuttering, while the latter deals with the person who stutters. Both perspectives have attracted sharp criticism, although thankfully the issue is not as divisive as it once was. However, there are some who believe that attitudinal adjustment must be made the central issue in stuttering therapy (and therefore in assessment also). For such people, objective behavioural analyses may be overlooked on the basis that there are so many problems which can affect reliability that the resulting data simply are not trustworthy (for example, Sheehan, 1984; see also chapter 7). Other commentators, who favour an operant approach to the treatment of stuttering have argued that attitudinal aspects lack objectivity and should not be allowed to carry any weight.

The rationale taken in this chapter is that although current approaches toward assessment of cognitive and motor speech aspects of fluency are both flawed, both have considerable merit also, and both are necessary to ensure a balanced perspective on the severity and impact of the disorder. Clinicians must recognize the limitations of both approaches, but if we do this we can use these procedures to get a clear picture of our clients' current status and needs. In addition, assessment materials can be used to drive the therapeutic process, and may be used at post-clinic and follow-up sessions to provide evidence of the effects of therapy.

We begin by outlining procedures that examine the overt behaviours of stuttering before moving on to ways of assessing cognitive aspects of stuttering. We then see how the various procedures are used amongst other assessment protocols for three types of assessment: those for preschool, elementary school and adolescents and adults who stutter.

Measurement of speech rate and speech fluency

The most commonly used method for collecting objective data on stuttering severity is the stuttering frequency count. This involves collecting a speech sample from the client, ascertaining the number of syllables or words spoken within the sample and then calculating the number of syllables or words which are stuttered. This figure is most commonly expressed as a percentage of stuttered syllables, or stuttered words (%SS; %WS) and usually accompanied by an analysis of speech rate expressed in the number of syllables or words spoken per minute (SPM, WPM). Figure 9.1 shows how speech fluency and speech rate can be calculated in this way. Counting stuttered syllables and rate in this manner is a well-established procedure and a supposed objective way of collecting data on the severity of stuttering. As we will see a little later in this section, however, there are a number of weaknesses and potential problems with this procedure. (See also Lees, 1994 for a critique of the syllable count.)

The fluency count

The fluency count is most commonly used as part of the information gathering process at assessment and at post-clinic and follow-up sessions, although it may be used throughout the therapeutic process to continuously monitor the client's progress (as is often the case on fluency shaping programs; see chapter 12). Most clinicians advocate that the speech sample comprises a minimum of two minutes of the clients talking time, excluding pauses. To accurately analyze the time taken during speaking, the talking time must be calculated using a stopwatch, which should be stopped when the client is either listening or considering a reply, as well as during pauses, but not where there is silence due to stuttering (for example, during a silent block). Simultaneously, the clinician must count each syllable whilst also making note of syllables which are stuttered upon. To do this accurately and reliably involves a number of skills. First, the clinician must be adept at counting syllables accurately at what may be a fast rate, whilst being able to recognize which of those syllables are stuttered. To this end, criteria as to what does and does not

1 Percentage of syllables stuttered (%SS)

Formula: <u>Total number of stuttered syllables</u>   x 100
             total number of syllables spoken

Worked example: <u>Total number of stuttered moments</u>   <u>52</u>
                    Total number of syllables   380

                    <u>53</u> x 100 = 13.68% SS
                    380

2 Speaking rate (in syllables per minute, SPM)

Formula: <u>Total number of all syllables spoken</u> x 60
             Total length of time (in seconds)

Worked example: <u>Total number of all syllables spoken</u>   <u>380</u>
                    Total length of time (in seconds)   120

                    <u>380</u>   x 60   = 190 SPM
                    120

3 Articulatory rate (in syllables per minute, SPM)

Formula: <u>Total number of nonstuttered syllables</u> x 60
             Total length of time taken (in seconds)

Worked example: <u>Total number of nonstuttered syllables</u>   <u>240</u>
                    Total length of time taken (in seconds)   120

                    <u>240</u>   x 60   = 120 SPM
                    120

Figure 9.1 Formulas for calculating frequency of stuttering and rate of speech.

constitute stuttering must be clearly defined and adhered to beforehand (see below). Second, this requires the physical manipulation of a stopwatch and possibly two event counters simultaneously.[1] All of this has to be done whilst paying attention to the client's speech. This can be tricky, particularly if the speech sample is taken from conversation, when turn taking can lead to lots of clicking on and off with the stopwatch. Once the speech sample data have been collected, the clinician uses the syllable count and stuttering count data

---

1 Event counters are small handheld devices which, when activated either mechanically or electronically, add a digit to a visual display. Thus, the clinician may use one to count fluent syllables and another to tally moments of stuttering.

to calculate rate of speech and the percentage of stuttering. The ability to rate speech samples accurately is a skill and can only be achieved through practice. Being able to rate samples accurately "online" and without later recourse to audio or video feedback is particularly difficult.[2] Ideally, a number of speech samples should be taken across a range of speaking situations. Commonly, these include conversation and monologue, and with older clients oral reading (where word avoidance cannot be hidden less easily) and telephone conversations.

What to count and what not to count

This can be awkward, both in terms of the units to be counted (syllables or words) and what is regarded as normal as opposed to stuttered. For example, some clinicians include all interjections and phrase revisions as stuttering in their fluency count as normal, whilst others may not. To complicate the matter further, it could well be that within the same speech sample the interjection might be seen as normal disfluency. "Oh . . . 26 multiplied by 20 is . . . er . . . 520", or stuttered as in "my name is . . . . er . . . John". Similarly, "he needs the will to live . . . the will to succeed" may sound plausible as attempting to repair a genuine slip of the tongue, whereas "I want to go to the . . . I want to watch a film" is more likely to be connected to word avoidance. For the clinician, the most important thing is to state explicitly the criteria on which the judgements of fluency and stuttering are made, and at the least to make a note of any behaviour which is considered unusual, even if the clinician is unsure as to whether it should be considered as genuine stuttering. Data then needs to be collected on the extent of each moment of stuttering; for example, the length of blocks, number of repetitions. (We return to this last issue in the section on fluency counts below.)

Syllables or words?

As far as the total count is concerned, a fundamental decision as to whether to work with words or syllables needs to be made. Inter-rater reliability in counting both words and syllables can be high (Ingham & Packman, 1999) when practised, although inter-clinic reliability can be a significant problem, as we will come to see. There is now an increasing trend toward using syllable counts which many clinicians and researchers believe to be more accurate.

---

2 The task of managing counters and stopwatches can be simplified through the use of a number of custom-made electronic devices that do away with the need to have a separate stopwatch. Here a stopwatch built into the calculator starts automatically when buttons used to count syllables are depressed and stops when the pressing has ceased. The clinician then only needs to press another button when a stuttering moment is recorded to complete the data collection. The device also gives online feedback as to rate of speech and also percentage of syllables stuttered.

For example, syllable counts compensate for the possibility of artificial differences in speech rate arising between speakers who use more multisyllabic words, and whose rate might appear slower simply because these take longer to produce than monosyllabic words. It also allows for the possibility of stuttering more than once on the same word. Once the clinician has made this decision, the next concerns what is chosen to be counted as stuttered.

Stuttering vs normal disfluency

This is a crucial but difficult area. In undertaking any analysis of the motoric disruptions seen in stuttering, clinicians need to distinguish what Yairi (1997) terms "stuttering-like disfluencies" (SLDs) from normal disfluencies (NDs). It is not always possible to categorically define certain disfluencies as either SLDs or NDs, but we know that certain types of disfluencies are more characteristic of stuttering than others. Normal disfluencies tend to be characterized by pauses, interjections and revisions (Yairi, 1997) while part-word and monosyllabic word repetitions when repeated once are common amongst 2- to 4-year-old children, and even multiple repetitions if shown infrequently need not be cause for concern. However, more consistent multiple repetitions are considered SLDs, and place the child at risk of stuttering, particularly if repetitions lack even rhythm and are at an increased rate, as do pauses which carry tension or respiratory struggle (Ambrose & Yairi, 1999; Starkweather, 1987). Yairi (1981) also suggests that younger preschool children showing less than 3 percent of disfluent words have comparable fluency to adults, and that those with 4–9 percent of disfluent words are only a little more disfluent than adults. Only those children with over 10 percent disfluent words may be at greater risk for stuttering. This "at risk" figure of 10 percent seems a little high, and clinicians may feel more comfortable with Conture's (1997) contention that upward of 3 percent disfluency, in the form of whole or part-word repetitions, together with a minimum of 3 units of repetition signals a child of between 2 and 5 years to be at risk of stuttering (see also Table 9.1).

For example, stuttering tends to be identified more by sublexical speech errors (particularly phoneme repetition, prolongations and blocks) while normal disfluency is usually associated more with word or phrase level repetition and revision[3] (Boehmler, 1958; Conture, 2001; Gregory and Hill, 1984; Johnson, 1959; Van Riper, 1982). It is also important to remember, though, that there may occasionally be instances where sublexical disfluencies are incorrectly perceived and supralexical disfluency incorrectly perceived as normal disfluency. There is to date remarkably little objective research as to how listeners make fine level judgements along the SLD/ND continuum. For

---

3 Although note that these types of disfluencies may very well be seen in cluttering (chapters 8, 17).

Table 9.1 Summary of normal and stuttering-like disfluencies seen in preschool children

Type of disfluency	Normal disfluency?	Stuttering-like disfluency?	References
Pauses, interjections, and revisions	Yes. The most common types of disfluency in young preschool children	No	Wexler & Mysak (1982)
Multisyllabic word repetition	Yes. Common at age 2–3	No	Bloodstein & Gantwerk, (1967); Yairi (1981)
Monosyllabic word repetition	Yes; common, but usually only one repetition each time (though occasionally may be up to 5)	May be of concern if there is an average of two or more repetitions per moment of disfluency, and repetitions are quick or arhythmic	Ambrose & Yairi, (1999); Bloodstein & Gantwerk (1967); Gregory & Hill (1984)
Part-word repetition	May be normal in children under the age of 3	Yes, if there is an increase in number, speed, or inconsistent rhythm of repetitions, and if target vowel is replaced with schwa	Gregory & Hill (1984); Yairi (1981); Yairi & Lewis (1984)
Phoneme repetitions and phoneme prolongations	No	Yes	Wexler & Mysak (1982); Yairi (1981)
Tense pauses	No; very rare	Yes	Ambrose & Yairi (1999)

example, the voice onset time[4] in a nonstuttered production of the word "pen" would be expected to last around 50 ms or $\frac{1}{20}$ of a second. Increasing this delay to 1000 ms (1 second) would very likely result in the word being judged as stuttered, but where exactly the change in judgement between fluent and stuttered within these extremes is made is unknown. Advances in automatic machine recognition of stuttering moments may point the way for the future in this area (for example, see Howell, Sackin, Glenn, & Au-Yeung, 1997).

---

4 Voice onset time is the time elapsed between release of the plosive (in this example /p/) and the onset of vocal fold vibration for the following vowel (/e/).

To make a decision about supralexical disfluency we need to consider a number of factors. One useful indicator is frequency of the repetition or revision: "it's it's over there" may be regarded as a normal disfluency, "it's it's it's it's it's it's over there" is less likely. Other important cues include tension and concomitant escape or struggle behaviour. Even a single repetition of a word will clearly be identified as stuttering if it is accompanied with excessive facial tension and head jerk.

Should nonstuttering disfluencies be included?

There may be occasions when a clinician would want to focus more on the client's overall fluency rather than stuttering alone. Here a case can be made for including nonstuttering disfluencies in the count alongside moments of genuine stuttering. In the majority of cases, though, the fluency count is used to identify stuttering alone. However, some disfluencies are not easily categorized. As we have seen above, interjections such as "um . . . er . . . OK" may or may not be examples of stuttering, depending on a number of factors. Even experienced clinicians might not agree as to their categorization by a given speaker. Indeed, it is perfectly feasible for "um" to present as both stuttering and normal disfluency on different occasions within a single speech sample.[5] If the interjection is being used to control or postpone a moment of stuttering there may be a case for counting all interjections as stuttering moments, or all as normal disfluencies. There may also be a case for including only some as stuttering. The reality is that there is no consensus as to how to deal with this issue. Some clinicians automatically include all interjections as stuttering, on the grounds of consistency, and that they are, in either case, impediments to fluent and articulate speech and as such factors which they would want to consider in therapy. In the end, the decision lies with the clinician. Once a decision has been made and justified, it is crucial to qualify findings from any subsequent fluency count with clarification of the criteria used.

Primary vs secondary stuttering

This is another potentially difficult area and there are different perspectives as to how moments of secondary stuttering that present as abnormal or superfluous motor behaviour should be dealt with in the fluency count (or even if such secondary stuttering should be included at all). On the one hand, it would seem wrong not to include secondary activity. After all, for a significant number of those with established speakers, these features may represent the most significant problems. On the other hand, the purpose of the fluency count is, after all, to obtain a measure of speech fluency. As is the case with

---

5 It is quite possible that the clinician would wish to target these interjections in therapy, irrespective of whether they are coded as moments of stuttering, or not.

nonstuttering disfluencies, there are methodological inconsistencies in procedures. Some clinicians count only primary stuttering behaviours. Arguably, the majority at least count verbal secondary responses, including the "ums, ers" and "OKs" we mentioned earlier if they are seen to be postponing devices. Video evidence here can uncover nonverbal secondary behaviours and may also help more clearly identify primary ones, too: for example, a fleeting silent block is more easily identified if video evidence also shows concomitant lip protrusion. When nonverbal secondary features appear alongside a motoric disruption to speech, for example, a head jerk coinciding with the termination of a block, there is no problem in identifying this as stuttering. However, categorizing a moment of eye avoidance when there is no disruption to speech fluency or scoring a moment of obvious circumlocution presents a greater difficulty. In this example, most likely, the eye avoidance would be noted but not scored as a moment of stuttering. Similarly, the word avoidance would be noted separately but would not constitute a moment of stuttering.

Speech rate

Speaking rate can be as revealing of a person's communication problem as the percentage of syllables which are stuttered, and it is important that these data are recorded accurately. Andrews and Ingham (1971) calculated a mean figure of 196 SPM and a standard deviation of 34 (therefore 162–230 SPM) for conversational speech of nonstuttering adult speakers, and these normative data have been universally accepted. This equates to a mean of 140 WPM with a standard deviation of 115–165 WPM. Reading rates have been found to be quicker, ranging between 210–265 SPM or 150–190 WPM (Darley & Spriestersbach, 1978). But here again we find potential sources of variability because, while this figure has been widely adopted, the methods and procedures that were used to arrive at this figure have varied substantially. One problem is how to incorporate natural pausing into the fluency count, and therefore how much time should be allowed for a pause before the rater stops the stopwatch, waiting for the speaker to begin again. Boberg and Kully (1985) suggest 3 seconds. But once again, there is no universally accepted norm for pause time into the syllable count and the potential discrepancies could be significant. For example, if two raters were both to calculate that a speech sample was spoken at exactly 200 SPM, during which time the speaker paused 4 times each minute, the difference between one rater waiting for 3 seconds and the other for 1 second would result in a 27 SPM discrepancy between the two calculations.

Articulatory rate and speaking rate

As we have seen from Figure 9.1, speaking rate refers to speech rate calculated from the total number of syllables spoken within a minute, whereas articulatory rate refers to the number of nonstuttered syllables spoken over the same time period. Figure 9.2 provides an illustration of how artifactual differences can appear in speech rate data, depending on the type of stuttering that occurs within the speech sample. In this example, both speakers have six target syllables. But speaker A is repeating syllables whereas speaker B is prolonging them. Speakers A and B both complete the phrase in the same length of time, and both have the same number of disfluencies (speaker A has three instances of part-word repetitions, speaker B has three instances of phoneme prolongation). In terms of communicative content, then, both speakers A and B have stutters of similar severity. If we are looking to calculate speaking rate though, speaker A will come out within the normal range, using the formula given in Figure 9.1 (thus 14 syllables/4 seconds × 60 = 210 SPM), whereas speaker B's rate will work out at an abnormally slow 90 SPM (6 syllables/4 seconds × 60). Obviously, this can be misleading. Substituting articulatory rate formulas for speaking rate ones resolves this problem. Alternatively, the rater can make a clear indication in the notes that in terms of communicative content the repetitive behaviour of speaker A is resulting in an inflated SPM figure. To summarize, then:

1 When calculating percentage of syllables stuttered, speaking rate (involving the counting all syllables) must be used.
2 The use of speaking rate over articulatory rate can sometimes give misleadingly high SPM figures when multiple repetitions of syllables and/or words is the primary stuttering feature, as opposed to prolongations and blocks.

Do fluency counts accurately reflect severity?

A common and justified criticism of the fluency count is that it only goes part-way in reflecting the severity of primary stuttering. Compare the hypothetical case of a speaker who produces one instance of single word repetition in a speech sample containing 100 syllables with that of another hypothetical speaker who again has one instance of stuttering in 100 syllables,

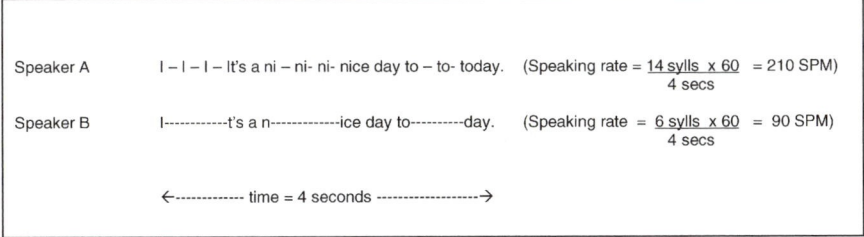

Figure 9.2 Identical length phrases with similar degree of stuttering and identical communicative content, but showing very different speaking rates.

but this moment of stuttering consists of a 20-second prolongation with accompanying head movements and tongue thrust. Despite the significant differences between the two speakers, the fluency count will only record that both had 1 percent SS. Clearly, the severity of the moments of stuttering must be considered alongside the frequency data. To deal with this, it is commonplace for clinicians to note, in addition to the frequency and syllable count data, the main characteristics of the stutter, and within each category (phoneme repetition, prolongation, etc.) to record the mean number of repetitions (or length of prolongation, etc.) alongside the most severe moments. A hypothetical example of such an adjunct might take the form shown in the box.

Stutter characterized by:

1 *Phoneme repetition.* Average number of repetitions = 4; greatest = 9

2 *Syllable repetition.* Average number of repetitions = 2; greatest = 3

3 *Silent blocks.* Average length of block = <1 second; greatest = 2 seconds

---

In an ideal world one would go into much greater detail, perhaps listing objective data on the proportion of stuttering within each subtype; the number of blocks, repetitions, prolongations, etc. represented as a percentage of the total amount of stuttering; loci of stuttering, and so on. Such data may be essential in certain research papers which are looking at stuttering characteristics, for example, but faced with the reality of time pressures in a busy clinic this is rarely possible. Instead, such information is likely to be noted informally alongside the fluency count data.

Reliability in calculating moments of stuttering and rate of speech

It is important that counting is done accurately, and we have already outlined a number of potential difficulties with the fluency count. To help ensure that the data are being collected in a systematic and accurate fashion reliability checks can be made. There are two basic types of reliability measures; intra-rater and inter-rater measures. Intra-rater reliability reflects how consistent a count is (of either rate of speech or stuttering severity) with another count made by the same person on the same data sample. Say, for example, a clinician analyzes a passage and records 30 moments of stuttering in 300 syllables (thus 10 percent SS). The clinician subsequently analyzes that same passage some time later but arrives at a slightly different number of stuttering moments; let's say 33 in this case. Running an intra-rater check would determine whether this discrepancy is acceptable, or not. Similarly, inter-rater reliability refers to the degree to which two (or more) independent raters arrive at similar results when calculating either rate or percentage of stuttering. Acceptability of error between two counts of the same data can be calculated using the formula given in Figure 9.3. Generally, for both inter-rater and intra-rater measures, the accepted minimum reliability figure is 90 percent (Boberg & Kully, 1985; Prins & Hubbard, 1990). Pearson product-moment correlations may also be applied to test inter-rater agreement. Druce, Debney, and Byrt (1997) suggest correlations above. 0.8 as being excellent, whilst Ryan and Van Kirk (1995) cite. 0.9. To return to our example, then, 30/33 × 100 = 90.9 percent agreement, which is satisfactory (although higher figures may be required for some research purposes). As we see from Figure 9.3 our independent raters here do not meet the 90 percent criterion, and the passage would need to be re-analyzed until a higher level of agreement is reached.

Kully and Boberg (1988) have pointed out that inter-rater, and particularly inter-clinic reliability is often poor. Nonetheless, highly trained judges can achieve consistently high levels of agreement between observers (e.g., O'Brian, Packman, Onslow, & O'Brian, 2004; Young, 1975). O' Brian et al. (2004) compared the reliability of the fluency count with a nine-point severity scale, finding very high levels of intra-judge and inter-judge agreement for both measures. Clinicians need to be aware that although two counts of the same data set may yield similar or even identical intra-/inter-rater figures, these do not necessarily represent the identification of the same moments of stuttering. So, theoretically, two raters might identify an identical number of disfluencies but with completely different loci, and this discrepancy would not be revealed by the reliability count. Event by event consistency is a significant difficulty and probably the best course of action is to have all inexperienced raters undergo repeated practice with highly

Procedure:	Collect the two calculations of the data. Divide the smaller of the two numbers by bigger number and then multiply by 100 to find the percentage.
Worked example:	Rater 1 calculates a total of 175 syllables spoken, rater 2 calculates 200 syllables.
Thus:	$\frac{175}{200} = 0.875$
	0.875 x 100 = **87.5%**

Agreement here is less than 90%. These two raters would need to look again at how they arrived at their figures, and to practise further counts to ensure higher levels of agreement.

Figure 9.3 The calculation of intra-speaker and inter-speaker agreement.

experienced raters until high level agreement on speech data with these expert raters is achieved.

Aside from the practical problems already mentioned, there are variables too relating to the difficulty of measuring a disorder whose severity is often subject to situational variability (Block, 2004; Ingham & Costello, 1984). It is quite common for people to attend clinic expressing embarrassment that their stuttering is not as severe as it usually is, and for some speaking to a clinician can be fluency enhancing in itself. On the other hand, it is sometimes the case that clients can be extremely anxious about coming for an assessment and this may be reflected in raised severity. It may also be the case that, for reasons which may or may not be obvious to the person concerned, they are having a good day or a bad day. The variability in severity is one of the defining characteristics of the disorder, and clinicians will need to look at their find-ings from fluency counts in the light of the client's and caregiver's comments as to general levels of severity. In some cases, it may be possible for the client to collect audio or videotaped evidence of speech which demonstrates differ-ent levels of fluency to those seen at the clinic. For example, a parent may bring in a tape of the young child playing at home, or an adult may record himself giving a presentation at work. Table 9.2 summarizes some of the difficulties inherent with the frequency count.

Interpretation of frequency counts

So, the baseline data have been collected. Speaking rate and percentage of syllables have been calculated, information qualifying the procedures that the clinician has followed has been noted, together with data on the severity of stuttered moments. What does all the data tell us? Well, obviously a person who either has no disfluencies or only has normal disfluencies should present with 0 percent stuttering. But as we have already mentioned, there will be some error in judging moments of stuttering (and normal disfluency). Clini-cians quite often use the range of 0–2 percent to indicate fluency within the normal range for older children and adults, although both the type of stutter-ing behaviour (lexical/supralexical vs sublexical) and the severity of the moments of stuttering would also need to be considered before judging that these infrequent disfluent moments constitute genuine stuttering. The clin-ician would also need to consider the person's fears and anxiety (see sections below) when coming to a final diagnosis.

The Stuttering Severity Instrument (SSI)

The SSI (Riley, 1972, 1994) is an established and standardized test which is unusual in that it combines both an objective analysis of motor speech flu-ency together with linguistic and nonverbal aspects of the disorder. It can be used with adults and children and has been validated for use with both. It does not deal with speech rate, but it does involve a fluency count, together

Table 9.2 Summary of some potential difficulties associated with undertaking a frequency count in free conversation

Problem	Example	What can be done
Inter-clinic variability in data collection criteria	Pause behaviour	Clearly specify measurement criteria used.
Intra-clinician variability	A clinician's analysis of the same passage of speech reveals very different fluency counts or rate calculations	As much practice as necessary to ensure that reliability is above 90%. Ensure consistent criteria are being applied for all analyses.
May be discrepancies between speech rate data depending on the type of disfluencies that are produced (see earlier example)	Comparing speaking rates for speakers who prolong or block vs those who repeat part words or words	Articulatory rate must be used for SPM calculations.
Problems with judging stuttering/normal disfluency	Clinician unsure as to whether single word repetition is stuttering or normal disfluency	Check: frequency of occurrence within the speech sample and concomitant signs of struggle or tension. Make mention of any uncertainty in the clinical notes.
Fluency count does not account for natural variability in fluctuation of severity	Person tells clinician that the stutter is usually much worse/ better than usual	Rather little, other than to recognize and acknowledge the problem. Note whether current fluency level is regarded as typical by speaker and/or caregivers. Undertake second assessment at different venue/ different time of day, if possible.
Does not measure severity of stuttered moments	Frequency of stutter does not always correlate with severity	Note severity of all stuttered moments, e.g., number of repetitions or length of blocks prolongations. Calculate mean scores and outliers for each stuttering subcategory.
Word avoidance	Client presenting with little or no overt stuttering	Frequency count needs to be taken during oral reading.

with data on severity of stuttered moments, not just frequency and concomitant secondary activity. The SSI breaks stuttering down into three components: frequency, duration, physical concomitants. Within each category, task scores are given to raw data, which are eventually totalled to give a single score. Although some have questioned the reliability of the test, it is generally well respected and very widely used.

Administration of the SSI

FREQUENCY

A speech sample of at least 200 words is needed for analysis. Depending on age, the client either reads aloud or interprets a story from a cartoon. They then either talk about their job or school. Again, this sample should comprise at least 200 words, and many clinicians prefer to continue for longer. Some clinicians collect data from more than one sample (for example, telephone conversations). The clinician then makes frequency counts of each of the speech samples, and under category 1 on the form translates these into the task score. For example, 9 percent SS on the conversation task would translate as a task score of 6. The same percentage in the reading task would work out as 5. The total would be recorded in the total frequency score. In our example then this would be $6 + 5 = 11$.

DURATION

Duration is assessed by finding the three longest stuttering moments and then calculating the mean length of time of these three. Like the raw figures on frequency of stuttering, this time, calculated in seconds regardless of the stuttering subtype, is then converted to a total duration score. In the original version, Riley advocated counting words and expressing the frequency count in terms of percentages of stuttered words. As already mentioned, this can create some problems when a person stutters more than once on a single word. The SSI-3 (1994) now requires calculations in syllables.

PHYSICAL CONCOMITANTS

This third section has the clinician evaluate a range of secondary stuttering behaviours, grouped into four subcategories on a scale of 0 (none) to 5 (severe and painful looking). The scores for each subcategory are then added together to make the physical concomitants score.

The frequency task score, duration score and physical concomitants scores are then totalled to give the total overall score. This score can then be measured against the severity ratings, ranging from 0 (very mild) to 45 (very severe) which are included in the SSI test.

Assessment of attitudes toward stuttering

From the late 1960s, the development of assessments devoted to the client's attitude toward stuttering began to be explored. One of the first and most enduring of these was the Perceptions of Stuttering Inventory (PSI; Woolfe, 1967). This assessment procedure looks at stuttering from three perspectives: struggle, expectancy and avoidance. A further and equally enduring cognitive assessment has been the S-24 scale (Andrews & Cutler, 1974). Although not as comprehensive as the PSI, the S-24 was faster to administer and has subsequently become arguably the most used "cognitive" assessment tool. Many clinicians have come to rely on it heavily (see below).

Another significant development in the 1980s came with the application of the Locus of Control of Behaviour checklist (Craig, Franklin, & Andrews, 1984) to the evaluation of stuttering. This questionnaire requires the person to respond to 17 questions using a 7-point scale and probes the degree to which the individual believes that situations related to his stuttering are under his control or due to external factors. In addition to providing useful background information, research has suggested this assessment also carries some predictive value, with those reporting a higher degree of internality more likely to maintain benefits gained in therapy than those who believe they have less control (or higher degree of externality). The mid-1980s also saw the development of the Self-Efficacy Scaling by Adult Stutterers (SESAS; Ornstein & Manning, 1985) which measures confidence in speaking across a number of situations. More recently, two new additions include the Wright and Ayre Stuttering Self-rating Profile (WASSP; Wright & Ayre, 2000) and the Overall Assessment of the Speaker's Experience of Stuttering (OASES; Yaruss & Quesal, 2004).

Modified Erikson Scale of Communication Attitude (S-24)

The S-24 represents the development and revision of an attitudinal assessment originally devised by Erikson (1969). The S-24 scale (Andrews & Cutler, 1974) has remained unchanged in 30 years. Despite the development of recent and more sophisticated assessment tools it is still widely used in clinics across the world. It requires respondents to answer 24 statements relating to how confident they feel in their verbal communication and how life events are implicated by the stutter. Interviewees are only given the option of responding either "true" or "false" to all 24 statements. When completed, the clinician allocates a score of 0 to each response that indicates a positive attitude toward speaking, whilst a score of 1 is given to each negative perception. For example, a client responding "false" to the question "I feel I am usually making a good impression when I talk" (question 2) would receive 1 point, while a reply of true would receive 0 points. Respondents must answer all questions. Thus the maximum score (indicating maximum negativity toward speech) is 24, whilst the minimum score is 0. A key problem with the S-24 is that many respondents find it difficult to be constrained by the binary answers they are required to give. For example, statement 16 – "I am embarrassed by the way I talk" – may be considered "true" in some circumstances but "false" in others. The respondent must decide which response is the most appropriate, allowing for the noted variability.

Table 9.3 shows the mean and standard deviation scores for a group of 36 adults who stutter at various stages in the therapeutic process and 25 control speakers, as reported by Andrews and Cutler (1974). The pattern of improved confidence immediately following treatment together with some regression as the speakers encounter difficulties during the transfer phase of therapy is a common one.

As with other cognitive self-assessments described in this section, the S-24, in addition to providing a useful baseline and post-therapy assessment tool, can also be used to help direct therapy. Note, however, that early claims that the S-24 could be used to predict therapeutic outcome have been strongly refuted (Ingham, 1984). Figure 9.4 shows a completed S-24 of an Apple House client. Despite having a very mild stutter perceptually and presenting as a very competent and articulate speaker, Andrew maintained a very poor perception of his speaking abilities, as shown in his baseline score of 24.

Therapy comprised a counselling approach directly addressing his responses to some of the S-24 questions, particularly those relating to avoidance. These responses were explored further to determine the underlying issues responsible for the skewing of his self-perception. A post-clinic score of 8 indicated his attitude toward his speech now approximated that of nonstuttering speakers (see Table 9.3), and a score of 10 at a final 12-month follow-up suggested that this new perception had stabilized.

Perceptions of Stuttering Inventory (PSI)

This questionnaire was developed by Woolfe (1967) and characterizes cognitive and affective components of stuttering in terms of struggle, avoidance and expectancy. This is one of the earliest examples of a way of measuring the effect of stuttering from the individual's perspective rather than that surmised by the clinician. Although again requiring binary responses, it is

Table 9.3 Mean and standard deviation figures of a group of 36 adults who stutter and 25 adults who do not stutter (adapted from Andrews and Cutler, 1974)

		Mean	*SD*
Adults who stutter	Pretreatment	19.22	4.24
	Posttreatment	14.27	5.73
	Posttransfer	9.11	5.18
Adults who do not stutter		9.14	5.38

The following statements are concerned with various aspects of communication. If a statement is true, or mostly true for you, tick the letter T. If a statement is false, or not usually true for you, tick the letter F. Please respond to every statement, and note that there are no right or wrong answers.

			Score
I usually feel that I am making a favourable impression when I talk.	T	F✔	1
I find it easy to talk with almost anyone.	T	F✔	1
I find it very easy to look at my audience while speaking to a group.	T	F✔	1
A person who is my teacher or my boss is hard to talk to.	T✔	F	1
Even the idea of giving a talk in public makes me afraid.	T✔	F	1
Some words are harder than others for me to say.	T✔	F	1
I forget all about myself shortly after I begin to give a speech.	T	F✔	1
I am a good mixer.	T	F✔	1
People sometimes seem uncomfortable when I am talking to them.	T✔	F	1
I dislike introducing one person to another.	T✔	F	1
I often ask questions in group discussions.	T	F✔	1
I find it easy to keep control of my voice when speaking.	T	F✔	1
I do not mind speaking before a group.	T	F✔	1
I do not talk well enough to do the kind of work I'd really like to do.	T✔	F	1
My speaking voice is rather pleasant and easy to listen to.	T	F✔	1
I am sometimes embarrassed by the way I talk.	T✔	F	1
I face most situations with complete confidence.	T	F✔	1
I talk easily with only a few people.	T✔	F	1
I talk better than I write.	T	F✔	1
I often feel nervous when talking.	T✔	F	1
I find it hard to make talk when I meet new people.	T✔	F	1
I feel pretty confident about my speaking ability.	T	F✔	1
I wish I could say things as clearly as others do.	T✔	F	1
Even though I know the right answer I often fail to give it because I am afraid to speak out.	T✔	F	1

Total S-24 = 24

Figure 9.4 A completed baseline S-24 for an adult Apple House client, Andrew.

more comprehensive than the S-24, comprising 60 questions to which the respondent must either "agree" or "disagree" that the statement is or is not characteristic of himself. See Table 9.4 for a comparison of the PSI to other cognitive/attitudinal assessments. The rationale is that stuttering can be defined as struggle, avoidance and expectancy. The assessment was developed with two principle objectives in mind: to facilitate a descriptive analysis of stuttering and to understand what stuttering means from that individual's perspective.

> It can be used to a) describe comprehensively what the stutterer does when he "stutters"; b) broaden the stutterer's definition of his problem; c) analyse the relationships among struggle, avoidance and expectancy; and d) formulate therapeutic goals and evaluate progress toward these goals.
>
> (Woolfe, 1967, p. 167)

Definitions

1   *Struggle*. Phonemic, phonatory and linguistic modifications and excessive tensions or extraneous movements in the speech mechanism or in other body structures.
2   *Avoidance*
   - avoiding speaking by withdrawing from a situation requiring speaking verbal participation
   - avoiding speaking through behaviour which reduces the likelihood of verbal involvement
   - avoiding linguistic elements.
3   *Expectancy*. The individual avoids anticipated failure by:
   - covert preparations prior to speech attempt
   - body movements or postures as speech is initiated
   - linguistic and nonlinguistic changes once speech has been initiated.

When analyzing SSI responses, the clinician must pay attention to the interpretation of both individual items as well as overall score. In addition the correlation between the clinician's perceptions and those of the client is seen as significant. The degree of agreement between the two is referred to as *perceptual congruence*. Symmetry amongst the three targeted areas is also considered important and a number of outcome profiles are possible:

1   Symmetrical high score; stuttering perceived as severe.
2   Symmetrical low score; stuttering is mild (which Woolfe, 1967 argues should lead to a favourable prognosis).
3   Asymmetrical profile 1; struggle scores are greater than avoidance/ expectancy scores. Clinician would need to consider whether all stuttering behaviour has been accurately reported.
4   Asymmetrical profile 2; avoidance/expectancy scores are greater than struggle scores. The diagnosis of interiorized stutterer would need to be considered here. Therapy would aim to restore symmetry across PSI scores.

PSI scores and levels of severity

below 7	mild
8–11	moderate
12–15	moderate-severe
16–20	severe

Overall Assessment of the Speaker's Experience of Stuttering (OASES)

The purpose of this instrument is to assess the overall impact of stuttering on both teens and adults who stutter, and to provide an outcome measurement system that allows comparison between different treatments across several relevant dimensions. The rationale is that clinicians need to base their treatment and assessments on multiple factors.

The starting point for OASES is the World Health Organization's *International Classification of Functioning, Disability, Health* (ICF). This describes disorders under three headings: (a) impairment in body function or structure; (b) contextual factors; (c) limitations or restrictions. For the person who stutters, impairment relates to the observable stuttering behaviours, contextual factors concern features such as avoidance and the effect of environment, while limitations or restrictions refers to the impact that the stutter has on daily living. Ignoring matters relating to *impairment*, the OASES questionnaire probes areas relating to *contextual factors* and *limitations/restrictions* by having participants circle a number on a five-point scale. Unlike some cognitive/affective questionnaires such as the S-24, items which do not apply to a particular individual may be left blank. The questionnaire comprises four parts: general information (total of 20 questions); your reactions to stuttering (25 questions); communication in daily situations (25 questions); quality of life (25 questions).

- *Part I: general information*. Comprises three subsections, the first two containing questions about the individual's knowledge of stuttering and stuttering support; the final testing perceptions as to previous therapy and perception as a speaker.
- *Part II: reactions to stuttering* Comprises three subsections. The first deals purely with affect, while the second probes secondary characteristics such as avoidance, facial grimacing and suchlike. The third deals with issues such as acceptance and confidence.
- *Part III: communication in daily situations*. Comprises four sections examining the difficulty of communicating: A general situations (e.g., talking under time pressure); B at work, C specific situations (e.g., ordering food in a restaurant); D at home.

- *Part IV: quality of life*. Contains five subsections: section A comprises three questions all asking how quality of life is negatively affected by stuttering, personal reactions to stuttering as well as others' reactions to the stuttering. The remaining parts all focus on how stuttering interferes with communication in various settings (section B), various relationships (section C), job and career (section D), personal life (section E).

Once the client has completed the form, scores from the four parts are totalled to give a final score. There are a number of examples of related questions being asked, in different parts, throughout the questionnaire, which allows for a more complete picture of the particular issue to be developed. For example, in Part I the client is asked "How often do you use techniques, strategies, or tools you have learned in speech therapy?" Later in the same part, the client is asked to rate "your ability to use techniques you have learned in speech therapy". Thus a mismatch of results here could show a lack of usage of skills, even if the individual feels perfectly competent to implement them.

The Wright and Ayre Stuttering Self-rating Profile (WASSP)

The Wright and Ayre Stuttering Self-rating Profile (WASSP; Wright & Ayre, 2000) represents another recent attempt to examine cognitive and affective variables amongst adults who stutter age 18 or over (see Figure 9.5). The profile has also been used with clients aged 14 to 18, but the authors suggest that not all clients of this age group will be able to use the profile effectively and the clinician should exercise her judgement on such cases. Like OASES, WASSP was developed with the help of feedback from clients who stutter. The questionnaire comprises 26 statements that examine the speaker's self-perceptions across five subscales. The first deals directly with the client's perception of their overt stuttering behaviour (nine items), the remaining sections consider thoughts about stuttering (three items), feelings about stuttering (six items), avoidance due to stuttering (four items), disadvantage due to stuttering (four items). For each item, clients are required to circle the number on a seven-point Likert type scale (where 1 = "none"; 7 = "very severe") which best describes each aspect of their stutter. In addition, at "time 1" (the beginning of a period of therapy) clients are encouraged to write down any aims or expectations they might have for a given block of therapy, and at "time 2" (completion of that period of therapy) to summarize what they feel has been achieved during that time period. The client and clinician then compare and discuss the two profiles to evaluate progress over that time period.

Included in the WASSP package are details on its development, sections on validity and reliability and instructions for use, together with an appendix, which includes completed profiles on two adults who stutter as well as the blank WASSP profile forms, which can be photocopied. WASSP covers a lot

WASSP Rating Sheet

Name _____   Date _____

Instructions: Please rate each of the following aspects of your stutter using a 7-point scale, 1 indicatiing 'none' and 7 indicating 'very severe'.

Place a circle round the number which you judge best describes each aspect of your stutter.

Stuttering behaviours	None						Very severe
Frequency of stutters	1	2	3	4	5	6	7
Physical struggle during stutters	1	2	3	4	5	6	7
Duration of stutters	1	2	3	4	5	6	7
Uncontrollable stutters	1	2	3	4	5	6	7
Urgency/fast speech rate	1	2	3	4	5	6	7
Associated facial/body movements	1	2	3	4	5	6	7
General level of physical tension	1	2	3	4	5	6	7
Loss of eye contact	1	2	3	4	5	6	7
Other (describe)	1	2	3	4	5	6	7
Thoughts about stuttering							
Negative thoughts before speaking	1	2	3	4	5	6	7
Negative thoughts during speaking	1	2	3	4	5	6	7
Negative thoughts after speaking	1	2	3	4	5	6	7
Feelings about stuttering							
Frustration	1	2	3	4	5	6	7
Embarrassment	1	2	3	4	5	6	7
Fear	1	2	3	4	5	6	7
Anger	1	2	3	4	5	6	7
Helplessness	1	2	3	4	5	6	7
Other (describe)	1	2	3	4	5	6	7
Avoidance due to stuttering							
Of words	1	2	3	4	5	6	7
Of situations	1	2	3	4	5	6	7
Of talking about stuttering with others	1	2	3	4	5	6	7
Of admitting the problem to yourself	1	2	3	4	5	6	7
Disadvantage due to stuttering							
At home	1	2	3	4	5	6	7
Socially	1	2	3	4	5	6	7
Educationally	1	2	3	4	5	6	7
At work	1	2	3	4	5	6	7

Time 1: Please write down any aims/expectations you have for this block of therapy.

Time 2: Please summarise what you feel you have achieved during this block.

Figure 9.5 Wright and Ayre Stuttering Self-rating Profile (WASSP).

of ground yet is easy to administer, taking most clients around five minutes to complete. It claims to be comprehensive and succeeds in many ways. However, some areas are not covered (for example, self-perception of speaking ability, confidence levels) and also some subscales are covered rather sparsely; but surely no profile that can be administered in such a short space of time could be truly comprehensive. In this respect it differs from OASES which is more thorough (containing 95 questions on affective, cognitive matters, as opposed to WASSP's 17), but takes longer to complete. WASSP has been standardized, albeit on a relatively small group. It is a useful clinical tool and again, like OASES, it elicits a more sensitive data set than can be derived from the binary responses elicited by the S-24, which takes roughly the same time to administer. (See Ward, 2002 for a review of the WASSP questionnaire.)

Table 9.4 Comparison of cognitive and affective measurement questionnaires that may be used in adult treatment programs

Assessment	*Format*	*Strengths*	*Weaknesses*
Perceptions of Stuttering inventory (PSI, Woolfe, 1967)	List of 60 questions comprising 20 questions (randomly distributed) on stuttering as struggle, avoidance and expectancy.	Detailed. Quite comprehensive. Opportunities to compare mismatch between 3 areas investigated.	Requires binary answers which limit sensitivity of responses; many respondents find great difficulty in arriving at definitive decision to questions which might be answered "yes" under some circumstances, and "no" under others.
Revised communication attitude inventory (S-24, Andrews & Cutler, 1974)	List of 24 questions on a speaker's confidence in speaking.	Norms for those who stutter and those who don't. Quick to administer.	Like the PSI, it requires binary "yes/no" answers. Questions not always the most pertinent for PWS.
Locus of Control of Behaviour (LCB, Craig, Franklin, & Andrews, 1984)	List of 17 questions probing the degree to which the speaker sees his speech behaviour as being a product of internally or externally controlled events.	Gives an index as to internal/ externality of control which can be helpful in determining cognitive goals in therapy and maintenance. Comparisons also possible with those who do not stutter.	Focuses only on locus of control, so will usually need to be presented with other cognitive assessments.

cont.

Table 9.4 continued

Assessment	Format	Strengths	Weaknesses
Wright and Ayre Stuttering Self-rating Profile (WASSP, Wright & Ayre, 2000)	List of 26 questions (17 on cognitive affective issues) across 5 areas; stuttering behaviours; thoughts about stuttering; feelings about stuttering; avoidance due to stuttering; disadvantage due to stuttering.	7-point Likert scale gives flexibility in response. Quickly administered. Standardized.	Lacks detail in some areas.
Overall Assessment of the Speaker's Experience of Stuttering (OASES, Yaruss & Quesal, 2004)	List of 95 questions under four subheadings: general information; your reactions to stuttering; communications in daily situations; quality of life.	Very comprehensive. Based on logical framework (WHO's IFC classification).	Not yet standardized. Takes a little more time than some others to complete.

Sheehan's iceberg model

Sheehan (1975) drew the simple but powerful analogy between stuttering and the form of an iceberg. To introduce this model, the clinician simply explains that, like the iceberg, stuttering has a visible component above the waterline, but also a greater and potentially more significant mass, hidden from view, underpinning the visible aspect. Clients then simply fill in a blank outline of an iceberg, itemizing stuttering components "above the waterline" including the blocks, prolongations and repetitions, alongside other visible struggle and escape behaviours that will be noticeable to others. Activity below the waterline relates to the cognitive and affective aspects that are not likely to be observed by listeners; for example, embarrassment, frustration, shame, fear, anger and avoidance, and these aspects too are recorded. The iceberg model differs from all those already described in that it helps only with identification. There is no objective measurement of any of the behaviours and cognitive/affective responses to stuttering that the client is listing. Also, it is the only procedure mentioned here that does not result in quantitative data. But it has many strengths. It is quick and easily administered. Also, either with or without prompting from a clinician (or perhaps other group members), completing an iceberg is of value both as a self-identification baseline measurement tool and as an empowering and liberating experience in its own right. This can be of value when it comes to desensitization aspects of therapy, as well as identification (see chapter 12) with regard to its usage in a number of programs. Finally, because of the clear and simple imagery it portrays between observable and attitudinal aspects, it is very suitable procedure to use with even younger children (as we do with our children at the Apple House stuttering centre in Oxford, see chapter 11).

Assessment of preschool stuttering

The nature and scope of the assessment of younger children varies from clinic to clinic and, understandably, tends to reflect the theoretical orientation of the therapeutic approaches that are used within that clinical setting. Having said that, there is pretty much a consensus as to a range of basic assessment procedures that should be applied in all cases when assessing a young child with a suspected stutter. Where opinion differs is over the need to apply certain procedures which may be regarded as essential in some clinics, but optional or even unnecessary in others. In the following chapter, we describe a very comprehensive approach to the assessment of preschool stuttering, based on the need to consider in fine detail the effects of the lived-in environment that subsequently underpins the therapeutic approach. Presented below is a more generic form of assessment procedures.

The most fundamental question that the assessment of the child first presenting at a clinic needs to answer is simply "Does the child stutter?" If assessment procedures indicate "yes" then the next question is "What is the risk that this stutter will persist?" If "no", the clinician needs to ascertain if there are any indications that the child is at increased risk of developing a stutter in the future. To answer these questions and to accrue enough information to develop a suitable therapeutic plan, the clinician must consider not only fluency measures but, since stuttering may be associated with other developmental speech and language problems, also be alert for a range of associated difficulties.[6] The following procedures will help the clinician to gain a picture of the relevant difficulties that a child is experiencing:

1   *Case history/parent interview*. This will elicit the parent's perceptions of the problems, and allows the clinician to collect background data on the child's development.

---

6 A number of approaches to the treatment of early stuttering stress the importance of environmental influences and these too are taken into consideration at assessment. We pursue this notion in the following chapter.

2   *Clinician and child interview.*
3   *Assessment of child's speech sample for speech rate and stuttering.*
4   *Assessment of parent–child interaction.* Here the clinician observes the child at play with either one but preferably both parents or caregivers. Some clinicians do not collect formal data on the parent–child interactions, whilst for others this procedure forms a considerable part of the assessment process. We look at parent–child interaction in the following chapter.

Case history

1   *Introduction.* Usually, we begin by asking the parents about the specific concerns that have brought them and their child to the clinic. This offers the parents an opportunity to present their perspective on the problem, together with a chance for them to explain their feelings about it. Only on rare occasions (perhaps when a parent is distressed that their child's stuttering is all their fault) would we stop to discuss any concerns at this point. Instead, we acknowledge that we have understood their concerns. We then state that we will be returning to address them at the end of the assessment, when we have had a chance to gather some necessary information.
2   *General development.* We continue by asking about the child's developmental milestones, beginning with pregnancy and birth, and moving on through motor development, asking how the child's development has compared with his siblings, and how they see the comparison at present. Similarly, we enquire about the child's language development. Although language and motor abilities are factors which we will assess with the child, it is often revealing to see how the parents' perceptions match (or mismatch) with the abilities we see when we are one-to-one with the child.
3   *Development of disfluency.* Here, we ask when they first had concerns regarding their child's fluency; how these fluency disruptions presented at that time and if they have now changed in what way. The purpose here is to discover whether these might be considered normal or stuttering-like disfluencies (SLD; see below). The latter may indicate a greater likelihood of genuine stuttering and may be of relevance to the eventual prognosis. For example, noting the time elapsed since the appearance of SLDs may also be significant. Spontaneous recovery in stuttering is more likely when there is a decrease in stuttering moments over the first year. Empirical evidence tells us that it is also important to know if the parents identified any noteworthy events or changes going on with the family at that time such as family upsets, new birth within the family, death of a relative, or with the child away from the family problems at nursery such as bullying at school, experiencing a moment of shock (Rustin, 1991; Rustin et al., 1996; Van Riper, 1982).

4   *Environment*. We explore here how the disfluency is affected in different circumstances. Are there any times or places where the fluency is improved (or even apparently goes completely), and does stuttering vary depending on who the child is speaking to? Relatedly, we ask about the family dynamics and how the child gets on with parents, siblings and his peers. Of interest here is whether there seems to be any association between fluency levels and favoured or disliked people. It is also important to ask whether the parents feel the child is aware of his stuttering. Is there any withdrawal? Is there any avoidance of words, situations or people? If the child is aware of stuttering, is this a subject that the parents have discussed with him, and if so what was the outcome of these discussions? Information should also be gained as to the child's general personality. Is he outgoing and happy-go-lucky, quiet, anxious, introspective? It is also important to know whether the parents have noticed any change in the child's personality since the development of disfluencies. Answers to these questions help determine the significance of secondary factors in the stutter and, relatedly, the degree these will need to be taken into account in any subsequent therapy.

5   *Concluding questions*. We need to know whether the child has been seen for therapy, or has been assessed elsewhere. If there has been previous treatment, the clinician needs to know as much about this as possible. Being able to access the child's clinical file from a previous therapist would obviously be of help when considering new treatment strategies. The parents' thoughts too as to how effective they perceived that therapy to be and the reasons why it was not continued would also need to be taken into consideration. We conclude by asking if the parents feel there is anything we have not covered that is of relevance to their child and his fluency.

Clinician and child assessment

This is where the clinician has a chance to see at first hand the issues which have come to light in the case history. The clinician uses age-appropriate play materials to engage the child's interest. A child who is quiet or nervous may initially be left to play on his own for a while before the clinician quietly joins in. An important objective is to ascertain whether the child is aware of his stuttering. The clinician must exercise judgement as to whether to actively pursue the issue, by asking whether the child knows why he has come today. Similarly, the clinician must be sensitive and adjust any terminology appropriately. Usually terms like "bumpy speech" and "getting stuck" can be used to direct the child to the fact that everyone gets stuck from time to time, and that the child is not alone in his difficulties. The clinician will also use this opportunity to note the child's motor speech and nonspeech motor control, as well as whether phonological and language skills appear age appropriate (see section below). During this session, the clinician will get some idea not only as to the child's fluency, but also to his general style of interaction.

It is often useful to ask the parents after the session if they felt that their child's behaviour and level and type of stuttering were typical. For example, a child may be going through a period of good fluency, but the parent might feel that there was increased stuttering at that session. (See next chapter for more discussion of these issues.) It is important to videotape (preferably) or audiotape this session. Video recordings often reveal significant but fleeting behaviours which can be missed on audiotape and allow the child's speech to be used as the basis for the speech sample (see below). Additionally, a videotape serves as a snapshot of the child's speech at that time (although we need to be aware of problems with reliability). It is therefore useful to keep this in the child's file as pre-clinic assessment data. On the basis of the clinician–child assessment, the clinician may feel that further (formal) assessments are warranted.

Receptive and expressive language

Poor language skills may be associated with stuttering behaviour (Stark-weather, 1997; Yaruss, 1999). These abilities may be tested using a number of the available standardized tests. Some commonly used examples in Britain include:

- *Word Finding Vocabulary Scale* (WFVS; Renfrew, 1988)
- *British Picture Vocabulary Scales* (BPVS; Dunn, Dunn, Whetton, & Burley, 1997)
- *Derbyshire Language Scheme Rapid Screening Test* (Masidlover & Knowles, 1982)
- *Clinical Evaluation of Language Fundamentals* (CELF; Wiig, Secord, & Semel, 2000)
- *Reynell Developmental Language Scales* (RDLS; Edwards, Fletcher, Garman, Hughes, & Sinka, 1997).

Phonology

Some researchers and clinicians believe there is a link between disordered and delayed phonology and stuttering (Bloodstein, 1995; Louko, et al., 1990; Kolk and Postma, 1997), although the evidence at present seems equivocal (Nippold, 1990). Some clinicians automatically screen for phonological problems, but it is more common to informally assess these abilities through observation, and to save formal testing for when this raises any suspicion of phonological delay or disorder. Commonly used tests in Britain include the *South Tyneside Assessment of Phonology* (STAP; Armstrong & Ainley, 1989) and the more complex *Phonological Assessment of Children's Speech* (PACS; Grunwell, 1985).

Motor control

The clinician should observe the child's ability to control at both fine and gross motor levels. The *Goodenough-Draw-a-Man Test* (Harris, 1963) provides one way of looking at both fine motor control and cognitive development simultaneously, although the issue of assessing cognitive abilities in younger children is notoriously difficult. Handedness should also be noted and parents consulted (and also the child if old enough) as to whether handedness is consistent across a range of tasks. (See chapter 2 for a discussion on the relevance of handedness, laterality and stuttering.)

Assessment of speech fluency and speech rate

We have covered the procedures involved in this in some depth earlier in this chapter. Many preschool children will show an increase in the number of disfluencies as a natural part of their speech and language development, so it is particularly important when assessing children of this age group to make sure that only moments of genuine stuttering and stuttering-like disfluencies are tallied, and that nonstuttering disfluencies are not included.

Secondary stuttering

As already alluded to in the introduction, both primary aspects of stuttering (the observable moments of stuttering) and secondary aspects (which may be both physical and emotional/cognitive) need to be considered at assessment. The identification of secondary features of the disorder such as struggle and avoidance tend to become more necessary for older children and adults because it is less usual for these features to present at the onset of preschool stuttering. Even if they are not apparent at assessment, it is important for the clinician to discover whether they are appearing away from the clinic. Usually information on the observable secondary aspects such as physical tension, struggle, tremor, eye avoidance, eye blinking and extraneous facial and body movements is captured informally during the clinician–child interview and the speech samples used for the analysis of overt stuttering. Similarly, the child's feelings and attitudes toward speech can be gleaned from these same interactions, together with the parent's responses in the case history.

Whether or not secondary (physical) behaviours are observed or reported, there is increasing evidence that some children as young as 3 years of age will already have significantly more negative self-perceptions than their fluent peers (Vanryckeghem, Brutten, & Hernandez, 2005). The observation of any such percepts should be noted at assessment. As yet, there are no standardized tests for examining self-perception in the preschool child, although a version of the Children's Attitude Test (CAT), called the KiddyCAT, has now been developed for use with younger children (Vanryckeghem et al., 2001, 2005).

Having gathered all this evidence, and analyzed the speech samples, the clinician now feeds back the findings to the parents, and appropriate plans for treatment, if indicated, are laid out. The treatment planning on the basis of assessment findings is covered in the following chapter.

Assessment of primary school age stuttering

Many of the assessment procedures outlined in the previous section will remain relevant to the assessment of the primary school age child. The clinician will need to collect a similar speech sample from which to calculate fluency and speech rate, and the interaction between child and parents will still need to be observed. It may also still be necessary to undertake formal testing of language functioning and, as with the preschool child, the child's general development and motor control abilities will need to be observed. The greatest changes concern the involvement of new professionals in the child's development, most obviously the schoolteachers, and this needs to be covered in both the case history and preferably through discussion with the teacher.

Case history

The case history in many ways follows a similar format as for the preschool child. The collection of details on general development, onset of the stutter, environmental factors and family dynamics will all be as relevant to the 5 year old, 7 year old or 10 year old as to the 3 year old. But the nearer we come to the upper end of this age range, the more the child's self-perception generally and of the impact he perceives his stutter to have specifically become issues. The child's environment will have broadened, and while school is the obvious new factor there may well be others in the form of afterschool activities and clubs. It is important that the assessment takes into account these new factors and that details about school, including teachers' perceptions, are taken into account. For example, does the child stutter more at home or at school? Is stuttering more severe with certain people at school (for example, with particular teachers or headteacher) or perhaps stuttering is more pronounced when speaking with their classmates? It is important to know whether the child is withdrawing at school, although this is a question that should also be asked of the school. At the end of the case history the clinician must allow enough time for the parents to ask questions.

It is important to have the opinions of the child's schoolteacher to add to that of the parent. If at all possible, a meeting with the teacher should be arranged, but if this cannot be managed, questionnaires may be sent out for completion and return. The problem with the latter arrangement is that the clinician will not have the opportunity to expand on any answers given and will be less able to advise the teacher as to some appropriate strategies to help with the child's management. The clinician needs to know about the child's involvement in class activities and whether he is talkative or not. A key issue is whether the child is being teased or bullied, and if so how he reacts and how the school manages the situation. Academic progress also needs to be reviewed (with particular interest on language comprehension and expression), and, alongside, this information as to whether the teacher believes the stutter is impeding the child's progress, and if so in what way.

Clinician and child assessment

At elementary school age, the child is better equipped to explain how he feels about stuttering than the preschool child, and the assessment can now more easily take the form of a discussion. There is also the advantage that the child will (in all likelihood) be aware of the stutter and, aided by the careful and considerate manner of the clinician, talking directly about it will generally be easier. The clinician needs to find out how the child feels about his speech generally: how it is at school, at home, with his friends, and how much of a problem the stutter is perceived to be. It is important to know whether any escape or avoidance tricks are being used, and if so whether the child is aware of them and willing to acknowledge them. It is also possible at this age to assess the child's reaction to any teasing or bullying. Throughout the session the clinician should be alert for signs of the stutter becoming increasingly established, including avoidance and increased levels of tension and, as before, videotaping the discussion is highly advisable.

There are few validated tools for the assessment of the school age child's feelings and attitudes toward speech, one notable exception being De Nil and Brutten's (1991) Childrens' Attitude Test (CAT) which comprises an S-24-like questionnaire. In addition, clinicians routinely develop their own informal assessment tools for probing this area. At the Apple House we require the older children to fill in simple questionnaires that probe their feelings and attitudes towards their stutter. We also use parents' responses from the case history together with careful and gentle questioning of children during their assessment to build a picture with the younger children.

An alternative method we have recently been using with success at assessment is to have the children draw their stutters. Simply providing coloured pencils and a sheet of paper, we deliberately keep the format as open as possible, saying something like "Can you draw how your stutter feels to you?" although we are happy to expand on this with children who are unsure. Unsurprisingly, responses are very individualistic. Some present their stutters as monsters from within, others have themselves attempting to hide from the stutter, while others draw contorted faces, caught and transfixed in silent blocks or repetitions. It is often startling, even with the younger children, to see how strongly some of these youngsters already conform to the stereotype of "the stutterer", with all the negative connotations that term can bring. The drawings while revealing in themselves also promote discussion, and the sharing of this information within a group can be particularly useful. It is often revealing to see how the childrens' drawings change when we ask them to redraw their stutters at the end of the therapy period.

Assessment of adolescent and adult stuttering

Many of the procedures relevant to the younger children will again be used with the adolescents and adults who stutter. However, the focus now is usually different. While the primary purpose of the assessment is still to diagnose whether the individual is stuttering or not, it is more often the case that the client has already been identified as stuttering, and more likely again that they will already have attended therapy.

Case history

As with the assessment of younger children, the clinician should collect information on the person's medical and linguistic background, so details on birth, together with a picture of speech/language and developmental milestones can be collected. Age of onset and if possible the type of stuttering at onset should also be recorded, as should any family history of speech/ language disorders in the family. Fluctuations in severity and any periods where the stutter has apparently disappeared, or has at least improved, should also be noted. Parents are likely to be the main source of information on early development, but the client himself will be the main focus for the majority of the clinician's questions. Any previous therapy should also be discussed, including the form it took (for example, fluency shaping/stutter more fluently/avoidance reduction), the length of time and scheduling of therapy (individual/weekly/intensive/group), and the perceived benefits if any.

With adolescents, it is helpful to have a parent assist with some of the details, particularly regarding early development. Adult clients usually have to rely on their own recollections (or recall the recollections of their parents) when it comes to early development issues, but supportive partners can play a useful role when it comes to more recent events. Quite often the mismatch between the client's perceptions and the partner's can be revealing in themselves. Note that where an adult or older teenager is presenting for the first time with a recent onset of stuttering, the clinician will need to consider the possibility of an acquired stutter (see chapter 16 regarding the differential diagnosis of this type of stuttering). In such cases, careful questioning will be needed to tease out whether the stutter can be linked to significant psychological events or to neurological damage, or whether the history better fits the possibility that this is a developmental stutter which has been dormant for a number of years and has become reactivated in recent times, or perhaps that it has never been a sufficient source of concern to seek therapy. In addition to undertaking a detailed review of circumstances linked to the onset of the stutter, the clinician will want to carefully consider the pattern of stuttering to help determine any similarities with subtypes consistent with acquired onset stuttering.

Adolescent and parent interview

This three-way discussion between client, parent and clinician leads on from the case history and provides an opportunity to hear the client's perspective on their difficulties and that of the parent. This part of the assessment often takes the form of a discussion and provides an opportunity to expand on the basic information gleaned earlier with regard to environmental influences. How are things at school? Is fluency improved at home, or with certain people? If so, with whom? When is it particularly problematic? It is comparatively rare to find an adolescent who stutters who does not avoid to some degree; whether this is at word or sound level, or with people or specific situations. Avoidance can be seen as one of the true measures of how entrenched the stuttering is, and all examples of avoidance need to be explored, including how the client feels about avoidance. This discussion gives the clinician the chance to informally assess the dynamics between parent and child and their interactional styles. It also helps the clinician ascertain the best approach to help the individual.

Client interview (adolescent)

We usually see adolescent clients for a one-to-one interview away from the parent(s). Here we discuss the client's perception of their problem, how the stutter has affected them at school and socially, and their reasons for attending this assessment. We also offer the client an opportunity to discuss in confidence any issues they feel uncomfortable talking about in front of their parents; or related problems that they do not wish their parents to know of, for example, problems at home and relationships with partners. Away from the influence of the concerned parents, a small number that we see concede that they are okay with their stutter, do not really want therapy and are here only because their parents have pretty much insisted upon it. Where this is the case, it is important to find out why there is a lack of motivation. Some may have felt that previous therapy had not been helpful and they do not want to undertake any more. In such cases, it is important to discuss various treatment possibilities and the fact that different approaches work for different people. For others it is also possible that an apparent lack of interest in stuttering therapy may indicate a type of avoidance masking deeper concerns about stuttering, which the person simply feels unable to address. Again, the clinician needs to be alert to this possibility and, in appropriate cases, talk through some of the issues involved, including possible approaches which might focus on avoidance and anxiety reduction. There might also be a genuine lack of concern from the client's perspective, and that other issues totally unrelated to stuttering are more pressing. The clinician must be honest and realistic as to what might be achieved in therapy, but should also attempt to demonstrate that therapy can be successful if the right approach is found. If, after discussion, the client still appears genuinely uninterested in therapy, there is no point in attempting to coerce the client to attend for therapy. It is important to let the person know that if there is a change in their thinking they can again come for an assessment. Sometimes the hardest part of the assessment procedure is explaining to a concerned parent that there is absolutely no potential in trying to force their son or daughter into attending speech therapy. It is also important to ask about the future. What are this person's plans? Do they wish to go on to further education after leaving school? Would they see their future differently were they not to stutter? One of the key outcomes of the assessment procedure must be to determine as accurately as possible how the individual sees his stutter in relation to past events, present status and future aspirations. There are a number of counselling techniques which can be useful in assembling such information (see chapter 13).

Client interview (adult)

This is usually more of an extension of the case history and, as with the adolescent assessment, takes the form of a discussion rather than a formal interview. As always, it is important that the clinician gains the person's confidence, and that the client feels able to discuss sensitive details relating to the stutter. The clinician will need to know how the stutter has changed since leaving school and whether any variability in severity can be linked to any tangible factors (perhaps an unwanted period of unemployment or divorce). It is also important to know the effect the stutter has played on the client's life choices. As always, there is great variability from client to client: some will have pursued careers which require a great deal of speaking in stressful situations (for example, lawyers and television presenters), whilst others may have chosen inappropriate careers purely because they did not involve speaking very much. One 42-year-old female client recently seen at the Apple House, intelligent, articulate, successful and with an interiorized stutter which would have been unnoticeable to almost all listeners, described how "I built my whole life around my stammer". From her early teens she had developed extensive and intricate pathways of avoidance at pretty much every level. Since that time, every upcoming situation, whether in the short, medium or long term was scanned for potential difficulty and strategies put in place to avoid words, subjects, people, situations and even careers. She came for assessment fatigued and drained after more than 30 years of extreme avoidance, and out of a need to relieve some of the pressure she felt by telling someone about the double life she felt she had been living.

Fluency count

It is quite possible that some adolescents may be attending a speech clinic for the first time and therefore have no previous speech and language diagnosis, although this is less common with adults. Thus, with the exception of those possibly presenting with late onset stuttering in early adolescence, the fluency and rate count will be used to determine type and severity of stuttering, rather than to confirm whether a diagnosis of stuttering is appropriate. The client should be recorded in conversation and during oral reading, the latter helping to uncover stuttering in those who are avoiding words or sounds in conversation. Some clinicians also like to record their clients in a phone conversation, although accruing enough of the client's talk time from which to undertake a fluency analysis can be problematic here. Making phone calls can also be distressing for some clients and some clinicians may prefer to avoid this. There are many adjuncts to these standard speech samples. For example, some clinicians collect data on confrontation naming and on automatic speech. The former can help determine the effects of time pressure on the stutter, the latter may be significant if there is a question of an acquired stutter (see chapter 16). Other clinicians may routinely compare fluency levels and speech rates between conversational and monologue speech samples to provide an indication as to influence of a more interactive discourse on fluency.

Attitudinal assessments

It is quite common, most notably in adulthood but also during adolescence, for the client's perception of and reactions to his problem to form the most significant part of the disorder. The fear of stuttering can actually present a greater difficulty and barrier to fluency than overt stuttering itself. If these aspects are to be dealt with, they first need to be properly identified at assessment. The section on the measurement of attitudinal factors covers some of the procedures more commonly used in clinics today. The extent to which these tools are used tends to vary dependent on the approach(es) offered at a given clinic. As indicated at the beginning of this chapter, those who favour a fluency shaping approach will spend little or no time assessing cognitive aspects. Conversely, those who take an avoidance-reduction approach may use cognitive assessments extensively, but may choose not to collect behavioural data such as rate and fluency counts. We have also said that it is common to collect data on both cognitive and speech fluency aspects of the stutter. We employ a range of attitudinal assessments at the Apple House, but routinely use the S-24 scale and the WASSP (described above), in addition to inhouse developed questionnaires.

Summation

Finally, the clinician will collate information from the case history, speech fluency data and interviews, summarizing the findings and impressions for the client when all the analyses have been completed. Although the clinician will now have a good idea as to the most appropriate course of action, the client should be involved in the decision-making processes. The effectiveness of previous therapies is something that will have already been discussed in the case history, but the present planned course of action needs to be made with the client's perceptions firmly in mind, although the majority of clients will be happy to pursue the clinician's plan. However, adults in particular will come with a variety of experiences of therapy. Some may have had none at all, whilst others may have a wide experience of a number of approaches and a very clear idea as to what they find helpful. Clinicians can use all of this information to develop an appropriate plan of intervention. The clinician must be aware of the needs of the client, but she must argue carefully and sensitively if she believes an alternative approach to one previously liked by the client to be the more appropriate course of action. Finding the time to discuss and explain why a new framework could be beneficial may be time consuming but necessary. Embarking on a program which the client does not understand or is resistant to is likely to meet with limited success and may even, in the longer term, be damaging.

Summary

The primary purpose of the identification procedure is to ascertain whether the client does indeed have a stutter. The assessment will need to include a comprehensive case history and we return to this issue in the following chapter. Procedures in the assessment of stuttering range from those which directly measure moments of stuttering to those which probe the client for his perceptions as to the impact the stutter has upon his life. The relative suitability of these will depend on a number of factors, the most fundamental being age of the client: for example, it is likely that assessment of very young clients will focus less on self-perception and more on the environment in which the child is existing. Stuttering may also be seen alongside other speech/language and behavioural problems. Particularly in younger children, these may need to be formally screened by use of the relevant tests (again see chapter 10 regarding the assessment of early stuttering). The assessment of an older child with a more established stutter is more likely to involve a greater consideration of the individual's feelings and responses to the stutter, in addition to the cognitive and behavioural considerations of the child's interactions at school and family dynamics.

With adolescent and adult clients, attitudinal profiling may form the most significant part of the assessment procedure, with the aim of restructuring and reconstruing negative perceptions as a major goal (see chapters 12 and 13). The range and type of assessments applied is also likely to be affected by the therapeutic procedures that will subsequently be offered. A clinic that offers an operant-based fluency shaping approach is likely to place greater emphasis on the assessment of motor speech breakdown, while clinics which take a more cognitive perspective, say offering a counselling approach, are more likely to be concerned with attitudinal aspects. With the increasing integration of cognitive and behavioural aspects in therapy (Guitar, 1998;

Peters & Guitar, 1991) it is to be hoped that increasingly factors relating both to the individual who stutters and the stutter itself will be explored at assessment.

Key points

- The fluency count is a supposedly objective way of measuring stuttering and does provide both qualitative and quantitative data. Although there are many potential problems with test–retest reliability, it remains the most commonly used procedure for evaluating moments of stuttering.
- The fluency count does not give any information as to the severity of the moments of stuttering. Data on severity needs to be collected alongside the frequency of stuttering data.
- The Stuttering Severity Instrument (SSI) is a well-known standardized assessment which holds an advantage over the fluency count in that it examines not only the frequency of stuttering but also severity and associated secondary movements.
- Attitudinal scales have been in existence for many years, but with increasing emphasis on client-centred therapies new assessment procedures are providing ever more sophisticated ways of evaluating how the individual is being affected by the stutter.
- Assessment procedures of children may include some or all of the following: tests of language, phonology, auditory processing, fine and gross motor skills, fluency and speech rate counts, attitudinal and cognitive scales.
- The identification of stuttering in older children and adults is likely to reflect an increased focus on cognitive, attitudinal and behavioural aspects associated with the disorder.

Further reading

Conture, E. (1997). Evaluating childhood stuttering. In R. F. Curlee and G. M. Siegel (Eds.), *Nature and treatment of stuttering: New directions* (pp. 237–256). Boston: Allyn & Bacon.

A comprehensive overview of a range of assessments and procedures available to the clinician. Conture is as keen as ever to avoid a "cookbook approach" and instead applies a problem-solving approach to the evaluation of stuttering in children up to the age of 7.

Gregory H. H., & Hill, D. (1999). Differential evaluation-differential therapy for stuttering children. In R. Curlee (Ed.), *Stuttering and related disorders of fluency* (pp. 23–44). New York: Theime.

I have mentioned throughout chapter 9 how different assessment procedures are associated with different therapeutic approaches. This chapter expands on how assessment influences treatment strategies in children who stutter.

Guitar, B. (1998) *Stuttering: An integrated approach to its nature and treatment* (pp. 151–211). Philadelphia: Lippincott Williams & Wilkins.

This large chapter covers assessment procedures together with sections on case history, and interviews for all age groups.

Manning, W. H. (1996). *Clinical decision making in the diagnosis and treatment of fluency disorders*. Albany, NY: Delmar.

Although much of the focus of this book is on the treatment of stuttering, there is also a great deal which is of relevance for the assessment of the child, adolescent and adult who stutters.

10 Treating early stuttering

Introduction

Research has consistently noted that for the majority of people who stutter, the onset of the disorder is preschool (Andrews & Harris, 1964; Conture, 2001; Dalton & Hardcastle, 1989; Gregory, 2003; Van Riper, 1982; Yairi & Ambrose, 1992b). The literature on therapy for younger children is considerable (see, for example, Adams, 1980; Bloodstein, 1993; Conture, 1990; Costello, 1983; Guitar, 1998; Onslow, et al., 1994, 2003; Pindzola, 1987; Rustin et al., 1996; Ryan, 1974; Shames & Florence, 1980; Shine, 1980, 1988; Van Riper, 1973; Wall, 1995). This chapter must by necessity, be selective. In order to try to characterize the breadth of therapeutic procedures currently available to clinicians, we focus largely on two approaches that illustrate very different rationales, methods and procedures for the treatment of early stuttering. One offers a motor speech explanation and a direct operant approach to deal with it. The other takes a more multifactorial perspective to aetiology, treating the problem from an (indirect) cognitive and interactional perspective. Both approaches are well established and widely practised. Between the range of possibilities exposed by these two therapeutic models, we can place the rationale and therapeutic procedures of the whole spectrum of integrated approaches that may be loosely labelled "mainstream therapies".

The decision-making process for therapy

Determining potential treatment approach from assessment

The first step toward effective therapy lies in conducting a thorough assessment of the child which has been described elsewhere (chapter 9). Having gathered information from formal and informal tests and the case history, the clinician must now form an opinion on the child. The following "stages of fluency" outline five potential outcomes from the assessment:

1   The child is not stuttering/beginning to stutter and is not perceived at being of increased risk to develop stuttering. Example behaviours:

disfluencies are infrequent and fall within normal disfluency parameters such as interjections, revisions and word repetition with only one repetition for each moment of disfluency; child is unconcerned about disfluencies; normal speech and language ability as recorded by standardized tests; positive speaking environment (explained below).

2   The child is not stuttering/beginning to stutter, but is perceived as being at increased risk of developing stuttering. There may be similar disfluencies to above, but may also have a positive family history of stuttering; greater exposure to negative speaking environments; presence of phonological disorder.

3   The child is showing some early signs of mild primary stuttering. This could include increased number of repeated units; greater percentage of disfluent syllables.

4   The child is showing signs of established stuttering. Behaviours might also include increased awareness of disfluencies; inappropriate pausing; blocking or prolonging; schwa insertion on repeated vowels.

5   The child is showing advanced signs of stuttering. In addition to behaviours noted in four, there may also be escape and avoidance behaviours: for example, word, sound, situation avoidance; facial grimacing; loss of eye contact; general withdrawal; obvious signs of embarrassment, frustration or fear.

If a diagnosis of stage 1 is made, there may be little to do other than to reassure parents that their child is not stuttering, nor is at any increased risk to eventually do so. Parents may be further reassured that if they continue to be concerned then they should again contact their clinician. Diagnosis of stage 2 might similarly involve counselling and, depending on the focus of the clinician's concern for increased likelihood of stuttering, she may also decide to employ an indirect approach (see below) to pre-empt it. Findings of stages three, four or five will in almost all cases result in the commencement of direct or indirect therapy just as soon as the caseload allows, although there may be circumstances where a delay in starting therapy is deemed necessary. One example might be where the family is about to move house and it is unlikely that the parents will be able to properly follow a direct intervention plan with the child during that time period.

Direct and indirect therapy

Fundamentally, treatment options fall within two parameters: direct and indirect approaches. The former involves active involvement of the clinician with the child, often in conjunction with the parents or primary caregiver. With an indirect approach the clinician seeks to establish fluency by first evaluating the effect that the environment is having on the child's fluency, and then manipulating this to provide a more supportive backdrop for fluency to increase. With direct therapy the child's speech is directly targeted by the clinician (rather than the environment in which the speech is produced), with systematic adjustments made to speech production in some shape or form. We illustrate both models below.

An indirect approach to therapy

Indirect approaches are based on the tenet that successful remediation can be achieved by manipulating the child's environment in such a way that will increase the likelihood of normal speech developing, and deprive the stutter of suitable environment for it to continue and flourish. Some simple examples of an indirect approach might include having the parents slow their rate of speech, finding more leisurely one-to-one time to spend with the child, asking fewer closed questions of their child, ensuring more consistent home routines. With this approach, there is no direct work on attempting to change or modify the child's speech patterns. We can see that if we place this approach within Starkweather's Demands and Capacities model (see chapter 1), onset is explained in terms of the reduced *capacity* (for example, apparent genetic susceptibility; reduced language skills) and that taking an indirect approach to therapy serves to reduce the external *demands* placed on the child's resources.

There are different schools of thought as to when to take an indirect or direct approach. Some clinicians prefer to utilize an indirect therapeutic approach with any preschool child who is showing signs of stuttering, regardless of whether the signs indicate a marginal stutter, or one that is already firmly established and advancing quickly (e.g., Rustin et al., 1996). Others may prefer to use an indirect approach with earlier stuttering, and adopt a more direct approach if this is not successful, or base their intervention strategies on the basis of a range of "severity" criteria (Conture, 2001). Still others advocate the use of a direct strategy with any preschool child who is showing signs of stuttering (Onslow, Costa, & Rue, 1990). It might be expected that consideration of the opposing theoretical stances represented in the different approaches and the presentation of the various arguments relating to them would be the significant factors in treatment program selection. In many cases, though, the choice has more to do with expediency, and it is simply the clinician's familiarity with a particular method that becomes the defining factor in the decision-making process.

The clinician may decide to take an indirect therapeutic approach to a child showing a stage 2 stutter. The first task may be to reassure the parents that their child is not stuttering, but at the same time it may also be appropriate to point out that there are certain factors which increase the likelihood that their child could begin stuttering. The scope of the advice will obviously depend first on the nature and extent of the perceived risk by the clinician, and second the degree to which the clinician feels the parents can take on board the advice in a way that will translate into a more positive environment for the child to speak in. The clinician needs to advise with great care. It is quite common for parents already to feel guilty that their child may be at risk, and perhaps even perceive it in some way to be their fault (for example, if there is some family history of stuttering).Where this is the case, it is important to dispel such fears and to provide reassurance. If anxiety or concern is felt by the parents and this translates into the home environment and interactions with the child, then this is going to be counterproductive to good fluency.

The clinician may initially wish to set three monthly review appointments with the parents of a child at stage 2, to check on progress and that the child is not developing abnormal disfluencies. As indicated earlier, the stage 3 and stage 4 child may also be considered a candidate for an indirect therapy approach, although some clinicians might also prefer to become actively involved in the direct treatment of such children.

Parent–child interaction approach

Parent–Child Interaction (PCI) therapy is a cognitive approach to the treatment of stuttering that can be used with both preschool and school aged children. It is based on the premise that stuttering is a heterogeneous disorder and must be treated as such. Accordingly, therapy should be shaped to meet the particular needs of each individual. Therapy involves modifying the child's environment, and particularly adjusting where necessary the interaction styles between parent(s) and child to provide an optimal opportunity for fluency to become permanently established. Originally used by clinicians following a Demands and Capacities approach to fluency therapy (Starkweather & Gottwald, 1990; Starkweather et al., 1990), therapists at the Michael Palin Centre (MPC) for stammering children in London have been developing their PCI approach over a number of years (Rustin, 1987, 1991; Rustin et al., 1996; Rustin, Cook, Botterill, Hughes, & Kelman, 2001).

I focus on this approach in some detail for two reasons. First, it is an established therapeutic approach which has been comprehensively described and is recognized internationally. Its philosophy is shared by many clinicians (e.g., Conture & Melnick, 1999; Manning, 1996; Starkweather et al., 1990; Zebrowski, 1997), although others have criticized the lack of objective data on its efficacy thus far (Ingham & Cordes, 1999; Onslow & Packman, 1999; Ryan, 2001). There is conflicting evidence as to whether parents' speech and language behaviours genuinely influence their children's stuttering (see Nippold & Rudzinsky, 1995). Work is being undertaken to address these issues and outcome data is beginning to emerge (e.g., Nicholas & Millard, 2003: Nicholas, Millard, & Cook, 2004).

A second reason is that PCI represents a good example of a cognitive-based approach to early stuttering, and as such provides an interesting alternative to operant approaches described later in this chapter. Further, the PCI approach, as used at the MPC, is not only employed when the child is at risk or has mild stuttering symptoms (the stage 2 and stage 3 children described above). The approach is outlined below.

Rationale

The theoretical stance taken by the MPC is that stuttering is multifactorial (Smith & Kelly, 1997; Starkweather & Gottwald, 1990), the causes of which, broadly speaking, can be seen to lie in four broad areas:

- *linguistic*, including developmental and current speech/language abilities
- *physiological*, relating to neurophysiological predisposition, fine and gross motor control outside the speech/language domain
- *environmental/sociocultural*, including family dynamics, child-rearing practices, second language issues
- *psychological/emotional*, comprising personality characteristics, causes of stress within the family unit (and coping strategies used to deal with such problems.

In viewing stuttering from a multifactorial perspective, there are similarities with Starkweather's Demands and Capacities model (Starkweather, 1987; see chapter 1) and the notion that stuttering is related to an inappropriate balance between those factors that can lead to abnormal disfluency, and those which help perpetuate the difficulties. Smith and Kelly's (1997) multifactorial model of stuttering is also consistent with this approach.

ASSESSMENT

Assessments and testing procedures reflecting this multifactorial model are extensive, requiring the child to attend the clinic with both parents, with the whole process taking the best part of a day. The assessment comprises three components: an assessment of the child without his/her parents; an assessment of the interaction between child and parent; an interview with the parents. The range of procedures is designed to probe the four areas of the model and aims to explain how difficulty in one area may impact on another. The following is a summary of the procedures used as described comprehensively by Rustin et al. (1996).

Child assessment

This comprises a set of assessments which, alongside stuttering, looks at the following:

- *Receptive and expressive language*: for receptive language (comprehension) data on length of utterance, syntactic complexity, semantic complexity and vocabulary are all collected using a variety of standardized tests. These include the *Derbyshire Language Scheme Rapid Screening Test* and the *British Picture Vocabulary Scales* (BPVS). Expressive abilities are recorded from Renfrew's (1988) Word Finding Vocabulary Scale

(WFVS). Additionally, analysis of linguistic form, content and usage is undertaken from the child's responses to stimulus "what's wrong" cards. Word-finding ability is also recorded.

- *Phonology*: MPC initially uses a simple phonology screen. If this uncovers a deviant pattern, more sophisticated tests such as Phonological Assessment of Child Speech (PACS; Grunwell, 1985) are undertaken.
- *Cognitive skills*: Organizational skills and problem solving are tested by having the child complete a series of graded tasks using an abacus. Factors such as the child's use of strategy and logical thought, ability to notice and correct errors, and willingness to ask for assistance are all noted.
- *Drawing*. The child completes the Goodenough Draw-A-Man Test and attempts to write his or her name. Pencil grip type, handedness and error patterns (for example, letter reversals for a school age child) are all noted.
- *Social skills*. This includes areas such as listening skills, ability to turn-take, animation of facial expression and use of gesture.
- *General behaviour*. The child's reaction to the *separation* from their parent for the assessment is noted. Child's compliance and *cooperation* with clinician and procedures; the *manner* in which the child engages in the tasks set by the clinician; levels of *anxiety* shown by the child; and the age-appropriateness of the attention level which the child shows.
- *Disfluency*. A disfluency count is also taken (see chapter 9 for a description of this procedure).

Child interview

- *Attitudes*. The child's attitudes and beliefs are sought from the child interview. Here, the clinician asks the child about his or her attitude to a variety of situations, for example, school or nursery. This may also include feelings towards friends and teachers.
- *Home/Family*. Relationships with siblings and parents, involving likes and dislikes.
- *Speech*. Includes questions on the perceived problem, perceived severity, coping strategies, whether the child wants help with speech.

The clinician then scores the tests and transcribes the speech sample. These data are used at the end of the parent interview as a part of the formulation process (see below).

Parent–child interaction assessment

The focus of this assessment is to observe the way the parent and child communicate with one another. The resulting therapy may focus, amongst other factors, on adapting parental interactive style, but the clinician must make it clear from the outset that there is no suggestion that the stutter has been caused by any inappropriateness of interaction. However, certain interactive styles can be responsible for maintaining the stutter; hence the initial need for assessment of these dynamics.

The data are collected from a video taken of each parent playing with the child for around 15 minutes. At the end of this, the clinician completes an interaction profile that comprises a template for summarizing the way in which the parent communicates both verbally and nonverbally with the child. Verbal factors include such aspects as turn-taking, speech rate, fluency, interruptions and complexity of language, while nonverbal attributes include listening skills, manner of speech, facial expression, position, and so forth. As Rustin et al. (1996) explain:

> The clinician will need to select and prioritise those aspects of parental style which may become targets for intervention. The items on the profile are not discrete and separate behaviours, they are part of a complex dynamic and bidirectional matrix, each item affecting other aspects of verbal and nonverbal language.
>
> It is therefore necessary to consider what effect a change in one behaviour would have on others, for example; if a parent who speaks rapidly, using few pauses and giving the child little time to imitate or respond reduces their rate of speech, an increase in pausing may occur thereby increasing initiation opportunities for the child.
>
> (p. 53)

Parent interview

This extensive interview with both parents provides a means of exploring in depth the subtle events which may be impacting, both positively and negatively on the child's stuttering. Originally, this procedure was scheduled to last for two and a half hours, but has since been adjusted to take into account the needs of parents and caregivers. Responses from mother and father are recorded separately throughout. Often a mismatch between the parent's perceptions can lead to some of the more significant findings. The first part of the interview is focused on the effect of the stuttering on the family, followed by a history of the child's general health as related to home routines. As the parents become more settled and comfortable in answering the questions, they are then asked about the child's personality as a lead-in to more sensitive areas concerned with family history. The interview subsequently returns to more concrete issues, such as developmental milestones and general development before concluding.

It is sometimes the case that parents, irrespective of any course of action taken over the child's stuttering, may be referred to other appropriate agencies (for example, counselling) to deal with issues that have come to light during the course of the interview.

Formulation

This stage provides the opportunity for the clinician to draw together all the assessment and interview findings and present them to the family. A summary chart (Figure 10.1) provides a pictorial representation of the four areas specified in the multifactorial model. Reviewing this with the family provides one way of making the link between the theoretical stance, the interview procedures and the relevance of the findings to that particular family.

The formulation process is therefore designed to explain the child's difficulties, as identified by the assessments and interview within context of a multifactorial view of stuttering to the family. In reviewing the assessments, the clinician identifies the significant findings and adds comments to the relevant area on the chart on which to place them, beginning with physiological and linguistic factors (some of which may be seen as *predisposing* factors to stuttering) before moving to the remaining two areas (psychosocial – emotional and environmental – sociocultural), which might be seen more as *perpetuating*

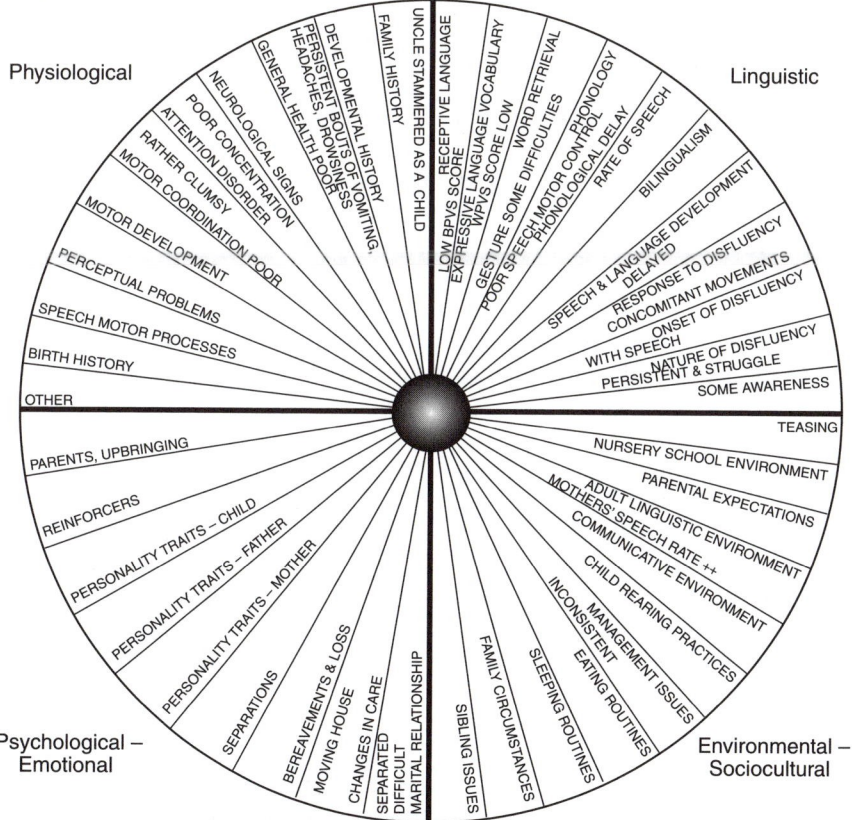

Figure 10.1 Summary chart of Chris age 5;4 (Rustin, Botterill, & Kelman, 1996. Reproduced with permission of the publishers).

factors. Thus the chart is used to demonstrate the multifactorial nature of the disorder and provides an aid for identifying the specific issues pertaining to the child which can be considered as factors in the child's stuttering. In giving feedback to the family, positive factors are also stressed, whether these relate to the child (for example, absence of any secondary stuttering), to the parents (for example, the parents are already using good rate of speech, or using nondirective and nonpejorative speech), or to parent–child interaction (for example, calm and easy manner with the child).

Parents of children who are beginning to stutter may be extremely concerned about the condition, but at the same time unsure of exactly what stuttering is, of how it may develop and, most importantly, confused as to the right and wrong ways of going about dealing with it. Presenting the evidence in this manner and finding the time to talk the parents through the relevant issues can in itself go a long way to alleviating the anxiety (and possibly guilt) that parents may feel over their child's condition.

Therapy

This comprehensive assessment procedure identifies clients as follows:

- Low risk of stuttering (minimal intervention required; corresponds to stage 1, described above).
- At risk of stuttering (delayed intervention, corresponds to stage 2). Delayed intervention may be appropriate when due to instability within the family there may not be sufficient time to devote to therapy. Such factors may include bereavement, moving house, birth of new baby.
- At risk of stuttering (intervention recommended; corresponds to stage 2). Experience shows that this group is the most likely outcome of assessment. Such children are then seen for a block of six once-weekly sessions of therapy (see below).

Additionally, although some factors that might inhibit effective therapy may be dealt with alongside therapy, there may be others which need to be dealt with prior to intervention. For example, it may be appropriate for a child with a severe language delay to be referred first for help with this. Alternatively, where there are particular difficulties with family dynamics (for example, going through an acrimonious divorce), parents might be referred to relevant professional agencies prior to the start of interaction therapy with the child.

Interaction therapy

This is an indirect method to the treatment of stuttering in children. Rustin et al. (1996) report that this method alone is very effective in dealing with stuttering, but also advocate the use of direct cognitive-behavioural therapy as an adjunct, in certain cases (see section below).

As stated above, the parent–child interaction observations will already have given the clinician an opportunity to evaluate family and parent–child dynamics. It should now be possible to ascertain the interaction style of the parents. A common problem is that because of concern about their child's stuttering but at the same time being confused by it, parenting styles may have been changed, sometimes negatively, in an attempt to control the stutter. For example, it is not uncommon for concerned parents to be more insistent on high levels of verbal performance, for example they might stop their child during a moment of stuttering, insisting that they pause, take a deep breath and start again. As Rustin et al. (1996) explain: "the principle aim of this therapeutic approach is to help parents restore confidence in their parenting skills, to understand the complexity of this disorder and to find ways of interacting with the child that will facilitate fluency" (p. 97). As a part of this process, the parents become used to monitoring their own interactive style and making the "small self-determined changes which are the cornerstone of this therapy" (p. 97).

Overview of therapy program

Children are seen for one-hour sessions weekly over a six-week period during which new interaction styles are established. This is followed by a six-week consolidation period, where the effects of the new interaction styles should become noticeable. Decisions as to the suitability of further therapy are made after the consolidation period.

Session 1 is given over primarily to the establishment of a five-minute "special time". The clinician explains that this constitutes a period of time set aside solely between parent and child, at home, between three and five days per week, depending on how practical a family will find it to free the necessary time. During the special time, the parent allows the child a play activity free from distractions and any input from siblings. Parent and child play, with the parent focusing attention on the child, and particularly the content of the child's speech, rather than the fluency of the output. The parent then records what happened during the time and reactions to it on a task sheet. The five-minute period must not be exceeded.

Session 2 begins with a review of feedback of the special times. This includes task sheet comments as well as "online" verbal feedback. Any difficulties in finding the time (or in keeping to the five-minute length) can be discussed. Parents are then individually videorecorded whilst playing with their child in a session modelled on the special time format. Each parent then reviews the video and comments are sought as to the interaction. Was the video typical of a normal five-minute session? Can the parents identify at least one positive feature of their interactive style and one aspect of behaviour which they might want to change? Parents are encouraged to comment on aspects such as naturalness, turn-taking, balance of talking time, and such like. Throughout this process the clinician acts as a guide, prompting and drawing out responses where necessary but always in a positive and supportive manner.

Parents are also asked to refer to a checklist of behaviours and identify one which is relevant to them. This procedure covers similar interaction issues to those noted in the interaction profile taken from the initial parent–child interaction video, which was recorded at assessment. Now, however, the clinician is working in conjunction with the parent to help identify interaction traits that are unhelpful, and also where possible to encourage the parent to self-identify difficulties, and equally importantly lead the parent towards proactive consideration as to how these traits can be changed.

Session 3 and subsequent sessions follow a similar format: the review of special time followed by video recording of play, together with subsequent review and analysis. Any changes in interactive style that are to be implemented are then noted for practice during the special time sessions in the coming week.

Consolidation period

During this additional six-week period, parents continue to use the special time periods as before. The weekly sessions at the clinic, however, are replaced with the parents returning the completed task sheets to the clinician, who reviews them at the end of each week. It is expected that during the consolidation period the child's fluency will increase. However, there may be circumstances perhaps unknown to the parents (such as problems at nursery which the child is not talking about at home) that are negatively affecting the child's fluency. Rustin et al. (1996) also note that as the child's fluency increases some parents become less consistent at providing the special time sessions. This can also lead to regression. Under these circumstances the parents are encouraged to make contact with the clinician. These issues can then be discussed in a further review appointment.

Direct approaches

As stated earlier, this is a cover-all term for therapies which target the act of stuttering directly, rather than those (such as the one described above) which facilitate increase in fluency by changing the environment in which the stuttering occurs. A significant number of established treatment programs for early stuttering combine direct and indirect approaches. However, the focus immediately below is on a comparatively recent direct treatment program which represents a significant breakthrough in preschool stuttering therapy.

The Lidcombe Program

Introduction

The Lidcombe Program (LP) is a parent-administered early intervention therapy for preschool children, based on principles of operant conditioning and fluency shaping. The goal is a speech output with less than 1 percent of syllables stuttered. With this approach, the child is praised for passages of fluent speech whilst stuttering is "punished" by having the child (fluently) repeat stuttered words. In fact, it is not so much a fluency shaping program, but more a fluency replacement program. Most of the outcome data collected have been on children up to 6 years old. While the program can be successful with school age children (Rousseau, Onslow, & Packman, 2005), there is some counter-evidence to suggest that it is most effective with the earlier age groups (Lincoln, Onslow, Lewis, & Wilson, 1996) and it is described specifically as a treatment for preschool children.

It is worth examining this program in some detail for a number of reasons: it has been shown to be highly successful, if controversial, in a number of areas, for example, in the use of parents as primary therapeutic providers. In this sense there is a similarity between the Lidcombe Program and parent–child interaction approaches, both of which have the parents as the primary deliverers of the therapy, with the clinician acting more in the role of a facilitator. The difference is that with a PCI approach the parental involvement involves adjustment of parental style and other environmental variables, whereas with the Lidcombe Program parents apply therapeutic strategies that have previously been considered solely the domain of the qualified speech language therapist/pathologist. In addition, the success of the program raises a number of interesting issues which challenge some of the established approaches to the treatment of early stuttering.

This response contingent stimuli (RCS) approach takes its name from the suburb in Sydney where early trials of the program were undertaken. While RCS therapies are plentiful amongst adult programs, they are rare amongst early intervention programs designed for preschool children. In a series of papers dating back from the early 1990s covering rationale, data outcome and new developments, Professor Mark Onslow and colleagues have put forward a compelling case for this operant-based approach to early intervention (Harris, Onslow, Packman, Harrison, & Menzies, 2002; Jones et al., 2005; Onslow, 1996; Onslow et al., 1996; Onslow, Menzies, & Packman, 2001; Onslow et al., 2003).

The rationale is that while stuttering can go on to develop into a complicated disorder, in its early stages it can be explained as a relatively simple problem of motor coordination. In one attempt to test this theory, Onslow, Stocker, Packman, and McLeod (2002) examined whether the LP facilitates change in motor speech function by measuring a number of acoustic durations pre and post clinic. No systematic differences between these two time frames were found. In fact, as we have seen from chapter 4, there is a reasonable body of evidence suggesting that stuttering is related to motor speech control deficits, but it does not obviously follow that a motoric explanation should underpin the success of the Lidcombe Program. This is because the approach does not work actively on changing motor speech patterns, or at least any more than it works on, say, changing linguistic or auditory processing. Although Lidcombe is a direct intervention program, there is actually no manipulation of vocal tract activity, so factors such as rate of speech, strength of articulatory contacts and force of laryngeal vibration and breathing patterns are all left undisturbed. Instead, stuttering is replaced with fluency by the systematic reinforcement of fluency and the gentle punishment of stuttering.

Although the program is assumed to work solely on the principle of operant conditioning, it is impossible to rule out environmental factors, such as increased talking time at home, more one-to-one time with the parent. A study is currently underway to define the most significant features of the program. Although some have speculated that the success of the operant is related to the neural plasticity seen in younger children (Rousseau et al., 2005; Venkatagiri, 2005), from an organic perspective the success of the Lidcombe Program is hard to explain. Nonetheless, two facts remain clear. First, regardless of the significant factors which underlie it, in its early years stuttering can be successfully treated as an operant. Second, those contingencies which bring about the change in fluency apparently need be little more than having the child self-correct moments of stuttering. This in itself is a hugely significant find and provides for a simple yet highly effective way of treating early stuttering.[1]

Onslow argues that if the program is administered correctly (and the delivery of the reinforcement in particular is seen as crucial) then a complete and permanent recovery from stuttering can be achieved. Indeed, the reported success, both in the short term and up to seven years post therapy is impressive (Lincoln & Onslow, 1997; Onslow et al., 1990, 1994). There may be a number of defining factors which determine levels of success of the Lidcombe approach. Children who start earlier on the program, have more motivated parents, have no second language difficulties, no dyspraxia and no coexisting speech and language problems may well do better, although objective data on this are lacking. Equally important will be the clinician's skill in administering the program. As one example, Onslow repeatedly states that if incorrect reinforcement procedures are used, the approach will not be successful and indeed may be damaging.

To ensure accuracy and consistency in the administration of the approach, all therapists must be Lidcombe qualified. This involves attending a five-day course run by recognized and accredited Lidcombe trainers.

When the Lidcombe Program was first introduced to the UK in the early to mid-1990s, it met with considerable resistance, particularly from clinicians who favoured a more cognitive approach to therapy, some of whom argued that the RCS therapy was too simplistic and inflexible to deal with a complex

---

1 Although operant programs can be very effective in controlling fluency in adults' speech, the particular contingencies used in the Lidcombe Program do not appear to work as effectively when applied to older children and adults who stutter.

disorder such as stuttering (e.g., Rustin & Cook, 1997). Gradually though it has become accepted and it now finds worldwide usage (see chapters 12 and 13 in Onslow et al., 2003 for clinicians' experiences of the program from around the world). With well-motivated parents and children, the opinion of a number of expert clinicians is that the program can produce impressive results and can eliminate stuttering in some younger children (see also Lincoln & Onslow, 1997).

Aspects of therapy

ASSESSMENT

Initially, the child is seen and assessed by the clinician and a case history is taken. As with most RCS programs the key assessment figure is percentage of syllables stuttered, although other behavioural and cognitive factors may be noted. The parent has the key points of the program explained, together with the idea that the parent will become the primary therapy provider, while the clinician will closely monitor progress during once-weekly sessions. The parent is then taught by the clinician how to give appropriate feedback and reinforcement to the child. Fluent speech is reinforced by praise, or by tangible rewards such as stickers, whilst stuttered moments are negatively reinforced; for example, the parent might say "Ooh, I think I heard a little bump on that word. Try and say it without the bump." (The child repeats fluently.) Parent – "That was great – I didn't hear any bump that time. Well done."

For children who present with higher severity ratings, the parent is taught not to negatively reinforce each stuttered moment. Generally, there should be five moments of positive reinforcement of fluency for every single moment of "punishing" (of stuttering). As such, the program is as much about maximizing fluent speech as it is about eliminating moments of stuttering. In the earlier stages of therapy the parent may also be taught how to constrain linguistic complexity in their child's speech so that high levels of fluency are consistently achieved from an early stage. This aspect of therapy is somewhat similar to another operant approach – Ryan's Gradual Increase in Length and Complexity of Utterance (GILCU) therapy (Ryan, 1984).

The parent is also taught how to record the child's level of stuttering on a record sheet (severity rating). Instead of having the parent learn to count syllables and relate this in terms of percentage of stuttered syllables, this is done on an impressionistic scale of one (no stuttering) to ten (worst stuttering that the child experiences). The clinician negotiates with the caregiver as to where the child is currently within this range (so, for example, a severity rating of 5 may equate to 9 percent SS for one child, but 7 percent SS or 14 percent SS for other individuals. After a short period of time to allow for familiarity in use, the parent should be able to report severity levels reliably, allowing both clinician and parent to produce similar severity ratings. At the second session, the parent may bring in a tape recording, demonstrating their attempts to use correct reinforcement, elicit appropriate length of utterance and record severity away from the clinic. The clinician will use the session to review the tape and help the parent with any problems relating to these aspects of the program.

ONLINE TREATMENT

Away from the clinic, the parent sets aside five-minute blocks of time each day where fluent speech is practised one to one with the child, keeping to the strict criteria regarding length of utterance and use of reinforcement. Each day the parent records the subjective severity ratings. No reinforcement is undertaken outside of these sessions, and away from the five-minute blocks the child's stuttering will not invoke parental comment. As fluency becomes established within the very structured sessions, so length of utterance is increased, by carefully adjusting the speech stimulus materials. Speech is also then encouraged in more spontaneous exchanges. During subsequent weekly meetings with the clinician, the parent will report on progress and the clinician will offer feedback as to both the child's progress and the parent's use of reinforcement during a trial session within the clinic. Depending on the issues arising from the parent's report, the clinician may model a session, or perhaps discuss ways of eliciting a longer length of utterance from the child. Both parent and clinician will agree on a severity rating figure for that session, as well as reviewing the daily stuttering severity charts the parent has been filling in. The time a child will spend at the online stage will vary from individual to individual, but the average is approximately 12 weeks. Once severity ratings (which will be agreed between parent and clinician) are consistently down to scores of either one or two, across a range of speaking situations, and remain consistent over a period of a few weeks, the clinician will embark on the second or "maintenance" phase of the program.

MAINTENANCE

In the maintenance phase the severity evaluations continue, but the speaking situations used to generate them become less and less structured as the fluent speech becomes established in a wider range of communicative contexts. Simultaneously, reinforcement will also be given less frequently. Assuming the fluency gains are maintained, contact with the clinician will gradually become less and less frequent, with visits to the clinic decreasing from weekly to bi-monthly and then monthly until no further input from the clinician is required. Clinicians and parents may also discuss the need for clinic visits by telephone. The phase two time period can vary considerably, but usually takes around 24 weeks, after which time children are usually discharged.

Summary

There is a growing body of evidence to suggest that the Lidcombe Program can be very effective in treating stuttering in young children. The premise that stuttering, at its inception at least, comprises a comparatively simple motor speech disorder is controversial and does not drive the therapeutic process, which works without manipulation of any motor speech variables. The success of the Lidcombe Program does serve to highlight significant differences between stuttering at onset and more established stuttering. Administering the program effectively is a complicated procedure, but at its core is the very basic premise that stuttering can be eradicated by simply telling the child to repeat a stuttered word fluently, and praising the child for fluency when this feedback is placed into an operant conditioning regime. Applying the same procedure does not work for older people who stutter, although, as we see elsewhere, operant techniques when applied to changing vocal tract dynamics can be effective in controlling adult stuttering.

It is also not clear how fluency is increased in the Lidcombe Program when, from a Demands and Capacities standpoint, it might appear to increase demand on speech (something the PCI approach works at eliminating). Ultimately, it may be that replacing stuttered speech which is effortful and may carry listener disapproval or concern with an output which is fluent and praised is an achievable and effective trade for the child. First, recall that the child is being praised for speech around five times as frequently as he is being told to repeat. Second, any extra "demand" in having the child repeat a stuttered word is done with sensitivity and in a linguistic environment where the child is able to succeed (and will again be praised for his success). Like any operant program, the success depends on the finer points as to how the reinforcement is administered. Onslow and colleagues have clearly stated that the success of the Lidcombe Program relies on the skill of the clinician (and parents) at administering such feedback.

Gradual increase in length and complexity of utterance

While the Lidcombe Program has received much attention over the last few years, there are a number of alternative fluency shaping approaches available. Of two (reported in a little more detail in Guitar, 1998), one uses token reinforcement together with carefully structured use of delayed auditory feedback to control rate and also continuous voicing as the main means of achieving fluency (Shames & Florence, 1980). Another (Shine, 1980) uses whispered speech early on in a seven-phase program to help establish fluency. This is later substituted with use of a slower rate and light articulatory contacts before a later phase further refines this into a pattern which is more normal sounding. Like the Lidcombe Program, Ryan's (1974, 1984) Gradual

Increase in Length and Complexity of Utterance (GILCU) approach works on the premise that speech is an operant, and that fluent responses can be elicited when appropriate rewards and punishments are administered. Note that the GILCU program is aimed predominantly at school aged children, but its significance as a precursor to the Lidcombe Program and its similarities warrant its inclusion here.

As is the case with all operant programs, therapy is very carefully controlled and highly structured as the child progresses through three phases: establishment, transfer and maintenance. This approach requires the child to work through a series of 54 steps. Step one of the establishment phase requires the child to speak one word fluently, ten times consecutively. When he is able to do this, he moves to step two (two words consecutively), step three (three words), and so on up to stage six. Stage seven comprises one sentence; stage eight, two sentences. At stage 11, 30 seconds of fluency speech is required. By stage 18 the child will be able to produce 5 minutes of fluent speech.

Throughout the establishment phase, the child responds to specific instructions, initially using single word utterances as in each of three modes, reading monologue and conversation. Stuttered responses are negatively reinforced, for example, "stop, speak fluently", and the child is required to repeat fluently before continuing. Fluent speech is rewarded with praise "good", and tokens which can later be exchanged for a tangible award are given. Note here the rather different implementation of reinforcement and punishment compared to the Lidcombe approach. Complete fluency is required before the child can progress to the next of the 18 levels which link start with single words and end with a 5-minute block of speaking time. The child moves on to the establishment phase once a five-minute block of speaking in each of the three modes has been completed with less than two stuttered moments within a two-minute period. Transfer consists of speaking fluently at home, at school, with different audience sizes and different physical settings. Again, small stepwise increments are reached before the child moves on to the next. The child is once again assessed across the three speaking modes, this time only one stutter per two minutes of speaking is allowed. Once this has been achieved, the child progresses to the maintenance phase. Here, the child is effectively put on review status, with clinical contact becoming less frequent as time progresses. The maintenance period concludes after 22 months. (See Table 10.1.)

The GILCU approach also provides the basis of a good many other operant programs currently used, one notably similar example being Costello's Extended Length of Utterance (ELU) program (Costello, 1983) which like the Lidcombe Program is still used widely today. (See also Ingham, 1984 for a review of operant approaches to the treatment of early stuttering, and also the selected reading list at the end of this chapter.)

Table 10.1 Similarities and differences between the GILCU approach and the Lidcombe Program

	GILCU	*Lidcombe Program*
Theoretical basis	Speech is an operant	Speech is (in its early stages at least) a motor-speech disorder and can be treated as an operant.
Goals	Normal-sounding spontaneous fluency	Normal-sounding spontaneous fluency.
Focus of reinforcement	Primarily punishment of stuttering and praise for fluency	Primarily praise for fluent speaking.
Type of reinforcement	Verbal and tangible	Verbal and tangible.
Parental involvement	Parents taught to identify and carry out treatment at home	Parents taught to identify and carry out treatment at home.
Use of gradual increase in length of utterance	Applied in a highly controlled manner. Child always begins at a one-word level – then two words etc.	Not controlled as rigorously as GILCU, e.g., child may start the program at 3–5 word level, even though the child may be younger than the school aged child on the GILCU program. There are no formal controls for length of utterance.
Setting for treatment	Treatment initially carried out in structured settings	Treatment carried out mostly at home, and in a variety of settings.
Contingencies for progression within the establishment phase of the program	Complete fluency required at each step before progression through to the next step can take place	No stages as such in phase 1 (establishment). Progression is monitored by severity ratings.
Fluency criteria to move from establishment phase of treatment	Five-minute blocks of speaking in each of three modes: conversation, monologue and reading with less than two stuttering moments within a two-minute speaking period	No formal timed test. Maintenance (phase 2) starts when the child is regularly achieving severity rating scores of 1–2.
Maintenance schedule	Child must achieve set levels of fluency within specific settings. Gradual withdrawal of clinical monitoring over 22-month period	No objectively measured goals for fluency within specific settings. Gradual withdrawal of clinical monitoring over 6–12 month period.

Integrated approaches

Van Riper's approach

To this point two supposed opposite approaches have been outlined. It is, however, quite possible to mix direct and indirect therapeutic strategies. One of the most enduring integrated approaches to preschool therapy was developed by Charles Van Riper and discussed in detail in his book *The Treatment of Stuttering* (Van Riper, 1973) long before the term "integrated" had been coined. The approach has two strands: it is indirect in the sense that there is no modification of moments of stuttering (as there is with his approach to treating established stuttering, see chapter 12); but it is direct in that the clinician works directly with the child as well as the child's family. Like Onslow and colleagues, Van Riper believed that a motor speech deficit was involved in stuttering, but, unlike Onslow, also cited the influence of faulty auditory feedback, as well as environmental factors such as negative emotion and stress as factors which needed to be addressed in therapy.

The overall goal of Van Riper's approach is the establishment of spontaneous fluent speech across all speaking situations. This is achieved by the establishment of "basal level of fluency" through the combined use of (a) modelling fluent speech, (b) reinforcing fluency in the child; (c) providing an optimum setting to allow fluency to develop within the clinic. Using the principles of learning theory, as he advocated in his approach to treating established and chronic stuttering, fluency is then developed by desensitizing the child to external fluency disrupters.

Direct treatment strategy

A key premise in this approach is that speech should be fun for the child, and indeed that the development of stuttering is strongly linked to the child's experiences of speaking most definitely not being an enjoyable experience. Related to this is the concept that speech that is fluent and enjoyable should be self-sustaining. Unlike his approach to treating established stuttering, Van Riper did not even advocate a formal maintenance phase to therapy. Establishing a positive relationship between child and clinician is also central and free play sessions with the child, where the clinician may initially need to say nothing, are advocated with a child who is showing signs of anxiety over his speech. Slowly, the clinician may introduce either symbolic noise sounds (for example, driving a car) and then one- or two-word phrases as the child becomes more comfortable and relaxed with the clinician's presence. As the relationship builds, play will become more interactive and the child will produce more language. All this helps to build a comfortable environment for the child in which fluency can develop.

The single word or short phrase comments and responses of the clinicians actually serve a second purpose: to provide a good speech model. In constraining language in this way Van Riper sought to minimize demands on the motor speech system that he considered underdeveloped. Van Riper was also keen to harness the use of natural fluency enhancers, such as supportive rhythmic stimuli (such as clapping) and echoic speech, both of which can be built into games. The second aim of reinforcing fluency is achieved by showing interest when the child is producing fluent speech, whilst appearing relatively disinterested in stuttered speech. Contrast this method of delivering feedback, where the child is unaware of the focus of the reinforcement, to that of the Lidcombe Program where, from a very early stage in therapy, the clinician and caregivers directly help the child to recognize moments of stuttering (through the use of negative comments) and fluency (through the use of praise and other tangible reinforcement).

Desensitization

Once the child is able to maintain fluency over a period of a few minutes, the clinician will deliberately start to interrupt the child's speech flow. This may continue until the clinician senses that the child is about to stutter, at which point the interruptions stop, allowing fluency to return. This pattern can then be repeated, with increased incidence as the child becomes more used to the interruptions, and fluency becomes less affected by them. Although there is no formal maintenance stage, in the latter stages of therapy the clinician may wish to change the child's negative reactions to moments of stuttering by rephrasing or summarizing after the child has shown anxiety and concern following a moment of stuttering. This approach is consistent throughout the treatment period, with the aim of replacing negative associations of speaking with pleasant ones.

Parent counselling

The legacy of Van Riper's approach to parent counselling is reflected in the parent–child interaction model described earlier in this chapter. Through discussion with the parents, the child's environment is modified to provide a setting that is optimally conducive to improved fluency. As noted earlier in this chapter, this not only involves interaction between parent and child, but may also include issues relating to the child as a part of the family unit, as well as at nursery school and in other related settings. Again, in direct contrast to the Lidcombe approach, the key is to avoid the child developing awareness of the stutter, and thus prevent the development of the secondary characteristics of struggle, escape and avoidance that can become associated with increased awareness of stuttering.

Integrated approaches tend to be used more with school age children than preschoolers (see chapter 11). Nevertheless, there are a number of established integrated approaches now used with younger children (for example, see

Adams, 1980; Conture, 1990; Gregory & Hill, 1980; Guitar, 1998; see also further reading).

Summary

Two models of preschool therapy have been outlined: direct and indirect approaches, together with one which combines both approaches. Within this framework, therapy for preschool children has been described from two supposedly opposing positions. One (cognitive) approach in the form of parent–child interaction deals with stuttering by changing the child's environment toward one that is highly conducive to the production of fluent speech. An alternative approach based on operant conditioning theory directly deals with stuttering by the careful rewarding of fluent speech and gentle verbal admonishment of moments of stuttering. While the two approaches are driven by different philosophies and take very different perspectives, there are some common features to both. Both models emphasize the importance of parental involvement, and parents play a critical role in administering therapy. Further, while the change in parent–child interaction is central to the PCI model of intervention, it may be that there are environmental forces at work within the Lidcombe framework also as the child enjoys specific talking time at home. Although classed as a direct approach to therapy, the Lidcombe approach does not directly modify motor speech patterning (again similar to PCI). As with integrated approaches used with older children and adults (see chapters 11 and 12), it is common to combine procedures that target speech modification with those that modify the child's environment.

So how can it be that one approach which directly and openly brings moments of stuttering to the child's attention and one which seeks to avoid the child becoming aware of his speech difficulties can both be effective? As yet there are no firm answers. Generally speaking, direct approaches are more likely to be used with children with more established and more severe stuttering, so perhaps direct comparisons cannot reliably be made because we are not comparing like with like. Also, despite the documented longer term success of the Lidcombe Program, the critical components of the approach have not yet been identified. For example, it is not yet absolutely clear as to the extent that the daily one-to-one time which the parent spends with the child is in itself a critical factor; thus potentially introducing elements of the PCI approach to the therapy. Conversely, a criticism of cognitive therapies such as PCI has been a lack of objective data-based evidence to support their effectiveness, although there is currently work in progress that aims to address this issue.

The Lidcombe and PCI approaches described above represent opposite philosophies on stuttering, and consequently offer different strategies as to how the disorder can best be dealt with. Comparisons of these approaches is intended to inform the reader of the range of thinking that exists on the subject of early intervention therapy. There are, of course, a great number of established therapies which combine cognitive and behavioural approaches to the treatment of early stuttering which we have not mentioned here. The reader is directed to a selection of these in the further reading section.

Key points

- Factors such as familial history of stuttering, poor language, phonological or motor speech skills, high parental expectation, extra demands placed on language processing, all increase the likelihood of eventual stuttering.
- The Demands and Capacities model provides a useful framework with which to explain why a child may be at risk of stuttering, or actually is stuttering, and also how therapy intends to deal with the issues. In the case of interaction therapy, this will be done by reducing the demands placed on the child, whose capacity for fluent speech and language has (for a number of potential reasons) been reduced. Whether the Lidcombe Program increases capacity or reduces demand awaits the outcome of studies currently underway to determine the exact underlying nature of the operant that the child responds to.
- Families of preschool children who are not stuttering but are at increased risk of doing so may benefit from a counselling approach to minimize realization of the increased risk.
- Therapy may take the form of indirect (environment modification) or direct (stuttering modification) approaches. The direct approaches include strongly operant regimes (for example, Lidcombe Program) and less rigorously enforced speech modification approaches (Van Riper, 1973; and see further reading).
- Although well described, there is comparatively little controlled outcome data on PCI therapy, but there is work in progress to address this issue.

Further reading

Conture, E. G. (1990). *Stuttering* (2nd ed.). Englewood Cliffs, NJ: Prentice-Hall.
Here Conture describes his stuttering modification approach to early onset stuttering in which he emphasizes the differences between causal and precipitating factors. Therapy combines direct stuttering approaches (modifying airflow and articulation (see following chapter) with PCI features, such as advising and encouraging parents. Particularly, Conture is keen to ensure that parents do not feel guilt toward their child's problems. The goal is to facilitate easy stuttering rather than to attempt to eliminate it.

Gregory H. H., & Hill, D. (1980). Stuttering therapy for children. *Seminars in Speech, Language and Hearing, 1*, 351–363.

This speech modification approach known as Easy-Relaxed Approach – smooth Movements (ERA-SM) is taught by modelling, which is gradually phased out as the child becomes skilled at using the techniques in extended speech sequences. Desensitization procedures are also applied, as is a parent counselling program which aims to help the parent identify the situations that result in increased stuttering.

Guitar, B. (1998). *Stuttering: An integrated approach to its nature and treatment* (chapter 13, pp. 337–366). Philadelphia: Lippincott Williams & Wilkins.

A direct treatment approach that primarily relies on fluency shaping strategies, but also combines some Van Riperian stuttering modification strategies and interactional components.

Rustin, L., Botterill, W., & Kelman, E. (1996). *Assessment and therapy for young disfluent children*. London: Whurr.

A thorough guide to the use of interaction therapy, as practised at the Michael Palin Centre for stammering children. The text is punctuated throughout with helpful case examples to illustrate assessment and therapeutic procedures.

Onslow, M., Packman, A., & Harrison, E. (2003). *The Lidcombe Program of early stuttering intervention: A clinician's guide*. Austin, TX: Pro-Ed.

This recent edited publication covers all aspects of the Lidcombe Program, both theoretical and practical, in great detail. This is the most comprehensive single source for information on this approach currently available. In addition to chapters by the editors on the development and procedures involved in the running of the Lidcombe Program, there are further chapters containing descriptions as to how the program is being developed worldwide.

Ryan, B. P. (1974). *Programmed stuttering therapy for children and adults*. Springfield, IL: Charles C. Thomas.

A strong advocate of operant conditioning in stuttering therapy, Ryan's long-established GILCU program takes an operant-driven fluency shaping approach to therapy (see section above). Some consider this book better than the second edition (Ryan, 2001), which is recommended reading in the following chapter.

Van Riper, C. (1973). *The treatment of stuttering*. Englewood Cliffs, NJ: Prentice Hall.

Van Riper's approach has been outlined above. This text provides the original source for his treatment of beginning stuttering.

11 The treatment of stuttering in school age children

Introduction

School brings a new environment, new challenges, new competitions, new friends, a new set of expectations and a whole new set of rules to the child. Some children may have already attended preschool nursery groups, but the atmosphere here is informal, and for many children primary school is the first time that they are aware of a need to be accepted by their peers. Even at this early age, children who are either rather tall, or rather short, have red hair, ears which stick out a little, wear glasses, or have any other feature that might be seen as distinguishing are very likely to have these aspects pointed out to them by their classmates. These observations may for the most part be good natured, but even well-intentioned comments can be upsetting, and barbed comments can positively hurt. Relatedly, the onset of school can also very quickly bring into sharp focus any difficulty that a child may have that may set him aside as being different in any way from the norm. Those with any form of obvious physical handicap are at risk, and children with stutters who experience physical difficulty in saying words may be particularly vulnerable. Now the child has to deal not only with a stutter, but the reactions of his peers and his teachers. Some children who stutter find little problem fitting in and making friends. For others, this can be a difficult and lonely time. At a period where it is likely the child is becoming more aware of his difficulty in speech, he now has to deal with negative reactions from his classmates (Franck, Jackson, Pimentel, & Greenwood, 2003), and social rejection and bullying can be a particular problem for many children who stutter (Davis, Howell, & Cook, 2002; Hugh-Jones & Smith, 1999; Langevin, Bortnick, Hammer, & Weibe, 1998). Unlike many with physical disabilities, the child with a stutter may to a greater or lesser extent be able to hide this problem. This in turn may lead to increased struggle, tension and escape behaviour, which may result in more stuttering and more unwanted attention focused on the lack of verbal acuity.

There may also be corresponding implications for school work. Some teachers, who are unsure as how best to help may unknowingly contribute to the problem by insisting he directly answers questions in front of the class.

Under such "demand speaking" situations, participation in class activities can diminish, and the child may start to develop ways to avoid responding to questions in class. We have seen a great many children, even at primary school level, who would prefer to be thought of as unintelligent, and uninterested, and will either avoid answering questions or answer with a shrug of the shoulders or give a deliberately incorrect answer to a question they knew the answer to, rather than be seen to stutter. This can lead to the teacher's misperception that the child is lazy or uninterested. Unfortunately there is some evidence to suggest that teachers view their stuttering pupils less favourably. This increases the sense of failure in the child and exacerbates levels of frustration which are already likely to be high. Subsequently, the child may either directly or indirectly convey his concerns to his parents, and some children may resort to tricks and even truancy to avoid school.

Of course, this rather negative scenario is not representative of the experience of all children who stutter, many of whom manage very well at school, and are little impacted by the changes school life brings, but there remains a significant number who, even by the age of 6, have already developed negative self-perceptions traditionally considered to develop later in childhood (Vanryckeghem et al., 2005). This is of particular concern because, although these struggle and escape behaviours are concerns in their own right, the building of these secondary behaviours indicates the establishment of the disorder and is not a good prognostic for recovery (Gregory, 2003). If not dealt with, they set the tone for increase in avoidance and struggle, and the further establishment of negative self-perception into later school life and adulthood. Like the primary characteristics of the disorder, they are more effectively treated if uncovered earlier rather than later.

Group therapy

As the child's social world starts to expand with the onset of primary school, and as social sophistication increases as he progresses toward adolescence, so different therapeutic formats can be introduced to deal with stuttering which may now be taking on a different form. Commonplace in adult therapy approaches (see chapter 12), group therapy is also used by some clinicians with adolescents and older primary school children (Baumeister, Casper, & Herziger, 2000; Boberg & Kully, 1985, 1994; Craig et al., 1996; Druce et al., 1997; Rustin, Cook, & Spence, 1995; Mitchell & Ward, 2005). With adult group therapy, groups which follow more of a fluency shaping approach tend to follow an intensive format running for seven or more hours per day, five days per week for two or three weeks, while those which take a stuttering modification perspective may use an extended time frame, with groups meeting for two hours or so once a week for up to a year (see chapter 12 on adult therapy). With adolescents and younger children, this split seems somewhat less clear. For example, while Boberg and Kully's (1985) fluency shaping based program does follow an intensive format, there are a number of operant-based programs which work on a one-to-one basis (e.g., Costello & Ingham, 1999; Ryan, 1984) and approaches which integrate stuttering modification and fluency shaping techniques which mix both group and one-to-one therapy (e.g., Mitchell & Ward, 2005).

Whether group therapy is long term or intensive it holds a number of advantages. From a clinician's perspective this can be a very time-efficient way of seeing those with fluency disorders (Druce et al., 1997). For some with busy clinics with long waiting lists, running groups can be one way of bringing down waiting time for therapy. Although seeing clients sooner rather than later would seem to make good clinical practice, expediency alone is not a reason for employing a particular therapeutic format, and there are associated benefits in seeing clients in a group.

First, each individual within the group is now no longer the only person with a "speech problem", and feelings of isolation are reduced (Bajina, 1995; Fawcus, 1995; Williams & Dugan, 2002). Group members can gain increasing confidence from being around others in the safe environment of the clinic where their speech may be no more or less remarkable than that of their peers. Particularly, there is the benefit of being able to explore both stuttering behaviours and reactions to stuttering amongst those who have experienced similar problems. To illustrate this point I recall a group of teenagers recently seen at the Apple House who were exploring their feelings and attitudes toward stuttering as a part of an identification phase of the course. As a result of this discussion, the subject of avoidance when speaking on the telephone came up. One group member who had been a little more reserved than others hesitatingly volunteered the fact that he would sometimes give himself another name rather than stutter on his real name when speaking on the telephone; a strategy he felt very unhappy about using. This was the first time he had disclosed this information to anyone, but on hearing this, to his great surprise, two rather more confident group members immediately spoke up, saying that they used the exact same strategy. All three had previously assumed that they were the only people who avoided in this way. The relief on their faces to learn otherwise was plain to see. So for the child, having one's peers help in the process of identifying both positive and negative aspects of speech can seem more relevant than having these things pointed out by a clinician. Intensive group therapy also can be highly motivating since rapid changes in fluency can be made within a short period of time (Druce et al., 1997).

While group work can carry many benefits, this therapeutic format is not without its problems. First, any group needs to be assembled with some care. For example, children presenting with co-occurring problems such as significant language delay or disorder or with cognitive impairment may do better with individual therapy, or within a group whose members have similar issues. Similarly, those also diagnosed with social phobia will feel more comfortable in a one-to-one setting. One criticism is that in following a set schedule for a group of individuals the individual needs of each member might not be met as effectively were they to be seen on a one-to-one basis. Some have also argued that the rapid changes that can be made with intensive approaches to group therapy may be equally quickly lost once the reinforcing effects of the group are suddenly withdrawn (Kroll, 2003). To counter these problems, it is common for intensive programs to include regular follow-up or "maintenance" sessions which follow the course. These meetings usually adhere to the group format and focus on consolidating the progress made in the earlier intensive part of the course. Some programs prefer to have individual follow-up sessions (Mitchell & Ward, 2005) to help individualize the carryover of gains made, whilst others, (e.g., Van Riper, 1973 when outlining his block modification program for adults) advocate a more even split between weekly group sessions and individual therapy (see next chapter).

Treatment of primary school age stuttering

Awareness of stuttering

Consistent with the need to fit in, school age children, who as preschoolers had perhaps enjoyed coming for therapy, may now show concern about being singled out for intervention, being seen as different or "having a problem". School age children may also differ from their preschool counterparts in that they may have already experienced therapy. Naturally, if they consider this to have been unhelpful, they are less likely to want to attend again. With increased awareness comes the unwanted correlate of the development of primary stuttering behaviours, and usually an increase in secondary behaviours. Although we see this in some preschool children, these problems are more commonly seen during the primary school years. Conture (2001), for example, suggests that these usually occur at age 9 to 10. This means that in addition to the word and part-word repetitions more typical of early onset stuttering, the clinician will now need to deal with the more established stuttering behaviours of sound prolongations and blocks (as in Van Riper's Track I development; see chapter 7). Similarly, secondary escape behaviours such as rapid blinking and head nodding may appear, as might the development of specific word, sound or person fears. Speaking situations both within school such as talking at show and tell, and at home such as talking on the phone may be avoided.

Maturation of the nervous system

A second issue that directly affects therapy relates to plasticity of the nervous system. During the preschool years and early primary school years the central nervous system seems more able to "automatically" take on and process novel information than later in life. So, while we have greater cognitive resources as adults than as children, we are likely to find it harder, say, to learn a second language at 35 than we are as a preschooler. This early ability to learn and assimilate new information in the early years seems particularly noticeable in the linguistic domain, and is important for us as clinicians. Whether for this reason or because of sociological or environmental influences, there is at least anecdotal evidence from a number of clinical centres to suggest that approaches such as the Lidcombe program are less effective with children at school and particularly those who are above age seven.[1] As we have seen in the previous chapter, early intervention is strongly favoured.

Summary

In sum, the early school years bring new challenges and pressures to the child who stutters. Peer group pressure may result in teasing, which in turn may lead to an increase in anxiety, avoidance and withdrawal. It may also lead to reluctance on behalf of the child to attend therapy sessions. As the child becomes older, peer group acceptance will become increasingly important. CNS maturational factors may also mean that therapeutic approaches that work very well in preschool children may be less effective when applied a few years later. On top of this, the disorder may now be more firmly established, with secondary behaviours increasingly evident. This increases the need for more complex treatment strategies which will need directly to take on board the child's feelings and attitudes towards his speech difficulties. It also indicates that the prognoses for complete recovery from the disorder, whether spontaneous or therapeutically induced, now becomes less favourable.

Vocal tract dynamics: a modular perspective to treatment

There are a great number of treatment approaches for primary school age children (Conture, 2001; Cooper & Cooper, 1985; Costello & Ingham, 1999; Gregory, 2003; Gregory & Campbell, 1988; Gregory & Hill, 1984; Guitar, 1998; Onslow et al., 2003; Pindzola, 1987; Rustin et al., 1996; Ryan, 1974; Wall & Myers, 1995; Williams, 1971), yet the components which make up therapy are drawn from a comparatively small array of therapeutic tools, and it is common to see similar techniques often appear in different programs under different guises. As is the case with the treatment of adult stuttering, therapy can usually be seen as comprising one of two approaches:

1   *Integrated approaches.* Here, there is consideration of the cognitive and affective issues which are associated with the child's experiences of having a stutter. There is also direct work on the modification of moments of stuttering. Cognitive components typically form a less significant part

---

1 Note that the Lidcombe Program was designed specifically for use with preschool children. In Australia, where the program was developed, preschool means up to the age of 6.

of the blend in the treatment of primary school children than with older children and adults.

2   *Fluency shaping approaches.* Here, the goal is not to modify stuttering, but rather completely to replace it (together with the restructuring of nonstuttered aspects of the child's speech). This is achieved by applying a range of fluency controlling techniques, usually implemented within a slow-speech framework, which fundamentally changes the way that respiration, phonation and articulation are coordinated for speech.

Although some of these techniques may be similar to those applied in integrated stuttering modification approaches, the significant difference lies with the fact that the aim of the fluency shaping approach is to rebuild all speech patterns, thus ensuring that stuttering simply does not arise. The purpose of the stuttering modification process, on the other hand, is to facilitate a more easy and controlled type of stuttering.

Below, first we describe a number of commonly used techniques to modify speech production before seeing the various ways these can be put to use in the treatment of primary school children who stutter.

Speech modification: rationale

The clinician has at her disposal a range of techniques that alter the way in which speech is coordinated. The speech modification approach has typically been associated with fluency shaping procedures, but increasingly these techniques form the building blocks of fluency in a number of programs, which use similar procedures but applied on a less rigorous basis. The underlying rationale for using speech modification techniques is that speech is directly controlled by three interlinked motor speech subsystems: those at a respiratory level where breathing for speech is generated; a laryngeal level where that air supply is turned into the voiced and voiceless sounds of speech;[2] and an articulatory level where control over structures such as the lips and tongue shape the sounds into recognizable units of comprehension – phonemes, syllables and words. In this model stuttering is considered to arise due to some incoordination: (a) within a given system; (b) between the relevant motor speech subsystems; or (c) arising from a combination of these two. As we have seen in chapter 4, there is evidence that all three motor speech subsystems can be affected in stuttered speech, but let's now look more closely as

---

2 Actually, the larynx (or more specifically the vocal folds within the larynx) is unique in that it functions not only at a phonatory level (as the sound generating device) but also at an articulatory level. For example, the glottal fricative [h] as in "hello" is produced by the partial adduction of the vocal cords, which constricts the airflow rising from the lungs, resulting in the friction needed to produce this sound. The larynx's primary function in speech, however, remains as a sound-source provider.

to how these aspects of speech production can be modified to produce a more fluent and less effortful output in a generic approach to stuttering modification.

Smooth airflow

The speech act starts with an intake of air followed by controlled exhalation. No matter how well controlled motor speech activity may be managed "downstream" of the lungs in the vocal tract, if the lungs are producing, say, spasmodic pulses of egressive air instead of a smooth and continuous output, then disrupted speech will inevitably result. In fact, a number of therapeutic approaches; for example, the Valsalva technique (Parry, 2000) and McGuire program (McGuire, 2003) base the speech modification aspects of their therapies solely on this area of vocal tract activity (see chapter 14).

The idea is that a smooth continuous airflow is prerequisite to produce fluent speech. Many airflow modification programs therefore start by looking at clients' breathing patterns. One commonly held starting point on the road to "smooth airflow" is the importance of using diaphragmatic breathing patterns. The basic principle here is that the lungs being pear shaped hold more air further down than at the more narrow part near the top. It is also the case that a significant number of children who stutter find a key feature is that they frequently run out of breath even close to or right at the beginning of a sentence, when a breath has only just been taken. For those who clearly have a particular problem with controlling exhalation for speech, focusing on improving control by accessing a more efficient use of lung air would seem to make perfect sense, but many clinicians advocate the use of diaphragmatic breathing as a matter of course for all clients, whether there appears to be a particular difficulty with breathing for speech or not.

Breathing diaphragmatically involves using the diaphragmatic muscle. This is a large sheet of muscle whose movement can be felt underneath the peripheral musculature at the front of the stomach, by applying light pressure of the hand at the midpoint between the xyphoid process (at the base of the sternum, or breast-bone) and the navel. When breathing in, the hand will be seen to rise as the diaphragm contracts, with the aerodynamic effect sucking air into the lungs. As the air is released, the hand placed on the stomach should slowly move back to its resting point. The clinician may model this type of breathing, contrasting it with the more shallow *clavicular* type of breathing, which is typical of the breathing patterns of many people who stutter (as well, we should add, of many people who do not stutter). Here, breathing occurs from higher in the chest and inhalation can be seen in the expansion of the rib cage and often raising of the shoulders (hence the reference to the clavical, a bone running somewhat parallel to the upper-most rib across the front of the shoulder). Clinicians will also demonstrate that with effective use of diaphragmatic breathing, the only movement will come from below the rib cage, and that any movement from the rib cage or shoulder area indicates a less effective and potentially more tense manner of breathing.

The instantiation of diaphragmatic breathing may be achieved in a structured manner using structured exercises. Initially, control of breathing may start with slow inspiration over a few seconds followed by slow exhalation over a similar time frame. As the client becomes more confident and adept, exhalation may be produced on a barely audible extended [s] and then [a]. These productions may be timed to provide objective measures of airflow control. It is important throughout that the client does not try to force out the last bit of lung air, and that he actively stops the exhalation before residual lung-air capacity is reached.

Diaphragmatic breathing is unquestionably a very effective method of breathing, but although an opera singer or a 100-metre runner may require the maximum air supply the lungs can produce, do we really need to have such large reserves of air in order to produce speech? One sentence may last less than one second, an average sentence only a few seconds. Clearly a great many people speak without using diaphragmatic breathing and have no difficulty either maintaining fluency or sufficient air supply. So why the importance of diaphragmatic breathing? First, if a person is breathing diaphragmatically, the extra lung air at the speaker's disposal may give the individual a greater time frame within which to implement fluency controlling techniques (see below). Second, people who stutter commonly report sensations of extra tension in the chest. In some cases this may be related to an increase in subglottal air pressure that can result from the air trapped in the lungs during a laryngeal block, but it may also occur in the form of general increase in levels of physical tension. Diverting the focus of breathing to the diaphragm can help dissipate this tension. Third, having greater lung-air reserves available to the speaker at least allows the option of using that supply to continue with speech, even if there is some stuttering which is resulting in an interruption to normal breathing patterns. Finally, stuttering occurs where there are natural breaks in the airflow. Encouraging smooth and continuous airflow helps demonstrate that there are no natural breaks between words in normal speech, and that a stoppage of air need only occur when a new breath group is started. Thus smooth airflow can be seen as the glue which (in motoric terms) binds the words together.

Soft glottal onsets

This technique builds on the basis of the smooth airflow techniques, combining with this a way of smoothly (or softly) initiating vocal fold vibration. Primarily used with words which start with a vowel or semi-vowel, the idea is first to make sure that a sufficient and effective air stream is initiated by use of smooth airflow techniques, and then vocal fold vibration for the word-initial vowel is then slowly brought in. As with the airflow technique, this is developed through a series of exercises. The fundamental point is that blocking on vowels is often associated with spasmodic laryngeal closure. When this occurs, the vocal folds are brought together abruptly and involuntarily, occluding the airway and prohibiting vocal fold vibration. (If they are brought together tightly, they cannot vibrate.) This is contrasted with an onset to the vowel where air is already moving between the vocal folds, and vocal fold vibration is built up from this position of an already moving airstream.

The clinician may begin by contrasting a "hard" glottal onset before a vowel with a "soft" one (for example [ʔa] as opposed to [ha]) and asking the client to identify differences. She may also explain and demonstrate that hard glottal onsets, when extended, will sound like laryngeal blocks. This is why a strategy that increases the size of the timing window in which the onset of airflow and vocal fold vibration is introduced is desirable. When in the early stages of learning this technique, the beginning of the word may also sound slightly stretched, thus a rather rudimentary soft glottal start will sound as if a [h] has been placed before the word initial vowel. In this way, *Amsterdam* might sound more like *hhaaaamsterdam*. In the early stages of acquiring this technique the word onset may be reduced in volume, which builds to a normal level over the first slightly elongated syllable. Initially, all this can sound rather clumsy and the [h] intrusive. A part of the development of skill with this technique is to establish steady yet inaudible airflow on which vocal fold vibration can be built.

Soft consonant contact

This technique focuses on reducing the force of articulatory contact and is applied particularly to word initial consonants, but also semi-vowels such as [j] as in "yes" and [w] as in "wood". Consonants are produced by the bringing together of two articulators, which may include the lips and teeth, the tongue, the hard and soft palates; either to the point where they form:

- *plosive or stop sounds*: with this class of sound the two relevant articulators form a complete occlusion in the vocal tract; for example [p, d, k].
- *fricatives*: here the articulators are brought close enough together for the airflow between them to produce audible friction; for example [v, s, θ]. All have an audible hissing type of quality to their production.
- *approximants or liquids*: these sounds are made by "approximating" two articulators, but not close enough to the point where friction is heard. This group includes sounds such as [r, w, j, l].[3]
- *affricates*: these comprise the combination of a plosive with a fricative

3 Some of these sounds, for example, /r/, /j/ (as in "yes") and /w/ are known as semi-vowels. This means that in addition to being used to describe consonants, they have a vowel-like quality, also. This becomes more obvious when the sound is stretched, so for example, /j/ will sound similar to the vowel in "bee" if it is extended.

made immediately afterwards and at the same place in the vocal tract. Examples of English affricates include the sounds at the beginning of the words "church" and "jam" respectively.

A soft contact, as the name implies, is produced by a gentle and tension-free contact between the articulators. Stuttering is strongly associated with increased levels of articulatory tension, and this new pattern involves reducing this to a bare minimum. Again, the basis of the soft contact approach lies in the initial use of a smooth airflow.

Approaches to building competence in use of soft contacts vary, but a common one is for the clinician to work through a sequence of simple nonwords which include a range of phonetic categories represented in word initial position, as we have briefly outlined above. Often, the clinician may choose to start with sounds which are made by the more visible articulators, i.e., the lips and teeth. The clinician may begin to introduce the soft/hard approach by producing simple words with varying degrees of tension. For example, "big" may be produced with exaggerated bilabial (lip) contact. The client will note the tension and the accompanying delay in releasing the lips for the following vowel, and the relationship between tension, delay and stuttering can be discussed. In contrast, an exaggeratedly soft production can then be produced, with the lips being brought together very lightly to produce a sound with no tension. The client can then experiment with their own productions using varying degrees of "softness" of contact, with very soft (or "light") contacts doing away with the complete occlusion and turning the plosive into a fricative. With the soft contact approach, as with soft glottal onset and smooth airflow, it is important that the client becomes attuned to identifying differences between different levels of articulatory tension if he is to be able to self-monitor and make the necessary articulatory adjustments away from the clinic and the feedback of the clinician.

Consonants tend to be stuttered on more than vowels and certain sound classes are more likely to be stuttered on than others. Plosives, as we have already mentioned in chapter 4, may be especially difficult, as they require a particularly precise timing relationship between airflow, phonatory onset and articulatory movement acting over a very short time period. The fact that airflow is completely stopped during their production also increases the likelihood of difficulty with these sounds. Particularly if a plosive occurs as sentence initial position, then speech involves combining airflow, phonation and articulatory movement from a preceding silence. Approximants, on the other hand, can be produced with a greater degree of temporal and articulatory imprecision, yet still be easily recognized.

Integration of speech modification techniques

These techniques are usually taught first at word level, then two word, phrase, sentence, and so on, mixing in increasing levels of motoric and linguistic difficulty as therapy progresses (i.e., using words with more complicated phonetic/phonotactic structures, together with less familiar and longer words and longer speech sequences). A slightly slower speech rate is often encouraged and to start with the emphasis is on the smooth initiation of initial word onset, which is usually where the great majority of stuttering is found. The child then practises longer speech sequences, learning to pause and repeat the process when a new breath is needed.

Adjuncts

The basic idea behind usage of these universally applied fluency techniques (or fluency skills, fluency enhancing gestures, speech skills, or whatever other name they may be called on any particular program) is very similar: they promote speech which is produced with reduced muscular effort and which is less tense. However, the schedule in which they are applied and the degree to which they are used varies considerably, and gives rise to the very varied speech modification programs which currently exist. Some programs use these approaches together with other fluency skills, which in effect are hybrids of the three already mentioned. For example, *blending* is a term used on some programs to describe the use of smooth airflow seamlessly to connect one word to another, but it is not a fundamentally new or different technique in itself. Note that this is another example of a technique that is merely making conscious a process which is natural and unconscious in normal speech, but which becomes disrupted due to stuttering.

Fluency shaping vs stuttering modification

These basic fluency skills can form the groundwork of either stuttering modification or fluency shaping approaches (see Figure 11.1). For example, many fluency shaping programs aimed at adolescents or adults use prolonged speech (Boberg & Kully, 1985, 1994; Craig et al., 1996; Ryan, 1974, 2001; Ward, 1992; Webster, 1980); requiring all techniques to be continuously employed. With programs for younger children, there is usually a smaller reliance on the overlearning of the fluency techniques. We do not generally use prolonged speech as a vehicle for learning speech control techniques on our treatment programs at the Apple House, and we do suggest that for many children there should actually be varying levels of control which can be employed. For example, it may be appropriate for some children to employ fluency techniques more rigorously in more difficult speaking situations (one common example being when introducing oneself to a stranger). Other children may benefit from using the techniques on a more regular basis. In our programs for secondary school children and adults these techniques may be applied on an "as needs" basis, with the client and clinician together determining when (and to what extent) these fluency aids should be used.

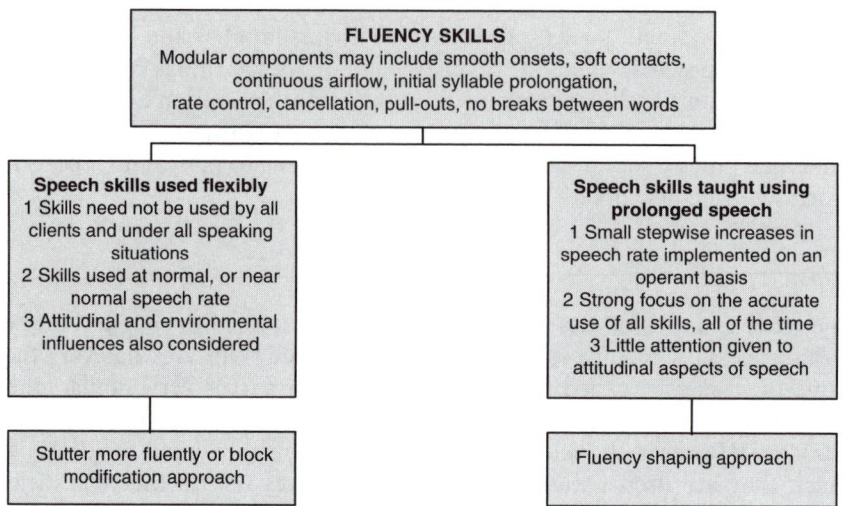

Figure 11.1 A modular perspective on the implementation of fluency skills.

The integration of speech modification and cognitive/attitudinal approaches

There is some consensus in the literature that treatment of school age children should be comprehensive, attempting not only to improve fluency but also communication skills more generally across a range of settings, not the least of these being in the classroom (Conture & Guitar, 1993; Williams & Dugan, 2002; Yaruss, 2002; Yaruss & Reardon, 2003). Programs which integrate aspects of fluency shaping techniques (e.g., Boberg and Kully, 1985; Neilson & Andrews, 1993) and stuttering modification (Van Riper, 1973) enable the child more readily to control and reduce the stutter, but at the same time address negative perceptions and attitudes about stuttering. Cooper and Cooper (1996), for example, consider Guitar's (1998) integrated approach to therapy the most efficacious. Integrated approaches also allow for flexibility in treatment to meet the varying needs of those attending for therapy (Healey, Scott, & Ellis, 1995; Mitchell & Ward, 2005; Ramig & Bennett, 1997).

The Apple House approach

We can demonstrate one way in which these generic stuttering modification techniques can be incorporated into an integrated fluency program by out-lining the group therapy approach taken in the treatment of primary school children at the Apple House. There is preliminary outcome data from 53 children who passed through the program between 2000 and 2005 that indicate this approach, which combines both cognitive and behavioural components, is effective in reducing severity of stuttering and improving positive perceptions of speech (Mitchell & Ward, 2005).

The policy at the Apple House is to see younger primary school children (5–7 year olds) individually, whilst 8- to 12-year-old children are usually seen for group therapy. There are sometimes compelling reasons why one-to-one contact may be desirable amongst these older children (for example with a child who has significant concomitant difficulties such as severe dyspraxia or being learning disabled). However, experience tells us that group therapy, which is a commonly used approach with older children and adults, can also be a very effective format for dealing with this younger age group.

Goals of the program

The goals of therapy are more attuned to those of stuttering modification rather than fluency shaping, although both approaches are used. The major aims are to provide the children with strategies to control their stuttering which are functional and sustainable; to increase confidence in speaking, and to eliminate avoidance and withdrawal behaviours. A further aim is to reduce stuttering, but where stuttering remains we place great importance on easy stuttering.

Parental involvement

Group therapy combines stuttering modification behavioural and cognitive management techniques in a program that runs over five full days, together with three individual follow-up sessions and a further group follow-up day at three months post clinic. Parents play an important role in therapy and consequently there is also a parents' group meeting a week before the course. This provides an opportunity for parents to tell us about the specific issues which concern them and their child. During this meeting we also outline the goals and features of the course, explain what we expect from the families and the children, and in return what the parents can expect from us and the program. We talk a little about possible causes of stuttering and stress the idea that while the course will provide the starting point for improved fluency, it may take considerable time before controlled stuttering will become truly established (or further improved).

We discuss any issues or problems with parents as they arise during the program, and in addition parents are actively involved in some of their child's home assignments during the course of the week. Teachers are contacted in advance of the course and feedback sheets on the teachers' perceptions are returned to the clinic. Wherever possible, a clinician will visit the school to discuss the child with the headteacher and teacher.

Assessment

Children are assessed for speech fluency and speech rate during spontaneous speech, confrontation naming, oral reading and a rote counting task. Clinicians later review the videotaped recordings and add comments on factors such as severity, tension levels, avoidance and other verbal and nonverbal behaviour. Children also complete in-house questionnaires as to how they feel about their fluency and how big a concern it is to them. The Children's Attitude Test (CAT; De Nil & Brutten, 1991) is also completed.

Identification: explaining stuttering

An important difference between school aged children and their younger counterparts is that now they are becoming increasingly aware of their difficulties. It is important for children to be active in the therapeutic process. This first involves bringing the stutter out into the open; for example, having a child with a covert stutter becoming more comfortable with stuttering openly, or encouraging a child with a more obvious stutter to better explain what is happening when he stutters. Note that even for those with quite severe stuttering, the stutter may be something that both he and his parents avoid discussing. It is not unusual for parents to apparently ignore their children's difficulties in the belief that bringing attention to it will exacerbate the problem.

The therapist must from the start develop a positive, understanding and trusting relationship. An important step toward increased fluency begins with discussing a little about what stuttering is. Using carefully worded language, the clinician explains that although nobody knows for certain why stuttering happens, we do know it is not the child's fault (which can be a surprisingly common misperception amongst a number of children). Some children want to know about what causes stuttering, whilst others are less interested in the details and really just want it fixed. With those who want to know more we explain that stuttering can run in families and that there may be differences in the way the brain deals with language (although we clearly point out that children who stutter are just as intelligent as their classmates who do not). We also talk about communication more generally, and what is good and bad communication. Importantly, we discuss the fact that stuttering need not get in the way of being a great communicator. Everyone including clinicians, we add, make mistakes in their speech and may get stuck from time to time. Related to this, we spend time talking about what is good communication and the use of such features as eye contact, turn-taking, body language, and such like. We finish this part of the session by making the point that a great many people who don't stutter are very bad communicators, and that many people who stutter, despite their difficulties and sometimes actually sometimes because of their difficulties, are very good communicators.

We then go on to talk about feelings associated with stuttering and any tricks that may develop alongside in attempts to hide or change the stutter. Like Fawcus (1995) we have found Sheehan's iceberg model of great value here (even some younger primary school children are able to use this to good advantage). Particularly, we have found that group icebergs (where individual contributions from the children are pooled to create a single iceberg) can be particularly revealing, with youngsters able, usually for the first time, to share the feelings they have about their stutter openly with others who are experiencing similar difficulties.

Desensitization

Once group members have had a chance to get to know each other, we have the children identify their stuttering during a short talk which is video-recorded. Before doing this we talk to the group, explaining that everybody has slightly different problems with their speech, and that the best way of trying to deal with those problems is by first being able to see exactly what they are. We also say that we want to look out for what is really good in their speech. When we play back the video, the child appearing on the video has the first opportunity to tell us about what he liked about the talk and what he didn't. Afterwards, clinicians and other group members may add their comments. This is often a good time to discuss the secondary behaviours that will be appearing on the screen. We discuss the fact that these are learned behaviours and can be changed. All this may sound a daunting task for young children, but almost invariably they find it a positive experience, with their peers quick to tell them what they thought was good about their performance. We also add how, by agreeing to do the video, they are already learning not to be intimidated by their stutter, which is a really important step in the process of change they have embarked on. By the end of the second morning of the course the children will know about their stutter, both primary and secondary behaviours, and are usually happy to be freely talking about them.

At this time we also talk about avoidance. (This will usually have already come up as an issue on the group iceberg.) Again the group format encourages the children to be more forthcoming when talking about this important aspect. As more children tell how they avoid certain situations, it is common for other quieter group members to join in, encouraged by the fact that others do similar things to avoid being seen to stutter.

Stuttering modification

We employ a number of fluency techniques, including all those described earlier in this chapter, to help control stuttering, although we use some different terminology, for example, "smooth start" instead of soft contacts. We refer to these various fluency techniques and others relating to more general communication skills such as good eye contact as "stammer stars".[4] We referred earlier to the idea of these techniques being modular, which is the basis they are used on this group program. It is explained that just as everybody's stutter is different, so different children will use different stammer stars to help with control. In addition to the techniques already mentioned we may add others: a slower speech may be useful to some children (although this does not mean prolonged speech) as may improved eye contact. We also find the use of cancellation and occasionally pull-outs help some children. (These stuttering modification techniques devised by Van Riper, 1973 are described in detail in the following chapter.) During the week, the children build up information in a folder. In addition to using the appropriate stammer stars, they have mnemonic stickers that they fix to the front of their folders. For example, there is a skateboard for those who are speaking too quickly and need to slow down.

Over the middle period of the week the children build skills in using these fluency techniques, slowly increasing length of utterance whilst maintaining control over their stuttering. To speed the process, we break the group into twos or threes and may even do one-to-one work with some children. This also allows us to help individualize the therapy process. Often, fluency levels are very high at this time and the children can see this improvement in the video presentations they are periodically asked to undertake. During the modification stage, we frequently return to the cognitive issues. As the children become more able to employ their control techniques, we discuss issues such as teasing and bullying and the best ways of dealing with these problems, all using smooth speech. As before, the group format helps considerably here. When talking animatedly about emotive subjects such as bullying, speech fluency is more likely to deteriorate. We alert the children to this and can move on to discuss the fact that stuttering is easier to control in the safe environment of the fluency clinic, and when the subject matter is less complex. These types of discussions also provide a lead-in to the transfer stage of the course.

Transfer

This is a crucial part of any stuttering therapy program and we are well aware that within the one-week group program there is only a limited time in which to help the children become more confident in using controlled fluency in more demanding settings. We would like to have the children based away from the Apple House for part of the penultimate day, but health and safety regulations currently make this very difficult. Instead, we have the children complete a number of transfer assignments on site. These are achieved through the use of structured role play and making phone calls of varying difficulty. Although we collect data on percentage of syllables stuttered and

---

4 The term "stammer" is still preferred in England and Wales.

speech rate, we do not set fluency targets for these with the children. Instead, we prefer to focus on the child's growing ability to use the fluency skills, and on the degree of control that the individual felt he had, together with his ability to self-analyze both positive aspects of his communication, together with those he might still want to change. Where possible, we use data collected at baseline to structure the transfer process in a helpful and hierarchical way, allowing children to follow individualized transfer programs.

Post-clinic assessment

At the end of the five days, the children repeat the same cognitive and speech fluency assessments taken at the beginning of the week. We also collect feedback on how enjoyable and helpful they found the course. At the follow-up parents' evening, parents view videos of their child giving a presentation toward the end of the week and we discuss their child's progress. This meeting also provides an opportunity for the parents to discuss with the clinicians how the fluency has stabilized following the end of the course.

Maintenance

The child is seen for three individual follow-up sessions over the next few weeks. This may be by either by a local clinician or a specialist Apple House clinician. At three months there is a follow-up day, attended by all the group, where there is reassessment of the children's fluency and their feelings and attitude towards it. If necessary, children may be seen for further one-to-one therapy after this time.

Fluency shaping and stuttering modification: what is what?

There are a number of published programs which integrate stuttering modification techniques together with the consideration of the primary school child's feelings and attitudes toward stuttering (Conture, 1990, 2001; Cooper & Cooper, 1985; Gregory, 2003; Gregory & Campbell, 1988; Gregory and Hill, 1984; Guitar, 1998; Starkweather, 1997; Wall & Myers, 1995). All use a similar range of controlling techniques, but apply them in slightly different ways. For example, Gregory's Easy Relaxed Approach – Smooth Movements (ERA-SM) has the child focus on the use of fluency skills at a slower rate, and only at the beginning of a sentence when there is likely to be greater difficulty. Wall and Myers (1995), on the other hand, focus mostly on a model of relaxed articulation, only looking to change phonatory and respiratory control if light articulation in itself is not successful. Van Riper's concepts of block modification are also used as therapy adjuncts.

As Guitar (1998) has pointed out, there is less of a difference between fluency shaping programs and stuttering modification programs for this age group than there is for adult clients. While agreeing somewhat, I would like to argue for a slightly different take on the situation. First, there are some programs for younger school children which remain heavily operant (Costello, 1984; Costello & Ingham, 1999; Ryan, 1974, 2001; Webster, 1980). For example, Ryan's (1974) preferred approach to treatment involves the use of an approach he terms Gradual Increase in Length and Complexity of Utterance (GILCU; see chapter 10). Costello's (1984) Extended Length of Utterance (ELU) program similarly has the child reduce speech rate, but without the use of delayed auditory feedback (DAF). Speech rate is slowly increased as the child moves through the program. Webster's (1980) program is an adaptation of his precision fluency program for adults, which again takes an operant approach. All of these programs focus on the "mechanics" of speech in a highly structured way and success is measured in behavioural terms. Attitudinal and cognitive aspects are given little attention.

Where I would agree with Guitar (1998) is that there is little difference between most programs which offer integrated perspectives on treatment and those which focus only on stuttering modification (as opposed to fluency shaping). An example can be seen here in Dell's (1993) approach, which Guitar (1998) cites as a primary example of a stuttering modification approach. Here, as with many integrated approaches, there is a strong focus on attitudinal aspects, together with components that turn hard stuttering into easy stuttering. Features such as voluntary stuttering also appear in integrated approaches, and Dell's approach does not seem appreciably different in ethos or in execution to Gregory's, or for that matter the Apple House program. Perhaps in the end we might simply recognize that some programs are "integrated" more toward the fluency shaping end of the continuum, and others more toward the stuttering modification end.

Treatment of secondary school age stuttering

The treatment of older children involves consideration of all of the issues already discussed in relation to the primary school age child who stutters, only now it is unlikely that the stutter can be resolved 100 percent with therapy. Now, the onset of adolescence adds further complexity to the picture. In addition to the problems already noted that stuttering can bring to the primary school pupil, the young person must now also deal with the change from child to adult with all the difficulties that time period can bring. We have mentioned some of the issues which need to be discussed already with reference to the assessment of adolescents who stutter, but the teenage years bring with them strong hormonal changes, together with an increased need for peer acceptance and conformity within the social group.

Stuttering and social anxiety

During this time of significant changes, there are greater pressures than ever on verbal performance. Within school, for example, giving verbal presentations in front of class is now a required part of the school curriculum in the UK. It is quite common for some adolescents who stutter to fake illness, or pretend not to have completed assignments, and use other avoidance techniques to avoid these presentations. Outside school, the pressures on verbal acuity are also increasing. Finding a partner involves talking, and typically talking which carries more meaning is harder for people who stutter. For some, the fear of stuttering in front of someone you want to impress may add further anxiety, and thus increase either the probability of more stuttering, the possibility of social withdrawal, or both. Although it is true that some adolescents who stutter manage the changing demands placed on communication in the teenage years with a minimum of difficulty, this is not the case for many, for whom this time may be characterized by increasing levels of anxiety.

With increasing levels of self-awareness (and self-consciousness) the individual is now likely to become more concerned about his difficulty in communicating and others' reactions to it. There is a growing body of evidence that children who stutter are perceived negatively even at primary school level (Langevin & Hagler, 2004) as well as secondary school and in adulthood (Cooper & Rustin, 1985; Crichton-Smith, 2002; Hayhow, Cray, & Enderby, 2002) and it is rare that stuttering does not have a detrimental effect on the child over the school years (Crichton-Smith, 2002; Hayhow et al., 2002). Given this situation, it would make perfect sense that stuttering leads to increased social anxiety, but the nature of the relationship is still not well understood and the reverse may also be true: that is, social anxiety leads to stuttering. Messenger, Onslow, Packman, and Menzies (2004) found that stutterers' anxiety was linked to the concept of expectance to social harm. Also anxiety is linked specifically to the social domain. Aside from the related effect of social withdrawal, there are direct ramifications for therapy, as anxiety is related to respiration. Messenger et al. (2004) referring to Larson (1988) point out that the limbic system is directly connected to brain centres that regulate vocalization and respiration, and suggest that a significant degree of anxiety is likely to destabilize the respiratory system. As Ezrati-Vinacour and Levin (2004) suggest, it is likely that anxiety will also produce qualitative changes in muscle activation in articulatory and phonatory systems. It is clear that stuttering is associated with disrupted motor activity in the vocal tract (see chapter 4). A further destabilized respiratory and articulatory system is likely to lead to greater stuttering.

As Messenger et al. (2004) explain, the direction of causality is potentially of clinical significance. If stuttering is the cause of the social anxiety (e.g., Alm, 2004a), then it would follow that successful treatment of the primary stuttering (thus removing the cause) should be sufficient remediation in itself. If on the other hand social anxiety causes stuttering, then management of the anxiety itself would need to be built into the therapeutic process. The problem is that while the removal of stuttering may be an achievable goal in early intervention programs, the emphasis when dealing with older children (and adults) is now on control of both the primary stuttering moments and the concomitant cognitive and emotional aspects. While very high levels of fluency might be achieved in therapy, a complete recovery from stuttering becomes increasingly unlikely as the disorder persists beyond adolescence (see chapters 1 and 9). It would therefore seem unlikely under Messenger et al.'s (2004) model that there would be complete resolution to the related issue of social anxiety. Those with interiorized stutters (see chapter 12) also provide compelling evidence that just because there is no overt stuttering does not mean there is no anxiety. For such people the fear of stuttering does not diminish, even when the stuttering is successfully hidden and avoided.

Assessment and planning therapy

We have discussed the various issues which need to be addressed in the assessment of teenage stuttering in chapter 9. If the client has previously undergone fluency therapy, he will be familiar with some of the assessment routines. Now, however, the clinician is more likely to focus on cognitive and affective factors than has previously been the case. Some standardized self-perception questionnaires may be appropriate, for example, as presented in WASSP (Wright & Ayre, 2000) or the CAT (De Nil & Brutten, 1991). It is possible that this is the first time the young person has been directly asked to consider his feelings and attitudes toward his speech and the way he perceives his world to be affected by it.

Stuttering modification approaches

The same issues that arise with the treatment of primary school children arise with secondary school children. Fundamentally, this means either taking a programmed (operant) approach targeting speech behaviour, a stuttering modification approach aimed at changing moments of stuttering to be less effortful, or an integrated approach to treatment. Note that with this age group "pure" cognitive approaches, that is, those which attend to cognitive and affective issues without some form of fluency modification, are extremely rare. As with the treatment of younger school age children, therapy can be seen as a modular process; that is, choosing from a selection of fluency enhancing strategies. This process starts with the clinician considering all the findings from the case history and assessment procedures that have been collected. It will have been important, during this time that the clinician has begun to develop a sense of trust with the young person, and to be as sure as possible that the responses to all the enquiries are genuine. The clinician will also have had an opportunity to listen to the client's perspective on his disorder and his personal goals for therapy. The clinician must then carefully talk through the possibilities for therapy, finally explaining to the child and parents the course of action which she believes will be most beneficial. Where either the client or parent has cited unrealistic goals, it is the clinician's job to gently explain the realistic possibilities as to what can be negotiated.

Three integrated approaches to the treatment of adolescent stuttering

As already mentioned, there are a considerable number of programs dealing with this age range which focus on the integration of cognitive and behavioural aspects. Although similar in the fact that they all "integrate", they vary in small ways in the degree to whether there is a slight cognitive or behavioural bias, although almost all feature an "easy speech" type component (e.g., Conture, 1997, 2001; Cooper & Cooper, 2004; Gregory, 2003; Gregory & Campbell, 1988; Guitar, 1998; Ramig & Bennett, 1997; Rustin et al., 1995; Wall & Myers, 1995). Gregory and Campbell's (1988) approach is somewhat different, however, in that to start with speech is initiated using his ERA-SM approach. Here, a speech sequence is initiated with a slightly slower speech rate and smooth changes between sounds and between words are made without reference to any specific fluency skills (such as soft consonants and gentle vowel onsets). Nonetheless, specific moments of stuttering may be modified if stuttering persists.

Apple House modular approach to adolescent stuttering

This will be a brief overview since I have already outlined our modular approach to the treatment of younger school children and there are a number of similarities to our program for older children. As before, there is contact with the childrens' schoolteachers and parents, and the latter are active in some therapeutic tasks. Again, we use a group format and the progression through identification, desensitization, modification and transfer remain similar. We find that with the older clients the sense of group identity develops quickly during the identification stage, when we often see relief on the faces of many who discover that coping strategies (for example, giving a different name when speaking on the phone) which they assumed to be unique to them were in fact used by others. Similarly, there is relief in the shared knowledge that feelings such as frustration, anger, anxiety and disappointment have been experienced by other group members. As before, there is integration of techniques which help improve speech fluency together with work on changing negative beliefs and self-perceptions, dealing with anxiety and avoidance. Perhaps the biggest difference between our younger and older school age groups is that with the latter there is a greater focus on cognitive aspects, and as such the client plays a more central role in his therapy. As with the younger groups, the split between time spent on behavioural and cognitive aspects of therapy will vary from client to client. This approach, like that of Kully and Langevin (1999), is comparatively unusual in that Van Riperian concepts such as cancellation are brought into both programs, although with our modular approach we may not consider all of these techniques suitable for all participants.

Michael Palin Centre approach

As with our previous example, this program developed at the Michael Palin Centre for stammering children in London takes a group approach to treatment. However, it may alternatively be implemented as a longer term approach. The program comprises six components: fluency control,[5] relaxation, social skills, problem solving, negotiation and environmental factors. These factors interrelate and may be taught simultaneously. As with their approach to the treatment of younger children (Rustin et al., 1996), which is outlined in some detail in chapter 10, the emphasis is on the interaction of the client with his environment. Although as before the main focus is likely to be on the involvement of the family, now partners and friends and the school are also involved in the therapeutic process. The most striking differences between the adolescent program and the parent–child interaction approach described in the previous chapter are that now direct work on fluency is also undertaken. The client takes on the responsibility of reducing stuttering and changing cognitive affective and emotional aspects of the disorder.

Guitar's integrated approach

Guitar (1998; Guitar & Peters, 1980) believes that stuttering arises through the combination of four components: altered neurological organization of speech and a vulnerable temperament, together with developmental and environmental factors. Guitar's most likely goal for the teenager who stutters is controlled fluency, as now the possibility of complete recovery with or without therapy is diminishing. Fluency is instated through the combined use of speech modification (such as cancellation and pull-outs) and fluency shaping techniques. Guitar refers to these techniques as fluency enhancing behaviours (FEBs). In addition, delayed auditory feedback (DAF) is also used as a therapeutic adjunct with some children. Children are initially taught to slow speech rate using DAF. Then through the clinician's modelling of a slower rate of speech, gentle glottal onsets and soft consonant contacts are subsequently introduced. Fluency is built up at word level and then short phrase using slow controlled rate of speech together with the FEBs. Once speech is consistently fluent at this level, the child moves on to structured conversation, spoken at 40 syllables per minute. Following this period, the FEBs are used to change from hard stuttering to easy stuttering, with changes in rate required when moments of stuttering are anticipated. Voluntary stuttering is also used at this stage to help show the client how to "downshift" his speech rate before he tries it with real stuttering moments.

---

5 This involves the identification of the client's own stuttering, together with a discussion of what is normal speech, and the introduction of fluency skills such as soft glottal onset, soft articulatory contact and slower rate.

Guitar also places importance on dealing with the client's negative emotions. Thus teasing is discussed, as is more general discussion of desensitization and avoidance. Openness about stuttering is encouraged and parent counselling is also integrated into the treatment program. Guitar's approach bears some similarity to that used by Kully and Langevin (1999). Like Guitar, Kully and Langevin use some Van Riperian techniques to modify stuttering, in addition to the consideration of cognitive aspects of the disorder. Also consistent with Guitar's approach, they use a slow prolonged speech rate to instantiate a range of fluency skills (although they do not use a DAF component to achieve this). In contrast, though, Kully and Langevin (1999) use an operant framework throughout their intensive program.

Fluency shaping approaches to the treatment of adolescent stuttering

There are a number of prolonged speech approaches to school age stuttering (Boberg, 1984;[6] Boberg & Kully, 1994; Craig et al., 1996; Druce et al., 1997; Hancock et al., 1998; Langevin & Kully, 2003; Ryan, 1974, 2001; Webster, 1979). Of note here is the similarity in approach of a number of clinicians to therapeutic strategies and procedures they use on their adult programs (e.g., Boberg & Kully, 1985; Ryan, 1974). Operant principles have been discussed earlier in this book (chapter 6) and also in relation to preschool therapy (chapter 10) and we come to it again in relation to adult therapy in the following chapter. Given the extensive overlap in the programmed approach between adolescent and adult therapies, we refer the reader to these other chapters whilst now focusing briefly on Ryan's long-established approach to the treatment of more persistent child stuttering.

Ryan's DAF-based therapy

In Ryan's view, speech is an operant and thus best treated by operant therapy (Ryan, 2001; see chapter 6). Although Ryan considers speech-related anxiety and attitudinal components also to be operant behaviours, these are not targeted in therapy, as it is assumed that they will improve alongside the improvement in primary stuttering.[7] Ryan prefers the use of his GILCU approach when dealing with primary school children, but where stuttering is

---

6 Boberg's (1984) approach to therapy can be considered as an integrated one, in that cognitive components are introduced into the framework. However, it is primarily an operant-based fluency shaping program. Integrated therapies mostly implement the use of (often similar) "fluency skills" in a less structured and more flexible way; for example, skills may not need to be employed 100 percent of the time.

7 Note that this perspective appears to assume that the act of stuttering is the (only) cause of anxiety in stuttered speech. Although there is a strong association between stuttering and anxiety, the direction of the relationship (or the possibility that it could be bidirectional) has yet to be established (see above).

more persistent and GILCU is insufficient to deal with the problem, he utilizes a similar DAF approach to that which he uses with adults (Ryan, 1974, 1984, 2001). This program incorporates 26 steps and differs from the GILCU version in which there is no manipulation of speech variables and fluency is achieved through praise for fluency and gentle admonishment for stuttering (see chapter 10). Instead, a slow prolonged speech pattern is instantiated, during an establishment phase, by using DAF (see chapter 3). Before therapy commences, parents and teaching staff are contacted and their help sought with home and school practice. Parents are also brought in to watch a therapy session to ensure they can accurately identify stuttering behaviours.

The establishment phase of the program begins with the child being taught how to produce slow prolonged speech before DAF is introduced at a 250 ms (¼ second) delay. Stuttering or an increase in speech rate is met with instruction to stop and to use the slow prolonged speech pattern. As the child moves through the steps, DAF delay is gradually decreased (in 50 ms increments) until the child is able to speak at a conversational level without any DAF. When the child has reached this stage, he must undertake 5 minutes each of oral reading, monologue and conversation with less than 0.5 percent stuttering. If the child achieves this, he moves to the transfer phase. If not, elements of the establishment phase must be repeated.

The structured transfer phase comprises speaking in a variety of settings, including the home, at school and on the telephone. All transfer tasks are carefully graded so, for example, telephone conversation transfer tasks range from a one-word comment spoken into an unplugged phone to a full three-minute conversation with a stranger. Transfer extends to fluent speaking at school (which is monitored by teaching staff) and at home (monitored by parents) with increasing numbers of family, friends and neighbours.

During the final maintenance phase, which lasts 22 months, the child is seen on 5 occasions, with fewer contacts toward the end of the maintenance phase. If the child is maintaining less than 0.5 percent stuttering at that assessment and reported to be maintaining high levels of fluency elsewhere, a further session is scheduled. If the child fails to meet these criteria, he must repeat earlier parts of the program. Typically, establishment requires ten hours, transfer requires nine hours and maintenance around two to three hours. Ryan (1984) claims that pooled data from a number of clinics on over 500 clients demonstrate that the average child commenced the course with 7 percent stuttering, and left with less than 1 percent stuttering. At one-year post clinic, more than 90 percent had maintained stuttering levels at 1 percent or below.

Is one treatment approach better than another?

As mentioned in chapter 15, making direct comparisons between approaches is not easy because of the difficulty in comparing programs which have different therapeutic goals. Although a reduction in stuttering frequency is generally associated with effective treatment (Thomas & Howell, 2001), consideration must also be given to the effect on communication more generally (Conture & Guitar, 1993; Kamhi, 2003). At present there are no reliable data that indicate one approach is more likely to produce lasting benefit than another, although it seems clear that some clients definitely fare better with particular approaches. There is, however, some data that compares the effects of three different treatment approaches over a four to six year follow-up period (Hancock et al., 1998). In this study, anxiety levels and speech naturalness data were collected alongside the usual speech fluency and speech rate information on three groups of 11–18 year olds who attended one of three therapeutic approaches. One followed an intensive prolonged speech format, the second took the form of a less intensive home-based parent–child interaction approach, while the third used electromyographic feedback to help reduce tension levels and thus levels of stuttering. Results from all three approaches showed a 75–80 percent reduction in stuttering immediately post clinic, and that similar levels of fluency were recorded between 2 to 6 years subsequently. Anxiety and speech naturalness also stabilized during this period.

Summary

Children who stutter will face a number of new challenges within the school setting. Now, moments of stuttering not only affect communication within the family and preschool friends, but the speaker is placed under greater strain in a more formal setting. The child may see the stutter as holding him back from making friends and from doing well at school. Teachers too may be unsure how to handle the child who is withdrawing because of stuttering, and may mistakenly view some of the escape and avoidance behaviours as laziness. Such difficulties in turn are likely to have repercussions when the child returns home from school. Thus, a change in the child's self-perception from having moments of stuttering to actually being "a stutterer" can present as the most striking feature of development at this time. Dealing with the child's new self-image and the negative self-perceptions which can quickly develop alongside may represent the greatest change that the clinician observes when assessing a school age children as opposed to preschool children. The available evidence shows that early intervention is most likely to be the most successful (see chapters 9 and 10). Thus the focus on therapy for the primary school aged child is likely to combine significant speech modification techniques. This of course will (by default) be the focus for all operant approaches, but those procedures that integrate operant and cognitive techniques usually combine direct treatment strategies. The approach may be different for older adolescents (say age 15–17) for whom recovery, either with or without therapy, is now unlikely. For secondary school children, dealing with the cognitive and affective issues may form the greater focus of the therapy for all except those taking an operant position on therapy.

Key points

- The challenges associated with beginning primary school may result in an increase in secondary stuttering behaviours.
- Direct therapy, in the form of either stuttering modification or fluency shaping, is more feasible at school age.
- Attempts at the reduction or elimination of disfluency through the use of verbal reinforcement (as in the Lidcombe program) do not appear to be as successful for school age children as for preschool children.
- As stuttering becomes more established, direct approaches for school age stuttering, whether fluency shaping or stuttering modification, now involve at least some manipulation of vocal tract activity (e.g., soft contacts, soft glottal onsets, smooth airflow, slow prolonged speech).
- For secondary school age children, there is likely to be an increased focus on dealing with cognitive/emotional and affective issues related to the stutter. Many treatment programs also place stuttering therapy within the more general context of communication skills.
- Unlike those programs for younger school age children, there are a number of programs for adolescents who stutter that combine operant fluency shaping approaches with stuttering modification and cognitive considerations.

Further reading

Boberg, E., & Kully, D. (1994). Long-term results of an intensive treatment program for adolescents who stutter. *Journal of Speech, Language, and Hearing Research 37*, 1050–1059.

Follow-up data are presented here on a group of adolescents who underwent the Comprehensive Stuttering Program (CSP) back in the mid-1980s. Since that time this clinic has revised its adolescent treatment program to include more cognitive aspects (see Kully & Langevin, 1999), but this still makes for an interesting read.

Guitar, B. (1998). *Stuttering: An integrated approach to its nature and treatment* (chapter 10: Intermediate stutterer). Philadelphia: Lippincott Williams & Wilkins.

A large chapter which outlines a range of treatment approaches for school age children.

Kully, D., & Langevin, M. (1999). Intensive treatment for adolescents. In R. Curlee (Ed.), *Stuttering and related disorders of fluency* (2nd ed.; pp. 139–159). New York: Thieme.

This chapter updates earlier descriptions of the three-week intensive teenage fluency therapy program offered at the Institute for Stuttering Treatment and Research

(ISTAR) in Edmonton, Canada. ISTAR has been diligently recording outcome data from its programs for many years and this program has received international recognition.

Rustin, L., Cook. F., & Spence, R. (1995). *The management of stuttering in adolescence: A communication skills approach*. London: Whurr.

This book comprehensively describes the Michael Palin Centre's approach to the assessment and treatment of adolescents who stutter. Consistent with this clinic's philosophy to treatment of younger children, the approach focuses on the significance of the individual's environment. Emphasis is placed on communication in general, as well as on stuttering specifically, together with the cognitive adjustments that may need to be undertaken to effectively cope with it.

Ryan, B. P. (2001). *Programmed stuttering therapy for children and adults* (2nd ed.). Springfield, IL: Charles C. Thomas.

This is an updated version of Ryan's seminal (1974) text of the same name. Some have commented that Ryan's continuing refusal to consider cognitive and affective aspects of stuttering in older children and adults is out of step with recent thinking. Ryan himself makes little attempt to hide his contempt for "unethical" non-operant approaches, and this is an uncompromising read. It is, however, a crystal-clear exposition on the operant perspective to stuttering treatment.

Stewart, T., & Turnbull, J. (1995). *Working with dysfluent children*. Bicester: Winslow Press.

This book provides some background on stuttering in childhood, but its main value lies in the range of clear and practical help it gives to clinicians. Amongst others there are particularly useful "hands-on" chapters on group therapy, and working together with schools and nurseries. A revised version is due to be published in 2006.

12 The treatment of stuttering in adults

Introduction

Once a stutter has persisted into adulthood, total recovery with or without therapy is very unlikely. For some, negative attitudes to speech and speech-related activity will have continued to build, particularly if earlier therapy has not been successful. Many of the issues that will have been of concern to the teenager will remain, but now new issues specific to adult life will have been added. Finding employment involves the often dreaded job interview. When a position has been found, posts which require a lot of talking place increasing pressures (or "demands" as they would be viewed in the Demands and Capacities model, chapter 1) on the individual.

Like early childhood and adolescence, adulthood too comprises periods of significant change, which affect people in different ways and at different periods; a point which is sometimes overlooked by commentators. Some may find their stutter stabilizes and even improves as they mature and find coping strategies that are beneficial. With changes in personal circumstance, others may notice fluctuations in levels of stuttering coincident with negative and positive changes in life events. Reflecting this diversity, adults refer for therapy for a wide variety of reasons, and at all ages. Unsurprisingly, necessity is a powerful motivator and it is common to have adults in their twenties and thirties coming for therapy, keen to improve their fluency in order to enhance their career prospects. Older adults may come for similar reasons, of course, but increasingly this may be to relearn techniques taught in earlier therapy whose effects have begun to wear off, or to try new therapeutic approaches. I have also had a number of referrals from recently retired people who now having more time on their hands have made the decision to seek help in improving their speech for the first time. Apart from the differences in age, adults will be referred with different levels of stuttering severity and avoidance, different attitudes to fluency and previous therapy, different personalities and self-perceptions, different levels of motivation and different goals.

Flexible therapeutic approaches are needed to deal with this diversity. As with the treatment of adolescent stuttering, so the tools used for the treatment of adult stuttering essentially borrow from one of two camps: those which target the immediate motor speech disruptions stuttering causes; and those which consider cognitive and affective issues that go hand in hand with living with a stutter. Clinicians also combine stuttering modification and fluency shaping techniques together with cognitive and affective factors in "integrated" approaches to treatment.

Stutter more fluently and speak more fluently approaches

For the first part of this chapter we focus on two approaches that represent well-reported and established procedures for the treatment of adult stuttering: Van Riper's (1973) stuttering modification approach and Boberg and Kully's (1985) comprehensive stuttering program (CSP). Both approaches continue to be used extensively and are widely respected. These approaches take different theoretical bases, yet in reality there is some common ground. Van Riper's approach emphasizes the goal of modifying stuttering, so that it is less effortful. Boberg and Kully's speak more fluently approach is based predominantly on an operant approach where the goals are to replace stuttering with a more fluent speech output. However, just as Van Riper's modification phase of therapy uses fluency enhancing techniques to control stuttering, so Boberg and Kully utilize stuttering modification procedures such as cancellation, and incorporate cognitive aspects into their program also. To illustrate a pure cognitive approach to therapy, I also outline Sheehan's (1975) approach-avoidance conflict therapy. Again, this approach has been chosen for its continuing influence and because it is respected and still much referred to even if, as we shall see, it takes what is still regarded by many as a rather radical stance over the issues that underlie stuttering. We return to this approach and pure fluency shaping perspectives later in this chapter. For the moment, though, we describe Van Riper's work on stuttering modification.

Modifying stuttering

Van Riper – stuttering modification

Arguably the most influential and widely used of all stuttering modification approaches to treatment was developed by Charles Van Riper. The program, also known as stutter more fluently or block modification therapy, was developed over a number of years, but is explained most fully in his seminal book *The Treatment of Stuttering* (Van Riper, 1973). A major focus of the therapy is to reduce the fear of stuttering by eliminating avoidance behaviours. People who stutter often report that the fear of stuttering leads to avoidance and increased anxiety. This in turn leads to increased stuttering. Van Riper's rationale is that by being able to modify stuttering into something less effortful, there will be reduced fear and avoidance, and this will lead to a decrease in stuttering. The decrease in stuttering will, in turn, result in less avoidance. Van Riper based his therapy design on his belief that stuttering, in part, arose out of a difficulty in the timing of speech events:

> Mistiming could be caused by an organic proclivity, emotional stress, or a malfunctioning servo system. The huge overlay of secondary symptoms are best explained with the principles of learning and conditioning. It is probable that stuttering grows and maintains itself largely through differential learning experiences.
>
> (Van Riper, 1982, p. 416)

Thus, therapy is based on the foundations of learning theory, servo theory and also aspects of psychotherapy. Learning theory principles can help the client unlearn old maladaptive responses to threat and to the experience of fluency disruption, and instead to learn new and more adaptive ones. The servo theory aspect refers to Van Riper's belief that stuttering was caused, at least in part, by a failure of the auditory processing system. In order to compensate for this deficit in processing, there is a need for the individual to "monitor his speech by emphasising proprioception thus bypassing to some degree the auditory feedback system" (Van Riper, 1973, p. 204). The time that Van Riper was developing the stutter more fluently approach coincided with a developing literature on possible auditory processing deficits, and particularly on the effects of altered auditory feedback of people who stutter. (We have considered stuttering as a disorder of auditory feedback in chapter 3.) The psychotherapeutic component concerns the individual's responses to core stuttering behaviour. Van Riper strongly believed that cognitive aspects of the disorder, such as frustration, anxiety, and fear, needed to be addressed with equal emphasis to the motoric aspects of the core stuttering. It is true that some of Van Riper's thinking is now regarded as outdated, but his influence on modifying stuttering has had and continues to have a very great effect on the work of many clinicians today.

Aims

With both cognitive and motoric aspects, the aims were similar; the individual should not use avoidance strategies and moments of stuttering should be modified and controlled so that stuttering is less effortful and less stressful. The term "stutter more fluently approach" thus contrasts with the "speak more fluently" alternatives which heavily targeted all motor speech behaviour, not just the moments in speech where stuttering occurred.

Schedule

In the original, Van Riper recommended a schedule that had the client attend an initial three- to four-month period of therapy comprising one-hour weekly of individual therapy and one hour of group therapy three times each week. Following this, there was a less time-intensive stabilization phase of a further three or four months comprising one or two one-hour weekly sessions of either group or individual therapy. There are now many variations on this theme. The schedule may be solely individual (once or twice weekly, usually taking between nine to twelve months) or once weekly in a group which occupies a similar time frame. For example, the City Lit Institute in London runs a number of courses based on the stutter more fluently approach (more commonly known as the block modification approach in Britain). These comprise both short-term intensive programs, usually running over a period of between four and nine days, and longer term once-weekly evening groups.

Therapy

Following assessment, therapy consists of a sequence of identification, desensitization, modification and stabilization, although these are not necessarily discrete stages and can overlap. For example, desensitization may be something that the client will continue to work on in the modification stage of therapy. Similarly, identification and desensitization stages may somewhat overlap.

Identification

The purpose of this phase is for the client to become aware of both primary and secondary features of the stutter. The focus throughout the period of therapy is on confrontation. Here the individual learns to understand both the motoric presentation of the disorder and his reactions to it. Acknowledging all the features of the stutter, increases the likelihood of approach, lessens avoidance (see also below Sheehan's approach and chapter 6). It will also help deal with any denial of aspects of the disorder, and increase awareness of the motoric events associated with the stutter. Identification targets include:

- core behaviours (e.g., blocks, prolongations, repetitions, tremor)
- avoidance or difficulty with specific linguistic stimuli (e.g., word and phoneme fears)
- avoidance of nonlinguistic stimuli (situational and person avoidance)
- sites of tension (e.g., neck, shoulders, entire body)
- post-stuttering reactions (e.g., embarrassment, shame)
- negative emotions prior to speech, during speech and following speech.

It is important that identification of stuttering should be structured in hierarchical order, starting with the least stressful, often easier moments of stuttering before moving on to more difficult secondary behaviours such as eye blinking or head nodding. Identification is achieved through use of a number of mechanisms. Clinicians may look through assessment material that has been collected during assessment and diagnosis. Self-assessment material such as the perceptions of stuttering inventory (Woolfe, 1967), the revised Erikson S-24 scale (Andrews & Cutler, 1974), the Overall Assessment of Stutterers' Experiences of Speaking (OASES; Yaruss & Quesal, 2004) and the Wright and Ayre (2000) stuttering self-rating profile may all provide useful material for the clinician to discuss with the client. (See chapter 9 for details on these procedures.) In addition, video feedback can be used to help identify primary stuttering moments. If therapy is within a group setting, other members may assist in the identification of stuttering.

Desensitization

Having identified the components of the stutter, the client now works on reducing the increased degree of emotional arousal that may have become established alongside the primary features of the stutter. There are a number of procedures that can help lessen the impact of the stutter and build up tolerance both to the client's feelings of frustration and toughening the client's feelings toward any negative listener reaction. Some of these might appear difficult to the client, so a skilled therapist with a positive therapeutic manner is important here. The positive outcome of the desensitization phase is that the client's stuttering response to certain situations is no longer viewed as being as feared. This may be achieved through a number of techniques:

OPEN STUTTERING

Here, the client may be asked to undertake a series of difficult speaking situations that otherwise would have been avoided. Similarly, an individual who has a covert stutter and is skilled at avoiding difficult words might be asked to confront difficult sounds and words – that is actively choosing stuttering over avoidance. As with all areas of stuttering modification therapy, this needs to be approached carefully and in a hierarchical way. Initially, encouraging the client to stutter openly in clinic may be the primary goal. The client might then progress to stuttering openly with closer friends or with colleagues at work before attempting more feared situations.

PSEUDOSTUTTERING

This technique, also known as voluntary stuttering, involves the client stuttering deliberately. There are different ways of approaching pseudostuttering, but the most common one has the client pretending to stutter, initially on a word which is not usually stuttered, and thus when the client is feeling secure. The sense of control over the voluntary stutter serves to decrease the sense of anxiety normally associated with stuttering activity, and so increases approach and lessens avoidance.[1] While doing this, the client observes the reaction of the listeners. It is often found that listeners are much less concerned about the stuttering than the client envisaged. This process also helps desensitize the client to the fact that he can keep calm even on the rare occasions when there is negative listener reaction. Clients usually learn to pseudostutter using easy repetitions, or sometimes prolongations. At first this is either one to one with the clinician, or within the confines of the group. By building up practice, confidence increases, and so the pseudostuttering is developed increasingly to approximate the genuine type of stuttering, including more feared words, and eventually in more feared situations. Van Riper suggests that the clinician should also practise pseudostuttering both within the clinic and on assignments.

FREEZING

This is a technique where, in the middle of a moment of stuttering, the client is called upon by the clinician to *freeze* the vocal tract and continue to hold the posture until told to release it. For example, a "frozen" prolongation would require a further stretching of the sound, whilst a block would continue to be held with the same degree of tension, in silence. To start with the moment of freezing is fleeting, but the length increases with practice. To help desensitize the client to listener reaction, the clinician may fake impatience or other negative behaviour into the reaction. Repeated practice of this routine helps the client become more tolerant of the core stuttering behaviours, and also to develop a resistance to the feeling of time pressure and the perceived need to move forward quickly with speech, even if this is likely to result in increased struggle and more stuttering.

Modification

This is the phase of therapy where "abnormal" stuttering is changed into a less effortful version. Rather than aiming directly for a reduction in the percentage of stuttered syllables, as is the case in many fluency shaping programs, the goal here is to promote "fluent stuttering" or controlled stuttering. The new type of stuttering is more desirable because it does not incur negative reactions either from the speaker or from the listener. The goals of this phase of treatment are:

---

1 The idea of increasing approach and reducing avoidance is a central theme in many approaches which aim to deal with the underlying belief systems that often serve to make stuttering worse. As we will see later in this chapter, approach avoidance itself forms the core issue of Sheehan's (1953) therapeutic approach, as well as his theoretical stance which views stuttering as approach-avoidance conflict. (We discuss this theory in chapter 6.)

- to condition more appropriate stuttering behaviour
- to eliminate previously learned stuttering behaviours
- to develop proprioceptive awareness of motoric aspects of speech.

We can see how the first two aims reflect Van Riper's belief that much of stuttering is learned, and how the third takes on board his servo model of stuttering; that is that stuttering is due in part to faulty feedback. Obviously, this is the phase which provides practical and direct strategies to help fluency, and a further aim during this phase, as is the case with others, is to help the individual alter negative self-perceptions.

Stuttering modification is achieved through the use of three techniques: cancellation, pull-outs and preparatory sets. Before starting on this phase of therapy, it is important that the client is prepared to take on feared words and that postponing devices, for example, extra words inserted to help run up to a feared word or sound, are not being used. Of course, these issues will have been tackled in the desensitization phase, but may need a little more work as speech modification techniques are implemented.

CANCELLATION

This is also known as post-block modification and is usually the first technique that is taught. Cancellation involves repeating a (completed) stuttered word using controlling strategies before continuing further with speech. To learn to cancel effectively, strict procedures need to be adhered to and three steps need to be followed:

Step 1   Following a stuttered word the client must:
- pause for a minimum of three seconds.
- replicate in pantomime a shortened version of the stuttering behaviour
- inaudibly articulate the word in a very slow and highly conscious manner. Sometimes a repetition of this substage is needed.

The idea of this is that it forces the client to confront the stuttering behaviour objectively.

Step 2   This is similar to step 1, but instead of miming the stuttered word, the word is repeated with a soft whisper.

Step 3   The stuttered word is now repeated aloud, but at a slow and highly controlled rate. This allows for some smoothing of sequential phones.

There are, in fact, some variations on this theme. A shortened version which is probably used more often goes as follows:

1   The client stutters. The stuttered word is eventually completed.

2 Deliberate pause for two seconds, during which time the client calms himself. The client repeats the stuttered word using easy stuttering (i.e., not fluently). (Easy stuttering requires the slow and deliberate articulation of the stuttered word using light articulatory contacts.)

3 Ongoing speech resumes.

Repeating the stuttered word often has a positive effect on associated secondary stuttering. For example, in controlling the stutter in a slowed repetition this might eliminate a jaw jerk which might have become associated with the rapid and over-tense muscular spasm associated with that behaviour, by adjusting the timing of the previously stuttered word. Cancellations are learned within the clinic to start with and are applied to situations of increasing difficulty as confidence in using the technique increases.

PULL-OUTS

This technique, also known as within block modification, involves a smooth withdrawal from an ongoing moment of stuttering. I give some examples of this with a range of stuttering behaviours below.

Pulling out of a prolongation initially involves prolonging further until the client becomes aware of the nature and location of the accompanying muscle fixation. This procedure uses the freezing technique already learned during desensitization. In doing this, the client becomes highly conscious of the physiological events associated with the stutter. The client then uses proprioceptive information from the frozen position to slowly change to a less tense and more normal articulatory posture. Initially, the client will work from this on command from the clinician. As proficiency in this process increases, the client will do this automatically.

Pull-outs from tremors may also be achieved by utilizing proprioceptive feedback. Here, the client slowly reduces the rate of oscillation and relaxes the point of tension during the moment of stuttering.

Laryngeal blocks may be modified by using low frequency and low amplitudinal vibration of the vocal cords. This mode of vibration, called vocal fry or creaky voice, differs from the chest-pulse register type normally associated with speech, in that it is achieved using lower subglottal air pressure, which in turn results in a more irregular opening and closing of the glottis, and reduced amplitude of vocal fold movement. With airflow moving slowly and in a controlled manner, full voicing can then be developed with practice.

Repetition of syllabic or phonemic units may be modified using a similar method to that used to control tremor. First, the rate of repetition is slowly decreased. The client then changes the slowed repetition into a prolongation of the sound. Adjustment of the articulatory posture may also be needed to move from the vowel centralization (schwa) which is a common feature of a more established stutter, and toward the original vowel target. To illustrate, a pull-out of a syllabic repetition on the word "blocking" might present as something like this:

Blu – blu – blu – blu – blu – blu – blo – blo ⟶ cking

The client should be able to use pull-outs before moving on to preparatory sets (see below).

Increasing proprioceptive awareness

As mentioned earlier, Van Riper believed that disturbed auditory feedback was a causative factor in stuttering. To counteract this, the client is encouraged to develop proprioceptive monitoring of motor speech activity. This blocking of auditory feedback helps the client focus on motor activity. Effective proprioceptive monitoring is seen in increased articulatory precision and exaggerated articulatory movement. Techniques to increase proprioceptive awareness include DAF, masking noise, pantomiming (exaggerated speech rehearsal) and visual monitoring. All these techniques were seen as drawing attention away from auditory processing. Some, such as DAF and masking, work by blocking out or changing this feedback route; others such as pantomiming actively increase motor speech activity and strength of motor speech movements. (We see this process in all three of the speech modification techniques.)

PREPARATORY SETS

This is also known as preblock modification. The term refers to a repositioning of the articulators immediately before a difficult or feared word. Van Riper's premise is that many who stutter develop abnormal preparatory sets. This can sometimes be observed as articulatory tension and struggle behaviour in moments immediately preceding a block. Preparatory sets replace these inappropriate postures which trigger stuttering with new positionings, or "sets" which stimulate slow motion speech and fluent stuttering. The new preparatory sets require careful initiation of airflow and voicing in conjunction with the light articulatory contact, or soft vowel onsets. The slowness of the production also gives a prolonged quality to the word. As with cancellation and pull-outs, preparatory sets are practised initially in easy nonconfrontational situations within the clinic, working through a hierarchy of less feared words toward more challenging assignments involving harder speaking situations and more difficult words.

Stabilization

The purpose of this phase of therapy is to strengthen the new fluent stuttering patterns and to ensure that these can be used across a range of different situations and speaking scenarios. During this final phase of therapy, the clinician's role becomes more one of a sounding board or consultant, as the client is encouraged more and more to become his own clinician, and slowly time spent with the clinician is reduced. Emphasis in the stabilization phase is also given to develop the client's ability to deal with stressful speech-related situations. This may be achieved first by continued practice of the fluency modification techniques in a variety of settings. On occasion, preparatory sets or pull-outs may fail to deal with a moment of stuttering, and a stuttered word is produced. The appropriate use of cancellation in particular is regarded as central here. As the name implies, a moment of stuttering can literally be cancelled out by this technique, and a sense of frustration or other negative emotions associated with a perceived failure to use a pull-out or preparatory set can be avoided. Doing this lessens the likelihood that the previous stuttering response will return. Pseudostuttering is also employed to practise and strengthen pull-out and cancellation procedures and can be used to tackle any remaining feared situations. As throughout the course of treatment, the client is encouraged to be open about feelings associated with stuttering.

The legacy of Van Riper's approach

The significance of Van Riper's approach to the treatment of stuttering cannot be underestimated. It is a testament to the efficacy of the approach that more than 30 years after the publication of *The Treatment of Fluency* many clinicians worldwide continue to follow the principles of the stutter more fluently philosophy, and Van Riper's therapeutic models, specifically. Particularly, many clinicians believe that there are significant advantages in making stuttering easier or "more fluent" rather than trying to eliminate it (e.g., Bloodstein, 1975; Conture, 2001; Gregory, 2003; Guitar, 1998; Hayhow & Levy, 1993; Manning, 1999; Starkweather, 1987). Although some of these clinicians integrate approaches rather than focusing exclusively on stuttering modification, all agree on the need to look hard at the relationship between environmental stimulus and the response of stuttering, and in changing belief systems which help perpetuate and exacerbate stuttering and shaping more appropriate responses, both cognitive and motoric.

Modifying behavioural, cognitive and affective responses to stuttering

Sheehan's approach-avoidance conflict therapy

Sheehan, whose theoretical stance on stuttering as approach-avoidance conflict has been described earlier in chapter 6, offers a strongly cognitive approach to therapy. For Sheehan, the modification of speech, whether achieved by stuttering modification or fluency shaping procedures, may be seen as superfluous. Instead, progress is measured in terms of how the client can come to manage avoidance of stuttering and stuttering-related scenarios. In this sense, it shares a similar philosophy to some of the counselling approaches outlined in chapter 13.

Briefly, Sheehan (1953, 1975, 1986) believed that stuttering moments occur when the person who stutters experiences an equal drive to talk together with an equal drive to remain silent, or avoid. A further premise (Sheehan & Sheehan, 1984) is that stuttering only becomes established in childhood when the child successfully learns how to suppress outward stuttering through use of avoidance techniques. Sheehan and Sheehan (1984) are careful to make the distinction between this suppression and both the frustration of stuttering and the learning of avoidance techniques which are related to it. Because of this, the theory is distanced from both Johnson's diagnosogenic theory, where the child stutters because there is expectancy to do so, and Bloodstein's anticipatory struggle hypothesis where it is the struggle itself which leads to stuttering (see chapter 6 for overviews of Johnson's and Bloodstein's theories). As Sheehan and Sheehan (1984) put it:

> Stuttering is perpetuated by the use of outward stuttering behaviour and by substitution of false fluency/inner patterns of stuttering.
>
> With some individual variability, stutterers appear to have the capacity to suppress the outward appearance of their stuttering, thus producing an apparent reduction in frequency. We assume that response suppression is a central continuing cause in maintaining stuttering behaviour. This suppression of outward stuttering may temporarily "make stutterers seem better;" actually, it moves them into a retreat position that makes ultimate recovery enormously more difficult.
>
> (p. 147)

The premise here is that people who stutter can overcome their difficulty if they can increase their approach tendencies, and relatedly if they can overcome their avoidance behaviour, whether this is avoidance from speaking in certain situations, avoiding certain words or sounds, avoidance of eye contact, and so on. As with Van Riper's approach, Sheehan and Sheehan describe their program as client focused, based on determining the needs of the person, rather than program focused. Consistent with Van Riper's approach, they divide their therapy into a number stages which may overlap.

Self-acceptance

The goal of this phase is for the client to accept himself as a person who stutters. That is not to say that the stuttering as it currently exists needs to be accepted, as this will be modified through therapy. The phase begins with the establishment of eye contact before speaking. The client is also encouraged to discuss both stuttering and therapy with a range of listeners. The client then notes their reactions and attitudes. Following a series of assignments involving meeting and discussing stuttering and stuttering attitudes, he explores his own feelings towards the disorder. This phase is somewhat analogous to Van Riper's identification and desensitization phases.

Monitoring

Here, the client continues to develop awareness of what he does when he stutters, and what devices are used to suppress stuttering. At this time there is no pressure to change any behaviour, but the client is encouraged to take responsibility for their speech behaviour. Sheehan's (1975) speech pattern checklist may be used during this phase to help with the identification process. This questionnaire is designed to confront the client with his stuttering and attitudes toward it.

Initiative phase

As the title suggests, the point of this stage of therapy is to have the client being proactive in the attempt to control avoidance. Rather than being fearful of stuttering-related variables, the client is encouraged to seek out fearful and difficult speaking situations, thus increasing approach and decreasing avoidance behaviours. In this way, the client becomes desensitized to situations that have in the past invoked fear. By speaking in these situations, even if there is stuttering, the fear factor will lessen:

> If you should stutter in the process, it will not be a tragedy, because stuttering is not a failure. Fear is not a failure, and by initiative you can give yourself more moments of stuttering with which to analyze and with which to modify.
>
> (Sheehan & Sheehan, 1984, p. 149)

Speech failures would include using avoidance techniques and other escape behaviours such as head nodding and foot tapping to maintain fluency.

Modification

This phase continues the theme of open stuttering, and increasing "approach" behaviour, but at the same time introduces some techniques that lead to more "easy" stuttering. As with Van Riper's approach in his modification stage, voluntary stuttering is used, but instead of having the client initially repeat the stuttering pattern, a technique called the "slide" is taught. This involves the prolongation of the first phoneme of the word followed by a smooth release into the following phoneme. The client must make sure the sound is held beyond the point it could be released, and then sliding to the next sound only when the sensation of tension has gone. As in earlier phases, the focus is on open stuttering, and clients are also encouraged to speak at a comfortable rate, resisting any perceived pressure to hurry. Here then we notice a big difference to Van Riper's approach, with very little emphasis placed on the direct adjustment of motor speech patterns associated with stuttering.

The safety margin

This final phase has the client build further resistance against avoidance behaviour by further developing tolerance of stuttering. This is achieved by reinforcing the idea of open stuttering by actually stuttering more (in a controlled and easy way) rather than stuttering less. Indeed, the client is encouraged to increase the amount of stuttering in his speech, and voluntary stuttering using the slide technique continues to be used on non-feared words so the listener is unaware of how fluent he can actually be. When the client reaches the stage where he is comfortable putting increased amounts of stuttering into his speech, Sheehan argues that a sense of security (or margin of safety) will have been achieved: "It is actually concealing some of the fluency instead of concealing some of the stuttering" (Sheehan & Sheehan, 1984, p. 150).

Sheehan's approach is often viewed as one of the strongest forms of the "cognitive" approaches. We see elsewhere (chapter 13) that a number of psychological frameworks have been used to structure therapy (for example, Kelly's humanistic approach, and Ellis' rational emotive behaviour therapy). It is a therapy that demands much of the clinician and even more of the client. Encouraging a client to take up an approach where they will be encouraged to stutter more, and to deliberately seek out difficult speaking situations without the safety net of controlling strategies, can be a difficult sell. For some clients, this prospect is just too difficult to take on and they may rather seek out alternative approaches: perhaps a highly structured one which specifically targets speech behaviours, as opposed to the psychological processes that influence their development and maintenance. These alternative approaches go by the generic name of fluency shaping therapies, and we come to them below. Like Van Riper and others who favour a stuttering modification approach, Sheehan has been criticized for not producing data on the effectiveness of his program. Sheehan, in turn, was often scathing in his criticism of the objectively measured fluency shaping efficacy data, as witnessed in his concluding paragraph on the subject in 1984:

> The data that are produced by many of the behavioral suppressors are not recovery figures – they are suppression figures. The indecent scramble for ever and ever higher percentages, like 90 or 89 or 93, becomes totally meaningless. We suggest that the figures published on the establishment of fluency are mostly behavioral suppression figures and not ultimately recovery figures, and that the more successful the suppression, the less the chance of eventual recovery.
>
> (Sheehan, 1984, p. 150)

Modifying speech: Fluency shaping approaches

This approach (also known as "speak more fluently") owes much to the development of operant conditioning and its application to stuttering theory and therapy in the late 1950s and subsequent development through the 1960s and 1970s (see also chapter 6). At the core of this approach lie two beliefs: first, that stuttering can be viewed as an operant response to an environmental stimulus and can be treated using operant principles; second, that fluency can be achieved by the implementation of motor control techniques which are then developed (or "shaped") to approximate normal sounding speech. Almost all fluency shaping programs for adults involve the use of a range of techniques to control respiration, phonation and articulation, which are implemented initially with stretched syllables spoken at a very slow speech rate.[2] These are the slow speech or prolonged speech programs. The therapeutic process involves slowly increasing speech rate, which is highly fluent, due to the use of speech controlling techniques until a normal or near normal rate is achieved. While fluency shaping techniques are used throughout the world, the majority of the research on their efficacy has come from North America and Australia. In the UK, speech modification procedures tend to dominate.[3]

There are a number of core characteristics which almost all fluency shaping programs adhere to, although older operant therapies have changed somewhat over the years. For example, consistent with operant research into the effects of altered auditory feedback at the time, some earlier programs used DAF to enhance fluency and to slow rate (e.g., Ryan, 1974). Punishment in the form of time-out contingencies has also been used.

Prolonged speech

Of the many contributions of the operant perspective on therapy, arguably the most significant has been in prolonged speech. As Ingham put it in 1984: "If a stuttering therapies 'hit parade' existed, then prolonged speech and its variants would currently top the chart" (p. 324). Perhaps the same cannot now be said of the programmed instruction approach exemplified in prolonged speech, and over 20 years later many clinicians are looking more toward consideration of cognitive and emotional aspects associated with stuttering. Nonetheless, prolonged speech is still very much in evidence in clinics all around the world. There are almost as many variants on the prolonged speech programs as there are programs themselves, and it will not be

---

2 Note that in contrast, operant approaches to the treatment of stuttering in preschool children do not involve any direct adjustment to vocal tract variables, and simply work by the reinforcement of fluent speech and gentle verbal correction of moments of stuttering.

3 This is the case for adult therapy at least. The success of the Lidcombe program can be seen as a recent example where this attitude is changing.

possible to cover the subtle differences which exist between them in a single chapter. However, before describing a generic prolonged speech program which works on the operant principles of response contingent stimuli (RCS), I first outline some similarities and differences between prolonged speech programs.

Theoretical underpinnings

Generally, the fluency shaping approach represents the perception that stuttering is a motor speech disorder (as we see from chapter 4). There are a number of versions of this theory, but all share the common belief that stuttering can be effectively treated as a disorder of motor speech timing. The idea is that speech, and therefore also stuttered speech, can be reconstructed by re-coordinating the motor speech subsystems subserving this function; namely, those systems controlling respiration, phonation and articulation.

It is also true to say that some variants on the prolonged speech therapies have been developed for reasons of expediency. They are highly structured and measurable although, as Sheehan (1984) and others have argued, the fact that there is objective measurement does not necessarily guarantee that what is being measured comprises what actually should be being measured. They can be, at least in the short term, very successful. (See chapter 15 for comment on the difficult issue of what constitutes successful treatment outcome.)

Finally, note that the prolonged speech approach has a very long history. Ingham (1984) cites a number of examples of this approach being used in the early part of the twentieth century (Bell, 1904; Bender & Kleinfeld, 1938; Gifford, 1939; Hahn, 1941). In fact the similarity of Hahn's approach in particular to many more recent therapies is remarkable. Going back further still and bearing considerable resemblance to therapies nearly 300 years later is the work of a medical practitioner named Cotton Mather (1724). Mather's description of his approach, cited by Borman (1969) in Ingham (1984) is worth repeating here:

> First use yourself to a very deliberate Way of Speaking, a Drawling that shall be little short of Singing. Even this Drawling will be better than Stuttering ... [as a result] ... the Organs of your speech will be so habituated into Right Speaking, that you will, by Degrees, and sooner than you imagine, grow able to speak as fast again, as you did when the Law of Deliberation first of all began to govern you. Tho' my Advice is, beware speaking too fast, as long as you live.
>
> (Mather, 1724, cited by Borman, 1969 in Ingham, 1984, p. 460)

Of interest here is not only the rather obvious way in which the technique mirrors those of even some very recent prolonged speech approaches, but also the notion that the retraining of motor speech patterns that takes place in these programs will become habituated over time, and that the new way of talking will become automatic. This has traditionally been seen as the case with more recent prolonged speech therapies, although many clinicians now using the approach are keen to stress that practice regimes will need to be invoked long after the period of therapy has ended. Not all observers are impressed by the fluency shaping programs and the resulting speech output. Amongst the loudest of dissenting voices is that of Kalinowski and colleagues who argue that this habituation of new motor speech patterns simply does not take place and the fluency that results from prolonged speech programs is false and will not be maintained (see chapters 3 and 14).

Main features of prolonged speech programs

The underlying principles have remained unchanged since the earliest published programs began back in the 1960s.

1   Not surprisingly, all prolonged speech programs share the common feature of stretched speech segments, brought about by extending vowels and, to varying extents, consonants. Note that prolonged speech is not necessarily slower than "normal" speech at the end of the treatment period, but it is introduced at the beginning of a program at a greatly reduced speech rate.
2   Speech rate used to be slowed by the use of delayed auditory feedback, but this has mostly given way to the introduction of a prolonged speech pattern which is modelled by the clinician.
3   Prolonged speech programs are most commonly used in an intensive group schedule. Most run over an eight-hour day for two or three weeks.
4   Clients work through a highly structured rate hierarchy, commencing with a very slow speech rate (often 60 syllables per minute, or slower), and then move through a series of incremental rate changes, eventually finishing with a rate that is either normal or near normal. The final rate may differ depending on the needs and abilities of each client.
5   Clients are taught a range of fluency skills (or fluency techniques) that are introduced alongside the initial slow speech rate. Skill usage must be maintained as rate is increased over the period of the program. Techniques include those as described in the previous chapter, such as continuous voicing, continuous airflow, soft articulatory contact, soft onset of vocal fold vibration.
6   Clients are required to use fluency skills within a stipulated range, and to keep to within a certain level of fluency during a given period of speaking time at each rate level, before being allowed to move on to the next rate. For example, within a speaking block of 5 minutes, a client may be required to keep to within +/− 10 syllables per minute of the target rate, whilst only making a maximum of 5 errors in fluency skill usage and maintaining 100 percent fluency. A client failing at a certain rate level may need to do more speaking practice, keeping within the required

fluency, rate and fluency skill criteria before being allowed to move on to the next rate.

7   The clinician's role is primarily one of feedback provider, and to closely monitor speech criteria throughout the program. A considerable amount of practice is required in order to be able to do this with consistency and accuracy. The clinician may need to simultaneously manipulate a stop-watch for each client in the group to record their speaking time, and to accurately count syllables per second and stuttered syllables, while noting down any errors in fluency skills and use of nonlinguistic communication. Electronic counters which automatically calculate ongoing speech rate and percentages of syllables stuttered (as identified by the clinician) are used by a number of clinics to help with these tasks.

Day 1   Baseline assessments, identification.

Day 2   Identification, early modification.

Day 3   60 SPM (introduction of fluency skills at 60 syllables per minute). Clients build up blocks of speaking time where the fluency skills must be maintained within certain levels. If the given number of fluency skill errors is exceeded, the client must repeat the block of speaking time.

Day 4   60 SPM & self-assessments (see below).

Day 5   90 SPM.

Weekend

Day 6   90 SPM, self-assessments, 120 SPM.

Day 7   120 SPM, self-assessments, 150 SPM.

Day 8   150 SPM, self-assessments, 190 SPM.

Day 9   Self-monitor, rate, assessment of transfer of fluency skills in conversation with a friend.

Day 10 Transfers of fluency skills with

  • a friend
  • a stranger.

Weekend

Day 11 Shopping transfer exercises, friend/survey transfers.

Day 12 Attitude session, stranger transfers.

Day 13 Maintenance talk, phone transfers.

Day 14 Maintenance talk, remaining transfers.

Day 15 Final presentation, post-clinic assessment.

Follow-up sessions are held at three months, six months and one year post clinic.

The box gives a brief summary of Boberg and Kully's (1985) comprehensive stuttering program (CSP). During week three, in particular, clients enter discussions on issues relating to the maintenance of fluency and on avoidance. Techniques such as cancellation may be employed when there are moments of stuttering. When cancellation has been used effectively, this is regarded as negating the moment of stuttering. Note that this practice would not occur on more pure operant fluency shaping programs. Table 12.1 summarizes some similarities between Boberg and Kully's (1985) CSP and Neilson and Andrew's (1993) program. Note that, consistent with recent thinking, they both incorporate some speech modification and cognitive components into their schedules. In this sense, they may also be regarded as integrated programs. However, the prolonged speech aspects and operant schedule predominates in both approaches.

Table 12.1 Comparison of two established operant-based fluency shaping programs

	Neilson & Andrews (1993)	*Boberg & Kully (1985)*
Program schedule	Three weeks, five full days per week	Three weeks, five full days per week plus some evenings
Speech rate		
Baseline rate	50 SPM	60 SPM
How slow rate is achieved	All phonemes are extended	Vowels are extended more than consonants
Rate increments	10 SPM. Final rate is 200 SPM	30 SPM. Final rate is variable, but usually around 180 SPM
Fluency factors		
Breathing	Relaxed natural breathing	Diaphragmatic
Prosody	Normal intonation taught when client has reached 100 SPM	Normal intonation taught from base rate of 60 SPM
Airflow/blending of words into phrases	Smooth and continuous breathing between words without pause	Similar
Phrase initiation with • Consonants • Vowels	• Soft articulatory contact made between the relevant articulators • Gentle voicing of vowels with smooth airflow	Similar
Prolongation	Monitored, but less formally than in the Boberg and Kully program	When a client fails to prolong even one or two syllables, this is still regarded as a fluency error, regardless as to whether this affects the overall rate (see below)

cont.

Table 12.1 continued

	Neilson & Andrews (1993)	Boberg & Kully (1985)
Fluency shaping procedures	Rating sessions: 7 minutes of stutter-free speech at the given rate during group conversation. Clinician gives feedback as to use of fluency skills and rate	Rating sessions: criteria varies from rate to rate using 0%–2% SS in five-minute conversation with clinician. May be in front of group. Fluency skills (e.g., soft articulatory contact) must be used within set guidelines and rate must be within + or − 10 SPM of target
Clinician's role	To monitor for each client: • Amount of speaking time taken • Accuracy of rate • Level of fluency	Similar to Neilson and Andrews, plus monitoring fluency skill usage
Progression to next speech rate	Ongoing: completion of seven-minute session with accurate rate and 0% stuttering required in group session. If client fails a session, the clinician restarts the seven-minute session again	Ongoing: successful completion of the between 3 and 5 five-minute blocks of speaking time within group setting (as above). Client must pass a one-to-one conversation in front of group members whilst maintaining fluency shaping criteria as above. Needs also to show self-awareness of any moments of stuttering and failure to use fluency skills
Transfer stage		
Onset of transfer stage	Starts at beginning of second week	Starts at end of second week
Procedures	Structured: both standard assignments (e.g., conversations with friends, phone calls) and advanced assignments (e.g., calling in to a radio show). Increasing emphasis on self-assessment	Similar standard assignments. Advanced assignments include giving a formal speech. Increasing emphasis on self-assessment and self-evaluation
Coping procedures used	Preparatory sets, cancellations	Mainly cancellations
Fluency criteria	Fluent normal sounding speech	Less than 1% SS

Fluency skills

Fluency skills include:

- normal intonation (this should be maintained as much as the slow speech will allow)
- smooth onsets (slow build-up of vocal fold vibration to start vowel sounds)
- soft contacts (smooth and light contact between articulators when starting consonants)
- smooth airflow (continuous use of airflow to connect syllables together)
- phrasing (the correct use of airflow over phrase length speech)
- speech rate (must be maintained within +/– 10 SPM of target rate over the duration of the block of speech)
- maintaining prolonged speech (momentary speeding up is counted as a fluency skill error)
- 0 percent stuttering (tolerance is increased to 1 percent at the beginning of the transfer stage)
- blending (the correct use of airflow to link words without pausing).

Self-assessments

After a block of speaking time at a given rate the client makes a two-minute video. The client must use fluency skills within a specified range and his evaluation of his performance must be similar to the clinician's. If these criteria are met, the client can then progress to the next rate.

Discourse format

Clients initially complete their blocks of speaking time with oral reading. As competence and familiarity with the speech rate and speech skills increase, sessions are then mixed with monologue, then conversation. (See Table 12.1.)

Thus far, we have made two underlying assumptions: first, that operant-based prolonged speech programs all entail the use of an intensive group format, second, that it is necessary to instantiate the fluency shaping skills via a programmed step-wise increase in rate, initially starting at an abnormally slow pace, in order for progress to be made. But variants on the intensive schedule have been tried. For example, Ward (1992) reported some preliminary data from a semi-intensive piloted version of Boberg and Kully's CSP called semi-intensive fluency therapy (SIFT). Instead of the three-week fully intensive program, Ward had his group of clients attend for two hours per evening, five days a week over a three-week period; each two-hour evening session roughly corresponding to the complete day's involvement on the fully intensive CSP. This schedule meant a reduction in the number of client–clinician contact hours normally used on the CSP from approximately 110 hours to 30 hours.

Although greater focus was placed on stuttering control rather than stuttering elimination, a major question was whether clients could achieve similar levels of post-clinic fluency control to the CSP with just over a quarter of the usual client–clinician contact time, using a schedule where during the day clients maintained their normal routine, and in the earlier stages without using the fluency skills. Results showed a drop in group mean percentage of syllables stuttered from 12.7 percent syllables to 3.2 percent at post-clinic assessment. A corresponding increase in self-perception was also recorded post clinic, with mean S-24 scores decreasing from the baseline of 17.75 to 8.75. The rather weak design (for example, the pilot study lacked a control group) means that these data need to be interpreted cautiously. Nonetheless, Ward (1992) questioned whether the amount of programmed instruction on some of the fully intensive fluency programs was always necessary to reduce stuttering levels to acceptable levels.

The Camperdown program

More recently, Harrison, Onslow, Andrews, Packman, and Webber (1998) used a somewhat different approach to reduce the number of clinical hours from an established 2-week prolonged speech program (Onslow et al., 1996) to a single 12-hour residential day. Despite the differences in schedule and the complete elimination of a transfer phase of therapy in the 12-hour program, the two schedules revealed very similar treatment outcomes. This led the researchers to query whether programmed instruction was actually necessary for prolonged speech to be successful, and to the development of Harrison et al.'s (1998) approach, which is now called the Camperdown program (O'Brian, Onslow, Cream, & Packman, 2001). Like Lidcombe, it takes its name from a suburb of Sydney where the program was piloted. This program consists of four phases: individual teaching sessions, a group practice day, individual problem-solving sessions, and a performance-contingent maintenance stage.

Individual sessions

Participants learn the prolonged speech pattern by imitating the speech of a speaker seen on video talking at 70 syllables per minute. The clinicians give feedback on the client's progress, but no direct reference is made to the techniques being used (such as soft contacts). Clients have up to five five-minute sessions in which to replicate the speech model in a three-minute monologue. Clients also learn how to use a nine-point Likert scale of stuttering severity in order to make self-evaluations as to their level of stuttering during the five-minute blocks of speaking time. When two clinicians agree that the client can produce stutter-free speech for the three minutes, he can progress to the next stage.

Group practice

Here, clients in groups of three practise controlling their speech, whilst simultaneously maintaining natural sounding speech output. Instead of the step-wise increase in rate of the normal prolonged speech programs, there is now a series of 14 "cycles" each of which contains three phases:

- the practising of the unnatural speech pattern
- speaking in monologue using this pattern, but attempting to improve naturalness of speech
- self-evaluation of level of stuttering and speech naturalness using nine-point scales.

Cycles 1 to 6 last for 15 minutes each and have one clinician paired with one client. In the remaining eight cycles the second phase is replaced by a group conversation. The aim is for clients to achieve naturalness scores within the range of 1–3 and severity scores of 1–2 by the end of the first day.

Individual problem-solving sessions

These are one-hour weekly sessions held subsequent to the group practice day. The focus is on helping clients develop generalization of their improved fluency, and dealing with particular difficulties that may be arising. In contrast to established prolonged speech programs, however, there are no programmed transfer tasks. Progression to the final stage of the program occurs when the client can: (a) maintain a ten-minute conversation (within the clinic); (b) hold a three-minute conversation outside the clinic; whilst maintaining severity ratings of 1–2 and naturalness ratings of 1–3 in both cases. Within clinic measures are taken at the beginning of each weekly clinical session. The beyond clinic measures are taken from recordings that the client has made during the week. When criteria are met over three consecutive weeks, the participants are allowed to progress to the final stage.

Performance-contingent maintenance stage (PCMS)

Follow-up sessions are based at intervals of 2 weeks, 4 weeks, 8 weeks, 12 weeks and 24 weeks. Should a client fail to meet the criteria at each stage (the same as for the entry criteria) that step is then repeated.

Treatment outcome

Treatment outcome data have been reported on 30 participants (O'Brian, Onslow, Cream, & Packman, 2003). Mean percentage of syllables stuttered dropped from 7.9 percent, pretreatment to 0.4 percent at the beginning of the PCMS stage of therapy with this figure remaining consistent at 0.5 percent

6 months post PCMS, and 0.4 percent at 12 months post PCMS. Speech rate also rose from 172 syllables per minute (SPM) to 199 SPM at entry to PCMS, and 209 SPM at 12 months post PCMS. Speech naturalness figures revealed that ten participants achieved naturalness ratings (as judged by independent raters) which were similar to their matched control subject, although there was a statistically significant group difference between participants and controls.

There is much to consider here. The program appears to achieve similarly high levels of success as other prolonged speech programs (e.g., Boberg & Kully, 1994; Onslow et al., 1996) but with considerably reduced clinician–client contact time. The program is simple. There is no programmed instruction, no specialist equipment, nor even formal learning of fluency techniques, such as soft contacts and gentle onsets, On this basis O'Brian et al. (2003) argue that it may be feasible for generalist therapists to implement the program. Yet there are some unresolved issues. The follow-up data reported by O'Brian et al. (2003) are on only 16 participants, about 50 percent of the original number of participants. Some withdrawals were clearly unavoidable, but one questions the genuine motives of at least some of those clients who dropped out. (One would imagine that with a program as immediately effective as this, there would be a strong motivation to persist with it.) It may also be significant that 55 percent of the remaining participants said that they would still prefer to stutter than to use an unnatural speech pattern at least some of the time, and that all but three participants responded with scores of 5–9 (where 1 is not at all and 9 is all the time) when asked how much they had to think about controlling their stuttering. These last two statistics may well be among the most significant for the long-term success of those who undertake the Camperdown program. The fact that such levels of controlled fluency can be acquired in a comparatively short space of time is certainly of importance. Ultimately, though, the ability to be able to apply controlling techniques on an ongoing basis after the program has ended is the real end-goal for prolonged speech programs. Here lies the major issue for all adult therapies, but particularly for those which shape fluency. Children undertaking the Lidcombe program are trading in stuttering for normal speech, and this for many children appears to be sustainable in the long term. This is a very different situation to adults who undertake fluency shaping programs in whatever form. Here, stuttering is traded for a speech pattern that, while offering high levels of fluency, is still intrinsically unnatural. Sustaining this in the long term is a different matter. Future studies will determine whether the Camperdown program can provide sustainable benefits in excess of those from already existing programmed therapy designs.

Prolonged speech programs and speech naturalness

This issue of the quality of the final speech product of prolonged speech programs tends to sharply polarize opinion. Prolonged speech programs can result in very high levels of fluency, but even at the normal or near normal speech rates often achieved at the end of these programs, speech can sound abnormal, which is a criticism often leveled at the fluency shaping approach. There may be two sources of any unnaturalness in speech.

First, there are the fluency techniques themselves. Many of these, as used in fluency shaping programs, represent the exaggerated application of what are essentially automatic "normal" speech production processes, and the bringing of these processes under conscious control. So, for example, continuous airflow is fundamental and automatic in normal speech, but this can be broken when stuttering. However, the heavy emphasis of "smooth airflow" techniques in prolonged speech programs can lead to an unnaturally breathy sounding output.

Second, there is the prolongation component itself. In one sense, this is the mode of speech on which the fluency techniques are developed and is not a technique in its own right; the idea being that the prolonged speech aspect is slowly faded out during the program, eventually leaving the unobtrusive use of the various fluency techniques. In reality, the prolonged vowel component of this approach can be noticeable as an increased stretching of syllables, even when speech rates are near normal. It is encouraging to see that clinicians using fluency shaping techniques are trying to address the issues of speech acceptability and are reporting objective data on the naturalness of speech in their outcome measures (Kully & Langevin, 1994; O'Brian, Packman, Onslow, & O'Brian, 2004; Ryan, 2001). Those who feel more comfortable with the sound of their speech are more likely to maintain benefits in fluency.

What is sometimes forgotten though is that even stuttering modification techniques can also affect naturalness and speech rate. Ward and Dicker (1998) monitored the speech rate of a group of clients who followed a stutter more fluently approach (Van Riper, 1973) over a ten-month period. They found a significant decrease in speech rate for all clients from the modification phase and at post clinic when compared to baseline measures, even though speech rate was not targeted in therapy.

Integrated approaches to the treatment of stuttering

So far, we have talked about stuttering modification and fluency shaping approaches as being opposed to each other, in terms of theoretical orientation, as well as therapeutic approach and structure. Let's summarize this before looking at the issue in a little more detail.

PHILOSOPHY

On the one hand we have stuttering modification approaches, where the goal is to produce a more acceptable form of stuttering, while on the other we have fluency shaping approaches which use fluency skills in an attempt to ensure that stuttering does not arise in the first place.

COGNITIVE ASPECTS

In addition to modifying moments of stuttering, stuttering modification approaches focus on the attitudes, feelings and beliefs of the individual. This is particularly evident when dealing with avoidance behaviours and negative perceptions toward stuttering.

THERAPEUTIC SCHEDULE

Typically (though not exclusively) fluency shaping programs are group based and run for two or three weeks on an intensive schedule. Stuttering modification programs can successfully run this way, but some clinicians prefer individual long-term or weekly groups as alternatives.

THERAPEUTIC STRUCTURE

Fluency shaping programs are heavily structured, where progress between the substeps within the course is determined by detailed and objectively measured criteria. Stuttering modification sessions are much more loosely structured and rely more on a counselling style of interaction between clinician and client, rather than programmed instruction. It is therefore comparatively easy to document sufficient detail on operant program structure to allow accurate replication of the program by others. Outlines on stuttering modification approaches, on the other hand, are usually less well defined and clinical judgement plays a greater role in the client's progression through the program.

TREATMENT OUTCOME MEASURES

Fluency shaping programs place great importance on the measurement of speech data, the most important of these being the frequency of stuttering moments as measured as percent syllables or words stuttered. Increasingly though, acceptability of the resulting speech output to the client is now being measured. Stuttering modification approaches result in changes in the client's behaviour which are not easily measured. Although increasingly cognitive aspects and self-evaluation are regarded as important components when measuring the successfulness of therapy, some still claim that it is unacceptable for programs not to contain behavioural measures as a part of clinical efficacy data (e.g., Ryan, 2001).

The case for integration

The past few decades have seen clinicians and researchers from both sides of the debate often heatedly argue their cases for their preferred approach. Critics of stuttering modification approaches argue that there is a lack of emphasis on the collection of objective data, particularly with regard to measuring cognitive aspects of the disorder (Ingham, 1998; Ryan, 2001). Ryan (2001) goes so far as to claim that the majority of these programs are unethical because of the lack of objective outcome data. Some are less than convinced about the underlying philosophy of the approach, claiming that it just produces "happy stutterers", and that the focus of treatment should be either to eliminate stuttering moments (preferably) or at the very least to minimize them. Conversely, fluency shaping approaches have been attacked for denying the importance of cognitive aspects of the disorder. Some have suggested that by controlling stuttering with the use of fluency shaping techniques, one is merely substituting one abnormal pattern of speaking for another, and that what results is not real fluency, but "pseudo fluency" (Dayalu, Kalinowski, & Saltuklaroglu, 2002). A large part of the problem is that it has been assumed by some that adults presenting for fluency therapy wish to focus only on improving just that – fluency – and that this can really only be dealt with by the application of operant procedures (Ryan, 2001). But this perception is changing. Onslow (2004a:357) puts the point succinctly in a review of Ryan's (2001) book when he writes:

> Ryan may be on solid ground in an argument that with preschool children all that matters is to stop stuttering, but these days that is far from what is thought to be the case with adults. It is clear that when stuttering goes the problem of stuttering is far from resolved.

But as we said at the beginning of the chapter, despite the differences that can be observed between the two approaches, there are also commonalties. Look at the stuttering modification techniques advocated by Van Riper and compare them with some of the fluency skills advocated in fluency shaping programs and you will see considerable overlap in the type of adjustments that are made to motor speech systems. For example, the preparatory set used by Van Riper has much in common with the ubiquitous soft contact or easy glottal onset used in fluency shaping approaches. Also, as we have already seen, some operant-based programs do acknowledge the importance of cognitive factors. For example, Boberg and Kully's (1985) program justifiably falls under the fluency shaping banner, but it not only contains components on attitude and avoidance, but also uses fluency modification techniques such as cancellation towards the end of the course. This cross-over can in fact be seen in a number of programs which integrate therapy approaches (Bloom & Cooperman, 1999; Cheasman, 1983; Conture, 1990; Gregory, 1979, 2003; Guitar, 1998; Manning, 1996, 1999; Neilson, 1999; Shames & Florence, 1980; Williams, 1979).

At the Apple House we offer both individual and group programs for adults who stutter. I have explained in previous chapters that while many programs take on board aspects of both approaches and sit at some point on the continuum between the two extremes, some may be nearer to one or other end, some may sit firmly in the middle. Our position is that most people will benefit from a mixture of cognitive and behavioural aspects, but that the therapeutic focus between these two aspects will need to vary from individual to individual. For example, a person with a covert stutter is likely to benefit more from an approach which targets cognitive issues relating to self-concept, avoidance and fear of stuttering than one where the focus is on rebuilding motor speech patterns. At the same time though, stuttering modification procedures may well form an important part of therapy in providing strategies for the control of the stuttering which has only just become "externalized". Conversely, a person who is completely unable to move speech forward due to a severe stutter may be better suited to a program which will allow him to initiate and join in conversations, even if this is at the cost of a slightly unnatural sounding speech output.

It is probably true to say that in Great Britain there has been a movement away from prolonged speech programs for the treatment of adults who stutter and towards a more integrated/cognitive approach over the last two decades or so. Particularly, counselling approaches are increasingly being taken up by clinicians (see chapter 13) and incorporated into popular integrated approaches. My impression is that while North America is experiencing a similar trend, this may not be as pervasive as it is in Britain, and that Australasia may be even less affected.

As for Britain, I have concern that some clinicians may now be a little too ready to dismiss prolonged speech models. Yes, there are significant problems with the long-term maintenance of a natural sounding speech output with this approach. Yes, I believe that we should also consider alternative approaches for our clients. And yes, there are undoubtedly many clients for whom this approach does not bring satisfactory results. Further, it is, I believe, of critical importance that those about to embark on a prolonged speech program must be given a very honest appraisal of the type of speech that is likely to result, and to allow time to reflect on whether that speech would be acceptable to them. Particularly, potential clients need to have a realistic model of what controlled fluency sounds like; to be aware that in order to maintain it fluency skills will need to be practised on a regular basis, and that even with practice the long-term maintenance is far from guaranteed. I think also that potential clients need to be made aware that if high levels of fluency are not maintained in the long term, this may have as much to do with the limitations of the program as with any perceived "failure" on behalf of the client.

Despite the problems, prolonged speech can and does work in the long term for some clients. One particular client with a severe stutter who had recently completed a stuttering modification approach program springs to mind. While he felt he had benefited significantly from therapy and particularly the attitude adjustment aspects, he remained somewhat dissatisfied with the controlled stuttering that he had gained with this approach. He was determined to achieve very high levels of fluency and enrolled on a fluency shaping program while in his late twenties. Thirty years later he is very happy using the controlled speech (as opposed to the controlled stuttering) that he learned all those years ago. His speech is highly fluent and normal sounding, and he claims that he can maintain this effortlessly and under all speaking situations. We need to know more about why some people are able to achieve this level of continued success and why others are not. The client himself puts it down to his own stubbornness and determination, but others with similar levels of motivation and diligence in practice are not able to sustain such levels of fluency.

Covert stuttering

We conclude this chapter with an overview of covert stuttering, also known as interiorized stuttering. This term can be applied to a significant subgroup of people who find, that as stuttering develops, they are increasingly able to avoid overt stuttering by skilful avoidance. This may include avoidance of words or sounds, certain situations, certain people, and so on. Avoidance skills can become so well practised and internalized that it may appear to others as if the stutter is resolving, and some children and adults can carry this off to the point where there is no discernable stuttering whatsoever. Some feel that this technique actually represents a type of self-administered therapy. After all, the point of therapy is to reduce stuttering, and unquestionably covert stuttering does reduce stuttering, so perhaps this simply represents a fluency enhancing technique. Surely, if so, that's all well and good? But usually, all is neither well nor good. "Interiorizing" the problem means that the moment of stuttering may be avoided, but the fear of stuttering is far from eliminated and becomes exacerbated. Now, all the negative associations built up between word and stuttering, people and stuttering, place and stuttering, situation and stuttering remain, and indeed build up, albeit in the absence of disfluency.

There is worse. As the speaker experiences increased success at hiding the stutter, so the act of stuttering becomes that much more unacceptable, and the possibility of being recognized as a stutterer something to be avoided at all costs. Fear then increases the likelihood of stuttering, thus giving the speaker grounds for further internalization, and so the cycle is repeated. Throughout all this there is often a tug of war going on within the speaker. There is the fluent persona that the world sees, and which the speaker wishes to maintain. On the other hand, there is the inescapable truth that the speaker is a person who stutters, and the fact that this reality is at odds with the fluent image presented results in more pressure and greater anxiety. Ultimately, we have a picture of a person who while demonstrating very little or no stuttering is nonetheless being controlled by the disorder in a very direct and damaging way. Stuttering is often effortful, but so is constructing ever more convoluted sentences in an effort to avoid the increasing number of words which give difficulty. It is also damaging to alter one's lifestyle to accommodate this fear of being seen to stutter.

An integrated approach to the treatment of covert stuttering

Some clinics run management programs specifically for this subgroup of people who stutter (e.g., Cheasman & Everard, 2005). Often, Sheehan's model of fluency therapy is one of the "mainstream" approaches followed by clinicians, but many of the counselling approaches outlined in chapter 13 may also be appropriate. Below is described a three-phase approach that we follow at the Apple House. It borrows both from the work of Levy (1987) and Cheasman and Everard (2005) as well as our personal clinical experiences.

Identification/desensitization

For this client group, identification and desensitization phases effectively run together. That is, the very act of identifying stuttering is likely to be an uncomfortable process for this client group. However, it is important from the outset that the client recognizes the need to change his perception of his stutter, and the fact that the successful attempts to hide it are ultimately self-defeating. This will involve bringing the stutter out into the open, and in a graded way attempting to eliminate the escape and avoidance behaviours that have built up over the years. Some clients come to therapy already realizing this and, although anxious about self-disclosure, are keen to work on changing their view on the necessity to hide stuttering. Others present in the hope that therapy will simply provide strategies that reduce any stuttering moments appearing in their speech. Either way, management will involve disentangling a whole range of negative emotions and inappropriate thinking on behalf of the client. Established negative concepts such as "I must not be recognized as stuttering, at any cost" and "avoiding is good because it means I don't stutter" need to be changed into positive ones such as "it doesn't matter if I stutter sometimes" and "I will not let my stutter control what I want to say". Working in groups can be particularly useful in implementing the process of cognitive change, and a sympathetic clinician is essential in establishing an atmosphere where the client can be open about his stuttering. Iceberg analyses can be useful to start the process of change, with clients using the above and below the waterline model to help understand the link between stuttering and feelings associated with (the fear of) stuttering.

While discussing these issues, the client should now be confronting his stutter in the therapeutic sessions and choosing moments of stuttering over avoidance. Client reactions to this differ, but unsurprisingly it is mostly an upsetting experience suddenly to have all moments of stuttering exposed, even if this is only with a clinician, or amongst supportive group members. At the same time though, the process can also be empowering, as clients for the first time in their memory use the words and phrases that they wish to say, rather than those which they feel they are constrained to say. It is also true that in some cases the level of stuttering experienced when not avoiding is lower than anticipated.

Working in small steps, the client slowly becomes more and more used to not using word avoidance in the clinic. Together with the clinician he identifies a ranked inventory of feared situations. Where there is one-to-one therapy, the client may be given daily assignments to complete at home, at work, or both, where he slowly but systematically confronts a range of feared speaking situations. Tolerance to moments of stuttering in some of these situations can be built up by using voluntary stuttering, where the client easily controls the faked moments of stuttering in situations which are initially comfortable but increase in difficulty.

Modification

Up until now, the client has been undertaking more and more speaking situations with "open stuttering", but without any means of controlling the blocks, repetitions and prolongations that will be occurring. This of course leaves the client feeling vulnerable and exposed, but most clinicians agree that it is necessary for clients to reach this stage before attempting to modify stuttering. Some, like Sheehan (see above), may choose to ignore any modification of speech at all. Others, however, feel that the modification of stuttering is an important part of the process. For example, Cheasman and Everard (2005) combine Riperean procedures with those of Sheehan in their group approach which runs for two hours per week over a two-term (24 week) period. Where stuttering modification is combined with approach-avoidance, the timing of the introduction of the modification components needs to be well considered. Starting on controlling stuttering too early in the therapeutic process can lead to an over-reliance on techniques, resulting in increased fears that they might not work and a quick return to the old covert stuttering pattern.

Stuttering modification approaches may be more appropriate than fluency shaping ones, in that the former results in controlled stuttering, and the fact that stuttering is more visible helps reinforce the importance of not hiding the stuttering. Approaches that "rebuild speech" (as opposed to controlling stuttering) essentially cover up stuttering, and this is at odds with the openness that is essential to the management of a covert stutter. Such approaches are more likely to lead to the older patterns of fear of stuttering arising again, and with it a return to covert stuttering. Approaches to stuttering modification have already been described above and the constructs can be used in a similar way with those who have covert stutters.

Transfer and maintenance

In one sense, the transfer of skills has already begun in the identification/ desensitization phase of the program, with the client becoming more used to stuttering openly. This process continues throughout the therapy period and beyond, but now the client will also be learning to establish stuttering modification techniques in a variety of nonclinical settings. The continued use of practice routines and regular follow-up meetings with clinicians and other group members can help ensure that both cognitive and behavioural gains made in therapy can be sustained in the longer term.

Summary

It is theoretically possible for there to exist an almost infinite range of therapeutic approaches, implemented on an individual or group basis, and either in intensive or long-term format. Approaches range from the purely operant fluency shaping versions (see Ryan, 2001), through integrated programs with a strong operant bias (e.g., Boberg and Kully, 1985); integrated programs with a speech modification bias (Gregory, 1979, 2003); integrated programs with a speech modification and cognitive bias (e.g., the approach for covert stuttering), and so on, all the way through to the "pure" cognitive approach where there is no manipulation of speech whatsoever (e.g., Sheehan, 1975). Increasingly, clinicians are taking on board the idea that the successful management of adult stuttering must involve consideration of the individual's feelings and attitudes toward the problem, regardless of any therapeutic bias toward an operant or cognitive model of therapy.

Adult clients demonstrate greater variability across a number of variables than other age groups, and different clients with different needs and goals will benefit from different approaches. Certainly, a large number of people who stutter are extremely knowledgeable about various treatment options, have tried a wide variety and know which works for them.

As yet, there are no empirical data to indicate which client will benefit in the long term from which approach. Generally, it is thought that those with more severe stutters (as identified by high percentage of syllables stuttered) are more likely to benefit from fluency shaping programs, while those who hold strongly negative perceptions of their speaking and high levels of speech-related anxiety (as identified by cognitive assessments such as the S-24 and PSI) are likely to benefit from a more cognitive approach. In fact, it is not clear whether even this generalization holds true. Neither is it clear that those undertaking fluency shaping programs are at greater risk of potential relapse following therapy than those following a stuttering modification approach. However, where there is relapse following a fluency shaping program, this does tend to be more visible, but this has more to do with the fact that levels of fluency will be more obviously affected by relapse than with the stuttering modification approaches, where high levels of fluency are not the main focus of therapy. What is clear is that, regardless of whether therapy is modifying speech, fluency, cognition or a mixture of these, it is essential that the client is very aware of the goals of therapy, that these goals are his goals, and that he is made as aware as possible of the likelihood of these goals being completely achieved.

Key points

- Two approaches to treatment can be identified: stuttering modification and fluency shaping. The former modifies moments of stuttering; the latter modifies the way that both normal and stuttered speech is produced.
- Stuttering modification approaches usually place importance on the cognitive and affective aspects of the disorder. Pure cognitive approaches, however, focus solely on such aspects, and in the complete absence of any modification to speech.
- Increasingly, there is a move to integrate stuttering modification, fluency shaping and cognitive approaches, but the relative prominence of the different components vary from program to program. Some more closely resemble fluency shaping approaches, while others have more in common with stutter more fluently programs.
- There is little objective data as to which type of individual will be best suited to which therapeutic approach. However, covert stuttering may best be managed either by cognitive or cognitive/stuttering modification approaches.
- Different clients will benefit from different approaches to therapy. The goal for the clinician is to work with the client to find the most appropriate one. For this to be achieved, the clinician's aims and objectives must be shared by the client.
- Many approaches appear successful in the short term. Relapse is a significant problem for all treatment programs.

Further reading

Gregory, H. H. (2003). *Stuttering therapy: Rationale and procedures.* Boston: Allyn and Bacon.
In chapter 6, Gregory explains his Easy Relaxed Approach – Smooth Movements to adult (and teenager) therapy.

Guitar, B. (1998). *Stuttering: An integrated approach to its nature and treatment* (chapter 9, Advanced Stutterer). Philadelphia: Lipincott Williams & Wilkins.
This chapter gives a very useful resumé of a number of well-known treatment procedures currently used by respected authors from North America and Australia.

Ingham, R. J. (1984). *Stuttering and behaviour therapy: Current status and experimental foundations.* San Diego, CA: College Hill Press.
This book provides very detailed accounts of all aspects of behaviour therapy.

Manning, W. (2001). *Clinical decision making in the diagnosis and treatment of fluency disorders* (2nd ed.). Albany, NY: Delmar.

An entire volume based, as the title suggests, on the perspective of treatment as arising from a series of problem-solving episodes. Issues relating to treatment efficacy arise throughout.

Ryan, B. P. (2001). *Programmed stuttering therapy for children and adults* (2nd ed.). Springfield, IL: Charles C. Thomas.

This book updates the first edition of Ryan's (1974) ground-breaking book on the use of operant conditioning in stuttering therapy. Ryan's view of those who do not take an operant line on treatment has not mellowed over the last 30 years and he continues to regard many who practise alternative treatments as unethical.

Sheehan, J. G. (1975). Conflict theory and avoidance-reduction therapy. In J. Eisenson (Ed.), *Stuttering: A symposium*. New York: Harper and Row.

A comprehensive introduction to Sheehan's approach-avoidance conflict therapy.

Van Riper, C. (1973). *The treatment of stuttering.* Englewood Cliffs, NJ: Prentice-Hall. The definitive text on Van Riper's stuttering modification approach.

13 Counselling approaches

Introduction

In the earlier chapters of part 2 we have outlined some of the basic concepts and procedures used in therapy and have described treatment programs which provide examples of how these concepts and procedures have been put to use. Although we discussed the therapeutic importance of considering a person's attitude toward their stutter, we have not looked at the different cognitive frameworks available to achieve this. We now consider a number of counselling approaches which have been applied to the treatment of child, adolescent and adult stuttering. As with just about every other means of treating stuttering, responses to counselling approaches tend to be highly individualistic. There are people who have been helped by all of the approaches outlined below, and there will be others who have found no gain in all of those we discuss. With all of these approaches there are no hard and fast rules when it comes to their application to stuttering, and the manner in which the therapist integrates any approach with other fluency enhancing procedures will vary widely. Some may avoid speech modification completely, others may blend counselling and fluency shaping approaches to form a more holistic approach.

Many student clinicians (and a number of experienced ones also) feel uncomfortable about undertaking a counselling approach to stuttering therapy, and that it is underrepresented on speech language therapy training programs. Some students even feel that it should not be within their remit as qualified therapists to attempt to implement such methods and procedures, and that this is best left to qualified psychologists. It is unfortunately true that counselling approaches tend to get rather short shrift on training programs, but this is usually out of a mixture of necessity (lack of available time) and a knowledge that the necessary skill level cannot be achieved in this specialist area within the time constraints of the training program. Yet these skills are crucial to the clinician who aims to provide a comprehensive approach to the treatment of stuttering. There is no substitute for experience here and shadowing expert clinicians is one way of gaining knowledge in counselling skills. In addition, there are generalized courses on the subject that can be undertaken post qualification. Many of the approaches below offer courses leading to formal qualifications to deliver a particular type of therapy.

Rogers' three conditions of the counselling relationship

We do not discuss here some of the older counselling procedures; for example, Freudian approaches, which now have a limited impact on stuttering therapy. Rather, given limited space and the burgeoning range of new counselling approaches, some of the more recent developments are outlined. Whilst approaches differ subtly or in some cases rather obviously, it may be helpful to begin by outlining some factors which are common to all. Rogers (1951) described three conditions of the counselling relationship pertinent to his person-centred therapy specifically, but which are considered to be representative of good counselling procedure generally. Listed here, they provide a point of general orientation as to the relationship between clinician and client before moving on to describe a number of counselling approaches and the facilitation of "change".

1   *Congruence or transparency*. This refers to the clinician being open and honest. Displaying this effectively requires skill and good judgement on behalf of the clinician. Developing a relationship in which change can flourish may require the clinician to probe deeply, yet the clinician must not be perceived as aloof and unapproachable. Self-disclosure on behalf of the clinician can be a useful counselling tool in achieving congruence, when used appropriately.
2   *Unconditional positive regard*. As the name suggests, the client must be seen in a positive light, unconditionally, rather than as a subject whose behaviour is to be manipulated. The client is valued for who he is, without resort to making judgements. As Gregory (2003) points out, this can be difficult, and it is natural for clinicians to be affected in some way if, for example, the person we are seeing reminds us of someone we have known in the past. The key is that the clinician is in partnership with the client, and that the type of teacher–pupil relationship (regardless of the age of the client) is avoided.
3   *Empathic understanding*. This has been described by Gregory (2003) as where "the clinician remains focused and attuned as accurately as possible to what the client brings to the encounter and especially to the underlying emotions" (p. 273). As Gregory points out, Rogers was keen to explain that being person-centred was in no way passive, but involved what he termed "active listening".

Cognitive therapy

This is really a cover term for a range of approaches that address the effects which cognitions, whether negative or positive, have on an individual's behaviour. As such all the sections below represent examples of cognitive therapy, but the premise underlying all is that cognitions (for us this particularly means those which relate to our self-perceptions as speakers) can be modified, when needed. While it is true that some people who stutter may not hold negative attitudes toward themselves and their speech, a great many do. Relatedly, such individuals may experience high levels of anxiety about speaking (Wright, Ayre, & Grogan, 1998). This in turn may be perceived in terms of a social cost (Fry & Farrants, 2003) and as social anxiety. In fact, recent research indicates that as many as 50 percent of those who stutter may warrant a diagnosis of social phobia (see also Kraaimaat, Vanryckeghem, & Van Dam-Baggen, 2002; Schneier, Wexler, & Liebowitz, 1997).

Cognitive therapy may address these issues in a number of ways, and in a recent paper Fry (2005) outlines a range of approaches. From the outset, clients are encouraged to confront and challenge their negative self-perceptions and to reconstruct or reframe them. The identification of negative automatic thoughts and emotions and their effect on fluency may be achieved through use of video taping to help the client observe the differences between his self-perceptions and the actual reality. Group work and role play can also play a significant part in this phase of therapy. Clients are also helped to offer alternative explanations for events to which they automatically assign negative perceptions. Communication skills, including aspects such as observation and assertiveness, are also targeted. The use of the latter can help in promoting a greater awareness of others' reactions, and helps the client to consider others' responses rather than his own (often irrational) predications as to how he is perceived. Cognitive therapy need not be undertaken as the sole method of intervention. Fry (2005) also advocates the use of cognitive approaches alongside fluency modification strategies, and also other counselling procedures such as brief therapy and personal construct therapy. (See Carolyn Gregory's excellent chapter on the use of counselling techniques and cognitive therapy in stuttering therapy; Gregory, 2003.)

Personal construct therapy

Personal construct therapy (PCT) is a therapeutic approach which has developed initially from the work of humanistic psychologist George Kelly (1955) and more latterly Fay Fransella (1972). Kelly's psychology is based on the assumption that man has the ability to change every aspect of his thought, emotion and behaviour. Our world is interpreted through the creation of an interlinked network of personal constructs built up through previous experience (both direct and vicarious). Constructs can be seen as a type of bipolar mental rating scale: good–bad, happy–sad, success–failure are three examples of constructs. Each individual judges every aspect of his environment – people, society, problems – through the use of constructs, with each person producing their own bipolar pairs. We then actively use these constructs, which consist of our theories about people, environment and situations, to anticipate the future and to help us to cope effectively with a variety of alternative scenarios. Our anticipation of how an event will be then allows us to test our coping strategies of the encounter in advance. If our construct system is correct, the reality of the event will conform to our expectations. If our construct system is incorrect we are likely to feel uncomfortable and possibly confused by the new experience. Both long-term and short-term goals are planned through our consideration of constructs, and we use these to anticipate potential problems in reaching our goals.

A key concept with PCT is that we should not need to rely solely on our past experience. If we accept that interpretations of past events may in some cases be incorrect, we can revise our construct system and achieve outcomes which otherwise would not be possible. So, with all constructs subject to the possibility of revision and change, we are not constrained always to play out the role which we had grown up with. Instead we have the ability to modify and adapt our beliefs about ourselves and others through the elaboration and modification of existing constructs and the addition of new ones.

PCT and stuttering

PCT may be used in a number of ways in the treatment of stuttering. It has been implemented with children, adults and adolescents (Botterill & Cook, 1987; Hayhow, 1987; Hayhow & Levy, 1993), offering a psychological framework from which the clinician and client can work together to alter the client's perception of himself with relation to the stutter, and to the world in which he and the stutter exists. Reconstruing may in itself lead to improvements in fluency, as more effective constructs develop and anxiety decreases, but PCT can also be used in conjunction with direct stuttering modification techniques (Botterill & Cook, 1987).

At a general level, most therapy focuses on the clinician's concern to understand the construct systems of the client in order to characterize and deal with their problems. Particularly, stuttering amongst some people may be associated with long-held "static" and often faulty constructs which the individual feels unable to modify. Fransella (1972) argues that people may choose to stutter because this is the most familiar and predictable role to play. It is the therapist's task to help the person discard the old and destructive construct systems and develop new ones. Stuttering is often linked with anxiety. In Kellian terms anxiety means realizing that the situations being faced lie for the large part outside one's construct system. As control over fluency and anxiety are incompatible, it is important to help the client reappraise his or her construct system to deal better with the effects of the stutter.

Therapeutic applications

Uncovering personal constructs

We have already briefly explained the nature of personal constructs. These vary in their importance and some are more core to a person than others. Constructs may also be nested, forming a subordinate pattern. The more core constructs are uncovered, the more we get to know the person's deepest and most significant feelings, fears, anxieties, beliefs. Reaching central constructions may be achieved with relative ease with some clients, while others may be less willing to share innermost thoughts. Thus, in some cases a clinician and client may interact at a core construct level; a more subordinate or peripheral level may be appropriate with others.

Techniques

The clinician's examination of the client's view of the world may be achieved by use of a number of techniques. Some, such as self-characterization where the client describes himself from the perspective of a third party, are commonly used as a part of the self-identification process across a range of therapy approaches. Others are used almost exclusively with PCT. With all, it is important that the clinician does not (knowingly or unknowingly) impose her own belief system on the client's constructions.

USING ELEMENTS (A TERM DESCRIBING ANYTHING THAT CAN BE CONTRUED)
TO ELICIT CONSTRUCTS

Kelly suggests selecting elements from one of 24 construct titles: for example: "Your mother (or the person who has played the part of your mother in your life)" and "Brother nearest your age (or the person who has been most like a brother)". The constructs may then be elaborated by use of additional statements such as:

- As I am now.
- As I would like to be.
- As I am when stuttering.
- As I think I will be after therapy.

The use of triads may now be employed to detect similarities and differences. For example, three constructs may be selected, and the client then considers a way in which the two are alike but different from the third. So, using the present example "mother" and "as I would like to be" might be put together because, perhaps they both understand the anxiety of stuttering while "brother" teases about stuttering.

A common approach to the structuring of constructs is called "laddering"

(Hinkle, 1965). This involves the clinician gently probing a particular construct, in reductionist fashion, so the client is in the end confronted with an irreducible statement and the core construct is elicited. Hayhow and Levy (1993) describe an example where the client is asked whether they would prefer to be a person who stutters or a person who speaks fluently, to which the client replies, "I'd prefer to speak fluently." The clinician responds, "Why would you prefer to be a person who speaks fluently?" The client replies, "Because I can say what I want to." The clinician continues probing in this manner, with the client giving reasons for wanting to be fluent moving from "being a more effective speaker" through being able to share with others and make friends to the final statement that "without relationships there's no point really".

Repertory grids

Another way of teasing out constructs is through the use of repertory grids. Here, an element (or elements) are presented with various constructs pertaining to that element rated on a scale below. The size of the rating scale will vary, depending on the construct which is being tested, but usually a seven-or nine-point scale is used.

The case below, described by Hayhow and Levy (1993), shows a grid pattern for the case of Sally (Table 13.1). Immediately striking is that her construct system is dominated by confidence. The *as I am* element contrasts sharply for this construct with almost all others (including *as I'd like to be*) which are perceived as strongly confident. In addition, a great number of the constructs are defined by extreme scores and these findings lead toward a number of suggestions for change. First, some way of breaking the "rules" of Sally's construct system needs to be found to change the apparent idea that one rule must automatically imply the other. This could be done by trying to have her think of a person who is both confident but not calm, or confident but unfriendly. Hayhow and Levy also suggest that constraining the extremes of Sally's judgements could be achieved by limiting the range of the constructs, for example, *more sensitive-less sensitive*. Most important to my mind from this example is the lack of correlation between the *fluent self* and *as I would like to be* elements. This strongly suggests that for this individual at least therapy will need to go beyond learning a fluency controlling technique, and that "Such change will need to be accompanied by major reconstruing of self and others" (Hayhow & Levy, 1993, p. 108).

Transactional analysis

This approach, developed by the Canadian psychotherapist Eric Berne, holds that we live out our lives according to scripts which are formed in childhood, but which continue to influence us and the life choices we make throughout our lives (Berne, 1968, 1991). An often cited example of a script is "Be Perfect"

Table 13.1. Repertory grid for Sally (from Hayhow & Levy, 1993. Reprinted with permission)

Key:
(1) = Mother; (2) = Father; (3) = Vince; (4) = Flora; (5) = As I am; (6) = As I'd like to be; (7) = Stuttering self; (8) = Fluent self; (9) = James; (10) = Carolyn; (11) = Anne; (12) = Kate

	Repertory grid: Sally Scale: 1–9	1	2	3	4	5	6	7	8	9	10	11	12
1	Strong character – weak character	1	7	1	1	8	1	9	3	1	3	2	1
2	Speaks their mind – passive	1	8	2	1	6	1	8	1	1	1	1	1
3	Stubborn – easygoing	1	1	2	3	5	5	8	5	1	5	5	1
4	Ambitious – unambitious	1	2	1	1	3	1	8	1	2	1	1	9
5	Talkative – quiet	1	7	6	2	5	2	8	2	1	3	2	1
6	Very sensitive – insensitive	9	8	7	7	1	7	1	7	9	7	8	9
7	Outgoing – introverted	2	8	4	2	7	2	9	7	1	3	1	3
8	Very assertive – unassertive	1	8	7	1	5	1	9	7	2	2	1	1
9	Very articulate – not articulate	1	5	2	2	4	1	9	2	2	1	1	2
10	Confident – lacking in confidence	1	3	3	1	8	1	9	3	2	2	1	1
11	Determined – undetermined	1	2	1	1	6	1	8	6	1	2	1	1
12	Very friendly – unfriendly	2	2	3	1	5	2	7	4	1	4	1	4
13	Calm – nervous	2	6	5	3	8	2	9	5	1	1	3	4
14	Socially acceptable – socially unacceptable	1	3	2	2	5	2	9	5	2	2	1	4
15	Doesn't experience fear – experiences fear	1	4	2	1	7	2	8	6	1	2	3	2

where we feel we should always be doing better. Therapy consists of gaining a deeper understanding of these scripts in order to change unwanted behaviour or feelings that arise because of them. Transactional analysis (TA) combines two elements; those of structural analysis which is a theory of personality, and transactional analysis which is a theory of communication. In therapy, the personality aspect of the theory, in the form of what Berne called an ego state model, must always precede the analysis of the transactions themselves. Transactions, Berne (1968) explains, are the result of a build-up of a series of exchanges or interactions (called strokes) between people. These strokes may be nonverbal and may be either positive (e.g., smiling) or negative (a common one for people who stutter is poor eye contact).

Each person may use one of three ego states within a transaction (let's focus here on verbal transactions). These three states comprise parent, adult, child. A complementary transaction occurs when, for example, a person addresses another from an adult ego state, and receives a response from an adult ego state. An example would be thus:

Q: *What time do we need to be at the Jones's tomorrow?*
A: *Around 7:15 in readiness for the 7:30 start.*

Consider if the same question (adult to adult) was asked, but this time the response is from a parent to adult state. Such a response might be:

A: *Around 7:15. You know, you really should have remembered that yourself.*

Conversely, a child to adult response might comprise something like this:

A: *Why is it that I have to remember everything?*

Complementary transactions do not necessarily require a response from the same ego state, but merely a response from the ego state that is intended by the person eliciting the response. Take the following exchange which has a child to parent statement met with a parent to child response:

Q: *What could I have done with my diary? I can't remember what time we are supposed to be at the Jones's.*
A: *That's OK. I'll phone them up and I'll check.*

An important part of TA philosophy is that of the contract between clinician and client. This involves equality and openness in the relationship. The client who stutters will be encouraged to set his own therapeutic goals and take on active responsibility in the quest to attain them. The clinician, on the other hand, takes on more of a role of facilitator in this process. Nonetheless the TA counsellor still has a more directive role in therapy than in some other counselling approaches. The crucial issue is the "cure", whereas in other approaches, for example, client-centred therapy, the relationship between the counsellor and client is the most important factor.

Rational emotive therapy

Sometimes referred to as rational emotive behaviour therapy, this approach was developed by Albert Ellis, a trained psychoanalyst who became interested in behavioural learning theory. As its name suggests, this approach not only considers the client's thinking, but also the emotions and behaviour which arise from it. It explores the close relationship between thinking and emotion. The major focus of therapy is to help clients change ineffective and irrational thinking, and to demonstrate to the client how these dysfunctional patterns of thinking may lead to emotional difficulties and self-defeating behaviour. In other words, it is not life events which constitute the main problem, it is in the ways to which those events are reacted (Ellis, 1990).

As far as stuttering is concerned, key to the theory is the idea that a build-up of negative information takes place in childhood. There may be a number of potential sources – parents, peer groups or society more generally. This leads to negative internal language or "self-scolding" behaviour. Unlike some other approaches (e.g., psychodynamic theory), the emphasis is less on the original source of the irrational thought, but more on how to deal with the difficulties which are currently presenting. Rational emotive therapy is therefore concerned with the way that the original problem of stuttering is perpetuated and exacerbated by ineffective and irrational thinking and internal verbalization. In addition, the client is helped to identify how the irrational thinking is contributing to the problem. A framework is provided to help reverse the process and lead the client toward more rational ways of thinking.

The ABC model

Therapy may utilize Ellis's ABC model (see Figure 13.1). Point A, represents an event to which the person who stutters might respond with negative self-talk or "catastrophizing" (point B). This in turn leads to a negative emotional consequence (point C) and then as a result a negative behavioural one.

In the case of our example below, rational emotive therapy would seek to rationalize the faulty internal dialogue seen in point B. The therapist might seek to discuss the possibility of having James look at the positive aspects of

---

A   James, who has a stutter is disfluent whilst introducing himself to Ben, a new work colleague.

B   James thinks, "That was terrible. Now he knows I have a speech problem. He must wonder what's going on. He probably thinks I have a really severe problem."

C   James feels depressed.

D   James now avoids speaking to Ben.

Ben notices this avoidance and takes it as an indication that James dislikes him. Ben now avoids meeting James wherever possible. James takes this as reinforcement that Ben thinks he (James) has a really severe problem with his speech.

Figure 13.1 Example of catastrophizing, using Ellis's ABC model.

the exchange (making good eye contact, smiling) as well as confronting the counterproductive and irrational belief that Ben must think negatively about him because of the stutter. In order to achieve this, James would need to change his internal dialogue. Techniques such as role play can provide useful platforms from which to practise this.

Neurolinguistic programming

This is arguably the most well known of the para-psychotherapies that has been applied to stuttering. It was developed in the 1970s by Richard Bandler (a mathematician and gestalt therapist) and John Grinder (a linguist). The original intention was to determine the processes by which some individuals became very successful whilst others did not. Bandler and Grinder closely examined the dynamics of successful therapists, including aspects such as thinking processes, movement and verbal and nonverbal communication. Their findings led to the establishment of neurolinguistic programming (NLP). NLP is unusual in that, unlike most other counselling approaches, it does not have a single theoretical/psychological starting point, but instead cherry-picks concepts from a number of other existing psychotherapeutic approaches. A number of people have expressed some concern over the title and even some qualified NLP practitioners who are very enthusiastic as to what can be achieved within this framework seem a little uneasy about it. Whether one is or is not at ease with the title, it certainly seems possible to take on board the basic concepts of NLP without having to accept the idea that we are all "neurolinguistically programmed" in any literal sense.

A basic feature of NLP is that for effective communication to take place one must be aware of which one of three "modes" they are operating in: visual, auditory or kinaesthetic. A breakdown in communication may occur if two (or more) speakers fail to recognize the mode which the other(s) is using. Thus, the person skilled in the use of NLP should be able to match the mode of their conversational partner by mirroring back the mode the other is using. For example, visual words and phrases include "I can *see* what you are getting at" or "*looking* at it from this perspective". An "auditory" person may use phrases like "I *hear* what you are saying", whilst a kinaesthetic person may use language such as "I *feel* that we're on the same track". NLP has been used widely, particularly across the private sector, where business may be conducted more efficiently and with less misunderstanding when people are more aware or tuned in to the modes of their colleagues and customers.

NLP and stuttering

Behind the NLP approach to stuttering lies the notion that it is strongly conditioned by anxiety and concern, which in turn lead to an increase in the disorder. As such, it is a perspective which can be applied more easily to established rather than early onset stuttering. Moreover, NLP argues that if thinking is appropriate, then there will be no stuttering. The fact that most people who stutter are fluent under certain circumstances when there is no pressure or anxiety, for example, when talking aloud to themselves or pets, is seen as evidence for this perspective. Writing in the British Stammering Association publication *Speaking Out*, Jones (1997) presents this perspective succinctly:

> It is my contention that "uneasy thoughts" about speaking situations create the physical and emotional effects we call stuttering. NLP made me realise that the way I had been thinking was not something that made my stammer worse or better, it was my stammer!
>
> My problem is having a stammer; knowing I've got "a stammer" makes me feel nervous; when I feel nervous I know I'll probably stammer. This is the dog chasing its tail! We have to turn it around and realise that "a stammer" is simply a linguistic label of complex mental/physical process triggered by specific stimuli. And that it is uneasy feelings, triggered by those stimuli that cause the stammering behaviour.

Bodenhamer (2004) makes a similar point, arguing that although organic factors may play a part in the original appearance of stuttering in childhood, the blocks that develop later do so due to negative associations built up over a period of years. Thus it is the semantics of the word (and the negative associations of having stuttered on that word before) which serve to underlie the problem, not the physical act of blocking itself. Therefore, to deal with stuttering one must first understand the existing "programs", that is, the ones giving rise to (or in Jones's terms actually *are*) stuttering. Some elements here bear similarity to Johnson's diagnosogenic theory. This will mean closely examining those negative feelings, and how they have become attached to specific speaking situations. Therapy then involves the reprogramming of these learned and established "uneasy thoughts", and in their place aims to instil the same feelings which arise under conditions where there is spontaneous fluency.

In many ways, this approach bears similarity to the relaxation/hypnosis model of stuttering rather than a "neurolinguistic" one. An example of this is reported in a case study of an adult stutterer whose fluency worsened under specific stressful situations (Binns & Phillips, 1997). Therapy centred on the premise that in order to feel anxiety and stress we turn our conscious attention inward upon ourselves. This focus then means we are unable to simultaneously attend to our environment and other people. To counteract this, the subject was taught stress reduction by actively focusing carefully on what other people were doing at these particular times. The subject reportedly found it impossible to do this whilst at the same time maintaining high levels of anxiety, which would normally have activated the stuttering. A second effect of this approach was that her perceptions of others around her at that time changed, finding them less threatening.

NLP as a part of an integrated approach to stuttering therapy

While some proponents of NLP find the procedures work well at reducing stuttering as a stand-alone technique, clinicians also combine it with fluency shaping and fluency modification techniques. For example, a common finding is that a range of behavioural techniques (particularly with older school age and adult clients) can result in quite high levels of fluency within the clinic, but that transfer of speech skills from the clinic to the outside world and subsequent establishment of these skills can be extremely difficult, and regarded by many as the hardest stages of the therapeutic process. Directly related to this is the issue that anxiety and stress levels, which may be well controlled in the clinic, rise significantly when the client is away from the fluency generating atmosphere of the clinic. Thus difficult transfer tasks such as phoning to a stranger may be completed with minimum difficulty in the clinic, but with extreme difficulty elsewhere. It is also common for clients to say that this failure is associated not so much with a failure of the techniques as such, but rather an inability to put them to use due to increased stress and anxiety levels. A range of NLP techniques may be useful in controlling these levels, to the point where any remaining fluency difficulties can be dealt with more effectively by the previously taught fluency techniques.

Brief therapy

Brief therapy (or solution-based therapy as it also known; Proctor & Walker, 1987) is a comparatively new approach which offers another problem-solving perspective to the disorder of stuttering. Like NLP, it borrows from other counselling procedures including the work of Rogers (1951) to provide a framework under which an individual can make self-determined changes to behaviour. It has at its core the need for understanding how communication between people causes problems to occur; the role which human communication plays in maintaining that problem, and how it can be a factor in problem resolution. As the name suggests, therapy can be successfully implemented over a short space of time, often within four to six sessions. However, this may extend to a matter of months for some people who stutter. An underlying premise to brief therapy is the notion that as a person becomes more aware of their failure to resolve a problem, the more difficult that problem is seen to be. This results in ever-increasing efforts being made to bring a resolution to the problem which in turn, Proctor and Walker (1987) argue, leads to a narrowing of the range of options an individual will consider to potentially ameliorate the situation. To this end, brief therapy focuses on the client and client-led personal change, rather than the moments of stuttering. The language used to try to bring about these changes is nondirective.

The fundamental focus underlying treatment is on solution and a shift from "problem talk" to "solution talk" (Burns, 2005; Cade & Hanlon, 1993; George, Iveson, & Ratner, 2001). The clinician's role is to guide and encourage the client towards finding his own way of changing and his own solutions; working to the client's individual's strengths and making positive use of his resources. Throughout, the focus is on achievement, what is going right and the future, rather than failure, what is going wrong and the difficulties of the past. In this sense, the approach turns on its head the "normative model", where stuttering is seen as a problem and where treatment is prescribed on the basis of the therapist's beliefs about it. The exact course that therapy takes varies from individual to individual, but the solution-based approach is concerned with building on fluency and situations under which increased fluency has been experienced in the past, rather than eliminating stuttering. Thus a common starting point lies in the identification of times and circumstances when fluency is improved. The client is then encouraged to build on this platform, all the time increasing awareness of the positive attributes and strengths that he brings to the process of change. Rating scales developed between the client and clinician are often employed to monitor the progress in change of behaviours. These may be related to levels of fluency or levels of cognitive adjustment.

Brief therapy can be used with younger clients and their parents. Hayhow and Levy (1993) offer a hypothetical case of a young child who has started to stutter where the child's parents' expression of their anxiety over the stutter only serves to maintain the problem. Accordingly, the clinician encourages the parents to keep a diary of the child's stuttering which will help better to understand the problem at their next meeting. Reframing the stutter could involve suggesting to the parents that the stutter may be due to the child's rapid increase in vocabulary. The idea is that now stuttering is not seen as negative, as it is associated with developing language skills, and this will lead to a reduction in stuttering. Hayhow and Levy (1993) refer to this process as "prescribing a symptom" and it needs to be maintained for some time even after any reduction in stuttering has been seen. As much as the approach in this example could be seen as a placebo (and some may feel uncomfortable with the idea that parents are being deceived), the argument is that the parents are no longer engaged in negatively affecting the stutter. Brief therapy can also be used effectively with adolescents and adults. As with Sheehan's approach-avoidance conflict therapy, and Van Riper's stuttering modification therapy (see chapter 12), the focus is on desensitization and open stuttering and the idea that the stuttering individual needs to be accepting of the disorder.

Summary

Counselling can be used with all age groups, and may be used as a stand-alone approach or can be combined with other procedures which more directly target the observable speech behaviours arising due to stuttering. We have seen in chapter 10 how the parent–child interaction (PCI) model uses a cognitive therapeutic framework to counsel the parents of preschool and school aged children who stutter, an approach also used in other established programs (for example, Hill, 2003). The focus of counselling in older children and adolescents, in addition to examining the child's feelings, beliefs and experiences, may require the clinician to draw in other professionals such as teachers, special educational needs workers and psychologists to provide a comprehensive therapeutic package which helps the child to deal with cognitive, affective and behavioural responses relating to stuttering and its effects, in various different environments. Adults too may benefit from counselling, and more and more clinicians are using such approaches as they seek to avoid "the fluency fallacy". (This term refers to the over-reliance placed on measuring stuttering only in terms of the percentage of syllables which are stuttered. See Sheehan, 1984 for a criticism of this.)

There is a growing recognition, even amongst those who favour a strong focus on motor speech aspects of management, of the importance of cognitive change (Onslow, 2004b). A counselling approach helps a person learn to live with a speech output which is disrupted, but in being able more easily to control the fear, avoidance and concern that has hitherto grown alongside the stuttering can help provide a more lasting solution.

Key points

- There are a number of cognitive psychological philosophies which have been applied to the treatment of stuttering. Some, like rational emotive therapy and personal construct therapy, work from a single underlying psychological perspective. Others, such as neuro-linguistic programming therapy and brief therapy, integrate a number of features from a range of approaches.
- All therapies, in varying manner, involve the client reframing his perceptions of himself as a person and the role of the stutter on life events.
- Counselling requires specific skills from the clinician which are not usually covered in speech language therapy training programs. There are many post-qualification courses which offer an opportunity to develop skills, both as a generic counsellor and more specifically with regard to a particular approach.
- Formal outcome data are lacking from all approaches, but the increase in uptake of these approaches by clinicians seems consistent with a general trend toward increased cognitive evaluation and treatment of established stuttering.
- The objective measurement of cognitive therapies is difficult (see chapter 9). There are no data as to the relative effectiveness of one

counselling approach over another. However, objective outcome measures could be obtained through the use of self-rating profiles such as the WASSP, OASES or PSI (see chapter 9).

Further reading

Burns, K. (2005). *Focus on solutions: A health professional's guide*. Chichester: Wiley.
A clear and thorough guide to solution-based therapy written by a London-based speech language therapist. This provides a very practical coverage of the subject matter and throughout the use of case examples helps illustrate the key points and concepts.

Flasher, C. V., & Fogle, P. T. (2004). *Counseling skills for speech language pathologists and audiologists*. New York: Delmar.
A very useful and practical guide to a range of counselling techniques.

Gregory, C. B. (2003). Counseling and stuttering therapy. In H. H.Gregory (Ed.), *Stuttering therapy: Rationale and procedures* (pp. 263–296). Boston: Allyn and Bacon.
An extensive chapter on counselling and stuttering. Rather than outline the differences between counselling approaches, this chapter looks at issues arising in stuttering treatment and shows how various counselling techniques can be used to shape cognitive, behavioural and affective responses to stuttering and the speaker's perception of speaking. The chapter is very thorough on older counselling frameworks (e.g., Rogers and Freud), but does not mention approaches such as NLP and brief therapy.

Hayhow, R., & Levy, C. (1993). *Working with stuttering: A personal construct approach*. Bicester: Winslow Press.
A clear and comprehensive workbook comprising ten chapters on the use of personal construct therapy with all age groups. This book is a recommended source for any clinician wishing to undertake this approach.

Hough, M. (1998). *A practical approach to counselling* (7th ed.). London: Longman.
Although focused on counselling rather than stuttering, this little book provides a very clear introduction to a wide range of counselling approaches. Case studies help provide practical examples as to how the techniques can be applied.

14 Alternative approaches to the treatment of stuttering

Introduction

The decision as to what to include under a heading of "alternative" treatment approaches automatically reflects on what can be considered "mainstream" therapy, and this must take the form of a somewhat arbitrary decision. Throughout chapters 10 to 13 I have referred to established approaches which have been based on interaction between a qualified speech and language therapist/speech and language pathologist (SLT/SLP) resting, broadly speaking, on the tenet that therapy can focus on: (a) altering vocal tract dynamics to increase levels of fluency; (b) changing the client's behavioural, cognitive and affective responses to stuttering; or (c) a combination of these two strategies. The approaches described in the present chapter appear because they fail, in various ways, to fulfil these assumptions. For example, altered auditory feedback therapy works on the basis that stuttering occurs as a result of faulty auditory processing, rather than faulty speech production. Although this is hardly a new idea (for example, Van Riper was making a claim for a faulty auditory processing component to the disorder over three decades ago), the form that therapy takes does not directly address these beliefs. On the other hand, the use of altered auditory feedback in the form described in this chapter looks to the feedback altering devices themselves to provide the fluency enhancing effects in the form of a prophylaxis. Their set-up requires either minimal or no input from a clinician.

The computerized devices described in a further section really constitute therapeutic adjuncts to the speech retraining type approach rather than an alternative treatment procedure. However, they receive a mention in this chapter because they are devices not commonly seen in fluency clinics. The next two approaches considered, botulinum treatment and drug treatments, look at stuttering from physiological and neurophysiological perspectives respectively. The future of botulinum treatment of stuttering is unclear at the moment, while attempting to control and reduce stuttering through the use of drug regimes has barely yet reached an experimental stage.

The final category comprises a consideration of some high-profile therapy programs, developed and implemented not by SLTs/SLPs but by people who themselves stutter. There has for some time been resentment among some people who stutter that treatment programs have mostly been developed and implemented by fluent clinicians who, whilst apparently knowing the theory about the disorder, lack the fundamental understanding of what it means to grow up and live with a stutter, and the way life can be affected by it. Of course, a great many highly distinguished qualified clinicians who have developed their own therapy programs have also stuttered; Einer Boberg, David Daly, Hugo Gregory, Barry Guitar, Wendell Johnson, William Perkins, Joseph Sheehan, and Charles Van Riper, to name but a few. However, this chapter focuses on those who have developed their own treatment programs in the absence of recognized SLT/SLP training, and often on the basis of life experiences and what has helped them, rather than what a textbook tells them should help them. SLTs and SLPs have traditionally been resistant to this development, due in many cases it has to be said to a sense of insecurity. I think too there is a sense of mistrust of such programs, which may be more evident in Britain than elsewhere. This may in some part be due to the fact that in Britain the vast majority of fluency therapy is provided free of charge under the auspices of the National Health Service. Those who run privately funded clinics are sometimes accused of placing a greater concern on generating income, rather than the ultimate well-being of their clients (regardless of whether the program directors are people who stutter or not). The different funding arrangements that exist for practising SLPs in the USA and elsewhere mean that this situation does not arise, at least not in the way that it does in Great Britain.

Altered feedback therapies

Introduction

As we have seen in chapter 3, a consistent finding over many years has been that most people who stutter find their fluency improves dramatically and effortlessly when singing or talking in unison. This increase in fluency has been credited to the influence on the speaker of the co-occurring speech signals picked up from the other speakers. Those altered feedback devices which utilize the effects of delayed auditory feedback (where the voice is heard a fraction of a second following its production) and frequency altered feedback (where the voice is heard with no time delay, but with a change in pitch) artificially attempt to recreate the exogenous speech signals that occur when speaking in time amongst others to enhance fluency. It is also known that when the speaker is less able to hear his own voice fluency typically improves. In addition, devices have been developed which utilize the masking of the speaker's speech signal to improve fluency. We begin, though, by looking at devices which effectively mimic others' speech signals.

Choral speech and shadowed speech

Under choral or unison speech the speaker produces the same words simultaneously alongside another model speaker. The fluency enhancing effects of this process can be quite dramatic for the majority of people who stutter, including those with severe stutters, resulting immediately in normal sounding and normal rate speech. Shadowed speech, which is very closely related to choral and unison versions, occurs where there is a slight delay between the speech of the model speaker and the shadower, as opposed to the simultaneous output produced during unison and choral speech. Like choral/ unison speech, shadowing can result in dramatic increases in fluency (Cherry & Sayers, 1956; Kelham & McHale, 1966), but like them also the gains in fluency tend to be lost once the stimulus of the model speaker has ended. Because of this, choral or shadowed speech in this form is of limited therapeutic value, but the effects can be harnessed in the form of delayed and frequency altered feedback to produce an effect which is more permanent.

Delayed auditory feedback therapy

The use of delayed auditory feedback (DAF) as a therapeutic device originates back to the 1960s. During this and the following decade, it was mostly used as part of an operant approach to therapy (e.g., Curlee & Perkins, 1973; Goldiamond, 1965; Perkins, 1973; Ryan & Van Kirk, 1974; Shames & Florence, 1980), although others less inclined towards the operant approach have also harnessed its effects (e.g., Van Riper, 1973; and see also Soderberg, 1969 for a useful review of 1960s DAF studies). Although DAF has also been used as an adjunct to therapy programs (e.g., Boberg & Kully, 1985), its use as a primary therapeutic tool declined as slow speech procedures took over as the established means of instantiating fluency in many operant type approaches. In addition, despite the dramatic increase in fluency that DAF could provide, there were still substantial difficulties in maintaining the positive effects after treatment. There was also the uncertainty among some researchers (at this time at least) that DAF worked not because it altered auditory feedback directly, but because the disruptive effects resulted in a slower speech output (see chapter 3).

However, in the 1990s a number of changes brought back DAF (and as we shall see later, also frequency altered feedback) as a viable therapeutic device. A primary force was the work of Kalinowski and colleagues, who demonstrated that DAF could work effectively at normal and even fast rates of speech (Kalinowski et al., 1993, 1995). An additional factor was that DAF devices were now becoming more portable, and tiny in-the-ear devices have become commercially available in recent years. The combination of these factors has led to a rather different approach to the use of DAF. As explained in chapter 3, traditionally therapy involved slowly decreasing DAF timing delays from an initial optimal setting for fluency to an eventual zero delay, at which point the client would need to work on maintaining fluency away from the clinic and away from the fluency enhancing effects of DAF. Now, the new smaller and more inconspicuous DAF devices may be worn and used continuously, thus obviating the need to have users become practised at maintaining fluency without the effects of the DAF. The procedure first requires the user to set the delay time of the device. In fact there is some disagreement as to what these optimal delay times are, but a delay of as little as 50 ms seems to be enough for some people to apparently perceive the altered speech stimulus as exogenous, and therefore to bring about increased fluency.

Both the positive effects and difficulties of DAF therapy can be seen in a recent study by Van Borsel, Reunes, and Van den Bergh (2003), who tested the effects of a largely self-administered DAF therapy regime on a group of nine adults who stuttered. Following an introduction to the use of the DAF equipment and the establishment of the subjects' preferred DAF delay settings, the speakers were tested for fluency under a range of speaking conditions, both under DAF and with no auditory feedback (NAF). DAF was found to significantly reduce the number of stuttered words across all speaking conditions. Subjects were then instructed to implement a self-practice routine involving daily DAF practice with a five-minute monologue, fifteen-minute conversation and five minutes of oral reading. They were also required to make telephone calls on a once-weekly basis, one to a fellow participant and one to a stranger in response to a newspaper advertisement. Data on the delay times used, together with speech rate, perception of fluency and emotional state, were recorded by each speaker in a diary during the three-month DAF therapy period. At posttest, Van Borsel et al. (2003) found that the number of stuttered words under NAF had decreased and there was no longer a significant difference between this and the number of stuttered words under DAF, for automatic speech, conversation, picture description, and repeating. However, a significant difference between fluency under NAF and DAF still existed for the oral reading contingency over that time period. A comparison of fluency under NAF found posttest speech to be significantly more fluent under all five speaking conditions, while a pre- and posttest comparison of fluency under DAF showed a posttest increase in stuttering compared to pretest across all conditions, although none of these increases were significant.

These findings highlight a number of features. First, although DAF decreased stuttering consistently amongst all speakers and across all conditions, the effects of feedback did not eliminate stuttering, even in the pre-clinic assessments.[1] Also, the post-clinic mean figures of stuttered words of around 16–17 percent for the conversation contingency are still very high,

---

1 It appears that DAF delay times for the pretest assessments were preset by the experimenters, based on the experiences of another group of people who stuttered. This may have resulted in less than optimal settings being used.

even given the fact that 7 of the 9 participants had stuttering severity instrument (SSI; Riley, 1972; chapter 9 this volume) classifications of "very severe", one of "severe" and only one of "mild". This clinically based finding is therefore consistent with those from laboratory studies (Kalinowski, Stuart, Wamsley, & Rastatter, 1999; Stuart, Kalinowski, & Rastatter, 1997). On the other hand, this clinical trial provides evidence that over an extended period DAF continues to elicit increased fluency, and, at the same time promotes increased levels of fluency (above baseline) even under NAF, and without the need to systematically reduce DAF levels toward zero feedback. The major question as to whether DAF would continue to work in the long term remains unanswered. Anecdotal reports from those who have tried DAF devices over a period of time are equivocal. Some have reported a continued but lessened benefit over a period of a few months, others found little benefit to start with, and did not continue with the device.

It is likely to be the case that a number of variables may be influencing treatment outcome. To start with, it seems that some people may simply be DAF positive and others DAF negative. That is, some (the majority) respond favourably to the technique, but others do not, despite having had the opportunity to experiment with a range of delay settings on the altered feedback devices. As yet, we do not know why. For example, Sparks, Grant, Millay, Walker-Batson, and Hynan (2002) found their two subjects with mild stuttering to be less susceptible to DAF conditions under both normal and fast speaking rates. However, the speaker with mild stuttering in Van Borsel, Reunes and Van den Bergh's study found no such effect. It is also currently unknown how different practice regimes with DAF might yield different results. Van Borsel et al.'s study revealed a modest correlation between the amount of practice that individuals undertook over the trial period and eventual levels of fluency, but more data are needed to confirm the effect of practice on the effect of sustained benefit.

Aside from the issue of size and general practicality issues with earlier devices, there have also been some practical difficulties in the development of DAF devices for therapeutic use, as opposed to those used in laboratory tests. Of particular note, first generation models of the Speech Easy® device failed to deal with the problem of the feedback loop; that is, the device cannot work until triggered by a speech sound and those who stutter, particularly those who tend to block on initial sounds, may not be able to produce this in the first place. The device would work well once speech was under way and the delayed speech signal was heard, but the silence preceding any new intake of breath posed problems for those who experienced silent blocks in sentence initial position.

Frequency altered feedback therapy

Frequency altered feedback (FAF) offers an alternative but related method of inducing fluency through altered feedback. Unlike DAF, the history of this approach is rather short, dating back only around ten years. Like DAF, it has been developed as a fluency prosthetic primarily through the work of Kalinowoski and colleagues (Armson & Stuart, 1998; Rastatter et al., 1998; Stuart, Kalinowski, Armson, Stenstrom, & Jones, 1996) although not exclusively (e.g., Ingham et al., 1997). Like DAF, FAF works by emulating the effects of having another person speaking at the same time. Here, though, altered pitch is the factor rather than altered timing of feedback of the speech signal, with the varying note that is produced in speech (intonation) being continually tracked by the user, but at a consistently different pitch. As with DAF, the change in signal needed for it to be effective varies from person to person. Setting up a FAF device for optimum effects is a process of trial and error. Generally, a pitch shift of half an octave or more seems to be sufficient. FAF on its own does not seem as powerful as DAF. One study found that only 50 percent of a group of people who stuttered improved their fluency under this condition as opposed to 100 percent whose fluency increased under DAF (Natke, 2000). However, research indicates that FAF is more effective when used in conjunction with DAF, as is possible with both the Fluency Master and Speech Easy devices. Generally speaking, available evidence suggests this combination brings about a 70 percent increase in fluency. A combination of DAF and FAF was found to reduce stuttering by about 70 percent in 11 adult females who stuttered (Grosser, Natke, Langefield, & Kalveram, 2001)[2] whilst Brenault, Morrison, Kalinowski, Armson, and Stuart (1995) and Zimmerman, Kalinowski, Stuart, and Rastatter (1997) noted improvements of around 80 percent and 60 percent respectively.

Masked auditory feedback therapy

There are a number of earlier reports of masking devices being used therapeutically (Derazne, 1966; Dewar & Barnes, 1976; Murray, 1969; Parker & Christopherson, 1963; Perkins & Curlee, 1969; Van Riper, 1965), based on the laboratory findings that many people who stutter are more fluent when their voice is masked by noise. Nowadays such devices tend to be overlooked in favour of those which alter DAF/FAF, and none remain in production now, but probably the most sophisticated masking feedback device made commercially available was the Edinburgh masker (Barnes, 1970; Birtles & Dixon, 1973). This device triggered a masking noise presented through a monaural earpiece, activated by a throat microphone, which could be concealed under a high-collared shirt.[3] There is a paucity of objective data on the effectiveness of

---

2 Note that a lesser reduction was found for the males in this study.

3 Following Birtles and Dixon's version of the Edinburgh masker, there were subsequent developments within the Edinburgh team, the most significant of which utilized a masking tone which could be locked to track the fundamental frequency of the speaker's voice. It is interesting that this development, which in one sense produced masking noise at the

this device but although, as with DAF, problems have been reported with carryover (Dewar & Barnes, 1976), one study found that 82 percent of a group of 67 users who had tried the device over a 6-month period said that unaided speech fluency had improved due to the use of the device (Dewar, Dewar, Austin, & Brash, 1979). Although later versions used rather clumsy looking binaural earpieces and a processor which was hardly inconspicuous, the Edinburgh masker was still portable and small enough to be used in a range of situations. The potential for indefinite usage obviated the need for carryover to be achieved. Some people still find the Edinburgh masker helpful, but many others found the effects wore off. Keyhoe (1998) has argued that successful usage, where carryover is successful, is achieved by those who combine therapeutic techniques with the use of the masker, and that decreased usage of the device over time occurs simply because it becomes superfluous.

Commercially available altered feedback devices

Fluency Master

This device works on the basis that people who stutter do not properly hear the vocal tone produced by their vocal cords. Vocal tone can be thought of as proprioceptive feedback and transmitted (mostly) via bone conduction to our ears when we speak. It equates to the feedback that we miss when we hear our voice played back on audiotape. The Fluency Master is a small device, similar in appearance to a hearing aid, which is worn behind the ear. It comprises a small microphone which picks up vocal fold vibrations and amplifies them. A small tube then carries the amplified signal to an earpiece fitted within the ear canal. The promotional material claims that across a group of 200 subjects a reduction in stuttering from 26.7 percent words stuttered (WS) to 2.3 percent WS was found. There are claims too that 80 percent of a group of 200 subjects achieved "lasting success" using the Fluency Master, although there is no explanation as to what "lasting success" really means. They also state that trials have been running for over three years. However, no figures are given as to levels of fluency maintained during this time period. A number of anecdotal reports from users suggest that the effects of the Fluency Master wear off over time. Some have also claimed that while the Fluency Master did initially improve their fluency, the gains were not as substantial as they had hoped and stuttering persisted, even wearing the device (it is produced by the National Association for Speech Fluency, 228 Birch Drive, New Hyde Park, New York, USA; www.stutteringcontrol.com).

same time as frequency altered feedback, did not produce more favourable results. However, the changing pitch of the device reportedly did make the instrument more easy to use over longer periods, due to the eradication of the monotone feedback, and it allowed effective masking to be achieved at lower sound levels.

Speech Easy device

This device, developed by Drs Kalinowski, Stuart and Rastatter at East Carolina University, USA represents the most sophisticated altered feedback device currently available. It went into commercial production in 2001 and currently costs around $3900 for the basic behind-the-ear model and up to $4900 for a more advanced version which has upgradable software options and is worn completely within the ear canal. The Speech Easy works by combining the effects of both DAF and FAF to simulate choral speech, and both parameters can be adjusted to maximize the fluency enhancing effect. Other features include suppression of feedback from more remote auditory sources, so only the speaker's altered feedback is heard. It is possible to program a number of different sound levels to adjust for both quiet and loud speaking environments. Kalinowski, Guntapalli, Stuart, and Saltuklaroglu (2004) reported survey-administered responses from 105 people who had used Speech Easy devices. Respondents claimed the device made a positive impact on a reduction in stuttering generally, as well as on speech naturalness, frequency of stuttering when speaking on the telephone and in conversation. Overall satisfaction was rated two on a scale where one is maximum positivity and seven maximum negativity.

Summary of the efficacy of altered feedback devices

There is a growing body of evidence to suggest that stuttering can be reduced by both DAF and FAF. The effects do appear to be highly individualistic. Some users have found no benefit (Armson & Stuart, 1998; Ingham et al., 1997) whilst others have been found to experience a reduction of fluency of between 40 to 80 percent (Armson, Foote, Witt, Kalinowski, & Stuart, 1997; Ingham, 1997; Kalinowski et al., 1993; Sparks et al., 2002). Further findings have shown that the effects are strongest when feedback is presented binaurally, whether for DAF or FAF (Stuart et al., 1997); that fluency can be improved at normal or even increased speech rates (Stuart et al., 1996) and that speech is perceived as being more natural than when there is no altered feedback (Stuart & Kalinowski, 2004), but that speech is still rated as less natural than that of nonstuttering speakers when experiencing the same feedback conditions.

However, in a recent critique of current research on the subject, Lincoln, Walker, and Brooks (2005) point out, that currently there are still significant gaps in our understanding of the effects of altered auditory feedback. In particular, they point out that the majority of findings have come from analysis of short segments of speech. When longer samples have been taken (for example, Armson & Stuart, 1998), this has resulted in a return to baseline levels of stuttering for 50 percent of the subjects within 10 minutes. Lincoln et al. (2005) speculate that the impact of altered auditory feedback on conversational speech might be much less than that experienced during oral reading. In addition, there is only one study to date (Armson et al., 1997) that has sampled speech in a more naturalistic setting away from the laboratory. Lincoln et al. (2005) also raise queries, as to the sustainability of increased fluency across a range of social environments. Finally, the greater amount of the work on altered auditory feedback has emanated from one laboratory – of Kalinowski and colleagues. Replication of findings by other labs would help.

Computerized feedback devices

Computer Aided Fluency Establishment and Trainer (CAFET) and Dr Fluency

These devices differ from altered feedback in that they do not directly affect speech output, but through the use of computer technology help the individual to increase control over physiological aspects underlying speech production by providing feedback on the control of respiratory and phonatory activity. So they may be of particular use when monitoring the usage of fluency enhancing techniques such as soft glottal onsets and soft consonants, where quite precise timing arrangements need to be made between breathing and vocal fold vibration. As such they are really adjuncts to therapist-led therapy, rather than therapy devices themselves. CAFET and Dr Fluency are two quite similar versions of this technology. Both are commercially available and may be used inside and outside the speech clinic.

With both devices, vocal intensity is monitored via a microphone and feedback includes data on the use of gradual onset. The computer reports whether intensity (loudness) is too low or high, or whether change in loudness is occurring too rapidly. The computer also alerts the user if his voice becomes too breathy. The microphone can also monitor the use of continuous voicing strategies. In addition to traces which monitor vocal intensity, breathing patterns are displayed onscreen from information received from a belt fitted around the chest.[4] This gives information on exhalation patterns, including gradual exhalation, prevoice exhalation, uncontrolled exhalation and attempts to speak on residual air. The idea is that the computer monitor provides instant and reliable visual feedback, thus freeing the clinician to focus on treating other aspects such as psychological aspects (Keyhoe, 1998). Efficacy data for these devices have not been well reported. As with more conventional feedback techniques, individuals need to keep up practice for them to be effective. Keyhoe (1998) suggests that one hour per day is optimal.

---

4 Dr Fluency has two belts to differentiate diaphragmatic breathing from clavicular breathing.

Drug therapy

We have already observed earlier (chapter 2) that stuttering can respond to a range of drugs. We also know that drugs have been used for many years in laboratory experiments into the nature of stuttering. Perhaps the most famous example of this is Jones's (1966) Wada test on a group of people who stutter. The procedure required injecting an anaesthetic (sodium amytal) into the carotid arteries of these subjects in order to isolate left and right hemispheres, and subsequently test these independently for linguistic function (see chapter 2). In the last 15 years or so the interest in treating stuttering through the use of drugs has intensified and a number of different types of drugs have now been tried by people who stutter. While as yet there is no drug currently available that is specifically developed to treat stuttering, some drug therapies have been developed in response to findings about chemical activity in the brains of those who stutter. Others work by alleviating symptoms associated with stuttering such as anxiety. It is important to bear in mind that to date there are no large-scale controlled studies on any of the drug therapies outlined below.

Dopamine blocking drugs

There is preliminary evidence that appears to link stuttering to the polygenic inheritance of dopaminergic genes, including D2 receptors (Comings et al., 1996; see chapter 2, this volume). D2 antagonists have also been implicated in recent studies which have found some people who stutter to have increased levels of dopamine (Wu et al., 1997).[5] A number of D2 receptor antagonist drugs have been tried to alleviate both primary and secondary symptoms of the disorder. Brady (1991) reported some success in the use of haloperidol to treat stuttering; particularly, secondary tic-like symptoms responded well to the medication. However, many patients discontinued the therapy due to unpleasant side effects. More recently, a new group of D2 drugs (called atypical neuroleptics or atypical antipsychotics) have been used to treat stuttering. Usually prescribed for the treatment of mania and schizophrenia, these drugs are generally better tolerated than the older D2 receptor antagonists in doses used to treat these disorders (*British National Formulary*, Mehta, 2003). Side effects in the smaller doses used to treat stuttering are still unconfirmed. A common version of this drug is called risperidone; others include clozapine and olanzapine. One double-blind study on 16 subjects who took 2 mg of risperidone per day found a significant reduction in mean syllables stuttered over those who took a placebo. Few side effects were reported and six of the eight subjects treated with the drug chose to continue with the regime

5 Although some have argued that both increased and decreased levels may be related to increased levels of disfluency (for example, Goberman & Blomgren, 2003; see chapter 2).

(Maguire et al., 1998). Some reports have indicated that D2 receptor antagonists can reduce stuttering by around 40–60 percent. We recently had a young adult client with a mild learning disorder referred for a stutter at the Apple House who had just been placed on risperidone for treatment of mania. No improvement in the stutter was recorded under the risperidone regime. Of course, this is an anecdotal and uncontrolled case report and the client carries the potentially confounding complication of a mental health diagnosis.

Serotonin-specific reuptake inhibitors

This group of drugs (SSRIs) includes variants such as clomipramine, fluoxetine, sertraline and paroxetine, which are commonly used in the treatment of obsessive-compulsive disorders and depression. As seen in chapter 2, there is evidence that fluoxetine and sertraline can induce stuttering in nonstuttering speakers, but confusingly there are also reports that this group of drugs may improve fluency amongst some people who stutter (Brady, 1998). Costa and Kroll (1995) reported the positive effects of sertraline on one stutterer in a controlled double-blind study. Gordon, Cotelingham, Stager, Ludlow, Hamburger, and Rapoport (1995) found clomipramine outperformed desipramine (an antidepressant which does not affect serotonin uptake) in a controlled study involving 17 adults who stuttered, whilst Lu, Gopal, Gooding, and Shiflet (2003) found no change in the speech fluency of a group of clinically depressed speakers who were receiving sertraline and fluoxetine. More recently, Stager et al. (2005) trialled paroxetine against the D2 antagonist pimozide in what was intended to be a double-blind placebo-controlled study of six subjects. The pimozide was found to significantly reduce severity of moments of stuttering and increase percentage of fluent speaking time, but no significant difference in estimated percentage of disfluencies per minute was recorded. Interestingly, a nonsignificant increase in general anxiety was recorded, together with a nonsignificant decrease in speech-related anxiety. No significant improvements in fluency were recorded for the paroxetine, leading the authors to conclude that D2 antagonists were superior to SSRIs for the treatment of stuttering. However, both drugs affect mood and the study had to be terminated due to severe side effects following the withdrawal of the paroxetine.

Beta-adrenoreceptor blocking drugs

These drugs, more commonly known as beta blockers, are most usually associated with controlling high blood pressure (hypertension), heart failure and heart attack (myocardial infarction), primarily by slowing heart rate. However, some of this group of drugs can work by blocking adrenoreceptors not only in the heart but also the pancreas, liver and, of particular interest here, the bronchi, where they may act on airway resistance. Varieties of beta blockers include atenolol, acebutolol and propranolol. These drugs may also be prescribed to alleviate some symptoms of anxiety, and palpitation, sweating, tremor and tachycardia. Given the increased likelihood of speech-related anxiety amongst those who stutter, it is not surprising that a number of this group have been prescribed these drugs, and their variants, to help control fear levels. Some use the short-acting variants on an as-needs basis. Others use the drugs on an ongoing basis. As with so many cases, proper controlled studies on the effects of these drugs are missing and most of the "evidence" is anecdotal. Some may benefit from beta blockers when combined with more conventional therapeutic approaches. A common problem with speech modification techniques is that anxiety levels can increase when away from the clinic to the point where well-learned fluency techniques which are effective in controlled circumstances become unuseable. Some have found that the lower tension levels experienced when taking beta blockers, can also help fluency enhancing techniques to be implemented more effectively.

Other drugs

The successful use of a temporary anaesthetic procedure with an adult diagnosed with a psychogenic stutter has also been reported (Dworkin, Culatta, Abkarian, & Meleca, 2002; see chapter 16). The technique required a single injection of lidocaine into the laryngeal area, with fluency enhancing strategies taught during the short period of time before the desensitizing effects wore off. The authors of this study were unable to ascertain whether the effectiveness of this treatment, which was maintained at subsequent follow-up sessions 18 months post treatment, was due to either a psychological or physiological response to the drug or an interaction between the two. Its potential for use with developmental stuttering is currently unknown and the nature of the response needs to be more clearly understood before its effect for developmental stuttering can be determined.

Summary of drug treatments

Drug therapy for stuttering is in its infancy. While a drug "cure" for stuttering may seem to be the holy grail for many people who stutter, the quest for effective controlling medications also attracts a lot of misinformation. Many of the treatment reports are anecdotal and offer nothing more than uncontrolled studies on one or two people which conclude that stuttering was reduced by around X percent. Aside from the lack of any rigorous attempt properly to verify the recorded increase in fluency, such reports also fail to point out that the trial was uncontrolled. Consequently there may be a number of alternative explanations for these apparent success stories. First, there may be a placebo effect. Second, a reduction in stuttering may be associated with factors relating more to physical and psychological variables which in the end relate to stuttering, rather than being a core component of it. Other people who stutter may or may not share these characteristics. As pointed out in chapter 2, the diverse effects that alcohol can have on levels of fluency provides an obvious example of how a commonly taken drug may differentially affect a population. Related to this is the fact that despite the range of drugs that have been reported to affect stuttering (either positively or negatively), remarkably little is known about the type of behavioural changes they bring about in stuttered speech. Van Borsel, Beck, and Delanghe (2003) undertook a review of the literature on pharmacological agents on stuttering specifically to find out whether the different drugs elicited different symptoms. The symptom most consistently affected by most drugs used in the treatment of stuttering was repetition, while some subjects also reduced the frequency of blocks and prolongations. Of drugs that induce stuttering, no particular relationship between drug type and fluency characteristic was found. Indeed, as we have already seen, drugs of the same class have been found to induce different symptoms.

At any rate, the likelihood that drugs can within the foreseeable future offer a "cure" is remote. Far more will need to be known about neurological functioning in those who stutter before this becomes any kind of a realistic possibility. Even with scientifically well-motivated drug regimes, as is the case with the D2 antagonists, the future is unclear. We do not yet know what percentage of people who stutter have excessively high levels of dopamine and what degree of variability in dopamine levels exist amongst this population. We also have limited information on the effects of these drugs on either fluency levels or side effects in the longer term for people who stutter. If there is a genetic component that codes (amongst other things) for elevated dopamine levels, then genetic engineering could in theory obviate the need for any D2 antagonist drug therapy. Recall also that no drug treatments can eliminate persistent developmental stuttering (although of course the same also applies for all other therapies).

To finish this section then, perhaps all that can be honestly said at the moment is that stuttering can be helped in some cases by some drugs. Whether the gains in fluency are permanent enough and of sufficient strength to make any side effects worthwhile, whether there would be adaptation to the drug after a period of time, and whether the side effects in the long term would be damaging are issues that as yet we do not have satisfactory answers for.

Botox treatment of stuttering

There are a limited number of reports of the use of Botox (Botulinum toxin) in the treatment of stuttering (Brin, Stewart, Blitzer, & Diamond, 1994; Ludlow, 1990; Stager, & Ludlow, 1994). Clinically Botox is usually indicated in the control of torsion dystonias and other involuntary movements, although more recently it has achieved a higher profile due to its usage in cosmetic surgery. It has also been used with success in the treatment of spasmodic dysphonia, which itself has been linked with stuttering. The procedure as a treatment for stuttering is primarily limited to those who experience laryngeal spasms (resulting in laryngeal blocks) as a significant feature of their disorder. It has also been used, albeit rarely, to control tremor and extraneous labial movements associated with disorder. The treatment of stuttering with Botox is still regarded as highly experimental.

The procedure involves the injection of Botox bilaterally, directly into the thyroaretynoid muscles within the larynx. The action of the substance is to reduce laryngospasm and thereby increase fluency. It is a procedure that needs repeating every few months to maintain any effect. Reports on its effectiveness vary. Ludlow (1990) found that her group of seven subjects experienced increase in speech rate, decrease in mean number of moments of stuttering and an increase in the percentage of fluent time. Despite elevated fluency levels, only four subjects decided to return for the follow-up injections four months later. Apart from complaints about the painful injections, side effects of breathy speech quality were consistently reported. This appeared to be a significant factor in subjects electing not to continue with the treatment. A few years later, Stager and Ludlow (1994) reported that their 19 subjects who underwent botulinum injection did experience a reduction in the severity of their blocks, but that in comparison with a second group who were being similarly treated for vocal tremor reported fewer days when they were benefiting from the procedure. Again, not all subjects took up the opportunity of follow-up injections. Professor Peter Ramig, an expert in communication disorders and himself a person who stutters was one of five subjects who experienced the effects of Botox during a study in the mid-1990s. Like some of Stager and Ludlow's subjects, he and his co-subjects found the injections painful and that there were only marginal gains to fluency. Ramig concluded that the impact of Botox is not as favourable for stuttering as it is for spasmodic dysphonia. In another study, Choi, Kim, Pyo, and Hong (2000) found that of their group of ten people who stutter, eight experienced some improvement in their fluency following Botox injection. They also reported that two further subjects who stuttered did not show any significant improvement of twitching of facial (perioral) muscles when the obicularis oris muscle was injected.

The results of these and other anecdotal reports on the use of botulinum toxin for the treatment of stuttering suggest that some benefit in fluency may be gained from the procedure. Unfortunately, the benefits are usually not substantial. Against this, the individual must weigh the side effects of breathy voice and occasionally lower pitch, coupled with painful injections which need to be repeated on an ongoing basis. These issues led a significant number of people to feel that the benefits do not outweigh the drawbacks. Denny and Smith (1997) conclude that "it appears that the use of botulinum toxin is a questionable treatment for stuttering" (p. 138).

Stutterer-led therapy

There are a large number of treatment programs run by people who stutter. Below I outline four such approaches. I have chosen to focus on these specific examples because they represent high-profile exponents of this type of approach. The McGuire program now has training courses worldwide, while Harrison's hexagon method is another example of an approach which has attracted considerable publicity. The Starfish method, which originated in Britain, is expanding rapidly. While Bell's stuttering cured course is perhaps less well known outside the Britain where it originated, it has nonetheless been running consistently for many years and has been the subject of much media attention.

The McGuire program

Introduction

This stuttering program has come about as a result of the experiences of a psychologist and person who stutters called Dave McGuire. He had earlier received considerable benefit from Sheehan's non-avoidance approach to stuttering (which we discuss in chapter 12), but found that his speech was still prone to relapse under critical moments. In 1993 McGuire attended a diaphragmatic breathing training program and found that applying this technique resulted in immediate fluency. Like the non-avoidance therapy, however, the diaphragmatic breathing method was prone to relapse. However, by using non-avoidance techniques, McGuire was able to recover quickly from these episodes and now considers himself to be totally fluent 99.9 percent of the time. The McGuire program was launched in 1994 and since that time many graduates (those who have completed the McGuire course) have themselves gone on to become instructors. The approach is now taught in a number of countries, including the UK, Ireland, USA, Norway and Australia.

Theory

McGuire takes on board both psychological and physiological perspectives and believes that both need to be addressed if the individual is to completely control stuttering. The psychological aspects of the approach are adapted from Sheehan's non-avoidance stance on stuttering theory. Whilst the second major component, diaphragmatic breathing, is also a technique which has been used in a great many therapy programs, McGuire's perspective on the theory differs substantially from earlier interpretations, however. Rather than focusing on costal (diaphragmatic) breathing as the desired method (as opposed to clavicular breathing, which tends to be the case in most programs where breathing is targeted) McGuire draws on accenting differences between the crural diaphragm and the costal diaphragm – two sets of muscles involved in the control of breathing that may function independently. The crural diaphragm contracts without our conscious control and is responsible for vegetative breathing and most breathing for speech. Costal breathing, on the other hand, results from the use of larger muscle sets and occurs when extra airflow is required, such as during more extreme physical exertion, when yawning, or when singing. This breathing pattern is usually under voluntary control. McGuire argues that because the crural diaphragm controls airflow for normal speaking, it is therefore this which spasmodically contracts in response to feared situations amongst people who stutter. Thus, in order to control stuttering, one can either retrain the crural diaphragm or work on desensitization to the fear, both of which may take considerable lengths of time. Alternatively, one can train oneself to use costal breathing.

Schedule and structure of program

The program is usually taught in a group format over a four-day intensive period. Follow-up weekends, refresher courses and an extensive support network help to maintain carryover of effects from the initial program. McGuire (2003) defines 11 levels through which the individual must pass, starting at "swamp of tricks and avoidance" (level 1), rising through levels such as "establishment" (level 3) and "mechanical fluency" (level 5) through to the highest level of "eloquence" (level 11). It is acknowledged that reaching the highest levels for most is a lifelong process.

Procedures and techniques

COSTAL BREATHING

Underpinning all the therapy is the idea of costal breathing (effectively, breathing from the rib cage rather than the abdomen). Before speaking, it is important to take a deep costal breath and then articulate immediately on exhalation. A belt worn around the rib cage is used to give feedback as to whether the desired breathing pattern is taking place. Alongside this a range of other speech modification techniques is employed.

HIT AND HOLD

Here, the initial sound is to be made with a clean start, or with "attack". There is no pause between a full (costal) inhalation and then exhalation for speech. The word initial sound is approached with aggression and articulated clearly. This sound is then extended (initially for around three seconds) before being released into the rest of the word. Clients then practise this technique across the range of vowels and consonants up at word level, and later phrase and beyond. The idea with the hit and hold technique is that, consistent with the McGuire policy of total non-avoidance, approach is strengthened and avoidance and struggle are weakened. It is acknowledged that, depending on the extent of the fast attack, it will not sound natural and need only be used under feared situations when a return to avoidance may otherwise result. Speakers are also encouraged to articulate with precision once the initial sound has been successfully produced. This is partly working towards a goal of "eloquent" speech and partly to reinforce non-avoidance.

DEEP BREATHY TONE

McGuire advocates the use of a lowered "tone" or pitch of the voice because increased pitch puts greater muscular strain on the vocal cords[6] (and unwanted pitch increases are often associated with moments of uncontrolled stuttering). Optimum pitch is as low as the speaker can go without straining. A breathy quality is then required to stop the low pitch sounding strained. McGuire argues that this is also a more "eloquent" and powerful way of speaking, and that it is linked with the necessary change in speaking personality that needs to take place. McGuire also believes that the lower tone takes the emphasis away from the larynx and articulators and places the focus firmly with the breathing apparatus. It is important to ensure that the speaker does not resort back to tricks to avoid speech, which inevitably affect the larynx and the articulators.

OTHERS

Speakers should develop assertiveness and self-acceptance. The McGuire philosophy is that speakers must take responsibility for their stutter, and also responsibility for overcoming it. They are encouraged not only to accept themselves as recovering stutterers, but to take an active part in demonstrating to others that they are working to overcome their difficulty. Other factors include learning to resist time pressure and overcoming the feeling that verbal response must be made immediately, even if this means that speech is rushed and poorly controlled.

PRACTICE

McGuire recommends two hours per day practice to ensure that speaking skills are maintained and developed.

---

6 McGuire does not elaborate on this assertion and it really needs at least some further qualification. It is true technically that higher pitch involves more tension in the vocal folds, in that they stretch and become tighter, but within the normal range of intonation that a speaker would use these differences in tension are minimal and should not be a factor. Only speaking with a pitch range that extends toward either the upper or lower limits of normal (chest pulse) register should aversely affect tension levels.

Summary

The McGuire program, like many other therapist-led techniques, comprises a range of approaches. Some of the components, such as non-avoidance, are familiar from the literature and well documented, whereas other techniques, such as the abrupt initial sound onset, fly directly in the face of fluency skills such as soft consonant onset. Although the costal breathing aspect is specific to the approach and cognitive components are included, the program can be seen primarily as a fluency shaping variant.

The McGuire approach tends to polarize opinion both from SLTs/SLPs and from graduates of the program. Generally speaking, therapists seem to have a number of reservations about the approach. Some claim that the need to be assertive in one's speech can lead to a speech output which, rather than sounding eloquent, may present to some as aggressive. Related to this, there are also claims that the program can even have a detrimental effect on those participants who for whatever reason, are unable to keep up or take on board the assertive approach. Some graduates have reported that they felt they had failed because they had been unable to master the breathing technique. Although the McGuire literature states otherwise, some former students have said they felt the ethos is that if the speaker follows the program's directives then he will become fluent. If he doesn't, then it is the fault of the speaker for not putting in the effort. Many too are sceptical about McGuire's take on the costal breathing approach and question the theory that underpins it.

On the other hand, there are a significant number of people who experience long-term benefit from the program, although it is difficult to objectively ascertain both the short- and long-term effects because researchers do not report scientific data on its effectiveness in peer reviewed journals. Whether the costal breathing technique works to bypass a compromised crural diaphragmatic system or whether it simply acts as a distractor, changes in fluency can be made using this technique. In addition the strong support networks built up in a number of countries offer good follow-up opportunities. While relapse is a common problem for all approaches to the treatment of stuttering, one could argue that a maintenance program where participants are required to practise two hours per day in addition to attending regular follow-ups is likely to sustain high success rates. One might also speculate that participants in other intensive programs which offered similar levels of post-clinic support might too experience continued high levels of fluency.

Harrison and the stuttering hexagon

We are already well aware of the idea of a "vicious circle" of stuttering. Indeed, a number of fluency therapies, both behavioural and cognitive, work on this very premise. A simple example of the vicious circle can be seen when a speaker stutters under a certain situation and experiences a range of negative emotions when doing so. When later called upon to speak again under similar conditions, recollections of the earlier event come to mind and the unwanted feelings such as anxiety, fear and even panic are again invoked, even in anticipation of the event. The increased levels of arousal which commonly involve increased tension are counterproductive to fluent speech, and the person may then find maintaining fluency even more difficult. This again leads to a subsequent increase in levels of stuttering, which in turn serves only to increase arousal of negative perceptions, so speaking becomes even more effortful. In this way the vicious circle becomes self-perpetuating. Harrison's approach seeks to reverse this process.

John Harrison is a person who stutters, and was recently program director for the National Stuttering Project in the USA. Harrison controls his stutter by using his hexagonal model of psychological and sociological systems, or as it is commonly known "Harrison's hexagon". In this model, the six points on the hexagon are represented by six basic components: intentions, behaviours, emotions, physical state, perceptions, beliefs. Lines connect each element to the other five, indicating that changes in one component will have an impact on others and can affect the dynamics of the entire system, either positively or negatively. The arrows, all pointing clockwise around the outside of the hexagon, show that changing one's hexagon, whether that change is positive or negative, begins with intentions, then behaviours, and continues in the order listed above. Harrison's argument is that if components are functioning positively, then this will have a fluency enhancing effect. The ultimate goal of self-actualization, therefore, is first to understand one's own hexagon and how the six components interact.

McGuire (2003) offers a nonspeech example of how the hexagon can work in describing a tennis match which he initially went into with negative *emotion* feeling depressed, which led to *perceptions* that winning did not happen when he felt that way. This correlated with the *beliefs* that he could not win, in turn resulting in negative *behaviours* such as poor concentration and preparation, and so on. McGuire worked on overcoming this particular negative hexagon by deciding he would do his best, and in focusing on positive thoughts that would help him perform better. He outlines the reverse (change from positive to a negative hexagon) in his tennis opponent that day. His initial *perception* was that he was definitely going to win, leading to the *belief* that he would easily beat McGuire, but this lead to negative *behaviour* in the shape of overconfidence and lack of concentration. Towards the end of the match he stopped *believing* he could win. It is easy to see how this "tennis match hexagon" can be related to a speech or "fluency hexagon".

Bell's stuttering cured course

Andrew Bell grew up with a developmental stutter, but now considers himself cured of the disorder. For over 20 years he has been offering intensive group courses which he claims can cure stuttering. The course, which takes place in Kirkcaldy, Scotland, runs for five full days between Monday to Friday.

Participants are not allowed to leave the venue (a hotel) during that time and distractions such as books and television are not allowed. On the website Bell claims that the course "takes a holistic approach to curing stammering, in dealing with all aspects of fluent speech, whilst instilling High Self Esteem and a High-Success Mental Attitude to bring about confident fluency of speech".

Procedures

The physical component of therapy largely comprises the practice of a forceful breathing technique which Bell calls the "vowel press". This is first produced using an isolated vowel to make a loud and "sharp" sound. Bell then uses the vowel press technique at phrase level. In real speech, the technique involves the omission of syllable initial consonants and the forceful stressing and stretching of vowel nuclei. This speaking pattern is learned and reinforced by multiple repetition. Any silence during the deletion of the syllable-initial consonant or consonant cluster is accompanied by head raising, while the stretched vowel is produced with a slow forward movement of the head. The stretching of vowels (up to four seconds, in the first instance) lends a prolonged speech component to the activity. The phrases used in practice, such as "My confident voice speaks for me", and even the slightly unsettling "I'm imposing my deep sharp voice on you", reflect an attempt to develop high self-esteem. Throughout the course, the notion is taught that participants should look up to no one. One participant later recalled that the group was encouraged to develop self-belief by reciting affirmations such as "Go back to the gutter where you came from" and "You are absolutely pathetic".

Scientific and peer reviewed data on the efficacy of this program is lacking. Unquestionably, some have found the program helpful, while others have not (e.g., Karia, 2002). Although there are doubtless many courses run throughout the world using somewhat similar techniques, I have chosen to outline this particular one for two reasons: first, it is comparatively well known across the UK; second, because of its title. Regardless of the reports of those who feel either positively or negatively about the course, I believe it is dangerous to use the word "cure" even in children's therapy programs, where permanent cessation of the disorder can be brought about. It is a positively misleading term for those therapies which address persistent adult stuttering. Therapy using many different procedures may help control, even to the point where an individual is able to consistently maintain normal sounding fluency across a range of speaking situations, but even those who are able to achieve these high levels of fluency are still not cured. Control strategies, regardless of how automatic they may become over time, are still control strategies.

The valsalva hypothesis

The valsalva manoeuvre comprises the abrupt co-contraction of the vocal folds in the larynx together with muscles of the abdomen and thorax.

Generally it occurs naturally, for example, when expelling bowel movements, but it is also triggered when exerting effort, such as when lifting heavy objects. Parry (1985) believes that there are multifactorial causes underlying stuttering behaviour, but proposes that certain common blocking activity in stuttered speech arises due to the inappropriate activation of this neuro-physiological phenomenon. Parry suggests that there might be inappropriate tuning of the valsalva mechanism in those who stutter, which is known to be triggered by increased subglottal air pressure, resulting in an oversensitive valsalva trigger mechanism. Thus, instead of airflow being initiated for speech, the valsalva manoeuvre triggers abrupt glottal closure. Parry (2003) believes that the same overactivation could also occur in the lips or the tongue.

Parry's argument is that established fluency techniques such as soft consonant contacts and soft glottal onsets work because of their indirect effect on the valsalva mechanism, but that a more efficient way to deal with the blocking is to tackle the underlying cause: the valsalva mechanism itself. Thus, it might be standard practice to work on reducing lip tension, but this will have limited effect without dealing with the physiological force that is causing the tension in the first place. Parry also observes that when there is a block at the lips, there is also muscular tension in the abdominal area, which he relates to an activated valsalva mechanism. Parry's answer, therefore, is to relax the abdomen by breathing abdominally, which will have the effect of tuning the laryngeal muscles for phonation, rather than the effortful closure associated with the valsalva mechanism. The effect of this should be to relax other structures further up the vocal tract. Similarly, Parry claims that a type of in-block modification can be applied by using this technique, and that articulatory blocks cannot be maintained if the abdomen is simultaneously relaxed. The precise relationship between abdominal tension and blocking is not clear, however. A block will back up air pressure into the lungs, so it seems perfectly possible that the abdominal muscle tension which many who stutter recognize could represent the effect of the block, rather than the cause of it.

The research to verify the effects behind the valsalva hypothesis is still lacking, but Parry is honest enough to admit this and at the same time is not suggesting that learning to control the valsalva mechanism will control all stuttering. Instead, he sees it as a technique that could and should be learned alongside other practices to control certain types of blocking behaviour. There seems little question that abnormal respiration is involved in stuttering (see chapter 4) and, as we have seen, both mainstream and non-mainstream approaches focus on relaxing thoracic muscle control. At present, objective evidence is lacking to determine whether gains made in controlling blocking by controlling abdominal muscle activity do so by suppressing the valsalva mechanism.

The starfish project

"Starfish" is an acronym for "Supportive Training And Recovery For Individual Stammerer's Harmony". In many ways the approach used by the founder, Anne Blight,[7] is similar to the McGuire program. The costal breathing method employed in conjunction with avoidance reduction therapy and positive attitude development are concepts which are already familiar components used on the McGuire approach.

The UK-based initial course is run over a three-day intensive period for which a fee is charged, but further refresher courses (which are optional) are free indefinitely. Additionally, the starfish project offers an impressive permanently available network of telephone support. Generally speaking, the tone of the initial group sessions appears more relaxed than that of the McGuire course. There is a greater emphasis on individuality and an acceptance that different people will move through the course at different rates, and indeed may have different goals. Similarly, with regard to maintenance of recovery, there seems to be a greater acceptance of those who do not or cannot keep up the high levels of practice needed to maintain high levels of fluency. Importantly, it is made clear at the outset that total fluency is not a goal. While three days does not give a great deal of time to change motor patterns and associated fears of stuttering, the short time frame does make it possible for more people to attend more easily. Those who have experienced success with breathing focused therapies in the past may find the initial three days sufficient to be able to begin to put the technique into practice on a reasonably permanent basis. Others may find they require more time. The frequency with which the courses run mean that attending a second program may be an easier (and for many a more appropriate) option than moving on to the follow-up sessions.

Summary

While many people who stutter are happy with the fluency therapy they receive from "mainstream" approaches, an increasing number seem to be considering alternative therapeutic options. This trend may be explained in a number of ways. First, there are probably now more therapeutic options than there have ever been: an increase in knowledge of stuttering from a neuro-chemical perspective has given rise to the treatment of stuttering using drugs that help reduce dopamine levels, whilst scientific and technological advances in auditory processing have directly led to the development of sophisticated and practical auditory feedback devices. Taking a rather different route, some prefer to pursue therapy programs led by people who have experienced

---

7 Anne Blight is a SLT, but the approach is included in this chapter as it is based on procedures developed by Dave McGuire and the support network is primarily maintained by those who have undertaken therapy, not SLTs.

therapy themselves and have gone on to develop their own approaches to therapy.

Second, the dissemination of knowledge on the subject has changed dramatically. Until recently, new advances in stuttering theory and therapy remained mostly in the domain of researchers in the field, primarily accessed by the academic journals, and through meetings at specialist conferences. Now, through the increasing number of self-help groups, access to the world-wide web and specialist email chat lists, more people have greater access to more knowledge and more quickly than ever before. Of course, as with mainstream therapy approaches, none of the alternatives outlined in this chapter provide totally satisfactory solutions to established stuttering.

Third, and related to the second point, many people who stutter are now more confident and questioning regarding the therapeutic options they are presented with by clinicians. It is increasingly the case that during the initial interview the clinician's role is, through discussion and careful questioning, to help the person find the program or approach that will be most beneficial, rather than to automatically enlist the person on the single option that is on offer at that clinic.

And what of the future? It is possible that as more is known about the brain and stuttering, effective treatment could be provided by drug therapy. More radically, if consistent structural neurological differences are confirmed amongst those who stutter, it is not inconceivable to imagine that surgery might provide one possible answer. Finally, an advanced understanding of a genetic underpinning to the disorder could lead to a genetic engineering resolution. These possible "hi-tech" solutions at present seem some way off.

Key points

- Feedback devices which mask, delay, or change the frequency of the speaker's speech signal can result in increased fluency. Newer devices that combine delayed auditory feedback and frequency altered feedback can, in some cases, result in immediate and effortless fluency with little or no input from a clinician.
- Altered feedback devices do not appear to work for everyone. Some users at least may adapt to the new feedback, thus losing the fluency enhancing effects.
- More long-term studies will be needed to test whether adaptation to altered auditory feedback (AAF) is a significant problem, and if so whether this can be overcome by altering the feedback settings of the devices. Similarly, there is a need to test the effects of AAF devices in more naturalistic settings and with longer speech samples.
- There are a number of alternative approaches to clinician-led flu-

ency therapy. Devices such as CAFET and Dr Fluency may be used to supplement clinician input and to help the client become more in tune with their new ways of controlling breathing and other speech-related activity.

- Currently, there is limited evidence that some people who stutter can be helped by drugs acting on either central neurological functioning (for example, related to dopamine levels in the brain), or on the relief of symptomatic features (for example, beta blockers for the treatment of anxiety). The treatment of stuttering with drugs is in its infancy and unlikely to develop significantly until there are more precise details on the neurological correlates of stuttering.
- Therapy led by people who stutter, like that provided by clinicians, may come in a variety of forms. The approaches described in this chapter all combine techniques used to control stuttering moments and procedures to reduce avoidance and improve self-image.

Further reading

Costa, D., & Kroll, R. (2000). Stuttering: An update for physicians. *Canadian Medical Association Journal, 162*, 1849–1855.
It is a reflection on the current state of knowledge of drug treatments for stuttering that I cannot point to any one particular text that comprehensively covers the subject. However, this paper by Costa and Kroll which gives an overview of recent theoretical and therapeutic advances also has a nice section on drug therapy.

Kalinowski, J., Armson, J., Roland-Mieszowski, M., & Stuart, A. (1993). Effects of alterations in auditory feedback and speech rate on stuttering frequency. *Language and Speech, 36*, 1–16.
There are a number of references to the work of Kalinowski and colleagues in the bibliography which I could have listed here. This was chosen because it was one of the first papers that dispelled the notion that DAF worked primarily because it slowed speech output.

McGuire, D. (2003). *Beyond stuttering: The McGuire programme for getting good at the sport of speaking*. London: Souvenir Press.
The clue is in the title. McGuire sees both speaking and sport as skills which can be perfected with application and continued practice, and there are numerous sporting analogies scattered throughout the text. The book describes the philosophy and therapy involved in the McGuire approach in some detail, and concludes with a number of reports from contented McGuire graduates.

Parry, W.D. (2000). *Understanding and controlling stuttering: A comprehensive new approach based on the valsalva hypothesis* (2nd ed.). Anaheim Hills, CA: National Stuttering Association.
This is Parry's definitive text on his valsalva hypothesis and contains details on both theory and therapy.

15 The efficacy of stuttering therapy

Introduction

It is increasingly the case that clinicians are being required to justify their methods of treatment. This demonstration of efficacy through the use of well-controlled clinical trials which report objective outcomes is also known as evidence-based practice (EBP), or as Finn (2003a, p. 209) puts it: "An evidence-based framework can be described as an empirically-driven, measurement-based, client-sensitive approach for selecting treatments." Professional bodies that govern clinical practice are increasingly taking on board EBP concepts. In the UK, the Royal College of Speech and Language Therapists has recently established clinical guidelines based on existing clinical practice which is well documented, and has built EBP-related aims into its strategic plan. Similarly, EBP has become central to the agendas of professional bodies in the USA (ASHA) and Canada (CASLPA, Canadian Association of Speech Language Pathologists & Audiologists), whilst Australia already has an established tradition of combining the efforts of clinicians, researchers and statisticians to produce EBP data, demonstrated in some recent publications. Examples of these include *Evidence-based Practice in Speech Pathology* (Reilly, Douglas, & Oates, 2004) and a recent edition of the national journal *Advances in Speech-Language Pathology* which featured a number of articles on the subject.

Of course it is absolutely right that those who employ the services of speech language therapists/speech language pathologists (SLTs/SLPs) and those who seek help from clinicians should know that the approaches being used have been demonstrated to be effective. But demonstrating efficacy creates a number of problems specific to the highly complex and variable disorder of stuttering. For example, at the inception of stuttering in the preschool years there is the fundamental issue as to how soon to start treatment. Are we wasting valuable resources treating children with newly identified stutters when we should in fact be waiting to see if spontaneous recovery is going to take place? What is the case for implementing a direct intervention technique over an indirect one? Consider, also the example of stuttering in adulthood. The stuttering behaviours are now more likely to be more complicated, with attitudinal, avoidance and escape behaviours more strongly established. We also have to deal with the added difficulty that stuttering can no longer be eliminated by therapy. What does efficacy mean here? One simple answer might seem to be to aim at reducing stuttering to a satisfactorily low and objectively measurable level. Of course a number of programs do this already, but what then of sustainability of progress made in treatment? What if our clients achieve our level of "X percent syllables stuttered", but then find over a period of months that higher levels of stuttering return? Is this acceptable? What if stuttering increases the following year, or the year after? If we take a more cognitive perspective on treatment, and record a number of positive changes in attitudinal adjustment over the therapeutic period, is that actually fluency therapy at all?

In sum, we need to consider the following questions. What do we mean by efficacy in stuttering treatment? Who decides on treatment goals? How do we define success? One fact is becoming clear from the increased focus on efficacy studies and the increased insistence on proper outcome measures: the client must be placed at the centre of the therapy. Once we as clinicians ensure that the therapeutic goals are also our clients' goals, we can at least begin to answer some of these questions in a meaningful way.

Problems in demonstrating treatment efficacy

It is generally agreed that there is an urgent need for research into the effectiveness of stuttering therapy (Bernstein-Ratner, 2005b; Ingham, 2003; Ingham & Riley, 1998). Although most programs are clinically evaluated by comparing clients' pre- and posttreatment performance across a range of tests, both behavioural and attitudinal, the open demonstration of efficacy using robust study designs as required by the peer reviewed journals is very much the exception rather than the norm. There are a number of reasons for this. First, and fundamentally, there are still strongly held views in opposing speech therapy camps as to what actually constitutes treatment, and consequently fundamental differences as to what constitutes effective and successful outcomes (Block, 2004). Reduction in the frequency of stuttering is generally considered to be associated with effective treatment (Thomas & Howell, 2001), although as we have seen in chapter 9, arriving at an agreement on measures such as percentage of syllables stuttered can be problematic (see also Block, 2004; Cordes & Ingham, 1998; Onslow, 1996), as is deciding what levels of remaining stuttering are acceptable posttreatment. Boberg and Kully (1985) put the figure at less than 2 percent whilst Davis, Howell, and Rustin (1999) suggest 2 to 4 percent. Despite these difficulties, it is certainly the case that the greater majority of available literature on efficacy centres on those programs which hold that therapy should first and foremost target speech fluency (e.g., Ingham, 1984; O'Brian et al., 2003; Onslow et al., 1990; Ryan, 1974). If there is overreliance on the percentage of syllables stuttered figure and that remaining stuttering consists of, for example, severe moments of stuttering and excessive tension, the true efficacy of the program must be questioned (Bernstein-Ratner, 2005b; Ingham & Costello, 1984; see also chapter 9). The issue of reliability in counting even objective outcome measures becomes problematic, since even these are inevitably (as Ingham and Riley, 1998, p. 757 put it) "filtered through the complexities of human perception", and thus leave much room for individual bias.

Although most authorities agree that there must be at least some objective data collected on speech fluency and speech rate measures (e.g., Conture & Guitar, 1993; Kroll, 2003) many researchers and clinicians believe that the treatment of stuttering must also address cognitive and affective aspects of the disorder, particularly with regard to the treatment of older children and adults (e.g., Bloom & Cooperman, 1999; De Nil & Brutten, 1991; Guitar, 1998; Rustin & Cook, 1995; Rustin et al., 1996; Sheehan, 1986; Van Riper, 1973). As we have seen in chapter 9, client self-measurement is being regarded as the central part of multidimensional outcome measures (Conture & Guitar, 1993; Finn, 2003a; Wright & Ayre, 2000; Yaruss & Quesal, 2004).

A second problem relates to the idea of the fluency program. In Guitar's excellent book (1998), *Stuttering: An Integrated Approach to its Nature and Treatment,* he acknowledges the increasing establishment of integrated approaches to the disorder within the clinic, a trend which is surely to be welcomed. However, I also wonder whether clinicians should attempt to go further and, particularly when treating an established stutter, aim not just to provide an approach which is integrated, but also to provide a range of therapies, each of which integrates cognitive, affective and behavioural aspects in different ways and to different degrees. Presenting a rather crude hypothetical example, we may have an integrated program which has (roughly) a 50–50 split of behavioural and cognitive processes (putting aside for the moment the issues as to how we might go about defining and measuring that). So, this is an "integrated" program and may serve a number of clients well. But should that clinician not also be able to adjust the therapeutic aspects to produce different percentages (or ratios) of the sub-components of therapy? Clients come to therapy with differing problems, and differing needs. While offering an integrated approach sounds impressive, perhaps clinicians should look at further tailoring aspects of therapy to the needs of the individual. In other words, clinics need to offer a range of integrated therapies rather than a single integrated therapy. The difficulty with this comes in defining the terms under which "success" (of which word more in a few moments) is achieved. Attempting to compare directly the effectiveness of one treatment approach against another, and particularly balancing the different weightings of cognitive and motor speech assessments across the different programs, would be fraught with difficulty. Effectively, this involves comparing apples with oranges.

There are problems too in demonstrating efficacy when seeing clients on a one-to-one basis. When there is likely to be more room for flexibility in approach and a greater opportunity to adjust treatment strategies "online" to accommodate the needs of the client, it becomes very difficult to tease out to what degree the various therapeutic components are effecting the change in behaviours.[1] Add to this the fact that different people will benefit differentially to subtle changes in procedures and we can see how difficult it becomes to produce a "program" that can be submitted to a journal under the guise of a single approach, where the contribution of the various components of the therapy can be interpreted objectively by others in any meaningful way. To put it another way, individualizing therapy to suit each person may be seen as good practice, yet this can lead to a catch-22 situation where deriving objective data as to the ratios to which the components are applied and which are helpful becomes almost impossible.

A third problem is a simple one of logistics. Many clinicians simply do not have the time to put into a study of sufficient weight, scope and scientific rigour to be considered by the academic journals. Particularly for those clinicians funded by government agencies such as the National Health Service in Britain, the remit, even for specialist posts in disfluency, is to assess, diagnose and treat. Research is often "encouraged", but in many cases time allowed for it comes down to no more than one or two days a year. Naturally as part of our job description we are required to document objective aims and objectives and audited to ensure that these are being met. However, this kind of evaluation is a long way from the kind of controlled study which would meet with peer approval in the journals.

It is true that often "external" funding can be found to help with this problem. The work of Kully, Langevin, and colleagues at the ISTAR centre in Edmonton, Canada provides one excellent example as to how a treatment-based centre can attract funding that allows the time for clinicians to undertake thorough and longitudinal analysis of treatment efficacy. It may also be possible for clinicians to work together with academic colleagues to spread the time burden. Surely though more of clinicians' time should be devoted to looking more thoroughly into the short- and long-term effects of their therapies? But for this practice to become more established, specialist fluency posts must come with a remit that efficacy must be given greater consideration than is often currently the case. This means building time for meaningful research concerning efficacy into the post description.

Efficacy in adult therapy: What constitutes successful treatment?

Reliable testing measures

As we have already seen, there is a need to have treatment strategies whose efficacy can be verified by the use of well-controlled outcome studies and measurement instruments whose validity and reliability have been rigorously

---

1 This may be particularly pertinent with counselling approaches to stuttering (see chapter 13).

tested. Even well-developed tests like the much used stuttering severity instrument (SSI-3; Riley, 1994) have been shown to have questionable rater reliability (Lewis, 1995), although a recent comparison between parents' subjective ratings and SSI-3 scores have been shown to yield high correlations for all but the concomitant behaviour subscale (Rosenthal, 2004). The modified Erikson S-24 scale (Andrews & Cutler, 1974) also has its critics (see Yaruss, 1997a for a comprehensive discussion of the measurement of stuttering).

In order to make any reasonable attempt at determining what constitutes success we must from the outset place the considerations and wishes of the client to the fore. Traditionally, clinicians have not always had a good track record in this regard.

The client as a consumer

We don't have to look back too far into the recent past to find a time when therapy goals were set solely by the clinician: clients followed that program and that pretty much was that. Over the last decade particularly, there are signs of a positive change in thinking from clinicians, prompted in part by the rise in equal accessibility of knowledge on the worldwide web on the subject to clinicians, researchers and people who stutter alike. This dissemination of knowledge has been accelerated by the increasing popularity of stuttering support groups and the development of email lists such as Stuttering Chat and Stutt L, to the point where people who stutter nowadays are not only much more aware of treatment options, but also have instant access to the opinions of their peers regarding them. This has led to an increase in people actively shopping around for a therapeutic approach that they think will suit them. While some clinicians have been reluctant to accept the role of the client as a consumer, many have welcomed this development.[2] With client and clinician actively engaged together in the process of finding a program which the client wishes to follow, we are far more likely to avoid a situation where the program's success criteria are met but the client's wishes are not. As a hypothetical example, let's take the case of an adult with a mild stutter (as measured by percentage of syllables stuttered) whose major concerns lie not so much with the moments of stuttering, which are fleeting, but with the very high levels of speech-related anxiety that he feels when he is fearful that he might stutter. This person attends an intensive fluency shaping program because this is the approach that the clinic adheres to and he is unaware of other treatment options elsewhere. He does well on the program and at post-clinic assessment easily exceeds the success criteria of less than 2 percent syllables stuttered. However, despite the high level of fluency, he continues

---

2 For example, we see this reflected in an increasing number of counselling approaches now being applied to the treatment of fluency disorders in which the client takes on a more active role in therapy (see chapter 13).

to experience elevated levels of anxiety and stress. After three months he experiences a significant relapse, associated with strong feelings that he has failed, which only serves to reinforce his negative self-perception as a person and as a speaker. Of course, relapse is a potential problem for all therapeutic approaches, but equally we could argue that this man might have been better served by an approach which dealt directly with his feelings towards the stutter and on reducing stress and anxiety levels. In sum, while in one sense this person met the targets for success for that particular program, these were not his own targets and goals.

The fact that clinicians now more than ever are prepared to work together with their clients to develop treatment plans which lead towards well-defined, mutually agreed goals which are both realistic and sustainable, gives us cause for optimism for the future. Quesal, Yaruss, and Molt (2004), for example, have expressed their concern that what tends to be measured in therapy (that is the primary behaviours) are inadequate and not necessarily the most relevant for many clients (see also Conture, 2001; Guitar, 1998). There are now increasing signs that the measurement of cognitive aspects of communication is being considered central to the measurement of stuttering behaviour (e.g., Wright and Ayre, 2000; Yaruss & Quesal, 2004) and establishment of the concept that client self-report collected over a long period of time can be viewed as important and meaningful data. Despite this welcome trend, it is demonstrably the case that stuttering modification approaches (including long-established procedures such as Van Riper's, and its subsequent variants) remain curiously underrepresented in the EBP literature (Bernstein-Ratner, 2005b; Kully & Langevin, 2005).

How long should therapy effects last to be considered "successful"?

Well, in one sense this is another "how long is a piece of string?" type of question. Certainly, there are different but equally awkward issues for efficacy claims, depending on the age of the client. As far as the treatment of the younger child is concerned, data on the long-term efficacy of treatment (the complete elimination of stuttering) is still clouded by our current lack of understanding of the role of spontaneous recovery (see chapter 7). Clearly, without this potentially confounding issue we can say that a treatment which removes all trace of stuttering in the long term is indeed successful. There are now some well-controlled studies that are beginning to provide such data (see below). The issues for adults and older adolescents who stutter are somewhat different, as now we are considering a disorder which is very unlikely to resolve completely, either with or without therapy. There are certainly examples of adults who have found (adult) therapy helpful, whether behavioural, cognitive or a mixture of both, and have felt no need to return for further therapy, regardless of whether that therapy takes a similar or different approach. In a review of 162 studies which encompassed a range of techniques from cognitive to behavioural approaches and from drug therapies to auditory feedback therapies, Bloodstein (1995) reported that around 95 percent resulted in significant reductions in stuttering frequency (usually defined as less than 3 percent of syllables stuttered).

The data on relapse stand in stark contrast to this figure, however. Craig and Hancock in their (1995) study place the relapse figure at above 70 percent; figures which are supported by earlier research (Boberg, 1981; Craig, 1998; Hancock & Craig, 1998). Consistent with this, all treatment approaches appear prone to relapse. Hayhow et al. (2002) found that no one specific approach could be identified as more effective than any other, with only 25 percent of those questioned reporting that rate control strategies were helpful, whilst Yaruss et al.'s (2002) survey found that only 40 percent of respondents were able to maintain fluency gains made using a wide range of treatment approaches. Only 52 percent said they were able to maintain fluency gains away from the clinic. The latter point about the difficulties associated with transfer of therapeutic techniques was echoed more recently in a paper by Stewart and Richardson (2004). As Guntupalli, Kalinowski, and Saltuklaroglu (2006, p. 3) point out in their review of these papers: "Their results highlight the significance of involving clients in the evaluation process and suggest that the gold standard for effectiveness should be one in which the client perceives the outcome as being of value." These findings highlighting the difficulties with relapse appear somewhat at odds with Guitar's (1998) statement of his integrated approach to adult therapy: that if the clinicians do their job well, the clients will not return. Bloodstein (1995), on the other hand, suggests that it is reasonable to expect treatment effects to last between two and five years.

Either way, the reality is that it is common practice for adult clients to continue to re-enlist on similar programs and/or explore various alternative treatment strategies over a number of years. Some people may feel they benefited a little from some approaches, perhaps not benefiting at all from others, whilst others might feel that any gains were either insufficient, short-lived, or both. For those who improved but did not achieve lasting benefit it is not uncommon for a number to repeatedly return to the same (or similar) program for top-up sessions over a period of years. Thus, the problem for efficacy is that we have a situation whereby it may be totally acceptable that "successful" treatment is repeatedly reapplied for the same individual over a number of years.

Efficacy of early treatment programs for children

Some preliminary considerations

One of the consistent findings in stuttering research is that the disorder increases in complexity and becomes harder to treat as it develops (see chapters 9, 10, 11). Studies have shown that children have greater plasticity of development in the preschool years than during school age years, affecting

such areas as motor control, emotional development and cognition. Specifically, the preschool period is particularly critical for speech and language
development (Krashen, 1973).

As we have also mentioned elsewhere, research supports the case for early
intervention of stuttering. Therapy is more effective when it is introduced
earlier: it requires fewer treatment hours (Onslow, Andrews, & Lincoln, 1994;
Starkweather & Gottwald, 1993); results in improved generalization from
clinic to natural environments (Curlee, 1984; Gregory & Hill, 1984); and
produces a more permanent remission of the disorder (Curlee, 1993; Onslow
et al., 2003). Despite this, there is disagreement as to exactly when therapy
should start, given that there is spontaneous recovery in between 74 percent
and 90 percent of those who have ever stuttered (Mansson, 2000; Yairi &
Ambrose, 1992b, 1999). It also seems that the younger the child, the more
likely the chance of recovery.

Of particular importance here is the finding that early treatment of stuttering can be successfully achieved through a number of different methods.
However, as suggested earlier, success and success rate data are not easy to
interpret. Starkweather (1999, p. 234) believes success rate to be "one of the
least meaningful of measures, depending, as it does on the definition of
stuttering, the definition of success, the skills of the clinician, and a host of
other factors".

Randomized control trial studies and single case methodology

Starkweather (1999) also makes the point that just because one technique
works well for one child, it does not mean to say that it will work well for
another. He goes on to advocate the use of individualized therapeutic strategies, following on from the careful assessment of both the child and his or
her environment to be successful. This in turn has implications for how we
measure outcomes from our therapies. There are implications here for
evidence-based practice and the use of what is commonly regarded as the
"gold standard" procedure (Ingham, 2003) for evaluating treatment effects;
that is, randomized controlled trial studies (RCTs; Jones, Gebski, Onslow, &
Packman, 2001; Schiaveti & Metz, 1996). The RCT method requires potential
clients to be randomly assigned to one of two or more groups; one group will
receive treatment, while another acts as a control group where there is
no treatment. A third group may also employed, for example, to receive a
placebo treatment. The performance of the (real) treatment group is then
compared over a period of time with that of the control group (and if used the
placebo group), to determine whether therapy alone is responsible for any
changes in the assessed behaviours.

However, there are problems with using this approach with younger children. First, there are ethical considerations. Clinicians and parents alike have
concerns about witholding therapy from a group of children, particularly
given the increasing data that indicate the importance of early intervention

(see chapter 10), even if therapy is eventually offered to the control group after the RCT period is over. The purpose of RCTs is to allow assertions to be made as to the benefits of treatment to any given population (or group). Such data is, of course, of great importance, but we must also be mindful that where more individualized approaches to therapy are being evaluated there is more likely to be individualized response, and that RCTs might conceal within-group variability to treatment methods. In such cases, an argument might be made for using a single case design or single subject A-B-A design (Bernstein-Ratner, 2005b; Breakwell, Hammond, & Fife-Schaw, 2000). Amongst the advantages of this approach are that it is more practical for those in routine clinical practice, and that it may allow easier identification of treatment components (Ingham & Riley, 1998; Thomas & Howell, 2001). In addition, some have argued that this design is more likely to uncover clinically significant findings (Finn, 2005), unobscured by statistical analyses (Ingham & Riley, 1998). But this approach too is not without its problems. Particularly, there will be difficulty in generalizing findings from an individual to a greater population. Work in the field of clinical psychology (Chambless & Ollendick, 2001) suggests that multiple single case studies can form an effective strategy here.

With the single case A-B-A design, a single person is selected for study. Data are collected on a number of occasions before the therapy period, a similar number during the therapy period, and finally data are again collected on a similar number of occasions following the completion of therapy. These procedures ensure that there is no spontaneous recovery prior to treatment (which otherwise might be ascribed to the treatment process itself). As we know, stuttering severity can be highly variable. Taking a number of measurements for a period of time post clinic, and comparing them with those measurements taken from earlier in treatment, helps cancel out the effects of natural variability in responses (and which, by definition, are not due to the effects of the treatment). Inferential statistical tests can then determine whether any changes in behaviour were genuinely due to the treatment process. A second advantage with the single case design is that, because each subject acts as his own control, there is no witholding treatment from another client.

One example of an individualized approach to early stuttering is the parent–child interaction (PCI) model (Rustin et al., 1996) described in chapter 10. Thorough assessments examine a range of features, motoric, genetic, linguistic, interactional, as well as environmental, that may be impacting on the child's disfluency. Careful consideration of the assessment data gives rise to an individualistic approach to treatment. Despite the establishment of parent–child interaction approaches, the comparative lack of data on their effectiveness has been commented on (Ingham & Cordes, 1999), although some single case study data is now appearing (Matthews, Williams, & Pring, 1997; Nicholas & Millard, 2003) and a larger scale group study data is also underway (Millard, work in progress).

In one sense, the antithesis of the individualized PCT approach can be seen in the highly structured Lidcombe program (chapter 10) where, in contrast, the same protocols are applied to each child. Here, environmental variables are much less of a concern to the therapist and family dynamics are largely seen as irrelevant to the therapeutic process, unless they are such that practice time cannot regularly be found. There is a great deal of published outcome data regarding the effectiveness of the Lidcombe Program (Jones, Onslow, Harrison, & Packman, 2000; Onslow et al., 1990, 1994), yet, as Bernstein-Ratner (2005b) has pointed out, these positive findings have been obtained in the absence of a solid understanding as to exactly why the program works. This issue has been taken up by the program authors, although in 2002 they were forced to conclude that "the mechanisms underlying treatment remain unknown" (Onslow et al., 2002, p. 29). A further attempt to ascertain "the active components" of the Lidcombe program (Harrison, Onslow, & Menzies, 2004) has also failed to answer these questions, although this study did conclude that the severity ratings played no significant role in affecting treatment outcomes. We are currently awaiting the results of a large new study of the Lidcombe therapy program which, in addition to providing more data on long-term outcome, will look at a range of factors to see if there are children who are failing to respond satisfactorily to the program, and what the significant factors behind this are. The study will consider both therapeutic components and environmental factors (Hayhow, work in progress).

To conclude, it is obviously of great importance that the efficacy of both direct and indirect approaches to treatment is demonstrated. But even this only tells us so much. What is equally needed is data from well-controlled studies as to why certain treatment procedures work better for some children than for others.

What constitutes good efficacy study design?

We have already mentioned the RCT model and the single case design approaches, and research design is a subject covered at length in a number of excellent texts (e.g., Bernstein-Ratner & Healey, 1999; Schiaveti & Metz, 1996). Below, we offer some preliminary thoughts on the subject based on Conture's (1999) helpful considerations as to weaker and stronger EBP designs. These are summarized below.

Two weak designs

One basic and unsatisfactory design has efficacy measured by assessing clients' abilities only once, immediately after a period of therapy. A number of problems arise from this design, the two major ones being: (a) because there is no pretreatment comparison measure we have no idea how clients were performing before the treatment; (b) because there is no control group, whether any change in behaviour can be reliably attributed to the therapy they received. A second and slightly more sophisticated version is the pretest–treatment–retest variant. This design is likely to be familiar to many clinicians as the type often used clinically to demonstrate program efficacy. Here at least we have information on the pretest (or baseline) performance from which to compare against the retest (post-clinic) assessment. As with the earlier example, however, there is no control group, so we cannot say with any certainty that the course of treatment alone was responsible for any change in performance.

Two stronger designs

Schiaveti and Metz (1996) offer two improvements over these designs: matched randomized pretest–posttest control groups and ABA time series. With the former, a group of individuals are gathered with matched profiles for a range of variables. These may include factors such as age, sex, pretreatment stuttering severity, attitudinal profiles, treatment history, and so on. (The exact range of variables that need to be controlled will depend somewhat on the type of features that the treatment program will be targeting.) The subjects are then randomly assigned to either the experimental group or a control group. Both groups are tested before therapy and after therapy, but those assigned to the experimental group are also assessed during the therapy period. Success in this design is determined by comparing any difference between control and experimental groups at pretest with any difference between the two groups at the end of the therapy period. There are also difficulties with this approach, including as mentioned earlier, deciding exactly what pertinent details need to be matched and the ethical problems associated with withholding treatment from those assigned to the control group. Although, as Conture points out, control group members may be offered treatment following completion of the study by means of compensation, this is not always seen as an attractive option to potential participants, particularly where younger children are concerned whose parents are well aware that treatment is more successful if started earlier.

An alternative to the matched randomized test–retest approach lies with the ABA time series design. Here there is just one experimental cohort, avoiding the need for a control group by having each participant act as his or her own control. Subjects are observed a number of times leading up to the therapy (A), again a number of times during therapy (B), and finally a number of times post therapy (A). The idea is that this design makes it possible to examine within-subject differences in performance before therapy, during therapy and after completion of the therapeutic period, all due to the multiple testing through each of these time periods. This technique carries the advantage of generating a considerable amount of detail from a small amount of subjects. A potential difficulty is that it may be difficult to generalize these findings to a wider population.

Documenting clinical outcome – a five-step program for clinicians

For reasons already stated, it may simply not be possible for many clinicians to attempt a thoroughly controlled study of treatment outcomes. However, Yaruss (1997b) has proposed a set of procedures which provide a five-step framework to the documentation of treatment efficacy in a meaningful but viable way, given constraints upon time and physical resources. Adherence to the procedures outlined below will at least allow the fluency program to be objectively judged and accurately replicated by others.

1 *Describe the nature of the treatment program.* There needs to be information on frequency and duration of treatment and number of hours of clinician–client contact as well as the ordering of treatment techniques. Any variations on the use of established techniques (for example, cancellation or airflow techniques) must be documented in sufficient depth that the program can be replicated by others.

2 *Define success clearly.* For some approaches, this may mean documenting more behavioural measurements (percent syllables stuttered), whilst for more integrated approaches, success may be defined by a reduction rather than elimination of stuttering, and comprise a greater focus on attitudinal and affective aspects of the disorder. Whatever the approach taken, there must be clarity as to exactly what is being measured, how it is being defined, and under what circumstance (for example, one criteria might be <2 percent syllables stuttered when speaking to strangers in conversation in a novel setting) and at what stages following therapy.

3 *Operationalize the clinical decision-making process.* This needs to be done to the point where treatment goals can be measured. Yaruss (1997b) says (and as also pointed out above) that this may present a bigger problem to treatment programs whose goals lie more towards changing attitudinal aspects, the measurements of which are not so easy to measure objectively. However, the recent development of OASES (Yaruss & Quesal, 2004) and WASSP (Wright & Ayre, 2000) now provide improved opportunities to reliably measure such variables.

4 *Measure the outcomes of treatment.* Consistent with our more robust research designs, Yaruss views the collection of pretreatment, during treatment and posttreatment data as essential in order to note changes in performance over time, and objective measurement of treatment outcomes would be expected in any treatment program. We have already mentioned the thorny issue of how long therapeutic effects might be expected to last. The issue of maintenance of long-term outcomes is obviously one that each clinician must individually address. Yaruss simply suggests that the client should remain in contact with the clinician for "an extended period of time following the termination of treatment" (1997b, p. 221), but when this extended period is really extended,

problems can arise. Onslow (2004a) has vented his frustration about journal editors who, while bemoaning the lack of long-term follow-up data on treatment efficacy, at the same time refuse to print findings from long-term studies because of difficulties in controlling variables associated with the time lag between the end of the program being studied and the follow-up period.

5   *Report all changes (both positive and negative) objectively.* This seems plain enough and simple enough, but the practice of reporting negative changes (or even no change) is all too frequently not adhered to. Yaruss is worth quoting directly on this important aspect:

> Unfortunately, it is all too tempting for practitioners to emphasize findings that highlight the benefits of their programs while minimizing less-than-satisfactory results. A pitfall of this approach is that the objective analysis of treatment outcomes may be blurred by dogma and strong opinions. In order to help clinical researchers better understand the stuttering disorder, however, it is crucial that treatment outcomes research be approached from a more objective perspective. This will allow other clinicians and researchers the opportunity to evaluate the treatments and determine which aspects of treatment may be most appropriate for their own clients.
>
> (Yaruss, 1997b, p. 221)

It would seem commonsense that those involved in the treatment of fluency, whether as clinician, person who stutters, researcher, or combination of these, would want to know not only what is effective, but what has been tried and found not to be as beneficial. Unfortunately, although perhaps understandable, it is all too often journal policy to reject articles where the findings are predominantly negative, and such data which may be potentially of great value may struggle to see print.

Summary

Clinicians face a number of significant problems when it comes to measuring the effectiveness of stuttering therapy. To start with, we currently lack a satisfactory definition as to what actually constitutes success in treatment. Indeed there may not be a single definition, and what might be seen as effective treatment may differ from client to client. At present, success is mostly taken to mean reducing (primary) stuttering to an acceptable level, as measured in syllables per minute, although such measurements may not always be the most important to a significant number who stutter. Clearly, there is a need to incorporate data on cognitive affective aspects of the disorder into assessment protocols. There are a number of new self-assessment tools which enable the collection of such information. It is also important to remember that even the most prestigious and well-reported treatment approaches, whether for children, adolescents or adults, will not suit all clients and there will be failures for all approaches. The long-term maintenance of gains made in therapy presents a further problem when attempting a definition of successful treatment. Relapse is a significant issue for all treatments and the gathering of long-term follow-up data, though necessary to determine the true value of therapy, is not easy to achieve. Of course, the longer the gains made in therapy persist, the more successful the program will be viewed, but these time frames will vary depending on the age of the client. Attempting to impose arbitrarily defined time periods which would signal a therapy as being "successful in the long term" is simply not feasible. There are other fundamental concerns too with having long-term follow-up data published, and with the fact that the majority of clinicians simply do not have the temporal resources needed to undertake stronger efficacy studies on their treatment approaches. Bernstein-Ratner (2005b, pp. 181–182) offers the following thoughts amongst her conclusions on the current status and future of EBP:

> We will probably not be able to change some of the inevitable differences in how scientists and clinicians view the major issues in EBP. What we need to do is find some basic concepts to agree on. Among them might first be an agreement that we need to keep working on the problem. It might be good to work together, since sample sizes required to show program component functionality may be enormous. . . . Second, it seems clear that we – scientific clinicians and clinical scientists alike – should keep better data. Further, we need to increase the rate at which successful therapists publish the data. Throughout all this, we must remember to report individual differences even as we evaluate the group data.

In defence of those who have failed to follow only those treatments which have been rigorously tested using objective measures, she adds:

> In this writer's opinion, the tone of some past debates is hardly likely to win over the non-believers (c.f. Ingham & Cordes, 1999). Rather than castigate researchers and clinicians who do not universally and exclusively endorse some of the approaches recommended by authors in 28/3, we should be proud of those who do not leap to administer treatments inconsistent with the emerging scientific understanding of the basis of stuttering. To me, it implies that such individuals are engaged in reflective thinking and would, therefore, be receptive to strengthened accounts of the causative mechanisms by which supposedly effective and efficacious programs achieve their ends.
>
> (Bernstein-Ratner 2005b, p. 182)

Despite the difficulties, there are positive signs. The issue of EBP is becoming increasingly high profile and, whatever the difficulties involved, the fact that the research and clinical community is increasingly being forced to face the issues of EBP is surely a good thing. However, for the foreseeable future it will be the case that even the most efficacious treatments will fail some clients. An important focus must therefore be to continue to learn why some clients benefit from some programs and not from others. The dissemination of data on approaches that have been found to be unsuccessful, can play an important part in working toward this goal.

Key points

- Clinicians may pursue a number of treatment strategies in the clinic. The recording of any treatment program should, as a minimum, comprise objective and measurable treatment aims against which treatment outcomes will be measured.
- The form that any therapy takes should be considered not only in light of the clinician's perceptions and perspectives but also that of the client.
- Determining what is best practice in the treatment of stuttering is made more difficult by the fact that there is divided opinion as to how treatment should be approached, and thus exactly what needs to be measured.
- Increasingly, clinicians are collecting data on the emotional and social consequences of stuttering. The importance of the client's self-perception as a tool for measuring treatment effectiveness is being increasingly recognized.
- There is no consensus as to what constitutes success in the long term (particularly with older clients).
- Well-controlled efficacy studies are time consuming and need to be longitudinal. There are significant practical difficulties for clinicians attempting to undertake such studies.

Further reading

Bernstein-Ratner, N., & Healey E. C. (Eds.). (1999). *Stuttering research and practice: Bridging the gap*. Mahwah, NJ: Lawrence Erlbaum Associates, Inc.
This comprises 16 chapters written by experts in the field. Many discuss efficacy in research. Of particular interest here are Conture's highly readable account of problems for research and efficacy, Ingham and Cordes' hard-hitting chapter on research trends and Starkweather's final chapter directly on treatment efficacy itself.

Block, S. (2004). The evidence base for the treatment of stuttering. In S. Reilly, J. Douglas, & J. Oates (Eds.), *Evidence-based practice in speech pathology* (pp. 83–109). London: Whurr.

Although Block's chapter will be of particular interest to fluency clinicians, the book in its entirety will be of benefit to those wanting to know more about EBP.

Cordes, A., & Ingham, R. I. (Eds.). (1998). *Treatment efficacy for stuttering: A search for an empirical basis*. San Diego, CA: Singular Publishing Group.

A 12-chapter volume written by a number of experts who discuss in depth a range of issues relating to this critical subject area. Be aware that some of the earlier chapters, though interesting in their own right, focus more on aetiological issues and are of less direct interest to the central focus of efficacy in treatment.

Various authors (2003) *Journal of Fluency Disorders, 28*, 3. An entire volume of *Journal of Disorders of Fluency* devoted to issues surrounding efficacy and evidence-based practice in stuttering.

16 Acquired stuttering

Introduction

In the vast majority of cases stuttering arises in childhood, most usually preschool and apparently without any physical reason. While such developmental stuttering (DS) may persist into adulthood, the onset of stuttering amongst the adult population is comparatively rare and can be identified in one of two forms: neurogenic stuttering (NS) which arises due to damage to the nervous system, or psychogenic stuttering (PS) which can arise following a traumatic experience. Some clinicians also argue for a third subcategory occult stuttering (see below). While the subtypes of acquired stuttering are now accepted as recognized forms of fluency disorders, opinion differs as to the extent these versions of stuttering are behaviourally related to the developmental condition, and how best these acquired disorders should be managed clinically. Compared with DS, acquired versions have been little studied and the data that exists is somewhat patchy. Some have claimed that acquired disfluency must be viewed pathophysiologically and dealt with therapeutically as distinctly different from the developmental condition.

The question of what exactly constitutes PS has also been contested and one of the most intriguing possibilities lies with the idea that some cases of late onset DS might actually better be described as types of PS. However, we begin by briefly mentioning occult stuttering.

Occult stuttering

This rather sinister sounding term was coined by Van Riper (see Van Riper, 1982) to describe an adult onset of a stutter with no obvious neurological or psychological cause. In some cases the onset may represent relapse in a recovered stutterer, or a failure to control overt stuttering in an individual who has for many years successfully hidden the problem. While it is not uncommon for individuals with these types of histories to present for therapy, one could question to what extent these examples truly reflect adult onset, rather than adult reappearance of a pre-existing disorder. The term is hardly ever used now and many clinicians are unaware of its existence as a potential stuttering subcategory.

Neurogenic stuttering

Although there is rather little data on acquired stuttering when compared to the developmental condition, it seems clear that stuttering subsequent to neurological trauma comprises the largest subgroup. The cause of NS (or SAAND; stuttering associated with acquired neurological damage, which is Helm-Esterbrooks' 1999 preferred term) can be varied. Most commonly, it arises from brain damage associated with stroke, but other causes include brain tumour, progressive supranuclear palsy, traumatic brain injury, Alzheimer's disease, Parkinson's disease, drug usage and renal dialysis (Brazis, Masdeu, & Biller, 1996; Christensen, Byerly, & McElroy, 1996; Helm-Esterbrooks, 1999; Heuer et al., 1996; Lee et al., 2001; Supprian et al., 1999). (See also chapter 2 for information on drugs that have been associated with increased levels of stuttering.) Although most authorities now agree that neurogenic stuttering exists as an independent and separate fluency disorder some older accounts have viewed it as a part of other speech and language disorders such as aphasia, apraxia of speech or dysarthria.

Stuttering subsequent to stroke

When stuttering is observed following a stroke, it may be associated with heterogeneous lesion sites in either hemisphere. In contrast to the limited number of regions identified as associated with DS, most cortical and subcortical areas, with the exception of the occipital lobe, have been implicated in NS.

Reported sites in the left hemisphere include the left supplementary motor area (Van Borsel, Van Lierde, Van Cauwenberge, Guldemont, & Van Orshoven, 1998), putamen and internal capsule (Harrison, 2004) and the striatum (Carleur, Lambert, Defer, Coskun, & Rossa, 2000). Stuttering associated with right hemispheric lesions has been reported (Ardila & Lopez, 1986; Fleet & Heilman, 1985; Harrison, 2004), and has also been described following lesions to right-sided subcortical areas (e.g. Horner & Massey, 1983; Soroker, Bar-Israel, Schechter, & Solzi, 1990). Neurogenic stuttering has also been reported with bilateral lesions (Balasubramanian & Haydn, 1996; Helm-Esterbrooks, 1993). Helm-Esterbrooks (1993) contends that unilateral lesions result only in transient stuttering, lasting no more than a few weeks, whilst bilateral damage results in a persistent version. Ciabarra, Elkind, Roberts, and Marshall (2000) report separate cases of stuttering associated with lesions to pontine nucleus, basal ganglia and left subcortical area. Others still have identified stuttering associated with lesions that link cortical and subcortical structures. Kono, Hirano, Ueda, and Nakajima (1998) report the case of a 54-year-old man who had a previous history of some stuttering associated with Parkinsonism, and lesions to the supplementary motor area and thalamus. This patient was admitted to hospital with right facial palsy and sudden onset of stuttering, without aphasia. MRI revealed an infarct extending from the putamen to the caudate nucleus in the left hemisphere. The authors argue that the stuttering related to damage to the basal ganglia circuits which link the cerebral cortex and basal ganglia. There are, in addition, reports of cases where lesions have led to the disappearance of a pre-existing stutter, and conversely to the re-emergence of a stutter that the individual had recovered from many years previously (Andy & Bhatnager, 1992; Helm-Esterbrooks, Yeo, Geschwind, Freedman, & Weinstein, 1996; Mouradian, Paslawski, & Shauib, 2000).

Some commentators believe that findings of stuttering associated with neurological underpinnings could potentially have important ramifications for our understanding of the developmental condition (Balasubramanian & Max, 2003), while others see the acquired and developmental versions as two separate entities, the neurologies of which cannot reliably inform the other (Watson & Freeman, 1997). It is interesting to note that there is comparatively wide variability in both sites of lesions (and also in the nature of the neurological damage) that can lead to NS when compared to the specific speech centres known to be affected amongst those with developmental stuttering (see chapter 2). Conversely, a defining feature of DS is its heterogeneity, whereas the symptoms experienced by NS sufferers apparently result in a more constrained set of motor speech disruptions, as we now see.

Characteristics of neurogenic stuttering

NS tends to be characterized by part-word or phoneme repetition. This ubiquitous finding is perhaps surprising given the breadth of causes and different lesion sites with which it can be associated. For example, Abe, Yokoyama, and Yorifuji (1993) observed this type of syllable-initial repetitive disfluency in a client suffering with lesions to the extra pyramidal tract pathways, arguing that lesions to subcortical areas such as the paramedian thalami and midbrain typically result in this type of repetitive behaviour. But as we have seen in chapter 2, stuttering can also be associated with activity in cortical as well as subcortical structures. Unlike the developmental version, NS also occurs on open as well as closed class words. This is in contrast to DS where, as we have seen in chapter 5, the onset of the disorder is characterized by stuttering on function words, with a strong tendency to switch to a content word locus at around age 8 to 9. Neither is stuttering restricted to initial syllables, as it tends to be in the developmental condition (unless the initial syllable does not carry primary stress, for example, in words such as attend) and may present on either stressed or unstressed syllables. NS is also associated with a relative lack of anxiety and tension and an absence of secondary symptoms (Ringo & Dietrich, 1995). Unlike DS, NS may frequently be associated with high levels of stuttering. It is not unusual for clients to present with over 50 percent of all syllables stuttered or above.

Despite the diverse neurological implications in acquired stuttering, those with a neurogenic version consistently respond negatively to a number of stimuli which promote fluency amongst the majority of those with the developmental condition. These include adaptation,[1] although the clarity of procedure in these studies has been questioned by some investigators (e.g., Ringo & Dietrich, 1995) and altered feedback, including delayed auditory feedback (DAF) and frequency altered feedback (FAF; Balasubramanian, Max, Van Borsel, Rayca, & Richardson, 1997). More studies are needed to confirm the consistency of these findings, but nonetheless these preliminary data appear to point toward a different neurological underpinning of developmental and neurogenic stuttering. With this regard, the study by Balasubramanian et al. (1997) is of particular note. Their adult subject's fluency actually worsened slightly under conditions of FAF at two different frequencies and DAF at 50 ms delay, yet this subject experienced developmental stuttering as a child. Were neurogenic and developmental stuttering to have a unifying pathology, some benefit from altered feedback might be predicted.

Nevertheless, while differences clearly exist between neurogenic and developmental conditions (see Table 16.1), some studies have commented on the similarities in symptomatology. Van Borsel and Taillieu (2001) found that even qualified clinicians failed to distinguish NS from DS from samples of connected speech. In fact, if we look at the evidence this is not perhaps as surprising as it might first seem. The repetitions which are characteristic of NS can and frequently do occur in DS. However, the blocks and prolongations of established DS tend not to occur in NS, which would not be picked up by a comparison of connected speech samples. Similarly, connected speech samples would not reveal the absence of most secondary behaviours, or the lack of adaptation and altered feedback effects which tend to separate the two disorders.

Psychogenic stuttering

Here, the onset of stuttering occurs as a result of emotional trauma, a stressful event, or series of events. Causes can vary widely, but death of a close friend or family member and break-up of a relationship are comparatively common reasons. Psychogenic stuttering may also occur as a psychological reaction to physical trauma. This can lead to complication in diagnosis amongst those who have developed stutters following head injury, resulting in uncertainty as to whether the stutter is due to the neurological trauma incurred (i.e., a neurogenic stutter), or the psychological impact of the traumatic event. Baumgartner and Duffy (1997) found

---

1 This is a phenomenon where fluency is temporarily improved by rote repetition of a word or phrase.

that 25 percent of cases diagnosed by them as psychogenic also evidenced neurogenic problems.

Some earlier accounts of the disorder refer to the term hysterical stuttering. Bleumel (1935) believed the cause to be inhibition; itself a form of hysterical conversion reaction. The tenet was that the sufferer was not a person who stuttered, but a hysterical person who responded to emotional trauma with "a broad pattern of disorganization consisting of excitement, restlessness, confusion, and perhaps hysterical vomiting or hysterical stuttering" (Bleumel, 1957, p. 45). Freund (1966) also subscribed to the idea of hysterical stuttering, listing among its features a lack of emotional reaction to the stutter; consistency of stuttering across a variety of situations; relative detachment of the stutterer from the stuttering (Deal, 1982); and late and sudden onset (Baumgartner, 1999). It is often the case that psychogenic stuttering is associated with clients who have an established history of visiting their general practitioner with a range of concerns, some of which may be considered to be psychosomatic. There also seems a more direct association between PS and complaints such as depression (Deal & Doro, 1984). In fact, applying the term "psychogenic stuttering" is becoming more problematic. The American Speech and Language Association guidelines in 1999 recommended that the use of the term must be restricted to disfluency which is associated with a diagnosed psychopathology. On the other hand, Baumgartner (1999) reports that a psychopathological diagnosis is not prerequisite.

Characteristics of psychogenic stuttering

Psychogenic stuttering can arise for a wide variety of reasons amongst people with very different backgrounds and of very different ages, so perhaps one of the most remarkable features of the disorder is the comparative homogeneity of its symptoms. This is in quite stark contrast to the variability in stuttering symptoms (between speakers) seen in those with the developmental condition. Deal (1982, p. 300) suggested seven elements that could be associated with "stuttering subsequent to psychological trauma":

- Sudden onset of stuttering.
- Onset of stuttering is related to a significant event.
- Disfluency is mostly represented by repetition of initial or stressed syllable.
- Fluency is little affected by choral reading, white noise, delayed auditory feedback, singing, or different speaking situations.
- Initially, there are no periods of stutter-free speech. Stuttering is experienced even on over-learned utterances (such as nursery rhymes) and automatic social responses ("hello" and "it's a nice day today").
- Initially, there is no interest in his or her stuttering.
- Same patterns of repetitions during mimed reading aloud as in conversational speech.

Some years later, Baumgartner and Duffy (1997) examined the abnormal fluency of a group of 49 clients with psychogenic stutters and found that the most frequent characteristic was sound or syllable repetitions. They also argued that these speech characteristics were more typical among those clients who had a history of stress disorders. A summary of symptoms occurring in NS, PS and DS can be seen in Table 16.1.

Late onset stuttering in children

As we have seen in earlier chapters, developmental stuttering usually starts in the preschool years. As mentioned in the opening chapter, the issue of later onset stuttering is one that presents us with something of a conundrum, both from a theoretical and clinical perspective, and there are a number of unresolved issues here. Some of these relate to adult onset and particularly the issue of whether some examples of late onset stuttering can be considered as some reactivation of a problem which has merely lain dormant and unrecognized in childhood (as suggested in Van Riper's occult stuttering). But here we are more concerned with the issue of whether a late onset of the disorder actually refers to a separate clinical entity. We have seen elsewhere that a number of researchers have apparently identified separate "tracks" of stuttering which start later in life (Van Riper, 1982 refers to later onset as being after 4 years old) and follow a rather different course of development to that assocated with the earlier onset variety (Van Riper, 1971). We have also noted that those who follow such patterns may be more difficult to treat successfully.

A thorny issue (and perhaps because of this an underresearched area) is how children who show a sudden onset of stuttering at age 10 or older should be diagnosed and consequently treated. At the Apple House, we see a small but significant number of children who present with later onset stuttering. Consistent with Van Riper's Track III and Track IV accounts, these children almost always report a rapid onset (a point always confirmed by the children's parents), usually with no periods of subsequent remission. There are sometimes elements of Track III behaviour, including the linking of the onset to a particular traumatic experience, and Track IV, including the stereotyped multiple syllable repetitions which are consistent with some reports of psychogenic stuttering which is usually diagnosed in adults. Indeed, Van Riper (1982) makes this point explicitly with regard to Track IV when he writes: "It is our impression that those who begin to stutter in adulthood are more likely to portray these behaviors than children. And the adults show very few changes once they begin to stutter this way. They continue to stutter much the same way they began" (p. 105).

So can these later onset children be considered as potential psychogenic stutterers rather than developmental ones? At what age (or age range) can one say that an individual is too old to be considered to start a developmental stutter, and the disorder consequently then needing to be considered as

Table 16.1 Comparison of some features of persistent developmental stuttering, neurogenic stuttering and psychogenic stuttering

	Onset and development	Presence of stutter when established	Susceptible to altered feedback	Adaptation effect	Stuttering behaviours	Struggle/secondary behaviours	Prognosis
Persistent developmental stuttering (PDS)	In childhood. Usually gradual; may be episodic	May vary depending on situation, conversational partner	Mostly, yes	Yes	Various – repetitions (phoneme, part word), prolongations, blocks, etc.	May be the most significant features of the disorder	No cure for adult stuttering, but may resolve spontaneously, or with therapy in childhood
Neurogenic stuttering	Sudden (if cerebral-vascular accident, CVA), though onset can be gradual for closed head injury. All types are nonepisodic, unless related to episodic drug use, when severity might vary	Situation independent	No	No	Usually phoneme, syllable or word repetition	Rare, if at all, but there may be frustration and anxiety	Variable: depends on the nature and extent of damage. NS associated with multiple lesions to both hemispheres tends to lead to persistent stuttering
Psychogenic stuttering	Sudden, coincident with traumatic event(s)	Situation independent	No	No	Typically syllable and word repetition	Rare, but there may be some situation avoidance	Variable. May resolve with resolution of the trauma, and often responds quickly but not always

Note that while symptomatology generally seems more consistent with NS and PS than DS, there is some inconsistency in reporting of symptoms, and not all findings are consistent with the above table. For example, Horner and Massey (1983) describe the case of a 62-year-old male who suffered diffuse damage to the right hemisphere as a result of a right middle cerebral artery infarct. Stuttering was characterized predominantly by word and phrase repetitions (although phoneme and syllable repetitions were also present), increased speech rate and reduced loudness. Oral reading and repetition were not as adversely affected as spontaneous speech, and singing and reciting familiar material were only slightly affected. Note, also, that Harrison (2004) provided an example of an adult with bilateral hemispheric lesions following stroke where familiar material was stuttered on with similar severity (although oral reading could not be tested due to co-occurring language problems).

psychogenic? It is understandable that most literature on stuttering focuses on the period at which developmental stuttering most commonly arises. Theories which consider developmental aspects are almost exclusively underpinned by the notion that stuttering is a preschool disorder: for example, linguistic and motoric perspectives (and those which integrate the two) take the bulk of their evidence from the time when these skills are rapidly developing in the preschool child. But such theories only add to the confusion when it comes to those who start to stutter long after these skills have been acquired.

Well, we could offer a Demands and Capacities perspective. Here, the individual might lack linguistic skill, motor skill and/or any combination of a range of factors that would place him at increased risk of stuttering. However, the child remains remain fluent during preschool and early school years, as level of demand is not yet above the threshold needed to activate stuttering. It might then only need a comparatively minor event (or traumatic period of time) later on to trigger the onset. There are as yet no reliable data which indicate that children with late onset stuttering do actually present with such linguistic, physiological, environmental or genetic profiles prior to the onset of the disorder.

Treatment of neurogenic stuttering

Assessment and diagnosis

The exact course that a first examination of a person suspected of having NS will take will vary significantly depending on the existing knowledge of the underlying neurological condition. This may appear comparatively straightforward, say, in the case of stroke, where there is sudden onset consistent of stuttering alongside the neurological trauma. It may be harder in the case of a person who presents with concerns that he has been experiencing increased disfluency over a period of some months (and at the assessment his disfluencies are consistent with NS), but has not yet sought the advice of his GP/physician. Suffice to say, in all cases, a full case history should be taken, gathering as much data as possible on a potential pre-existing stutter, including perspectives of close friends or relatives as to any observed changes in speech fluency. It would be important also to note whether the type of stuttering could be consistent with a psychogenic stutter. Careful questioning should explore this possibility and access to any relevant GP notes would also be required. Clearly, the key factor in the diagnosis of a neurogenic stutter is the presence of neurological damage or neurological trauma associated with the onset of stuttering behaviours. Diagnosis of NS cannot be made in the absence of hard medical evidence, whether in the form of a brain scan for a stroke, epilepsy, or tumour, or positive test results for a movement disorder such as Parkinson's disease, or a degenerative disease such as multiple sclerosis. Having said that, even this evidence may not provide conclusive proof that NS can in all cases be differentially diagnosed from PS.

Even when there is evidence to support the NS diagnosis, it may be impossible to rule out, in addition, a reaction to the neurological trauma in the form of psychogenic stuttering. Although there are some differences recorded between the two acquired stuttering subtypes, they also share a lot of common features and differences may not be apparent in all cases. Thus, differentially diagnosing the two can be very difficult. It is common practice that when stuttering presents alongside medical evidence of neurological trauma, the condition is diagnosed as NS, even when the trauma of undergoing a stroke could in itself be sufficient to result in a psychogenic onset, and effectively there could be a dual cause.

Generally speaking, a different approach to therapy will be required, depending on the medical diagnosis underlying the stuttering. Particularly, the therapist will need to consider whether that condition is likely to: (a) completely resolve, as could, for example, be the case for some drug-related stuttering once the substance is no longer being taken; (b) persist, as in the case of severe stroke; (c) worsen, as in the case with degenerative diseases such as multiple sclerosis and Parkinson's disease. Additional factors will include the site and extent of lesion(s), if appropriate, and the relevance of co-occurring conditions, whether speech related or not.

Let us take as a hypothetical example the case of a client who has just suffered a stroke, identified by magnetic resonance imaging (MRI) as the result of multiple lesions to the left temporal-parietal area. As he slowly begins to recover physical, cognitive and speech and language functions over the days following the incident, disfluencies start to appear in his speech. The first task for the clinician is to see the extent and range of the speech and language difficulties that present. Does the patient show evidence of aphasia, dyspraxia or dysarthria? All of these disorders have implications for fluency and we need to know whether the difficulties seen in our client can be explained in terms of these other disorders. Maybe the disfluencies are better explained in terms of the broken and telegraphic speech of a Broca's type aphasia? Perhaps the loss of fluency is associated with word-finding difficulties? Are the disfluencies more representative of a dyspraxic's repeated attempts at accurate phoneme production than a primary loss of fluency?

Here lies the first problem. "Pure" NS following stroke is comparatively rare, and the greatest likelihood is that it will appear alongside other speech and language disorders rather than in isolation. At this stage we need to gather as complete a case history as possible. In particular, we need to know whether there is any history of childhood or early onset stuttering, any other speech and language disorders, or any history of stuttering amongst relatives. It is also important to gather information concerning any premorbid history of psychological disturbances, including evidence of neuroticism. While we may now be in a position to consider the stutter as an acquired phenomena, we still need to be alert to the possibility that the stutter could be a reflection of the psychological trauma he has experienced rather than the physical one, and that this could be PS instead of NS.

Treatment

It is possible that this individual who has a single-sided cortical lesion may not be a candidate for fluency therapy, regardless of the presence of any co-occurring aphasia, at least in the first instance. First, where there is co-occurring aphasia, it is usual for this to form the more significant barrier to communication and for the sufferer to be more concerned about the aphasia than the stutter. Second, even if there is no evidence of aphasia (or other speech/language disorder) it may be appropriate, given the diagnosis of uni-lateral lesion, to wait to see if spontaneous remission takes place, and instead to reassure the client that there is a good likelihood of complete recovery of normal speech. The final decision as to whether to delay therapy would need to be considered in the light of the client's concern over his condition together with other factors such as severity of the stutter and competing cases on the caseload.

Prognosis will, in part, depend on the underlying neurological pathology, as well as the fluency diagnosis, the general health of the client, and the extent of any co-occurring disorders, whether outside the speech and lan-guage domain or not. Treatment may take the forms of speech modification, although speech pacing and relaxation may also be valuable components (Helm-Esterbrooks, 1999). Similarly, block modification techniques may be applied, and the slide in particular can be effective in dealing with multiple word initial repetitions. In some cases, for example, where NS occurs sub-sequent to multiple bilateral lesions, the prognosis for spontaneous recovery tends to be poor (Helm-Esterbrooks, 1986).

Harrison (2004) reported the case of a person who was referred for "stut-tering" at ten months post onset to a stroke. MRI scans revealed bilateral lesions affecting the left posterior parietal lobe and areas around the right caudate head, putamen and internal capsule. Speech was characterized by aphasia together with NS symptoms including multiple syllable and word repetitions on both function and content words, and a fluency count of around 55 percent SS. Speech rate was normal at around 200 syllables per minute. Therapy focused on slowing speech rate and relaxing speech musculature; the latter strategy meeting with little success due to problems with co-occurring oral apraxia. A pacing board approach was also unsuccess-ful. At ten-year follow-up, the patient presented with similar reading and writing difficulties. However, although "stuttering-like" disfluencies persisted, these were now less frequent. Despite this, some avoidance behaviour had started to emerge.

Let us consider a further example of a client diagnosed with Parkinson's disease. To start with, stuttering associated with this disorder may be difficult to diagnose. For example, the run-on (or festinant) speech characteristic of this type of (hypokinetic) dysarthria can lead to quick part-word repetitions which may appear similar to stuttering, but can also sound similar to clutter-ing. In any case, the rate control procedures seen in some stuttering and cluttering therapies may be helpful in reducing rate and number of repetitions and improving clarity. As with other neuromotor disorders, the use of aids such as pacing boards may be helpful in controlling speed and speech rhythm. Either way, the long-term prognosis here is not favourable. As the Parkinson's disease progresses, so motor control generally will decline, and with it, over a period of months or years, the quality of speech and language, and with that, fluency. We should also consider the possible role of medication in the stutter in this example. D2 antagonists used in the treatment of Parkinson's disease could be a contributory factor to increased disfluency (see chapter 2). It may be possible to get an idea as to the likelihood of this effect from considering the onset of the stuttering symptoms in relation to the implementation of levadopa medication.

Even if a link between the two is suspected, there may be little alternative but to continue with the drug. Ward and Wardman (2005) reported the case of a man who developed a stutter two years after the diagnosis of Parkinson's disease and treatment of this with Madapar (a D2 antagonist; see also chapter 2). Stuttering was characterized by multiple repetitions of syllables on both function and content words, in the absence of any physical struggle or tension. Speech rate was normal and regularly paced despite 35 percent of syllables being stuttered in conversation. It was clear that these symptoms were very different to those he experienced in his mild developmental stutter, which was characterized primarily by short blocks. The developmental condition had not concerned him, and his professional life, which involved a considerable amount of public speaking and chairing meetings, had not been affected by it. In contrast, this client was very anxious about the new stuttering and felt frustrated and embarrassed by it. The new stuttering symptoms seen in this client did not seem consistent with the types of fluency disturbances typical of Parkinson's speech (such as festinant speech and disturbed rhythm and speech rate), nor did the individual profile or stuttering onset pattern fit the diagnosis of a trauma-based psychogenic stutter. It was therefore hypothesised that the stutter may be related to the levadopa therapy, although objective testing of this was not possible because a withdrawal of the drug was not an option. Therapy comprised a mixture of airflow techniques and in-block modification (see chapter 12) to control the repetitions, together with some relaxation techniques. After five 45-minute therapy sessions, severity of stuttering had dropped to less than 2 percent SS, the number of repetitions on the remaining moments of stuttering had significantly reduced and there was normal sounding speech. Good carryover of the improved fluency was reported subsequently. Future follow-up sessions will indicate whether this progress can be maintained in the long term.

A rather different approach to treatment of NS has been offered by Andy and Bhatnager (1992) who outline the case of four clients diagnosed with mesothalamic damage. These individuals received mesothalamic stimulation to relieve pain, and this procedure also had a positive effect in reducing levels of stuttering. Andy and Bhatnager (1992) suggest that both chronic pain and stuttering may be triggered by similar electropathogenic generators (as identified by abnormal EEG signals) and that the acquired stuttering may be seen as a single component of a bigger syndrome. This notion is currently untested, but it begs some definition as to the nature and scope of this bigger syndrome, and is a point to which I return below.

Treatment of psychogenic stuttering

There is limited data on efficacy of treatment for this group of people who stutter. Response tends to be individualistic, based on a number of factors. In some cases, stuttering very obviously seems to represent an automatic response, and one that even goes unnoticed by the speaker, to an extreme psychological trauma. However, there are cases where there may be a very acute awareness, to the point where the original trauma itself resolves quickly, and instead the individual rapidly identifies the stutter as the over-riding concern (as in the case example below). There are different perspectives on treatment procedures, and different approaches may be pertinent to different cases. Clinicians may elect to treat PS using many of the procedures already used in the treatment of DS, and approaches that target motor speech alongside those which look at psychological influences may be integrated in a similar way. Depending on the nature of the onset, it may be important for the clinician to work in collaboration with a psychologist to try to resolve the psychological issues which underpin the stutter. Spontaneous recovery is also not uncommon in PS, but does not seem easily predictable from the nature of the psychogenic underpinning. In some cases PS does resolve completely, either with or without therapy: for example, stuttering associated with a bereavement may resolve after a period of grieving and adjustment to that person's loss. Baumgartner (1999) notes that around two-thirds of PS cases achieve completely normal or nearly normal sounding fluency within two therapeutic sessions. However, stuttering can persist long after the trauma is apparently no longer a factor, and it can last indefinitely. The reasons for this inconsistency are currently unknown, but are likely to be multifactorial, taking into account both the nature of the underlying trauma together with the individual variability in psychological response to dealing with life events. We can illustrate this variability in presenting the following examples.

Some case examples

Roth, Aronson, and Davis (1989) examined 12 cases of psychogenic stuttering. In contrast with Deal's assertions, the stuttering in most cases was variable in severity. Stuttering returned to normal either spontaneously or with therapy. They also found that all 12 cases complained of neurological symptoms that transpired to be nonorganic. Such an association between physical trauma representing as psychogenic stuttering is explained by the *DSM-III-R* (APA, 1987) classification of psychogenic stuttering as a conversion reaction. A conversion disorder is one where there is a physical manifestation, suggesting an organic disorder, but which in fact occurs due to psychological conflict. Two more examples of this can be seen in a study by Mahr and Leith (1992) who presented four cases of psychogenic stuttering. Case one identified a 44-year-old man who was severely injured and rendered unconsciousness when a truck reversed into him, pinning him against his own truck. On recovering consciousness, his speech was characterized by the syllable repetitions (as predicted by Deal, 1982) on approximately 80 percent of words. Other features included a high-pitched voice and rapid rate of speech. Mental status examination was normal. The stutter, rate and high pitch all responded to 9 months of twice-weekly 30-minute periods of therapy, and normal speech was maintained at a 2-year posttreatment follow-up.

A second case concerned a 39-year-old female undergoing a medical procedure under local anaesthetic. She became anxious when the effects of the anaesthetic began to wear off during the operation and was then placed under general anaesthetic. While recovering from this, she subsequently experienced post-operative confusion lasting two or three hours. After surgery, speech was hesitant and mildly disfluent, but began to worsen after a period of two months. After five months the diagnosis changed to "severe stuttering". As with case one, stuttering consisted of syllable repetition (up to 5 seconds of repetition) on approximately 90 percent of words. Again, speech rate was rapid but there was no struggle behaviour and she remained apparently unconcerned by her speech. Neurological exam was normal, but histrionic personality traits, including memory loss, auditory and visual hallucinations and sense of depersonalization were all present. After two and a half years, fluency therapy was abandoned due to lack of progress.

The two further cases both related to people who had a history of emotional problems: one involving bipolar depression related to physical abuse; the other recovering from physical and sexual abuse by her former husband. Of particular interest is that both started stuttering as therapy involved the individual in becoming more able to talk about the distressing episodes, and did not coincide with the period of abuse itself. In both instances, stuttering behaviour changed from mild to severe, including "secondary" symptoms not typically associated with a psychogenic stutter such as knee slapping, foot movements and head nodding. Also, both speakers experienced context-dependent stuttering, again untypical of a psychogenic onset. Both patients' stutters resolved with fluency therapy and psychotherapy. In one case, recovery took only a matter of a few weeks and focused on the patient becoming less anxious when recalling traumatic episodes. The other slowly came to accept the termination of the relationship with her husband and stuttering resolved as divorce proceedings were planned.

One case recently seen at the Apple House concerned a 54-year-old man whose onset of stuttering could be directly related to a very stressful period of time at work as a security guard. The stutter was consistent with Deal's list of features associated with PS, aside from strong awareness and concern about the stutter and instantaneous onset. He had a history of anxiety, had had two heart attacks and was now taking a range of drugs to control for hypertension. He presented at assessment with abnormally rapid and agitated speech, characterized by multiple syllable initial repetitions. A modified Erikson S-24 score of 21 revealed very negative self-perceptions as a speaker, and he expressed high levels of frustration and concern over his current difficulties with communication. At assessment over 60 percent of syllables were stuttered in conversational speech. Therapy focused on reducing speech rate to a normal speed together with relaxation and diaphragmatic breathing techniques. This approach resulted in normally fluent and normal sounding speech returning within one session, but while there was palpable relief at the return of his earlier levels of fluency, anxiety levels remained very high and transfer of fluency away from the clinic proved difficult.

As already noted above, it has been suggested that acquired stuttering may be triggered by a similar mechanism to that which signals pain (Andy & Bhatnager, 1992). This is an intriguing proposition, albeit one that has not been verified scientifically, or yet experientially. However, just occasionally cases occur where stuttering does seem to be related to intense pain. Perino, Famularo, & Taroni (2000) report the case of an individual who developed transient stuttering alongside a migraine attack. In addition, I can recall the recent case of a man in his mid-eighties who had damaged his back, with the consequence that he now experienced continuous and often severe back pain. Until this point he had always enjoyed good physical and mental health and had no personal or familial history of stuttering or other speech/language disorder. Surgery to the back was not a favoured option, largely due to his age, and instead the condition was controlled with pain-killing drugs. Stuttering, almost exclusively in the form of multiple and easy initial syllable repetitions, built up over a period of a few weeks alongside the back pain. Although this man was never totally free from the stutter, it varied in severity, which appeared heavily dependent on the degree of pain relief afforded by the drugs. From a diagnostic perspective the type of stuttering was mostly consistent with psychogenic stuttering, but there were some inconsistencies. Right from the outset, and more obviously still at times when the pain-relieving drugs allowed him to consider his stuttering more, he expressed concern and embarrassment over his stutter and avoided situations where he had to speak. He was very keen to work on improving his fluency and made significant progress simply using a slide approach (see chapter 12) to break the pattern of syllable repetitions, to the point where the syllable stuttered percentage dropped from over 35 percent to under 3 percent in conversation over a period of four one-hour sessions. Although very pleased with these results, this client found it almost impossible to maintain control over his fluency when pain levels increased, and this resulted in fluctuating levels of fluency on a day-to-day basis. Of course, it is possible that the trauma relating to the back pain and the ramifications for him and his wife were responsible for the stuttering, rather than the pain directly, in which case this might seem quite straightforwardly a case of PS. However, the assessment did not seem to fit the PS profile. The case history showed no evidence of previous anxiety-related illness, which can be a feature of those with PS. Relatedly, this individual appeared pragmatic about his acute back pain, which while evidently highly unpleasant was not considered by the medics as likely to worsen, or to carry a threat to life. In addition, the fact that the stutter varied according to pain levels is not consistent with a purely psychogenic diagnosis.

Anaesthesia treatment

There is one recent report of successful treatment of psychogenic stuttering by using a temporary anaesthetic to desensitize the larynx (Dworkin et al., 2002). This involved the case of a 39-year-old male subject who experienced whiplash injuries following a motor vehicle accident. There was no loss of consciousness, and thorough medical and physical investigations all failed to reveal any abnormality. Four weeks following the accident he spontaneously developed a severe stutter. Subsequent neurological and psychiatric investigations failed to provide an organic cause for the speech difficulty. He attended five sessions of conventional speech language therapy before the sessions were discontinued. Consistent with many reports of psychogenic stuttering, the client presented with multiple syllable repetitions and short blocks on initial phonemes. Singing or using prolonged speech failed to improve fluency. Laryngoscopy revealed a range of abnormal laryngeal activity, including intermittent supraglottal sphincteric contractions, coincident shimmying of the laryngeal framework and dyssynchronous vocal fold movement patterns.

Further assessment revealed a very slow speech rate due to a high number of multiple syllable repetitions (69 syllables per minute, SPM) and a high level of stuttered moments (45 percent syllables stuttered, percent SS). These factors, taken into consideration alongside an otherwise normal case history, the sudden onset, lack of periods of fluency and lack of neurological symptoms, led Dworkin et al. to conclude a diagnosis of psychogenic disfluency, possibly based on a marked emotional reaction to the car accident and hospitalization.

Lidocaine injection procedure

The researchers concluded that there might be an underlying laryngeal condition to the client's speech and proposed a technique which had previously yielded good results with clients with psychogenic muscle tension dysphonia (Dworkin, Meleca, Simpson, & Garfield, 2000). This involves an injection of an aneasthetic, lidocaine, into the subglottic airway via the cricothyroid membrane. The injection triggered a cough reflex which caused the solution to cover subglottal, glottal and supraglottal mucosa. For a 15-minute period following the injection the client showed a range of reactions not commonly associated with lidocaine, including mutism, dizziness, drooling, perspiration and dysponea.

As soon as these reactions diminished, the client immediately undertook fluency enhancing exercises. Strategies such as easy onset, light articulatory contact and smooth breathing techniques were introduced, initially in single words, then short phrases, sentences and finally conversational speech. This fluency training session lasted only 15 minutes and was the only behavioural intervention used. Fluency immediately increased from 45 percent disfluency to 5 percent following this period of therapy and speech rate increased to 82 SPM. At one-week post injection, these figures had changed to 4 percent SS and 127 SPM while at one-month posttreatment no disfluency was recorded and speech rate had increased substantially to 183 SPM. Further follow-up sessions taken over an 18-month period posttreatment all revealed fluency parameters within normal limits.

Explanations for recovery of fluency

Dworkin et al. (2002) offer three possible explanations as to why this procedure was so effective. First, a psychological perspective – here the stutter represents a conversion response to the emotional trauma of the accident. (See also Deal, 1982 and Roth et al., 1989 for similar explanations of psychogenic stuttering.) They argue that the strong nervous reaction to the lidocaine injection could indicate that the sudden improvement in fluency represented a counterbalancing of one traumatic status (the stuttering) with another traumatic event (the medical procedure). Dworkin et al. (2002) speculate as to whether a placebo would have given the same effect. If such a procedure could ever ethically be justified and similar results obtained with a saline solution, then, as Dworkin et al. (2002) suggest, the case for a conversion reaction would be overwhelming. It is worth noting that a placebo trial was implemented with Dworkin et al.'s (2000) muscle tension dysphonia group and it proved therapeutically ineffective.

A second explanation is that the fluency represents a sensorimotor response. This client exhibited laryngeal activity somewhat consistent with those noted in the psychogenic muscle dysphonia patients with whom the lidocaine procedure had been successful in an earlier experiment. Thus, the desensitization of the mechanoreceptors in the laryngeal areas in itself could be responsible. A final theory combines both psychologic and physiologic explanations. That is, the anaesthetic released the hypertension in the larynx, which gave the client just enough time to build confidence in his ability to maintain fluency in increasing length of utterances during the subsequent short period of therapy. As such, this allowed him to overcome the strong psychological reaction he had previously when unsuccessfully attempting similar exercises immediately prior to the lidocaine injection.

It will be interesting to see if any future anaesthetic techniques yield similar results, and to what extent it might become a recognized option for the treatment of psychogenic stuttering. In fact, in their conclusion, Dworkin et al. (2002) hint that that the process could even be used to treat developmental stuttering:

> Whether or not this form of treatment would work equally well with other disfluent patients, regardless of etiology, remains to be evaluated. It is conceivable that disfluent patients who are found to exhibit abnormal phonation subsystem features would be the best candidates and benefit the most from the current management approach.
>
> (Dworkin et al., 2002, p. 224)

If future research finds the procedure to consistently benefit those with psychogenic stuttering, and that the basis for the success is found to be physiological rather than psychological, it is a very different proposition in attempting to treat a developmental disorder, which appears to have an organic basis in this way, as opposed to an acquired disorder where the onset is linked to psychological trauma. Although similar in some respects, these two disorders have many significant differences.

Summary

Half a century ago, psychogenic and neurogenic stuttering were not considered to be "legitimate" fluency disorders: the former was seen as a part of a conversion neurosis, the latter explained merely as features of other speech and language disorders. The change (comparatively recently in the case of PS) to the present situation has allowed us to consider and treat acquired stuttering from a more objective viewpoint. Even so, the study of acquired stuttering is still in its infancy. There is a paucity of data on the subject and it will be interesting to see, as more becomes known, whether identifiable subgroups within PS and NS can be identified. For example, the issue of late onset stuttering is a confusing one, and most of the data on DS have looked at stuttering as occurring during the preschool or early school years. As we see throughout this book, many theories as to the development of stuttering have been based on data relating to this age group. Yet there is a small but substantial number of individuals who do not start to stutter until they are in their early teens, and who are currently being left out of the equation when it comes to considering how stuttering arises and develops. It may be stretching things a bit to suggest that this group potentially represents a type of PS subgroup, but data either supporting or refuting the idea are currently missing. Similarly, we might also consider the issue of pain as a factor in a potential PS subgroup. Turning to the neurological condition, we see that NS symptomatology is arguably more varied than PS. It may be that different subgroups of NS naturally arise from quantitative studies of the different neurological conditions that can be associated with the disorder. The answers to these questions currently await the findings of further research.

Key points

- Acquired stuttering refers to two main subgroups of stuttering. Neurogenic stuttering (NS) can result from a variety of neurological traumas including stroke, brain tumour, head injury, degenerative disease, drug usage. Psychogenic stuttering (PS) arises from a psychological trauma, including the death of a close friend or relative, physical attack.
- The different behavioural and cognitive profiles exhibited by those with a neurogenic and psychogenic onset suggest that the acquired versions of stuttering are distinct and separate from the disorder of developmental stuttering.
- Treatment strategies for PS and NS usually follow those used for the treatment of the developmental condition. In contrast to the adult form of developmental stuttering, the treatment of PS and NS can bring about a complete recovery (although see next point).
- Both spontaneous and treatment aided recovery from NS is variable, depending on the type and extent of neurological damage. Recovery from PS is also variable, the reasons for which are currently unknown and likely to be multifactorial.
- The successful treatment of PS by temporarily anaesthetizing the larnyx has been reported in one case report. This study may have implications for the medical treatment of PS and have theoretical implications as to why PS arises in the first place.

Further reading

Acquired stuttering has not received the attention afforded to the developmental version and much of the work in this area has involved small-scale studies. The references below have been selected for their breadth, and because they draw together knowledge on the subject in a practical way which will directly benefit the clinician.

Baumgartner, J. (1999). Acquired psychogenic stuttering. In R. F. Curlee (Ed.), *Stuttering and related disorders of fluency* (pp. 269–288). New York: Thieme.
This chapter discusses both the aetiology and therapy of psychogenic stuttering. A good and comprehensive source on the subject.

Helm-Esterbrooks, N. (1999). Stuttering associated with acquired neurological disorders. In R.F. Curlee (Ed.), *Stuttering and related disorders of fluency* (pp. 255–269). New York: Thieme.
Comprehensive on the causes of neurogenic stuttering, but this chapter, written by one of the foremost experts in the field, is also good on a range of treatment approaches. An earlier book chapter (Helm-Esterbrooks, 1986) also offers useful insights into both theoretical and clinical issues.

Roth, C. R., Aronson, A. E., & Davis, L. J. Jr. (1989). Clinical studies in psychogenic stuttering of adult onset. *Journal of Speech and Hearing Disorders, 54*, 634–646.
A useful review of psychogenic stuttering that illustrates the breadth of problems which can underpin the disorder and the differential responses to its treatment.

17 Assessment, diagnosis and treatment of cluttering

Introduction

We have already discussed the nature of cluttering and how cluttering presents in part one of this book. We know that the symptoms of cluttering can be diverse, with some features bearing similarity to those often associated with normal nonfluency, whilst there may be commonalities with stuttering, aphasia and apraxia of speech, amongst others. In addition, diagnosis can be complicated by the presence of coexisting speech and language disorders, and the concept of cluttering syndrome disorder has been introduced in an earlier chapter as one way of acknowledging and characterizing this variability. Objective data is currently lacking on issues such as effectiveness of therapy and whether factors such as spontaneous recovery can play a role, as it can with stuttering. The issues surrounding efficacy are compounded by the fact that there is still no universally agreed definition on the disorder. The current chapter considers the disorder from a modular perspective. That is, cluttering can be viewed as comprising a number of components, some of which may be considered "core" (for example, abnormally fast speech rate and inappropriate pausing), and others which may be regarded as more peripheral (for example, poor short-term memory, and poor motor control outside the speech domain). It is considered likely, however, that many of the areas implicated will be interlinked, and this will need to be taken into consideration when planning and structuring therapy.

Assessment of cluttering

Introduction

A comprehensive assessment is essential if an informed diagnosis is to be made. The exact form the assessment will take depends on the age of the client, but procedures will need to include a comprehensive case history, assessments (formal or informal) of language function, oromotor speech, articulation, rhythm, rate and fluency. When assessing a suspected clutter in a young child, the clinician may need to separate related disorders from the diagnosis, such as tachylalia, developmental language disorder, dyspraxia and stuttering. Information on behaviour will also need to be gathered and, again depending on the age of the individual, input from other professionals such as teachers, special educational needs care workers and psychologists may be needed. In some cases (usually involving older children and adults) a neurologist's report may be required, together with brain scan evidence in order to rule out the possibility of neurological trauma as a causal factor in the disorder.

Referral sources

Unlike stuttering, it is comparatively unusual for a person who clutters to come for an assessment out of their own concern about their speech. With children, the referral is often from either a parent or healthcare professional, initially for stuttering (which assessment may or may not find to coexist). Older children and adolescents may be reluctant attendees, initially at least, brought along by parents who are concerned that their children are mumbling and not easily understood. A common referral route with adults is one initiated by a senior work colleague, who is concerned that this person's poor communication skills may be affecting his chances of promotion. A quite frequent corollary of this is concern over the potential impact of the poor communication skills at an impending interview.

The case history

This will need to be as comprehensive as it would be for a person suspected of stuttering. Actually, given the fact that the two disorders often coexist, there is a reasonable likelihood that stuttering may be implicated as well. The clinician will need to gain the client's perspective on his or her speech difficulty, regardless of the source of the initial referral. It is recommended that the clinician begins by asking why the person has come to seek the advice or help of a speech language therapist/pathologist at this time, and what they perceive the main issues to be. The taking of the case history can then commence.

History of speech or language disorders in the family?

It is important to specifically enquire about stuttering at this point, as well as cluttering, and other developmental speech or language disorder. For example: "Did anyone in your family ever find difficulty in expressing themselves clearly – perhaps with words getting jumbled up, or speech being a little fast or unclear?"

Onset and background

Cluttering usually develops in the preschool years, although the data on this is somewhat less conclusive than for stuttering. Because the effects tend to be less obvious than those of stuttering, there may be a period of time when the clutter is developing unnoticed. Also, as we have already said, for many clutterers unawareness of the problem is a defining feature, so quite often the individual will be unaware of the time of onset. He may even have difficulty with this when accompanied at assessment by caregivers who have known him or her since birth because at that time and subsequently over a number of years the speech has not been regarded as abnormal. A little probing on behalf of the clinician can be helpful here with questions such as: "Did people ever comment on how fast you were talking when you were just beginning school?" or "Do you remember having difficulties saying long words?" (When assessing a young client, the clinician may need to direct such questions to the parent.)

Linguistic development

Children who clutter are typically late in achieving linguistic milestones. Onset of babbling, single words and two-word phrases may be slow to appear. The clinician needs to ascertain if caregivers or teachers ever expressed concerns over any aspect of speech and language as the individual developed, and any speech and language or hearing referral should be noted.

Primary and secondary school development

It may also be useful to ask about behaviour at school, as well as level of achievement academically. Some authorities believe that clutterers are poorer in arts subjects, whilst stronger in maths (Daly, 1996). This suggestion awaits further confirmation, but clutterers typically exhibit both poor reading and writing skills, although the clinician will want to test for these later. Children who clutter may also demonstrate (or have at some time demonstrated) behavioural problems, often associated with a natural impulsiveness and short attention span that tends to be associated with the cluttering stereotype. There may also be a history of restlessness. Particularly when discussing secondary school with an older client, it will also be useful to find out whether at that time the individual was aware of any speech difficulty, or if there was any negative reaction from his or her peers about speech output. A surprising number of clutterers do not appear to experience teasing about their speech at school. Those who do mostly say that it was good-natured and, as is so often not the case with stuttering, tend not regard this as cause for concern.

Motor skills

As Weiss (1964) and others have observed, the clumsiness that can be observed in the articulation of cluttered speech is often seen outside the speech domain. Children who clutter may have been described as poorly coordinated, awkward and weak in both gross motor and fine motor coordination. The clinician should be alert to these features in the presenting client. The general clumsiness may go hand in hand with the impulsiveness shown by many younger children who clutter, which in some cases can almost border on the compulsive, with some showing almost a constant need for movement. This may be more readily apparent in younger children, but poor coordination can be observed in adults as well. Once again, if the client is an adult, help from a parent or primary caregiver may be needed to confirm any such behaviour in childhood.

Medical history

Check here for serious medical events, including stroke and any head injury. Adult clutterers who show a preponderance of linguistic deficits may sometimes initially present with aphasic type difficulties. These difficulties, together with the disruption to thought processing prior to speech, can quite closely mimic the cognitive and high-level linguistic deficits seen amongst some closed head injury clients and right hemisphere stroke victims (Ward, 2004; and see below).

A list of prescribed medication should also be taken, as should any history of recreational drug usage. There is presently no reliable record of cluttering being effectively controlled by medication but, as we have seen with regard to stuttering, fluency can be affected both positively and negatively by a range of drugs. Consider the possibility of any drugs, whether prescribed or recreational, as potential influential factors.

Previous treatment

Information as to any previous speech language therapy should be gained. Details regarding the nature and focus of the therapy together with perceptions as to perceived efficacy should also be gathered. Where possible, case notes from earlier treatments should be collected.

Assessment procedures

It is recommended that the following procedures are videotaped.

Oral reading

Have the client read a passage out loud. If the client is school aged, it may be worth starting with a piece which is age appropriate and noting how the child manages. Do not persist with this if the child is struggling with the text. Instead make a note of this fact, which may in itself be significant for the diagnosis, as cluttering is often associated with poor reading skills. Change to reading material that is one year (or more, if necessary) below the age-appropriate norm. For nonreaders, have the client retell the story of a short and simple cartoon strip, or describe a picture. Remember also that, unlike stuttering, clarity of speech and language performance is likely to improve with increased formality. It may be that as the client becomes accustomed to the reading task more cluttering is found. Because of this, it may be worthwhile to leave the video running after the end of the reading if it is suspected that the client is controlling his or her cluttering in the hope that it will go unnoticed, and the client will give a more representative display of their usual speech and language characteristics. Daly and St Louis (1998) actively recommend pretending to the client that the video has not been working properly and continue to record the following "informal" exchanges that take place.

The nature of the oral reading task will limit the possibilities for language formulation difficulties that might be present in the clutter, but missed function words, and particularly pronouns, may still be a feature. The clinician should also be alert for other features of cluttered speech such as accelerated speech rate and articulation deficiencies. The clinician needs to note the client's awareness of any errors. It can be enlightening to gain the client's perspective on their performance by asking very general open-ended questions such as "How did you feel that went?" If a more focused response is sought, then prompt more specifically, for example, asking whether they felt they missed any words at all in the passage.

Retelling the story

When the passage has been read, the clinician should then ask the client to retell the story from memory. Typical language difficulties may include: muddled narrative; transposition of the sequence of events; over-elaboration of unimportant detail; omission of some central aspects of the story; rambling or "maze" behaviour; an inability to produce a coherent explanation of the story. Motor speech, rhythm and fluency difficulties may also be observed.

Spontaneous speech sample

The case history will have already provided a speech sample of sorts, but it is important to engage the client in a more relaxed speech exchange on a subject that is of interest to them which they are keen to talk about. As mentioned earlier, the more relaxed the client feels and the more informal the atmosphere, the greater the likelihood of "uncontrolled" cluttering. For younger children, talking about a favourite computer game, animal or cartoon character may be good sources of discourse. With adults, hobbies, vacations or work may be good subjects. A sample of three minutes of the client's talking time is recommended. During the speech sample (which should be captured on video or DVD if possible, but at the very least on audiotape) the clinician should be observing both speech and language components of the sample.

Fluency

Disturbances to speech rate and speech rhythm and fluency should be noted. Speech rate can be recorded in terms of syllables per minute although a potential problem here is that any fast bursts of speech may be counteracted by excessive (inappropriate) pausing, resulting in a slower than expected rate. To deal with this, some authorities advocate counting syllables per second during moments of rushed speech, and then converting these data to syllables per minute (St Louis et al., 2003). St Louis et al. cite norms for adult speakers of 6–7 syllables per second. Fluency can be measured in terms of percentage of syllables cluttered, using procedures described for stuttering in chapter 9. Further, a member of St Louis's team is currently developing software that will calculate cluttering in terms of a percentage of total speaking time.

Articulation

This can begin with an oral examination and an assessment of oromotor ability, including diadochokinetic rates. Testing automatic speech capabilities (e.g., counting days of the week, months of the year) as well as examining articulation in increasingly complex words are also recommended. Having the client attempt tongue-twisters can also be revealing. I have described more fully in chapter 8 the disturbances to articulation, language and other nonverbal characteristics that have been associated with cluttering and the reader is referred there for greater detail.

Language

I have already outlined in chapter 8 the type of linguistic deficits that may be seen either alongside or in the absence of articulatory problems. The clinician should be alert to these language errors, and particularly to a lack of coherence in discourse. Amongst other features there may be word-finding difficulties, increased presence of normal types of nonfluency such as phrase and word repetition, incomplete sentences, and particularly phrase and word revision.

Writing

Writing errors may mimic difficulties in the speech domain, so ask the client to write a short paragraph, looking for untidy or illegible writing, weak spelling, poorly constructed grammar, and transposition, elision and omissions of letters as evidence of cluttering-related activity. It has been my experience that a number of adults who clutter are reluctant to write, and many express some embarrassment about their abilities to do so. Some use either unjoined writing or write only using capital letters. In many such cases, it has been difficult to ascertain whether the unjoined script has been due to personal preference, or whether it has been prompted by others who have found their writing difficult to understand. Bearing in mind that poor handwriting is one of the earlier behaviours associated with cluttering, and that children are formally assessed on their writing skills from an early age at school, it would be interesting and potentially of great value to ascertain whether the separated handwriting represents a conscious coping strategy, brought about by others' inability to understand the handwriting. Given that those who clutter typically do not use controlling strategies with their speech proactively, then if proven this would represent a clear difference on behalf of the speaker between awareness of and reaction to the written and spoken forms of language.

Fine and gross motor control

Clinicians may want to test nonspeech motor control informally. Fine motor control ability can be observed when the client is writing, and degrees of clumsiness may be recorded. It is possible that the clinician may want to ask younger children to undertake some simple tasks to test coordination more formally. However, the more general lack of coordination seen in some younger children who clutter is less likely under such circumstances. As with speech output, difficulties are more likely to appear when the child is relaxed and unaware that he is being assessed.

Cluttering checklists and self-assessments

In sum, throughout the data collection process the clinician should be alert for a range of cluttering symptoms. Table 17.1 has been developed from a number of sources (including Dalton & Hardcastle, 1989; Daly, 1996; Myers & Bradley, 1992; St Louis & Myers, 1997; Weiss, 1964) as well as my own clinical experience. It can be used simply as a checklist to describe cluttering behaviour at assessment, or to provide a profile which may be used to focus therapeutic intervention. In addition to Daly's (1996) cluttering treatment planning profile which is completed by the clinician, he also includes a similar self-assessment sheet for completion by the client called the Checklist for Possible Cluttering. This contains identical assessment criteria to the

Table 17.1 Checklist of cluttering behaviour (based on Dalton & Hardcastle, 1989; Daly, 1996; Myers & Bradley, 1992; St Louis & Myers, 1997; Weiss, 1964, and clinical experience).

1 = Within normal limits
2 = Somewhat abnormal
3 = Markedly abnormal

		1	2	3	Notes
Speech rate and speech fluency	Excessively fast speech rate				
	Short bursts of fast speech				
	Unable to maintain natural speech rhythm				
	Inappropriate pausing				
	Inappropriate breathing patterns				
	Phoneme repetition				
	Part-word repetition				
	Word repetition				
	Phrase repetition				
Articulation	Mumbling/low volume indistinct speech output				
	Excessive coarticulation				
	Cluster reduction				
	Weak syllable deletion				
	Festinant speech (speech becomes faster and more mumbled over a sentence or phrase)				
	Transposition of phonemes (spoonerisms)				
	Anticipatory coarticulation errors				
	Mispronunciations				
	Speech characterized by a lack of physical tension				
Language, and linguistic fluency	Confused wording				
	Unfinished sentences				
	Revised sentences/phrases				
	Word retrieval difficulties				
	Inappropriate pronoun usage				
	Use of nonspecific words "thing"				
	Use of interjections and fillers – "um," "er," "well," "you know"				
	Poor syntax				
	Empty speech/maze behaviour				
	Repetition and revision of words and phrases				
	Semantic paraphasias – magazine for paper				
	Unfinished sentences				
	Possible high level comprehension difficulties				
	Unconcerned/unaware of speech and language errors				
Disorganized thinking	Reduced ability to sequence significant events in a story (also may give prominence to unimportant details when storytelling)				
	Gives inappropriate level of detail				
	Goes off topic/tangential speech				
	Unaware of fluency/speech/language errors				

cont.

Writing	Poor handwriting Written errors mimic speech errors, including: missing or transposed characters, lack of consistency in letter height Careless spelling errors				
Attention	Short attention span Easily distracted Forgetful				
Other nonverbal attributes	Poor gross and fine motor control				
Other					

Note: Some commentators have included a lack of musicality as a characteristic symptom of cluttering (e.g., Daly, 1996; St Louis & Myers, 1997). Similarly, Daly (1996) includes "superficial" and "short tempered" as features of those who suffer from the disorder.

clinician's assessment, except the presentation order of the 33 criteria is randomized. The client scores between 0 and 4, depending on whether they feel the statement applies "not at all" or "very much". The clinician's version scores on a six-point scale ranging from "undesirably different from normal" to "desirably different from normal", this latter phrase allowing for the possibility that some aspects of speech might sound distinctive from a non-cluttering speaker, but actually better.

Comparing the client and clinician's perceptions at baseline assessment can be enlightening. Some clinicians use Woolfe's (1967) Perceptions of Stuttering Inventory (see chapter 9). I also use the WASSP (Wright & Ayre, 2000) in this way. Where there are questions relating to matters of fact – for example, some questions on the WASSP and PSI relating to the physical aspects of disfluencies – the clinician can make direct comparisons between their own observations and those of the client. Where there are matters of feelings and attitudes – including those addressed in the S-24 and subsections of WASSP and the "expectancy" and "avoidance" statements on the PSI – the clinician can go through the responses together with the client once the client has completed the assessments. There is no reason why the present model (as in Table 17.1) could not also be presented in similar fashion. One small problem with Daly's version is that in an effort to maintain the similarity between the client and clinician's version, some vocabulary and wording may be a little obscure for some clients, e.g., "tachylalia", "anomia" and "inappropriate reference by pronoun is common".

Differential diagnosis

As we have seen in chapter 8, one of the problems in diagnosing and treating cluttering is that it often presents in conjunction with other disorders, some of which are speech/language based and others which are not. The clinician must judge whether assessment data point to a diagnosis of person who clutters. If the clinician is unsure as to whether the cumulative data warrant this diagnosis, she may wish to consider the diagnosis of cluttering syndrome behaviour (see chapter 8). This latter term may also be useful if cluttering behaviours appear alongside other speech and language problems.

Cluttering and stuttering

This is the most likely single combination seen in adults with a suspected clutter. Recall that some estimates suggest that as many as two-thirds of adult clutterers also stutter (see chapter 8). The pairing of stuttering with cluttering may well present in younger children too, but with a greater likelihood that other disorders may also be involved. Below we outline some similarities and differences between the two disorders.

Speech rate and fluency

1   Stuttering is usually associated with slower rates of speech, although the range is wide, and some people who stutter may speak quickly but without cluttering. Cluttering is often associated with rapid speech rate and some believe it to be a core symptom of the disorder.
2   The underlying rhythm of speech is affected in stuttering by the interruptions due to stuttered moments. Speech rhythm is often affected in cluttering, but this may be due to a more fundamental difficulty in maintaining rhythm and can occur even when there is no physical fluency disruption.
3   Fast bursts of speech are not characteristic of stuttering, although there can be cases where a speaker who stutters may rush to say more on one breath, fearful that a pauses would lead to greater stuttering.
4   Sublexical errors generally tend to be associated with stuttering rather than cluttering and particularly, blocks and sound prolongations are not features of cluttering. However, there are exceptions to this rule – notably sound and part-word repetitions are commonly seen in cluttering.
5   Phrase repetitions often occur in cluttered speech, but are less typical in stuttering. If they do appear in stuttered speech they are more likely to be accompanied by indications of frustration, anxiety and a sense of lack of control. Cluttered versions, typically, are unaccompanied by fear and often any awareness.

Articulation

Stuttering can copresent with articulation problems in younger children (e.g., Bernstein-Ratner, 1997), so a diagnosis of stuttering with cluttering should not be made on this basis alone. The clinician should look at the range of articulatory behaviours, together with rhythm and nonverbal factors, to make an informed diagnosis of cluttering in such cases. Adult stuttering is only rarely associated with articulation difficulties of any kind.

Language

1   Stuttering is not associated with disturbances to language function in adults, as can be the case for cluttering, but it can be associated with language disturbances in children. The situation is therefore somewhat analogous to that of articulation. A diagnosis of stuttering with cluttering in children should therefore not be made solely on the basis of a stuttering existing together with a co-occuring language problem. Bear in mind also that an established stutter may be associated with apparent maze behaviour when an individual is using circumlocution to avoid a problematic word or sound. This may be seen more frequently in the speech of some teenagers and adults.
2   Fillers may be a feature of both disorders (although some authorities, for example, Myers & St Louis, 1992, claim otherwise). Certainly, I would agree that they arise for different reasons. Fillers in stuttering may be used to postpone a difficult word, whereas fillers in cluttering may either be a part of the disorganized speech generally, or more specifically a device to help deal with word-finding difficulties.

Disorganized thinking

This is not a feature of stuttering, although the speech of some who stutter may appear disorganized due to linguistic avoidance strategies and use of inappropriate fillers and starter phrases.

Other

Stuttering, unlike cluttering, is not associated with any particular personality traits (see chapter 8). Cluttering is not associated with secondary behaviours, but can often present alongside poor eye contact. However, this is related to poor communication skills more generally and is not contingent on moments of disfluency, as it tends to be with stuttering.

Cluttering and neurological disorders

I have reported in an earlier chapter that cluttering has some speech and language features that are consistent with a neurological diagnosis. The articulatory disturbances have been likened to apraxia of speech (De Hirsch, 1961) and language disturbances to those of aphasia (Luschinger & Landolt, 1951). Usually, these acquired neurological disorders can quite easily be separately identified from cluttering, not least on the basis of hard neurological evidence such as brain scans. Note, however, that there have been some reports of cluttering associated with the onset of neurological damage (Hashimoto et al., 1999; Lebrun, 1996; Thacker & De Nil, 1996). The possibility that cluttering subsequent to brain damage could comprise a separate (although related) disorder is one which awaits the findings of further research.

Cluttering and apraxia of speech

As we have seen, articulatory difficulties associated with cluttering may share some similarities to apraxia of speech, however, others do not. Slow speech rate is characteristic of apraxia, while the reverse is true of cluttering. Patterns of articulatory errors may be similar across the two disorders (such as anticipatory errors, sound reversals, etc.) but cluttering errors tend to decrease with repetition and conscious effort, whereas apraxic speakers may continue to make multiple and inconsistent errors when asked to repeat the same word or phrase. Neither is the frustration and struggle behaviour seen in apraxia present in cluttering. Indeed, as most authorities concur, the reverse is typical.

Cluttering and aphasia

In most cases, cluttering presents as a mixture of articulation/fluency problems together with language difficulties, the balance between the two areas varying from individual to individual. Aphasia, on the other hand, is by definition purely a language disorder. This in itself may be enough to avoid any confusion between the two disorders. There are, however, a very small number of cases where cluttering can appear apparently in the absence of articulatory, rhythmic or fluency difficulties (e.g., Ward, 2004). In these cases, the resulting speech can appear very much as an expressive type of aphasia.

Ward's (2004) case concerned a 30-year-old man who had presented initially with aphasic-like symptoms, but in the absence of any neurological diagnosis. At assessment he presented with severely restricted expressive language characterized by very slow verbal response times, multiple aborted attempts at answering questions, short and often unfinished responses, limited word usage with excessive use of filler phrases. Word-finding difficulties, maze behaviour and lack of struggle were all strongly evident, but in the absence of elevated speech rate. There was no evidence of stuttering and language comprehension appeared normal. A functional magnetic resonance imaging (fMRI) scan revealed no abnormality, as did a psychological evaluation. This man made significant gains in a therapeutic approach that targeted sentence completion, concise speech and sequencing tasks (see below), but interestingly, as his language abilities improved and speech rate increased, motoric signs of cluttering began to appear in the form of overcoarticulation and speech dysrhythmia, even at normal speech rates. One interpretation of this is that the language elements of this speech could be explained in terms of cluttering syndrome behaviour (see chapter 8), even at the slow speech rates initially observed, and that more visible motoric and rhythmic elements to the cluttering came about due to a reduced capacity to maintain motoric fluency coincident with the subsequent increase in rate of speech.

Treatment of cluttering

A synergistic approach to remediation

Cluttering therapy presents us with a conundrum. On the one hand, the various areas of articulation, rate, fluency, language and nonverbal communication may be viewed as modular – communication-related areas that interrelate but can also be described in stand-alone terms. Indeed, we have presented them as such when discussing them above. On the other hand, there are relationships between deficits copresenting in a number of areas. For example, increased speech rate results from a relative shortening of vowel length compared to consonant length (O'Shaughnessy, 1987). Thus, weak syllable deletion may result from an inability to deal with an increased speech rate. This has led some clinicians to take a synergistic approach to cluttering (Myers, 1992; Myers & Bradley, 1992), which St Louis and Myers (1997, p. 324) outline thus:

> Synergism has to do with different parts of the communication system working together in a highly coordinated and well timed or synchronous manner. One consequence of this synergistic and synchronous interaction is that different parts of the system affect others. When rate is too fast or not well modulated with linguistic or thought units, discourse loses coherence.

So while taking heed of the various components that may characterize any given clutter, it is also important to consider the interrelated nature of the various components of the disorder when developing a treatment plan. Cluttering is a multifaceted disorder and there is no single method of intervention, so an individualized treatment plan needs to be developed for each client. The direction of the treatment plan will be determined by a number of factors. The clinician should already have gathered information from a number of sources: case history, reports from parents, teachers and perhaps other professionals such as special educational needs coordinators (SENCOs) in addition to data on speech, articulation, language and so forth, as outlined in the assessment section above.

It is important that the client is aware of his problem. Identification provides the starting point for therapy. But as we will see, it is a theme that runs all the way through the therapeutic process as well. Described below is an approach to cluttering therapy that, drawing on the work of Daly, St Louis, and others, I have developed at the Apple House. With minor modification, this can be applied to younger children, adolescents and adults. There is current work in progress to provide objective findings as to the efficacy of this approach.

Identification of cluttering

One important piece of data that the clinician will need to consider initially is why the person has presented for assessment (and potentially for therapy) at this particular time. As we have said earlier, unlike stuttering, where the vast majority of people attending assessments do so because they personally have concerns about their fluency, people who clutter may be attending because they have perhaps been coerced into doing so. This may be because of concerns raised by schoolteachers or parents, or in older clients by managers who feel that a difficulty with communication is holding their juniors back from promotion.

As with stuttering therapy, intervention must primarily address the client's concerns and therapy must work toward goals mutually agreed between the client and the clinician. In order for this to take place, the client needs to be aware of the problems with his or her speech. I have mentioned before that lack of awareness of the problem by the client is a strong characteristic of the disorder. However, I disagree with Daly (1996) who believes it to be a mandatory symptom. Some cluttering clients actually do have good awareness and present at clinic frustrated by their inability to communicate clearly. Others have some insights and may or may not feel that the problem warrants help from a speech/language professional. At the other end of the spectrum, others may still actively resent the idea that there is something wrong with their speech, and rather choose to believe that any difficulty lies with conversational partners who do not listen properly. My point here is simply that addressing the basic concerns of the client may present a strong initial challenge to the clinician dealing with those clients who do not consider themselves to have a problem.

This rather fundamental issue needs to be addressed with care. Where there is a lack of awareness, it is the clinician's first priority to bring the fundamental elements of the cluttering to the client's attention in a confident, clear but sympathetic way. Even those who are aware of their difficulties are likely to be confused as to what is wrong. One way in which this can be approached is to tell the client that he does have a fluency problem; that it is not stuttering but instead a disorder which is less well known called cluttering. It may be useful to discuss some of the basic issues of cluttering with the client or client's parents, although the extent of the detail of the information given will vary from client to client. It may be useful, though, to mention straightaway that the exact cause of the problem is not known, but people who clutter have the same spread of intelligence as those who do not. The clinician can also add that it is a problem that can respond well to therapy, although this will depend somewhat on the outcome of the assessments. The prognosis for severe cluttering is less favourable and severe cluttering may be intractable. The identification process can then proceed with an outline of the major symptoms of the disorder. Having the client complete the cluttering checklist (Table 17.1), or going through the clinician's findings from the list with the client provide alternative ways of doing this.

If it is implemented with assuredness and calm confidence, there is almost always a positive response to this type of approach, even amongst those who have been reluctant initially either to believe they have a problem, or that they need help to overcome it. It can actually be empowering for those clients who sensed that something is wrong with their speech to realize that they are suffering from a recognized speech/language disorder that can be treated. The client can also gain confidence from knowing that there are facets of the disorder which are not significant in his particular case. For those who present with poor awareness, there is likely to be only minimal breakthrough in their understanding of their difficulties thus far. The real focus up to this point has been getting the client "on board" with therapy and, importantly, getting them to gain confidence in your assessment and evaluations.

Monitoring and self-awareness

Once a positive attitude has been established, try moving on further with identification. Have the client watch a video of himself and ask him to note any behaviours that you have described as cluttering which relate to his performance. Initial reaction to this exercise can be wide ranging, from great awareness "Wow, I never knew I talked so fast!", to poor awareness "I can't see much wrong there", to apparent gross indifference "I wish I had chosen a different sweater today." I include this last inappropriate comment as an example of the type of poor pragmatic skills that can be seen in some cluttering behaviour. It is important that the client becomes aware, through the use of video and audio playback, of the reasons why his speech is difficult to understand. It may take a few sessions to reach this stage of awareness. Some clients may even become frustrated that they want to really "get started" in therapy, unaware that they already have. It is important to make clear from the beginning that being able to accurately self-monitor and critically analyze speech and language performance is absolutely central to therapy. It will not be possible to change behaviours which go unrecognized in the first place. The development of self-awareness is a factor that runs all through the therapeutic process. While self-monitoring is a skill that will develop over time, there is a need, at a fundamental level at least, for the client to recognize that their speech is difficult to understand, and for them to have the confidence in your ability to help them improve the situation. When the client has come this far, therapy is underway.

Modification

The exact direction that the next phase of therapy will take depends on findings from the case history, assessment and identification stages. As I have already said, most people who clutter will display a range of symptoms across a number of areas. In the modification stage of therapy it is best to focus on a limited number of areas, probably a maximum of two or three in the first place. Unless there are compelling reasons to the contrary, start with the areas which are causing the most problems for intelligibility. Daly (1996) outlines four areas: modifying speech rate and regularity; promoting relaxation and mental imagery; increasing awareness of cluttering; improving attention span. One could perhaps add a fifth: increasing effective language usage. When developing your treatment program you will be aware of the interrelated nature of the areas you will be addressing, but at the same time you will need to explain your plan in simple terms to a younger client. For example, you will know that inappropriate pausing is resulting in disfluency, but you may need to explain your plan to work on normalizing speech rhythm in terms of "trying to make speech a little more smooth".

There are many ways of breaking down the various cluttering components into (semi) discrete areas. The key to success lies in structure. Good progress is made by making a series of carefully structured small steps, all carefully monitored by the clinician.

Excessively fast speech rate

Here, as with so many other areas, speed of improvement depends largely on the ability of the client to self-monitor. You will already have begun to address this with earlier identification, but now these skills need to be developed more sharply. For almost all adult clients, and many younger ones also, I have found that talking specifically about speed of utterance in terms of syllables per minute (SPM) or syllables per second (SPS) helps to clarify the goals. It also gives the client an objective measure to aim for in therapy, which can feel empowering. Initially, we discuss baseline rate of speech in terms of SPM. We then relate this to a normal speech rate using Andrews and Ingham's (1971) figures of 190–210 SPM which the clinician then models.[1] Once this speech rate can be readily identified, a slower rate of around 160 SPM is also modelled. The client may then be presented with speech sequences produced at three randomly selected different speech rates

---

1 A useful memory aide for the client can be to have him count out loud in seconds, using a stopwatch as a guide. Then have the client count one-two-three for each second. A normal rate is fractionally faster than this speed, being around three and a half syllables per second, although this figure allows for occasional pauses to speech flow featuring in the equation.

160 SPM, 200 SPM and 300 SPM, and asked to identify which speed corresponds with which sequence. Once the client is able to reliably distinguish these three rates, we talk about how at 300 SPM some of the sounds become blurred or even lost altogether. At this point, I sometimes ask a question using rapid speech together with overcoarticulation resulting in an unintelligible output. As the client tries in vain to make sense of the utterance, I explain what I was doing: my speech rate was around 300 SPM; there was very little movement from my lips and tongue when making the words; and that there comes a point in anyone's speech where intelligibility cannot be maintained due to an increase in rate. I also explain that speech rate becomes habituated over time. Some people naturally have faster speech rates, others naturally have slow ones. The natural tendency is for all of us to believe that our speech rates are "normal" until we have objective evidence to show otherwise.

The client can now try aiming for a normal speech rate. It may be helpful to ensure that the speaking context is closely controlled, beginning with non-propositional speech. Reading from a simple text can be a good place to start. Workbooks on cluttering, stuttering and even dyspraxia with pages of phonetically balanced sentences of increasing length provide a good source (e.g., Daly, 1996; Turnbull & Stewart, 1999). Fast bursts of speech are characteristic of cluttering, so have the client aim for consistency of rate as well as an accurate mean rate. Use modelling initially to ensure the client is aware of the correct speed. If necessary have them repeat a phrase before attempting controlled new phrases. Encourage the client to listen to their speech as they talk, and have them analyze their performance for rate and consistency of rate after each attempt. To this end, it is important either to audiotape or videotape all attempts and use playback to resolve any discrepancies between your perception of the client's performance and their own. Some severe clutterers will have problems in achieving a consistent normal rate of speech, even given this careful structuring. If this is the case, try using choral reading or even syllable timed speech initially to encourage the new rate of speech. A number of clinicians have also utilized delayed auditory feedback.

A common finding is that even though clients may achieve success in reducing rate to within normal parameters, there is unease that it feels unnaturally slow. It is the clinician's job to reassure that the speech may feel slow because of the natural tendency towards rapid rate, but that it will not be perceived as slow by listeners. Back this up by having the client listen to a passage of normal rate speech spoken by another person and ask if this too feels slow.[2] The further clients get into therapy and the more self-monitoring

---

2 Using recordings of TV or radio news presenters can be a good source. These tend to maintain a steady slow-normal speech rate and are almost invariably evaluated as being clear and effective speakers, but without being regarded as being slow.

skills improve, the greater their awareness that the original cluttering speech feels uncomfortable and out of control. I focus the client on the idea that therapy is concerned with regaining control over speech and the speech apparatus. It is beneficial for some clients to model genuinely slow rates of around 160 SPM or even 120 SPM rate, again using short read phrases or sentences. When this has been achieved with around 90 percent success, we then return to a normal rate. For many speakers, this helps them put the 200 SPM rate into a different perspective and it no longer feels quite as abnormal. I explain that this is just a practice exercise, but that there may be times when slowing to a subnormal speech rate can be very useful. A commonly used analogy here is with gears in a car. Different gears are useful in different circumstances, and having them at your disposal all adds to the amount of control you have. A useful extension of this analogy is that if you are in too high a gear you are likely to go too fast, lose control and crash.

Once normal rate speech has been consistently achieved in short sentences, the clinician might move on to practise with longer passages of oral reading, perhaps a paragraph from a book. This often brings new problems for the client. First, the extra sentences are likely to trigger faster rates of speech as the client focuses more on the semantics of the passage and less on self-monitoring. Second, this fast rate can be exacerbated by problems with breathing, where the client accelerates speech in an effort to produce as much speech on one exhalation as possible. It may be helpful to forewarn the client that this might happen, and to remind about the use of self-monitoring skills to help keep rate in check. Marking appropriate pausing and breathing points in the text will also help prevent the "run-on" type of speech that can be prevalent in the speech of many clients who clutter.

Speech rhythm and intonation

Use this level of material to control for any rhythmic disturbances – keeping an even pace within each breath group, and also to deal with monotony in speech production. If these are particularly strong features of the disorder, try using simple nursery rhymes or limericks to help establish appropriate stress, rhythm and intonation. Appropriate stress may involve modifying up to three parameters – loudness (intensity), pitch (fundamental frequency) and vowel length (vowel duration) – all of which can be affected in cluttered speech. With older clients, you can explain the importance of word stress, with examples where stress alone determines the meaning of word. For example, placing stress on the first and second syllables of *pervert* results in completely different meanings (and also, in this case, different word class; noun vs verb). More complex poetry and play readings can also provide a good source of material and a higher level challenge, as the client may cease to self-monitor as effectively when cognitive focus turns more towards content and away from speech control.

Once the client is able to maintain a normal speech rate, together with appropriate rhythm and intonation in oral reading, the next step is to move into spontaneous speech. There are a number of ways to do this: a simple question and answer exercise may be a good starting point. Remember that cluttering has been linked with disturbance to the thinking that precedes speech. Now that the required speech is spontaneous, more planning for speech will need to be done. Effective planning is automatic in normal speech, but it is something that needs to be brought under more voluntary control for some people who clutter (see below). Ensure that the client's speech when giving either questions or answers is preceded by the necessary mental planning, where the client holds in memory the exact response he is going to say. Fairly simple syntax can be used and to start with the utterance should fall comfortably within one breath. As always, encourage the client to self-monitor and objectively analyze following the completion of a question or answer. Also, tape these exchanges so an accurate record of progress is available for feedback to the client. For some clients, you may wish to practise changing rates from 200 SPM down to 160 and 120 SPM during the questions and answers to emphasize the control they now have. When the client is able to achieve normal rate speech with good intonation and normal speech rhythm with these simple structures, follow this with extended dialogue, using extended syntactic structures. This in turn can later be extended to more propositional dialogue through activities such as role play or group discussions and, when appropriate, carefully graded transfer tasks.

Articulation

Dalton and Hardcastle (1989) coin the term "overcoarticulation" to describe the almost dysarthric type of articulation commonly associated with cluttering. Quite often, the compression of consonant clusters, syllabic elements, or elision of consonant singletons that result in this type of speech can be traced to an over-rapid speech rate. For many clients then, successfully modifying rate control is the key to increased intelligibility. While rate control is often very effective on its own for dealing with the telescoping of words that leads to loss of phonemes and syllables, it is not uncommon for some clutterers to still have problems with overcoarticulation. If rate stabilization alone does not bring about the necessary improvement in clarity, articulation may be worked on directly. One way of doing this is to take an articulation drill approach, similar to that used in dyspraxia therapy. The approach advocated for cluttering involves practice of specific speech targets in a highly structured and systematic manner. This involves having the client repeat fully voiced bisyllabic structures following a clinician's model. Initially work from nonsense syllables, with the phonological structures becoming more complex as the client's accuracy of production improves. Real words may then be substituted, usually at a two or three word level, and an appropriate rate introduced as skill increases and longer utterances are attempted.

Overcoarticulation/mumbling

Quite often, a mumbling type of delivery is seen together with overcoarticulation. However, they are not exactly the same thing. Overcoarticulation may be seen, for example, in the word television being produced as "tevision" (an example which here has actually led to weak syllable deletion), but it is still possible for this reduction to be articulated with good volume and reasonable clarity amongst the remaining syllables. Mumbling, on the other hand, implies a consistent and full-time lack of articulatory movement together with reduced volume. Mumbling may also be a feature associated with festinant speech. Where mumbling is a feature of the cluttering, the client may also need to be encouraged to produce an increased range of articulatory movement. Starting with phonemes that are more visible (bilabial, labiodental and perhaps linguadental sounds), have the client practise short phrases whilst making exaggerated mouth movements in front of a mirror. If you can illustrate with a phrase that has already appeared on an assessment video, you can use this to point out the difference in clarity between the two versions. Daly (1996) also advocates the use of a chewing technique to deal with mumbled articulation. Here, the client imagines he has a piece of chewing gum in his mouth. While chewing on the imaginary gum, with teeth apart, he begins to hum for 5–10 seconds at a time. This method has its basis in the work of Froeschels in the 1930s and later in the 1950s (Froeschels, 1952), where the "breath chewing technique", as it has subsequently been referred to (e.g., Van Riper, 1982), was used with stutterers to improve rhythmic and timing abilities. For present purposes, the technique can exercise and relax the oral-motor mechanism. It also helps promote greater jaw movement and provides a template for a more consistent rhythmic basis to speech.

Language problems

A large number of clutterers have problems with lexical access. For some, this may be because there are competing ideas and thoughts which result in almost a "freezing" of linguistic fluency. This can clearly affect the rest of the intended sentence, with the individual either repeating a postponing word or phrase, or attempts at phrase revision, to repair the sentence which now cannot be completed as originally planned. More damagingly still, some clutterers appear not only to have moments where a word cannot be accessed, but times when a given train of thought can be completely blanked out – an experience which some have likened to "being like a rabbit in the headlights". With this comes an inability to progress the sentence further. This can sometimes result in maze behaviour as the client attempts to keep language flowing, whilst having little idea as to what the original intended message was, or where the sentence is leading. Again, this phenomenom may be seen to reflect a breakdown between thinking for speech and language formulation.

As before, awareness and acknowledgement of these deficits and difficulties by the client is most important. Even the knowledge that these difficulties represent strands of a recognized speech and language disorder can bring some relief. In fact, regardless of whether these problems arise due to disrupted thought processing prior to speech, or defective speech/language processing itself, having the client slow speech rate will allow more time for effective word finding and also syntactic processing to take place. Where sentences may run on, are revised or tail off with no ending, the clinician might wish to encourage the use of shorter sentences and less complicated syntax to start with. As a preliminary step, it may even be worthwhile to practise exercises with the client where he plans out succinct responses word for word from the beginning of the sentence to the end prior to speech. For this to be effective, the client should have a precise mental picture of the complete sentence before attempting an utterance.

Narrative and sequencing of information

As we have seen earlier, a common language difficulty for those who clutter lies with the telling or retelling of narratives. Coherence and cohesion can be increased by explaining that for any narrative there is a hierarchical structure which needs to be followed. An example below is taken from a client whose clutter was characterized by profound difficulties with language organization, and is a response to the question what do you do for a living?

A: Well, you know – er – well there's the exhausts – the exhausts come in –
   well, they – they come come in on the lorry and they you know – get put in
   – in the different bays. Well, sometimes they er go to the wrong one. . . .

In one sense this client was describing exactly what he was doing in his job, but he had completely neglected to say that he was working for a company that supplied and fitted exhaust systems and tyres, and that his position as stacker involved ensuring that deliveries were put away in the correct places. One helpful way I have found in dealing with this is to introduce a pyramid model to structure language (Ward, 2004). At the top of the pyramid are short, concise sentences, containing essential information, which gives the listener the initial crucial introduction. It is important that the client resists any urge to start to expand on more minor details straightaway, and that there is clarity in the shorter and direct statements. The next layer down the pyramid may carry either a similar or slightly lower level of propositionality, but the trend is that as the narrative develops so one works down the pyramid, adding detail as the client reaches further down the structure (Figure 17.1). Clarity is usually achieved (at least early on in therapy) by increasing the number of short sentences, rather than increasing the length of sentences, so the clinician is likely to need to specify the need for short sentences, carrying comparatively simple syntactic structures, which need to have beginnings and ends. Depending on the severity of the problems, the clinician may wish

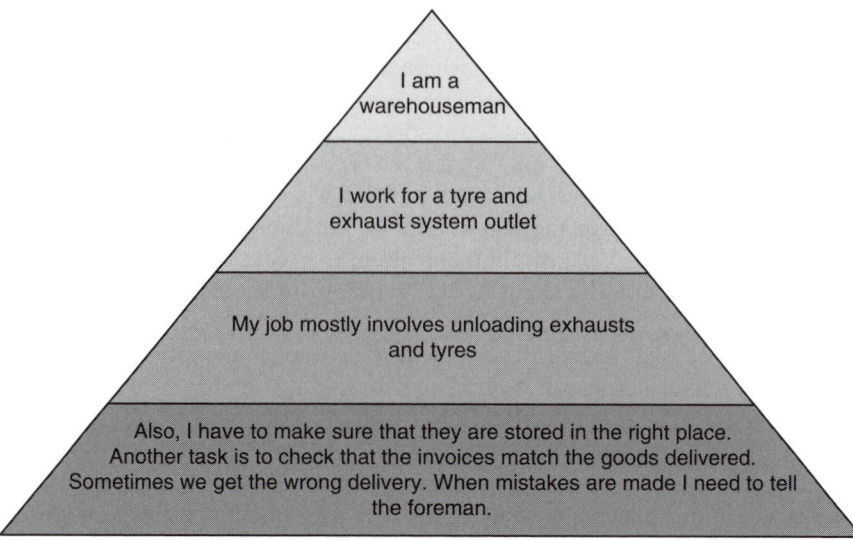

Figure 17.1 Pyramid model of narrative structure.

to work on either constraining or developing length and complexity of utterance.

Implicit in this approach is the idea that clutterers have difficulty in sequencing verbal information. Clients may be asked to sequence a series of cards that tell a story. Having a short cartoon strip cut up and then reassembled by the client is a good alternative here for younger clients. Ask the client to tell the story of the cartoon, sequencing each picture at a time, building up the narrative, using carefully constrained sentence structures, as appropriate. Once an appropriate storyline has been defined, ask the client to retell the story from memory, using the controls on syntax and appropriate level of detail. Here, as ever, use video or audio feedback to demonstrate how controlling linguistic output can bring significant benefits in terms of increased clarity and intelligibility.

Pragmatics

Let us briefly return to our hypothetical person who clutters, who on seeing himself on video at assessment remarked about his sweater rather than his speech. Whether this comment was the result of divergent thought processing, more to do with a short attention span, or simply embarrassment, it is sometimes the case that clutterers lack the social awareness that acts as the glue to coherence in conversational speech. This may result in a failure to pick up the verbal and nonverbal cues from the listener that the message has not been understood. Again, much of therapy here centres around increasing awareness, the difference being in this case that it is not only awareness of their own speech that needs to be considered, but awareness of others' reactions to it. Role play can be a useful device to help bring the conversational partner's verbal and nonverbal responses into focus for the individual who clutters (eg., St Louis & Myers, 1997).

Relaxation

Some authorities, most notably Weiss (1964, 1967), have asserted that people who clutter by nature lack awareness. However, while lacking an understanding of what is actually wrong with their speech, some are aware that it can evoke negative listener reactions. It is also true that some clients become agitated and even aggressive when they fail to be understood and are asked to repeat (Daly, 1996). This presents two problems: one is that the listener may be surprised to find themselves on the receiving end of the person who clutter's frustration; second, attempting to improve on an unintelligible output is likely to be unsuccessful given an increasingly heightened emotional state. Learning to deal calmly with the frustration of failing to be understood can be an important therapeutic component for some. Such clients are encouraged to see requests to repeat as useful triggers to aid recall of the modifications to speech and language that they have been working on in therapy, and as such to turn a negative response into advantage. Alongside this, learning to apply relaxation techniques, whether these are muscle specific or more generalized relaxation procedures, can be helpful in dissipating unwanted tension. Calm responses are far more likely to be more controlled, and therefore understandable, than angry ones.

Delayed auditory feedback

In addition to the methods and procedures outlined above, some clinicians have experienced success using delayed auditory feedback, a procedure well known for its efficacy in treating stuttering (see chapters 3 and 16). St Louis et al. (1996) reported that two subjects who underwent a DAF program both reduced their cluttering to satisfactory levels while using the device. However, both experienced difficulties in transferring the success when the altered feedback was withdrawn.

Maintenance of fluency

There are as yet no reliable data as to the efficacy of cluttering therapy, but once cluttering has become established in adulthood the emphasis will be on controlling and containing the symptoms. As with chronic stuttering, there is no "cure" for cluttering in adulthood. Control over an extended time period rests on the individual's ability to self-monitor, and to put into practice the techniques and procedures learned in therapy. In this respect, there is a further similarity with stuttering treatments that target fluency control. The ability to control cluttering in the long term may well be related to the range and severity of the problems encountered by each individual. It would also seem likely that those who are more motivated to maintain higher levels of fluency will put more effort into maintenance exercises than those who are less concerned.

We can speculate on a number of reasons as to why this might be. First, the strategies needed may not be as taxing cognitively as those required to control stuttering. For those with milder cluttering control may only need to be at a subliminal level. For example, managing rate control may be one fundamental aspect of some stuttering therapies, where adjustments to vocal tract coordination, in the form of soft consonant contact, soft glottal onset, smooth airflow may predominate, yet slowing rate may well be the overriding technique for those who clutter. Second, cluttering is unaccompanied by the extreme fears, anxieties and range of negative emotions often experienced by those who stutter. Thus, even if increased cluttering starts to occur at some point following a successful period of therapy, this is usually not accompanied by a sense of failure, anxiety, shame, anger or other negative emotion that may be felt by a stutterer who experiences fluency breakdown after a period of good control. In fact, this lack of fear together with increased awareness can be used to the individual's advantage, as the increased cluttering signals that more control is again needed. In the absence of significant negative emotions, increasing control once more may be quite possible.

While there are no published data on the maintenance of cluttering therapy, it has been my experience that while some people who clutter return for "top-up" therapy, there are fewer proportionally than those who return having earlier attended stuttering therapy. Most appear able to deal with any periods of difficulty and "relapse" does not really seem to happen in the same way as it can with stuttering. Of course, it is possible that this apparent success represents nothing more than the individual again returning to higher levels of cluttering but without feeling the need to return for treatment. However, there are undoubtedly those who have severe clutters (without stuttering) who do not respond to therapy and continue to clutter, despite the best efforts of both themselves and their clinicians. My experience has been that these people appear simply to be unable to slow speech rate and at the same time maintain natural speech rhythm. Attempts to do so invariably result in a disintegration of fluency, resulting in a speech rate that can be lowered only at the cost of exaggerated syllable separation and markedly abnormal intonation. There are other informal reports of intractable cluttering and we need more data in order to define whether a particular subgroup is less likely to benefit from cluttering therapy.

Treating cluttering and stuttering

This is an area which has been remarkably underresearched. It is of some concern because, as we have seen, cluttering often co-occurs with other speech and language disorders. Weiss (1964) has argued that cluttering under-lies most stuttering. Some have commented on the possibility that the treat-ment of stuttering may lead to the discovery of an underlying clutter (St Louis et al., 2003). Although this can certainly be the case, the reverse can also be true. It is not unusual to treat cluttering with success only to find that a coexisting stutter now becomes more visible. Often, cluttering in the form of fast bursts of speech and uncontrolled rate actually appears to directly lead to moments of stuttering, apparently being triggered by the preceding uncontrolled rush of speech. Thus, where a stutter is less visible and not viewed as a big problem to the client, it may be worth dealing with cluttering first and then addressing the stutter afterwards. This cluttering/stuttering model bears similarity to Van Riper's (1973) Track II model of stuttering (see chapter 7).

Where stuttering and cluttering coexist and where the cluttering predomi-nates, I have found that dealing with the cluttering can be effective in clearing the way for further work with the stuttering. Often, where rate is implicated in the clutter (the vast majority of occasions) work on rate reduction carries the additional benefit of allowing more time for the client to spontaneously modify moments of stuttering. There are some problems though. For example, the treatment of overcoarticulation may involve the use of tech-niques to increase articulatory precision, while treating blocking in stuttering may require sounds to be approached with a more relaxed and less tense articulatory posture. Nonetheless, people who clutter can and do benefit from treatment programs that are aimed at those who stutter. In fact, it seems quite likely that for many years a large number of such speakers will have simply been misdiagnosed as "pure" stutterers and treated as such. On the other hand, some people who clutter have deliberately been put in groups with people who stutter to good effect.

One example of this is described by Langevin and Boberg (1996) who report the successful use of the comprehensive stuttering program (Boberg & Kully, 1985) with a group of adults who both stuttered and cluttered. This intensive program incorporates fluency shaping techniques together with atti-tude adjustment and speech modification techniques (see also chapter 12). Therapeutic success was measured by percentage improvement in the number of syllables stuttered, stabilization of speech rate in syllables per minute, together with nonspeech measures; the Perceptions of Stuttering Inventory (PSI; Woolfe, 1967); the S-24 and the Self-Efficacy Scaling by Adult Stutterers (SESAS; Ornstein & Manning, 1985). Significant gains were made by all clients during the program, although these were generally less robust for the cluttering and stuttering speakers when compared to pure stuttering speakers, and were maintained one year post clinic. This finding is encour-aging. However, all four adults who cluttered were selected for inclusion first on the basis of a fast rate of speech, while two showed problems with language. It might seem likely that a program whose major therapeutic component is rate control could be effective for dealing with this type of cluttering and stuttering. It would be interesting to see if "pure" clutterers with more significant language-based difficulties and less significant rate problems would similarly benefit from such an approach.

Summary

There is no one treatment method for cluttering. Effective treatment begins with a thorough case history, together with assessments which probe across a range of speech, language and nonspeech variables. From this, the clinician can ascertain first whether the client is a "person who clutters" as opposed to a normal speaker with only very minor cluttering symptoms. At the present time, there is no objective way of drawing a line between these two diagnoses. In recognition of this fact the term borderline cluttering has often been used, although I have suggested that the term cluttering spectrum behaviour may be a better descriptor for such people. Regardless of the terminology used, the clinician will need to consider which (if any) components of the problem need to be addressed, and whether there are other concomitant speech/language and nonspeech issues which need to be taken into consideration. Clients may benefit from a synergistic approach to treatment, where treatment in one area may have a positive effect in others. Even amongst those who demonstrate some awareness of their difficulties at assessment, building up the client's understanding and acknowledgement of his problems is likely to be at the centre of almost all therapeutic programs. Treating cluttering/stuttering clients can prove difficult when an approach which reduces cluttering may be needed but is contra-indicated for stuttering. However, there is evidence to suggest that rate control components of cluttering can be successfully addressed in programs originally designed to deal with stuttering. A significant problem is that there is no objective data on treatment efficacy. This is likely to remain the case for some time due to the multifaceted nature of the disorder and the difficulty in arriving at a widely accepted data-based definition of cluttering.

Key points

- Cluttering is a developmental fluency disorder that is related but different to stuttering. In childhood it is often seen alongside disorders such as ADHD, articulation disorders, language disorders, stuttering, and also learning disabilities.
- While there is a general consensus as to the verbal and nonverbal features associated with the disorder, authorities differ on the question of the core characteristics. Cluttering is usually diagnosed by expression of the following features: excessively fast speech rate;

particularly fast bursts of speech; inappropriate pauses; jumbled articulation; overcoarticulation; repetition of sound units (particularly at word level or above); difficulties with language formulation including word finding; excessive use of interjections; poor syntax; unfinished sentences; poor social interaction skills. Nonlinguistic symptoms are lack of awareness of the problem, poor attention, poor memory.

- Unlike stuttering, cluttering can be seen as a disorder that sits on a normal not-normal continuum. That is, much cluttering behaviour may be regarded as normal (or within normal limits) if it is seen infrequently in speech. Conversely, even small amounts of genuine stuttering may be regarded as pathological.

- The term cluttering syndrome behaviour (CSB) can be used to describe cases where there are elements of cluttering, but the clinician is not convinced that a diagnosis of person who clutters is appropriate.

- Cluttering therapy for either linguistic or motoric factors is centred on increasing the client's perception of the disorder and then modifying the abnormal speech or language factors in small stages. The prognosis for controlled fluency among most clutterers is good if self-awareness and self-monitoring skills can be developed. Severe and chronic cluttering can be very resistant to therapy.

Further reading

Daly, D. A. (1996). *The source for stuttering and cluttering.* East Moline: IL: LinguiSystems.
I have made a number of references in the present chapter to this excellent workbook on cluttering. It includes case studies and exercises to work on motor speech aspects of the disorder.

Daly, D. A., & Burnett, M. L. (1999). Cluttering: Traditional views and new perspectives. In R. F. Curlee (Ed.), *Stuttering and related disorders of fluency.* New York: Thieme.
A comprehensive source written by acknowledged experts in the field.

Myers, F. L., & St Louis, K. O. (Eds.). (1992). *Cluttering: A clinical perspective.* Kibworth: Far Communications.
Although nearly 15 years old, this book contains a tremendous amount of information and is still very well worth reading.

St Louis, K. O., & Myers, F. L. (1997). Management of cluttering and related fluency disorders. In R. F. Curlee & G. M. Siegal (Eds.), *Nature and treatment of stuttering: New directions* (2nd ed., pp. 312–332). Boston: Allyn & Bacon.

This chapter presents clear rationales and outlines for cluttering therapy, and it is also good on theoretical aspects. It is not the purpose of the book to go into too much detail on treatment strategies, so look elsewhere (e.g., Daly, 1996) if you need a high level of information on practical aspects of therapy.

Various authors and various titles (1996). *Journal of Fluency Disorders, 21*, issues 3–4. A whole volume of *Journal of Fluency Disorders* devoted to cluttering. This contains a substantial amount of information on both theory and therapy.

References

Abe, K., Yokoyama, R., & Yorifuji, S. (1993). Repetitive speech disorder resulting from infarcts in the paramedian thalami and midbrain. *Journal of Neurology, Neurosurgery, and Psychiatry, 56*, 1024–1026.

Abwender, D.A., Trinidad, K.S., Jones, K.R., Como, P.G., Hymes, E., & Kurlan, R. (1998). Features resembling Tourette's syndrome in developmental stutterers. *Brain and language, 62*, 455–464.

Adams, M.R. (1974). A physiologic and aerodynamic interpretation of fluent and stuttered speech. *Journal of Fluency Disorders, 1*, 35–47.

Adams, M.R. (1980). The young stutterer: Diagnosis, treatment, and assessment of progress. *Seminars in Speech, Language, and Hearing, 1*, 289–299.

Adams, M.R. (1987). Voice onsets and segment durations of normal speakers and beginning stutterers. *Journal of Fluency Disorders, 12*, 133–139.

Adams, M.R., & Haydn, P. (1976). The ability of stutterers to initiate and terminate phonation during production of an isolated vowel. *Journal of Speech and Hearing Research, 19*, 290–296.

Adams, M.R., & Popelka, G. (1971). The influence of "time out" on stutterers and their disfluency. *Behaviour and Therapy, 2*, 334–339.

Adams, M.R., Runyon, C., & Mallard, A.R. (1975). Airflow characteristics of the speech of stutterers. *Journal of Fluency Disorders, 1*, 3–12.

Agnello, J.C. (1975). Voice onset and termination features of stutterers. In L.M. Webster & L. Furst (Eds.), *Vocal tract dynamics and dysfluency* (pp. 940–954). New York: Speech and Hearing Institute.

Agnello, J.C., & Wingate, M.E. (1972). *Some acoustical and physiological aspects of stuttered speech.* Paper presented at the American Speech and Language Association, Chicago.

Alfonso, P.J. (1991). Implications of the concepts underlying task-dynamic modelling on kinematic studies of stuttering. *Haskins Laboratory Status Report on Speech Research, SR–107–108*, 93–110.

Alm, P.A. (2004a). Stuttering, emotions, and heart rate during anticipatory anxiety: A critical review. *Journal of Fluency Disorders, 29*: 123–133.

Alm, P.A. (2004b). Stuttering and the basal ganglia circuits: A critical review of possible relations. *Journal of Communication Disorders, 37*, 325–369.

Alm, P.A. (2005). On the causal mechanisms of stuttering. PhD thesis, University of Lund, Sweden.

Ambrose, N.G., Cox, N.J., & Yairi, E. (1997). The genetic basis of persistence and recovery in stuttering. *Journal of Speech, and Hearing Research, 40*, 567–580.

380 References

Ambrose, N.G., & Yairi, E. (1999). Normative disfluency data for early childhood stuttering. *Journal of Speech, Language, and Hearing Research, 42*, 895–909.

Ambrose, N.G., Yairi, E., & Cox, N.J. (1993). Genetic aspects of early child stuttering. *Journal of Speech and Hearing Research, 36*, 701–706.

American Psychiatric Association (APA, 1987). *Diagnostic and statistical manual of mental disorders* (3rd ed.). Washington, DC: American Psychiatric Association.

Amman, J.O.C. (1965). *A dissertation on speech.* New York: Stechert-Hafner. (Original work published 1700)

Anderson, J.D., & Conture, E.G. (2000). Language abilities of children who stutter: A preliminary study. *Journal of Fluency Disorders, 25*, 283–304.

Anderson, J.D., & Conture, E.G. (2004). Sentence structure priming in young children who stutter. *Journal of Speech and Hearing Research, 47*, 552–571.

Anderson, J.M., Hughes, J.D., Rothi, L.J., Crucian, G.P., & Heilman, K.M. (1999). Developmental stammering and Parkinson's disease: The effects of levadopa treatment. *Journal of Neurosurgery and Psychiatry, 66*, 776–778.

Andrews, G. (1984). The epidemiology of stuttering. In R.F. Curlee & W.H. Perkins (Eds.), *Nature and treatment of stuttering: New directions.* San Diego: College Hill Press.

Andrews, G., Craig, A., Feyer, A.M., Hoddinott, S., Howie, P., & Neilson, M. (1983). Stuttering: A review of research findings and theories circa 1982. *Journal of Speech and Hearing Disorders, 48*, 226–246.

Andrews, G., & Cutler, J. (1974). Stuttering therapy: The relation between changes in symptom level and attitudes. *Journal of Speech and Hearing Disorders, 39*, 312–319.

Andrews, G., & Harris, M. (1964). *The syndrome of stuttering.* London: Spastics Society Heinemann.

Andrews, G., & Ingham, R. (1971). Stuttering: Considerations in the evaluation of treatment. *British Journal of Disorders of Communication, 6*, 427–429.

Andrews, G., Morris-Yates, A., Howie, P., & Martin, N. (1990). Genetic factors in stuttering confirmed. *Archives of General Psychiatry, 48*, 1034–1035.

Andrews, G., Quinn, P.T., & Sorby, W.A. (1972). Stammering: An investigation into cerebral dominance for speech. *Journal of Neurology, Neurosurgery and Psychiatry, 35*, 414–418.

Andy, O.J., & Bhatnager, S.C. (1992). Stuttering acquired from subcortical pathologies and its alleviation from thalamic perturbation. *Brain and Language, 42*, 385–401.

Ardila, A., & Lopez, M.V. (1986). Severe stuttering associated with right hemisphere lesion. *Brain and Language, 27*, 239–246.

Armson, J., Foote, S., Witt, C., Kalinowski, J., & Stuart, A. (1997). Effect of frequency altered feedback and audience size on stuttering. *European Journal of Disorders of Communication, 32*, 359–366.

Armson, J., & Stuart, A. (1998). Effect of extended exposure to frequency altered feedback on stuttering during reading and monologue. *Journal of Speech, Language, and Hearing Research, 41*, 479–490.

Armstrong, S., & Ainley, M. (1989). *South Tyneside assessment of phonology.* Ponteland: Stass.

Arnold, G. (1960). Studies in tachyphemia: 1. Present concepts of aetiologic factors. *Logos, 3*–23.

Atkinson, C.J. (1952). Vocal responses during controlled aural stimulation. *Journal of Speech, and Hearing Disorders, 17*, 419–426.

Au-Yeung, J., & Howell, P. (2002). Non-words reading, lexical retrieval and stuttering:

Comments on Packman, Onslow, Coombes and Goodwin (2001). *Clinical Linguistics and Phonetics, 16*, 287–293.

Au-Yeung, J., Howell, P., & Vallejo-Gomez, I. (1998). Phonological difficulty and stuttering. A comparison between Spanish and English. *Journal of Speech, Language, and Hearing Research, 41*, 1019–1030.

Au-Yeung, J., Vallejo-Gomez, I., & Howell, P. (2003). Exchange of disfluency with age from function words to content words in Spanish speakers who stutter. *Journal of Speech, Language, and Hearing Research, 46*, 754–765.

Backus, O. (1938). Incidence of stuttering among the deaf. *Annals of Otology, Rhinology, and Laryngology, 47*, 632–635.

Bajina, K. (1995). Covert aspects associated with the stuttering syndrome: Focus on self-esteem. In M. Fawcus, (ed.), *Stuttering: From theory to practice*. London: Whurr.

Balasubramanian, V., & Haydn, P. (1996). Acquired stuttering following bilateral parietal lobe lesion: A case report. In C.W. Starkweather & H.F.M. Peters (Eds.), *Proceedings of the 1st World Congress on Fluency Disorders* (pp. 617–620). Nijmegen: Nijmegen University Press.

Balasubraminian, V., & Max, L. (2003). *Auditory feedback and adaptation effect in adults with neurogenic stuttering*. Paper presented at the 4th World Congress on Fluency Disorders, Montreal, Canada.

Balasubramanian, V., Max, L., Van Borsel, J., Rayca, K.O., & Richardson, D. (1997). Acquired stuttering following right bilateral and frontal pontine lesion: A case study. *Brain and Cognition, 53*, 185–189.

Barasch, C.T., Guitar, B., McCauley, R.J., & Absher, R.G. (2000). Disfluency and time perception. *Journal of Speech Language, and Hearing Research, 43*, 1429–1439.

Barber, V.A. (1940). Studies in the psychology of stuttering: XV chorus reading as a distraction in stuttering. *Journal of Speech Disorders, 4*, 371–383.

Barnes, H.E. (1970). *Gunning vacation bursary report*. Department of Physiology, University of Edinburgh.

Barr, D.F., & Carmel, N.R. (1969). Stuttering inhibition with high frequency narrow band masking noise. *Journal of Auditory Research, 9*, 40–44.

Batik, J., Yaruss, J.S., & Bennett, E. (2003). *A preliminary investigation of the co-occurrence of word-finding disorders in children who stutter*. Paper presented at the 4th World Congress on Fluency Disorders, Montreal, Canada.

Baumeister, H., Casper, F., & Herziger, F. (2003). Treatment outcome study of the stuttering therapy summer camp for 200 children and adolescents. *Psychotherapie, Psychosomatik, Medizinische, Psychologie, 53*, 455–463.

Baumgartner, J. (1999). Acquired psychogenic stuttering. In R.F. Curlee (Ed.), *Stuttering and related disorders of fluency* (pp. 269–288). New York: Thieme.

Baumgartner, J., & Duffy, J. (1997). Psychogenic stuttering in adults with and without neurogenic disease. *Journal of Medical Speech-Language Pathology, 5*, 75–95.

Bell, A.M. (1853). *Observations of defects of speech, the cure of stuttering, and the principles of elocution*. London: Hamilton-Adams.

Bell, A.M. (1904). *The faults of speech*. Washington: The Volta Bureau.

Bender, J.F., & Kleinfeld, V.M. (1938). *Principles and practices of speech correction*. New York: Pitman.

Benson, D., & Geschwind, N. (1968). Cerebral dominance and its disturbances. *Pediatric Clinics of North America, 15*, 759–769.

Berne, E. (1968). *The games people play*. Harmondsworth: Penguin.

Berne, E. (1991). *Transactional analysis in psychotherapy*. London: Souvenir Press.

Bernstein, N. (1981). Are there constraints on childhood disfluency? *Journal of Fluency Disorders, 6*, 341–350.

Bernstein-Ratner, N. (1997). Stuttering: A psycholinguistic perspective. In R.F. Curlee & G.M. Siegel (Eds.), *Nature and treatment of stuttering: New directions* (pp. 99–127). Boston: Allyn and Bacon.

Bernstein-Ratner, N.E. (1998). Linguistic and perceptual characteristics of children at stuttering onset. In E.C. Healey & H.F.M. Peters (Eds.), *Proceedings of the 2nd World Congress on Fluency Disorders* (pp. 3–6). Nijmegen: Nijmegen University Press.

Bernstein-Ratner, N.E. (2000). Performance or capacity, the model still requires definitions it doesn't have. *Journal of Fluency Disorders, 25*, 337–346.

Bernstein-Ratner, N.E. (2005a). Is phonetic complexity a useful construct in understanding stuttering? *Journal of Fluency Disorders, 30*, 337–341.

Bernstein-Ratner, N.E. (2005b). Evidence based practice in stuttering: Some questions to consider. *Journal of Fluency Disorders, 30*, 163–188.

Bernstein-Ratner, N., & Benitez, M. (1985). Linguistic analysis of a bilingual stutterer. *Journal of Fluency Disorders, 10*, 11–19.

Bernstein-Ratner, N., & Healey, E.C. (Eds.). (1999). *Stuttering research and practice: Bridging the gap*. Mahwah, NJ: Lawrence Erlbaum Associates, Inc.

Biggs, B., & Sheehan, J. (1969). Punishment or distraction? Operant conditioning revisited. *Journal of Abnormal Psychology, 74*, 256–262.

Binns, F., & Phillips, B. (1997). What if stammering were a skill, and not a disability? *Speaking Out* (Journal of the British Stammering Association), spring.

Birtles, C.J., & Dixon, K.L. (1973). Simple dual-purpose device for the treatment of stutter. *Medical and Biological Engineering, 11*, 651–653.

Bleumel, C.S. (1913). *Stuttering and cognate defects of speech, Vol. I*. New York: Stechert.

Bleumel, C.S. (1935). *Stuttering and allied disorders*. New York: Macmillan.

Bleumel, C.S. (1957). *The riddle of stuttering*, Danville, IL: Interstate Publishing.

Block, S. (2004). The evidence base for the treatment of stuttering. In S. Reilly, J. Douglas, & J. Oates (Eds.), *Evidence based practice in speech pathology*. London: Whurr.

Blood, G.W., Ridenour, C. Jr., Qualls, C.D., & Hammer, C.S. (2003). Co-occuring disorders in children who stutter. *Journal of Communication Disorders, 36*, 427–488.

Bloodstein, O. (1960). Development of stuttering. *Journal of Speech and Hearing Disorders, 25*, 219–237.

Bloodstein, O. (1975). Stuttering as tension and fragmentation. In J. Eisenson (Ed.), *Stuttering: A symposium* (pp. 1–96). New York: Harper & Row.

Bloodstein, O. (1984). Stuttering as an anticipatory struggle disorder. In R.F. Curlee & W.H. Perkins (Eds.), *Nature and treatment of stuttering: New directions* (pp. 171–186). San Diego: College Hill Press.

Bloodstein, O. (1987). *A handbook on stuttering* (4th ed.). Chicago: National Easter Seal Society.

Bloodstein, O. (1993). *Stuttering: The search for a cause and cure*. Boston: Allyn and Bacon.

Bloodstein, O. (1995). *A Handbook on stuttering* (5th ed.). San Diego, CA: Singular Publishing Group.

Bloodstein, O., Alper, J., & Zisk, P. (1965). Stuttering as an outgrowth of normal disfluency. In D.E. Barbara (Ed.), *New directions in stuttering: Theory and practice*. Springfield, IL: Thomas.

Bloodstein, O., & Gantwerk, B.F. (1967). Grammatical function in relation to stuttering in young children. *Journal of Speech and Hearing Research, 10*, 786–789.

Bloodstein, O., & Grossman, M. (1981). Early stutterings: Some aspects of their form and distribution. *Journal of Speech and Hearing Research, 24*, 298–302.

Bloom, C., & Cooperman, D. (1999). *Synergistic stuttering therapy: A holistic approach,* Boston: Butterworth-Heinemann.

Boberg, E. (1981). *Maintenance of fluency.* New York: Elsevier.

Boberg, E. (1984). Intensive adult/teen therapy program. In W.H. Perkins (Ed.), *Stuttering disorders* (pp. 161–172). New York: Thieme-Stratton.

Boberg, E., & Kully, D. (1985). *Comprehensive stuttering program.* San Diego, CA: College Hill Press.

Boberg, E., & Kully, D. (1994). Long-term results of an intensive treatment program for adolescents who stutter. *Journal of Speech Language, and Hearing Research, 37*, 1050–1059.

Boberg, E., Yeudall, L.T., Schopflocher, D., & Bo-Lassen, P. (1983). The effect of an intensive behavioural program on the distribution of EEG alpha power in stutterers during the processing of verbal and visuospatial information. *Journal of Fluency Disorders, 8*, 245–263.

Bodenhamer, R. (2004). *Mastering blocking and stuttering: A cognitive approach to achieving fluency.* Carmarthen: Crown House.

Boehmler, R.M. (1958). Listener responses to nonfluencies. *Journal of Speech, and Hearing Research, 1*, 132–141.

Borden, G. (1988). Commentary on J. Harrington's paper: Stuttering, delayed auditory feedback and linguistic rhythm. *Journal of Speech and Hearing Research, 31*, 136–137.

Borg, E., & Zarkrisson, J. (1975). The activity of the stapedius muscle in man during vocalization. *Acta Otolaryngologica, 79*, 325–333.

Borman, E.G. (1969). Ephphatha, or, some advice to stammerers. *Journal of Speech and Hearing Research, 12*, 453–461.

Bosshardt, H.G. (1998). Speech fluency under dual task conditions. In E.C. Healey & H.F.M. Peters (Eds.), *Proceedings of the 2nd World Congress on Fluency Disorders.* Nijmegen: Nijmegen University Press.

Botterill, W., & Cook, F. (1987). Personal construct theory and the treatment of adolescent dysfluency. In L. Rustin, H. Purser, & D. Rowley (Eds.), *Progress in the treatment of fluency disorders* (pp. 147–165). London: Taylor & Francis.

Boutsen, F.R., Brutten, G.J., & Watts, C.R. (2000). Timing and intensity variability in the metronomic speech of stuttering and nonstuttering speakers. *Journal of Speech, Language, and Hearing Research, 43*, 513–520.

Brady, J.P. (1998). Drug induced stammering: A review of the literature. *Journal of Clinical Psychopharmacology, 18*, 50–54.

Bray, M. (2003). The nature of dysfluency in Down's syndrome. *Royal College of Speech and Language Therapists Bulletin*, March, 8–9.

Bray, M. (2005, June). *Awareness and anxiety: What evidence is there of either in young adults with Down's syndrome who are dysfluent?* Paper presented at the 7th Oxford Dysfluency Conference, Oxford.

Brayton, E.R., & Conture, E.G. (1978). Effects of noise and rhythmic stimulation on the speech of stutterers. *Journal of Speech and Hearing Research, 15*, 483–486.

Brazis, P.W., Masdeu, J.C., & Biller, J. (1996). *Localization in clinical neurology* (3rd edn.). Boston: Little, Brown.

Breakwell, G., Hammond, S., & Fife-Schaw, C. (2000). *Research methods in psychology* (2nd ed.). London: Sage.

Brenault, L., Morrison, S., Kalinowski, J., Armson, J., & Stuart, A. (1995). *Effect of altered feedback on stuttering during telephone use*. Poster presentation, American Speech-Language Hearing Association convention, Halifax, NS, Canada.

Brin, M.F., Stewart, C., Blitzer, A., & Diamond, B. (1994). Laryngeal botulinum toxin injections for disabling stuttering in adults. *Neurology, 44*, 2262–2266.

Brookshire, R., & Martin, R. (1967). The differential effects of three verbal punishers on the disfluencies of normal speakers. *Journal of Speech and Hearing Research, 42*, 3–28.

Brosch, S., Haege. A., Kalehne P., & Johannsen, H.S. (1999). Stuttering children and the probability of remission – the role of cerebral dominance and speech production. *International Journal of Pediatric Otorhinolaryngology, 47*, 71–76.

Browman, C.P. and Goldstein, L.M. (1986). Towards an articulatory phonology. *Phonology Yearbook, 3*, 219–252.

Browman, C.P., & Goldstein, L.M. (1995). Dynamics and articulatory phonology. In T.van Gelder & R.F. Port (Eds.), *Mind as motion: Explorations in the dynamics of cognition* (pp. 173–193). Cambridge, MA: MIT Press.

Brown, S.F. (1937). The influences of grammatical function on the incidence of stuttering. *Journal of Speech Disorders, 2*, 207–215.

Brown, S.F. (1938). A further study of stuttering in relation to various speech sounds. *Quarterly Journal of Speech, 24*, 390–397.

Brown, S.F. (1945). The loci of stuttering in the speech sequence. *Journal of Speech Disorders, 10*, 181–192.

Brown, T., Sambrooks, J.E., & MacCulloch, M.J. (1975). Auditory thresholds and the effect of reduced auditory feedback on stuttering. *Acta Psychiatrica Scandinavia, 51*, 297–311.

Brutten, G.J., & Shoemaker, D.J. (1967). *The modification of stuttering*. Englewood Cliffs, NJ: Prentice-Hall.

Bryngelson, E., & Rutherford, B. (1937). A comparative study of laterality of stutterers and nonstutterers. *Journal of Speech Disorders, 2*, 15–16.

Burke, B.D. (1969). Reduced auditory feedback and stuttering. *Behaviour Research and Therapy, 7*, 303–308.

Burns, K. (2005). *Focus on solutions: A health professional's guide*. Chichester: Wiley.

Byrd, K., & Cooper, E.B. (1989). Expressive and receptive language skills in stuttering children. *Journal of Fluency Disorders, 14*, 121–126.

Cade, B., & Hanlon, W.O. (1993). *A brief guide to brief therapy*. New York: Norton.

Cady, B.B., & Robbins, C.J. (1968). *The effect of the verbally presented words "wrong", "right" and "tree" on the disfluency rates of stutterers and nonstutterers*. Convention address, American Speech and Hearing Association.

Campbell, J.H., & Hill, D. (1987). *Systematic disfluency analysis*. Paper presented at the annual convention of the American Speech-Language Hearing Association, New Orleans.

Campbell, J.H., & Hill, D. (1993). *Application of a weighted scoring system to systematic disfluency analysis*. Paper presented at the annual convention of the American Speech-Language Hearing Association, Anaheim, CA.

Carleur, L., Lambert, J., Defer, G.L., Coskun, O., & Rossa, Y. (2000). Acquired and persistent stuttering as the main symptom of striatal infarction. *Movement Disorder, 15*, 242–246.

Carr, B.M. (1969). Ear effect variables and order of report in dichotic listening. *Cortex, 5*, 63–68.

Caruso, A.J., Abbs, J.H., & Gracco, V.L. (1988). Kinenatic analysis of multiple movement coordination during speech in stutterers. *Brain, 111*, 439–455.

Caruso, A.J., Gracco, V.L., & Abbs, J.H. (1987). A speech motor control perspective on stuttering: Preliminary observations. In H.F.M. Peters & W. Hulstijn (Eds.), *Speech motor dynamics in stutterers.* Wein: Springer-Verlag.

Chambless, D. L., & Ollendick, T. H. (2001). Empirically supported psychological interventions: Controversies and evidence. *Annual Review of Psychology, 52*, 685–716.

Chandra, R. (1987). *Introductory physics of nuclear medicine.* Philadelphia: Lea & Febiger.

Chang, S.E., Ohde, R.N., & Conture, E.G. (2002). Coarticulation and formant transition rate in young children who stutter. *Journal of Speech and Hearing Research, 45*, 676–688.

Cheasman, C. (1983). Therapy for adults: An evaluation of current techniques for establishing fluency. In P. Dalton (Ed.), *Approaches to the treatment of stuttering* (pp. 76–105). London: Croom Helm.

Cheasman, C., & Everard, R. (2005, June). *Interiorised/covert stammering – a group therapy programme – clients' and therapists' perspectives.* Paper presented at the 7th Oxford Dysfluency Conference, Oxford.

Cherry, E.C., & Sayers, B.M. (1956). Experiments on the total inhibition of stuttering by external control, and some clinical results. *Journal of Psychosomatic Research, 1*, 233–246.

Choi, H.S., Kim, Y.H., Pyo, H.Y., & Hong, W.P. (2000). *Effect of botulinum toxin injections on adult stuttering patients.* Poster presentation, IFA 3rd World Congress on Fluency Disorders, Denmark.

Christensen, R.C., Byerly, M.J., & McElroy, R.A. (1996). A case of sertraline-induced stuttering. *Journal of Clinical Psychopharmacology, 16*, 92–93.

Ciabarra, A.M., Elkind, M.S., Roberts, J.K., & Marshall, R.S. (2000). Subcortical infarction resulting in acquired stuttering. *Journal of Neurosurgery and Psychiatry, 69*, 546–549.

Colcord, R.D., & Adams, M.R. (1979). Voicing durations and vocal SPL changes associated with stuttering reduction during singing. *Journal of Speech and Hearing Research, 22*, 468–479.

Comings, D.E., Wu, S., Chiv, C., Ring, R., Gade, R., Ahn, C., et al. (1996). Polygenetic inheritance of Tourette's Syndrome, stuttering, attention deficit, hyperactivity, conduct and oppositional defiant disorder: The additive and subtractive effect of the 3 dopaminergic genes – DRD2, D beta H and DAT 1. *American Journal of Medical Genetics, 67*, 264–288.

Conture, E.G. (1974). Some effects of noise on the speaking behaviour of stutterers. *Journal of Speech and Hearing Research, 17*, 714–723.

Conture, E.G. (1990). *Stuttering* (2nd ed.). Englewood Cliffs, NJ: Prentice-Hall.

Conture, E. (1997). Evaluating childhood stuttering. In R.F. Curlee & G.M. Siegel (Eds.), *Nature and treatment of stuttering: New directions* (pp. 237–256). Boston: Allyn and Bacon.

Conture, E.G. (1999). The best day to rethink our research agenda is between yesterday and tomorrow. In N. Berstein Ratner & E.C. Healey (Eds.), *Stuttering research and practice: Bridging the gap.* Mahwah, NJ: Lawrence Erlbaum Associates, Inc.

Conture, E.G. (2001). *Stuttering: Its nature, diagnosis, and treatment*. Boston: Allyn and Bacon.

Conture, E.G., & Guitar, B. (1993). Evaluating efficacy of treatment of stuttering: School-age children. *Journal of Fluency Disorders, 18*, 253–287.

Conture, E.G., & Melnick, K.S. (1999). Parent–child group approach to stuttering in preschool children. In M. Onslow & A. Packman (Eds.), *The handbook of early stuttering intervention* (pp. 17–52). San Diego: Singular Publishing.

Conture, E.G., & Zackheim, C.T. (2002). *The long and winding road of developmental stuttering: From the womb to the tomb*. Paper presented at the 6th Oxford Dysfluency Conference, Oxford.

Conture, E.G., Zackheim, C.T., Anderson, J., & Pellowski, M. (2004). Lingusitic processes and childhood stuttering: Many's a slip between intention and lip. In B. Maassen, R.D. Kent, H.F.M. Peters, P.H.H.M. van Lieshout, & W. Hulstijn (Eds.), *Speech motor control in normal and disordered speech* (pp. 253–281). Oxford: Oxford University Press.

Conway, J.K., & Quarrington, B.J. (1963). Positional effects on the stuttering of contextually organized verbal material. *Journal of Abnormal and Social Psychology, 67*, 299–303.

Cooper, E.B., & Cooper, C. (1985). *Personalized fluency control therapy*. Allen, TX: DLM.

Cooper, E.B., & Cooper, C. (1996). Clinicians' attititudes towards stuttering: Two decades of change. *Journal of Fluency Disorders, 21*, 119–135.

Cooper, E.B., & Cooper, C. (2004). Treating fluency disordered adolescents. *Journal of Fluency Disorders, 28*, 125–142.

Cooper, E.B., & Rustin, L. (1985). Clinician attitudes toward stuttering in the United States and Great Britain: A cross-cultural study. *Journal of Fluency Disorders, 10*, 1–17.

Cooper, E.B., Cady, B.B., & Robbins, C.J. (1970). The effect of the verbally presented words "wrong", "right" and "tree" on the disfluency rates of stutterers and nonstutterers. *Journal of Speech and Hearing Research, 13*, 230–244.

Cooperman, D. (2003). Personal communication, email correspondence to the author, October.

Cordes, A., & Ingham, R.J. (1998). *Treatment efficacy for stuttering: A search for empirical bases*. San Diego, CA: Singular Publishing Group.

Coriat, I.H. (1943). Psychoanalytic concept of stuttering. *The Nervous Child, 2*, 167–171.

Costa, D., & Kroll, R. (1995). Sertraline in stuttering. *Journal of Clinical Psychopharmocology, 15*, 443–444.

Costa, D., & Kroll, R. (2000). Stuttering: An update for physicians. *Canadian Medical Association Journal, 162*, 1849–1855.

Costello, J. M. (1983). Current behavioral treatments for children. In D. Prins & R.J. Ingham (Eds.), *Treatment of stuttering in early childhood: Methods and issues*. San Diego: College Hill Press.

Costello, J.M. (1984). Operant conditioning and the treatment of stuttering. In W.H. Perkins (Ed.), *Stuttering disorders*. New York: Thieme Stratton.

Costello, J.M., & Ingham, R.J. (1999). Behavioral treatment of younger children who stutter: An extended length of utterance method. In R.C. Curlee (Ed.), *Stuttering and related disorders of fluency* (2nd ed., pp. 80–109). New York: Thieme.

Cox, N.J., Kramer, P.L., & Kidd, K.K. (1984). Segregation analysis of stuttering. *Genetic epidemiology, 1*, 245–253.

Cox, N., Roe, C., Suresh, R., Cook, E., Lundstom, C., Garsten, M., et al. (2005, June). *Chromosomal signals for genes underlying stuttering: A preliminary report.* Paper presented at the 7th Oxford Dysfluency Conference, Oxford.

Craig, A. (1998). Relapse following treatment for stuttering: A critical review and correlative data. *Journal of Fluency Disorders, 23*, 1–30.

Craig, A., Franklin, J.R., & Andrews, G. (1984). A scale to measure locus of control of behaviour. *British Journal of Medical Psychology, 57*, 173–180.

Craig, A., & Hancock, K. (1995). Self-reported factors related to relapse following treatment for stuttering. *Australian Journal of Human Communication Disorders, 23*, 48–60.

Craig, A., Hancock, K., Chang, E., McCready, C., Shepley, A., McCaul, A., et al. (1996). A controlled clinical trial for stuttering in persons aged 9–14 years. *Journal of Speech and Hearing Research, 39*, 808–826.

Craig. A., Hancock, K., Tran. Y., Craig. M., & Peters, K. (2002). Epidemiology of stuttering in the communication across the entire life span. *Journal of Speech Language and Hearing Research, 45*, 1097–1105.

Crichton-Smith, I. (2002). Communicating in the real world: Accounts from people who stutter. *Journal of Fluency Disorders, 27*, 333–352.

Cross, D.E., & Cooke, P. (1979). *Vocal and manual reaction times of adult stutterers and nonstutterers.* Paper presented at the annual convention of the American Speech Hearing Association, Atlanta.

Cross, D.E., & Luper, H.L. (1979). Voice reaction time of stuttering and nonstuttering children and adults. *Journal of Fluency Disorders, 4*, 59–77.

Cross, D.E., Shadden, B.B., & Luper, H.L. (1979). Effects of stimulus ear presentation on the voice reaction times of adult stutterers and nonstutterers. *Journal of Fluency Disorders, 4*, 45–58.

Crowder, J.E., & Harbin, R. (1971). The effect of punishment on stuttering: A case study. *Psychotherapy: Theory, Research and Practice, 8*, 179–180.

Cuadrado, E.M., & Weber-Fox, C.M. (2003). Atypical syntactic processing in individuals who stutter: Evidence from event-related brain potentials and behavioural measures. *Journal of Speech, Language, and Hearing Research, 46*, 960–976.

Cullinan, W.L., & Springer, M.T. (1980). Voice initiation and termination times in stuttering and nonstuttering children. *Journal of Speech and Hearing Research, 23*, 344–360.

Curlee, R. (1984). Stuttering disorders: An overview. In J. Costello (Ed.), *Speech disorder in children.* San Diego, CA: College Hill Press.

Curlee, R. (1993). Identification and management of beginning stuttering. In R. Curlee (Ed.), *Stuttering and related disorders of fluency.* New York: Thieme.

Curlee, R.F., & Perkins, W.H. (1969). Conversational rate control therapy for stuttering. *Journal of Speech and Hearing Disorders, 34*, 245–250.

Curlee, R.F., & Perkins, W.H. (1973). Effectiveness of a DAF conditioning program for adolescent and adult stutterers. *Behaviour Research and Therapy, 11*, 395–401.

Curlee, R., & Yairi, E. (1997). Early intervention with early childhood stuttering: A critical examination of the data. *American Journal of Speech-Language Pathology, 6*, 8–18.

Curry, F.K.W., & Gregory, H.H. (1967). *A comparison of stutterers and nonstutterers on three dichotic tasks.* Convention report, American Speech and Hearing Association.

Dalton, P., & Hardcastle, W. (1989). *Disorders of fluency and their effects on communication*. London: Elsevier.

Daly, D.A. (1986). The clutterer. In K.O. St Louis (Ed.), *The atypical stutterer: Principles and practices of rehabilitation*. New York: Academic Press.

Daly, D.A. (1992). Helping the clutterer: Therapy considerations. In F.L Myers & K.O. St Louis (Eds.), *Cluttering: A clinical perspective*. Kibworth: Far Communications.

Daly, D.A. (1993). Cluttering: Another fluency syndrome. In R.F. Curlee (ed.), *Stuttering and related disorders of fluency*. New York: Thieme.

Daly, D.A. (1996). *The source for stuttering and cluttering*. East Moline, IL: LinguiSystems.

Daly, D.A., & Cantrelle, R. P. (2006). Cluttering: Characteristics identified as diagnostically significant by 60 fluency experts. Paper to be presented at the 6th IFA World Congress on disorders of fluency, Dublin, July.

Daly, D.A., & Burnett, M.L. (1998). Cluttering: Traditional views and new perspectives. In R. F. Curlee (Ed.), *Stuttering and related disorders of fluency* (2nd ed.). New York: Thieme.

Daly, D.A., & Cooper, E.B. (1967). Rate of stuttering adaptation under two electro-shock conditions. *Behaviour Research and Therapy, 5*, 49–54.

Daly, D.A., & Kimbarrow, M.L. (1978). Stuttering as an operant behavior: Effects of "wrong", "right" and "tree" on the disfluency rates of school-age stutterers and nonstutterers. *Journal of Speech and Hearing Research, 21*, 581–597.

Daly, D.A., & St Louis, K.O. (1998). Videotaping clutterers: How to do it – what to look for. In E.C. Healey & H.F.M. Peters (Eds.), *Proceedings of the 2nd World Congress on fluency disorders* (pp. 233–235). Nijmegen: Nijmegen University Press.

Daniels, E.M. (1940). An analysis of the relation between handedness and stammering with special reference to the Orton-Travis theory of cerebral dominance. *Journal of Speech Disorders, 5*, 309–326.

Darley, F., & Spriesterbach, D. (Eds.). (1978). *Diagnostic measures in speech pathology*. New York: Harper and Row.

Darwin, E. (1800) *Zoonomia*. London.

Daskalov, D.D. (1962). On the problem of the basic principles and methods of prevention and treatment of stuttering. *Zhurnal Nevropalatogii I Psikhiatrii imeni S', Korsakova, 53*, 1047–1052.

Davis, S., Howell, P., & Cook, F. (2002). Sociodynamic relationships between children who stutter and their non-stuttering classmates. *Journal of Child Psychology and Psychiatry, 43*, 939–947.

Davis, S., Howell, P., & Rustin, L. (2000). A multivariate approach to diagnosis and prediction of therapy outcome with children who stutter: The social status of a child who stutters. In K.L. Baker (Ed.), *Proceedings of the 5th Oxford Dysfluency Conference*, Oxford.

Dayalu, V., Kalinowski, J., & Saltuklaroglu, T. (2002). Active inhibition of stuttering results in pseudo fluency: A reply to Craig. *Perceptual Motor Skills, 94*, 1050–1052.

De Ajuriaguerra, J.R., Diakine, H., Gobineau, S., Narlian, & Stambak, M. (1958). Le bégaiement. *Presse Médicale, 66*, 953–956.

Deal, J.L. (1982). Sudden onset of stuttering: A case report. *Journal of Speech and Hearing Research, 47*, 301–304.

Deal, J.L., & Doro, J. (1984). Episodic hysterical stuttering. *Journal of Speech and Hearing Disorders, 52*, 299–300.

Deecke, L., Kornhuber, H.H., Lang, W., Lang, M., & Schreiber, H. (1985). Timing function of the frontal cortex in sequential and motor learning tasks. *Human Neurobiology, 4*, 143–154.

De Hirsch, K. (1961). Studies in tachyphemia: 4, diagnosis of developmental language. *Logos, 4*, 3–9.

Dell, C. (1993). Treating school-age stutterers. In R.Curlee (Ed.), *Stuttering and related disorders of fluency*. New York: Thieme.

Dell, G., & Julliano, C. (1991). Connectionist approaches to the production of words. In H.F.M. Peters, W. Hulstijn, & C.W. Starkweather (Eds.), *Speech motor control and stuttering*. Amsterdam: Exerpta Medica.

De Nil, L. (2004). Recent developments in brain imaging research in stuttering. In B. Maassen, R.D. Kent, H.F.M. Peters, P.H.H.M. van Lieshout, & W. Hulstijn (Eds.), *Speech motor control in normal and disordered speech* (pp. 113–138). Oxford: Oxford University Press.

De Nil, L., & Brutten, G. (1991). Speech associated attitudes of stuttering and normally fluent children. *Journal of Speech and Hearing Research, 34*, 60–66.

De Nil, L., Kroll, R., & Houle, S. (2001). Functional neuroimaging of cerebellar activations during single word reading and verb generation in stuttering and nonstuttering adults. *Neuroscience Letters, 302*, 77–80.

Denny, M., & Smith, A. (1997). Respiratory and laryngeal control in stuttering. In R.F. Curlee and G.M. Siegel (Eds.), *Nature and treatment of stuttering: new directions* (pp. 128–142). Boston: Allyn and Bacon.

Derazne, J. (1966). Speech pathology in the USSR. In R.W. Reiber & R.S. Brubaker (Eds.), *Speech pathology*: Philadelphia: Lippincott Williams & Wilkins.

Dewar, A., & Barnes, H.E. (1976). Automatic triggering of automatic masking in stuttering and cluttering. *British Journal of Disorders of Communication, 11*, 19–26.

Dewar, A., Dewar, A.W., Austin, W.T., & Brash, H.M. (1979). The long-term use of an automatically triggered auditory feedback masking device in the treatment of stammering. *British Journal of Disorders of Communication, 14*, 219–229.

DiSimoni, F. (1974). Preliminary study of certain timing relationships in the speech of stutterers. *Journal of the Acoustical Society of America, 56*, 697.

Dorman, M.F., & Porter, R.S. (1975). Hemispheric lateralization for speech perceptions in stutterers. *Cortex, 11*, 181–185.

Douglas, E., & Qarrington, B. (1952). The differentiation of interiorized and exteriorized secondary stuttering. *Journal of Speech Disorders, 17*, 372–388.

Druce, T., Debney, S., & Byrt, T. (1997). Evaluation of an intensive treatment program for stuttering in young children. *Journal of Fluency Disorders, 28*, 209–218.

Dunlap, K. (1932). The technique of negative practice. *American Journal of Psychology, 55*, 270–273.

Dunn, L.M., Dunn, L.M., Whetton, C., & Burley, J. (1997). *British Picture Vocabulary Scales* (2nd ed.). Windsor: NFER Nelson.

Dworkin, J.P., Culatta, R.A., Abkarian, G.G., & Meleca, R. J. (2002). Laryngeal anesthetization for the treatment of acquired dysfluency: A case study. *Journal of Fluency Disorders, 27*, 215–226.

Dworkin, J.P., Meleca, R.J., Simpson, M., & Garfield, I. (2000). Use of topical lidocaine in the treatment of muscle tension dysphonia. *Journal of Voice, 14*, 567–575.

Dworzynski, K., & Howell, P. (2004). Cross-linguistic factors in the prediction of stuttering across age groups – the case of German. In A. Packman, A. Meltzer, &

H.F.M Peters (Eds.), *Theory, research and therapy in fluency disorders, proceedings of the 4th world congress on fluency disorders* (pp. 382–388). Nijmegen: Nijmegen University Press.

Dworzynski, K., Howell, P., & Natke, U. (2003). Predicting stuttering from linguistic factors for German speakers in two age groups. *Journal of Fluency Disorders, 28*, 95–113.

Eaves, L., Kendler, K., & Schulz, C. (1986). The familial vs. sporadic classification: Its power for the resolution of genetic and environmental etiologic factors. *Journal of Psychiatric Research, 20*, 115–130.

Edwards, S., Fletcher, P., Garman, M., Hughes, A., & Sinka, I. (1997). *The Reynell Developmental Language Scales III*. Windsor: NFER Nelson.

Eisenson, J., & Wells, C. (1942). A study of the influence of communicative responsibility in a choral speech situation for stutterers. *Journal of Speech Disorders, 7*, 259–262.

Ellis, A. (1990). *Reason and emotion in psychotherapy*. New York: Citadel Press.

Erikson, R.L. (1969). Assessing communication attitudes among stuterers. *Journal of Speech and Hearing Research, 12*, 711–724.

Ezrati-Vinacour, R., & Levin, I. (2004). The relationship between anxiety and stuttering: A multidimensional approach. *Journal of Fluency Disorders, 29*, 135–148.

Fagan, L.B. (1931). Graphic stuttering. *Psychology Monographs, 43*, 67–71.

Fairbanks, G. (1954). Systematic research in experimental phonetics – 1. A theory of the speech mechanism as a servomechanism. *Journal of Speech and Hearing Disorders, 20*, 142–153.

Fawcus, M. (Ed.). (1995). *Stuttering: From theory to practice*. London: Whurr.

Felsenfeld, S. (1995). *Speech outcomes in adopted children with a positive and negative parental history of speech disorder*. Paper presented at the annual meeting of the Behaviour Genetics Association. Richmond, VA.

Felsenfeld, S. (1996). Progress and needs in the genetics of stuttering. *Journal of Fluency Disorders, 21*, 77–103.

Felsenfeld, S. (1997). Epidemiology and genetics of stuttering. In R.F. Curlee & G.M. Siegel (Eds.), *The nature and treatment of stuttering: New directions* (2nd ed.). Boston: Allyn and Bacon.

Felsenfeld, S. (1998). What can genetics research tell us about stuttering treatment issues? In A. Cordes & R.J. Ingham (Eds.), *Treatment efficacy for stuttering: A search for empirical bases* (pp. 51–65). San Diego, CA: Singular Publishing Group.

Felsenfeld, S. (2002). Finding susceptibility genes for developmental disorders of speech: The long and winding road. *Journal of Communication Disorders, 35*, 329–345.

Felsenfeld, S., & Drayna, D. (2001). Stuttering and genetics: Our past and our future. In S.E. Gerber (Ed.), *The handbook of genetic communicative disorders*. New York: Academic Press.

Felsenfeld, S., Kirk, K.M., Zhu, F., Statham, D.J., Neale, M.C., & Martin, N.G. (2000). A study of the genetic and environmental etiology of stuttering in a selected twin sample. *Behaviour Genetics, 30*, 359–366.

Ferreira, F. (1991). Effects of length and syntactic complexity on initiation times for prepared utterances. *Journal of Memory and Language, 30*, 210–233.

Finn, P. (1998). Recovery without treatment: A review of conceptual and methodological considerations across disciplines. In A. Cordes & R.J. Ingham (Eds.), *Treatment efficacy for stuttering: A search for empirical bases* (pp. 3–26). San Diego, CA: Singular Publishing Group.

Finn, P. (2003a). Evidence based practice treatment of stuttering: II. Clinical significance of behavioral stuttering treatments. *Journal of Fluency Disorders, 28,* 209–218.

Finn, P. (2003b). *Self-change from stuttering during adolescence and adulthood.* Paper presented at the 4th World Congress on Fluency Disorders, Montreal, Canada.

Finn, P. (2005). The epigenisis of stuttering. *Journal of Fluency Disorders, 30,* 163–188.

Flanagan, B., Goldiamond, I., & Azrin, N.H. (1958). Operant stuttering: The control of stuttering behaviour through contingent consequences. *Journal of Experimental Analysis of Behavior, 1,* 173–177.

Flanagan, B., Goldiamond, I., & Azrin, N.H. (1959). Instatement of stuttering in normally fluent individuals through operant procedures. *Science, 130,* 979–981.

Flasher, C.V., & Fogle, P.T. (2004). *Counseling skills for speech language pathologists and audiologists.* New York: Delmar.

Fleet, W.S., & Heilman, K.M. (1985). Acquired stuttering from a right hemisphere lesion in a right hander. *Neurology, 35,* 1343–1346.

Flugel, F. (1979). Erhebungen von Personlichkeitsmerk-malen an Muttern stotternder Kinder und Jungendicher. *Dsh Abstracts, 19,* 226.

Forster, D.C., & Webster, W.G. (1991). Concurrent task interference in stutterers: Dissociating hemispheric specialization and activation. *Canadian Journal of Psychology, 45,* 321–335.

Forster, D.C., & Webster, W.G. (2001). Speech-motor control and interhemispheric relations in recovered and persistent stuttering. *Developmental Neuropsychology, 19,* 125–145.

Foundas, A.L., Bollich, A.M., Corey, D.M., Hurley, M., & Heilman, K.M. (2001). Anomalous anatomy of speech-language areas in adults with persistent developmental stuttering. *Neurology, 57,* 207–215.

Foundas, A.L., Bollich, A.M., Feldman, J., Corey, D.M., Hurley, M., Lemen, L.C., et al. (2004). Aberrant auditory processing and atypical planum temporale in developmental stuttering. *Neurology, 63,* 1640–1646.

Foundas, A.L., Corey, D.M., Angeles, V., Bollich, A.M., Crabtree-Hartman, E., & Heilman, K.M. (2003). Atypic adults with persistent developmental stuttering. *Neurology, 61,* 1378–1385.

Fowler, C.A. (1980). Coarticulation and theories of extrinsic timing. *Journal of Phonetics, 8,* 113–133.

Fox, P.T., Ingham, R.J., Ingham, J.C., Zamarripa, F., Xiong, J.H., & Lancaster, J.L. (2000). Brain correlates of stuttering and syllable production. A PET performance-correlation analysis. *Brain, 123,* 1985–2004.

Franck, A., Jackson, R., Pimentel, J., & Greenwood, G. (2003). School age children's perceptions of a person who stutters. *Journal of Fluency Disorders, 28,* 1–15.

Fransella, F. (1972). *Personal change and reconstruction.* New York: Academic Press.

Freeman, F.J. & Ushijima, T. (1978). Laryngeal muscle activity during stuttering. *Journal of Speech and Hearing Research, 21,* 538–562.

Freund, H. (1952). Studies in the interrelationship between stuttering and cluttering. *Folia Phoniatrica, 4,* 146–168.

Freund, H. (1966). *Psychopathology and the problems of stuttering.* Springfield, IL: Charles C. Thomas.

Froeschels, E. (1952). Chewing method as therapy. *Archives of Otolaryngology, 38,* 427–434.

Froeschels, E. (1955). Contribution to the relationship between stuttering and cluttering. *Logopaedic en Phoniatrie, 4*, 1–6.

Froeschels, E. (1964). *Selected papers (1940–1964)*. Amsterdam: North-Holland.

Fry, J. (2005, June). *The cognitive model of social anxiety and its application to stuttering*. Paper presented at the 7th Oxford Dysfluency Conference, Oxford.

Fry, J., & Farrants, J. (2003). What's at stake? Adolescents' perceptions of the consequences of stuttering. *Proceedings of the 6th Oxford Dysfluency Conference* (pp. 275–278). De Montfort University: KLB Publications.

Fukawa, T., Yoshioko, H., Ozawa, E., & Yoshida, S. (1988). Difference of susceptibility to delayed auditory feedback between stutterers and nonstutterers. *Journal of Speech and Hearing Research, 31*, 475–479.

Garber, S.R., Siegel, G.M., Pick, H.L., & Alcorn, S.R. (1976). The influence of selected masking noises on Lombard and sidetone amplification effects. *Journal of Speech and Hearing Research, 19*, 523–535.

Garrett, M. (1991). Disorders of lexical selection. In J.M. Levelt (Ed.), *Lexical access in speech production* (pp. 143–180). Cambridge, MA: Blackwell.

George, E., Iveson, C., & Ratner, H. (2001). *Problem to solution*. London: Brief Therapy Press.

Gifford, M.F. (1939). *Correcting nervous speech disorders*. New York: Prentice-Hall.

Gifford, M.F. (1940). *How to overcome stammering*. New York: Prentice-Hall.

Glauber, I.P. (1958). The psychoanalysis of stuttering. In J. Eisenson (Ed.), *Stuttering: A symposium*. New York: Harper and Row.

Goberman, A.M., & Blomgren, M. (2003). Parkinsonian speech disfluencies: Effects of L-dopa related fluctuations. *Journal of Fluency Disorders, 28*, 55–70.

Godai, U., Tatarelli, R., & Bonanni, G. (1976). Stuttering and tics in twins. *Acta Genetica Medicae et Gemellologiae (Roma), 25*, 369–375.

Goldberg, G. (1985). Supplementary motor area structure and function: Review and hypotheses. *Behavioural and Brain Sciences, 8*, 567–615.

Goldiamond, I. (1965). Stuttering and fluency as manipulable operant response classes. In U. Krasner and L. Ullman (Eds.), *Research in behaviour modification*. New York: Holt, Rinehart and Wilson.

Goldman, R. (1967). Cultural differences on the sex ratio in the incidence of stuttering. *American Anthropologist, 69*, 78–81.

Goodstein, L.D. (1956). MMPI profiles of stutterers' parents, A follow-up study. *Journal of Speech and Hearing Disorders, 21*, 430–435.

Goodstein, L.D., & Dahlstrom, W.G. (1956). MMPI differences between parents of stuttering and nonstuttering children. *Journal of Consulting Psychology, 20*, 365–370.

Gordon, C.T., Cotelingham, G.M., Stager, S., Ludlow, C.L., Hamburger, S.D., & Rapoport, J.L. (1995). A double-blind comparison of clomipramine and desipramine in the treatment of developmental stuttering. *Journal of Clinical Psychiatry, 59*, 5–14.

Gottwald, S. and Starkweather, C.W. (1995). Fluency intervention for preschoolers and their families in the public schools. *Language, Speech, and Hearing Services in Schools, 26*, 115–126.

Gracco, V.L. (1986). Timing factors in the coordination of speech movements. *Society for Neuroscience Abstracts, 12*, 971.

Gracco, V.L., & Abbs, J.H. (1986). Variant and invariant characteristics of speech movement. *Experimental Brain Research, 65*, 156–166.

Gray, M. (1940). The X family. A clinical and laboratory study of stuttering family. *Journal of Speech Disorders, 5*, 343–348.

Gregory, C.B. (2003). Counseling and stuttering therapy. In H.H. Gregory, *Stuttering therapy: Rationale and procedures* (pp. 263–296). Needham Heights, MA: Allyn and Bacon.

Gregory, H.H. (1964). Stuttering and auditory central nervous system disorder. *Journal of Speech and Hearing Research, 7*, 335–341.

Gregory, H.H. (1968). *Stuttering: Differential evaluation and therapy*. Austin, TX: Pro-Ed.

Gregory, H.H. (Ed.). (1979). *Controveries about stuttering therapy*. Baltimore: University Park Press.

Gregory, H.H. (Ed.). (2003). *Stuttering therapy: Rationale and procedures*. Boston: Allyn and Bacon.

Gregory, H.H., & Campbell, J.H. (1988). Stuttering in the school-age child. In D.E. Yoder & R.D. Kent (Eds.), *Stuttering, then and now*. Columbus, OH: Charles E. Merrill.

Gregory H.H., & Hill, D. (1980). Stuttering therapy for children. *Seminars in Speech, Language, and Hearing, 1*, 351–363.

Gregory H.H., & Hill, D. (1984). Stuttering therapy for children. In W. Perkins (Ed.), *Stuttering disorders* (pp. 77–98). New York: Thieme-Stratton.

Gregory H.H., & Hill, D. (1999). Differential evaluation-differential therapy for stuttering children. In R. Curlee (Ed.), *Stuttering and related disorders of fluency* (pp. 23–44). New York: Thieme.

Griggs, S., & Still, A.W. (1979). An analysis of individual differences in words stuttered. *Journal of Speech and Hearing Research, 22*, 572–580.

Grosjean, M., Van Galen, G.P., de Jong, W.P., van Lieshout, P.H.H.M., & Hulstijn, W. (1997). Is stuttering caused by failing neuromuscular force control? In W. Hulstijn, H.F.M. Peters, & P.H.H.M. Van Lieshout (Eds.), *Speech production: Motor control, brain research and fluency disorders* (pp. 197–204). Amsterdam: Elsevier.

Gross, M.S., & Holland, H.L. (1965). The effects of response contingent electroshock upon stuttering. *American Speech and Hearing Association, 7*, 376.

Grosser, J., Natke, U., Langefeld, S., & Kalveram, K. (2001). Reduction in stuttering by delayed and frequency shifted auditory feedback: Effects of adaptation and sex differences. In H.G. Bosshardt, J.S. Yaruss, & H.F. M. Peters (Eds.), *Fluency disorders: Theory, research, treatment, and self-help. Proceedings of the 3rd world congress of fluency disorders*. Nijmegen: Nijmegen University Press.

Gruber, L., & Powell, R.L. (1974). Responses of stuttering and nonstuttering children to a dichotic listening task. *Perceptual and Motor Skills, 38*, 263–264.

Grunwell, P. (1985). *Phonological assessment of child speech*. Windsor: NFER Nelson.

Guillaume, J.G., Mazars, G., & Mazars, Y. (1957). Epileptic medication in certain types of stuttering. *Revue Neurologique, 99*, 59–62.

Guitar, B. (1975). Reduction of stuttering frequency using anolog electro/myographic feedback. *Journal of Speech and Hearing Research, 18*, 672–685.

Guitar, B. (1998). *Stuttering: An integrated approach to its nature and treatment*. Philadelphia: Lippincott Williams & Wilkins.

Guitar, B., Guitar, C., & Neilson, P.D. (1988). Onset sequencing of selected lip muscles in stutterers and nonstutterers. *Journal of Speech and Hearing Research, 31*, 28–35.

Guitar, B., & Peters, T.J. (1980). The high school and adult stutterer. In *Stuttering: An integration of contemporary therapies* (pp. 31–47). Memphis: Speech Foundation of America.

Guntupalli, V.K., Kalinowski, J., & Saltuklaroglu, T. (2006). The need for self-report data in the assessment of stuttering therapy efficacy: Repetitions and prolongations of speech. The stuttering syndrome. *International Journal of Communication Disorders, 41*, 1–18.

Haefner, R. (1929). *The educational significance of lefthandedness*. New York: Columbia University Press.

Hahn, E.F. (1941). A study of the effect of remedial treatment on the frequency of stuttering in oral reading. *Journal of Speech Disorders, 6*, 29–38.

Hall, J., & Jerger, J. (1978). Central auditory function in stutterers. *Journal of Speech and Hearing Research, 21*, 324–337.

Hancock, K., & Craig, A. (1998). Predictors of stuttering relapse one year following treatment for children aged 9–14 years. *Journal of Fluency Disorders, 23*, 31–48.

Hancock, K., Craig, A., Campbell, K., Costello, D., Gilmore, G., McCaul, A. et al. (1998). Two-six year controlled-trial outcomes for children and adolescents. *Journal of Speech, Language and Hearing Research, 41*, 1242–1252.

Hand, C.R., & Luper, H. L. (1980). Durational characteristics of stutterers' and nonstutterers' fluent speech. *American Speech and Hearing Asociation, 22*, 709.

Hanley, T.D., & Steer, M.D. (1949). Effect of level of distracting noise on speaking rate, duration and intensity. *Journal of Speech and Hearing Research, 21*, 324–337.

Hannley, M., & Dorman, M. (1982). Some observations on auditory function and stuttering. *Journal of Fluency Disorders, 7*, 93–108.

Harms, M.A., & Malone, J.Y. (1939). The relationship of hearing acuity to stuttering. *Journal of Speech Disorders, 4*, 363–370.

Haroldson, S.K., Martin, R.R., and Starr, C.D. (1968). Time out as a punishment for stuttering. *Journal of Speech and Hearing Research*, 11: 560–566.

Harrington, J. (1988). Stuttering, delayed auditory feedback and linguistic rhythm. *Journal of Speech and Hearing Research, 31*, 36–47.

Harris, D.B. (1963). *Goodenough-Harris Drawing Test*. New York: Harcourt-Brace Johanovich.

Harris, V., Onslow, M., Packman, A., Harrison, E., & Menzies, R. (2002). An experimental investigation of the impact of the Lidcombe Program on early stuttering. *Journal of Fluency Disorders, 27*, 203–214.

Harrison, E., Onslow, M., Andrews, C., Packman, A., & Webber, M. (1998). Control of stuttering with prolonged speech: Development of a one-day instatement program. In A.C. Kordes & R.I. Ingham (Eds.), *Treatment efficacy for stuttering: A search for empirical bases* (pp. 191–212). San Diego, CA: Singular Publishing Group.

Harrison, E., Onslow, M., & Menzies, R. (2004). Dismantling the Lidcombe program of early stuttering intervention: Verbal contingencies for stuttering and clinical measurement. *International Journal of Language and Communication Disorders, 39*, 257–267.

Harrison, J. (2004). Two very different cases of adult onset stuttering. In A. Packman, A. Meltzer, & H.F.M Peters (Eds.), *Theory, research and therapy in fluency disorders. Proceedings of the 4th World Congress on Fluency Disorders* (pp. 499–504). Nijmegen: Nijmegen University Press.

Hashimoto, R., Taguchi, T., Kano, M., Hanyu, S., Tanaka, Y., Nishizawa, M. et al. (1999). A case of dementia with cluttering-like speech disorder and apraxia of gait. *Rinsho Shinkeigaku, 39*, 520–526.

Haydn, P.A. (1975). *The effects of masking and pacing on stutterers' and nonstutterers' speech initiation times.* Unpublished doctoral dissertation, Purdue University, USA.

Hayhow, R. (1987). Personal construct therapy with children who stutter and their families. In C. Levy (Ed.), *Stuttering therapies: Practical approaches.* London: Croom Helm.

Hayhow, R., Cray, A.M., & Enderby, P. (2002). Stammering and therapy views of people who stammer. *Journal of Fluency Disorders, 27,* 1–16.

Hayhow, R., & Levy, C. (1993). *Working with stuttering: A personal construct approach* (2nd ed.). Bicester: Winslow Press.

Healey, E., Scott, L., & Ellis, G. (1995). Decision making in the treatment of school-age children who stutter. *Journal of Communication Disorders, 39,* 107–124.

Hedge, M.H. (1971). The effect of shock on stuttering. *Journal of the All India Institute of Speech, 2,* 104–110.

Hejna, R. (1955). A study of the loci of stuttering in spontaneous speech. *Dissertation Abstracts, 15,* 1674–1675.

Helm-Esterbrooks, N. (1986). Diagnosis and management of neurogenic stuttering in adults. In K.O. St. Louis (Ed.), *The atypical stutterer: Principles and practices for rehabilitation* (pp. 199–213). New York: Academic Press.

Helm-Esterbrooks, N. (1993). Stuttering associated with acquired neurological disorders. In R.F. Curlee (Ed.), *Stuttering and related disorders of fluency* (pp. 205–219). New York: Thieme.

Helm-Esterbrooks, N. (1999). Stuttering associated with acquired neurological disorders. In R.F. Curlee (Ed.), *Stuttering and related disorders of fluency* (pp. 255–269). New York: Thieme.

Helm-Esterbrooks, N., Yeo, R., Geschwind, N., Freedman., M., & Weinstein, C. (1996). Stuttering: Disappearance and reappearance with acquired brain lesions. *Neurology, 36,* 1109–1112.

Henrikson, E.H. (1936). Simultaneously recorded breathing and vocal disturbances of stutterers. *Archives of Speech, 1,* 133–149.

Heuer, R.J., Sataloff, R.T., Mandel, S., & Travers, N. (1996). Neurogenic stuttering: Further corroboration of site of lesion. *Ear Nose and Throat Journal, 75,* 161–168.

Hill, D. (2003). Differential treatment of stuttering in the early stages of development. In H.H. Gregory, *Stuttering therapy: Rationale and procedures* (pp. 142–185). Boston: Allyn and Bacon.

Hillman, R.E., & Gilbert, H.H. (1977). Voice onset time for voiceless stop consonants in the fluent reading of stutterers and nonstutterers. *Journal of the Acoustical Society of America, 61,* 610–611.

Hinkle, D. (1965). *The change of personal constructs from the viewpoint of a theory of construct implications.* Unpublished doctoral thesis, Ohio State University.

Hirschberg, J. (1965). Stuttering. *Orvosi Hetilap 106,* 780–784.

Horner, J., & Massey, E.W. (1983). Progressive dysfluency associated with right hemisphere disease. *Brain and Language, 18,* 71–85.

Hough, M. (1998). *A practical approach to counselling* (7th ed.). London: Longman.

Howell, P., & Au-Yeung, J. (1995). Syntactic determinants of stuttering in the spontaneous speech of normally fluent and stuttering children. *Journal of Fluency Disorders, 20,* 317–330.

Howell, P., & Au-Yeung, J. (2002). The EXPLAN theory of fluency control and the diagnosis of stuttering. In E. Fava (Ed.), *Pathology and therapy of speech disorders* (pp. 75–94). Amsterdam: John Benjamins.

Howell, P., Au-Yeung, J., & Pilgrim, L. (1999). Utterance length and linguistic properties as determinants of lexical dysfluencies in children who stutter. *Journal of the Acoustical Society of America, 105*, 1–10.

Howell, P., Au Yeung, J., & Rustin, L. (1997). Clock and motor variance in lip tracking: A comparison between children who stutter and those who do not. In W. Hulstijn, H.F.M. Peters, & P.H.H.M. Van Lieshout (Eds.), *Speech production, motor control, brain research and fluency disorders* (pp. 573–578). Amsterdam: Elsevier.

Howell, P., Au-Yeung, J., & Sackin, S. (1999). Exchange of stuttering from function words to content words with age. *Journal of Speech, Language, and Hearing Research, 42*, 345–354.

Howell, P., Davis, S., Cook, F., & Williams, R. (in preparation) *What determines whether a child who stutters at age eight will continue to do so at teenage?*

Howell, P., & Dworzynski, K. (2005). Planning and execution processes in speech by fluent speakers and speakers who stutter. *Journal of Fluency Disorders, 30*, 343–354.

Howell, P., El-Yaniv, N., & Powell, D.J. (1987). Factors affecting fluency in stutterers when speaking under altered auditory feedback. In H. Peters & W. Hulstijn (Eds.) *Speech motor dynamics in stuttering* (pp. 361–369). New York: Springer Press.

Howell, P., Ruffle, L., Fernandez-Zuniga, A., Gutierrez, R., Fernandez, A.H., O'Brien, M.L., et al. (2004). Comparison of exchange patterns of stuttering in Spanish and English monolingual speakers and a bilingual Spanish-English speaker. In A. Packman, A. Meltzer, & H.F.M Peters (Eds.), *Theory, research and therapy in fluency disorders, Proceedings of the 4th World Congress on Fluency Disorders* pp. (415–422). Nijmegen: Nijmegen University Press.

Howell, P., Sackin, S., Glenn, K., & Au-Yeung, J. (1997). Automatic stuttering frequency counts. In H.F.M. Peters, W. Hulstijn, & P.H.H.M. Van Lieshout (Eds.), *Speech production: Motor control and fluency disorders* (pp. 395–404). Amsterdam: Elsevier.

Howell, P., & Vause, L. (1986). Acoustic analysis and perception of vowels in stuttered speech. *Journal of the Acoustical Society of America, 79*, 1571–1579.

Howell, P., Williams, M., & Vause, L. (1987). Acoustic analysis of repetition in stutterers' speech. In H. Peters & W. Hulstijn (Eds.), *Speech motor dynamics in stuttering*. New York: Springer Press.

Howie, P.M. (1981). Concordance for stuttering in monozygotic and dizygotic twin pairs. *Journal of Speech and Hearing Research, 24*, 317–321.

Hubbard, C.P., & Prins, D. (1994). Word familiarity, syllabic stress pattern, and stuttering. *Journal of Speech and Hearing Research, 37*, 564–571.

Huchinson, J.M., & Navarre, B.M. (1977). The effect of metronome pacing in selected aerodynamic patterns of stuttered speech. *Journal of Fluency Disorders, 2*, 189–204.

Hugh-Jones, S., & Smith, P. (1999). Self-reports of short and long term effects of bullying on children who stutter. *British Journal of Educational Psychology, 69*, 141–158.

Humphrey, D., and Reed, D. (1983). Separate cortical systems for control of joint movement and joint stiffness: Reciprocal activation and coactivation of antagonist muscles. In J. E. Demedt (Ed.), *Motor control mechanisms in health and disease* (pp. 347–352). New York: Raven Press.

Ingham, R.J. (1983). Stuttering and spontaneous remission. When will the emperor realize he has no clothes on? In D. Prins & R. Ingham (Eds.), *Treatment of stuttering in early childhood: Methods and issues* (pp. 113–140). San Diego, CA: College Hill Press.

Ingham, R.J. (1984). *Stuttering and behavior therapy*. San Diego, CA: College Hill Press.

Ingham, R.J. (1998). On learning from speech-motor control research. In A. Cordes & R.J. Ingham (Eds.), *Treatment efficacy for stuttering: A search for empirical bases* (pp. 67–101). San Diego, CA: Singular Publishing Group.

Ingham, R.J. (2003). Evidence based treatment of stuttering: I. Definition and application. *Journal of Fluency Disorders, 28*, 197–207.

Ingham, R.J., & Cordes, A.K. (1999). On watching a discipline shoot itself in the foot. In N. Bernstein-Ratner & E.C. Healey (Eds.), *Research and practice: Bridging the gap* (pp. 211–230). Mahwah, NJ: Lawrence Erlbaum Associates, Inc.

Ingham, R.J., & Costello, J. (1984). Stuttering treatment outcome evaluation. In J. Costello (Ed.), *Speech disorders in children*. Windsor: NFER-Nelson.

Ingham, R.J., Fox, P.T., Costello Ingham, J., & Zamparripa, F. (2000). Is overt stuttered speech a prerequisite for the neural activations associated with chronic developmental stuttering? *Brain and Language, 75*, 163–194.

Ingham, R.J., Fox, P.T., & Ingham, J.C. (1994). *Brain image investigation of the speech of stutterers and nonstutterers*. Paper presented at the Annual Convention of the American Speech-Language-Hearing Association, New Orleans.

Ingham, R.J., Moglia, R.A., Frank, P., Ingham, J.C., & Cordes, A.K. (1997). Experimental investigation of the effects of frequency-altered auditory feedback on the speech of adults who stutter. *Journal of Speech, Language, and Hearing Research, 40*, 361–372.

Ingham, R.J., & Packman, A. (1999). Treatment and generalization effects in an experimental treatment for a stutterer using contingency management and speech rate control. *Journal of Speech, Language and Hearing Disorders, 42*, 394–407.

Ingham, R.J., & Riley, G. (1998). Guidelines for documentation of treatment efficacy for young children who stutter. *Journal of Speech, Language and Hearing Research, 41*, 753–770.

Jakielski, K.J. (1998). *Motor organization in the acquisition of consonant clusters*. Unpublished doctoral thesis, University of Texas, Austin.

Jäncke, L., Hänggi, J., & Steinmetz, H. (2004). Morphological brain differences between adult stutterers and non-stutterers. *BMC Neurology, 4*, 23.

Janssen, P., Kraaimaat, F., & Brutten, G. (1990). Relationship between stutterers' genetic history and speech-associated variables. *Journal of Fluency Disorders, 15*, 39–48.

Jasper, H.H. (1932). A laboratory study of diagnostic indices of bilateral neuromuscular organization in stutterers and normal speakers. *Psychological Monographs, 43*, 172–174.

Jayaram, M. (1984). Distribution of stuttering in sentences: Relationship to sentence length and clause position. *Journal of Speech and Hearing Research, 27*, 329–338.

Jeffers, S. (1992). *Feel the fear and do it anyway*. London: Random House.

Jezer, M. (1997). *Stuttering: A life bound up in words*. New York: Basic Books.

Johnson, W. (1946). *People in quandaries*. New York: Harper.

Johnson, W. (1959). *The onset of stuttering. Research findings and implications*. Minneapolis: University of Minnesota Press.

Johnson, W. (1961). *Stuttering and what you can do about it*. Garden City, NY: Doubleday.

Johnson, W., et al. (1959). *The onset of stuttering*. Minneapolis: University of Minnesota Press.

Johnson, W., & Brown, S.F. (1935). Stuttering in relation to various speech sounds. *Quarterly Journal of Speech, 21*, 481–496.

Johnson, W., & King, A. (1942). An angle board and hand usage study of stutterers and nonstutterers. *Journal of Experimental Psychology, 31*, 293–311.

Johnson, W., & Rosen, L. (1937). Effects of certain changes in speech patterns upon the frequency of stuttering. *Journal of Speech Disorders, 2*, 192–195.

Johnston, S.J., Watkin, K.L., & Macklem, P.T. (1993). Lung volume changes during relatively fluent speech in stutterers. *Journal of Applied Physiology, 75*, 696–703.

Jones, M. (1997). Towards re-programming the stammering mind. *Speaking Out* (Journal of the British Stammering Association), Winter.

Jones, M., Gebski, V., Onslow, M., & Packman, A. (2001). Design of randomized controlled trials: Principles and methods applied to a treatment for early stuttering. *Journal of Fluency Disorders, 26*, 247–267.

Jones, M., Onslow, M., Harrison, E., & Packman, A. (2000). Treating stuttering in young children: Predicting treatment time in the Lidcombe Program. *Journal of Speech, Language, and Hearing Research, 43*, 1440–1450.

Jones, M., Onslow, M., Packman, A., Williams, S., Ormond, T., Schwarz, T., et al. (2005). A randomized controlled trial of the Lidcombe Programme of early stuttering intervention. *British Medical Journal, 331*, 7518.

Jones, R.K. (1966). Observations on stammering after localized cerebral injury. *Journal of Neurology and Neurosurgery, 29*, 192–195.

Kadi-Hanafi, K., & Howell, P. (1992). Syntactic analysis of the spontaneous speech of normally fluent and stuttering children. *Journal of Fluency Disorders, 17*, 151–170.

Kalinowski, J., Armson, J., Roland-Mieszowski, M., & Stuart, A. (1993). Effects of alterations in auditory feedback and speech rate on stuttering frequency. *Language and Speech, 36*, 1–16.

Kalinowski, J., Armson, J., Stuart, A., Hargrave, S., Sark, & MacLeod, J. (1995). Effect in alterations in auditory feedback on stuttering frequency during fast and normal speech rates. In C.W. Starkweather & H.F.M. Peters (Eds.), *Stuttering: Proceedings from the 1st World Congress on Fluency Disorders*. Nijmegen: Nijmegen University Press.

Kalinowski, J., Dayalu, V., Stuart, A., Rastatter, M.P., & Rami, K. (2000). Stutter-free and stutter-filled speech signals and their role in stuttering amelioration in English speaking adults. *Neuroscience Letters, 293*, 115–118.

Kalinowski, J., Guntapalli, V.K., Stuart, A., & Saltuklaroglu, T. (2004). Self-reported efficacy of an ear-level prosthetic device that delivers altered auditory feedback for the management of stuttering. *International Journal of Rehabilitation Research, 27*, 167–170.

Kalinowski, J., Stuart, A., Rastatter, M.P., Snyder, G., & Dayalu, V. (2000). Inducement of fluent speech in persons who stutter via visual choral speech. *Neuroscience Letters, 281*, 198–200.

Kalinowski, J., Stuart, A., Wamsley, L., & Rastatter, M.P. (1999). Effects of monitoring condition and frequency-altered feedback on stuttering frequency. *Journal of Speech Language, and Hearing Research, 42*, 1347–1354.

Kamhi, A. (2003). Two paradoxes in stuttering treatment. *Journal of Fluency Disorders, 28*, 187–196.

Kant, K., & Ahuja, Y.R. (1970). Inheritance of stuttering. *Acta Medica Auxologica, 2*, 179–191.

Karia, M. (2002). *Does it work? Andrew Bell's stammering cured course.* http://www.stuttering-cured.com

Kelham, R., & McHale, A. (1966). The application of learning theory to the treatment of stuttering. *British Journal of Disorders of Communication, 1*, 114–118.

Kelly, G. (1955). *The psychology of personal constructs.* New York: Norton.

Kelso, J.A.S., & Tuller, B. (1987). Intrinsic time in speech production: Data and theory. In E. Keller & M. Gopnik (Eds.), *Motor and sensory processes in language.* Hillsdale, NJ: Lawrence Erlbaum Associates, Inc.

Kent, R.D. (1984). Stammering as a temporal programming disorder. In R.F.Curlee & W. Perkins (Eds.), *Nature and treatment of stammering: New directions* (pp. 283–301). San Diego, CA: College Hill Press.

Kent, R.D. (2000). Research on speech motor control and its disorders: A review prospective. *Journal of Communication Disorders, 33*, 391–428.

Keyhoe, T.D. (1998). Computers and electronic devices for stuttering therapy. In E.C. Healey & H.F.M. Peters (eds.), *Proceedings of the 2nd World Congress on Fluency Disorders* (pp. 262–266). Nijmegen: Nijmegen University Press.

Kidd, K.K. (1977). A genetic perspective on stuttering. *Journal of Fluency Disorders, 7*, 97–104.

Kidd, K.K. (1984). Stuttering as a genetic disorder. In R.F. Curlee & W.H. Perkins (Eds.), *Nature and treatment of stuttering: New directions.* San Diego, CA: College Hill Press.

Kidd, K.K., Heimbuch, R.C., & Records, M.A. (1981). Vertical transmission of susceptibility to stuttering with sex-modified expression. *Proceedings of the National Academy of Sciences, USA, 78*, 606–610.

Kidd, K., Kidd, J.R., & Records, M.A. (1978). The possible causes of the sex ratio in stuttering and its implications. *Journal of Fluency Disorders, 3*, 13–23.

Kidd, K.K., Reich, T., & Kessler, S. (1973). A genetic analysis of stuttering suggesting a single major locus. *Genetics, 74*, 137.

Kimura, D. (1961). Cerebral dominance and the perception of verbal stimuli. *Canadian Journal of Psychology, 3*, 166–171.

Kimura, D. (1963). Speech lateralization in young children as determined by an auditory test. *Journal of Comparative Physiology and Psychology, 56*, 899–902.

Kimura, D. (1967). Functional asymmetry of the brain in dichotic listening. *Cortex, 13*, 163–178.

Kinsbourne, M., & Hicks, R. (1978). Functional cerebral space: a model for overflow, transfer and interference effects in human performance: A tutorial review. In M. Kinsbourne (Ed.), *Asymmetrical function of the brain.* Cambridge: Cambridge University Press.

Kinsbourne, M., & McMurray, J. (1975). The effect of cerebral dominance on time sharing between speaking and tapping by preschool children. *Child Development, 46*, 240–242.

Kistler, K. (1930). Linkshändigkeit und sprachstörungen. *Schweitz-Medizini Wochenschrift, 11*, 32–34.

Kleinow, J., & Smith, A. (2000). Influences of length and syntactic complexity on the speech motor stability of the fluent speech of adults who stutter. *Journal of Speech, Language, and Hearing Research, 43*, 548–559.

Kloth, S., Janssen, P., Kraaimant, F., & Brutten, G. (1995). Speech-motor and linguistic skills of young stutterers prior to onset. *Journal of Fluency Disorders, 20,* 157–170.

Kolk, H., & Postma, A. (1997). Stuttering as a covert repair phenomenon. In R.F. Curlee & G.M. Siegel (Eds.), *Nature and treatment of stuttering: New directions* (pp. 182–203). Boston: Allyn and Bacon.

Kono, I., Hirano, T., Ueda, Y., & Nakajima, K. (1998). A case of acquired stuttering resulting from striocapsular infarction. *Rinsho Shinkeigaku, 38,* 758–761.

Kraaimaat, F.W., Vanryckeghem, M., & Van Dam-Baggen, R. (2002). Stuttering and social anxiety. *Journal of Fluency Disorders, 27,* 319–331.

Kramer, M.B., Green, D., & Guitar, B. (1987). A comparison of stutterers and non-stutterers on masking level differences and synthetic sentence identification tasks. *Journal of Communication Disorders, 20,* 379–390.

Krashen, S. (1973). Lateralization, language learning and the critical period: Some new evidence. *Language Learning, 23,* 63–74.

Kroll, R. (2003). LPV forum – letter to the editor. *Logopedics, Phoniatrics, Vocology, 28,* 92–93.

Kroll, R.M., De Nil, L.F., Kapur, S., & Houle, S. (1997). A positron emission investigation of post-treatment brain activation in stutterers. In W. Hulstijn, H. F. M. Peters, and P. H. H. M. Van Lieshout (Eds.), *Speech production, motor control, brain research and fluency disorders.* Amsterdam: Elsevier.

Kully, D., & Boberg, E. (1988). An investigation of inter-clinic agreement in the identification of fluent and stuttered syllables. *Journal of Fluency Disorders, 13,* 309–318.

Kully, D., & Langevin, M. (1999). Intensive treatment for adolescents. In R. Curlee (Ed.), *Stuttering and related disorders of fluency* (2nd ed., pp. 139–159). New York: Thieme.

Kully, D., & Langevin, M. (2005). Evidence-based practice in fluency disorders. *The ASHA Leader,* 10–11, 23.

Lai, C.S.L., Fisher, S.E., Hurst, J.A., Vargha-Khadem, F., & Monaco, A.P. (2001). A forkhead-domain gene is mutated in severe speech and language disorders. *Nature, 413,* 519–523.

Langevin, M., & Boberg, E. (1996). Results of intensive stuttering therapy with adults who clutter and stutter. *Journal of Fluency Disorders, 21,* 315–327.

Langevin, M., Bortnick, K., Hammer, T., & Weibe, E. (1998). Teasing/bullying experienced by children who stutter: Toward the development of a questionairre. *Contemporary Issues in Communication Science and Disorders, 25,* 12–24.

Langevin, M., & Hagler, P. (2004). Development of a scale to measure peer attitiudes toward children who stutter. In A.K. Bothe (Ed.), *Evidence-based treatment of stuttering: Empirical issues and clinical implications* (pp. 139–171). Mahwah, NJ: Lawrence Erlbaum Associates, Inc.

Langevin, M., & Kully, D. (2003). Evidence based treatment of stuttering III. Evidence based practice in a clinical setting. *Journal of Fluency Disorders, 28,* 219–236.

Langova, J., & Moravek, M. (1964). Some results of experimental examinations among stutterers and clutterers. *Folia Phoniatrica, 16,* 290–296.

Langova, J. & Moravek, M. (1970). Some problems of cluttering. *Folia Phoniatrica, 22,* 325–336.

Lankford, S.D., & Cooper, E.B. (1974). Recovery from stuttering as viewed by parents of self-diagnosed recovered stutterers. *Journal of Communication Disorders, 7,* 171–180.

Larson, C. (1988). Brain mechanisms involved in the control of vocalization. *Journal of Voice, 2,* 3–10.

LaSalle, L., & Carpenter, L. (1994). *The effect of phonological simplification on children's fluency.* Paper presented at the America Speech-Language-Hearing Association Convention, New Orleans.

LDA (1988). *What's Wrong Cards.* Cambridge: Living and Learning.

Lebrun, Y. (1996). Cluttering after brain damage. *Journal of Fluency Disorders, 21,* 289–295.

Leder, S.B. (1996). Adult onset of stammering as a presenting sign in a Parkinsonian-like syndrome: A case report. *Journal of Communication Disorders, 29,* 471–477.

Lee, B.S. (1951). Artificial stutter. *Journal of Speech and Hearing Disorders, 16,* 53–55.

Lee, H.J., Lee, H.S., Kim, L., Lee, M.S., Suh, K.Y., & Kwak, D.I. (2001). A case of risperidone-induced stuttering. *Journal of Clinical Psychopharmacology, 21,* 115–116.

Lees, R. (1994). Of what value is a measure of the stutterer's fluency? *Folia Phoniatrica et Logopaedica, 46,* 223–231.

Lemert, E.M. (1962). Stuttering and social structure in two Pacific societies. *Journal of Speech and Hearing Disorders, 18,* 168–174.

Levelt, W.J. (1989). *Speaking: From intention to articulation.* Cambridge, MA: MIT Press.

Levelt, W.J. (1992). Accesssing words in speech production: Stages, processes and representations. *Cognition, 42,* 1–22.

Levelt, W.J. (1998). *Speaking: From intention to articulation* (2nd ed.). Cambridge, MA: MIT Press.

Levy, C. (1987). Interiorised stuttering: A group therapy approach. In C. Levy (Ed.), *Stuttering therapies: Practical approaches.* London: Croom Helm.

Lewis, J., Ingham, R., & Gervens, A. (1979). *Voice initiation and termination in stutterers and normal speakers.* Paper presented at the annual American Speech and Language Association convention, Atlanta.

Lewis, K.E. (1995). Do SSI-3 scores adequately reflect observations of stuttering behaviors? *American Journal of Speech-Language Pathology, 4,* 46–59.

Lincoln, M., & Onslow, M. (1997). Long-term outcome of an early intervention for stuttering. *American Journal of Speech-Language Pathology, 6,* 51–58.

Lincoln, M., Onslow, M., Lewis, C, & Wilson, L. (1996). A clinical trial of an operant treatment for school-age children who stutter. *American Journal of Speech-Language Pathology, 5,* 73–85.

Lincoln, M., Walker, C., & Brooks, T. (2005, June). *What is known and unknown about altered auditory feedback as a treatment for stuttering,* Paper presented at the 7th Oxford Dysfluency Conference, Oxford.

Lindsley, D.B. (1940). Bilateral differences in brain potentials from the two cerebral hemispheres in relation to laterality and stutterering. *Journal of Experimental Psychology, 26,* 211–225.

Loban, W. (1976). *The language of elementary school children.* Champaign, IL: National Council of Teachers.

Logan, K.J. (2001). The effect of syntactic complexity upon the speech fluency of adolescents and adults who stutter. *Journal of Fluency Disorders, 21,* 85–106.

Logan, K. (2003a). The effect of syntactic complexity upon the speech of adolescents and adults who stutter. *Journal of Fluency Disorders, 26,* 85–106.

Logan, K. (2003b). The effect of syntactic structure upon speech initiation times of stuttering and nonstuttering speakers. *Journal of Fluency Disorders, 28*, 17–35.

Logan, K., & LaSalle, L. (1999). Grammatical characteristics of children's conversational utterances that contain disfluency clusters. *Journal of Speech, Language, and Hearing Research, 42*, 80–91.

Louis, E.D., Winfield, L., Fahn, S., & Ford, B. (2001). Speech dysfluency exacerbated by levadopa in Parkinson's disease. *Movement Disorders, 16*, 562–565.

Louko, L., Conture, E.G., & Edwards, M.L. (1999). Phonological characteristics of young stutterers and their normally fluent peers. *Journal of Fluency Disorders, 15*, 191–210.

Louko, L., Edwards, M.L., & Conture, E.G. (1990). Treating children who exhibit co-occuring stuttering and disordered phonology. In R. Curlee (Ed.), *Stuttering and related disorders of fluency* (pp. 124–138). New York: Thieme.

Love, G., & Webb, W. (1996). *Neurology for the speech language pathologist*. London: Heinemann Butterworth.

Lu, F.L., Gopal, K., Gooding, H., & Shiflet, K. (2003). *Effects of selective serotonin reuptake inhibitors (SSRIs) on speech fluency*. Paper presented at the 4th World Congress on Fluency Disorders, Montreal, Canada.

Lucero, J.C., Munhall, K.G., Gracco, V.L., & Ramsey, L.O. (1997). On the registration of time patterning of speech movements. *Journal of Speech, Language, and Hearing Research, 40*, 1111–1117.

Ludlow, C. L. (1990). Treatment of speech disorders with botulinum toxin. *Journal of the American Medical Association, 264*, 2671–2675.

Ludlow, C.L. (1999). A conceptual framework for investigating the neurobiology of stuttering. In N. Bernstein-Ratner & E.C. Healey (Eds.), *Stuttering research and practice: Bridging the gap* (pp. 63–84). Mahwah, NJ: Lawrence Erlbaum Associates, Inc.

Luessenhop, A.J., Boggs, J.S., Laborwit, L.J., & Walle, G. (1973). Cerebral dominance in stutterers determined by Wada testing. *Neurology, 23*, 1190–1192.

Luschinger, R., & Arnold, G.E. (1965). *Voice-speech-language: Clinical communicology: Its physiology and pathology*. Belmont, CA: Wadsworth.

Luschinger, R., & Landolt, H. (1951). Electroencephalographische untersuchungen bei stotteren mit und ohne polterkopnenete. *Phoniatrica, 3*, 135–151.

Maassen, B., Kent, R.D., Peters, H.F.M., van Lieshout, P.H.H.M., & Hulstijn, W. (Eds.) (2004). *Speech motor control in normal and disordered speech*. Oxford: Oxford University Press.

MacNeilage, P. (1970). Motor control and the serial ordering of speech. *Psychological Review, 3*, 182–196.

Maguire, G.A., Gottschalk, L.A., Riley, G.D., Franklin, D.L., & Potkin, S.G. (1998). Risperidone in the treatment of stuttering: A double-blind placebo-controlled study. *New research program and abstracts of the American Psychiatric Association annual meeting* (p. 207, May–June). Toronto, Canada.

Maguire, G.A., Riley, G.D., Franklin, D.L., & Gottschalk, L.A. (2000). Risperidone for the treatment of stuttering. *Journal of Clinical Psychopharmacology, 20*, 479–482.

Mahr, G., & Leith, W. (1992). Psychogenic stuttering onset. *Journal of Speech and Hearing Research, 35*, 283–286.

Manning, W.H. (1996). *Clinical decision making in the diagnosis and treatment of fluency disorders*. Albany, NY: Delmar.

Manning, W.H. (1999). Management of adult stuttering. In R.F. Curlee (Ed.), *Stuttering and related disorders of fluency* (pp. 160–180). Albany, NY: Delmar.

Manning, W. (2001). *Clinical decision making in the diagnosis and treatment of fluency disorders* (2nd ed.). Albany, NY: Delmar.

Mansson, H. (2000). Childhood stuttering: Incidence and development. *Journal of Fluency Disorders, 25*, 47–57.

Maraist, J.A., & Hutton, C. (1957). Effects of auditory masking on the speech of stutterers. *Journal of Speech and Hearing Disorders, 22*, 385–389.

Martin, R., & Haroldson, S. (1979). Effects of five experimental treatments on stuttering. *Journal of Speech and Hearing Research, 22*, 132–146.

Martin, R., & Lindamood, L. (1986). Stuttering and spontaneous recovery: Implications for the speech-language pathologist. *Language, Speech, and Hearing Services in Schools, 17*, 207–218.

Martin, R., & Siegel, G. (1975). The effects of response contingent shock on stuttering. *Journal of Speech and Hearing Research, 2*, 340–352.

Masidlover, M., & Knowles, W. (1982). *Detailed test of comprehension: Derbyshire Language Scheme*. Derby: Derbyshire County Council.

Mastrud, B. (1988). *The Oxfordshire fluency programme for adolescent stutterers*. Paper presented at the 2nd Oxford Dysfluency Conference, Oxford.

Matthews, S., Williams, R., & Pring, T. (1997). Parent–child interaction therapy and dysfluency: A single case study. *European Journal of Disorders of Communication, 32*, 346–357.

Max, L. (2004). Stuttering and internal models. In B. Maassen, R. Kent, H.F.M. Peters, P.H.H.M.van Lieshout, & W. Hulstijn (Eds.), *Speech motor control in normal and disordered speech*. Oxford: Oxford University Press.

Max, L., Gracco, V.L., & Caruso, A.J. (2004). Kinematic event sequencing in stuttering adults: Speech, orofacial nonspeech, and finger movements. In A. Packman, A. Meltzer, & H.F.M Peters (Eds.), *Theory, research and therapy in fluency disorders: Proceedings of the 4th World Congress on Fluency Disorders* (pp. 315–322). Nijmegen: Nijmegen University Press.

Max, L., & Yudman, E.M. (2003). Accuracy and variability of isochronous rhythmic timing across motor systems in stuttering and nonstuttering individuals. *Journal of Speech, Language, and Hearing Research, 46*, 146–163.

Mayberry, R.I., & Shenker, R.C. (1997). Gesture mirrors speech motor control in stutterers. In H.F.M. Peters, W. Hulstijn, & P.H.H.M. Van Lieshout (Eds.), *Speech production: Motor control and fluency disorders* (pp. 183–190). Amsterdam: Elsevier.

McCall, G., & Rabuzzi, D. (1973). Reflex contraction of middle ear muscles secondary to stimulation of laryngeal nerves. *Journal of Speech and Hearing Research, 16*, 56–61.

McClay, H., & Osgood, E.I. (1959). Hesitation phenomena in spontaneous English speech. *Word, 15*, 18–44.

McClean, M.D., Goldsmith, H., & Cerf, A. (1984). Lower lip EMG displacement during bilabial dysfluencies in adult stutterers. *Journal of Speech and Hearing Research, 27*, 342–349.

McClean, M.D., Kroll, R.M., & Loftus, N.S. (1990). Kinematic analysis of lip closure in stutterers' fluent speech. *Journal of Speech and Hearing Research, 33*, 755–760.

McClean, M.D., Levandowski, D.R., & Cord, M.T. (1994). Intersyllabic movement timing in the fluent speech of stutterers with different disfluency levels. *Journal of Speech and Hearing Research, 37*, 1060–1066.

McClean, M.D., Tasko, S.M., & Runyan, C.M. (2004). Orofacial movements associated with fluent speech in persons who stutter. *Journal of Speech, Language, and Hearing Research, 47*, 294–303.

McFarland, D.H., & Moore, W.H., Jr. (1982). *Alpha hemispheric assymetrics during an electromyographic feedback procedures for stuttering.* Paper presented at the Annual Convention of the American Speech and Hearing Association, Toronto, Canada.

McFarlane, S., & Shipley, K. (1981). Latency of vocalization onset for stutterers and nonstutterers under conditions of auditory and visual cueing. *Journal of Speech and Hearing Research, 46*, 307–311.

McGuire, D. (2003). *Beyond stuttering. The McGuire programme for getting good at the sport of speaking.* London: Souvenir Press.

Mehta, D.K. (Ed.). (2003). *British National Formulary.* London: Pharmaceutical Press.

Melnick, K.S., & Conture, E.G. (2003). Phonological priming in picture naming of young children who stutter. *Journal of Speech, Language, and Hearing Research, 46*, 1428–1443.

Merits-Patterson, R., & Reed, C.G. (1981). Disfluencies in the speech of language-delayed children. *Journal of Speech and Hearing Research, 24*, 55–58.

Messenger, M., Onslow, M., Packman, A., & Menzies, R. (2004). Social anxiety in stuttering: Measuring negative social expectancies. *Journal of Fluency Disorders, 29*, 201–212.

Metz, D.E., Conture, E.G., & Caruso, A. (1979). Voice onset time, frication and aspiration during stutterers' speech. *Journal of Speech and Hearing Research, 22*, 649–656.

Mitchell, P., & Ward, D. (2005, July). *The Oxford stammer programme's intensive group treatment programs for eight–twelve year old children: Course outline and outcome data.* Paper presented at the 7th Dysfluency Conference, Oxford.

Molt, L. (1996). An examination of various aspects of auditory processing in clutterers. *Journal of Fluency Disorders, 21*, 215–225.

Molt, L. (2003, August). *Competition effects on AERP in stutterers.* Paper presented at the 4th World Congress on Fluency Disorders, Montreal, Canada.

Moncur, J.P. (1952). Parental domination in stuttering. *Journal of Speech and Hearing Disorders, 17*, 155–165.

Monroe, S., & Simmons, A. (1991). Diathesis-stress theories on the context of life stress research: Implications for the depressive disorders. *Psychological Bulletin, 110*, 406–425.

Moonen, C.T., van Zijl, P.C.M., Frank, J.A., Le Bihan, D., & Becker, E.D. (1990). Functional magnetic resonance imaging in medicine and physiology. *Science, 250*, 53–60.

Moore, W.H. (1984). Central nervous system chaarcteristics of stutterers. In R.F. Curlee & W.H. Perkins (Eds.), *The nature and treatment of stuttering: New directions* (chapter 4). San Diego, CA: College Hill Press.

Moore, W.H., Jr., Craven, D.C., & Faber, M.M. (1982). Hemispheric alpha asymmetries of words with positive, negative and neutral arousal values preceding tasks of recall and recognition: Electrophysiological and behavioral results from stuttering males and nonstuttering males and females. *Brain and Language, 17*, 211–224.

Moore, W.H., Jr., & Haynes, W.O. (1980). Alpha hemispheric asymmetry and stuttering: Some support for a segmentation dysfunction hypothesis. *Journal of Speech and Hearing Research, 23*, 229–247.

Moore, W.H., Jr., & Lang, M.K. (1977). Alpha asymmetry over the right and left hemispheres of stutterers and control subjects preceding massed oral readings: A preliminary investigation. *Perceptual and Motor Skills, 44*, 223–230.

Moore, W.H., Jr., & Lorendo, L.C. (1980). Hemispheric alpha asymmetries of stammering males and nonstuttering males and females for words of high and low imagery. *Brain and Language, 17*, 211–224.

Mori, K., Sato, Y., Ozama, E., & Imaizumi, S. (2004). Cerebral lateralization of speech processing in adults and child stutterers: Near infrared spectroscopy and MEG study. In A. Packman, A. Meltzer, & H.F.M. Peters (Eds.), *Theory, research and therapy in fluency disorders. Proceedings of the 4th World Congress on Fluency Disorders* (pp. 323–330). Nijmegen: Nijmegen University Press.

Morovak, M., & Langova, J. (1962). Some electrophysiological findings among stutterers and clutterers. *Folia Phoniatrica, 14*, 305–316.

Mouradian, M.S., Paslawski, T., & Shauib, A. (2000). Return of stuttering after stroke. *Brain and Language, 73*, 120–123.

Murphy, M., & Baumgartner, J.M. (1981). Voice initiation and termination in stutterers and nonstutterers. *Journal of Fluency Disorders, 6*, 257–264.

Murray, E. (1932). Disintegration of breathing and eye movements in stutterers during silent reading and reasoning. *Psychological Monographs, 43*, 218–275.

Murray, F.P. (1969). An investigation of variably induced white noise upon moments of stuttering. *Journal of Communication Disorders, 2*, 109–114.

Murray, H.L., & Reed, C.G. (1977). Language abilities of pre-school stuttering children. *Journal of Fluency Disorders, 2*, 171–176.

Myers, F.L. (1992). Cluttering, a synergistic framework. In F.L Myers & K.O. St Louis (Eds.), *Cluttering: A clinical perspective*. Kibworth: Far Communications.

Myers, F.L., & Bradley, C.L. (1992). Clinical management of cluttering from a synergistic framework. In F.L Myers & K.O. St Louis (Eds.), *Cluttering: A clinical perspective*. Kibworth: Far Communications.

Myers, F.L., & St Louis, K.O. (1992). Cluttering: Issues and controversies. In F.L Myers & K.O. St Louis (Eds.), *Cluttering: A clinical perspective*. Kibworth: Far Communications.

Natke, U. (2000). Stotterreduktion unter verzögerter und frequenzverschobener auditiver Rückmeldung (Reduction of stuttering frequency using frequency shifted and delayed auditory feedback). *Folia Phoniatrica et Logopaedica, 52*, 151–159.

Natke, U., Sandrieser, P., van Ark, M., Pietrowsky, R., & Kalveram, K.T. (2004). Linguistic stress, within-word position, and grammatical class in relation to early childhood stuttering. *Journal of Fluency Disorders, 29*, 109–122.

Neilson, M. (1980). *Stuttering and the control of speech: A systems analysis approach.* Unpublished doctoral dissertation, University of New South Wales, Australia.

Neilson, M. (1999). Cognitive-behavioral treatment of adults who stutter: The process and the art. In R. Curlee (Ed.), *Stuttering and related disorders of fluency* (2nd ed., pp. 181–199). New York: Thieme.

Neilson, M., & Andrews, G. (1993). Intensive fluency training of chronic stutterers. In R. Curlee (ed.), *Stuttering and related disorders of fluency* (pp. 139–165). New York: Thieme Stratton.

Neilson, P., Quinn, P., & Neilson, M. (1976). Auditory tracking measures of hemispheric asymmetry in normals and stutterers. *Australian Journal of Human Communication Disorders, 4*, 121–126.

Neilson, M., O'Dwyer, N., & Neilson, P. (1988). Stochastic prediction in pursuit tracking: An experimental test of adaptive model theory. *Biological Cybernetics, 58,* 113–127.

Neumann, K., Euler, H.A., von Gudenberg, A.W., Giraud, A.L., Lanfermann, H., Gall, V., et al. (2003). The nature and treatment of stuttering as revealed by fMRI. A within – and – between group comparison. *Journal of Fluency Disorders, 28,* 381–410.

Nicholas, A., & Millard, S. (2003). Effectiveness of parent–child interaction therapy. In K.L. Baker (Ed.), *Proceedings of the 6th Oxford Dysfluency Conference* (pp. 145–158). Oxford: KLB Publications.

Nicholas, A., Millard, S., & Cook, F. (2004). Parent–child interaction therapy: Child and parent variables pre and post therapy. In A. Packman, A. Meltzer, & H.F.M. Peters (Eds.), *Theory, research and therapy in fluency disorders. Proceedings of the 4th World Congress on Fluency Disorders* (pp. 108–116). Nijmegen: Nijmegen University Press.

Nicolosi, L., Harryman, E., & Kresheck, J. (1996). *Terminology of communication disorders* (4th ed.). Baltimore, MD: Williams and Wilkins.

Nippold, M.A. (1990). Concomitant speech and language disorders in stuttering children: A critique of the literature. *Journal of Speech and Hearing Disorders, 55,* 51–60.

Nippold, M.A., & Rudzinsky, M. (1995). Parents' speech and childrens' stuttering: A critique of the literature. *Journal of Speech, Language, and Hearing Research, 38,* 978–989.

Oates, D.W. (1929). Left-handedness in relation to speech defects, intelligence and achievement. *Forums of Education, 7,* 91–105.

O'Brian, S., Onslow, M., Cream, A., & Packman, A. (2001). A replicable, non-programmed, instrument-free method for the control of stuttering with prolonged speech. *Asia-Pacific Journal of Speech, Language, and Hearing Research, 6,* 91–96.

O'Brian, S., Onslow, M., Cream, A., & Packman, A. (2003). The Camperdown program: Outcomes of a new prolonged speech treatment model. *Journal of Speech, Language, and Hearing Research, 46,* 933–946.

O'Brian, S., Packman, A., Onslow, M., & O'Brian, N. (2004). Measurement of stuttering in adults: Comparison of stuttering-rate and severity-scaling models. *Journal of Speech Language, and Hearing Research, 47,* 1081–1087.

Ohashi, Y. (1973). The development of stuttering in children. *Japenese Journal of Child Psychiatry, 14,* 142–166.

Ohman, S.E. (1967). Numerical model of coarticulation, *Journal of the Acoustical Society of America, 41,* 310–320.

Ojemann, R.H. (1931). Studies in handedness; III. Relation of handedness to speech. *Journal of Educational Psychology, 22,* 120–126.

Onslow, M. (1992). Choosing a treatment procedure for early stuttering: Issues and future directions. *Journal of Speech and Hearing Research, 35,* 983–993.

Onslow, M. (1996). *Behavioral management of stuttering.* San Diego, CA: Singular Publishing Group.

Onslow, M. (2003). Evidence-based treatment of stuttering: IV. Empowerment through evidence-based treatment practices. *Journal of Fluency Disorders, 28,* 237–245.

Onslow, M. (2004a). The bitter sweet tale of empiricism in stuttering treatment research. In A. Packman, A. Meltzer, & H.F.M Peters (Eds.), *Theory, research and therapy in fluency disorders. Proceedings of the 4th World Congress on Fluency Disorders* (pp. 3–12). Nijmegen: Nijmegen University Press.

Onslow, M. (2004b). Ryan's programmed therapy for stuttering in children and adults. *Journal of Fluency Disorders, 29*, 351–360.

Onslow, M., Andrews, C., & Lincoln, M. (1994). A control/experimental trial of an operant treatment for early stuttering. *Journal of Speech and Hearing Research, 37*, 1244–1259.

Onslow, M., Costa, L., Andrews, C., Harrison, E., & Packman, A. (1996). Speech outcomes of a prolonged speech treatment for stuttering. *Journal of Speech and Hearing Research, 39*, 734–749.

Onslow, M., Costa, L., and Rue, S. (1990). Direct early intervention with stuttering: Some preliminary data. *Journal of Speech and Hearing Disorders, 55*, 405–416.

Onslow, M., Menzies, R., & Packman, A. (2001). The Lidcombe program: Development of a parent conducted operant early intervention for stuttering. *Behaviour Modification, 25*, 116–139.

Onslow, M., & Packman, A. (1999). *The Lidcombe program of early stuttering intervention*. In N. Bernstein-Ratner & E.C. Healey (Eds.), *Stuttering research and practice: Bridging the gap*. Mahwah, NJ: Lawrence Erlbaum Associates, Inc.

Onslow, M., & Packman, A. (2002). Stuttering and lexical retrieval: Inconsistencies between theory and data. *Clinical Linguistics and Phonetics, 16*, 295–298.

Onslow, M., Packman, A., & Harrison, E. (2003). *The Lidcombe program of early stuttering intervention: A clinician's guide*. Austin, TX: Pro-Ed.

Onslow, M., Stocker, S., Packman, A., & McLeod, S. (2002). Speech segment timing in children after the Lidcombe program of early stuttering intervention. *Clinical Linguistics and Phonetics, 16*, 21–33.

Ornstein, A., & Manning, W. (1985). Self-efficacy scaling by adult stutterers. *Journal of Communication Disorders, 18*, 313–320.

Orton, S.T. (1927). Studies in stuttering. *Archives of Neurology and Psychiatry, 18*, 671–672.

Orton, S.T., & Travis, L.E. (1929). Studies in stammering; IV. Studies of action currents in stutterers. *Archives of Neurology and Psychiatry, 21*, 61–68.

O'Shaughnessy, D. (1987). *Speech communication: Man and machine*. New York: Addison Wesley.

Packman, A., & Onslow, M. (1999). Fluency disruption in speech and in wind instrument playing. *Journal of Fluency Disorders, 24*, 293–298.

Packman, A., Onslow, M., Coombes, T., & Goodwin, A. (2001). Stuttering and lexical retrieval. *Clinical Linguistics and Phonetics, 15*, 487–498.

Panelli, C., McFarlane, S., & Shipley, K. (1978). Implications of evaluating and intervening with incipient stutterers. *Journal of Fluency Disorders, 3*, 41–50.

Parker, C.S., & Christopherson, F. (1963). Electric aid in the treatment of stutter. *Medical Electronics and Biological Engineering, 1*, 121–125.

Parry, W.D. (1985). Stuttering and the Valsalva mechanism: A hypothesis in need of investigation. *Journal of Fluency Disorders, 10*, 317–324.

Parry, W.D. (2000). *Understanding and controlling stuttering: A comprehensive new approach based on the Valsalva hypothesis* (2nd ed.). Anaheim Hills, CA: National Stuttering Association.

Parry, W. (2003). *Reducing stuttering blocks by relaxation of the valsalva mechanism*. Paper presented at the 4th World Congress on Fluency Disorders, Montreal, Canada.

Perino, M., Famularo, G., & Taroni, P. (2000). Acquired transient stuttering during a migraine attack. *Headache, 40*, 170–172.

Perkins, W.H. (1973). Replacement of stuttering with normal speech: II. Clinical procedures. *Journal of Speech and Hearing Disorders, 38*, 295–303.

Perkins, W.H., & Curlee, R.F. (1969). Clinical impressions of portable masking unit effects in stuttering. *Journal of Speech and Hearing Disorders, 34*, 360–362.

Perkins, W.H., Kent, R.D., & Curlee, R.F. (1991). A theory of neuropsycholinguistic function in stuttering. *Journal of Speech and Hearing Research, 34*, 734–752.

Peters, H.F.M., & Boves, L. (1988). Coordination of aerodynamic and phonatory processes in fluent speech utterances of stutterers. *Journal of Speech and Hearing Research, 31*, 352–361.

Peters, H.F.M., Hietkamp, R.K., & Boves, L. (1993). Aerodynamic and phonatory processes in dysfluent speech utterences of stutterers. *American Speech and Hearing Association, 35*, 144.

Peters, H.F.M., Hulstijn, W., & Starkweather, C.W. (1989). Acoustic and physiologic reaction times of stutterers and non stutterers. *Journal of Speech and Hearing Research, 32*, 668–680.

Peters, H.F.M., Hulstijn, W., & Van Lieshout, P.H.H.M. (2000). Recent developments in speech motor research into stuttering. *Folia Phoniatrica et Logopaedica, 52*, 103–119.

Peters, H.F.M., & Starkweather, C.W. (1989). Development of stuttering throughout life. *Journal of Fluency Disorders, 14*, 301–321.

Peters, H.F.M., & Starkweather, C.W. (1990). The interaction between speech motor coordination and language processes in the development of stuttering: Hypotheses and suggestions for research. *Journal of Fluency Disorders, 15*, 115–125.

Peters, T., & Guitar, B. (1991). *Stuttering: An integrated approach to its nature and treatment*. Baltimore, MD: Williams and Wilkins.

Pierce, C.M., and Lipcon, H.H. (1959). Clinical and encephalographic findings. *Military Medicine, 12*, 511–519.

Pindzola, R. (1987). *SIP: Stuttering intervention program*. Austin, TX: Pro-Ed.

Poole, K.D., Devous, M.D., Freeman, F.J., Watson, B.C., & Finitzo, T. (1991). Regional cerebral blood flow in developmental stutterers. *Archives of Neurology, 48*, 509–512.

Postma, A. (2000). Detection of errors during speech production: A review of speech monitoring models. *Cognition, 77*, 97–132.

Postma, A., & Kolk, H. (1992). Error monitoring in people who stutter: Evidence against auditory feedback defect theories. *Journal of Speech and Hearing Research, 35*, 1024–1032.

Postma, A., & Kolk, H. (1993). The covert repair hypothesis: Prearticulatory repair process in normal and stuttered disfluencies. *Journal of Speech and Hearing Research, 36*, 472–478.

Poulos, M., & Webster, W. (1991). Family history as a basis for subgrouping people who stutter. *Journal of Speech and Hearing Research, 34*, 5–10.

Preus, A. (1981). *Identifying subgroups of stutterers*. Oslo: Universitetsforlaget.

Preus, A. (1992). Cluttering or stuttering: Related, different or antagonistic disorders. In F.L Myers & K.O. St Louis (Eds.), *Cluttering: A clinical perspective*. Kibworth: Far Communications.

Prins, D., & Hubbard, C. (1990). Consistency of interstress intervals in the fluent speech of people who stutter during adaptation trials. *Journal of Speech and Hearing Research, 25*, 799–804.

Proctor A., Duff, M., & Yairi, E. (2002). Early childhood stuttering: African Americans and European Americans. *ASHA Leader, 4*, 15, 102.

Proctor, H., & Walker, G. (1987). Brief therapy. In E. Street (Ed.), *Family therapy in Britain*. New York: Harper and Row.

Prosek, R.A., Montgomery, A., Walden, V.E., & Schwartz, D.M. (1979). Reaction time measures of stutterers and nonstutterers. *Journal of Fluency Disorders, 4*, 269–279.

Quarrington, B. (1965). Stuttering as a function of the information value and sentence position of words. *Journal of Abnormal Psychology, 70*, 221–224.

Quarrington, B., Conway, J., & Siegel, N. (1962). An experimental study of some properties of stuttered words. *Journal of Speech and Hearing Research, 5*, 387–394.

Quesal, R.W., Yaruss, J.S., & Molt, L. (2004). Many types of data: Stuttering treatment outcomes beyond fluency. In A. Packman, A. Meltzer, & H.F.M Peters (Eds.), *Theory, research and therapy in fluency disorders. Proceedings of the 4th World Congress on Fluency Disorders* (pp. 218–224). Nijmegen: Nijmegen University Press.

Quinn, P.T. (1972). Stuttering – cerebral dominance and dichotic word test. *Medical Journal of Australia, 2*, 639–642.

Quist, R., & Martin, R. (1967). The effect of response contingent verbal punishment on stuttering. *Journal of Speech and Hearing Research, 10*, 795–800.

Ramig, P.R. (1993). High reported spontaneous stuttering recovery rates: Fact or fiction? *Language, Speech, and Hearing Services in Schools, 24*, 156–160.

Ramig, P., & Bennett, E.M. (1997). Clinical management of children: Direct management strategies. In R.F. Curlee & G.M. Siegel (Eds.), *Nature and treatment of stuttering: New directions* (2nd ed.). Boston: Allyn and Bacon.

Rastatter, M.P., Stuart, A., & Kalinowski, J. (1998). Quantitive electroencephalogram of posterior cortical areas of fluent and stuttering participants during reading with normal and altered auditory feedback. *Perceptual Motor Skills, 87*, 623–633.

Records, M.A., Heimbuch, R.C., & Kidd, J.R. (1977). Handedness and stuttering: A dead horse? *Journal of Fluency Disorders, 2*, 271–282.

Reilly, S. Dougles, J., & Oates, J. (Eds.) (2004). *Evidence-based practice in speech pathology*. London: Whurr.

Renfrew, C.E. (1988). *Word Finding Vocabulary Scale*. Oxford: Renfrew.

Riaz, N., Steinberg, S., Ahmad, J., Pluzhnikov, A., Riazuddin, S., Cox, C., et al. (2005). Genomewide significant linkage to stuttering on chromosome 12. *American Journal of Human Genetics, 76*, 647–651.

Riley, G.D. (1972). A stuttering severity instrument for children and adults. *Journal of Speech and Hearing Disorders, 37*, 314–322.

Riley, G.D. (1994). *Stuttering severity instrument for children and adults* (3rd ed.). Austin, TX: Pro-Ed.

Riley, G.D., & Ingham, J.C. (2000). Acoustic duration changes associated with two types of treatment for children who stutter. *Journal of Speech Language, and Hearing Research, 43*, 965–978.

Riley, G., & Riley, J. (1986). *Oral motor assessment and treatment: Improving syllable production*. Austin, TX: Pro-Ed.

Riley, G.D., Wu, J.C., & Maguire, G. (1997). PET scan evidence of parallel cerebral systems related to treatment effects. In W. Hulstijn, H.F.M. Peters, & P.H.H.M. Van Lieshout (Eds.), *Speech production: Motor control, brain research and fluency disorders* (pp. 321–327). Amsterdam: Elsevier.

Ringel, R.L., & Steer, M.D. (1963). Some effects of tactile and auditory alterations on speech output. *Journal of Speech and Hearing Research, 6*, 369–378.

Ringo, C.C., & Dietrich, S. (1995). Neurogenic stuttering: An analysis and critique. *Journal of Medical Speech Language Pathology, 3*, 111–122.

Robb, M., & Blomgren, M. (1997). Analysis of F2 transitions in the speech of stutterers and nonstutterers. *Journal of Fluency Disorders, 21*, 1–16.

Rogers, C. (1951). *Client centered therapy*. Boston: Houghton-Mifflin.

Rommel, D. (2001). The influence of psycholinguistic variables on stuttering in childhood. In H.G. Bosshard, J.S. Yaruss, & H.F.M. Peters (Eds.), *Fluency disorders: Theory, research, treatment and self-help. Proceedings of the 3rd World Congress on Fluency Disorders*. Nijmegen: Nijmegen University Press.

Rommel, D. (2004). The influence of syntactic variables on the development of stuttering. In A. Packman, A. Meltzer, & H.F.M Peters (Eds.), *Theory, research and therapy in fluency disorders. Proceedings of the 4th World Congress on Fluency Disorders* (pp. 406–414). Nijmegen: Nijmegen University Press.

Rosenfield, D.B., & Goodglass, H. (1980). Dichotic testing of cerebral dominance in stutterers. *Brain and Language, 11*, 170–180.

Rosenfield, D.B., & Jerger, J. (1984). Stuttering and auditory function. In R.Curlee & W.H. Perkins (Eds.), *The nature and treatment of stuttering: New directions* (pp. 73–88). San Diego, CA: College Hill Press.

Rosenthal, W.S. (2004). Tracking the progress of stuttering treatment using subjective parent ratings. In A. Packman, A. Meltzer, & H.F.M Peters (Eds.), *Theory, research and therapy in fluency disorders. Proceedings of the 4th World Congress on Fluency Disorders* (pp. 225–231). Nijmegen: Nijmegen University Press.

Roth, C.R., Aronson, A.E., & Davis, L.J., Jr. (1989). Clinical studies in psychogenic stuttering of adult onset. *Journal of Speech and Hearing Disorders, 54*, 634–646.

Rousseau, I., Onslow, M., & Packman, A. (2005, June). *The Lidcombe program with school-age stuttering children*. Paper presented at the 7th Oxford Dysfluency Conference, Oxford.

Rustin, L. (1987). *Assessment and therapy program for dysfluent children*. Windsor: NFER-Nelson.

Rustin, L. (1991). *Parents, families and the stuttering child*. London: Whurr.

Rustin, L., Botterill, W., & Kelman, E. (1996). *Assessment and therapy for young dysfluent children*. London: Whurr.

Rustin, L., & Cook, F. (1995). Parental involvement in the treatment of stuttering. *Language, Speech and Hearing Services in Schools, 26*, 138–150.

Rustin, L., & Cook, F. (1997). Commentary on the Lidcombe programme of stuttering intervention. *European Journal of Disorders of Communication, 32*, 250–258.

Rustin, L., Cook, F., Botterill, W., Hughes, C., & Kelman, E. (2001). *Stuttering: A practical guide for teachers and other professionals*. London: David Fulton.

Rustin, L., Cook, F., & Spence, R. (1995). *The management of stuttering in adolescence: A communication skills approach*. London: Whurr.

Ryan, B.P. (1974). *Programmed stuttering therapy for children and adults*. Springfield, IL: Charles C. Thomas.

Ryan, B.P. (1984). Treatment of stuttering in school children. In W.H. Perkins (Ed.), *Stuttering disorders* (pp. 95–105). New York: Thieme-Stratton.

Ryan, B.P. (1990). *Development of stuttering, a longitudinal study: Report 4*. Paper presented at the American Speech-Language Hearing Association Convention, Seattle.

Ryan, B.P. (2001). *Programmed stuttering therapy for children and adults* (2nd ed.). Springfield, IL: Charles C. Thomas.

Ryan, B.P., & Van Kirk, B. (1974). The establishment, transfer and maintenance of fluent speech in 50 stutterers using delayed auditory feedback and operant procedures. *Journal of Speech and Hearing Disorders, 39*, 3–10.

Ryan, B.P., & Van Kirk, B. (1995). Programmed stuttering treatment for children: Comparison of two establishment programs through transfer, maintenance and follow-up. *Journal of Speech and Hearing Research, 38*, 61–75.

Salihovic N., & Sinanovic, O. (2000). Stuttering and lefthandedness. *Medical Archives, 54*, 173–175.

Salmelin, R., Schnitzler, A., Schmitz, F., Jäncke, L., Witte, O., & Freund, H.-J. (1998). Functional organization of the auditory cortex is different in stutterers and fluent speakers. *Neuroreport, 9*, 2225–2229.

Schiavetti, N., & Metz, D. (1996). *Evaluating speech research in speech pathology and audilology* (3rd ed.). Boston: Allyn and Bacon.

Schneier, F.R., Wexler, K.B., & Liebowitz, M. R. (1997). Social phobia and stuttering. *American Journal of Psychiatry, 154*, 131–132.

Siegel, G.M. (2000). Demands and capacities or demands and performance? *Journal of Fluency Disorders, 25*, 321–327.

Selkirk, E. (1984). *Phonology and syntax: The relation between sound and structure.* Cambridge, MA: MIT Press.

Shahed, J., & Jankovic, J. (2001). Re-emergence of childhood stammering in Parkinson's disease: A hypothesis. *Movement Disorders, 16*, 114–118.

Shames, G.H. & Florence, C.L. (1980). *Stutter-free speech: A goal for therapy.* Columbus, OH: Charles E. Merrill.

Shames, G.H., & Sherrick, C.E. (1963). Discussion of nonfluency and stuttering as operant behaviour. *Journal of Speech and Hearing Disorders, 28*, 3–18.

Shapiro, A. (1980). An electromyographic analysis of the fluent and dysfluent utterences of several types of stutterers. *Journal of Fluency Disorders, 5*, 203–231.

Shaywitz, B.A., Shaywitz, S.E., Pugh, K.R., Constable, R.T., Skularsky, P., Fulbright, R.K., et al. (1995). Sex differences in the functional organization of the brain for language. *Nature, 373*, 607–609.

Shearer, W., & Simmons, F. (1965). Middle ear activity during speech in normal speakers and stutterers. *Journal of Speech and Hearing Research, 8*, 203–237.

Sheehan, J.G. (1953). Theory and treatment of stuttering as an approach avoidance conflict. *Journal of Psychology, 36*, 27–49.

Sheehan, J.G. (1954). An integration of psychotherapy, and speech therapy through a conflict theory of stuttering. *Journal of Speech and Hearing Disorders, 19*, 474–482.

Sheehan, J.G. (1958). Projective studies of stuttering. *Journal of Speech and Hearing Disorders, 23*, 18–25.

Sheehan, J. (1970). *Stuttering: Research and therapy.* New York: Harper and Row.

Sheehan, J.G. (1975). Conflict theory and avoidance-reduction therapy. In J. Eisenson (Ed.), *Stuttering: A symposium.* New York: Harper and Row.

Sheehan, J.G. (1984). Problems in the evaluation of progress and outcome. In W.H. Perkins (Ed.), *Stuttering disorders.* New York: Thieme-Stratton.

Sheehan, J.G. (1986). Theory and treatment of stuttering as an approach-avoidance conflict. In G.H. Shames & H. Rubin (Eds.), *Stuttering then and now*. Ohio: Charles E. Merrill.

Sheehan, J.G., & Martyn, M.M. (1966). Spontaneous recovery from stuttering. *Journal of Speech and Hearing Research, 9*, 121–135.

Sheehan, J.G., & Sheehan, V.M. (1984). Avoidance-reduction therapy: A response suppression hypothesis. In W.H. Perkins (Ed.), *Stuttering disorders*. New York: Thieme-Stratton.

Shine, R. (1980). Direct management of the beginning stutterer. *Seminars in Speech, Language, and Hearing, 1*, 339–350.

Shine, R. (1988). *Systematic fluency training for young children* (3rd ed.). Austin, TX: Pro-Ed.

Shockey, L. (2004). *Sound patterns of spoken English*. Oxford: Blackwell.

Siegel, G.M. (2000). Demands and capacities or demands and performance? *Journal of Fluency Disorders, 25*, 321–327.

Silverman, E.-M. (1972). Generality of disfluency data gathered from preschoolers. *Journal of Speech and Hearing Research, 7*, 381–388.

Skinner, B.F. (1957). *Verbal behavior*. Englewood Cliffs: Prentice-Hall.

Slorach, N., & Noehr, B. (1973). Dichotic listening in stuttering and dyslalic children. *Cortex, 9*, 295–300.

Smith, A., Denny, M., Shafer, L. & Kelly, E.M. (1996). Activity of intrinsic laryngeal muscles in fluent and disfluent speech. *Journal of Speech, Language and Hearing Research 39*, 329–348.

Smith, A., & Goffman, L. (2004). Stability and pattering of speech movement sequences in children and adults. In B. Maassen, R.D. Kent, H.F.M. Peters, P.H.H.M. van Lieshout, & W. Hulstijn (Eds.), *Speech motor control in normal and disordered speech* (pp. 227–252). Oxford: Oxford University Press.

Smith, A., Goffman, L., Zelaznik, H., Ying, G., & McGillem, C. (1995). Spatiotemporal stability and patterning of speech movements. *Experimental Brain Research, 104*, 493–501.

Smith, A., Johnson, M., McGillem, C., & Goffman, L. (2000). On the assessment of stability and patterning of speech movements. *Journal of Speech Language, and Hearing Research, 43*, 277–286.

Smith, A., & Kelly, E. (1997). Stuttering: A multifactorial dynamic model. In R.F. Curlee & G.M. Siegel (Eds.), *Nature and treatment of stuttering: New directions* (pp. 204–217). Mahwah, NJ: Lawrence Erlbaum Associates, Inc.

Smith, A., & Kleinow, J. (2000). Influences of length and syntactic complexity on the speech motor stability of adults who stutter. *Journal of Speech Language, and Hearing Research, 43*, 513–520.

Soderberg, G.A. (1966). The relations of stuttering to word length and word frequency. *Journal of Speech and Hearing Research, 9*, 585–589.

Soderberg, G.A. (1967). Relations of word information and word length to stuttering disfluencies. *Journal of Communication Disorders, 4*, 9–14.

Soderberg, G.A. (1969). Delayed auditory feedback and the speech of stutterers: A review of studies. *Journal of Speech and Hearing Disorders, 33*, 3–10.

Sommer, M., Koch, M.A., Paulus, W., Weiller, C., & Büchel, C. (2002). Disconnection of speech-relevant brain areas in persistent developmental stuttering. *The Lancet, 360*, 380–383.

Sommers, R.K., Brady, W.A., & Moore, W.R. (1975). Dichotic ear preference of stuttering children and adults. *Perceptual and Motor Skills, 41*, 931–938.

Soroker, N., Bar-Israel, Y., Schechter, I., & Solzi, P. (1990). Stuttering as a manifestation of right hemisphere subcortical stroke. *European Neurology, 30*, 268–270.

Spadino, E.J. (1941). *Writing and laterality characteristics of stuttering children.* New York: Columbia University Press.

Sparks, G., Grant, D.E., Millay, K., Walker-Batson, D., & Hynan, L.S. (2002). The effect of fast speech on stuttering frequency during delayed auditory feedback. *Journal of Fluency Disorders, 27*, 183–201.

Stager, S.V., Calis, K., Grothe, D., Bloch, M., Berensen, N., Smith, P., et al. (2005). Treatment with medications affecting dopaminergic and serotonergic mechanisms: Effects on fluency and anxiety in persons who stutter. *Journal of Fluency Disorders, 30*, 319–335.

Stager, S.V., Denman, D.W., & Ludlow, C.L. (1997). Modifications in aerodynamic variables by persons who stutter under fluency-evoking conditions. *Journal of Speech Language, and Hearing Research, 40*, 832–847.

Stager, S.V., & Ludlow, C.L. (1994). Responses of stutterers and vocal tremor patients to treatment with botulinum toxin. In J. Jankovic & M. Hallett (Eds.), *Therapy with botulinum toxin* (pp. 481–490). New York: Marcel Dekker.

Starkweather, C.W. (1985). The development of fluency in normal children. In H.H. Gregory (Ed.), *Stuttering therapy: Prevention and intervention with children* (pp. 9–42). Memphis: Speech Foundation of America.

Starkweather, C.W. (1987). *Fluency and stuttering.* Englewood Cliffs, NJ: Prentice-Hall.

Starkweather, C.W. (1997). Therapy for younger children. In R.F. Curlee & G.M. Siegel (Eds.), *Nature and treatment of stuttering: New directions* (2nd ed., pp. 259–279). Boston: Allyn and Bacon.

Starkweather, C.W. (1999). The effectiveness of stuttering therapy. In N. Bernstein-Ratner and E.C. Healey (Eds.), *Stuttering research and practice: Bridging the gap.* Mahwah, NJ: Lawrence Erlbaum Associates, Inc.

Starkweather, C.W., & Gottwald, S.R. (1990). The demands and capacities model II: Clinical application. *Journal of Fluency Disorders, 15*, 143–157.

Starkweather, C.W., & Gottwald, S.R. (1993). A pilot study of relations among specific measures obtained at intake and discharge in a program of prevention and early intervention for stuttering. *American Journal of Speech-Language Pathology, 2*, 51–58.

Starkweather, C.W., & Gottwald, S.R. (2000). The demands and capacities model: Response to Siegel. *Journal of Fluency Disorders, 25*, 369–375.

Starkweather, C.W., Gottwald, S.R., & Halfond, M.H. (1990). *Stuttering prevention: A clinical method.* Englewood Cliffs, NJ: Prentice-Hall.

Starkweather, C.W., Hirschmann, P., & Tannenbaum, R. (1976). Latency of vocalization onset: Stutterers versus nonstutterers. *Journal of Speech and Hearing Research, 19*, 181–192.

Starkweather, C.W., & Myers, N. (1978). *The intervocalic interval in stutterers and nonstutterers: A close analysis.* Paper presented at the Annual Meeting of the American Speech and Language Association.

Stevens, M.M. (1963). *The effect of positive and negative reinforcement on specific disfluency responses of normal speaking college males.* Unpublished doctoral dissertation, State University of Iowa.

Stewart, J.L (1960). The problem of stuttering in certain North American Indian societies. *Journal of Speech and Hearing Disorders, monograph supplement, 6*, entire issue.

Stewart, T., & Richardson, A. (2004). A qualitative study of therapeutic effect from a user's perspective. *Journal of Fluency Disorders, 29*, 95–108.

Stewart, T., & Turnbull, J. (1995). *Working with dysfluent children*. Bicester: Winslow Press.

St Louis, K.O. (1992). On defining cluttering. In F.L. Myers & K.O. St Louis (Eds.), *Cluttering: A clinical perspective*. Kibworth: Far Communications.

St Louis, K.O. (1998). Linguistic and motor aspects of cluttering symptoms. In E.C. Healey & H.F.M. Peters (Eds.), *Proceedings of the 2nd World Congress on Fluency Disorders* (pp. 40–43). Nijmegen: Nijmegen University Press.

St Louis, K.O., & Hinzman, A.R. (1988). A descriptive study of speech, language, and hearing characteristics of school age stutterers. *Journal of Fluency Disorders, 13*, 331–356.

St Louis, K.O., Hinzman, A.R., & Hull, F.M. (1985). Studies of cluttering: Disfluency and language measures in young possible clutterers and stutterers. *Journal of Fluency Disorders, 10*, 151–172.

St Louis, K.O., & Myers, F.L. (1997). Management of cluttering and related fluency disorders. In R.F. Curlee & G.M. Siegal (Eds.), *Nature and treatment of stuttering: New directions* (pp. 312–332). Boston: Allyn and Bacon.

St Louis, K.O., Myers, F.L., Cassidy, L.J., Michael, A.J., Penrod, S.M., Litton, B.A., et al. (1996). Efficacy of delayed auditory feedback for treating cluttering: Two case studies. *Journal of Fluency Disorders, 21*, 305–314.

St Louis, K.O., Myers, F.L., Faragasso, K., Townsend, P.S., & Gallaher, A.J. (2004). Perceptual aspects of cluttered speech. *Journal of Fluency Disorders, 29*, 213–235.

St Louis, K.O., Raphael, L.J., Myers, F.L., & Bakker, K. (2003). Cluttering updated. *ASHA Leader, 18*, 4–5, 20–21.

Streifler, M., & Gumpertz, F. (1955). Cerebral potentials in stuttering and cluttering. *Confinia Neurologica, 15*, 344–359.

Stromstra, C. (1957). A methodology related to the determinations of the phase angle of bone-conducted speech sound energy of stutterers and nonstutterers. *Speech Monographs, 24*, 147–148.

Stromstra, C. (1972). Interaural phase disparity of stutterers and nonstutterers. *Journal of Speech and Hearing Research, 15*, 771–780.

Stuart, A., & Kalinowski, J. (1996). Fluent speech, fast articulatory rate, and delayed auditory feedback: Creating a crisis for a scientific revolution. *Perceptual Motor Skills, 82*, 211–218.

Stuart, A., & Kalinowski, J. (2004). The perception of speech naturalness of post-therapeutic and altered auditory feedback speech of adults with mild and severe stuttering. *Folia Phoniatrica et Logopaedica, 56*, 347–357.

Stuart, A., Kalinowski, J., Armson, J., Stenstrom, R., & Jones, K. (1996). Fluency effect of frequency alterations of plus/minus one half and one quarter octave shift in auditory feedback of people who stutter. *Journal of Speech Language, and Hearing Research, 39*, 396–401.

Stuart, A., Kalinowski, J., & Rastatter, M.P. (1997). Effect of monaural and binaural altered feedback on stuttering frequency. *Journal of the Acoustical Society of America, 101*, 3806–3809.

Stuart, A., Kalinowski, J., Rastatter, M.P., & Lynch, K. (2002). Effect of delayed auditory feedback on normal speakers at two speech rates. *Journal of the Acoustical Society of America, 111*, 2237–2241.

Subirana, A. (1964). The relationship between handedness and language function. *International Journal of Neurology, 4*, 215–234.

Subramanian, A., Yairi, E., & Amir, O. (2003). Second formant transitions in the fluent speech of persistent and recovered preschool children who stutter. *Journal of Communication Disorders, 36*, 189–208.

Supprian, T., Retz, W., & Deckert, J. (1999). Clozapine-induced stuttering: Epileptic brain activity? *American Journal of Psychiatry, 156*, 1663–1664.

Sussman, H.M., & MacNeilage, P.F. (1975). Hemispheric specialization for speech production and perception in stutterers. *Neuropsychologia, 13*, 19–27.

Taylor, I.K. (1966). The properties of stuttered words. *Journal of Verbal Learning and Behaviour, 5*, 112–118.

Teigland, A. (1996). A study of pragmatic skills of clutterers and normal speakers. *Journal of Fluency Disorders, 21*, 201–214.

Thacker, R.C., & De Nil, L.F. (1996). Neurogenic cluttering. *Journal of Fluency Disorders, 21*, 227–238.

Thomas, C., & Howell, P. (2001). Assessing efficacy in stuttering treatments. *Journal of Fluency Disorders, 26*, 311–333.

Throneburg, R., and Yairi, E. (1994). Temporal dynamics of repetitions during the early stage of childhood stuttering. *Journal of Speech and Hearing Research, 37*, 1067–1075.

Timmons, R.J. (1966). *A study of adaptation and consistency in a response-contingent punishment situation*. Unpublished doctoral dissertation, University of Kansas.

Travis, L.E. (1928). A comparative study of the performances of stutterers and normal speakers in mirror tracing. *Psychological Monographs, 39*, 45–51.

Travis, L.E. (1931). *Speech pathology*. Englewood Cliffs, NJ: Prentice-Hall.

Travis, L.E., & Herren, R.Y. (1929). Studies in stuttering: V. A study of simultaneous antitropic movements of the hands of stutterers. *Archives of Neurology and Psychiatry, 22*, 487–494.

Travis, L.E., & Knott, J.R. (1936). Brain potentials from normal speakers and stutterers. *Journal of Psychology, 2*, 137–150.

Trotter, W.D. (1959). Relationship between severity of stuttering and word conspicuousness. *Journal of Speech and Hearing Disorders, 21*, 198–201.

Tudor, M. (1939). *An experimental study of the effect of evaluative labeling on speech fluency*. Unpublished Masters' thesis, University of Iowa, Iowa City.

Turnbull, J., & Stewart, T. (1999). *The dysfluency resource book*. Bicester: Winslow Press.

Van Borsel, J., Beck, C., & Delanghe, J. (2003). *Stuttering and medication: A look at the symptoms*. Paper presented at the 4th World Congress on Fluency Disorders, Montreal, Canada.

Van Borsel, J., Goethals, L., & Vanryckeghem, M. (2003). *Dysfluency in Tourette syndrome*. Paper presented at the 4th World Congress on Fluency Disorders, Montreal, Canada.

Van Borsel, J., Reunes, G., & Van den Bergh, N. (2003). Delayed auditory feedback in the treatment of stuttering: Clients as consumers. *International Journal of Language and Communication Disorders, 38*, 119–129.

Van Borsel, J., & Taillieu, C. (2001). Neurogenic stuttering versus developmental stuttering: An observer judgement study. *Journal of Communication Disorders, 34*, 1–11.

Van Borsel, J., Van Lierde, K., Van Cauwenberge, P., Guldemont, I., & Van Orshoven,

M. (1998). Severe acquired stuttering following injury of the left supplementary motor region: A case report. *Journal of Fluency Disorders, 23*, 49–58.

Van Borsel, J., & Vanryckeghem, M. (2000). Dysfluency and phonic tics in Tourette syndrome: A case report. *Journal of Communication Disorders, 33*, 227–240.

Van Lieshout, P.H.H.M. (1996). From planning to articulation in speech production: What differentiates a person who stutters from a person who does not stutter? *Journal of Speech, Language, and Hearing Research, 39*, 546–564.

Van Lieshout, P.H.H.M. (1997). Higher and lower order influences on the stability of the dynamic coupling between articulators. In H.F.M. Peters, W. Hulstijn, & P.H.H.M. Van Lieshout (Eds.), *Speech production: Motor control and fluency disorders* (pp. 161–170). Amsterdam: Elsevier.

Van Lieshout, P.H.H.M. (1998). Linguistic and motor determinants of speech fluency. In E.C. Healey & H.F.M. Peters (Eds.), *Proceedings of the 2nd World Congress on Fluency Disorders* (pp. 15–23). Nijmegen: Nijmegen University Press.

Van Lieshout, P.H.H.M., Hulstijn, W., & Peters, H.F.M. (2004). Searching for the weak link in the speech production chain of people who stutter: A motor skill approach. *Journal of Fluency Disorders, 25*, 337–346.

Van Lieshout, P.H.H.M., Rutjens, C.A.W., & Spauwen, P.H.M. (2002). The dynamics of interlip coupling in speakers with a repaired unilateral cleft-lip history. *Journal of Speech Language and Hearing Research, 45*, 5–19.

Van Riper, C. (1935). The quantitive measurement of laterality. *Journal of Experimental Psychology, 17*, 327–332.

Van Riper, C. (1937). The growth of the stuttering spasm. *Quarterly Journal of Speech, 23*, 70–73.

Van Riper, C. (1965). Clinical use of intermittent masking noise in stuttering therapy. *American Speech and Language Association, 6*, 381.

Van Riper, C. (1971). *The nature of stuttering*. Englewood Cliffs, NJ: Prentice Hall.

Van Riper, C. (1973). *The treatment of stuttering*. Englewood Cliffs, NJ: Prentice-Hall.

Van Riper, C. (1982). *The nature of stuttering*. Englewood Cliffs, NJ: Prentice-Hall.

Van Riper, C. (1992). Foreword. In F.L. Myers & K.O. St Louis (Eds.), *Cluttering: A clinical perspective*. Kibworth: Far Communications.

Vanryckeghem, M., Brutten, G., & Hernandez, L.M. (2005). A comparative investigation of the speech-associated attitude of preschool and kindergarten children who do and do not stutter. *Journal of Fluency Disorders, 30*, 307–318.

Vanryckeghem, M., Hernandez, L.M., & Brutten, G. (2001). The KiddyCAT: A measure of speech-associated attitudes of preschoolers. *ASHA Leader, 6*, 136.

Venkatagiri, H. (1981). Reaction time for voiced and whispered /a/ in stutterers and nonstutterers. *Journal of Fluency Disorders, 6*, 265–271.

Venkatagiri, H. (2005). Recent advances in the treatment of stuttering: A theoretical perspective. *Journal of Communication Disorders, 38*, 375–393.

Viswanath, N.S., & Rosenfield, D.B. (2000). Preponderance of lead voice onset time in stutterers under varying constraints. *Communication Disorders Quarterly, 22*, 49–55.

Wada, J. (1949). A new method for the determination of the side of cerebral dominance: A preliminary report on the intercaratoid injection of sodium amytal in man. *Medical Biology, 14*, 221–222.

Wada, J., Clarke, R., & Hamm, A. (1975). Cerebral asymmetry in humans. *Archives of Neurology, 32*, 239–246.

Wada, J., & Rasmussen, T. (1960). Intracarotid injection of sodium amytal for the lateralizarion of cerebral speech dominance: Experimental and clinical observations. *Journal of Neurology and Neurosurgery, 17*, 266–282.

Wall, M.J. (1977). *The location of stuttering in the spontaneous speech of young child stutterers.* Unpublished doctoral dissertation, City University of New York.

Wall, M.J. (1980). A comparison of syntax in young stutterers and nonstutterers. *Journal of Fluency Disorders, 5*, 345–352.

Wall, M.J. (1995). *Clinical management of childhood stuttering* (2nd ed.). Austin, TX: Pro-Ed.

Wall, M.J., & Myers, F.L. (1995). *Clinical management of childhood stuttering* (2nd ed.). Austin, TX: Pro-Ed.

Ward, D. (1990). Voice onset time and electroglottographic dynamics in stutterers' speech: Implications for a differential diagnosis. *British Journal of Disorders of Communication, 25*, 93–104.

Ward, D. (1992). Outlining semi-intensive fluency therapy. *Journal of Fluency Disorders, 17*, 243–255.

Ward, D. (1997a). Intrinsic and extrinsic timing in stutterers' speech: Data and implications. *Language and Speech, 40*, 289–310.

Ward, D. (1997b). Stuttering and articulator sequencing: Intrinsic and extrinsic timing perspectives. In H.F.M. Peters, W. Hulstijn, & P.H.H.M. Van Lieshout (Eds.), *Speech production: Motor control and fluency disorders* (pp. 171–176). Amsterdam: Elsevier.

Ward, D. (2002). WASSP: Wright and Ayre stuttering self-rating profile review. *International Journal of Language and Communication Disorders, 37*, 493–495.

Ward, D. (2004). Cluttering, speech rate and linguistic deficit: A case report. In A. Packman, A. Meltzer, & H.F.M Peters (Eds.), *Theory, research and therapy in fluency disorders. Proceedings of the 4th World Congress on Fluency Disorders* (pp. 511–516). Nijmegen: Nijmegen University Press.

Ward, D., & Arnfield, S.A. (2001). Linear and nonlinear analysis of the stability of gestural organization in speech movement sequences. *Journal of Speech Language, and Hearing Research, 44*, 108–117.

Ward, D., & Dicker, P. (1998). *The motoric, linguistic and psychological effects of block modification therapy.* Paper presented at the bi-annual meeting of the Royal College of the Speech and Language Therapists, Liverpool.

Ward, D., & Wardman, N. (2005, July). *Acquired stuttering subsequent to Parkinson's disease and levadopa therapy in a person with developmental stuttering.* Paper presented at the 7th Oxford Dysfluency Conference, Oxford.

Watanabe, E., et al. (1996). Non-invasive functional mapping with multi-channel near infra-red spectroscopic topography in humans. *Neuroscience Letters, 16*, 41–44.

Watkins, R.V., Yairi, E., & Ambrose, N.G (1999). Early childhood stuttering III: Initial status of expressive language abilities. *Journal of Speech, Hearing, and Language, Research, 42*, 1125–1135.

Watson, B., & Alfonso, P. (1982). A comparison of LR and VOT values between stutterers and nonstutterers. *Journal of Fluency Disorders, 7*, 219–241.

Watson, B.C., & Freeman, F.J. (1997). Brain imaging contributions. In R.F.Curlee & G.M. Siegel (Eds.), *Nature and treatment of stuttering: New directions* (pp. 143–166). Boston: Allyn and Bacon.

Watson, B.C., Freeman, F.J., Devous, M.D., Chapman, S.B., Finitzo, T., & Pool, K.D. (1994). Linguistic performance and regional cerebral blood flow related to acoustic laryngeal reaction time in adult developmental stutterers. *Journal of Speech Language, and Hearing Research, 27*, 1221–1228.

Weber-Fox, C., Spencer, R.M.C., Spruill, J.E., & Smith, A. (2004). Phonologic processing in adults who stutter: Electrophysiological and behavioral evidence. *Journal of Speech, Language, and Hearing Research, 47*, 1244–1258.

Webster, R.L. (1979). Empirical considerations about stuttering therapy. In H. H. Gregory (Ed.), *Controversies about stuttering therapy*. Baltimore: University Park Press.

Webster, R.L. (1980). Evolution of a target based behavioral therapy for stuttering. *Journal of Fluency Disorders, 5*, 303–320.

Webster, R.L., & Lubker, B.B. (1968). Interrelationships among fluency producing variables in stuttered speech. *Journal of Speech and Hearing Research, 11*, 754–766.

Webster, W.G. (1985). Neuropsychological models of stuttering – 1. Representation of sequential response mechanisms. *Neuropsychologia, 23*, 263–267.

Webster, W.G. (1986). Response sequence organization and reproduction in stutterers. *Neuropsychologia, 24*, 813–821.

Webster, W.G. (1988). Neural mechanisms underlying stuttering. Evidence from bi-manual handwriting. *Brain and Language, 33*, 226–244.

Webster, W.G. (1989a). Sequence reproduction deficits in stutterers tested under nonspeeded response conditions. *Journal of Fluency Disorders, 14*, 79–86.

Webster, W.G. (1989b). Sequence initiation by stutterers under conditions of response competition. *Brain and Language, 36*, 286–300.

Webster, W.G. (1990). Evidence in bi-manual finger tapping of an attentional component to stuttering. *Behavioural and Brain Research, 37*, 93–100.

Webster, W.G. (1997). Principles of human brain organization related to lateralization of language and speech motor functions in normal speakers and stutterers. In W. Hulstijn, H.F.M. Peters, & P.H.H.M. Van Lieshout (Eds.), *Speech production: Motor control, brain research and fluency disorders* (pp. 119–139). Amsterdam: Elsevier.

Weiss, D. (1964). *Cluttering*. Englewood Cliffs, NJ: Prentice-Hall.

Weiss, D. (1967). Similarities and differences between cluttering and stuttering. *Folia Phoniatrica, 19*, 98–104.

Weiss, D., & Zebrowski, P. (1992). Disfluencies in the conversations of young children who stutter: Some answers to questions. *Journal of Speech and Hearing Research, 35*, 1230–1238.

Westby, C.E. (1974). Language performance of stuttering and nonstuttering children. *Journal of Communication Disorders, 12*, 133–145.

Wexler, K.B., & Mysak, E.D. (1982). Disfluency characteristcs of 2–4 and 6 year old males. *Journal of Fluency Disorders, 7*, 37–46.

Wiig, E., Secord, W., & Semel, E. (2000). *Clinical evaluation of language fundamentals (pre-school)* (3rd ed.). London: Psychological Cooperation.

Wiig, E.H., & Semel, E. (1984). *Language assessment and intervention for the learning disabled* (2nd ed.). Colombus, OH: Charles E. Merrill.

Williams, D.E. (1971). Stuttering therapy for children. In L.E. Travis (Ed.), *Handbook of speech pathology* (pp. 1073–1094). New York: Appleton-Century-Crofts.

Williams, D.E. (1978). The problem of stuttering. In F. Darley & D. Spriesterbach (Eds.), *Diagnostic measures in speech pathology* (pp. 284–321). New York: Harper and Row.

Williams, D.E. (1979). A perspective on approaches to stuttering therapy. In H.H. Gregory (Ed.), *Controveries about stuttering therapy*. Baltimore: University Park Press.

Williams, D.E., & Dugan, P. (2002). Administering stuttering modification therapy in school settings. *Seminars in Speech and Language, 23*, 187–194.

Williams, D.E., & Kent, L. (1958). Listeners' evaluations of speech interruptions. *Journal of Speech and Hearing Research, 1*, 124–136.

Wingate, M.E. (1964). A standard definition of stuttering. *Journal of Speech and Hearing Disorders, 29*, 484–489.

Wingate, M.E. (1969). Sound and pattern in "artificial" fluency. *Journal of Speech and Hearing Research, 12*, 677–686.

Wingate, M.E. (1970). Effect on stuttering of changes of audition. *Journal of Speech and Hearing Research, 13*, 861–873.

Wingate, M.E. (1976). *Stuttering: Theory and treatment*. New York: Irvington.

Wingate, M.E. (1979). The first three words. *Journal of Speech and Hearing Research, 22*, 604–612.

Wingate, M.E. (1984). Stuttering events and linguistic stress. *Journal of Fluency Disorders, 9*, 295–300.

Wingate, M.E. (1988). *The structure of stuttering: A psycholinguistic analysis*. New York: Springer-Verlag.

Wingate, M.E. (2002). *Foundations of stuttering*. San Diego, CA: Academic Press.

Witelson, A., & Pallie, W. (1973). Left hemisphere specialization for language in the newborn: Neurological evidence of asymmetry. *Brain, 96*, 641–646.

Wohl, M.T. (1970). The treatment of non-fluent utterances: A behavioural approach. *British Journal of Disorders of Communication, 5*, 66–76.

Wolk, L., Edwards, M.L., & Conture, E.G. (1993). Coexistence of stuttering and disordered phonology. *Journal of Speech and Hearing Research, 36*, 900–917.

Wood, F., Stump, D., McKeehan, A., Sheldon, S., & Proctor, J. (1980). Patterns of regional cerebral blood flow during attempted reading aloud by stutterers both on and off haloperidol medication: Evidence for inadequate left frontal activation during stuttering. *Brain and Language, 9*, 141–144.

Woolfe, G. (1967). The assessment of stuttering as struggle, avoidance, and expectancy. *British Journal of Disorders of Communication, 2*, 158–171.

World Health Organization (WHO, 1992). *International statistical classification of diseases and related health problems, tenth revision* (ICD-10). Geneva: World Health Organization.

Wright, L., & Ayre, A. (2000). *WASSP: Wright and Ayre Stuttering Self-Rating Profile*. Bicester: Speechmark.

Wright, L., Ayre, A., & Grogan, S. (1998). Outcome measurement in adult stuttering therapy: A self-rating profile. *International Journal of Language and Communication Disorders, 33*, 378–383.

Wu, J.C., Maguire, G., Riley, G., Fallon, J., LaCasse, L., & Chin, S. (1995). A positron emission tomography [18F] deoxyglucose study of developmental stuttering. *Neuroreport, 6*, 501–505.

Wu, J.C., Maguire, G., Riley, G., Lee, A., Keator, D., Tang, C., et al. (1997). Increased dopamine activity associated with stuttering. *Neuroreport, 8*, 767–770.

Wyneken, C. (1868). Über das Stottern und dessen Heilung. *Zeitschrift für rationelle Medizin, 31*, 1–29.

Wyrick, D.R. (1949). *A study of normal nonfluency in conversation*. Unpublished Masters thesis, University of Missouri.

Yairi, E. (1981). Disfluencies of normally speaking two-year-old children. *Journal of Speech and Hearing Research, 24*, 490–495.

Yairi, E. (1997). Home environment and parent child interaction in childhood stuttering. In R.F. Curlee & G.M. Siegel (Eds.), *Nature and treatment of stuttering: New directions.* Boston: Allyn and Bacon.

Yairi, E., & Ambrose, N. (1992a). A longitudinal study of stuttering in children: A preliminary report. *Journal of Speech and Hearing Research, 35*, 755–760.

Yairi, E., & Ambrose, N. (1992b). Onset of stuttering in pre-school children: Selected factors. *Journal of Speech and Hearing Research, 35*, 782–788.

Yairi, E., & Ambrose, N. (1996). Erratum. *Journal of Speech and Hearing Research, 39*, 836.

Yairi, E., & Ambrose, N. (1999). Early childhood stuttering I: Persistence and recovery rates. *Journal of Speech Language, and Hearing Research, 35*, 755–760.

Yairi, E., & Ambrose, N. (2005). *Early childhood stuttering.* Austin, TX: Pro-Ed.

Yairi, E., Ambrose, N.G., & Cox, N.J. (1996). Genetics of stuttering: A critical review. *Journal of Speech and Hearing Research, 39*, 771–784.

Yairi, E., Ambrose, N., Paden, E., & Throneburg, N. (1996). Predictive factors of persistence and recovery: Pathways of childhood stuttering. *Journal of Communication Disorders, 29*, 51–77.

Yairi, E., & Lewis, B. (1984). Disfluencies in the onset of stuttering. *Journal of Speech and Hearing Research, 27*, 154–159.

Yamashita, Y., Maki, A., & Koizumi, H. (1996). Near infrared topographic measurement system: Imaging of absorbers localized in a scattering medium. *Review of Scientific Instrumentation, 67*, 730–732.

Yaruss, J.S. (1997a). Clinical measurement of stuttering behaviors. *Contemporary Issues in Communication Science and Disorders, 24*, 33–44.

Yaruss, J.S. (1997b). Treatment outcomes in stuttering. In A.K. Cordes & R.J. Ingham (Eds.), *Treatment efficacy in stuttering: A search for an empirical basis.* San Diego, CA: Singular Publishing.

Yaruss, J.S. (1999). Utterance length, syntactic complexity, and childhood stuttering. *Journal of Speech, Language, and Hearing Research, 42*, 329–344.

Yaruss, J.S. (2000). The role of performance in the demands and capacities model. *Journal of Fluency Disorders, 25*, 347–358.

Yaruss, J.S. (2002). Facing the challenge of treating stuttering in the schools. *Seminars in Speech and Language, 23*, 153–159.

Yaruss, J.S., & Conture, E. (1993). F2 transitions during sound/syllable repetitions of children who stutter and predictions of stuttering chronicity. *Journal of Speech, Language, and Hearing Research, 36*, 883–896.

Yaruss, J.S., La Salle, L., & Conture, E.G. (1998). Evaluating stuttering in young children: Diagnostic data. *American Journal of Speech-Language Pathology, 7*, 62–76.

Yaruss, J.S., & Quesal, R. (2002). Academic and clinical education in fluency disorders: an update. *Journal of Fluency Disorders, 27*, 4–63.

Yaruss, J.S., & Quesal, R.W. (2004). Overall assessment of the speaker's experience of stuttering (OASES). In A. Packman, A. Meltzer, & H.F.M Peters (Eds.), *Theory, research and therapy in fluency disorders. Proceedings of the 4th World Congress on Fluency Disorders* (pp. 237–240). Nijmegen: Nijmegen University Press.

Yaruss, J.S., Quesal, R.W., Reeves, L., Molt, L., Kluetz, B., Caruso, A.J., et al. (2002). Speech treatment and support group experiences of people who participate in the National Stuttering Association. *Journal of Fluency Disorders, 27*, 115–134.

Yaruss, J.S., & Reardon, N. (2002). Successful communication for children who stutter: Finding the balance. *Seminars in Speech and Language, 23*, 195–204.

Yaruss, J.S., & Reardon, N. (2003). Fostering generalization and maintenance in school settings. *Seminars in Speech and Language, 24*, 33–40.

Yeudall, L.T., Manz, L., Ridenour, C., Tani, A., & Lind, J. (1991). Variability in the central nervous system of stutterers. In E. Boberg (Ed.), *Neuropsychology of stuttering* (pp. 129–164). Alberta: University of Alberta Press.

Young, M.A. (1961). Predicting ratings of severity of stuttering. *Journal of Speech and Hearing Research, Monograph Supplement, 7*, 31–54.

Young, M.A. (1975). Observer agreement for marking moments of stuttering. *Journal of Speech and Hearing Research, 18*, 530–540.

Zackheim, C.T., & Conture, E.G. (2003). Childhood stuttering and speech disfluencies in relation to children's mean length of utterance: A preliminary study. *Journal of Fluency Disorders, 28*, 115–142.

Zebrowski, P. (1997). Assisting young children and their families: Defining the role of the speech-language pathologist. *American Journal of Speech-Language Pathology, 6*, 19–28.

Zenner, A.A., Ritterman, S.I., Bowen, S.K., & Gronhovd, K.D. (1978). Measurement and comparison of anxiety levels of parents of stuttering, articulatory defective and normal speaking children. *Journal of Fluency Disorders, 3*, 273–283.

Zhou, Y., Denny, M., Bachir, N.M., & Daubenspeck, J.A. (1995). Laryngeal responses to single breath expiratory and inspiratory loads. *FASEB Journal*, A567.

Zimmerman, G.N. (1980a). Articulatory behaviors associated with stuttering: A cinefluorographic analysis. *Journal of Speech and Hearing Research, 23*, 108–121.

Zimmerman, G.N. (1980b). Articulatory dynamics of the fluent utterances of stutterers and nonstutterers. *Journal of Speech and Hearing Research, 23*, 95–107.

Zimmerman, G.N. (1984). Articulatory dynamics of stutterers. In R.F. Curlee & W.H. Perkins (Eds.), *Nature and treatment of stuttering: New directions*. San Diego, CA: College Hill Press.

Zimmerman, S., Kalinowski, J., Stuart, A., & Rastatter, M. (1997). Effect of altered auditory feedback on people who stutter during scripted telephone conversations. *Journal of Speech Language, and Hearing Research, 40*, 1130–1134.

Zocchi, L., Estenne, M., Johnston, S., del Ferro, L., Ward, M.E., & Macklem, P.T. (1990). Respiratory muscle coordination in stuttering speech. *American Review of Respiratory Disease, 141*, 1510–1515.

Author index

Subject index

Date Due